D1599095

THESE MEN
HAVE SEEN
HARD SERVICE

★ ★ ★ ★ ★ ★ ★ ★ ★

THESE MEN
HAVE SEEN
HARD SERVICE

The First Michigan Sharpshooters
in the Civil War

RAYMOND J. HEREK

WAYNE STATE UNIVERSITY PRESS DETROIT

GREAT LAKES BOOKS

*A complete listing of the books in this series
can be found at the back of this volume*

PHILIP P. MASON
Editor
Department of History, Wayne State University

DR. CHARLES K. HYDE
Associate Editor
Department of History, Wayne State University

Copyright © 1998 by Wayne State University Press,
Detroit, Michigan 48201

02 01 00 99 98   5 4 3 2 1

Library of Congress Cataloging-in-Publication Data

Herek, Raymond J., 1945–
    These men have seen hard service : the First Michigan
Sharpshooters in the Civil War / Raymond J. Herek.
        p.   cm. — (Great Lakes Books)
    Includes bibliographical references and index.
    ISBN 0–8143–2672–2 (alk. paper)
    1. United States. Army. Michigan Sharpshooters Regiment, 1st
(1863–1865). 2. United States—History—Civil War, 1861–1865—
Regimental histories. 3. Michigan—History—Civil War, 1861–1865—
Regimental histories.   I. Title.   II. Series
E514.9.H47   1998
973.7′474—dc21   97–24303

To My Father and Mother

RAYMOND V. AND LOUISE HEREK

✷ ✷ ✷ ✷ ✷ ✷ ✷ ✷ ✷ ✷

Contents

★ ★ ★ ★ ★

Illustrations and Maps
★ ★ ★ ★ ★

Maps

Photographs

Preface

✯ ✯ ✯ ✯ ✯

The first time I visited my wife's hometown of Harbor Springs, Michigan, I found it interesting, enchanting, and filled with the history and quaint charm all small towns should have. A quarter-mile from the farm on which she lived, down a gravel road overhung with magnificent spruce trees planted a century before and past another delightful farmstead surrounded by 80-year-old maples, lay Lakeview Cemetery, a graveyard unlike any I had ever seen. A large meteorite-like boulder marked the grave of one of the town's leading businessmen. A statue marked the plot of a boy just graduated from school. A unique catafalque memorialized a local man called "Michigan's Indian Poet."

I saw the final resting place of my wife's great-grandfather, who had served in the Michigan legislature in the 1870s. Next to his grave is a stone marking the memory of one of his grandsons who was killed in the Meuse–Argonne in World War I. He isn't there—he was buried in France; his grief-stricken parents erected the stone to remind themselves that a plot in France is forever a part of America.

I stood over the graves of her grandparents, and I learned that her grandpa was a stone mason who left his physical mark on stone walls and sidewalks all around the town. In all, three generations of my wife's family are buried in the cemetery.

Scattered throughout the burying ground were scores of government headstones commemorating the service of men to their country. Regardless of all the twentieth century's wars, it seemed that the Civil War predominated. Engineers, cavalrymen, artillerymen, and infantrymen from Pennsylvania, Missouri, Ohio, Illinois, and the state of Michigan settled there after the war, and they died there.

What really caught my eye, though, were the Indian graves. Most of them were off to one side of the cemetery, segregated in death as they were in life. Five of them were surmounted by white government headstones. All had belonged to Company K of the First Michigan Sharpshooters. Of the dozens of Civil War veterans interred in Lakeview Cemetery, no more than two or three even belonged to same regiment; but here were five men—

John Shomin, John B. Shomin, Leon Otashquabono, Augustus Boushaw, and John Tabyant—all Native Americans, who had served in the same company in a regiment whose history I knew nothing about. What did these Sharpshooters do? Where did they fight? How did it happen that only Indians served in this one company? No book covered their exploits, and at the time I could find very little factual material. The seed of wanting-to-know-more started to germinate.

Over the years I have returned with my wife many times to plant fresh flowers on the graves of her parents and the earlier generations. And every time we put in the marigolds and impatiens and other annuals, I looked over at those five Indian graves, wondering what knowledge was buried with those men.

After more than a quarter-century of research through scores of books, dozens of rolls of microfilm, in college libraries, private collections, the National Archives, and on the battlefields where the 1,300 men of the First Michigan Sharpshooters fought, after years of writing and being prodded to produce a history of those men, many of whom I now feel as if I had known, I present this narrative of the events commemorating the actions of the First Regiment of Michigan Sharpshooters.

I owe so much to so many relatives, friends, acquaintances, and friendly and helpful professionals who guided me and helped me in too many ways to mention. Without the help of John Buckbee, who graciously lent me the papers of his great-grandfather, Julian Edward Buckbee, this history would be woefully inadequate. Leland Thornton of Centreville, Michigan, and Buckbee read parts of the manuscript. Their comments and notations were well appreciated. Gerald Pergande of Bay City waded through the entire narrative, marking my deficiencies and buoying me up. I cannot adequately convey my thanks for his insights and corrections.

I wish to thank Emily Evans Walsh of Howell, Michigan, and her brother, David J. C. Evans, of Connecticut for sharing the papers of their great-grandfather, Ira L. Evans. The encouragement in Emily's letters always pushed me ahead.

Dr. Marjorie Downie Banks of the Shrine to Music Museum at the University of South Dakota in Vermilion shared her knowledge of Charles G. Conn. My cousin Anthony Herek made a number of trips to the Library of Michigan for me. So did Christopher Behmer, who copied pages of material that I would otherwise have missed. Dr. William Mulligan of Negaunee, Michigan, sent me some material on William H. H. Beadle. The late Floyd Haight, a most gracious and admirable man, told me a fascinating story of his great-uncle who won the Congressional Medal of Honor at the Battle of the Crater. Judge Robert Crary of Jackson, Michigan, spent an afternoon showing me the sights of old Jackson and telling me stories of his great-grandfather, James S. DeLand. He also informed me that his forbear's surname is pronounced "DEE-Land."

Lee Hadden of Sterling, Virginia, let me read his manuscript on the Fourth Virginia Infantry, a most interesting fighting unit on the "other" side; and he showed me some fascinating tidbits on the Fourteenth Virginia Infantry. Scott Cumming of Bay City, Michigan, sent me copies of the *Official Records* when I needed them. Jerry Roe of Lansing, Michigan, gave me a few citations on the Sharpshooters's monument on the Capitol lawn. Chris Czopek of East Lansing made some great modern photos of items dealing with the Sharpshooters. His ongoing interest in the regiment, especially Company K, is quite keen.

Dr. Warren C. Young of the Northern Baptist Theological Seminary in Lombard, Illinois, sent me some wonderful material on the Sharpshooters' chaplain, Dr. David Heagle. Dr. Jerome Fallon and Dr. Arlan K. Gilbert of Hillsdale College cleared up some misinformation I had about a few of the Civil War graduates of their esteemed institution. Dale Niesen, a collector *par excellence* of Civil War photos, graciously put any and all of the pictures in his collection at my disposal. Robert M. Coch, another avid collector of Civil War memorabilia also shared the likenesses in his vast collection with me. Art Kniep of Harrisville, Michigan, spent much of his free time developing copies of photographs for this enterprise. Jan House and Robert C. Myers of the 1839 Courthouse Museum in Berrien Springs, Michigan, sent some material on Capt. George Murdoch. Mrs. Arlene Lavigna of the Kimball House Historical Society in Battle Creek, Michigan, made available to me an article on the Sharpshooters's most memorable fight.

I owe debts of gratitude to the staff members at the Alcona County Library in Harrisville, Michigan. They have honored scores of requests for books and microfilm over the years. The professional people at the Clarke Historical Library, Central Michigan University, Mt. Pleasant, and at the Western Regional Library, Western Michigan University, Kalamazoo, especially

Mrs. Phyllis Burnham, were always helpful. My thanks go out to the staff at the Bentley Historical Library, Michigan Historical Collections, University of Michigan, Ann Arbor, for their constant and avid attention. Likewise, the staff at the State Archives of Michigan in Lansing were always courteous and quick with their assistance.

Ruth Bender at the Elkhart Public Library, Elkhart, Indiana, sent me information on Charles G. Conn. The staff at the United States Military History Institute, Carlisle Barracks, Carlisle, Pennsylvania, especially Dr. Richard Sommers, were always cordial and quick with the appropriate information. Dr. Sommers cleared up a real sticking point regarding the commander of the Sharpshooters.

My utmost gratitude goes out to my wife, Druane, who has heard me brag and wonder about the Sharpshooters for more than a score of years. Her encouragement in my research and writing knew no bounds. And to our son, Ray: I really appreciated the times we played catch in the summers after I had worked on this book. It took me from the computer and my desk, cleared the cobwebs from my head, and gave me a fresh outlook at things.

I truly owe all of you a great debt. Thank you very much.

Introduction

★ ★ ★ ★ ★

Colonel Charles V. DeLand, the original commander of the First Michigan Sharpshooters, always wrote both romantically and paternalistically of his old regiment in his post-Civil War remininscences. "It has the distinction," he boasted, "of losing more men in battle in eleven months than any other [Michigan regiment] in the army, and more than many lost during the entire war."[1] He vaunted the casualties of the regiment: 144 killed in action or died of wounds, 273 wounded in action, 142 died in rebel prisons, more than 90 died of some disease. He further listed the more than 130 men and two sets of colors captured by the regiment. He said a "distinguished Major General" called the record of the Sharpshooters "second to none in the service."[2]

In the same breath, DeLand chastised the media, the army, and politicians for denigrating the reputation of *his* regiment. He constantly complained, "because disappointed, ambitious, jealous & shirking peace holders *in the rear* have deliberately falsified us."[3] He said the Sharpshooters did not have the glory due them "because the facts are not known or fairly stated."[4]

DeLand believed "a fair accounting of its history in the field . . . will establish its reputation."[5] Unfortunately, neither he nor any of the Sharpshooters wrote a history of the organization. The survivors of the regiment scattered over a dozen states. Most of them, if they wrote anything at all, recorded nothing of their service in the Civil War. They worked and raised their families and went to weddings and funerals. Some attended regimental reunions. They shared their memories with each other, but, by and large, they took those same memories to their graves.

It is difficult to understand why the memory and exploits of the regiment faded into the mists of time. The First Michigan Sharpshooters is enshrined in Fox's *Three Hundred Fighting Regiments*.[6] Its monument, one of the most conspicuous in the state, stands on the grounds of the state capitol.

The recruitment of the Sharpshooters began inauspiciously in the winter of 1862–1863. Thousands of men had already enlisted in Michigan regiments the previous summer and fall, and a smaller pool of available men stymied the efforts of those trying to sign up volunteers. Patriotism still stirred emotions, but they were tempered with the realities of long casualty lists from the war zones. Bounties—money payments to induce enlistments—helped convince others to join the army. Older men, many in their forties, felt justified leaving their families with a small nest egg while they fought for their country. Native Americans were actively recruited for the simple reason that the regiment was a difficult one to raise. All in all, herculean labors were expended to recruit the regiment.

Because the Sharpshooters were kept in backwater areas during the first fifteen months of their existence, desertions cut deep swaths into their numbers. Guarding an arsenal and rebel prisoners for more than a year, learning that they were to be armed with the standard infantryman's weapon instead of modern target rifles, forever drilling and mounting guard were not conducive to good morale.

Much of the history of the Sharpshooters included duty at the Dearborn arsenal just outside of Detroit, and Camp Douglas in Chicago. Since they remained such a long time at those two places, it was imperative that the entire story of their early months be included in the narrative. Too many habits, ideas, and feelings—in short, the myriad of personal traits that infused the Sharpshooters—took root in those fifteen months before they saw actual combat. When the regiment finally did reach the front, during Ulysses S. Grant's Overland Campaign of 1864, it had trouble adapting. Stymied in their first attempts to prove themselves, the Sharpshooters eventually showed their mettle at Spotsylvania and the battles around Petersburg, Virginia.

Receiving but little official praise for its part in the Civil War, and all but forgotten in the century since the war, the Sharpshooters' contribution was nonetheless impressive. Still, the 1,300 men who constituted the regiment, and their exploits, are forgotten. Their own grandchildren grew up knowing little, if anything, about the Sharpshooters. When their grandfathers died and were buried in the local cemetery, a headstone later arrived from the government with the old veteran's name, his company designation and the strange initials: "1st Mich. S.S."

It was almost as if a conspiracy of silence kept the First Michigan Sharpshooters from ever getting their due. Over the last quarter of a century I have looked for the scattered facts, slim as they were in some cases, and now "a fair accounting of its history" can be told.

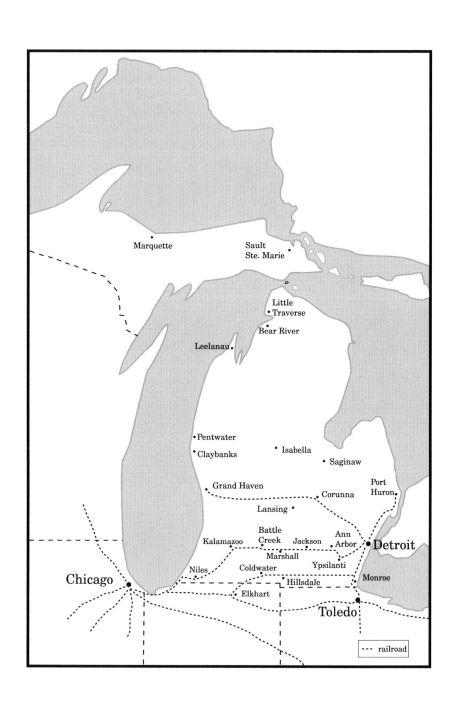

Marquette

Sault
Ste. Marie

Little
Traverse

Bear River

Leelanau

Pentwater

Claybanks

Isabella

Saginaw

Grand Haven

Corunna

Port
Huron

Lansing

Battle
Creek

Ann
Arbor

Jackson

Detroit

Kalamazoo

Marshall

Niles

Coldwater

Ypsilanti

Chicago

Hillsdale

Monroe

Elkhart

Toledo

--- railroad

CHAPTER 1

Down with Treason

The Newspaperman from Jackson

Colonel DeLand anticipated a difficult situation awaiting him at Camp Chandler in Kalamazoo. Believing that 500 officers and men of his new regiment—the First Michigan Sharpshooters—expected his arrival at the rendezvous camp, the former newspaperman, politician, and veteran volunteer soldier quickly discovered that he had not properly prepared himself. Arriving at the former county fairgrounds on a cold 16 January 1863, DeLand immediately found himself besieged by a full regimental complement of would-be officers who eagerly and noisily waved lists of volunteers' names.

Instead of the expected files of hundreds of stalwart men, DeLand learned he had only a paper command; 400 men had been enlisted, but only 225 had gathered, and 80 of them claimed to be holding commissions, both real and promised.[1]

Examining the credentials of his erstwhile officers, DeLand found that some of them had been recruiting for months. A number had tried unsuccessfully to obtain commissions in other regiments but had been willing to settle for this one. Some had enlistment papers for 20 to 100 men. Others did not have a single enlistee in camp; their recruits had either secured their bounties, enlisted in other regiments, or deserted. DeLand's anxious anticipation crumbled to ashes. "The prospects of the Sharp-shooters was [*sic*] not encouraging," he understated.[2]

An ambitious man with fine civilian, political, and military credentials, Charles Victor DeLand seemed an excellent choice to command the new regiment. A respected newspaperman, De-Land had joined the army soon after the First Battle of Bull Run convinced the Union that the war would not be a short one. He had better than average political connections, most notably with Michigan's Republican war governor, Austin Blair, and with the state's newest senator, Zachariah Chandler.[3]

Descended from a French Huguenot family that had emi-grated to America in 1634, DeLand was born in North Brookfield, Massachusetts, on 25 July 1826, the oldest son of a War of 1812 veteran. Four years later his parents moved to Jackson, Michigan, which at that time was little more than a wilderness outpost.[4]

In 1836 "Charlie" started working as a printer's devil at the Jacksonburg *Sentinel*, the local newspaper, where he learned that a newspaperman took a clear stand on the issues of the day. He cultivated an attitude that was "independent but with Whig pro-clivities," both echoing and influencing the self-reliant nature of his frontier readers.[5]

In 1843 DeLand began to travel as a newspaper journey-man. For four years he honed his journalistic skills in Detroit and in Buffalo and Rochester, New York. In 1848, after buying out the assets of his hometown newspapers (including those of the old *Sentinel*), he established the Jackson *Citizen*. Outspoken-ness being a hallmark of the pioneer newspaperman, the *Citizen*'s editor became a vociferous critic of all that was wrong with the world. DeLand, used to personal and professional confronta-tions, developed an abrasive personality. He became so positive of his own convictions that anyone who dared disagree with him was considered a charlatan, an imposter, a liar. He was a formi-dable opponent, but also a strong supporter of causes he consid-ered worthwhile.[6]

The controversy over slavery found DeLand on the side of the abolitionists.[7] His father's house near Jackson was a station on the Underground Railroad. "The negroes used to come in in-stallments of one to half a dozen, always in the night," he wrote years later:

> and were secreted during the day[,] and the next night forwarded
> to the next station. . . . Many a weary night's ride fell to my lot,

along the new and rough roads, across [the neighboring towns of] Leoni and Waterloo, to aid these poor fugitive slaves on their way to freedom."[8]

By the mid 1850s DeLand, together with Henry Barnes of the Detroit *Tribune*, and George A. Fitch of the Kalamazoo *Telegram*, were known quantities. They and other influential Whig newspaper editors in the state of Michigan were the first to call for a mass meeting in Jackson on 6 July 1854 to set forth the political program to deal with the nation's mounting ills.

Gathering in a large park "under the oaks" (no building in town could accommodate the vast crowd), Northern reformers, Whigs, and Free Soilers set up a political organization called the Republican Party. The delegates demanded a new agenda for the new party: Slave territories will not exist in the West; the odious Fugitive Slave Law will be repealed; and "the abomination of slavery shall no longer be perpetuated under the sanction of the federal Constitution."[9] From that point on, DeLand's *Citizen* echoed Republican feelings in Michigan.[10] After serving several years in county and city offices, DeLand won election from the Twelfth State Senatorial District in 1860. While running his paper and serving in the Michigan Senate, the Civil War erupted. The first state legislator to join the army, DeLand did not resign his political office, but he did sell his newspaper and raise a company of men from the Jackson area, to which he was elected captain. Calling themselves the "Jackson County Rifles," Captain DeLand and his recruits joined the regiment then forming at Fort Wayne in Detroit in early September 1861.[11] There, they were mustered into the Ninth Michigan Infantry as Company C, the color company.[12]

In October 1861 the Ninth Michigan, 913 strong and led by Col. William W. Duffield of Detroit, left the state for Kentucky and the Army of the Cumberland to become the first regiment from Michigan "to enter upon active service in the western departments of the army."[13] Eventually the regiment moved farther south to Tennessee. While stationed at Murfreesboro, Captain DeLand had temporarily reverted to his former occupation. With borrowed type he ran off a few editions of a sheet called the *Union Volunteer*, ostensibly to convert the "heathen 'Secesh" and let them see the error of their ways.[14]

In Tennessee DeLand saw slavery first-hand. He already possessed a healthy hatred for slave owners; that feeling was now renewed. One March morning he encountered "two gents of the Secesh school" hunting for "niggers." As officer of the day, DeLand decided who did and who did not enter his regiment's encampment.

> I politely informed them there were no niggers in the camp of the 9th Regt. & if there was they [the slave hunters] could not be admitted without a pass from Gen. Buel [*sic*], and that we did not intend either to steal or chase their property.[15]

The colonel ordered DeLand to throw the slave catchers out of the camp, "which duty I performed with a hearty good will," declared DeLand, "amid the cheers of the whole regiment."[16]

DeLand's vehemence hit a more strident note in a letter to his former paper in Jackson. Whenever he wrote for the public, he used his "editorial voice," one honed to perfection on the pages of his beloved *Citizen*. He would "condemn the institution [of slavery], in toto," he remonstrated:

> and make every traitor feel the full force of his treason, and drink to the very dregs the fruits of his folly. . . . the Federal Government . . . must pursue a policy that is both physically and financially crushing to this class of people. . . . To the leaders, the corrupt aristocracy, the arch leaders of treason, I would not extend a single favor or indulge in a single attempt at condolence or sympathy. My motto is, down with treason, and the most ample and severe punishment to all traitors and perjurers.[17]

DeLand did not just grandstand for the sake of public adulation. The editor from Jackson fully adopted the abolitionist crusade; he truly believed in the Union cause and in the agenda of the Republican Party.

On 5 May 1862 the Ninth Michigan fought a spirited contest with Confederate cavalry led by Gen. John Hunt Morgan in Lebanon, Tennessee. But the regiment's most memorable fight was on 13 July 1862, when six companies battled an overwhelming enemy force headed by Gen. Nathan Bedford Forrest. After holding off the rebels for eight hours and losing a third of their men, with no additional help forthcoming, the Ninth Michigan was forced to surrender.

In his after-action report Colonel Duffield singled out Captain DeLand for special recognition because of the latter's "cool and gallant conduct throughout the action, and the fearless manner in which he led his company as skirmishers in pursuit of the enemy when [the rebels were first] repulsed."[18]

The victorious Southerners marched their prisoners to McMinnville, a 44-mile trek, then shipped them by train to Madison, Georgia, where they confined them in an old "cotton factory." DeLand never forgot the treatment he received, nor the poor sustenance doled out—rotten pork "abounding in worms" and what passed for bread, a concoction made of corn and wheat and no leavening, "and consequently about as capable of digestion as the same quantity of bricks."[19]

Paroled in early October 1862, and suffering from scurvy and chronic diarrhea, DeLand returned to Jackson and remained there until 20 November, when he learned of his formal exchange.[20] In the meantime he pulled all the strings he could. Being a junior officer was not to his liking, not when there were colonelcies available. Fortunately, he knew the "right" people. Within a year after moving his family to Michigan, his father, William DeLand, had been appointed justice of the peace by the territorial governor, Lewis Cass. After statehood in 1837 the elder DeLand held a number of local political offices. He was elected probate judge in 1840 and served in that position for the next eight years. Everyone, even his son in his letters home, referred to him as the "Judge." He wielded plenty of political clout, even in 1862.[21]

Also, as one of the charter members of the Michigan Republican Party, DeLand basked in the good graces of some of the giants in the party. Austin Blair, Michigan's current Republican governor, lived in Jackson and had a law practice there. He and DeLand had known each other for years. Zachariah Chandler, one of the emerging leaders of the Republican Party nationwide, had attended the formation of the party "under the oaks" in 1854 and knew the newspaperman well.[22]

His political friends went to work for him, and by November 1862 DeLand was assured of a colonelcy. In the middle of that month, after his formal exchange as a prisoner of war, he received official authority to raise a regiment of sharpshooters. DeLand was then 36 years old and a bit tall for the mid 1800s at five feet, ten inches, which he carried on a spare frame. His blue eyes glared out of a stern face, and his black hair and wiry beard added to his dark looks.[23]

Michigan's Contribution to the War Effort

Discouragement reigned supreme in the northern states by the middle of 1862. Union armies had sustained in excess of 46,000 casualties in the first half of the year. The war in the West had seemingly bogged down after the costly victory at Shiloh in April. In the East, the Army of the Potomac retreated from a series of Confederate hammer-blows called the Seven Days' Battles. Washington politicians feared a rebel onslaught against the nation's capital. In that apprehensive atmosphere Pres. Abraham Lincoln issued a call for 300,000 additional men for the country's defense. Each state was assigned a quota based on its population.[24]

By 1 July 1862, Michigan had furnished more than 25,000 men to the war effort. Sixteen infantry regiments, three cavalry regiments, eight six-gun batteries, and a regiment of engineers and mechanics were already at the front.[25] Through tremendous effort an additional seven infantry regiments were readied for the field of battle 30 days after Lincoln's call.[26] At no other time during the Civil War had so many of Michigan's sons joined the colors. While the seven infantry regiments were being sent to the war zones, new rendezvous camps were being established for even more regiments.

The Seventeenth Michigan Infantry was recruited throughout the state, while the six successive regiments of infantry were raised respectively in each of Michigan's six congressional districts.[27] The citizens of Detroit petitioned to raise a unit of their own, and the Twenty-fourth Michigan Infantry, soon to join the famed "Iron Brigade," began drilling at Fort Wayne.

The response to calls for enlistment was so great that more companies were raised than could be immediately accommodated. These surplus companies were assigned by the state adjutant general's office to two new infantry units, the Twenty-fifth and Twenty-sixth.[28] Cavalry units were recruited at the same time. The Fourth, Fifth, and Sixth Michigan Cavalry Regiments were organized in the summer of 1862 and also sent to the field. Every regiment was fully equipped by the state.[29]

Michigan's allotment, set by the war department in a 9 August 1862 memorandum, was still 11,686 men short. Governor Blair ordered township and ward officers to complete a census of men of military age and return it to their respective county clerks on or before 10 September 1862. The results were eye-opening. There were still 91,071 men not in uniform living in the state,[30] so the state made preparations to encourage more men to volunteer. Local bounties—money payments generally raised through popular subscription or local taxes and given to prospective recruits—were offered by individuals, wards of larger cities, certain towns, townships, and counties.[31]

Governor Blair did not care for "the vicious but well intended system of citizens' bounties." He considered the local governments' attempts a source "of endless trouble." "In my opinion," he stated, "this whole system of bounties has been carried to a great excess, resulting in excessive taxes, with great demoralization of the people, and with no corresponding benefit to the government or to the soldier himself."[32] Men traveled to wherever the bounties were highest. Towns and counties in a bidding frenzy offered higher bounties than they normally would. Some men enlisted, then deserted at the first opportunity.[33] Blair suggested a uniform state bounty of $50 be offered in lieu of any local inducements. The enlistee would receive the money once his regiment was formally mustered into the service of the United States.

Even as late as November 1862, Michigan still needed to provide more than 4,000 men. To help induce enlistments, the federal government had already authorized bounty payments and one month's advance pay to volunteers. Potential officers of proposed organizations began enlisting men. The Twenty-seventh Infantry took shape, many of its enlistees coming from the Upper Peninsula. The Seventh, Eighth, and Ninth Cavalry regiments were recruited. Another infantry regiment, the Twenty-eighth, was proposed as an Irish unit.[34]

The Governor from Jackson

The First Michigan Sharpshooters, one of the most difficult regiments to raise in the state, would have some problems not endemic to earlier regiments. Too many new units were recruiting in the state in late 1862, leaving a smaller pool of able-bodied and willing enlistees for DeLand's recruiters. Furthermore, older Michigan regiments that were already in the field were constantly recruiting in the state in order to replenish their numbers. Early in the war Governor Blair had decided to put fewer regiments into the field and to keep them filled with recruits, rather than raising new regiments every time a new quota was levied from Washington.

A politically expedient mode of raising new regiments (from colonel to drummer boy) was favored by certain Union states, notably New York, Pennsylvania, Ohio, Indiana, and Illinois. Governors repaid political debts by appointing party cronies to regimental commands.governor Blair, however, believed *esprit de corps* was fostered by reinforcing older units. "New recruits put into old organizations," he told the state legislature, "under trained and competent officers, are of such greater value to the service than if organized into new bodies, with officers unused to war. They quickly catch the spirit, and acquire the skill of old soldiers."[35]

Blair found himself severely chastised by his fellow Republicans for selecting regimental commanders without regard to party. He was constantly pressured by party hacks, professional politicians, and office seekers to appoint "favorite sons" to positions of command. Although censured as a political Benedict Arnold, Blair maintained his policy of trying to find the most qualified man for the job.[36]

Blair had come to Michigan in 1840 after his graduation from Union College and Albany Law School. Elected to the Michigan legislature on the Whig ticket in 1846, as a freshman lawmaker he "made a report in favor of removing the word 'white' from the [state] Constitution, as a qualification for suffrage, which caused his defeat the next year [1848] on the charge of being 'an abolitionist.'" In 1848 Blair joined the Free Soil Party. In 1854 he helped inaugurate the Republican Party, and in 1860 he attended the convention that nominated Abraham Lincoln for the presidency.[37]

Blair would lead the state through the turmoil of the Civil War. The preservation of the Union was at stake, he remonstrated in countless speeches:

> When the Southern traitors commenced this bloody contest, they did it wholly without excuse; and upon their guilty heads must rest forever the responsibility of that enormous crime. Not a groan escapes from a dying Union soldier on the field or in the hospital, that is not a cry to God for vengeance against them.

To Blair, as to many Northerners, the war was a holy quest, a vindication of the principles of the United States of America.

"The best and bravest of our people fight in the ranks of its armies," he told the legislature. "Scarce a battle-field of the war but has drunk of Michigan blood, and the graves of our men mark the camping-ground of every army of the Union." It was a war of retribution against the Southern renegades. "Every despairing wail wrung from the hearts of countless widows and orphans they have made," he thundered, "appeals to same high throne against them."[38] Austin Blair's sympathies were to his country and his adopted state. Cost him what it might, he did not waver from the task confronting him.

A New Regiment Takes Shape

A regiment of sharpshooters was proposed to facilitate the recruiting of an extra thousand men from the state. The color, the dash, the individual "on his own hook" should appeal to these independent Westerners. Colonel Hiram Berdan's two regiments of U.S. Sharpshooters, which had been recruited throughout the Northern states, supplied the "dash and color" in opposition to infantry regiments, which constituted the backbone of the Union armies. A sharpshooter belonged to an elite unit. Some state officials believed recruits would want to belong to such a band of riflemen.[39]

Colonel DeLand, writing years after the war, gave another reason for his regiment's beginnings. Since "there appeared to be still a surplus of men offered who could not be put into service as Infantry, [after the Seventeenth through Twenty-seventh Infantry regiments were recruited in 1862,] the project of organizing them into a battalion of Sharpshooters was adopted."[40] If that were true in late 1862, it dissipated by early 1863. The well had run dry. Winter was not a good time for enlistments, and it soon became apparent that supplying the needed men for a full regiment of sharpshooters would be difficult, if not impossible.

Actually, back in late November 1862 the secretary of war had telegraphed Governor Blair asking if a battalion of four or five companies of sharpshooters could be raised in the state. Blair returned such a spirited reply that a decision was made to enlist a full regiment. Because the recruiters would not be able to be as selective as Colonel Berdan, Michigan's sharpshooter regiment was enlisted using simpler, baser principles. Certain counties were behind in their quota for raising troops; they would be thoroughly canvassed for recruits. If fewer men responded than were needed, drafted men would be used to fill the regiment from the sluggish counties.[41] DeLand's regiment, then, might not be the choice unit he had envisioned. Rather, the exigencies of war forced him to accept men who would have to be converted into sharpshooters.

The Officers

If any one quality personified most (if not all) of the officers of the First Michigan Sharpshooters, it would have to be ambition. Those vying for positions in any command structure have to be ambitious, but some of the officers in this new regiment elevated ambition to an art form. As in all regiments, some of the officers in the Sharpshooters became very good; others either worked hard to maintain their status or found themselves in over their heads. Unfortunately, there were some who never should have worn shoulder straps. Time and the requirements of warfare would winnow some out and cast others into roles they found exhilarating. They would all be tested—by themselves, by others in and out of the regiment, and by the ruthlessness of war.

Levant C. Rhines, a Battle Creek lawyer, brought the largest contingent of men to Camp Chandler in January 1863. The young attorney evidently showed promise. Maj. John Piper, every inch the soldier himself, considered Rhines "far the superior of any Line Officer in the Regiment."[42] He and his lieutenants, George C. Knight and Guy Newbre, recruited more than 80 men in and around Battle Creek; all of them were present to greet Colonel DeLand at his arrival at Camp Chandler.[43]

Rhines had converted his Battle Creek law office, which was located over C. B. Parker's Hat Store, into a recruiting depot. He admonished potential volunteers to enlist and to pick up a bounty before the draft nabbed them (a draftee did not receive a bounty).[44] An indefatigable worker, purposeful, but with fewer contacts than DeLand, Rhines enlisted "able-bodied men and those who are good marksmen" by promising them their bounties within 48 hours of enlistment. He obviously paid them out of his own pocket, expecting to be repaid when their bounties came in. Rhines also had his men examined by a local physician, Dr. Z. T. Slater, to weed out those who were not "able-bodied."[45] Calhoun County and its largest city, Battle Creek, contributed 145 men to the ranks of the new regiment. Additionally, eight of the original officers hailed from the county.[46]

Asahel Nichols of Lansing began enlisting men in October.[47] By early December 1862 Nichols had signed up 60 men from the area around Jackson. Recruitment for the new sharpshooter regiment was aided by the local newspaper through enticing notices:

> This is a very desirable arm of the service, as there is less of the laborious duties, and more active military duty than in any other corps. . . . all those who prefer light and active service in a new regiment to enduring the miseries of the draft and hard service in the old regiments should make haste to enroll themselves in this new and favorite regiment.[48]

The first lieutenant for Nichols's company entered with a sterling military record. Ira L. Evans of Niles had served as a corporal of the color guard in the Second Michigan Infantry since its inception in 1861. He brought much-needed experience into the fledgling regiment and a maturity that steadied those around him at perilous moments. Twenty-seven years old in 1863, Evans represented the best the officer corps needed.[49]

Henry Hinckley, the man about to become Nichols's second lieutenant, had some handsome backing, but there were lingering doubts about him. The editor of the Lansing *State Republican*, John Allen, touted 32-year-old Hinckley. Hinckley had told Allen of recently being "unanimously elected Captain" of his company in the Twentieth Michigan Infantry, but he wanted to join the Sharpshooters instead. In actuality, Hinckley had served in the Twentieth as a sergeant, and nothing more than raw ambition pushed him to transfer to the new regiment. It also helped that Hinckley was Nichols's brother-in-law.[50]

A dark cloud seemed to follow Hinckley's career in the Sharpshooters. He and Nichols did not get along with Colonel DeLand. In a regiment that would have a horrific turnover in junior officers because of battle injuries, Hinckley was the only charter officer to muster out at the end of the war at the same rank with which he was originally mustered in.

Few others were as enterprising as Nichols and Rhines. In fact, DeLand was taken aback at the schemes of some men who craved a commission in the regiment. In answer to one man who wished to purchase a commission for $100, Deland—exasperated at such gall—said he would only "give offices to *working* men without regard to their money."[51] He further stated that if the inquirer recruited 30 men, he would receive a first lieutenancy; for 20 men, a second lieutenancy; for 10 men he would make first sergeant of a company.[52]

"I expended all my time and a large amount in private means in trying to fill up and organize the Regt," DeLand explained. He later estimated his personal expenses up to the time of the regiment's muster in July 1863 to have been $3,000. Since he expected such dedication from all his officers, his irritation with the would-be commission buyer was understandable.[53]

Lucien Meigs of Reading and his associates, Thomas R. Fowler of Jonesville and Albert Porter Thomas of Allen, signed up 76 recruits in Hillsdale County. Extolling the benefits of being a sharpshooter, Meigs and his colleagues advertised in the local paper in the hope of luring new men into the regiment:

> It is an active branch of the service, always in light marching condition, with the best arms, and long range, with each man fighting on his *"own hook"* than infantry or cavalry; giving an opportunity for the exercise and the same skill and shrewdness exhibited in the hunting sports in our western forests.[54]

All told, 129 sharpshooters would come from Hillsdale County, and the three recruiters were mustered as officers for Company C.[55] Meigs, the oldest line officer in the regiment at age 42, had come to Michigan in 1842 from New York. He was a school teacher; now he would be teaching a more serious subject.[56]

In adjoining Branch County, 38-year-old Andrew J. Hall of Coldwater beat the drum until 30 men joined the colors.[57] One of Hall's recruits was a tall, dark-complexioned 33-year-old named Henry Cleavland. A rugged man with coarse features, Cleavland had served a one-year sentence in Jackson Prison for stealing cattle in 1859. Tattoos ran up and down both arms. He had the look of a man to be avoided.[58]

Elmer C. Dicey of Grand Haven had already enlisted 14 men from his home town. Dicey had had a bad time in the Fifth Michigan Cavalry. He enlisted as an officer but was appointed supernumerary second lieutenant, a superfluous position. Having no command, he resigned. Now he was taking no chances. His men, the "Ottawa Wildcats" (named after their home county), would see to it that he served as captain.[59]

With so many regiments having already attracted most of

the state's available pool of enlistees, the gleanings for some hopeful officers were slim indeed. Competition between would-be commanders was intense. William Clark and Eugene Rowlson opened a recruiting office in Hillsdale in early December 1862. Rowlson had served several months in Berdan's First U.S. Sharpshooters. Clark went on to become a lieutenant in the new regiment's Company B, but Rowlson never entered it.[60]

One of Clark's first enlistees was 44-year-old George Washington Warren of Hillsdale. Warren's son and namesake had been wounded while serving with the Twentieth Indiana Infantry on the Peninsula. Even though he had lost a leg, the younger Warren remained an avid patriot. He wanted to "get a cork leg and go back to fight the traitors again, before the War was over."[61] His father sincerely regretted "that I have not one whole regiment of just such dear ones to furnish my country in this hour of her peril."[62] Having no other sons to send to the conflict, the elder Warren offered himself and signed on with the Sharpshooters.

Frank Whipple, soon to be a second lieutenant in the new regiment, had already served a year and a half in the First U.S. Sharpshooters. He had fought in the Seven Days' Battles, the Second Battle of Bull Run, and Antietam. A commissary sergeant when he resigned to join DeLand's regiment, the 25-year-old Whipple already possessed the expertise of a veteran and the methodical manner of a businessman.[63]

No man tried harder than William H. Randall of Pittsfield to become an officer in the regiment. Randall was a 21-year-old veteran, having served in the First Michigan Infantry (3 months) and having fought in the First Battle of Bull Run. When the regiment disbanded after its three-month enlistment, he was so ill he did not muster with the three-year First Michigan Infantry. In the summer of 1862, Randall, now recovered from his illness, received permission from the governor to recruit. He assisted in raising two companies for one regiment but was thwarted in his attempt to secure a position of authority in that unit. He then threw in his lot with the Twenty-eighth Michigan Infantry. After many of his friends signed on with the First Michigan Sharpshooters, Randall asked Governor Blair to transfer him.

Even though he found it difficult to procure enlistees, Randall still was able to report to Camp Chandler with 8 or 10 men. Taking a cue from Samuel Hudson, who had raised his quota from the Port Huron area, Randall went to the same town and signed up 25 men. Fully expecting to be mustered as an officer in one of the new companies, Randall "found foul play was the order of the day" when he learned that Colonel DeLand had appointed his cousin, Hooker A. DeLand, as captain of the latest company. Bitter at this turn of events, Randall believed that Hooker De-Land did not recruit a single individual.[64] Randall finally received his second lieutenant's commission, but only after he convinced Governor Blair and State Adjutant General Robertson to look over the enlistment papers recording the names of those who had signed up the recruits. He was the last original line officer mustered into the regiment.[65]

Hooker Ashton DeLand, another of the regiment's veterans, had served in the First Michigan Infantry as a sergeant. He had seen plenty of action in the Peninsula Campaign, the Second Battle of Bull Run, and Fredericksburg. The editor of the Jackson *Citizen* believed his cousin would "make a capital officer" in the new regiment. Additionally, the editor of the Democratic Jackson *Eagle* endorsed the younger DeLand. "He has risen from the ranks," the comment read, "and by his bravery earned his present position long ago." Regretfully, the experience he brought with him would serve neither him nor the Sharpshooters well. Hooker DeLand would cast a disreputable shadow over both the regiment and his own future.[66]

Joseph O. Bellair of Detroit became the first lieutenant of Hooker DeLand's company. He, too, had a modicum of military experience. He had helped organize the Lyon Guard, a militia unit in his home town, and had drilled in its ranks for a year, eventually becoming a lieutenant. But the Lyon Guard was for homebodies; Bellair wanted more action than the local militia unit could provide.[67]

Two of the toughest and most unsavory volunteers in the regiment served in Hooker DeLand's company. They were the Snay brothers, Richard and Moses. Richard was 24; Mose (as everyone called him) was 21. Richard was a dark-complexioned man with a similar past. His black hair and dark hazel eyes masked a street tough from Detroit. He sported a tattoo of a sailor on his right arm and an anchor on his left. His brother Mose feared no man and gave scant respect to few. Belligerent and insubordinate in camp, both brothers nevertheless turned out to be good, steady soldiers on the firing line.[68]

Lt. Thomas Gaffney of Niles resigned his commission in the Ninth Michigan Infantry (Colonel DeLand's old outfit) and threw his lot in with the Sharpshooters, where a captaincy awaited him. Moses Powell, a former deputy sheriff from Gaffney's home town, joined him as first lieutenant. Admired by some of the officers as having potential for greatness, Powell possessed a martial bearing and an enviable record as a lawman. He would disappoint all of them when the regiment marched into combat. Charles G. Conn, another veteran, who had served in the Fifteenth Indiana Infantry as a musician, rounded out the line officers in the company.

The Adjutant from Chicago

Edward J. Buckbee, pining for adventure with the yearning romanticism of a teenager, had drilled with a militia unit in Chicago before the war, even though he was under age. Immediately after the First Battle of Bull Run, he tried to join the Nineteenth Illinois Infantry:

> My sister insisted that I should not go, and cried. Mr. Jansen [her husband] scolded and called me a fool, and then wrote to my mother, who started the law after me in the person of my [other] brother-in-law, Henry M. Cheever, who came at once to Chicago and informed Capt. Hayden that I was under age and my mother being a widow, I could not go without her consent.[69]

Being forcibly removed from the army "was a terrible mortification to me," lamented Buckbee, but his brother-in-law advised him to have patience. Cheever was a personal friend of Governor Blair of Michigan, and felt certain he could obtain a commission for Buckbee in a future Michigan regiment.[70]

For one long teenage year Buckbee stewed over the turn of events, but Cheever kept his word. Governor Blair's office notified Buckbee on 18 November 1862 to report to Lt. Col. John R. Smith in Detroit. Smith, "a gruff-spoken and severe looking . . . one-armed veteran of the Mexican War," was the military commander of the state of Michigan and a Regular Army officer. He mustered Buckbee as first lieutenant and adjutant of the First Michigan Sharpshooters. Taken aback at the lad's lack of military expertise, Smith softened a bit when he learned that the young adjutant, who was only 18 years old at the time, did know company drill from his pre-war militia experience. "Well," Smith rationalized, "I guess you know about as much about the matter as some of the officers will."[71]

After leaving Smith's office, the euphoric Buckbee went directly to a bookstore to buy every volume on military training he could find. In short order he opened an office in Ypsilanti and began procuring volunteers.[72]

About a month later Buckbee received a letter from Colonel DeLand, whom he had heard about but had not yet met. The two came face to face at the Michigan Exchange, Detroit's largest and finest hotel. It was not an amicable conference. DeLand had requested someone else as regimental adjutant; specifically, he desired a friend to have the appointment, a friend with military know-how.[73] Not realizing DeLand's disposition, Buckbee was:

> somewhat anxious as to the impression I would make on my Colonel. He greeted me rather stiffly, asking me numerous questions about my habits, studies, etc., which I could not see had any particular bearing upon my new position. Finally, he commenced to talk of military affairs, and told me of the amount of service he had seen, and asked me what I considered as my qualifications to fill the position of Regimental Adjutant. Of course, I had no answer to make as to the duties in the office of Adjutant. I, therefore, after squirming about in my chair for a while, told him that I could handle the musket with any man and was perfectly familiar with Company-drill, and that I liked it. At this, he softened up a little and said, "Well, that's good, anyway, for with the exception of the men who are appointed Lieutenant Colonel and Major, I do not know of one who has any knowledge of Company-drill"; and, he informed me that he could use me in that line and "probably teach me as to the office business." [74]

DeLand and Buckbee never became friends but always treated each other with military courtesy. Many men would help to shape the fortunes of the First Michigan Sharpshooters, but these two very different personalities, who met at this chilly reception in the waning days of 1862, would have a most profound influence on this regiment.

The lieutenant colonel mentioned by DeLand was William Henry Harrison Beadle. Born in Indiana in 1838, Beadle attended the University of Michigan, specializing in civil engineering, and graduated in 1861. He immediately entered the army as first lieutenant of Company A, Thirty-first Indiana Infantry. He was promoted to captain but resigned his commission in February 1862. For a few months he helped organize and train the Twenty-sixth Michigan Infantry. He toyed with the idea of becoming adjutant of the Twenty-sixth, but threw in his lot with the Sharp-shooters instead. He received his appointment as lieutenant colonel on 1 January 1863, his twenty-fifth birthday.[75]

Maj. John Piper of Battle Creek rounded out the list of field officers. He had originally enlisted in Company D, Fourteenth Missouri Infantry, as captain in September 1861. A famous outfit in the Western theater of the war, the regiment became known as Birge's Western Sharpshooters. Piper had raised the company exclusively in southwestern Michigan but was unable to obtain admission into a Michigan regiment at the time.[76] Birge's Sharp-shooters saw action at Fort Donelson, Shiloh, Iuka, and Corinth. In November 1862 the regiment's designation changed from the Fourteenth Missouri to the Sixty-sixth Illinois Infantry. The 26-year-old Piper resigned his commission in January 1863; he brought a wealth of practical soldiering to Camp Chandler.[77]

Opening a recruiting office over Raymond & Hall's Grocery in Battle Creek, Piper and Martin Wager advertised for volunteers between the ages of 18 and 45, promising $150 bounty—$75 to be paid when mustered in, the balance when mustered out. He told his potential enlistees they would be armed with sporting rifles, "which will make them part of the most efficient corps in the service." The officers (he told them) were "men of ability and experience," and "are capable of instructing or leading them in any emergency."[78]

One of the finest officers in the regiment was one who would not lead men into battle, but who took care of their most trying physical needs. He was chief surgeon, Dr. Arvin F. Whelan of Hillsdale. Born in Oneida County, New York, in 1831, Whelan came to Michigan in 1853, entering the University of Michigan's medical department the next year. Graduating in 1856 with an M.D. degree, he started his practice in Otsego and moved to Hillsdale in 1857. Whelan enlisted in the Eleventh Michigan Infantry as an assistant surgeon in November 1861. After a year he resigned that position and entered the ranks of the Sharpshooters.[79] A highly conscientious physician, Whelan brought with him the good wishes of the Eleventh Michigan Infantry: 20 officers of his former regiment had signed a personal testimonial on his behalf. The Sharpshooters were getting a skillful, personable, and gracious doctor.[80]

Dr. George L. Cornell, the assistant surgeon, studied medicine at Michigan Central College in Spring Arbor. He learned the profession from his father, Dr. Jerry G. Cornell of Spring Arbor, and Dr. Moses Gunn, surgeon at the University of Michigan and chief surgeon for the Fifth Michigan Infantry. The younger Cornell practiced his profession while collector of customs at St. Clair, Michigan. A War Democrat, the 34-year-old physician exhibited "rare skills as a surgeon" and brought to the fledgling regiment a mature outlook in both politics and medicine.[81]

The Draft

In his first order to the men under his command, issued 5 January 1863, Colonel DeLand directed his recruiters to cease signing up men by 12 January and to report with their enlistees to Camp Chandler by the 15th.[82] DeLand found himself snared in a dilemma not of his making. John Robertson, the state adjutant general, had ordered all enlistments to stop. Governor Blair had sent Robertson a directive halting all recruiting for new Michigan regiments until the older ones had signed up enough men to achieve minimum strength.

A "draft" was blowing across the state, and Robertson wanted an accounting from each county and regiment. Depending on its population, a county had to furnish a specific number of men to the army. Every time a man enlisted, he was credited to a certain county. Robertson now had to work through a mountain of paperwork, making sure the credits for enlistments tallied with what the counties claimed. Each county knew how many men it was to contribute; if a county did not yield enough recruits, a draft of the available manpower would make up the difference. Once the paperwork ended and assessments were made, enlistments for the new regiments would be allowed to continue.[83]

The first tally of those counties not affected by the draft came from Robertson's office on 3 February 1863. Other lists followed in quick succession. Recruiting was allowed only in those counties which appeared on the record. When a full list was published, the draft was inaugurated in counties still in arrears.[84]

It would take Michigan most of 1863 (using a complicated formula that factored in the length of each volunteer's enlistment) to fully implement the draft. In the meantime, the legislature inaugurated a state bounty system to prod lukewarm or undecided patriots to sign up, even though local communitites had already proffered money payments to volunteers for more than half a year.[85]

Fraud and Deceit

As commanding officer, Colonel DeLand had to move the mountains of red tape associated with starting a new regiment. He kept up a constant correspondence with Lt. Col. John R. Smith in Detroit, pleading that his enlistees be mustered.[86] Only a specifically designated member of the Regular Army could muster volunteers into the service, so it was imperative to DeLand that such a representative visit Camp Chandler. Worse yet, soldiers received no pay until they were mustered. There was bounty money, though. The federal government offered $100 to new recruits, $25 upon enlisting and the balance when mustered.[87]

The state of Michigan began offering a $50 bounty in March 1863. The payment of bounties caused many men to weigh the odds of enlisting. Private soldiers received $13 a month, not a munificent sum even in those days. But $100 and any local bounty money, plus the monthly wage a man could send home to his loved ones, would be enough to see his family through hard times.

The federal government decided how many men each loyal state would furnish for the war effort. If a state could not produce the requisite number of enlistments, the remainder would be drafted. Drafted men did not receive a bounty, but they could hire substitutes to serve in their places.[88]

Uncertainty of the law spawned problems. Moscow (in Hillsdale County) was unable to defray the bounties its committee had promised volunteers for the First Michigan Sharpshooters. Men were duly enlisted, but they balked at military service when their local bounties were not paid. Because they were enlisted under false promises, DeLand agreed to plead their case to a higher authority. Irritated by such fraud, he complained to his superiors that "There has been more trouble and shuffling in Hillsdale [County] than all the other counties in the State."[89]

Following Moscow's lead, the town fathers of Camden (also in Hillsdale County) pulled the same shenanigans. Four Camden men enlisted in the Sharpshooters with the promise of a local bounty. Once accepted into the regiment, the men requested their bounties from the town board, only to be refused.

Lieutenant Colonel Smith called the system "cruel," and declared that such communities should have their names published so that other men would not be duped. Nonetheless, he continued, the men who volunteered and were sworn into the service were still required to serve. There was no appeal, he went on, because the "Government cannot be considered as a party to such a transaction. Government officers and agents have no authority to make provisions, or enter into obligations, which the Government is not bound to fulfil [*sic*]." Newspapers published the facts of the case to alert volunteers. Unfortunately for the men involved, the local communities of Moscow and Camden never made good on their promises.[90]

Desertions

In the overall recruiting structure, someone (in the case of the First Michigan Sharpshooters it was DeLand) was empowered by the government to delegate authority for recruiting soldiers. These recruits were then to be collected into companies and sent as an entity to the rendezvous camp. All transportation costs were borne by the government.

The recruiter was subject to a series of risks, not the least of which was the loss of funds incurred by faulty recruiting procedures. He could also forfeit his anticipated commission by taking too much time enlisting the requisite number of men. If the time limit expired, the recruits could be transferred to another company, and the recruiter lost both his investment and his expected rank in the regiment.[91] DeLand knew the law and worked hard to keep his regiment and his rank.

No sooner had the recruiting officers reported to Camp Chandler than desertions ate into the regiment like a cancer. Men were issued uniforms, and then they took "French leave." During their stay at Camp Chandler the Sharpshooters lost at least 45 men who left the regiment for good.[92] Some of the deserters had run up bills while at Camp Chandler, telling their officers to deduct the money from their future bounty payment.[93]

Circumstances were not conducive to keeping men at the camp. Previous regiments had been raised and mustered within a month or two, most of them in the warmer months. Colonel DeLand complained that "desertions began to become so frequent that they fully counterbalanced the increase by recruits."[94] He blamed the weather: "the winter was cold and dreary, [and] the barracks utterly unfit for winter quarters."[95] DeLand had to send officers he could hardly spare to apprehend the deserters.[96] At other times he sent letters asking some authority to detain suspected or actual deserters.[97] He also demanded that men who were paid bounties to join the Sharpshooters be delivered to him by officers commanding other regiments.[98]

In one case DeLand threatened prosecution. Wesley Cross of South Haven had helped his son Alpheus desert and flee to Canada. DeLand gave the elder Cross an option. Either:

> return the deserter inside of thirty days to this Camp, & he will be received as absent without leave, or I will lay the matter before the U.S. Attorney and move for your speedy prosecution for the offense.[99]

Despite the threat, Alpheus Cross never returned to the regiment.

Rank and File

Colonel DeLand originally intended that the Sharpshooters be made up of young men.[100] Recruits had to be 18 years old, but circumstances permitted younger boys to volunteer. Musicians and drummers, if they received their parents' permission, were allowed to join; some, though, failed to obtain the requisite concession. Three boys—William M. Squires, Henry Elliott, and Albert Rickard—all of whom were underage, were discharged after their parents "made personal applications for their discharge." [101]

Out of the 1,300 officers and men who would serve in the regiment, at least 41 were under the age of 18. How many more lied about their age will never be known. Two of them were only 13 when they enlisted. William Duverney, the youngest of the volunteers, came into the regiment as a musician. He and his half-brother, 18-year-old John Kedgnot, enlisted from Grand Haven in December 1862. The two young enlistees were also the first Indians in the Sharpshooters. Both would serve in Company B.[102]

George W. Stone, the other 13-year-old, joined Company D on 6 March 1863. His was a unique history. Born in New Bern, North Carolina, as George W. Timmons, he somehow wound up New York as a young child; he was sent to Michigan in 1857 with 30 other boys and girls. Sponsored by the Children's Aid Society, orphaned and abandoned children from the East were transported west with the hope that they would be adopted by loving families. Arriving on "Orphan Trains," these youngsters were generally trotted off to a nearby church where they were chosen by the local citizens. It was an idealistic venture that continued into the twentieth century.

The 8-year-old Timmons found a home with the Simeon Stone family of Albion. As he grew older, the lad became a favorite of George N. Davis of the same town. When Davis began recruiting for the Sharpshooters, he enlisted the boy. Their lives became "closely connected" from that time on. Stone would survive the war, missing only one engagement with the enemy. He would go on to revel in the Grand Army of the Republic, rarely missing any kind of encampment, and he would die celebrating the end of another war.[103]

Eli Nichols came next in age. Just 14 when he enlisted in Company I in August 1863, he, too, would survive the war, being mustered out as a corporal in July 1865.[104]

On the other side of the regimental ledger were 102 men over the age of 40. The oldest "official" recruit was Evon B. Webster, who enlisted in January 1864, when he gave his age as 50. Battle wounds cut short his army career, and he was discharged for disability in October 1864.[105]

All told, the average age in the regiment was 25. Colonel DeLand was 36. His field and staff officers ranged in age from 19 to 45. Ed Buckbee, the adjutant, was the youngest; Jacob Mc-Nett, second assistant surgeon, was the oldest.[106] Among the line officers, Capt. Lucien Meigs was the oldest at 42, and the youngest was 2nd Lt. William Randall at 20.[107] The average age of the company officers was 29.

At least 69 families were represented by two or more men in the First Michigan Sharpshooters. There were fathers and sons, such as 44-year-old Clark Fox, Sr., and his sons 16-year-old Clark, Jr., and 18-year-old Charles. Sets of brothers—James, John, and Samuel Harper of Emmett; Marion and William Northrup of Kalamazoo; John and Louis Shomin of La Croix; and Albert, Charles, and Stephen Quance of Camden—left home together for the great adventure of soldiering.

Older men now had a real chance to enlist. The local, state, and federal bounties would provide the needed sustenance for the loved ones left behind. A husband was assured of his wife's economic well-being. Two or more brothers saw the bounties as an opportunity to leave the family farm. The money they received would enable their parents to hire help or buy goods while they were away in the army.

Typical of many recruits were the Stephens brothers from Assyria Township in Barry County. John, 18, enlisted in Company A, putting away his studies for the duration of the war. His younger brother Charles, 16, went into Company A as a musician. Otis F. Kimball, 17, of Calhoun County also joined the same company. His father had served as a drummer boy in the War of 1812, and his grandfather fought in the Revolution. Martial derring-do stirred his blood, and Kimball was one of the earliest recruits in the regiment. He would also be one of the first casualties in a wooded tract called the Wilderness.[108]

The Sharp brothers, Mathew and Warren, of Scipio, enlisted two days after Christmas 1862. Their nephew, Zena Ransom, signed his enlistment papers the same day in Jonesville. All served in Company C under Captain Meigs. Only one would survive the war.

At least 37 officers and men brought with them experience from previous war service. Of the officers, 12 (including the three field officers) were old campaigners who had experienced the war first-hand; they had "seen the elephant." Most of the enlisted veterans had been discharged for various disabilities but had sufficiently recovered to join the colors again. A majority of them became noncommissioned officers; their knowledge of war and army know-how was readily put to use.

Joseph Stevens of Company B was a good example. Born in Yorkshire, England, in 1842, he came with his family to Hillsdale, where they settled. In June 1861 he enlisted in the Fourth Michigan Infantry. Captured during the Seven Days' Battles on the Peninsula in 1862, Stevens wasted away in Libby Prison until his exchange. Hospitalized, then discharged for chronic illness, he waited only one week in Hillsdale before joining the Sharpshooters. He entered as a sergeant and became a rock upon which many Company B men depended.[109]

Leverette N. Case of Jonesville had served with the Seventh Michigan Infantry for a year until his discharge for disability in July 1862. A year later he signed up with the Sharpshooters. Promoted through the ranks, by the end of the war he was a brevet major.[110]

The Indians

Although most of Michigan's regiments came from existing militia units, major cities, or a single congressional district, recruiters for the First Michigan Sharpshooters had to canvass the entire state. No part of the state was left untouched, yet finding enough men to fill the ranks remained difficult. Fortunately, there was still a relatively numerous group of men untapped by previous regiments. Michigan's Native Americans were not citizens of the United States, unless by Act of Congress or some other special exemption. Neither were they subject to the draft.[111] There were some overtures to recruit them early in the war, but in general Indian volunteers had been rejected out of hand.

George Copway, a Chippewa Indian and Methodist minister, actually made a proposition to the federal government in May 1861 to raise a regiment of Indians from the Great Lakes area, "not to be employed for using the tomahawk or scalping knife upon the people of the South but as scouts and runners for the army. They will be young men, inured to hardship, fleet as deers [*sic*], shrewd and cautious."[112]

Copway was a well-known missionary in the Michigan region, his territory extending into Minnesota, Wisconsin, Illinois, and Iowa. He had traveled widely in Europe and numbered among his friends the poet Henry Wadsworth Longfellow. Copway had authored five books, which mainly detailed Native American life, and was an able spokesman for the Indians of the state.[113] The national government quickly ended Copway's plan. His scheme to recruit Indians for the Union army "under the auspices of Michigan" was quietly shelved.[114]

While Copway was talking to officials in Washington, the Indians of northern Michigan had a gathering near the Straits of Mackinac. Two hundred of them "offered there [*sic*] services to fight for the Stars and Stripes."[115] A half-dozen Chippewa Indians, led by an immense, heavily-muscled 25-year-old named Thomas Ke-chi-ti-go, tried to enlist in Saginaw, but they, too, were refused.[116]

The ultimate decision to include Indians in the ranks rested with the Michigan legislature, not with the war department in Washington, DC. The days when red men and white had fought each other on Michigan's frontier were not that distant. Even though there had been no hostilities between the two groups since the War of 1812, the very idea of having "uncivilized" men participate in a "civilized" war rankled not a few minds. The Detroit *Free Press*, which continually spouted the rhetoric of the Democratic Party, reported that Copway's proposal was:

> fortunately nipped in the bud by the legislature. Every man knows the system of warfare adopted by these demi-savages, and the civilized people of the northern states will hardly consent this year [1861] to become responsible for the performance of such allies.[117]

Even the Republican-backed Detroit *Advertiser and Tribune* in mid 1863 did not enthusiastically endorse the idea of Indians representing Michigan on the battlefield:

> as a race, they [the Indians] have not yet reached that degree of civilization which should entitle them to all the rights, and place on them all the responsibilities of citizenship. Very few of them can read, and by far the greater portion neither speak nor understand our language. At the best they are but semi-civilized. . . . They are a poor, ignorant and dependent race.[118]

But the situation in 1863 had changed dramatically from that of mid 1861. Men were desperately needed—all men! Thousands of Indians lived on the fringe of white settlements in Michigan. Prejudice finally gave in to common sense, and the legislators came to realize that Indians could make good soldiers. After all, many were excellent marksmen. They had to be; in the woods a man's family depended on his unerring aim to put food on the table. At the same time, the lawmakers were giving in to the county officers who were clamoring for some relief from the draft. As long as *any* man enlisted from a particular county, that county's board would not have to draft another white man.

To forestall the state from taking any more men via the draft, the board of supervisors in northern Michigan's Oceana County in late 1862 informed the appropriate authorities that 94 white men, "Citizens of the county of Oceana," enlisted together with "thirty-four Indians whom we regard as citizens of said county." The Indians may not have been allowed to vote or hold public office, but they were not subject to the draft, either. The supervisors saw to it that those "thirty-four Indians" in the army saved a like number of their white neighbors from the draft.[119]

CHAPTER 2

Other Important Work

Camp Chandler

Herculean labors awaited the Sharpshooters at Camp Chandler. New enlistees had to be transformed into soldiers. Men were separated into barracks, company officers began to assert themselves, and the seemingly endless train of paperwork was processed.[1] With company rolls completed, officers drew clothing allotments for their men from the regimental quartermaster.[2] Everything was done "by the book."

To curtail any adverse actions by the men in his command, DeLand issued orders forbidding more than five men of the same detachment to leave the camp in a group, "and these to have the written permit of the officer in charge."[3] A daily schedule was posted:

Reveille and Roll	7:00 AM
Breakfast	8:00 AM
Squad Drill	9:00-10:00 AM
Company Drill	10:30-12:00
Dinner	12:30 PM
Squad Drill	1:00-2:00 PM
Company Drill	1:00-4:00 PM
Supper	5:30 PM
Roll Call	8:00 PM
Lights Out	9:00 PM[4]

Realizing that most of his officers possessed little familiarity with conducting drill, Colonel DeLand soon added an hour of "Officer Drill" in the morning. Immediately thereafter, the officers imparted their fresh knowledge to their respective commands.[5]

The new officers not only had difficulty drilling their recruits, they also had trouble controlling them. The men were getting acclimated to army life, and some did not like it much. DeLand ordered the reporting of all "discourteous behavior[,] disobedience of orders or using improper or impudant [sic] language" expressed by the enlistees when charged to perform military duties by a noncommissioned officer or guard.[6] Men continued to leave the compound regardless of orders, so Colonel DeLand demanded that all written permits to do so be countersigned by the lieutenant colonel or himself.[7]

Some of the rank and file, being in a strange place beset with outlandish regulations, felt the rules of propriety did not apply to them. Rambunctious recruits broke boards in some of the barracks buildings. Instead of using "sinks" (actually nothing more than small sheds over large holes in the ground), men relieved themselves anywhere in the camp.[8] Not that Camp Chandler was in pristine condition when the Sharpshooters entered it. Three other regiments had previously used it as a rendezvous point, the last one having vacated the premises the previous September.[9]

While on leave in Kalamazoo, some of the men took advantage of the fact that they were unknown to the general populace; they habitually insulted the local citizenry, committing what the commanding officer termed "gross outrages upon citizens, particularly female." All he could do without named culprits was to fret and threaten.[10] When a malefactor was discovered, justice was swift. Charles Foote, one of the recruits, was remanded to the civil authorities on a charge of "larceny from dwelling house in day time." Tried and convicted, Foote was sentenced to three years in Jackson Prison.[11]

Colonel DeLand advised his officers to "crack down" on men illegally absenting themselves from camp and to withhold passes from those men "guilty of improper conduct while absent or returns [sic] in a state of intoxication."[12] Company commanders delegated authority to their noncommissioned officers and made sure all squads were thoroughly drilled in military courtesy. Talking back to an officer—commissioned or noncommissioned—had to be immediately reported to the officer of the day, and the miscreant was arrested and confined in short order.[13]

Courts-Martial Begin in Earnest

Toward the end of February a regimental court-martial board was convened to hear a docket of charges against members of the regiment. The regimental quartermaster, 1st Lt. David G. Palmer, acted as board president; 2nd Lts. Asahel W. Nichols and Robert F. Hill took their places as the other two members of the board. Capt. Levant H. Rhines served as judge advocate.[14]

Sgt. Charles G. Conn was the first man in the regiment to appear in front of the court-martial board. Charged with "Maliciously injuring the property of private citizens" and then overstaying the limits of his pass from camp on 18 February, the court found Conn guilty of only the second charge. His punishment was a public reprimand from Colonel DeLand during a regimental dress parade.[15] Sergeant Conn's two companions in crime, Pvts. Daniel Gore and Benjamin F. Waters, received reprimands from the court and were returned to their detachments, their behavior being blamed on Conn's bad example.[16]

Pvt. William Gerrington left camp without obtaining a pass and was sentenced to two days in the new guardhouse. Soon after his release, Gerrington disappeared from the regiment. Pvt. Luke Hatch, accused of "running the guard" and eluding the patrol sent to search for him, also received two days in the lockup.[17] Charges leveled against Pvt. William Wheadon included the same brought against Hatch. He, too, was remanded to the custody of the jailer.

Lastly, the case against Pvt. Edgar O. Freeman, charged with being absent from camp for three days before being apprehended by civil authorities, was heard. Pleading guilty, he occupied the guardhouse for three days, and $10 was deducted from his pay to cover the cost of his arrest. To forestall any escape attempts, the prisoners had to surrender all matches and knives before their incarceration.[18]

At the next session of the court, held on 21 February 1863, Pvt. Charles Wheeler admitted his guilt for being absent without leave; after being "deprived of matches and cutting instruments," he was confined in the guardhouse for two days.[19]

Absences from camp continued. Three more privates soon occupied the guardhouse. A patrol guard picked up Pvts. Wallace

Ibbotson, Frank Wagoner, and Charles B. Johnesse for overstaying their leave time. The court-martial board sentenced each to only twenty-four hours confinement, but on bread and water rations.[20] Serving in the army was still a lark for the trio. The future held unknown horrors enough for them. Johnesse would soon cause the death of a friend, and Wagoner would die facing the enemy in some rain-soaked woods in Virginia.

The New Chaplain

David Heagle, a 26-year-old Baptist minister, joined the regiment as its chaplain. Originally from Montgomery County, New York, he had recently graduated from Union College and Rochester Theological Seminary. Destined to live a long and productive life, Reverend Heagle would survive all the field officers and most of the line officers. His reports to the Detroit *Advertiser and Tribune* kept the home folks attuned to the fortunes of the Sharpshooters after they left Michigan.[21]

With the arrival of Heagle, much of the drill that daily occupied the soldiers' lives was omitted on the Sabbath. Officers and men were expected to attend divine services at 2:00 PM "in the large building" in Camp Chandler. The officer of the day saw to it that the structure was heated and further readied for the observance of the Lord's day.[22]

During January Colonel DeLand managed to sort out his company commanders from the aspiring officers who had besieged him at his reception earlier that month. By the beginning of February only one full company (officially commanded by Capt. Levant C. Rhines) occupied the camp. Other companies had to be consolidated, making for some heated debates.[23] The changes meant hard feelings on the part of a number of officers, but it could not be helped. If certain individuals wanted to be commissioned officers, it was imperative that they enlist more men.

To further streamline the daily routine, DeLand ordered the quartermaster to issue cooking paraphernalia—plates, eating utensils, and other sundry kitchen items—to each company commander. "Raw rations" entered the vocabulary of the regiment. Two men from each company were detailed as cooks. By this method the regiment saved government money. Fewer rations would be wasted, DeLand believed, if smaller batches of men were accountable for the amount of food prepared.[24]

Whether they liked it or not, the men slowly grew accustomed to taking orders. They did things they had no idea were covered by army regulations. One day, because of an outbreak of smallpox in the Kalamazoo area, Colonel DeLand ordered his entire command vaccinated against the disease. Officers and men were further prompted to report all new recruits to the surgeon for vaccination.[25]

Camp Chandler continued to remain a cold purgatory for enlistees and officers alike—the temporary housing, the trickle of new men into the regiment—any place would have been better. Developing events on the other side of the state slowly brought change to the regiment.

Copperhead Territory

Detroit was a sharply divided city. True, Wayne County voted Republican in 1860, but the Democrats had always enjoyed a healthy majority there. The area was ready to return to the Democratic fold.[26] Because of its proximity to Canada (only a few minutes away by ferryboat), Detroit was a deserter's dream. "Copperheads" were much in evidence. The Detroit *Free Press*, a very vocal Democratic organ in an age of rabidly partisan politics, continually lambasted the Lincoln administration and vilified the very idea of abolitionism.

There had been an altercation of considerable importance back in July 1862. At a public recruitment meeting on the Campus Martius, the open area adjoining City Hall in downtown Detroit, a mob tried to attack the speaker's dais, on which was seated a number of Detroit's premier politicians, including Mayor William C. Duncan; Congressman William A. Howard, a friend of Colonel DeLand; Detroit's richest citizen, Eber B. Ward; and former Territorial Governor, Senator, Secretary of State, and Minister to France Lewis Cass, the grand old man of Michigan's Democratic Party. There was a lively round of shouting, swearing, and fisticuffs before hecklers were dispersed.[27]

A worse affair—a race riot—took place in early March 1863. Negro-hating whites beat and burned their way through Detroit's "Colored" district. At least two people died in the riot, and more than 30 dwellings were destroyed. Detachments from the

Nineteenth U.S. Infantry (stationed at Detroit's Fort Wayne) and from the Twenty-seventh Michigan Infantry (then being recruited at Ypsilanti) were hustled off to Detroit to quell the disturbance. An inquiry into the origins of the riot found much of the citizenry opposed to the Lincoln administration's view of civil rights. A racist mood, encouraged by the editor of the Detroit *Free Press*, pervaded the town.[28]

The Dearborn Arsenal

The adjutant general of Michigan needed guards at the United States Arsenal at Dearborn, a small settlement twelve miles west of Detroit, and the Sharpshooters fit the bill. In early February newly acquired stores were added to those already in place at the arsenal. Thousands of modern Enfield and Springfield rifles were warehoused there.[29]

The arsenal consisted of eleven brick buildings arranged around a 360-foot square. Built in 1833, it was used as a munitions depot for Detroit and other military posts throughout the Old Northwest. The rifles, packed twenty to a box, were stacked in the main three-story building. A Captain J. Peel and a few soldiers of the Regular Army guarded the grounds. Such a small military detachment in charge of so many weapons attracted attention from all quarters.

In late February a detachment of Sharpshooters was ordered to Dearborn to protect the arsenal and the weapons stored there. Accordingly, Colonel DeLand detailed Captain Rhines's company, under the command of Maj. John Piper. Quartermaster Palmer issued all necessary food, clothing, and equipage to the departing men, who were eyed with envy by those left behind. Jacob McNett, second assistant surgeon, provided the requisite medical stores and accompanied Rhines. They left Kalamazoo by train on the night of 26 February.[30] Just over 300 men remained at Camp Chandler.[31] As a group, they detested the place.

During April the Sharpshooters sustained 20 more desertions.[32] Colonel DeLand's irritation with the weather, the condition of the buildings, and the complaints of his officers and his men became more aggravated by the desertion rate. His regiment did not seem to grow; the desertions balanced out the new recruits.[33] He finally and plaintively asked the adjutant general to move all the Sharpshooters to Dearborn, and permission was soon granted. At the end of April 1863 the Sharpshooters packed their bags and loaded their knapsacks, bid Camp Chandler a hearty good riddance, and departed by train for the Dearborn arsenal. The move, reported Chaplain Heagle, was "favorable for the regiment, and wise for the State."[34]

As soon as they reached their new quarters, DeLand strongly enjoined the rank and file not to deface or destroy any government property. Officers and noncommissioned officers learned they would "be held personally and strictly responsible for the conduct of their men in these matters."[35] To end any problem before it even began, the colonel commanded his men not to commit any "personal and public nuisance." DeLand wanted no repeat of the odious acts committed by the recruits when they first reported to Camp Chandler.[36]

The arsenal in Dearborn was truly "a very great improvement" on Camp Chandler. Chaplain Heagle's articles in the Detroit *Advertiser and Tribune* not only kept the public abreast of regimental activities, but his attitude mirrored that of his colonel. A loyal subordinate, Heagle always reflected the official position of the regiment, which of course was that of its commander. Dearborn was small and clean, announced Heagle, "no detriment, but a great advantage to the regiment." Morale was good and "Everything looks prosperous." So prosperous, in fact, that 16 new men joined the colors only one week after the Sharpshooters moved to the arsenal.[37] Heagle ended his report with news that could have come only from Colonel DeLand: "It is hinted now that this regiment will probably remain in the State for some time to come."[38]

As soon as the Sharpshooters set up shop at Dearborn, they had their first brush with a Copperhead. An old resident of the area, Cyrus Randall, approached various guards around the encampment and harangued them on their political views. Officially, Randall used "opprobrious & treasonable language . . . towards the sentinels & in their presence."[39] In actuality he let the Sharpshooters know that he definitely sided with the rebel cause.

For a number of days and nights Randall harrassed the guards with his outbursts. He sought them out time after time, and involved himself in "hurrahing . . . for Jeff Davis and the success of the rebellion, and in the very faces of our soldiers, denouncing the work in which they are engaged."[40] To some of the Sharpshooters, Randall's platitudes were nothing less than insults to their patriotism, and according to military law were liable to punishment.[41]

Lt. Guy Newbre, the officer of the guard, finally arrested Randall on the orders of DeLand. The old rebel found himself hauled into camp, jailed for a few hours, then brought into De-Land's presence. Putting on a show for the unwitting victim, the colonel vigorously questioned Randall and then "magnanimously" released him, but not before forcing him to take the oath of allegiance. Chastised, Randall did not bother the guards again.[42]

Recruiting Continues

Colonel DeLand had much more on his mind than some harmless old Copperhead. His regiment was woefully under-strength; he had to recruit actively. To that end he saturated the state with recruiters. He sent no less than 54 men on recruiting duty in Michigan, 13 of whom had a double tour; 17 officers of the regiment had to take their turn, a number of them twice. Included in the total were nine men not in the regiment who hoped for commissions by enlisting others. As with these volun-teer regiments, any man who enlisted the requisite number was eligible to become a line officer.[43]

Of the nine recruiters not in the regiment, not one raised enough men to obtain a commission. Some were unique in their approach, though. James Walton of Lenawee County received permission to sign up men for the Sharpshooters: "All recruits reported by said Walton are to be assigned to his son for the purpose of obtaining for him a commmission & discharge from the Regt of which he is now a member."[44]

Caleb A. Ensign of Jonesville, also not a member of the Sharpshooters, received authorization to recruit men, for which he was to receive a second lieutenant's appointment. Ensign never completed his assignment and was never mustered into the Sharpshooters. He was more successful raising men for the First Michigan Engineers and Mechanics, and was commissioned a sec-ond lieutenant in that organization in December 1863; he ad-vanced to first lieutenant four months later.[45]

Professor John A. Banfield, former principal of the Dow-agiac Union School, tried his hand at earning a commission in the Sharpshooters by enlisting "teachers and students." He was not heard from again.[46]

Believing Hillsdale County to be fertile ground for enlist-ments, Harry W. Horton obtained permission to recruit men there. He was "authorized to raise a *full company* provided the same be *completed* and *mustered* within *forty days*," an utterly impossible order, given the success of the previous recruiters and the rather slim pickings left there. Horton did not receive a commission either.[47]

The Indians Begin to Arrive

Although DeLand's recruiters combed the length and breadth of Michigan, there were relatively few enlistees except for a new group, Indians. One of the first to join was Thomas Ke-chi-ti-go of Saginaw. Ke-chi-ti-go, who had been refused enlistment in 1861, brought some men with him. An extremely strong and large man, he was called "Big Tom" by the white Sharpshooters who were hard put to remember the names of the Native Americans. He received one of the sergeants' positions.[48]

Another early Indian enlistee was Payson Wolfe of Northport. Thirty years old in 1863, Wolfe had always been a man to lead the crowd, rather than one to follow anonymously behind. When 19, he married the 15-year-old daughter of the local white Protestant missionary.[49] In the 1856 election, Wolfe, who was an American citizen, was the only Indian to vote the Republican ticket. His father-in-law, Rev. George N. Smith, noted that the others "voted Democratic out of fear of the [government] Agent who would take their tickets and give them [a] Democratic ticket and he put them in such fear that they could not resist him."[50]

When the war began in 1861, Wolfe's wife made a Union flag, four feet by eight feet. Wolfe painted the stars on the flag and he and his father-in-law "got a pole and raised the flag on the north end of our house."[51] There was no doubt as to Payson Wolfe's sympathies. When he left home to join the Sharpshooters, 19-year-old Charles Allen accompanied him. Young Allen would become Company K's original first sergeant. He would also be the first in the company to give his life for his country.

On 1 June 1863 Lts. William J. Driggs and William S. McClelland, the latter never receiving a commission in the Sharpshooters, assisted by William Collins, an interpreter and enlisted Indian from Isabella, were detailed on "Recruiting Service among the Indians in northern Michigan," with headquarters at Pentwater.[52] Driggs was then 24 years old. A sickly man, he had previously enlisted in the Sixth Michigan Cavalry as a private in

August 1862 and then transferred to the Seventh Michigan Cavalry as a corporal a month later. Discharged from the service on 8 December 1862, he turned up as a recruiter for the Sharpshooters. His father was a respected Republican congressman from Saginaw, which may have played some role when the younger Driggs sought a commission in the Sharpshooters.[53]

The two lieutenants were empowered by DeLand to offer the Indians the same benefits bestowed on white soldiers. Since the new state bounty act was passed in March 1863, each new recruit was given $50, "to be paid as soon as mustered." Another $25 U.S. bounty would be paid as soon as the company was organized. Each soldier would also be paid $13 per month "and all necessary clothing & subsistence during his term of enlistment as is provided by Law."[54] DeLand took considerable pains to ensure that Driggs explained to the Native Americans exactly what they needed to know. "Great care," he told his officers, "will be taken in enlisting Indians to give them all necessary & correct information upon all subjects, relating to pay, bounties, &c."[55]

On the Fourth of July quite a celebration was held on the reservation in Oceana County.[56] The principal speaker was Capt. Edwin V. Andress, who looked resplendent in his officer's uniform. Andress would ultimately command the Indian company. Louis Genereau, who had considerable influence with this band of Ottawas although he was only half Indian, interpreted Andress's remarks for the crowd. Also backing up Andress was Chief Paw-baw-me, one of the Ottawa subchiefs. Both orators urged the young men to enlist. Led by young Louis Genereau, Jr., the 18-year-old son of the interpreter, 25 men joined the colors. All would serve in Company K, the "Indian company."

The next day Captain Andress led his enlistees, accompanied by nearly the entire reservation, to the dock at Pentwater. The departure was filled with the pathos, fear of the unknown, and anxiety attendant to such spectacles. The young men boarded the steamboat, and were soon off on their great adventure.[57]

Other Indians were recruited at Little Traverse Bay, from the settlements at Bear River, Little Traverse, and La Croix, and the Mackinac region. Some came from the Isabella Reservation in the center of the state, others from the Saginaw area. Recruiting in the Saginaw region evidently progressed well, for Lieutenant Driggs passed through Detroit on 22 May with 24 Native Americans he had enlisted there.[58]

Second Lt. Garrett A. Graveraet led a recruiting drive at

Little Traverse. One of those he signed up was an Ottawa chieftain, Daniel Mwa-ke-wenah, or Daniel Wells, who lived across Little Traverse Bay at Bear Creek.[59] Graveraet, scion of a well-known fur-trading family in northern Michigan, is referred to in the records as a "halfbreed," and he exhibited the best of both worlds. His education was prodigious; fluent in English and Chippewa, as well as other modern languages, he was a talented musician, teacher, and artist.[60] Although only 23 years old, he was already well known in the region.[61]

One of the lieutenant's recruits was his own father, 55-year-old Henry Graveraet, who gave his age as 45. Formerly the probate judge of Emmet County, the elder Graveraet was mustered in as a sergeant of Company K;[62] he was the only non-Indian enlisted man in the company.[63] Another of the Indian recruits had recently finished a term as the Emmet County registrar. Francis Tabasasch, 38 years old, signed his papers in La Croix, along with a number of his neighbors.[64]

Every week or so the Detroit newspapers mentioned "another fine little squad" of Sharpshooters, usually under the charge of Major Piper, making the trip from Dearborn to Detroit to be mustered into the service at Col. J. R. Smith's office.[65]

As they would be throughout their military career, the Indians were singled out in the press. No other Michigan regiment had such a concentration of Native Americans. This group was indeed unique. Colonel Smith (the mustering officer), liking what he saw, said, they are "nearly all tall and good-looking fellows. They are the stuff, no doubt, of which good sharpshooters can be easily made."[66]

The line officers of Company K entered the regiment with good credentials. Captain Andress and Second Lieutenant Graveraet spoke a number of languages, including French and local Indian dialects. First Lieutenant Driggs, whom one white enlisted man called "a typical English dude," at least had previous military experience and was "a good fellow and a good officer."[67]

From the beginning there was little social intermingling between the whites and Indians of the regiment. Charles Bibbins of Company E later reminisced about the Indians:

> Very few of them had any knowledge of the English language, which made it very hard to drill them like the other soldiers, and they often rebelled in many little things they were required to do, and had to be handled with soft gloves, so to speak, in order to

keep them in line with the other soldiers. The idol of their company was Big Tom, an Indian Sergeant of immense proportions, and it was thru this Sergeant that the officers of the company were able to handle them.

These Indians made fairly good soldiers, but could not be trusted with any special duty on account of their limited knowledge of English. They never associated with the other soldiers, always keeping strictly to themselves from the time they joined the regiment until they were mustered out.[68]

Recruiting continued briskly. On 3 June Hooker A. DeLand was mustered as captain of Company F. That meant six companies were filled, or almost filled. At that time it was hoped that two companies of Indians would be raised, thus making only one other full company of whites to be recruited.[69]

Captain DeLand received quite a bit of help from his cousin, the colonel. Unassigned recruits were placed under the younger DeLand's "control and instruction."[70] Some officers thought he did not merit his appointment, but the newspapers reported none of that. The reporters saw a raw body of men fast becoming a fighting unit. "The regiment . . . has already attained," reported the *Advertiser and Tribune*, "in discipline a good degree of perfection."[71] That good news probably came from the chaplain.

More Courts-Martial

Soon after the Sharpshooters' arrival at the arsenal, several complaints made their way to the regimental headquarters. A few enterprising soldiers had either passed or attempted to pass some worthless bank notes onto the local citizenry.[72] In another case, Pvt. Edward Terwillager (a wagoner in Co. E) was court-martialed and found guilty of stealing a shirt, coat, "and other articles of value" while on duty at the Old Capital Building in Detroit. He had to make restitution and was sentenced to five days at hard labor. On 7 May 1863 Pvt. Luke Hatch of Company E was convicted of sleeping on guard duty. Previously he had "run the guard." The court forced him to do "hard labor with ball and chain [for] ten days and a stoppage of twenty days['] pay.[73]

The misuse of alcohol contributed continual offenders to the guardhouse. On the same day that Private Hatch began serving his sentence, Pvt. Charles M. Wheeler of the same company found himself under "close confinement on bread and water for ten days and to the stoppage of one month['s] pay" because he was so drunk that he could not even report for guard duty.[74]

At times the court-martial board varied its punishment. Pvt. Lawrence Banks had to spend four days in the guardhouse for drunkenness, except for two hours on each of those days "when he shall be publicly paraded wearing a barrel labeled 'The Price of Whiskey.'"[75] Pvt. Frank Shields was so intent on deserting while intoxicated that he had to be physically restrained. After serving his sentence of being shackled to a ball and chain for fifteen days and losing one month's pay, he deserted at the first opportunity.[76]

Colonel DeLand finally initiated a "black list" of offenders to forestall the plethora of violations of furlough and pass privileges. Any soldier overstaying his leave would see his name posted on the regimental black list. No leave of any kind would be issued to anyone whose name appeared on the list for 30 days thereafter.[77] A week later Pvt. Thomas Allyn (Co. D), at 45 one of the older men of the regiment, attempted to bring liquor into camp. His name topped the black list.[78]

The provost marshal for Detroit, Capt. John Newberry, having had too many errant Sharpshooters brought before him, was finally exasperated. Any excuse a soldier could make up was used by DeLand's men when the provost guard apprehended them. "I was separated from my officers; I missed my train," those arrested would plead. "They clearly are such deserters," Newberry reported. "Please control your charges," he demanded. A harried Colonel DeLand sent another order out to his men, particularly the officers. Company commanders were to keep full records on all their men. Furloughs must list the "name, company, date, destination, age, height, description of person, when expires, and when returned." Stoppage of pay would result from days not accounted for. Such unexpired absences must stop, DeLand insisted again;[79] but transgressions continued unabated.

After Pvt. George Wyant spent five days in the guardhouse on a diet of bread and water, he served five more days in solitary confinement. All this was the result of his cursing at, and then attacking and beating Pvt. Wilson Ryan. Wyant bided his time and deserted a month later. Ryan went on to fight the rebels; captured at Petersburg, he later died of starvation and disease in the infamous Andersonville prison pen.[80]

A bigger fight broke out a couple of weeks later. Three soldiers, Pvts. Byron E. Potter, William Van Dusen, and Charles Wheeler (the last no stranger to the court-martial board) were brought up on charges of "disorderly and unsoldierly conduct." "Potter[,] for not using his influence to quell the riot in which the others were engaged," received a public reprimand. Van Dusen and Wheeler found themselves confined to camp for the next month.[81]

The First Casualty

By far the most serious breach of discipline occurred on 11 May when Pvt. Abel Shaw was mortally wounded while standing guard.

The enlisted men, being hard-pressed for excitement, invented little entertainments. The guards at the arsenal camp walked their posts with unloaded weapons.[82] At times, before a soldier mounted guard, his messmates would secretly load his piece. Then, coming off duty, the guard would snap the lock on the cap and the weapon would fire, startling the man and provoking hysterical laughter among his friends. At other times a handful of sand would be poured down a friend's musket barrel. When the officer of the guard checked the weapons, extra punishment would be doled out to the owner of the dirty musket, all to the merriment of the unfortunate soldier's friends. But what happened on 11 May caused grief all around.

Someone had loaded Pvt. Abel Shaw's weapon with powder and ball. Then Pvt. Charles Johnesse entered the picture. A friend of Shaw's, Johnesse played the unwitting murderer. Shaw stood idly talking to some friends with his upper arm resting on his rifle muzzle. Johnesse crept up behind him and snapped the lock on the guard's gun, hoping that the cap would fire and startle the unsuspecting Shaw.[83] To his horror, the musket fired; the ball tore through Shaw's shoulder, smashing the humerus.

Surgeon Arvin Whelan, aided by Dr. Moses Gunn of the Fifth Michigan Infantry, resectioned Shaw's arm, a daring procedure for the time.[84] The doctors removed the damaged bone, but instead of amputating the arm, the ends of the remaining bones were made adaptable, resulting in (if all went well) a much less serviceable and shorter arm. Shaw suffered for almost a month. He died on 5 June, the first regimental casualty to a bullet.[85]

DeLand was livid with rage. While blaming Johnesse, "a

thoughtless and wayward boy," the colonel said:

> he is guiltless compared with the wreatch [*sic*] who had converted
> the gun into an infernal machine to deal death and misfortune
> upon an innocent man. . . . Let this sad causality [*sic*] be a lesson
> to all, not to repeat the carelessness of which to day we have had
> so severe a lesson.[86]

Johnesse, whatever his punishment, had to live with his
own conscience. He served until the end of the war. The other
"wreatch" was never officially named.[87]

Loose Discipline

DeLand warned his men in May that "there is too much
looseness and inaccuracy in the discharge of their duties."[88] Some
days prior to that admonition, the colonel had started classes for
his officers. As of 8:30 AM on 12 May, the regiment's officers received their military education via *Casey's Tactics*, the official drill
manual for the army. DeLand also met with them "at 7:30 p.m. for
instruction in drill & regulations."[89] The officers then used their
knowledge to drill the recruits in both military movements and
deportment.

Disciplinary matters came to a head again on the night of
25 May. Three prisoners—William C. Raymond, Francis Shields,
and Alonzo Smith—broke out of the guardhouse and made good
their escape. A squad picked up Raymond shortly afterward. He
had only recently been brought back under guard after being
away from camp for two weeks. A court-martial board dismissed
him from the service. Shields also was recaptured, only to desert
again a few months later. Smith got away altogether.[90]

Scapegoats were easy to find. The escape was blamed on "a
gross degree of carelessness on the part of guards & officers on
duty at the time," read the official inquiry. "The practice of officers
retiring to their quarters while on duty is all wrong and will not
be hereafter tolerated. Neither will non-commissioned officers be
allowed to exchange duties or act for each other." Only two enlisted men, Cpls. John Mahan and Rasmus Oleson, were chastised
for allowing the escape. No officer was named in the report.[91]

Although desertion kept chipping away at the ranks, there
were bright moments when the prodigals returned, some under

guard and some by their own volition. John Detro of Captain Rhines's company came back after his travels (to where, only he knew) on 21 April. Detro had little of the warrior in him. The 30-year-old became a cook, and he stayed a cook. He must have been better than average, because a year later he was still preparing meals at division headquarters.[92]

Presentations

Regardless of the problems in the regiment, as a rule there was good will between the officers and the men. Familiarity may breed contempt, but it also fosters respect and friendship. There were innumerable testimonials presented to the officers by the men of their companies. Capt. Asahel W. Nichols received "a very splendid regulation sword" from his company.[93] Not to be outdone by the men of Company E, Capt. George Davis became the recipient of "a very beautiful sword, sash and belt, costing the handsome sum of $75."[94] Davis's Company D epitomized the volunteer nature of the new army. Said the author of the newspaper article commemorating the event:

> Appropriate speeches were made by Private E[dward]. F. Ro[d]gers and Capt. Davis, and many loud cheers were given by the happy boys, and the usual number of *smiles* returned by the officers. The Captain is among the popular ones in the regiment.[95]

Not a week passed before 1st Lt. Samuel Hudson received "the same kind of magnificent offering" from the men of Company D.[96] A day later the third line officer in the company, 2nd Lt. Cyrenius B. Knight of Newton, accepted "an elegant sword, sash, and belt" from his men. The Hillsdale County recruits of Capt. Lucien Meigs's company presented him with "a very beautiful sword, sash and belt, the gift of confidence and respect from the boys in his company."[97] Lt. Col. William H. H. Beadle even received a horse from the men in the regiment.[98]

Arming the Regiment

In the midst of the presentations a real morale killer struck the regiment. Colonel DeLand kept dunning the authorities in

41

Washington, asking for the appropriate weapons to outfit a sharp-shooting regiment. Time after time they refused him. Some men in the regiment had served in Berdan's U.S. Sharpshooters or Birge's Sharpshooters and knew the effect of target or deer rifles against the rebels. Again at Dearborn DeLand fired off another request to the war department, asking for Sharps rifles for his command. The Sharps rifle was a single-shot weapon, but it was a breech-loader, which made it faster to reload than the standard muzzle-loading Springfield rifle. The war department told Governor Blair that "other important work" would be retarded if Sharps rifles were to be procured.[99] Springfield rifles, the standard arm of the common infantryman, would be good enough, the war department affirmed. After all, the Sharpshooters were guarding thousands of them.

The .58 calibre Springfield rifle was the basic infantry weapon of the common footsoldier in the Civil War. A good man could muzzle-load and fire an aimed shot three times in a minute. When a rifle was fired, the hollow base of the bullet expanded to fit tightly against the rifled grooves in the barrel. The rifling and the snug fit of the bullet made a more accurate weapon. The conical-shaped bullet of soft lead, or minié ball, was a frightening missile of destruction. Crashing through muscle and bone, the low-velocity missile left horrendous wounds. A sharp-eyed rifleman could hit an eleven-inch bull's eye at 300 yards. Even at 500 yards the slug could rip through six inches of pine wood.

Near the end of May officers tried to explain the situation to the men in the ranks. Many had signed up for a sharpshooting outfit, not an ordinary infantry regiment. Disappointing as it must have been—and strange as it seems—only one man made a fuss over the matter. Pvt. William J. Ross (Co. F) rejected the Springfield issued to him. "I refuse to take the gun," he told his lieutenant and then Colonel DeLand. "I enlisted for a Sharp Shooter and won[']t take that anyway and I never take anything back, you can put me in the Guard House and be damned."[100]

Although DeLand's sympathy lay with Ross, the recruit had to be dealt with before the affair got out of hand. A court-martial board found Ross guilty of insubordination and sentenced him to fourteen days in the guardhouse, the first two on bread and water and the rest at hard labor.[101] After having second thoughts about his actions (and probably a visit from his commanding officer to talk over the dilemma), Ross apologized to the colonel for his outburst and returned to his company.[102]

The Colors

A week after Ross's release from captivity, one of those grand events occurred which was long remembered by the men of the regiment. Immediately following dress parade on the evening of 4 June, Lieutenant Colonel Beadle ordered Captain Dicey's Company B to the front of the battalion, where the men formed two platoons facing each other. Dr. Jacob McNett, the assistant surgeon, then presented a national flag donated by the Albee family of Grand Haven. Both McNett and Dicey called Grand Haven home, as did many of the Company B recruits. Receiving the proffered national colors, Dicey responded to the regiment:

> I cheerfully accept this beautiful suit of colors in behalf of my company, with the terms proposed "that we should never disgrace them." When I think of the patriotic motives that prompted the company I represent to enlist in the service of their country, I have no fears that they will ever disgrace the old flag.[103]

The flag presentation helped boost the morale of the regiment. The colors were the focus of the unit, the modern counterparts to the sacred Roman standards. They represented the pride of the regiment and were a rallying point in battle. The enemy drove for that point of the regiment. The men defended the flag, their honor, their pride, and their hope for a better Union. From now on the men would dress on the colors at every drill session and parade. At every regimental formation, the Stars and Stripes would fly. It was a perilous time for the United States, and unabashed patriotism was the norm for the regiment. It can be imagined that more than one man swelled with pride while gazing on the symbol of the nation at the presentation.

A few weeks later the Sharpshooters received their second flag, the state colors, from Mrs. Austin Blair, the governor's wife. Accepting the gift for the regiment was Color Sgt. George A. Caine. Another of the veterans, Caine had served in Mulligan's Irish Brigade (an Illinois unit) for seven months in 1861. No sooner was he mustered out than he joined Yates's Sharpshooters—the Sixty-fourth Illinois Infantry. He was elected second lieutenant and then promoted to captain in August 1862. Resigning for reasons of disability in September 1862, Caine enlisted in the Sharpshooters the following May. He was only 20 years old.[104] The colors were put into good hands. Almost one full year from the date he received them, Caine would save them from certain capture in a murderous fight with the enemy in front of Petersburg, Virginia.

The Brass Band

Even with the new flags, morale was noticeably ebbing. Desertions were still too frequent, and knowing they would be just another infantry regiment did not help. Besides, many of the Sharpshooters had received no pay except the original bounty payment, and some were four, five, or six months in arrears. There were definite rumblings in the ranks. DeLand realized "a feeling of dissatisfaction was growing into open mutiny."[105] Even the officers were discouraged by the turn of events. At his daily lessons in *Casey's Tactics* the colonel sought the advice of his junior officers. What could be done to alleviate the malaise in the regiment?

> Among the experiments hit upon to revive an interest and inspire confidence among the men, the idea of a Brass Band was suggested and at a meeting of all the officers . . . it was voted to have a Brass Band. In fulfilling this request of the officers I adopted the plan.[106]

Regimental bands were commonplace early in the war. Dozens of regiments actively recruited musicians. All regiments had drummers or fifers. Oftentimes they would be grouped together to form a regimental band. There were so many bands in the Union army that in 1862 Congress passed a law providing for only one band per brigade.

Colonel DeLand, in trying to boost morale, was operating outside the official pale. He would be called to task on this matter later in the war, but for now bands were morale builders, and he meant to have one. Marching or drilling to band music was easier than without it. Listening to the band play in the evening was a pleasant diversion from the daily grind. Some men were detailed from the ranks, and others still had to be recruited. Soon there were 13 musicians involved in the new brass band. All would belong to Company G, the company then being completed.

The First Review

Until they were mustered into service as full companies, the unorganized companies trained at Fort Wayne in Detroit; Maj. John Piper commanded there. The other six companies drilled at the Dearborn arsenal. When the battalion at Dearborn was sufficiently drilled, the colonel received word that the governor and other dignitaries were coming to review the Sharpshooters. The six companies and their officers made ready to meet the officials at 8:30 on the morning of 16 June.[107]

DeLand was anxious to show off the battalion. Still chagrined at the slow progress of recruiting, he knew that:

> When full, the Sharpshooters in point of soldierly-looking men, efficiency in discipline under their officers, and real solid worth, will stand second to no regiment that has been raised in the State. Michigan may well be proud.[108]

He hoped that the display would impress the right people.

The men decorated the camp with small trees and boughs for the occasion. At 9:00 AM the battalion met the governor's train at the Dearborn depot. There were more celebrities than most of the men among the blue-clad group had ever seen at once. Gov. and Mrs. Austin Blair led the delegation. Sen. Jacob M. Howard, State Adj. Gen. John Robertson, State Q.M. Gen. William Hammond, and other military men and their ladies completed the party.[109]

After conducting the guests of honor to their camp, the Sharpshooters were shown off by their colonel. DeLand had them march up and down the review field a number of times, executing various maneuvers for the onlookers. He then joined the governor's party at the reviewing stand and told Adjutant Buckbee to parade the men past the stand. Buckbee did not yet know it, but he would definitely impress the colonel this day.

The young adjutant walked out to the companies standing in the sun and saw that the men were not aligned as they were supposed to be. The marching and countermarching had put the left in place of the right of each company, and the front rank where the rear rank should have been. Not knowing how to gracefully realign the men, Buckbee strode back to Colonel DeLand and hastily explained the situation. Up to this point the two officers had not gotten along too well. Buckbee had received his commission from the governor over objections from the colonel. Ever since that time, DeLand had bombarded the governor's office with requests to transfer the young adjutant to another regiment so DeLand could replace him with a man more to his liking. Now, hearing Buckbee's anxious plea, DeLand solemnly told him, "Adjutant, I am going to take my position with the Governor and his Party; you will march the column by in review."[110]

After some quick thinking on his way back to the battalion, Buckbee about-faced the men, and then marched and countermarched them a little to get them arranged correctly. His intense study of company and battalion maneuvers served him well. He then paraded the men past the reviewers, as proud as he could be. Even the colonel was impressed. Years later Buckbee learned that from that time forward Colonel DeLand had stopped importuning the governor to find a new adjutant.[111]

The battalion stood inspection for the governor and his party, and then there were the inevitable speeches. Governor Blair surprised the men in the ranks by addressing them, not their officers. "It was my desire," he told them, "to see those members of the regiment who carry the musket."[112] The men gave him three rousing cheers at the close of his talk, and then they settled down to hear some remarks from Senator Howard.[113]

Newspaper coverage of the event buoyed Colonel DeLand. He was touted for being *just the right man in the right place. No other man but he would have had the indomitable will—the almost super-human perseverance, to have raised a regiment as he has in these times."*[114]

DeLand, however, remained frustrated with his officers, his superiors, and his regiment, which tried his patience in a thousand ways. Lieutenant Colonel Beadle, noted in the papers for his education and prior military experience, was privately denigrated by his commander. Praised in the press for his gallantry in the field and for "being very prepossessingly military in appearance," Beadle aroused ire in DeLand, because the latter always looked on the Sharpshooters as being "his" regiment. He considered Beadle a fifth wheel. DeLand resented his second-in-command because Beadle was mustered in the middle of May as a lieutenant colonel, while he was still trying to bring the regiment to minimum strength so he could be officially mustered as colonel. Not only was Beadle mustered, griped DeLand, he also "drew pay from the U.S. while doing little or no duty, . . . [although DeLand was] in command all the time."[115]

Even after the governor's review, the colonel found the battalion lacking in military bearing. Too much time "is allowed to run to waste" during drill, he complained. The men took "long rests under shade trees"; the officers were prone to "shirk labor." Both "discipline and order" had to be preserved. The double-quick step must be employed more often. "The sucess [sic] and discipline of a Regiment demands very largely, in fact, almost wholly, upon the proper discipline, instructions and efficiency of the Companies, and Officers."[116]

Thankfully, thought the Sharpshooters, the colonel's days were considerably brightened by the birth of his daughter on 18 June, two days after the governor's review. The colonel's wife, Mary, in residence at the Dearborn arsenal, presented DeLand with his second daughter. Surgeon Whelan was the physician in attendance. The little girl, named Dell Whelan DeLand, received the appellation "Daughter of the Regiment" many years later when the Sharpshooters held their first reunion. Of course, by that time the dull duty of drill had been superseded by the glory attained on the battlefield. Young Dell's birth had coincided with the birth of the regiment itself; being the colonel's daughter also helped.[117]

The Fourth of July

Quite a festive event, with the Sharpshooters as the focus, was planned for the nation's eighty-seventh birthday. Friends and relatives from as far away as Battle Creek packed picnic baskets with all sorts of delicacies. Railroad fares to Dearborn to attend the celebration were half price. All in all, "a great gala-day shall be made."[118]

The Fourth of July began cooler than expected. During the late morning hours a heavy haze blotted out the sun and a breeze blew in from Lake Erie. The Sharpshooters, decked out in their finest, paraded for the benefit of the admiring visitors and the local residents in attendance, and then they drilled for the enjoyment of the spectators. In the afternoon the men wilted as an oppressive sun burned through the haze. They stood in sweaty formation as local dignitaries delivered the mandatory patriotic addresses. Finally, the regiment stepped through a "Fancy Drill & Dress Parade." The day's festivities were capped by a fireworks display.[119]

Earlier, Colonel DeLand had warned his men to behave like true soldiers and promised "the severest punishment" to those who circumvented his orders.[120] The day's programs proceeded well, and the colonel complimented the officers and men on their martial decorum. He was proud, he said, of their conduct, which became "the occasion and the Regiment."[121] The colonel, the men learned, could be as quick with a compliment as he was with a condemnation.

Still, DeLand and his men yearned for action. None of them had joined the army to put on parades in Michigan. In the East, the Army of the Potomac had fought and won the great Battle of Gettysburg, but the Sharpshooters had played no part in the victory. Down South, the Mississippi River ran "unvexed to the sea" since the fall of Vicksburg to Union arms, and the Sharpshooters had had nothing to do with that victory either. Some of the men had signed the roster eight months before, and they had not yet left the state. The regiment had been exercised five hours a day while at Dearborn. They maintained a rigorous schedule and had been hardened for the tough marches down "the long pikes of Tennessee or the bad roads of Virginia."[122] Yet the war had a good chance of ending before they entered it.

The regiment (or rather the six companies endlessly drilling at Dearborn) had received its marching orders three times already and just as many times had them canceled. Continually being kept on the edge of anxiety, some of the officers hoped for any kind of action. "Governor [Blair] says he will send us to Indiana to enforce the draft if he can—I hope he will," wrote Adjutant Buckbee to his sweetheart, Mollie. Even that sort of bland operation was preferable to the interminable drill at Dearborn.[123]

CHAPTER 3

We Could Have Whipped You

Morgan's Raid

On 2 July 1863, the Confederate general John Hunt Morgan and 2,500 rebel cavalrymen crossed the Cumberland River in Kentucky and headed north toward Indiana. On 4 July, while the Sharpshooters entertained their friends and relatives at Fort Dearborn, Col. Orlando Moore and 200 men of the Twenty-fifth Michigan Infantry held up Morgan's force at Tebb's Bend on the Green River in Kentucky. After a four-hour fight, Moore refused to surrender, uttering a memorable reply: "this being the Fourth of July I cannot entertain the proposition." [1]

Morgan's raiders drew off and effected a crossing at another ford. The delay cost the rebels more than twelve hours and at least 71 men. The Twenty-fifth Michigan suffered 6 killed and 23 wounded. [2]

The next day, 5 July, after light skirmishing, Morgan easily took Lebanon and Bardstown and continued to move north. At noon the same day, John Robertson, Michigan's adjutant general, received a hurriedly dictated telegram from Brig. Gen. Orlando B. Willcox, the U.S. commander of the military district of Indiana and Michigan: "Morgan is in Kentucky[.] Has captured Lebenon [sic][.] Please get them [sic] Sharpshooters ready to come at once"[.][3] By the following day, Willcox was almost frantic: "Please send all the Michigan troops down, to report to me as quick as possible. . . . Loose [*sic*] no time"[.][4]

DeLand saw the Morgan raid as a chance to obtain from Willcox and the Regular Army those things which so far had been denied him and his regiment. DeLand was never to be a favorite of Willcox's, and the problems between the two men may have started at this time. Some of the Sharpshooters had not been paid since their enlistment, in some cases since the waning months of 1862. The colonel now demanded that the paymaster from Detroit formally muster in a dozen men at Dearborn and that all of his men be paid.

Not knowing what to expect from the advancing gray host, Willcox found himself forced into a corner and had to accede to DeLand's requirements: "If the Sharp Shooters can certainly get off by Tomorrow night [7 July] I will consent to that much delay for their payment[.] They should be paid at once," Willcox wired to Robertson.[5]

DeLand knew army regulations stated that a colonel of a volunteer regiment could be mustered into the service only when a regiment attained minimum strength. Since only 400 men made up the regiment, the unit did not officially merit a colonel as commanding officer. In his third telegram to Detroit, Willcox put the reponsibility on Governor Blair's shoulders: "If it be the wish of the Governor that Col DeLand accompany the Sharp Shooters in command, you will please direct the recruiting officer in my name to muster him in."[6] DeLand hurriedly contacted the adjutant general's office in Detroit. A quick exchange of telegrams with the governor ensued, and a letter "requesting" DeLand's muster as colonel "on behalf of the Governor of the State" was carried to Col. John R. Smith's office the same day. Smith accordingly mustered DeLand as colonel of the First Michigan Sharpshooters.[7]

Colonel DeLand and his regiment, six small companies, were now in the service of the U.S. government. Enough men or not, DeLand was officially a colonel and the Sharpshooters were a regiment, at least for the present.

General Willcox kept frantically calling all available regiments to Indianapolis to repel the gray invaders. In the meantime, mountains had to be moved in Dearborn. Orders effectively canceled all leaves. Absent men hurried back to the arsenal. A few men hastily wrote letters to loved ones, and everyone checked and rechecked his equipment. Major Piper retained command of the four understrength companies at Fort Wayne. Quartermaster Palmer readied five days' rations in bulk for the men, and all company commanders made sure their men had two days' cooked rations.[8] Colonel Howard, the U.S. paymaster at Detroit, assembled the Sharpshooters and paid them their due.[9]

DeLand told his men they were ordered to report to Louisville to repel Morgan's invaders; but even as the Sharpshooters left Dearborn aboard the Michigan Central Railroad on the afternoon of 8 July, the rebels were crossing the Ohio River into Indiana. The Sharpshooters' route took them through Jackson, where the train made a short stop. Their arrival was anticipated, and a number of "friends of the boys were at the depot to see them off for the war."[10]

Guards were placed at the end of each car to stop any man from leaving the coach. Mose Snay, one of the toughest men in the regiment, demanded to be let out. A native of Detroit, Snay was one of the earliest recruits for Company F, having enlisted on Christmas Day, 1862. Six feet tall and 21 years old, strongly muscled and a bully, Snay was a man most stepped away from. "He had a bad reputation when he entered the Regiment," remarked one officer. The guard refused Snay's request and held the door closed. Enraged, Snay broke the window in the door with his elbow. The glass shattered and a small shard of it struck the guard's eye. A quick examination showed a serious wound. Some felt the guard might lose his eyesight. As it was, a piece of glass did cut the eyeball, but the man's sight was not affected.

Someone called 1st Sgt. Edwin O. Conklin of Snay's company to deal with the miscreant. Although the Detroit tough "had bullied and snubbed a number of the non-commissioned officers," Conklin always stood up to him. Conklin called the sergeant major, related the problem, and requested some handcuffs. Snay glared at Conklin and said he would kill the man who tried to handcuff him. Conklin looked right at Snay and declared, "Mose, I'm going to put these hand-cuffs on you and if you make the least bit of trouble, there are men enough of us here to hang you up—not by your neck, that would not be necessary, but by your hand-cuffs."

Snay grudgingly submitted to the handcuffs, but refused to go to his seat. Sergeant Conklin spoke quietly to Snay. The big man then walked to his seat and let his fellows tie his arms down. Snay could have been court-martialed, but Conklin interceded on his behalf to the colonel. From that time forward, Snay caused no particular problems.[11]

On the afternoon of 9 July the regiment reached Indianapolis. That evening the Sharpshooters proceeded by train to Seymour, a town about 50 miles south of the capital. Awaiting word of the whereabouts of the rebels, the Sharpshooters cooled their heels in Seymour until Saturday morning, 11 July. They then traveled by rail to North Vernon, a village 14 miles to the east, where Morgan's men had been sighted. At Seymour a couple of companies of Indiana militia had joined the Sharpshooters. Adjutant Buckbee took note of the Hoosiers:

> On this jaunt through the country, the Indiana fellows certainly enjoyed themselves. A number of them I saw fire from the top of the boxcars at the cattle (their neighbors' cattle) in adjoining fields. What, with the motion of the train, and their own clumsiness with the musket, they did not seem to be able to hit a cow at twenty rods distant.[12]

A pilot engine preceded the train carrying the Sharpshooters and the Indiana militia. With the exception of an engineer and a fireman, only Adjutant Buckbee was on board. Colonel DeLand ordered him to ride the engine and signal the troop train if he sighted Morgan's men. Feeling the weight of the world on his young shoulders, Buckbee mounted the pilot engine, but soon realized that he could not view the countryside as well as he thought he could. He then crawled on top of the engine; finding he could not stand securely on the swaying machine, he lay down.

> The engineer said something to me, but I could not make out what it was and leaned over the edge of the cab and asked the fireman what he meant. The fireman stuck his head out of the window and I could only distinguish the words "damn fool."[13]

Without sighting the rebels, the Sharpshooters detrained at North Vernon.[14] Apprised by local farmers that Morgan was at Vernon (only about four miles south), DeLand ordered his men to the latter place on the double-quick.

The day was a hot one, but the colonel urged his men forward. Sand filled the shoes of the Sharpshooters. "We had not run probably a mile when the Indiana militia fellows took to the shadow of a rail fence and rested," recalled the adjutant.[15] Exhausted, the six companies finally entered Vernon at 4:00 PM and were met by what seemed to be the entire population of the town. Dozens of townspeople joyfully welcomed the sweating Sharp-shooters with pails of ice water. It took the combined efforts of all the officers, backed by their noncommissioned staffs, to forestall their men from drinking themselves sick. A guard was quickly set up, and the ladies of Vernon were allowed to give each man only a cup of water.[16]

The Sharpshooters happened to enter Vernon just when Morgan's men were demanding the surrender of the place. Their offer was declined by General Love, who commanded all Federal forces in the area.[17] As a consequence, Love had 35 minutes to send away all noncombatants. Colonel DeLand agitated for an immediate attack but was sharply overruled.[18]

Not knowing the full status of the enemy confronting him but believing they outnumbered his men, Morgan utilized another weapon—subterfuge. While the larger part of his force tore up the railroad tracks around the town and then retreated to Dupont (10 miles south) to feed and rest their mounts, other smaller units kept the Union soldiers busy by appropriating horses from local farmers and leaving their pickets in full view of the Sharpshoot-ers in Vernon.[19]

Colonel DeLand realized the situation resembled the one at Murfreesboro the year before. He knew that reinforcements, or the threat of them, would keep the enemy at bay. Issuing orders to his officers to cover all roads into Vernon, DeLand retained all his drummers as well as some 300 armed civilians in the town as a reserve. At nightfall he sent teams of horses down the road to North Vernon; when they returned he had the drummers play as if more troops were arriving.[20] He figured that the Confederates would think too many Union soldiers were in town and leave.

General Love's Hoosiers set up two pieces of artillery near the church. After placing his pickets, Adjutant Buckbee wandered to the churchyard but decided not to sleep there.

> After taking a look at those guns, I took my blanket and moved away for nearly forty rods, calculating that the pieces of an exploded cannon would not reach me that far, for the guns were old, rusty affairs, loaded to the muzzle, and they certainly looked dangerous.[21]

While Colonel DeLand deployed his nervous troops and made ready for the inevitable attack by Morgan's men, Adjutant

Buckbee received orders from General Love to report to the telegraph station in North Vernon. From that point he was to relay messages received from Gen. Lew Wallace's office in Indianapolis to General Love in Vernon. Within two hours after seating himself in the office, telegrams began to come in from the state capital. Generally, the messages had the same import: Hold the position at Vernon. Do not pay attention to rumors brought in by local farmers. All troop movements will be reported to you by Wallace's office.[22]

Early the next morning, after copying a communication, the puzzled telegraph operator asked, "I wonder what this means? Here's a dispatch saying 'Good night, I hope you have enjoyed yourself.'"[23] Perplexed by the message, the two men looked at each other, but soon resumed their business of waiting for more news. Several hours passed before the next telegram began clicking its bulletin across the wire. The authorities in Indianapolis wanted to know why no communications had emanated from North Vernon during the night.

Then the light dawned on Buckbee. Morgan's raiders had put one over on the Federal forces. They had cut and tapped the telegraph wire north of North Vernon, so they could intercept messages from Indianapolis and feed all sorts of fictitious information to the Union commanders. By the same token, the Confederates had received and answered all of Love's telegrams. No one on the the Union side was blamed, although enough laughter and derision resulted from the officers and men who heard the story.[24]

The Sharpshooters kept squads on every road into Vernon and a few of them even saw some action against the enemy. At 4:00 in the morning—about the same time Morgan's telegrapher bade everyone a good night—2nd Lt. Cyrenius B. Knight and his squad of pickets fired at a group of horsemen approaching them. At the sound of the shooting, the rebels hurried off. At daylight the body of "a young fellow—a mere boy" was found on the road.[25] As the Sharpshooters moved out, most of them stared at the first casualty they had caused in this war.

The main party of rebels was gone, and the few Confederates who were captured were dog-tired from the effects of the raid. What really impressed the captured rebels was the small number of Federals in Vernon. They thought the town was full of Union infantry. "We could have whipped you'uns in ten minutes," the raiders said.[26] It was the first place they had not attacked on their foray through Indiana, and it was no more defended than other places had been. Actually, hearing that Vernon was heavily defended, Morgan had made up his mind to bypass the town as soon as he sighted it. Skirmishers had ringed the hamlet while the main body of raiders set off for Dupont.

Morgan's demand for the surrender of Vernon immediately before the arrival of the Sharpshooters was a deception. He knew the odds and had bluffed, so that he could form his column beyond Vernon. General Love's plea for two hours to remove all noncombatants had played into Morgan's hands. Explained Basil Duke, one of the raiders close to Morgan: "Humane considerations are never inopportune."[27]

The Sharpshooters captured 16 rebels in all, including a Negro servant of a Confederate major, and a large number of jaded horses released by the raiders.[28]

Morgan's main force was already in Ohio, but scattered bands still plagued southern Indiana. Consequently, DeLand marched his men 25 miles eastward to Sunman Station, arriving there on Tuesday, 14 July. They stayed in the vicinity for two days, then received orders to return to Indianapolis. By the time the Sharpshooters reached the capital, the harried rebels of Morgan's command were bone-weary from their ride through Yankeedom. Exhausted and hemmed in, the rebels found their way barred across the Ohio River. In a running battle they suffered more than 800 casualties, including 700 captured. A week later, deep in Ohio, Morgan was surrounded and hopelessly outnumbered; he surrendered the remnant of the 2,500 men who had left Tennessee full of dash and promise at the beginning of the month.

The danger was over. DeLand submitted no after-action report but did write an article for the Detroit *Advertiser and Tribune*. Never one to shove his light under a bushel, DeLand praised the regiment in superlatives. In his history of the campaign, he stated that soon after the Sharpshooters entered Vernon, they:

> were anxious to attack the rebels at once, and had it not been for the order of the Commanding General to the contrary a more general engagement would no doubt have been brought on; and, as our forces had greatly the advantage as to grounds, perhaps greater laurels would have been won by them.[29]

In retrospect DeLand was wrong. Leaving the defenses in the town and fighting in the open would have been more advantageous to Morgan's cavalry. Besides, DeLand did not know he was facing a vastly inferior force, because Morgan had pulled most of his men off to Dupont, 10 miles away. And lastly, as Adjutant Buckbee realized, "If we had succeeded in heading him [Morgan] off, I am quite sure he would have had some fun at our expense," for the Sharpshooters were still new at this game.[30]

Nonetheless, Colonel DeLand heaped plaudits on his men:

> One thing developed by this little adventure of theirs is the fact that the Sharpshooters can fight. . . . Their desire to be let loose upon Morgan there at Vernon, gives us some glimpses of the kind of spirit which they possess; and their patient endurance of the long march to Sunmanville, as well as their conduct on the night of the 11th inst., prove their competency for the field, or any other kind of military service.[31]

The Momentous Return to the Arsenal

The trip back to Dearborn was an adventure that no one planned, a hurry-up affair due to a potential flare-up in Detroit. Rumor had it that the Copperheads in Wayne County planned to take over the Dearborn arsenal.[32] General Willcox, now back at his headquarters in Detroit, relayed word to Indianapolis to get the Sharpshooters back immediately.

Being camped near a railroad yard, it did not take the regiment long to entrain the men, the officers' horses, and their equipment for Michigan. Colonel DeLand understood the railroad authorities to say that the train was a "through" to Detroit. It was Saturday evening, 18 July.

Just after daylight on Sunday the Sharpshooters arrived at the switch-off in Sidney, Ohio. From there the intersecting tracks led to Toledo, then Detroit. No train was waiting. The impatient conductor told DeLand to unload his men and baggage as quickly as possible. DeLand refused; he wanted to know how he and his men were to get to Detroit. The conductor assured him that it was not his problem.

DeLand fumed. At 9:00 AM, when the local telegraph office opened, he wired Indianapolis, calling on both the railroad and the military authorities, demanding to know what was happening. The railroad officials told the conductor to proceed on his way and told DeLand to find his own transportation to Detroit. As a gesture of good will, the baggage cars, containing five horses belonging to the field officers and the regimental equipment, were uncoupled from the train before it departed.

DeLand then telegraphed Dayton to have a Dayton and Michigan Railroad train pick up his men. "Nobody had any notice of our coming and nothing was in preparation," he complained.[33] He was informed that no train was available. Furious, DeLand told the D & M people of the urgency of his orders to get to Detroit. The railroad company managed to put together a train of boxcars, but it would not leave Dayton before noon that day.

At 6:00 PM the train finally puffed into Sidney. Hauling six heavily-laden boxcars, it had taken six hours to come 35 miles. At Sidney ten more boxcars were coupled to the train, and the Sharpshooters climbed aboard. No passenger cars were available; DeLand dispersed his officers and men on the tops of the freight cars. In this manner the Sharpshooters traveled to Toledo, over 100 miles away. During the night it started to rain, adding to everyone's misery. Some of the men lost their rifles, and about half the ammunition was ruined.

Arriving at Toledo at 1:00 AM on Monday, 20 July, DeLand faced another dilemma. Again, no train was immediately ready to transfer the Sharpshooters to another line. All the officials of the next line were then in Michigan, and the telegraph office did not open until 7:00 AM. The Sharpshooters protected themselves as best they could from the rain. Permission from the railroad superintendent was finally secured at 8:00 AM, and the men boarded a mail train for Detroit; their horses, tents, freight, and baggage were left in Toledo to be sent the next day. The Sharpshooters arrived at Detroit, their final destination, at 3:00 that afternoon, after 54 hours on the road.

Colonel DeLand immediately proceeded to General Willcox to explain what had happened, hoping for some justification. What truly galled DeLand was that a special train of passenger cars had been sent expressly by Willcox to Indianapolis to pick up the Sharpshooters, but it returned empty to Detroit, arriving 12 hours before DeLand's regiment. Someone in Indianapolis had decided to move the Sharpshooters by another route before the arrival of the other train, causing unneeded confusion, short tempers, fatigue, and waste.[34]

Meanwhile, the editor of the Detroit *Free Press* made a veiled admonition to the local Copperheads. He warned them not to meet openly, for General Willcox had forbidden such gatherings.[35] They were said to have convened in four towns outside of

Detroit, including Dearborn. There it was decided to seize the arsenal, since the Sharpshooters were still in Indiana. But the regiment returned. "Since then they [the Copperheads] have been a woebegone and forlorn-looking set—their last hope has vanished."[36]

According to DeLand, the Copperheads were caught off-guard when his regiment showed up in Dearborn. "What brought them damned Sharpshooters back here?" was heard, although much of what the Copperheads were up to was so much hot air. Ostensibly, the Sharpshooters headed back to Michigan to disrupt any plans made by the Knights of the Golden Circle (as the rebel sympathizers were known) to attack the Dearborn arsenal. The rumor of a Copperhead conspiracy to attack the arsenal was bandied about by the press during and after the Morgan raid. "A gigantic plot" involving the Knights of the Golden Circle in and around Dearborn was foiled by "several stout loyal hearts" in the vicinity and more especially by the return of the Sharpshooters, according to an editorial in the Grand Rapids *Eagle*.[37]

Colonel DeLand had no trouble fixing the blame for his regiment's problems in transit on the U.S. Army quartermaster department in Indianapolis. To him, the result was traitorous, because "there was momentary and immenent [sic] dangers of a Riot in the City of Detroit, which was alone restrained by the expectation of the arrival of the Regiment on Sunday evening as it should have arrived, instead of being delayed until Monday afternoon by the route alloted by you."[38] No riot took place, and no Copperheads attacked the arsenal. The Sharpshooters again took up their lodgings at Dearborn.

Company K

During the absence of the six companies, recruiting had continued; 24 Indians from the Saginaw area enrolled the day before Colonel DeLand led the six companies to Indiana,[39] and 23 others had already been mustered by the end of May.[40] Before the Sharpshooters entrained for Indiana in July, there were almost 80 Indians in the regiment.[41] By the time DeLand returned, a full company had been mustered and was training.[42] For a while it was thought that two companies of Indians would serve with the Sharpshooters, but by August the well had run dry. Another 50 would trickle in by twos and threes for the rest of the war as replacements, but no more large contingents of 20 or 30 came through.

Recruiting parties continued to travel to the Indian settlements. Sgt. Henry Graveraet of Company K accompanied Richard Cooper, a civilian agent and recruiter in early August, but they had only limited success.[43]

In the middle of July, while DeLand chased Confederates in Indiana, Chief Nock-ke-chick-faw-me, a Saginaw Chippewa, journeyed to Detroit to speak to the young warriors of his tribe. He exhorted them to be brave and honorable by reminding them of their heritage: "We are descendants of braves, who united with our younger brothers, the Ottawas, drove the powerful tribes now beyond the *great river*' from these *our once beautiful hunting grounds.*" He wanted them to "be heroic and brave. Have confidence in the Great Spirit, and when you die your forefathers will welcome you to the spirit land as brave sons." Then he mentioned the loyalty of the young warriors before him and why they enlisted: "If the South conquers you will be *slaves, dogs.* There will be no protection for us; we shall be driven from our homes, our lands and the graves of our friends."[44]

The chief's counseling words embodied the reasoning behind the Indian enlistments. Whereas the whites joined the colors to put down the rebellion, to free the slaves, and for lesser motives (the adventure of being in a war, the bounty money), many of the Indians joined because they believed the South was out to enslave all of them. The young warriors were going to fight for their own freedom, their homes, and their lands, where the graves of their families were located.

Discipline Problems

Even before the Sharpshooters returned after their Indiana excursion, Captain Dicey's Company B was ordered on detached duty to Fort Wayne.[45] The military authorities in Detroit were still nervous over the "Copperhead Conspiracy." Three thousand stands of small arms were removed from Fort Wayne and stored at the Dearborn arsenal, but Company B stayed at Fort Wayne. To guard against any encroachment by the Copperheads, double pickets were stationed around the fort.[46] Colonel DeLand detailed 2nd Asst. Surg. Jacob B. McNett and Charles A. Hudson, a hospital steward, for duty with Dicey's company.[47]

At the arsenal the Sharpshooters settled down to the usual routine, but the unusual soon cropped up. Almost immediately several civilians complained of seeing soldiers bathing within sight of the main road outside the camp.[48] Negative reports involving Sharpshooters on leave came from U.S. Army headquarters in Detroit as well, and DeLand had to come down on his men again.

A couple of young recruits from Company F, George Sidney and Charles Johnesse (the latter no stranger to trouble), left the regiment when it returned from Indiana. For a few days they enjoyed themselves immensely in Detroit until the provost marshal picked them up.[49] Two corporals, Enos Bolton and Elihu Powers, had deserted while the regiment chased the rebels through the Hoosier state. Capt. Lucien Meigs and Sgt. Immanuel Brown had to go to Indianapolis and apprehend them and any other deserters from the regiment they could find.[50] Some men, still believed to be in Indiana, simply could not be located. After the regiment's return to Dearborn, others took French leave. Colonel DeLand, encountering pressure from his superiors to find the root causes of the plethora of desertions, again blamed "the loose company discipline which is prevalent and the worse than careless manner in which the general duty of the camp is performed."[51]

Corraling deserters required a major effort. Oftentimes DeLand sent Sgt. John Morey (Co. C) across the river into Canada to apprehend deserters. Morey's methods were so effective that General Robertson of the adjutant general's office also employed him in that capacity.[52]

Company officers generally followed the leads on the American side of the river. Thirty-year-old Merrick Bradley of Battle Creek left Dearborn under orders to "arrest any and all deserters" from the Sharpshooters or any other regiment. He was not the only one so empowered.[53] Lt. Ira Evans and Sgt. W. J. Lee, together with Sergeant Major Quackenbush, were ordered to arrest three known deserters and two supposed ones, "who are reported to have left Detroit this day noon, upon the steamboat for Saginaw."[54] On that same day DeLand preferred various charges against seven enlisted men and remanded them to the custody of Col. J. R. Smith in Detroit.[55] By 12 August thirteen men, all considered deserters (including Corporals Bolton and Powers), found themselves confined in the "Detroit city prison."[56] Of the thirteen, only three eventually deserted for good, while another three would eventually be thrown out of the service after being court-martialed for various offenses.[57]

Willis S. Coon and his son Lewis of Company E, both of Rives Township in Jackson County, deserted from Camp Chandler on 12 April after only two months of "soldiering." Both had collected about $400 in bounty money, and DeLand thought Uncle Sam should have his money's worth. In July the local provost marshal caught up with the elder Coon and returned him to the Sharpshooters. They never apprehended Lewis, but another son, James, remained with the regiment. Willis would be caught by the rebels in another year; eventually he gave up more than his freedom.[58]

Despite the desertions, the regiment was actually increasing in size. Only 400 Sharpshooters chased Morgan through Indiana in July, but by the beginning of August there were 800 men in the ranks.[59] Recruiters (especially those who wanted a commission) combed the state. By twos and threes the new men showed up at Fort Dearborn.

Wallace Woolsey and his friend Douglas Hazel, both from Northport, left their homes near the end of July aboard Woolsey's boat. The two 18-year-olds left word that they were sailing to "salt water," and they did not want their parents to follow. In a few weeks the folks at home learned that the boys had enlisted in Company I.[60] Within a month, Hazel deserted from the regiment; maybe he made it to salt water. Woolsey would serve out his enlistment.[61]

Another new enlistee was Cyrus Perrigo of Arbela Township in Tuscola County. Only recently turned 18, the young Perrigo was one of Lt. William Randall's prospects. His older brother Simeon was currently with the Tenth Michigan Infantry.[62] Perrigo would not only participate in all the escapades of the regiment but would be the last survivor of all the men who served in the Sharpshooters.

The increased enlistments would have cheered any colonel, and DeLand must have been extraordinarily pleased to see the new men. When mustered in as colonel of the First Regiment Michigan Sharpshooters on 6 July, DeLand had been told by General Willcox, his department commander, that the rank was "conditional." If the regiment did not reach minimum strength, DeLand's contingent was in danger of being parceled out to other regiments then being raised.[63]

Special Duties

Being the only regiment-in-training in the vicinity, the Sharpshooters had the dubious honor of furnishing ceremonial guards for all occasions, and August proved to be a busy month for them.

Henry Kessler of Company G, a 45-year-old member of the band, died early in the month. Lieutenant Conn, the entire band (including Kessler's son Thomas), and a detail of eight men under Sgt. Daniel Gore accompanied the remains to Kessler's home in Elkhart, Indiana, where they attended the funeral.[64]

On 13 August Lt. Col. Mark Flanigan of the Twenty-fourth Michigan Infantry, who had lost his left leg at the Battle of Gettysburg, was feted in Detroit. Company B, under Captain Dicey, turned out for the reception. The local reporter was impressed by the appearance of the Sharpshooters. "They have gained a precision in military evolution that does them credit."[65]

Another funeral took place in Ann Arbor on 16 August; quite a turnout of Sharpshooters, commanded by the adjutant, attended the affair. Forty-six men, six noncommissioned officers, and the brass band under Lieutenant Conn traveled by special train to the obsequies.[66]

Small details chipped away at the command. Pvt. Peleg A. Briggs (Co. D) went to Detroit, having been detailed as an orderly for General Willcox.[67] Other, more odious details had to be handled as well. On 15 August 2nd Lt. Cyrenius Knight (Co. D) returned to Detroit with his small detachment of Sharpshooters. They had taken 40 Union deserters from Detroit and Cairo, Illinois, and turned them over to military authorities at Memphis, Tennessee. Some of the deserters were "hard cases," having skipped three or four times already. Perceiving no problems with this group, Knight said "he would either bring back a receipt for each man returned to his regiment or a receipt for his death."[68] Knight's squad experienced few difficulties with its task.

Only days before, Lieutenant Colonel Beadle had finally felt well enough to resume some of his duties. While escorting a batch of prisoners to Vicksburg, Mississippi, Beadle severely injured his left leg, just above the knee. Beadle was "one of those ever active, living, stirring, energetic men who can never rest on any account," according to the optimistic Chaplain Heagle. The wound had kept him from his daily chores, and he resented the inactivity.[69] So did the rest of the regiment.

The war continued without the Sharpshooters. They had chased after John Morgan and his will-o'-the wisp horse thieves, but things had again settled down to the dull routine of arsenal life. They hungered for action. As usual, though, higher authorities thwarted their expectations.

CHAPTER 4

I Do Not Like This Camp

Arrival at Camp Douglas

Sunday, 16 August 1863, turned out to be the busiest day since the Sharpshooters had left Michigan a month before. Early in the morning Colonel DeLand received a telegram from Brig. Gen. Orlando B. Willcox, commander of the Department of Indiana and Michigan. The orders were explicit. The Sharpshooters were to vacate the Dearborn arsenal and to proceed immediately to Camp Douglas in Chicago. Company commanders assembled their men at 3:00 PM and told them to be ready to leave in five hours.[1]

Seven companies (A, C, D, E, F, G, and K) gathered their belongings and stuffed them into knapsacks and haversacks, checked their weapons, wrote quick letters to loved ones, and formed in the arsenal yard for last-minute instructions. Captain Dicey readied his Company B at Fort Wayne to "march with his whole command, take the train at the Junction, and join the Regiment."[2] All the men carried one day's cooked rations; the quartermaster prepared five days' rations in bulk to be shipped with the regiment.[3] Companies H and I remained at the arsenal under the command of Lieutenant Colonel Beadle; when they reached minimum strength, they were to join the rest of the regiment at Camp Douglas.

Before the seven arsenal companies departed, Colonel De-
Land addressed them. He paternally admonished the men to
avoid straggling and to stay on the train. Any "strolling from the
command will be surely punished," he told them. "It is hoped that
the hurtful, and disgraceful practice of whiskey drinking will be
discontinued, that the disgraceful scene of our former march may
be avoided."[4] Those who had chased Morgan's horse thieves
through Indiana understood DeLand's allusion. Adjutant Buckbee then called the assemblage to attention and presented Major
Piper with a sword, sash, and belt. Donations for the gift had
come from the men in the ranks. Piper, always crisp and terse,
accepted the gift, delivered a brief speech of thanks, and the
seven companies marched out of the arsenal.[5]

An enlisted man wrote, "We were loaded in good passenger
cars before nine [PM] and were on our way rejoicing. What a
grand idea to go to Camp Douglas—the renowned camp."[6] Buckbee and a number of others felt far from elated. "We were all
eagerly looking forward to the time when we would go to the
front; and, in a short time received orders—but, alas! not to go to
the front—but to Chicago."[7]

Camp Douglas had been inaugurated in 1861 as a mobiliza-
tion center for troops from the 24 northern counties of Illinois.
Located about three and a half miles south of Chicago, the land
belonged to the Stephen A. Douglas estate. An Illinois judge and
senator and Democratic presidential contender, Douglas had died
in June 1861. The tracks of the Illinois Central Railroad ran near
the edge of Lake Michigan, just alongside the camp.[8]

All told, about 25,000 Union soldiers trained at Camp
Douglas during the Civil War.[9] Rebel prisoners from Ulysses S.
Grant's victory at Fort Donelson arrived there in March 1862. By
July 7,850 Confederates occupied the stockade.[10] In the fall of
1862, 8,000 Union soldiers who had been captured and paroled
by the Confederates at Harpers Ferry, Virginia, were sent there.
Because the Union prisoners had been paroled (it was still an
innocent time, and men gave their word not to fight against their
captors until duly exchanged), they ultimately went off to garrison forts on the western frontier, where they could still be used
to fight Indians. All the paroled soldiers had left by April 1863.[11]

In May 1863 most of the rebel prisoners were removed from
the camp, leaving only those too sick to be transported.[12] It was
at this juncture that Colonel DeLand received orders to invest
Camp Douglas. He became overall commander of the camp, while

Major Piper commanded the Sharpshooters who would guard the Confederate captives.[13]

There were essentially three separate areas to the camp.[14] The eastern part faced the road; it held the camp headquarters, a parade ground known as "Garrison Square," and barracks for the officers and men guarding the camp. Adjutant Buckbee, like many of his men, remembered the camp well long after the war:

> The buildings were all one story, except the headquarters, which was a story and a half building[;] not far from the main entrance and just in front of the headquarters was the band stand and flag staff. The barracks for Company officers and their men were on the North, West and South frontages of this square. Back of the barracks on the South side of the square was a large space occupied by teamsters, servants, etc.[15]

Just south of that area was the hospital complex, and west of the headquarters was the prison camp proper. The parade ground used by the guards for training purposes encompassed 20 acres. Outside and across the road from the main gate was a tower; Chicago's citizens would climb the tower for a fee to look at Union soldiers in training or Southern boys in captivity.

A 14-foot-high board fence, three miles in circumference, surrounded the entire camp. When the Sharpshooters took over the camp, nothing separated the prisoners from Garrison Square except a line of guards; no fence had been erected there yet.[16] Guards walked a beat of 120 feet each along the fence surrounding the prison yard. A "dead line" existed just inside the fence; any prisoner who stepped over it was fair game for the pickets. In this case, the dead line was a ditch. No one was permitted in it.[17]

Stepping off the train at 10:00 Monday morning, 17 August 1863, the seven companies of Sharpshooters looked across at their new quarters. Their trip to Chicago had been uneventful except for frequent stops. At 2:00 AM Monday there was a 20-minute layover in Marshall, Michigan.[18] At 6:30 AM the regiment arrived with the morning light at Niles, Michigan.[19] Three and a half hours later they rolled into Chicago. Their reception was not auspicious. One of the Sharpshooters noted their "welcome":

> There had been a heavy rain during the night and in consequence of which water was standing on the ground within the camp. When

it was seen by the "sojers" their ambition in a measure subsided. We were kept as in parade nearly half an hour until our quarters were assigned, when we marched to them, unstrung knapsacks, and began to do duty, cleaning up dirt and "graybacks" (vermin).[20]

Word quickly spread that the new regiment at Camp Douglas included a detachment of Indians. "No company has excited more curiousity than they," related one of the Sharpshooters. "The Chicagonians seem to be all eager to see them." Enthused at the welcome experienced by the regiment and its "celebrity" company, the chronicler commented further on Company K: "The Indians seem to be 'all the go' with them, and make good soldiers." He did not neglect the rest of the regiment: "Send the Sharpshooters more soldiers, just such soldiers as the number at present here, and Michigan will be honored still more than she has been."[21]

Only 49 rebels occupied the camp when the Sharpshooters detrained.[22] They were the sick who had to be left behind when most of the others were transferred out. The next day 600 Confederate prisoners entered the camp, and the day after that another 560 joined them. These were Morgan's men, the same Confederates who had led the Sharpshooters on a merry chase a month before. It must have felt like sweet justice to the Michigan boys.[23]

One rebel from an Alabama regiment remembered that when he and his fellow prisoners arrived at Camp Douglas the night of 24 August, a heavy frost covered the ground. "We fared tolerably well for a time as to rations, but most of us were thinly clad and in poor shape for the approaching winter."[24] A Sharpshooter agreed: "The 'rebs' are a rough looking set," he noticed, "clothed in all sorts of colors and styles, mostly in cotton. The cold nights has [sic] brought them to a realizing sense of their condition, and they are often seen hovering around a fire like 'chickens around a dough dish.'"[25]

In just a few more days the total rebel population of Camp Douglas reached 1,600. Colonel DeLand was overwhelmed by the position he now occupied. "It is an immense job for me with my small force of men," he wrote his wife only three days after his arrival. "We mount now 200 guards daily. The officers & men go on duty every day, and I work from 5 in the morning till midnight." Finishing the letter, an annoyed and bone-tired DeLand added, "It is now 12 at night & there are 600 more prisoners at the landing coming in to night."[26]

Reverend Heagle, in a cheerful letter to the Detroit *Advertiser and Tribune*, saw the colonel differently; he described DeLand at this stage as a "take charge" commandant. "With his coat off, though, and that extraordinary manner of his in dispatching undertakings, he has succeeded already in accomplishing wonders. The chaotic camp of yesterday is at this time one of the strictest order." [27]

A week later there were so many more rebel prisoners that it took half the Sharpshooters to mount guard, "making it rather hard for the boys, having to go on every other day," remarked an enlisted man.[28] To at least one young Sharpshooter—19-year-old Amos Farling (Co. G)—life was a lark, even at Camp Douglas. Hardships and work were aspects of life that had to be endured, but there was also time for frivolity, and Farling chronicled much of it. Even though the men stood guard every other day, "nevertheless we had a jolly time," he related.[29]

Much of the first month's duty for the Sharpshooters included not only guarding and taking care of the prisoners, but also reconstructing much of the camp's facilities. Barracks had to be rebuilt and the campgrounds improved; in fact, the entire camp had to be fixed up. Many of the bunkhouses had no windows, beds, or stalls; everything was covered in dust and grime.[30]

By the end of August more than 3,500 Confederates were incarcerated at Camp Douglas, and much work needed still to be done. Fortunately, Company H, under Capt. Andrew J. Hall, was now at the camp. Leaving Dearborn on 27 August, the new men arrived the next day. Only Company I was still at the arsenal.[31]

According to Chaplain Heagle:

> Col. DeLand's treatment of rebel prisoners is remarked to be very different from that which he himself experienced when a prisoner in Georgia . . . [;] the fact that a large sewer is being constructed under his direction for the draining of the camp—a thing that has long been very much needed—illustrates his regard for the sanitary welfare of his men.[32]

As a token of esteem for their commander, the officers of the regiment presented DeLand with a "very handsome watch" on the evening of 23 September.[33]

September was obviously the month for testimonials. Back at the arsenal, Lieutenant Colonel Beadle accepted a "beautiful silver mounted breech loading rifle." Lt. Robert F. Hill presented the weapon on behalf of Company I.[34] During the same month Capt. Thomas Gaffney (Co. G) received quite a tribute from his hometown folks in Niles, a silver-hilted sword and belt that cost more than $100. Gaffney was one of the veterans; he had entered the Ninth Michigan Infantry, DeLand's old regiment, in August 1861. By the following March he wore a second lieutenant's shoulder straps. He fought well at the Battle of Murfreesboro and was wounded in the fray. He and DeLand obviously got along well; the latter wrote a fine biography of Gaffney in his history of Jackson County four decades later.[35]

Overcrowding (in excess of 5,000 prisoners at the beginning of October) so strained the camp's resources that DeLand received an official chastisement from Col. William H. Hoffman, the U.S. Commissary General of Prisoners.[36] Hoffman's acting medical inspector, Surg. A. M. Clark, examined Camp Douglas in October and found much to complain about. Only the rations were "abundant and good," all else was in arrears. The water supply and sewage disposal were wanting, there was no general cleanup of the camp, and discipline was poor. The prisoners' barracks were not heated, most of the prisoners were filthy, and they were inadequately clothed.[37]

DeLand defended himself vigorously. He insisted the problems were not his fault: "the camp has here-to-fore been a mere rookery; its barracks, fences, guard houses, all a mere shell of refuse pine boards; a nest of hiding places, instead of a safe and compact prison." He also contended that he was doing all in his power to alleviate the problems, but more money and manpower were needed.[38]

Lieutenant Randall blamed the rebels for the unsanitary conditions in the barracks: "The prisoners had plenty of water, yet they allowed their quarters to become very filthy. This was their own fault for they had nothing else to do but clean quarters."[39]

Progress continued. Sanitary facilities were deemed "very good" after another inspection in December. Drains were dug throughout the camp to alleviate the problem of standing water. Soon after, coal stoves heated all the barracks, and appropriate clothing was provided all the prisoners.[40]

In late October a measles epidemic hit the camp. The regimental surgeons were assisted by nurses from the prison population and from the Sharpshooters. Captain Rhines started a medical corps for the prisoners. He found ten Confederates in the camp "who had left home and practice of medicine to fight in line for Dixie," and he put them in charge of all the sick rebels. At first, the medical corps went from barracks to barracks to minister to the ill. Later, an old chapel was partially renovated and appropriated for the use of the ill; 70 sick men were put there.[41]

The Invalid Corps

The manpower situation was alleviated somewhat when 400 men of the Eighth and Fifteenth Invalid Corps arrived at Camp Douglas in the middle of November. Made up of Union soldiers considered physically unfit for active field duty, the Invalid Corps did duty guarding camps, arsenals, hospitals, and military offices. They were men who still wanted to serve. Suffering from wounds or sickness, they were incapable of active field service but could perform lighter work, such as guarding prisoners or arsenals.[42] Officers who opted for the Invalid Corps were demoted one grade. A major became a captain, a captain a lieutenant, and so on.

The name "Invalid Corps" really rankled the men in the organization (only a rare individual wishes to be pointed out as deficient in any regard). It was bad enough that their rebel charges in Camp Douglas and other prison pens called them "Condemned Yankees."[43] That their own government should inflict such a derisive sobriquet on them was a cruel joke. Eventually, the name was changed to "Veteran Reserve Corps," a title deserving respect. After all, they were men who had "seen the elephant" in all its trappings. They were veterans proud enough to stay in the army and serve their country, even though many of them surely belonged in hospitals themselves.

These veterans wore distinctive uniforms of a light blue, the color of a robin's egg, which shouted at the beholder that the wearer was some sort of anomaly; they hated the color intensely. Finally, the powers in Washington relegated the new uniforms to the bonfire, and the veterans exchanged them for the standard type.[44]

The last company of Sharpshooters stationed at the Dearborn arsenal finally joined the rest of the regiment at Camp Douglas in early November. One company of the Invalid Corps relieved them at Dearborn, and Lieutenant Colonel Beadle led Company I onto the train bound for Chicago.[45] They arrived at the camp on Wednesday, 4 November. For the first time DeLand's command was assembled as a unit. The next day Beadle assumed command of the entire regiment, since DeLand was in charge of the post itself. In addition, on 1 December DeLand took over as military commander at Chicago.[46]

With the regiment now filled at least to the minimum, many officers believed they would soon be transferred to active service in the field.[47] They were mistaken. Another rumor making the rounds was that they would soon be issued new Spencer repeating rifles; after all, they *were* Sharpshooters. This, too, was only more wishful thinking.[48]

The Rebel Prisoners

Visitors to the camp remained a constant source of irritation to the guards. One of the Sharpshooter officers vented his anger and frustration over his duties to a friend back in Hillsdale:

> We are in the *delightful* business of guarding rebel prisoners, some 4,000, nearly all of whom are Morgan's men, and mostly from Kentucky, and are a better class of prisoners, as far as size and intelligence are concerned, yet meaner and harder to get along with—demanding more privileges than others. We are annoyed very much by their friends coming from Ky. to see them. Ex-Governor Magoffin of Ky. has been here four days trying to see his son and succeeded to-day.
>
> I do not like this camp, it is low and dirty and the sand flies continually. The rebs are a dirty, lousy set of fellows and have a good many sick. This cold weather pinches them terribly as they are poorly clad and have no blankets.[49]

Lieutenant Randall of Company I concurred when he wrote that "the border States men are more bitter towards us than those from the Gulf States."[50] An enlisted man related that the guards "are not allowed to converse with them now, nor even patronize the same sutler."[51]

Once the rebels realized where they were and learned the routine of camp life, the more industrious among them began making plans to escape. No scheme seemed too daring. Some tried to bribe their way out, but the Sharpshooters figured that one out quickly. In at least one instance a guard took a bribe, then reported it, but kept the trust of the rebel. The prisoner was allowed to pass, but—lo! and behold!—another guard picked up the prisoner, returning him to the stockade. What happened to the Confederate's money was not related.[52]

A prisoner bribing a guard or attempting to escape was punished in any number of ways. One of the most common was to tie the offender up by his thumbs so that his toes barely touched the ground. It was an innocuous-sounding chastisement, but one guaranteed to make some men deathly ill after a few hours.[53]

Because of the extent of the camp, outsiders prowled about the high board fence almost at will. At times, articles were thrown over the fence to be picked up by the rebels inside. In mid September six prisoners (among them young Magoffin) tried to escape. The attempt was thwarted, but a waiting carriage was noticed outside the fence. Conicidentally, ex-Governor Magoffin of Kentucky, the lad's father, was in Chicago at that time.[54]

By early October the new sewer was completed and two Confederates (there were now 5,782 present) escaped through it. It took them 16 hours to churn their way through the three-quarters of a mile length of it. Then they celebrated their escape in grand style, trying to drink their way through Chicago's saloons; only one eluded capture.[55]

In the middle of October, 26 prisoners escaped. Worse yet, they broke out of the "White Oak," the camp's dungeon. A small building set aside to confine those guilty of various infractions (in particular, escape attempts), all of the White Oak's present occupants had tried to escape before; now they pooled their talents. Confined in an upper story, they cut their way through the floorboards to the room below, then pried up floorboards and dug a tunnel 25 feet to the fence. "The impracticability of the affair increases still more," recalled one of the Sharpshooters who later discovered the escape, "when we remember that they had no suitable instruments to dig with; [all] they had were some old broken [tin] plates and the fingers God gave them."[56] They picked a dark, cold, and stormy night to go under the wall—a perfect setup.

The escapees moved so stealthily that a guard stationed outside the door of the White Oak remained unaware of the escape until morning. Some were retaken after the hue and cry was raised, but others remained on the loose. "All of them might be captured, or would have been brought back into camp before this, if there were no copperheads to assist them," related one of the Sharpshooters.[57]

Because of DeLand's complaints, a new fence was built around the entire camp; it was scheduled for completion in November. Two coats of whitewash, inside and out, were applied, so as to better see the outlines of unauthorized personnel at night.[58]

In November six barracks burned down. The fires stemmed from overheated stoves, and 400 feet of fence also burned. One evening while on guard, Private Farling saw fire licking out the window of a barracks where surplus rifles were stored. Discharging his weapon, he yelled for the corporal of the guard. In a moment bugles rang out. Extra sentries ran hastily to posts encircling the camp. Maybe, the men thought, the fire was a ruse to mask another escape attempt. Fire engines arrived from the city, but 120 feet of barracks was a smoking ruin, as were the muskets inside. As a result the camp became so crowded that 1,000 captives were transferred to another prison at Rock Island, Illinois.[59]

On the foggy evening of 3 December, 65 of John Hunt Morgan's men escaped through another tunnel; 57 feet long, it started beneath a bunk in one of the barracks alongside the fence and ended just outside the perimeter of the fence. Thirty of the escapees were apprehended by the next afternoon, picked up at various railroad stations in Chicago. Some turned up in a couple of Chicago hotels; others were brought in during the next few days, apprehended while making their way south. Only a few evaded capture.[60]

The Boredom of Camp Life

In mid November orders arrived from Maj. Gen. Henry Halleck, general-in-chief of the armies, telling DeLand to report with his men to the Army of the Cumberland in southern Tennessee. As soon as the six Invalid Corps companies were reinforced at Camp Douglas, the regiment could depart; but reinforcements did not show up and the order was rescinded two weeks later. The Sharpshooters roundly damned the fates that ruled them.[61]

The rumor mill ground out another story—four companies of the Invalid Corps were due to arrive on 16 December, with six more to follow the next day. "This looks like the departure of the Sharpshooters for the front," Chaplain Heagle gleefully informed the readers of the Detroit *Advertiser and Tribune*. But no, it proved to be more gossip bandied about by hopeful souls. It was back to drill and guard duty. The front seemed very, very far away.

No competent army allows its component parts to idle away; too many problems arise. Knowing that, the men were kept busy by their officers in a series of duties besides guarding prisoners. Major Piper drilled the men mercilessly. All Civil War regiments received drill instruction; some became quite proficient in military maneuvers, but few were drilled as long as the Sharpshooters. They had been in some camp or other learning soldierly responsibilities since January 1863, principal among them being drill, drill, drill. Except for the few weeks spent chasing Morgan's horse thieves in Indiana, they drilled. Now, besides guarding rebel prisoners, they drilled again.

While some of the men drew guard duty, others met in Garrison Square. Major Piper set the tone in October. Squad drill ran from 10 to 11:00 AM; company drill followed in the afternoon from 1:30 to 2:30. Every line officer and enlisted man not on guard duty or excused by the surgeon or the commanding officer of the regiment "must be present for these drills." Men and officers were subject to inspection at both drills, and particular attention was paid to unmilitary appearances. Sure to rankle the major, a stickler for military protocol, was sloppy dress; his unmitigated wrath fell on those privates guilty of "the practice of wearing the pants in the boots, and of going with the coat unbuttoned," and crushing in the of tops of their caps to look like veterans.[62] After one inspection, Piper caustically remarked that there were only two or three hats in the regiment that looked "regulation." He informed the company officers that such behavior "destroys their uniformity & looks," and it would not be tolerated.[63]

As odious as drill could be, some of the men took pride in their unit's appearance. One Sharpshooter regaled the homefolks with such a description:

> As they form into line now, on dress parade, in the evening, it does not need a very skillful eye to tell where the line is; but every man is in his place, and the line is a straight one, and the "Order arms," "shoulder arms," "present arms," etc., are all executed "decently and in order"—the thumps of the muskets along on the ground are all together as one thump, and the presentations &c., are all correct and in unison.[64]

Cottage Grove

There were also days off for some of the men. It did not take them long to learn of a popular watering hole known as Cottage Grove, located three-quarters of a mile south of Camp Douglas. A horse-drawn streetcar ran from the camp to the place. Actually, it was "a poor excuse for a grove," being a series of beer gardens and some bowling alleys scattered among some scrub oaks. But it was the closest thing to a saloon for the thirsty soldiers, and they had some merry times there.[65]

Several complaints had already been made about some drunken Sharpshooters. In September a number of them got into a fight at a German picnic not far from the camp.[66] Cottage Grove, though, was the primary place habituated by the off-duty Sharpshooters, and the men used every dodge and stratagem to spend time there. Some even exchanged uniforms with the Invalid Corps guards in order to pass their own guards at the camp gates.[67]

A few of the regimental officers were roughed up one night at Cottage Grove. The following evening some of the rank and file went back to reciprocate. Some of "the Germans lost the shape of their faces, and the contents of their grand saloon were demolished and strewn over the floor," recalled Amos Farling, who definitely had a hand in the fray.[68]

Boredom and Idleness

Back at the camp there were problems in the ranks again. The novelty of Camp Douglas wore off quickly. For whatever reason, Pvt. Henry Smith (Co. H), a 42-year-old enlistee from Coldwater, put an end to his life. Just relieved from guard duty, the poor soul walked off to a secluded corner and shot himself in the head on the evening of 25 September. No one knew the motivation for the act. Amos Farling's only comment was that Smith "was deranged."[69]

Forty-nine Sharpshooters deserted while the regiment was stationed at Camp Douglas. The boredom inherent in guarding prisoners and in repeated drill broke down morale.[70] Desertion, the great plague of the Sharpshooters, began gobbling up the men soon after they reached Camp Douglas. An enlisted man observed in late August:

> This regiment has been a long time getting up and is not full yet. There is [sic] a great many desertions. Last night a parole [patrol] was bringing them in that had got out of camp one way and another, and one made an excuse to go a little aside from the guard

when he took bail for security, as the saying is, and after refusing to halt at the word of command was fired at, the ball taking effect in the calf of the leg making quite a serious wound. He is now in the hospital.[71]

In late August DeLand detached a noncommissioned officer by the name of McCormick to pick up some deserters thought to be in Detroit. McCormick found them, but he let them go without reporting to the proper authorities. The suspicions of the deputy provost marshal in Detroit were finally confirmed when McCormick was identified by a man from Rochester, New York, as a deserter from a New York regiment. His arrest effectively removed him from the ranks of the Sharpshooters.[72] Merrick Bradley was another one. Having already seized a number of deserters from Camp Douglas, Merrick decided that he had had enough of army life, and he left the regiment for good at the end of September.[73]

At Camp Douglas, the Sharpshooters witnessed first-hand the effects of a major court-martial sentence. On 17 January the regiment, less those on duty in the camp, lined up on the parade ground and observed two of their own drummed out of camp. Toward 4:00 PM, with the Invalid Corps also drawn up in line, the Sharpshooters awaited the spectacle. The two miscreants, Pvts. William H. Wilder (Co. G) and John C. Miller (Co. F), were marched to Garrison Square. These two living examples of military justice became a crude warning to the rest of the regiment. Pvt. Daniel S. Robbins (Co. B) described the exhibition with appropriate editorial comments to the folks back home:

> the culprits appeared, hand-cuffed, with a board bound upon their backs, upon which was enscribed the word *deserter*, escorted by a guard of six men at charge bayonets, marching to the head of the column from there proceeded by the field band playing the Rogues' Band they was marched around the battalion, and from thence out of camp, with the finger of scorn pointed at them from every one, and from this place they was [*sic*] sent to work on fortifications for the period of two years, without pay.[74]

The colonel and his staff obviously hoped that the spectacle would have the appropriate effect on his men.

Bouts with the Bottle

Colonel DeLand deplored drunkenness. He had had trouble many years before with a whiskey faction in Jackson, and the very idea that some men allowed themselves to become slaves of John Barleycorn both amazed and dismayed him. The last man demoted at Camp Douglas was Sgt. Richard Freeligh (Co. F). For "repeated drunkenness and violation of standing orders of camp," Freeligh was reduced to the ranks in February 1864.[75] One of the Indians, Pvt. Sash-ko-bon-quot, a 45-year-old enlistee from Pinconning, died when he was crushed between two railroad cars. Subsequent investigations showed him to have been drunk at the time.[76]

First Lt. Ira Evans (Co. E) also had a weakness for the bottle. Lt. Col. Beadle was ready to dismiss Evans from the regiment for the latter's repeated forays with the whiskey jug. Beadle was more of a disciplinarian than DeLand. After being besieged by "the earnest appeals of the friends of Lieut Evans to overlook his offenses and by his personal pledge that hereafter he will entirely refrain from the use of intoxicating liquors," DeLand ordered Evans's release from arrest and his return to duty.[77]

The colonel cited certain "mitigating circumstances" in his release order. He admired Evans's previous military service; the lieutenant "has earned his promotion by his faithful service in the field and by personal bravery in the hour of Battle."[78] Evans was one of the veterans in the Sharpshooters, and he had an exemplary war record. For almost two years he had fought as part of the regimental color guard of the Second Michigan Infantry in all of its battles, from First Bull Run through the Peninsula Campaign of 1862.[79] To be selected for the regimental color guard was a mark of honor, a recognition by one's officers for being a brave and gallant soldier, and a distinction not bestowed lightly. DeLand's confidence in Evans would prove to be correct.

The colonel considered alcoholism as the "worst fault and most glaring defect" of the regiment; "officers cannot restrain men who themselves indulge in such vices," he counseled. He forbade the presence of any intoxicated soldier—enlisted man or officer—and further required that anyone shielding another member of the Sharpshooters known to be habitually intoxicated to be arrested. DeLand wanted no repetitions of the offense, but liquor never completely disappeared from the regiment. Its possession simply became more secretive.[80]

Captain Gaffney's Sin

Arrested and charged with "conduct unbecoming an officer and a gentleman to the prejudice of good order and military discipline," 25-year-old Thomas H. Gaffney (Co. G) found a more serious crime laid at his doorstep.[81]

Camp Douglas was only a few hours by train from the homes of many of the Sharpshooters, so friends and relatives frequently dropped by. One of the visitors—the wife of an enlisted man in Company G—evidently caught the eye of Captain Gaffney. Sarah Frost of Hudson, Michigan, often visited her husband William. Gaffney became enamored of Mrs. Frost; he "trumped up some charge against her husband and managed to have him thrown into the guard-house, where he remained for four weeks." In this manner (so stated an article in the Chicago *Times*, one of the foremost Democratic weeklies in the country), Gaffney managed to prey on the young wife who was trying to get her husband released from imprisonment. At Gaffney's insistence, she saw him daily in his quarters. One of the Indians reported Gaffney's behavior, and an investigation revealed the officer's culpability. Frost was freed from captivity; Gaffney was arrested on orders from the lieutenant colonel on 4 January. Unlike Evans, Gaffney found no savior. He did manage to stay with the regiment, although his status remained in limbo.[82]

A Journalistic Enemy

Wilbur F. Storey, the editor of the Chicago *Times*, was an old adversary of Colonel DeLand's. From Vermont, Storey came to Jackson, Michigan, in 1845 and started the Jackson *Patriot*.

In 1853 Storey became editor and proprietor of the Detroit *Free Press*. The paper was virulently Democratic in politics, in keeping with Storey's motto: "Print the news and raise hell." A strict constitutionalist, he hated abolitionists and saw the North as dragging the South into conflict. Seeking a bigger outlet for his political theories, Storey moved to Chicago in June 1861, where he bought the *Times* and made it a premier weekly and "the most outspoken anti-war and anti-administration newspaper in the country."[83]

Complaining about the anti-administration press occupied much of Colonel DeLand's time. As a former editor/publisher he knew the business well. Newspapers during the Civil War were notoriously biased; in the North the papers were either pro-Lincoln or anti-Lincoln, either partisan Republican or Democrat. There seemed to be no middle ground. DeLand always supported the Republican cause, regardless of where it led: Preserve the Union, prosecute the war, emancipate the slaves. His old Jackson *Citizen* kept the faith, unlike the Jackson *Eagle*, which adhered more to the Democratic way of thinking. In Detroit, the *Advertiser and Tribune* echoed the sentiments of President Lincoln's party, and the *Free Press* opposed the Republican handling of the war.[84]

A newspaper masthead could confuse the reader. The Niles *Republican* had Democratic leanings and reprinted many articles from the Chicago *Times*. The Marshall *Democratic Expounder* also quoted liberally from the *Times* and printed letters from Sharpshooters with Democratic proclivities, but without appending their names. The enlisted men expected chastisement from DeLand if their letters appeared in the Copperhead press, so the editors usually appended only an initial or two after each letter.

Because of DeLand's total dedication to the Republican Party, he was drubbed more than once by the opposition press. No sooner had the Sharpshooters arrived at Camp Douglas than the colonel forbade the Chicago *Times* in camp. That paper was acknowledged as a bitter foe of the Lincoln administration and as a solace to the rebels—it published news they liked to read.[85] At least one Sharpshooter complained of this in a letter to his hometown newspaper, the Marshall *Democratic Expounder*. More copies of the *Times* were sold in Camp Douglas than any other paper before the arrival of the Sharpshooters, "as the news-boy told me repeatedly," wrote the soldier identified only as "E." After enlisting, doing duty, guarding prisoners and the like—"are those that do all this to be deprived of that one trifling luxury?"—what was the harm in reading the *Times*?

> They have claimed that it discouraged enlistments. Under that head does it discourage enlistment, now that we have enlisted? Did it discourage us before enlisting? If it did why are we here? We read it before, and we enlisted. Not only three or four of us, but more, which fact I claim breaks down their argument.[86]

DeLand's attitude made him and his regiment a recipient of Wilbur Storey's venom. This was unfortunate, because many of the Sharpshooters were dyed-in-the-wool Democrats who followed Storey's view of the Lincoln administration. When DeLand forbade the circulation of the *Times* in the camp, Storey repaid the compliment, excoriating his old enemy with a blast entitled, "Colonel DeLand Rampant":

> It [DeLand] was formerly editor of an unknown sheet in Jackson, Michigan, and obsequious in performing dirty work for Blair, the abolition Governor of that State and a resident of that village, whence its commission and title as colonel.[87]

It is no wonder that DeLand tried to keep the *Times* out of the camp; he and Storey had neither love nor respect for one another.

False Witness

On the evening of Wednesday, 21 October, a pair of men representing themselves as Detroit detectives came to Camp Douglas and asked to see Colonel DeLand.[88] The two detectives, who gave their names as Smith and Green, produced various warrants, affidavits, and other documents. According to the detectives, two of DeLand's men—Pvt. Henry B. Cleavland and 1st Lt. George Fowler of Company H—had participated in a murder the previous September.

John C. Depew, an "old and respected citizen" of Chelsea, Michigan, and a dealer in agricultural machines, disappeared the night of 10 September 1863. Earlier that day Depew had sold some machinery; when he started for home that evening (a short distance from the village), he held a hefty amount of cash. He never arrived. The next day search parties combed the area; his body was not found until three days later. Found just outside of town near the railroad depot, the body had been robbed and the man's head crushed on one side.[89]

After holding them at arm's length, DeLand learned that Smith and Green would go over his head, to his department commander, if he did not voluntarily turn over the two Sharpshooters. The detectives took DeLand into their confidence. They:

> did not think that Cleveland [*sic*] & Fowler were guilty, but . . . they could do nothing further until these parties were produced, and . . . they would pledge me their sacred honor that the suspected parties should have a fair trial.[90]

Somewhat convinced, DeLand delivered up Cleavland, but refused to hand over Fowler unless the former were convicted, and then only if Fowler's presence was demanded by the court. Cleavland was taken to Ann Arbor, jailed, and arraigned.

Only later, when he learned the date of the murder, did DeLand realize he had been duped by Smith and Green. Cleavland supposedly had killed the man on 10 September 1863, but the soldier's company (H) had left Dearborn on 27 August and arrived at Camp Douglas the next day. Records showed that Cleavland was with his company; he had no furlough, nor was he absent from Camp Douglas for any 24-hour period between 27 August and the date he was arrested. Furthermore, Cleavland's whereabouts on 9 and 10 September were completely verifiable. On 9 September (the day before the murder), DeLand learned that Cleavland:

> "ran the guard," . . . and was seen outside in a drunken brawl, by Surgeon A. F. Whelan, who reported the fact to me; & I ordered Lt Fowler to send a guard for his arrest. Sergt. Charles Bragdon, Company H, with a squad of men was sent to arrest him, did so, & lodged him in the "guard house." He was released from Guard House at 8 o'c on the morning of the 10th of September & placed on guard [as punishment]. His name was duly entered on the Guard Report Book for that day as on duty on "Post No. 8, 3d Relief of 2d Division." Post No. 8 was a very important place, by an opening in the yard, and I went to the Officer of the Guard [Lt. George C. Knight] and rebuked him for putting Cleveland [*sic*] on that post, knowing he had been drunk the day before, and he replied that he had two good men each side of him who would watch him. . . . He was discharged from guard on the 11th of Sept at 9 1/2 o'c A.M. & on the 2d and 3d roll calls of that day, marked present with his company.[91]

DeLand immediately telegraphed the court to hold up the examination of Private Cleavland; he also, at his personal expense, sent two sergeants with the company roll book to Ann Arbor. Depositions were taken from both sergeants. DeLand further wrote to the court-appointed attorney for Cleavland, asking that depositions be taken from various Sharpshooters, because the presence of the defendants in Ann Arbor was well nigh impossible given the nature of their duties at Camp Douglas. The attorney, complained DeLand, dragged his feet, "paid no attention to the case," and did next to nothing to defend Cleavland. To add insult to injury, Smith and Green attacked DeLand's character by inserting "scurrilous reports" in the Ann Arbor paper.

When Cleavland's trial finally came up, the Sharpshooters were under marching orders to join the Army of the Potomac, and not a soldier could be spared to attend the proceedings. Cleavland was sentenced to the state prison at Jackson for life. "So far as I have learned," DeLand later wrote in a plea for clemency to Michigan's governor, Henry H. Crapo, "the evidence was all from beginning to end, manufactured by the detectives Green and Smith. The counsel assigned Cleavland did nothing to insure him a fair trial, and his conviction was a fraud and injustice."[92] Cleavland found himself convicted "on the testimony of a woman, supposed to be a harlot."[93]

Unfortunately, Cleavland had already served a term in prison. In October 1859 he had been convicted of larceny in Ingham County and had served the sentence in Jackson.[94] The exigencies of military life proscribed any action DeLand could take on Cleavland's behalf. Not until January 1865 did DeLand make another attempt to right what he knew was a wrong. Remonstrating with Governor Crapo, DeLand cited chapter and verse regarding Cleavland's innocence, but that letter and any attendant evidence failed to secure Cleavland's release. Henry Cleavland served the sentence handed down by the Washtenaw County court (solitary confinement in Jackson Prison) until the governor inexplicably pardoned him on 20 February 1867. He had served two years and eleven months, less one day, for a murder committed by someone else.[95]

Galvanized Yankees

Life was drab for the Sharpshooters, but even more so for the rebel prisoners. Boredom was their constant companion. "A few days ago a 'reb' thought to 'do something,'" wrote a Sharpshooter to his home folks:

> and got on top of the barracks. The report of a gun, the whistling of a bullet within a foot of his rebelship, brought him down, and with the remark that he had been in war but was never so scared in his life as he was then.[96]

Some of the Kentucky boys even asked to take the oath of allegiance so they could quit the prison and go home.[97] Captain

Rhines of Company A actually enlisted rebel prisoners for the Union army. Although he had no authority from Washington to do so, over 100 had been signed up.[98] Eventually termed "Galvanized Yankees," these Southerners obviously enlisted to get out of the prison pen, but they did not enlist to fight against the Confederacy. They joined Regular Army units to fight Indians on the plains and to keep the peace out West.[99]

The attitude of the Confederates changed, though, after prisoners from the Battle of Chickamauga entered the camp. A rebel victory, Chickamauga signaled a virtual end to "good Union men" in the Southern ranks. One of the Sharpshooters wrote home of 50 rebels being put under armed guard:

> A Union man belonging to the mess had his life threatened by them; the reason for the arrest was that he had manifested a desire to leave them by taking the oath of allegiance. He never was a rebel but [was] conscripted into their service. The intention of the authorities is to keep that squad there until the men who uttered the threat are given up.[100]

For the rebels who did not enlist, there were precious few ways of getting out of Camp Douglas. The most popular was to escape, or to die in the attempt. On New Year's Day 1864 the thermometer hit 38 degrees below zero. The howling wind sweeping across Lake Michigan drove snow through every crack in every barracks building. Guards were relieved every hour, yet they could barely move once they came off duty. During the night the wind and cold continued unabated. Dozens of the guards complained of frozen hands and feet. Two of the Sharpshooters were so stiff, "incapable of moving a foot or raising a hand," that it was not sure if they would recover.[101]

The men in the guardhouse ran out of coal that night; they kept the fire burning by breaking up whatever boards could be stripped from the inside of the building.[102] One of the sentries spied a ladder near the inside fence, but the weather was just too frightful to send a party to apprehend escapees. In the morning the guards found two rebels frozen stiff only a few yards outside the fence. Two more men were caught, cold and exhausted, some distance from the camp.[103]

A Night on the Town

At one and a half stories, the headquarters building at Camp Douglas was the tallest structure in the camp. The two rooms on the upper story were appropriated for the use of Adjutant Buckbee. The adjutant's responsibility centered on the paperwork of the regiment, and there was always plenty of it. Buckbee also had formidable authority; his orders were to be obeyed implicitly by the company commanders, even though they outranked him. In battle situations the adjutant carried the colonel's orders to the commanders. Although the orders were delivered by the adjutant, they emanated from the colonel.

The paperwork endemic in running the regiment and with the camp of prisoners was prodigious. The burden was such that a number of civilian clerks were employed at the headquarters building in addition to soldiers detailed from the ranks. Also enjoined in such work were two young Confederates, formerly of Morgan's command.[104] Buckbee "became very much attached to one of these men, and was a good friend to both of them." [105]

Having lived in Chicago before the war, Buckbee knew the city intimately. His sister was "one of the society ladies of the city," and consequently, "I was invited here and there and was kept on the continual go." [106]

During the Sharpshooters' stay at Camp Douglas, Edwin Booth, the noted tragedian and older brother of John Wilkes Booth, appeared at McVicker's Theatre in Chicago. One of Buckbee's Confederate clerks maintained that John Wilkes was the better actor of the two, but the young adjutant demurred, for he had seen both act. To end the argument, he asked the rebel clerk if he would accompany him to Chicago to see the elder Booth perform. "How on earth am I to go to the City and see a theatrical performance?" asked the Southerner. Buckbee's answer was as logical as it was daring:

> There is no reason on earth why you should not spend a night with me in my room up stairs. I can furnish you with clothes, and can walk you out of this camp without any questions being asked; and we can come back together—without any questions being asked.[107]

Unbelievably, the two carried out the plan without a hitch. Not only did they attend the performance, they also enjoyed an after-theater dinner at the home of Buckbee's sister. The two subsequently returned to Camp Douglas and Buckbee's quarters for the balance of the night. "I appreciate the fact that I was laying myself open," wrote an older and wiser Buckbee more than 40 years later, "not only to censure but probably to a court martial." In that, he was undoubtedly correct, but, as he remembered, "no questions were ever asked, and no complaints were made." [108]

The Brass Band

The brass band caused DeLand more trouble than he thought possible. It was created to solve a problem, not to provoke more headaches. During the Sharpshooters' stay at Dearborn, one of the officers had suggested a brass band to prop up morale. [109] At first, five fifers selected by Fife Maj. Odoniram J. Pettengill (Co. D) and four drummers chosen by Drum Maj. Albert W. Jacobs (Co. A) formed a "Music Corps" to be commanded by Pettengill. At the same time each company commander had to provide, procure, or enlist (however he saw fit) a bugler to be included in the drum corps. Practice sessions were relegated to four hours per day with mandatory daily appearances at reveille, dinner, and tattoo. [110]

No sooner did the proposition of a brass band evolve than the six companies left Dearborn to chase Morgan's horse thieves out of Indiana. When DeLand and the six companies took over Camp Douglas, the band was finally organized and later joined the bulk of the regiment along with Company G. [111]

Second Lt. Charles G. Conn (Co. G), excused from his regular duties, oversaw the education of the band members. An accomplished cornet player, Conn had originally served in the Fifteenth Indiana Infantry as a musician. After that band mustered out, the 18-year-old joined the Sharpshooters. [112] Colonel DeLand made a choice appointment by selecting Conn for this position. The young officer first set to work procuring acceptable musicians. In all, 13 men composed the brass band, although not all played at the same time. Strict rules governed those chosen for the available positions. Conn gathered his charges about him and the group practiced four hours per day, two in the morning and two in the afternoon. Exempt from regular duty, the band members nevertheless had a full schedule. Their presence was expected at all parades and inspections, including daily dress parade, Sabbath services, and at nightly concerts (weather permitting, of course) at

7:00 PM, at which they had to play at least four tunes for the regiment's enjoyment.[113]

While at Camp Douglas, one of the rebel prisoners joined the brass band. Emil Geyer, a German immigrant, had played in a band belonging to a Georgia regiment before his capture. A music teacher in the South before the war, he was an accomplished violinist. Geyer became friendly with Lieutenant Randall of Company I and often played the violin in the officer's quarters. Randall maintained that Geyer, after the latter took the oath of allegience, "was appointed leader of the Brass Band."[114]

Some trouble with the band developed at Camp Douglas. Colonel DeLand, in a letter of defense to the U.S. adjutant general's office on 10 April 1864, stated that the band had rendered no service since the first of the year.[115] Months later he sang another tune. Being chief administrator of Camp Douglas, he said, occupied all his time. When he took command of the regiment again in March, just before the transfer to the front, he called the officers of the regiment together to learn the status of the unit. When the subject of the brass band arose, there was some shuffling around of the blame for the state of affairs to which it had descended.

The band members had a set routine, but the terrible winter weather cut into their performances. Actually, the band had outlived its usefulness. No longer did the musicians play as often or as long as at Dearborn. Some of the members were chronically ill, and others actually refused to play at guard mounting or at any occasion at all. The officers agreed to discontinue its existence.

The regiment still needed qualified drummers and buglers. These were formed into a regimental music corps, commanded by 30-year-old Drum Maj. Abner Thurber of Three Rivers, Michigan. He saw to it that the buglers and drummers were properly instructed and that they practiced with their instruments. Furthermore, DeLand wanted to weed out all slackers. "Company Musicians and Buglers who are not prepared for duty, through neglect of officers or loss of their instruments will be placed upon duty as private Soldiers."[116]

More Deserters

Aside from the "irksum [*sic*] duty," as Pvt. Dan Robbins put it, of guarding prisoners and "drill, drill, drill," there were some official duties the Sharpshooters performed to alleviate the monotony of Camp Douglas.[117] Since September, details of Sharpshooters had been entrusted with delivering groups of Union army deserters apprehended in the Chicago area to Cincinnati. The men in the details had a chance to escape the humdrum of camp life and to see a bit of the world. Traveling by train, they would turn their charges over to the provost marshal in Cincinnati, explore the city, spend the night at the local soldiers' home, and return to Chicago the next day. It was an outing looked to with excitement.

Deserters were hunted or escorted only by men who were fully trusted by their commanders; one such man was Sgt. Joseph Stevens of Company B. A deserter named Charles Wheeler had sent his superiors a mocking letter, informing them that he actually helped some rebels escape while on guard duty, "and that they paid him well for his services." Stevens was ordered to find the ne'er-do-well and bring him back to face charges. Wheeler was picked up near Hillsdale and returned to Camp Douglas in the custody of the no-nonsense Stevens. The chagrined 20-year-old now told a different story; he was just tall-talking, he informed his superiors. They must have accepted his new version, because Wheeler was allowed to transfer to the Ninth Indiana Infantry a month later. Wheeler served in the Hoosier regiment for the remainder of the war, mustering out in September 1865.[118]

Another deserter, H. Sayers (Co. H), almost succeeded in reaching the safe haven of Canada. Arriving at Detroit from Camp Douglas, Sayers tried to steal a boat one night in the middle of March. His intrusion caused a barking dog to alert the boat's owner. Sayers drew a revolver, but the other man grabbed it from him, and a guard eventually took Sayers into custody.[119]

New Recruits

When assigned to Camp Douglas in August 1863, the First Michigan Sharpshooters had only the minimum number. During the fall and winter 50 men deserted and another 20 died; at the same time the regiment enlisted 62 men.[120] The relative numbers, then, remained essentially the same. Men arrived singly or in small groups during the winter to augment the ranks of the Sharpshooters. Often the hometown newspapers reported that a "squad in charge of Capt. A. J. Hall . . . left here on Monday morning"; more often than not, the departures were probably noticed only by a few loved ones.[121]

One of the new recruits was a man destined to bring glory to the Sharpshooters. He was Colonel DeLand's younger brother, James Speed DeLand. Jim was born in Jackson, Michigan, on 10 November 1835, "the first white boy born in the city limits."[122] At the age of 15 he went to work for his older brother in the office of the Jackson *Citizen*. For ten years the two brothers worked side by side, and then Jim went to Minnesota for a year. In 1862 he became part owner of the *Citizen*, and remained with it until the fall of 1863. In December he enlisted as a private in Company F, his cousin Hooker's company. A bit shorter than his older brother, Jim was balding and did not have the colonel's abrasiveness. Of the three DeLands in the Sharpshooters, Jim's reputation always remained sterling. Doubtless his relationship to the colonel helped get him promoted, but his conduct on and off the battlefield proved he deserved each promotion.[123]

One of the veterans to sign up with the Sharpshooters at Camp Douglas was a 17-year-old from Coldwater. John Rainbow had already served a year with the Seventy-fifth Illinois Infantry, and had participated in the Battles of Perryville and Stones River. Laid low by the measles, Rainbow left the army, but in October 1863 he signed enlistment papers with the Sharpshooters.[124]

Nineteen-year-old James B. Haight of Camden signed the Company E roster on 23 February 1864. His younger brother Sidney had been in the regiment since the previous October. The two boys visited a photographer a few weeks later, had their likenesses taken, and sent a copy home to their parents. They stared into the camera and posterity as they were about to embark on the great adventure of their lives.[125]

The Lieutenant Colonel Drills the Men

Ever since his arrival in November with Company I in tow, Lieutenant Colonel Beadle kept the men of the regiment drilling. There were squad and company drills in the morning, and for two hours each afternoon the men were put "through a most rigorous 'course of sprouts'" in battalion drill. Officers were not exempt; they had to report *in writing* to Beadle each morning the movement to be practiced by their men that same morning.[126]

Being responsible for their men learning the myriad drills, company officers shuffled them through *Casey's Tactics* at all hours of the day and night, in all sorts of weather. I "drilled my company many a day in the hours when [Camp] Douglas sleeps," remembered Lieutenant Randall.[127]

This routine "afforded my Regiment an opportunity to become most superbly efficient in battalion maneuvers,"[128] wrote Adjutant Buckbee. Lieutenant Randall bragged on the efficiency of the regiment: "It was not an uncommon thing for the Regt to form 'Hollow Square' from line of Battle in 30ty seconds."[129] The Hollow Square was a useless maneuver that was rarely used in battle, although the rapidity with which a regiment could form one did impress commanding officers. The Sharpshooters, like almost every other regiment in both armies, practiced it.

A no-nonsense disciplinarian, Beadle expected perfection from both his officers and his men, with particular onus being heaped on the officers if they neglected their duties or performed them inadequately. Years later Lieutenant Randall remembered Beadle; he had made quite an impression on the young officer: "I have often seen him halt the Reg't and call a delinquient [*sic*] officer to the front, damn him off soundly, and send him to his Qts. [quarters] under arrest."[130] Beadle was not to be trifled with; his regiment was going to be second to none in any endeavor.

Because so many Sharpshooters fell ill in the early weeks of January, the healthy men had to stand guard as often as every other day.[131] The new board fence surrounding the camp was almost completed, and it had an elevated walkway on the outside for the guards.[132] New hospital buildings being constructed under the supervision of Dr. Arvin Whelan, the chief surgeon, were fast approaching completion. Three Sharpshooters died in January— Cpl. Cornelius Montgomery (Co. E) from a measles relapse, Pvt. George Haulterbaum (Co. H) from typhoid pneumonia, and Cpl. Charles Nichols (Co. H) of "fits." Thirty-seven men were confined to the hospital with a variety of ailments, including pneumonia, frostbite, diarrhea, and vaccination complications, even though the chaplain asserted that the number of sick was drastically reduced from two weeks previously.[133] There were then 5,581 prisoners confined at Camp Douglas; 55 of them died in January.[134]

Dr. George L. Cornell of St. Clair left the regiment at the end of January, his resignation from December finally having been accepted. This left the Sharpshooters with only two doctors.[135] To make matters worse, payday came and went in January, but no pay came with it. "There is nothing said about going to the field," was an oft-repeated message of discouragement.[136] The last time the Sharpshooters heard anything different was just before Christmas, but they were still at Camp Douglas a month later.[137]

Target Practice

By February the Sharpshooters had begun target practice; after all, they were Sharpshooters even if they had been issued standard infantrymen's rifles. Besides battalion, company, and skirmish drill, and guarding the rebels, time was allotted for marksmanship.[138]

When the daily target practice commenced, the results amazed all onlookers. In order to qualify as a sharpshooter (according to War Department procedures), a man had to make a "string of five shots, 100 yards off hand or 200 yards at rest, not to exceed 25 inches."[139] In other words, after a soldier took his five shots at the target, the officer certifying the shots had to measure the distance from the bull's eye for each bullet. If the total sum was more than 25 inches, the soldier did not qualify as a sharpshooter.[140]

Capt. Andrew J. Hall of Company H took charge of target practice and certified each target.[141] In a letter extolling the merits of the regiment's shooting prowess, the readers of the Detroit *Advertiser and Tribune* learned that "Colonel DeLand has a regular shooting school, and every man is carefully instructed in all the details of using and managing a gun, and in target shooting."[142] One of the main problems in raising the regiment was that the men had to be marksmen. The proof of the pudding was now being tested. "Thus far," added the reporter, "but two men in [the] regiment have failed to make the required test on the first trial. I saw yesterday at the camp a large number of shots made at 40 rods[,] the average string being less than 15 inches." In fact, most were under 10 inches. [143]

On a different note, the writer remarked that the Sharpshooters "are heartily tired of 'home guard' duty," especially since winter was almost over, and the spring campaign would soon begin.[144] They had only to wait a little longer.

The War Beckons

Marching orders finally reached the Sharpshooters on Saturday, 12 March.[145] Colonel DeLand knew of the change as early as the middle of February, but he needed to have a replacement at Camp Douglas. That change came on 3 March when Col. James C. Strong of the Fifteenth Invalid Corps formally took command of the post from DeLand and his regiment.[146] Orders left the War Department on 8 March, commanding the Sharpshooters to report to Annapolis, Maryland, "without delay." Annapolis was designated the rendezvous point for all regiments of the Ninth Corps commanded by Maj. Gen. Ambrose Burnside.[147]

The Sharpshooters were on their way to war. They were so sick and tired of "home guard" duty that the news of their transfer "created a perfect *furore* of happiness and pleasure" among them.[148] "I can hardly depict the exuberance with which we received this information," commented Adjutant Buckbee. "It did not require any stimulating drinks to raise our feet and walk on air."[149]

CHAPTER 5

A Good "Breaking In"

The Road to Annapolis

The war beckoned the Sharpshooters, and the men and
boys gladly departed Camp Douglas for the front and
all its unknowns. Baggage packed and men ready, Colonel De-
Land ordered the regiment aboard the 22 cars of the Michigan
Southern Railroad on the afternoon of St. Patrick's Day, 17
March 1864.[1] The Sharpshooters had no regrets upon leaving
their home of seven months; 800 men piled aboard the cars. The
sick stayed behind. All the officers save one (Lieutenant Randall
was then home in Michigan on leave, and would join the regiment in Annapolis) accompanied their men.[2]

In a way, it was *déjà vu* for some of the veterans in the
regiment. In 1861, when the war still conjured thoughts of a
romantic quest and the slaughter of tens of thousands was a
horrible nightmare yet to come, young warriors on their way to
the front had received accolades and applause, handshakes and
kisses, cakes and pies, and every sort of "God bless you" and "Get
a rebel for me" at each whistle stop. Three years of interminable
bloodshed later, the mind-numbing sights of empty sleeves and
vacant chairs around family tables had sobered such overt outgo-
ings in all parts of America. But this was a new Michigan regiment going off to war in this spring of 1864. Yes, sir, it was one of

ours, and at every town along the Southern Michigan Railroad route, "we were greeted and feted," reported Chaplain Heagle.[3] Even after three heartbreaking years of grim war, Michigan still cheered on her sons.

Major General Burnside

The secretary of war had designated Annapolis, Maryland, as the "depot and rendezvous" for the Ninth Corps. Old regiments were ordered from Tennessee and new regiments from their respective states.[4]

The Ninth Corps was always linked to the name of its long-time commander, Maj. Gen. Ambrose E. Burnside. Burnside graduated from West Point in 1847, saw action in the Mexican War, and then fought Indians in the early 1850s. He resigned from the army in 1853 and involved himself in the manufacture and sale of a breech-loading rifle he had invented. After incurring heavy debts, he sold his patent. Ironically, the firm that bought the rights to the rifle sold thousands of these superior weapons to the U.S. government during the Civil War.

After the failure of his business venture, Burnside became a railroad administrator in Illinois. At the outbreak of the war he was appointed colonel of the First Rhode Island Infantry. Commanding a brigade at the Battle of Bull Run in July 1861, he received his first star. In 1862 he defeated a rebel force on the coast of North Carolina and won his second star and command of the Ninth Corps. He performed poorly at the Battle of Antietam, where he showed little initiative and clung to a conservative action when dash was needed.

Appointed commander of the Army of the Potomac (a job he did not want), Burnside had his army attack rebel entrenchments at Fredericksburg, Virginia, in December 1862. The battle was an abject defeat for the Union, a total debacle, and proved that Burnside was not the man the occasion merited. He was affable and courtly, well liked by his men, but events seemed to control him rather than the other way around.

Burnside was relieved of command of the Army of the Potomac, but retained control of the Ninth Corps. He also took over the much smaller Army of the Ohio, which was stationed at Cincinnati. In 1863 he kept the Confederates at bay in Tennessee, defeating them at Knoxville in a campaign that won laurels for him. In the spring of 1864 Burnside was transferred back East; he gathered together the disparate parts of his Ninth Corps at Annapolis.[5]

At this point in time Burnside's corps was not yet officially part of the Army of the Potomac, although it would act with that army. Actually, Burnside was superior in rank to the commander of the Army of the Potomac, Maj. Gen. George G. Meade. Meade could not just order the Ninth Corps around. Lt. Gen. Ulysses S. Grant accompanied the Army of the Potomac, issuing orders to Meade and Burnside and coordinating the movements of the Ninth Corps with the Army of the Potomac and thereby keeping the chafing to a mimimum.[6] Long after the war, one Ninth Corps officer even congratulated the magnanimous Burnside for putting aside rank to rally to the support of the republic.[7]

The train carrying the Sharpshooters passed through Ohio with no incidents to report, other than a change of cars at Cleveland. As the men neared Pittsburgh, the train ran off the tracks, "causing injury to no one and delaying us but two hours."[8] Nothing more about the trip was reported as the men sped through Harrisburg and then on to Baltimore. There they transferred to a ship, and reached Annapolis at 7:00 PM on 21 March. They disembarked and marched three miles northwest of the city to the Paroled Prisoners Camp, where they were put into standing barracks for a few days until tents could be provided for them.[9]

With the attendant confusion in the move from Camp Douglas, a few men came up missing. Pvt. Richard Johnson (Co. F) eluded the guards on the train, managed to stray from the regiment, and avoided the war.[10] Someone remembered Pvt. Edward C. Byrnes (Co. B) getting off the train in Elkhart, Indiana, but no one noticed him climbing aboard again. Byrnes was one of those men who needed watching. In April 1863, only two months after enlisting, he ran off, not returning to the regiment until 27 February 1864. Now he was gone for good.[11]

Getting Acclimated to the Army

The weather was none too kind to the Sharpshooters; it rained for two weeks after their arrival, making it miserable for the boys in their tents.[12] H. J. Gray, a representative of the Michigan Soldiers' Relief Association in Baltimore and Annapolis, and

Chaplain Heagle tendered a list of 47 Sharpshooters in different hospitals, "who are suffering from indisposition brought on by the late severe weather."[13] Included on the list was the bedridden Lieutenant Colonel Beadle, who was recovering from pneumonia. Captain Rhines (Co. A) had been stricken with smallpox. Also listed as sick were Capts. Andrew J. Hall (Co. H) and George N. Davis (Co. D). In addition, Charles Fox (Co. B), a 19-year-old farmer from Reading, had already died from typhoid pneumonia. So had Silas D. Fegles of Niles, Michigan, but his was a special case.

Fegles, one of Company A's first enlistees, had left the regiment while on leave in June 1863. On the books as a deserter since that time, he had been arrested in January by a local provost marshal and sent to Annapolis soon after the Sharpshooters arrived there. While incarcerated, Fegles came down with typhoid pneumonia. He died of its effects on 23 April 1864 without being tried. They laid his remains to rest in the national cemetery at Annapolis.[14]

The First Michigan Sharpshooters was now part of the Ninth Corps; as part of a larger unit, the regiment had to provide men for a myriad of corps details. First off, though, the regiment needed a sergeant major. The previous one, John Quackenbush, had been "relieved from duty" on 1 April, "Reduced to the Ranks[,] and ordered to report to Adjutant E. J. Buckbee in arrest."[15] The replacement—a good choice as future events unfolded—was the colonel's younger brother, Jim DeLand.[16]

The Sharpshooters were visibly impressed with the immensity of the Ninth Corps camp. "In every direction from our camp, as far as we can see," commented George Warren, the hospital steward, "are outspread the white tents of accumulating regiments, so that there seems to be only an itinerant city of active and stirring soldiers."[17]

While in camp near Annapolis, the Sharpshooters saw the sights, made acquaintances in the other regiments assigned to the Ninth Corps, and performed the duties and extra details inherent in all armies. A month after their arrival, the Twenty-seventh Michigan Infantry came into camp; a new regiment, the Twenty-seventh contained a host of boys from Hillsdale County. Home was not so far away after all.[18]

As in all armies, there were unending chores. The first sergeants looked over their books and assigned unpleasant duties to unlucky soldiers. Cpl. William Buchanan (Co. A), one of three brothers from Burlington, was told that he was now Major Piper's hostler; Pvt. William Hatch went to the hospital as a cook; and 34-year-old Pvt. William Cady (Co. C) became Quartermaster Palmer's orderly.[19]

Orders from Ninth Corps headquarters detailed Sharpshooters for "Special Service." Led by Capt. Edwin V. Andress, 96 enlisted men were assigned duty as a "Police Party" on 14 April,[20] and 22 more joined the party the next day.[21] A day later 20 extra men left under the command of Sgt. Alonzo Walls (Co. C) and Cpl. Jeremiah O'Leary (Co. H) to report to the U.S. General Hospital at the Naval Academy for "permanent guard duty." Knowing they would be gone for a while, the men were supplied "with a tent, a proper number of camp kettles and mess pans." [22] Ten more men (the regiment's quota) set out for fatigue duty, manhandling supplies of all kinds at the Ninth Corps depot, for the day of 17 April.[23] The next day a man from each company, commanded by Cpl. Thomas Blake (Co. F), reported for duty at the Ninth Corps provost marshal's office.[24] Another order commanding ten men under Corporal Quackenbush (formerly the sergeant major) to "report with either an ax or a spade" as a detail for the regimental "Pioneer Corps" came through channels on 22 April. Definitely not a choice assignment, one man from each company received the bad news from his first sergeant and reported (no doubt with appropriate epithets) to Corporal Quackenbush.[25]

Not being on his own hook any longer, Q.M. Sgt. Milo Dyer found that he had to go through more channels to procure and store supplies for the regiment. Pvts. Fred Smith, George W. Barnes, Obediah Gleason, and John Waters were assigned to Dyer, whose problems were just beginning.[26] Heretofore, with the exception of when the Sharpshooters were chasing Morgan's men through Indiana, their home base had been static. Now the regiment followed the fortunes of the Ninth Corps, which was shortly to join the Army of the Potomac. Dyer's duties would soon become manageable, but for the interim he needed extra help.

Problems arose in the medical section as well, but they were quickly resolved. George Warren, the steward responsible for the regimental hospital stores, requested assistance; 43-year-old Pvt. Wesley Sage, previously detailed as a nurse, stayed on as Warren's assistant.[27]

The regiment still had two qualified surgeons. Assistant Surgeon George Cornell left the regiment, and Dr. Asahel B. Strong of Reading, Michigan, joined it in January. Strong came into the regiment with a personal recommendation from the regiment's chief surgeon, Arvin Whelan. They had practiced together a number of years, and Strong's skills were well appreciated by Whelan.[28] There was a problem, though. Strong had not been formally mustered, nor had he yet been paid, despite Colonel DeLand's pleas that the situation be rectified. While in Annapolis, DeLand managed to have Dr. Strong formally mustered, and the surgeon's commission was backdated to January 1864.[29]

The appointment of Strong released Dr. McNett from the service. Although in poor health, McNett stayed on until the new surgeon's nomination became final. McNett had been with the regiment since its inception, and his resignation left Dr. Whelan with just one assistant again.[30]

Few of the men or officers in the regiment had much rest after reaching Annapolis. As the ranking officer, Colonel DeLand met the commanders of nearby regiments, carefully noting who had superior rank. Even though the Sharpshooters had only joined the Ninth Corps within the past month, there were colonels of inferior grade in older regiments; DeLand's commission dated from July 1863 when the regiment had chased Morgan across Indiana. DeLand made his rounds, measuring the worth of each officer he met.

A month after leaving Camp Douglas, the Sharpshooters' numbers were augmented with 16 recruits. Due to army red tape, these new men had been shunted around unnecessarily from one point to another. They enlisted in Michigan in January and early February, were duly gathered together in Grand Rapids for transportation to Camp Douglas, and then, inexplicably, were sent to Camp Nelson, Kentucky, just outside Lexington. DeLand sent a request through Ninth Corps channels, asking that the recruits be assigned to his command in Maryland. Finally, during the second week of April, the newcomers arrived at Annapolis and took their places in the ranks.[31]

As their regimental name indicated, the Sharpshooters were deadly with their rifles. Unlike most units, which rarely employed target practice, the Sharpshooters regularly trudged off to the target range to enhance their marksmanship. Amid other diversions, Pvt. Amos Farling and the rank and file "had a very fine time at target practice," while awaiting orders to move out against the rebels.[32]

Even with men assigned to the myriad duties and details, the most essential item did not escape those in command—drill. At Annapolis a new wrinkle was thrown in. The Sharpshooters were already more than proficient in drill, so much so, bragged Adjutant Buckbee, "that when we went to the front, men who at first looked on us as new troops were disconcerted to find that we could out-maneuver any Regiment in our Corps, not only in battalion movements, but on a skirmish line."[33] At Annapolis each company commander was ordered to employ a "competent bugler" for skirmish details. Since the men on the skirmish line were spread out and hence difficult to give orders to, bugle calls made the task much simpler.[34]

The Sharpshooters were justly proud of their prowess on the drill field. In that era of linear formations, a battalion or regiment was judged by its smooth order and quick movements on the field. On Wednesday, 13 April, Lieutenant General Grant and Major General Burnside, together with Q.M. Gen. Montgomery C. Meigs, inspected the present regiments of the Ninth Corps. For most men in the regiment it was the first time they had seen such important military figures, and, Lieutenant Randall remembered, "there was much enthusiasm[,] the boys greeting them with loud cheers."[35]

George Warren concurred and believed that the "demonstrations of confidence in Gens. Grant and Burnside, by the soldiers, were universal and joyous, and gave favorable indications of future success."[36] Thirty-five regiments were present, and many of the Sharpshooters believed their regiment shone the brightest. Warren wrote to the folks back home: "Col. DeLand has good reason for a military pride in his command in the field, and with his love of order, and just sense of discipline, will surely have one of the best regiments in this department."[37]

The Ninth Corps

On 22 April the regimental clerk dipped his pen in his inkwell and wrote "Hd. Qrs. 1″ M.S.S. 2″ Brig. 3″ Div 9″ A.C." for the first time. The First Michigan Sharpshooters were now officially part of a larger whole.[38]

Beefed up for the new campaign, the Ninth Corps was an imposing force. Burnside commanded 42 infantry regiments, 3 cavalry regiments, and 15 artillery batteries.[39] At the threshold of the spring campaign, the corps numbered 24,000 men. Made up of four divisions (three white and one black), there were as many new men as veterans in the corps. Brig. Gen. Thomas G. Stevenson commanded the First Division, Brig. Gen. Robert B. Potter the Second, and Brig. Gen. Orlando B. Willcox the Third.

The Fourth Division—officially called "Colored Troops" and unofficially termed "Smoked Yankees" by many of the white soldiers—was under Brig. Gen. Edward Ferrero.[40] The fighting qualities of the black soldiers were grounds for much speculation. They had not yet had a chance to prove themselves, although confidence in their commander was high. Noted a veteran of the Second Michigan Infantry about the Negro troops: "They are a good looking body of men, commanded by General Ferrero, who commanded our division in East Tennessee, and if any Gen. gets fight out of them, General Ferrero will."[41]

Willcox's Third Division contained the only western soldiers in the corps. Of his eleven regiments, six hailed from Michigan and one from Ohio. In addition, two each came from New York and Pennsylvania.

General Willcox's career spanned the entire war. Born in Detroit in 1823, he attended West Point, graduating eighth in the class of 1847 (other notables in the same class were A. P. Hill, John Gibbon, and Ambrose Burnside). Willcox had served in both the Seminole and Mexican Wars. Still only a first lieutenant in 1857, he resigned from the service and became a lawyer in Detroit, joining his brother's practice. At the advent of the Civil War, Governor Blair appointed Willcox colonel of the First Michigan Infantry, a three months' regiment. Wounded and captured while commanding a brigade during the First Battle of Bull Run, he was finally exchanged in August 1862. He received his first star and took over a division in the Ninth Corps in time for the battles at South Mountain and Antietam. When Burnside became commander of the Army of the Potomac, Willcox took over the Ninth Corps. His superiors constantly cited him for gallantry in action, including the campaign just ended at Knoxville.[42] Most of Willcox's regiments had seen plenty of action on quite a few fronts—in Maryland, Virginia, the Carolinas, Mississippi, and Tennessee.

Willcox's division was divided into two brigades. Col. John F. Hartranft commanded the first, made up of the Second, Eighth, Seventeenth, and Twenty-seventh Michigan, 109th New York, and Fifty-first Pennsylvania (his old regiment). The 109th was the largest regiment in the division. Although organized in August 1862, the unit had done almost no fighting since its muster; instead it had guarded railroads and performed garrison duty in the District of Columbia.[43]

The Second Brigade, commanded by Col. Benjamin C. Christ, had five regiments: the First Michigan Sharpshooters, Twentieth Michigan, Seventy-ninth New York, Sixtieth Ohio, and Fiftieth Pennsylvania (Christ's former regiment).

The Fiftieth and Fifty-first Pennsylvania (both of which were always associated with Burnside's corps) had similar histories. Both regiments hailed from the Harrisburg area, the Fiftieth having mustered on 1 October 1861, and the Fifty-first six weeks later. They had taken part in the South Carolina expedition in April 1862, then Second Bull Run, South Mountain, and Antietam. In the last battle the Fifty-first Pennsylvania (with the Fifty-first New York) had taken Burnside Bridge. After Fredericksburg, both Pennsylvania regiments went with the corps to Vicksburg and then to East Tennessee. The men of both regiments comprised the material from which a good fighting army is made. They had seen war and had made it a most terrible enterprise.[44]

The "fresh fish" in the Second Brigade were the Sharpshooters and the Sixtieth Ohio. The Ohio boys related a sad history. The original regiment had been part of the 12,000-man force that surrendered at Harpers Ferry in September 1862. All the men were paroled, but, according to the rules of the time, they had to be formally exchanged before they could take up arms again. The Buckeyes were sent to Camp Parole in Annapolis, then to Camp Douglas. Finally, the regiment mustered out in November 1862. In February 1864 it was reorganized in Cleveland and Columbus, leaving Ohio for Alexandria, Virginia, on 21 April to join the Ninth Corps.[45]

Most of the regiments in Willcox's division had been together for years. The new ones were bigger, but the old veterans were long on experience. In particular, Willcox was partial to three of the Michigan regiments—the Second, Seventeenth, and Twentieth—and the Seventeenth was his "pet." [46] All three were brigaded together for quite some time. The Seventeenth, also known as the "Stonewall" Regiment, fell under Willcox's command at the time he took over the division just before the Battle of South Mountain in 1862. Charging a stone wall behind which a rebel regiment was firing, the green unit sustained 141 casualties but drove out the Confederates. Ever since then Willcox had looked after them.[47]

The Second Michigan was the first three-year regiment the state sent to the front. Its original colonel, Israel Richardson, sustained mortal wounds as a division commander at Antietam. The unit's first action was at Blackburn's Ford at the First Battle of Bull Run. In the Seven Days' Battles in front of Richmond, the Second lost 178 men. Transferred with the Ninth Corps to the West in 1863, the Second fought a bloody engagement at Jackson, Mississippi, and a brilliant encounter at Knoxville, Tennessee.[48]

The Twentieth Michigan saw minor action at the Battle of Fredericksburg, then shipped out when the Ninth Corps went west. At a place called Horse Shoe Bend on the Cumberland River in Kentucky, the regiment beat back an attack by Gen. John Morgan, in "one of the most notable minor actions of the war." Outnumbered eight to one, the Twentieth severely punished the enemy. Engaged at Campbell's Station, Knoxville, and Fort Saunders (all in Tennessee), the regiment fought well, and was always cited in division reports.[49]

The Twentieth's commander, Byron M. Cutcheon, graduated from the University of Michigan. In 1862 he resigned as principal of Ypsilanti High School and joined the Twentieth as a second lieutenant. His rise in rank was meteoric; he became captain, major, then lieutenant colonel in quick succession. Cited continually for bravery in action, Cutcheon received the Medal of Honor for "distinguished gallantry" at Horse Shoe Bend, Kentucky, on 10 May 1863.[50]

The Eighth Michigan Infantry spent its first months on the coast of South Carolina. On 16 June 1862 the unit assaulted a rebel fort at Secessionville, James Island, South Carolina, losing 182 men in the process. The regiment fought at Second Bull Run, Chantilly, and South Mountain. Transferred to the Western army, the Eighth fought in all the Ninth Corps engagements. The Eighth was a two-year regiment; in January 1863, 283 men reenlisted as veteran volunteers.[51]

The Twenty-seventh Michigan was organized at the same time as the Sharpshooters, and three companies were raised in Michigan's Upper Peninsula. Joining the Ninth Corps at Vicksburg in June 1863, the regiment participated in various battles and skirmishes but did not play a major role. The original enlistees made up only eight companies, and the regiment existed in that form until March 1864, when the final two companies joined it. An additional two companies of sharpshooters were made part of the the Twenty-seventh when the regiment rendez-voused at Annapolis under its commander, Maj. Samuel Moody. This beefed up its personnel to 864.[52]

The Seventy-ninth New York, also known as the Highland-ers, was the sister regiment of the Eighth Michigan Infantry. The Eighth's surgeon, Wells B. Fox, claimed that no two regiments in Burnside's corps "loved each other better than these two."[53] Or-ganized in New York City in May 1861, the Seventy-ninth fought at the First Battle of Bull Run, then went with Burnside's am-phibious operation to the Carolinas. At Secessionville, the Sev-enty-ninth came to the rescue of the Eighth Michigan. The regiment also saw action at the Second Battle of Bull Run, Fred-ericksburg, and the siege of Vicksburg. After following Burnside's campaign in East Tennessee, it rendezvoused with the Ninth Corps at Annapolis. Its term of service, though, would be com-pleted on 29 May.[54]

The old regiments had warm feelings for General Burnside, regardless of his reputation in the rest of the army. "The boys almost worship him, and well they may for he is a good man and Jenl [*sic*]," wrote one of the Twentieth Michigan veterans.[55]

Now that they were in the Ninth Corps, the Sharpshooters began looking the part. They lost no time attaching the corps badge to their hats. Beginning in 1862, the various corps in the Union army distinguished themselves by using certain symbols as their special identification. The Second Corps used a trefoil, the Fifth a Roman cross, the Sixth a Greek cross, and the Ninth a shield on which was a crossed cannon and fouled anchor.

Because there were three divisions in a corps, each division was further delineated. The first division had a red corps badge, the second a white one, and the third's badge was blue. If a corps contained four divisions, the last one used green as its color. The badge for enlisted men usually was a piece of wool cloth cut in the appropriate shape. Those officers who could afford it pur-chased a gilt corps badge.

Another Try for Better Weapons

So much of the Sharpshooters' drill included skirmishing—in keeping with their name—that it was obvious they should be used in that capacity. Believing that his men should be well armed for their deadly business, Colonel DeLand again tried to requisition weapons commensurate with his regiment's official designation. He put in a request for 700 Henry rifles. A repeating rifle, the Henry was a .44 caliber weapon capable of holding 15 rounds in its magazine, with another in its chamber. "Men are apt to waste ammunition unless they are pressed for time to load," DeLand wrote to Brig. Gen. George D. Ramsay, the U.S. chief of ordnance:

> The Henry can be loaded with safety on the double quick. . . . Skirmishers should always be free to watch the enemy and the advantage of starting in with sixteen loads in the magazine is an incalculable one and does much to promote care, steadiness, composure and confidence.[56]

DeLand was more astute in this matter than quite a few commanders superior to him. He realized that better weapons made better soldiers. DeLand also knew that a repeating rifle was best for the job his men were trained to do, but narrow-minded heads prevailed and the First Michigan Sharpshooters never received Henrys.

The First March

Orders read to all Ninth Corps units on 22 April included the admonition to cook enough rations to last five days.[57] The entire corps made last-minute arrangements to join the Army of the Potomac some 44 miles away. All extra baggage was sent by boat to Alexandria, Virginia, and trains moved supplies to the front. The men were to "foot it" to their new location;[58] the veterans reckoned "it would be a good 'breaking in' of the new regiments."[59]

Sick men stayed behind, and Lieutenant Colonel Beadle said his final goodbye to the regiment. Very ill with typhoid fever, Beadle would never rejoin his men; a respected officer, his loss would be felt. Lieutenant Randall considered him "our most Efficient Experienced man thoroughly posted in discipline." Randall found him not only "responsible for the efficiency and good conduct of the men[,] yet securing always the good will of his Comd." The men would miss him. He later transferred to the Veteran Reserve Corps, where he rendered valuable service.[60]

On 23 April bugles sounded "Strike Tents" and awakened the men at 4:00 AM, but it was not until after 11:00 AM that Colonel Christ's brigade moved out. The veteran regiments blamed the newcomers for the delay.[61] The day was hot for April, and considerable straggling was evident.[62] Private Farling recalled that 16 men went down with sunstroke.[63] Colonel Cutcheon of the Twentieth Michigan noted that the Sharpshooters were encumbered with "enormous knapsacks."[64] Chaplain Heagle left little out of his description: "The endurance of the regiment has been tried," he wrote. Inside of two days the men would march almost 50 miles. But, he maintained, the Sharpshooters did well, considering:

> that it was the regiment's first march of any importance, and that the roads were considerably heavy, one day on account of rain and mud and heat, and the other on account of heat. . . . None of the officers faltered, and but few of the men. The Indians did marvellously—not a man of them behind.
>
> A good deal of clothing and luggage in general was thrown away on the road, strength being unequal or least unwilling to the burden. About all the luggage any of us have now is what could not conveniently be despensed [sic] with. Only half a "dog tent," a blanket, a rubber [blanket], and an extra shirt.[65]

Randall also noticed that "most of the boys threw away their O'coats or blankets to lighten their heavy Knapsacks. I carried one heavy blanket, one piece of D'Abri tent, 5 days rations, Haversack, canteen, Sword & belt."[66]

Reviewed by the President

A severe thunderstorm drenched the Ninth Corps during the night of 24 April. The next morning the men marched ten miles over muddy roads and through a creek to Washington, DC. Just outside the capital city the corps halted, the men stacked arms. They were told to make themselves presentable, for they were going to pass in review in front of the president. They scraped mud from uniforms and shoes, and polished buttons and brass.

Feeling better about themselves, they continued the march. Willcox's Third Division led the corps down New York Avenue to Fourteenth Street. At this juncture the entire corps closed up and then turned onto Pennsylvania Avenue.[67]

Crowds awaited the marching soldiers. One would think that the people of Washington had seen enough soldiers during the past three years; but they had never seen regiments of "Colored" troops, nor had they witnessed a full company of Indians on their way to war. "Congress and the President were eager to witness the movement." All the Ninth Corps soldiers gloried in the adulation.[68]

Two blocks from the White House stood the magnificent Willard Hotel. Some wits believed that more important political business was conducted at the Willard than in the Capitol Building. Frequented by congressmen, cabinet members, and assorted lobbyists (in fact, the term began there), the hotel thronged with the important people of the day.

President Lincoln stood on a balcony overlooking Pennsylvania Avenue. With him were his secretary of war, Edwin McM. Stanton, and General Burnside. They were joined by Willcox as his division marched by. The president looked unwell to the men: "pale and careworn," wrote Lieutenant Randall.[69] The president's face "was drawn, careworn and white," reiterated Adjutant Buckbee; "there was a set look in his eyes, I do not think that he saw us at all."[70]

Quite a bit of bantering was kept up as the sweaty soldiers paraded down the avenue, many of the remarks being directed at the commander in chief. One Sharpshooter declared that "the president was very careful to keep out of harm's way" up there on the balcony, away from the crowds. Another nearby averred, "If the President was down South he would dodge behind every tree he came to." To that Amos Farling waggishly retorted, "I would like to be there when the dodging was going on, he would never dodge behind the second tree." Although Farling had said it only in jest, word of his comment reached his superiors.[71]

A number of the college students in the Second and Twentieth Michigan and First Sharpshooters had decided earlier to serenade President Lincoln as they paraded past Willard's and its regal onlookers:

We are coming, Father Abraham,
 Three hundred thousand more,
  Shouting the Battle Cry of Freedom!
And we'll fill the shattered ranks,
 Of our brothers gone before,
  Shouting the Battle Cry of Freedom![72]

Marching in step down the main avenue of the nation's capital—with the president, the secretary of war, and their general officers gazing down on them—various regiments sent up cheer after cheer. The Eighth Michigan gave them "three times three and a tiger." Groups of men sang the martial tunes of the day. This was all part of the glory of being a soldier.[73]

The feeling was euphoric, and the fatigue of the past day and a half was temporarily forgotten as they marched under the eyes of their commanders. With the pride of men who knew the fate of the republic depended on them, they saluted their leaders and felt like nothing could stand in the way of their quest for the Holy Grail.

But this was no sightseeing venture, and the corps "passed wearily" over the Long Bridge and onto Virginia's bloody soil. A wave of nostalgia hit Lieutenant Colonel Cutcheon of the Twentieth Michigan as he remembered his regiment traversing the very same ground back in 1862, when it had first arrived as a green outfit. Now only 325 men followed its colors.[74]

After crossing the Long Bridge, the corps worked its way toward Alexandria, but stopped short of the town by a mile and a half.[75] The end of any march is a welcome relief, and this surely was no exception. The men were stripped to their essentials, and the road from Annapolis was littered with their excess baggage. The 44-mile march in hot, rainy, and humid weather made the new men realize just what "essentials" were.

When the Sharpshooters reached their camp and the men were dismissed to their various tasks, Cpl. Cyrus W. Hall stalked up to Amos Farling and told him to consider himself under arrest for using "disrespectful language toward the President." Farling refused to go. Striking at the private with his rifle, Hall missed and fell, and Farling clipped him with his own weapon. A squad arrested Farling and took him to Colonel DeLand, who had already been apprised of the private's remarks when the regiment passed the president in review. DeLand called Farling a Copperhead, but Farling retorted, "I am no more a Copperhead than you." DeLand countered, "You have tried to kill Corporal Hall, and I shall see that you are punished."

That night five men with blackened faces took Farling from his guards and escorted him out of camp. One of his abductors slipped a noose over the prisoner's head. Immediately, a rush of bodies moved on Farling and his captors. A short but vicious fight ensued. Someone cracked Farling over the head; when he came to, he found himself back in camp, among friends. Whoever was involved in the plot to teach Farling a lesson kept quiet about it. As for Farling, he had his hearing, but when it was learned that others had said just as much or more about the president, and since the spring offensive was only beginning and every man was needed, he was released from custody.[76]

Early on the morning of 27 April, General Ferrero's division of "Colored" troops joined the rest of the Ninth Corps. The seven large regiments were mainly composed of ex-slaves from Virginia and the Carolinas. "They were well clothed and armed, and seemed to take pride in making a good appearance," related the commander of the Twentieth Michigan.[77] One veteran of the Second Michigan saw a more warlike quality in these men:

> These negroes will remember Fort Pillow [where many Colored soldiers were murdered by the rebels after having surrendered]; no taking prisoners on their side, and if you should hear of some deeds committed on their side, which will be shocking to human nature, don't wonder. The rebels have called up the ghost, now let them free him. They have commenced a game at which two can play.[78]

More than a week later, that same soldier watched the First Michigan Colored Infantry (soon to be rechristened the 102nd U.S.C.T.) sail from Annapolis to Hilton Head. There was another reason for his interest in Michigan's sable regiment. His unit, the Second Michigan, had furnished six officers for the Colored regiment. "We shall follow their footsteps with a great deal of interest," he concluded.[79]

To the Rapidan River

Reveille came early on 27 April, but as before (complained Colonel Cutcheon), "the corps was a long time getting straightened out." No progress was made on the road till late morning.[80]

The men marched through Alexandria; a flood of memories hit Lieutenant Randall when they bypassed Sutor's Hill on the outskirts. He and the rest of the First Michigan had camped there before the First Battle of Bull Run several years ago. "Noticed that the fine grove covering Shuters [sic] Hill had been cut down to give full sweep to the artillery from Fort Ellsworth," he mused.[81]

Tramping over sandy roads for 14 miles that day, the men passed Annandale and continued to Fairfax Courthouse. The Sharpshooters reached the courthouse about 11:00 PM, and "in the darkness turned off the road and bivouacked at will, wherever we could find a spot."[82]

An eerie incident took place in the camp of the Twenty-seventh Michigan that night. Picking up whatever wood they found in the darkness, a group of them hastily made a few small fires and brewed coffee before retiring. The next morning, one of them recalled, "we found that our camping ground was a grave yard and that we had been using headboards to light our fires, which made us new men feel very sensative [*sic*]."[83]

The men in the ranks had no idea where they were going, "unless to meet the rebels up on the Rapidan," guessed the chaplain. "The impression is that there is to be a big fight shortly."[84] The chronicler of the Second Michigan felt the same way: "The blow will soon be struck hereabouts; everything indicates it."[85]

So far, the Ninth Corps had supported the Army of the Potomac in a reserve position. While Grant moved the Army of the Potomac south to hit the Confederates, Burnside's corps guarded the railroad lines in the rear of the Union army from rebel attack. If and when Grant needed him, Burnside was to abandon the railroad and make haste to the Army of the Potomac.

Time after time the Union armies in the East had lost the edge against the Confederates. Their lackluster commanders had been either too timid to attack or too obstinate to change their plans when the occasion demanded it. In planning his campaign, Grant had called in all available men. Department commanders had to strip their standing garrisons; that was the reason the Sharpshooters were released from guarding prisoners at Camp Douglas. Heavy artillery regiments, which guarded the forts encircling Washington, DC, were given rifles and parceled out to the army. The 109th New York undoubtedly missed its comfortable lodgings in the District of Columbia.

Some of those regiments had been in the army for two years but had never heard a shot fired in anger. They had enjoyed permanent quarters, ample food, and no danger. Those days were over. Cavalry regiments found themselves dismounted and treated as infantry. Washington was primarily guarded now by the "condemned Yankees" of the Veteran Reserve Corps. All able-bodied men were either at the front or on their way to it.[86]

There was a late reveille the morning of 28 April, giving the men time to write home. They were told "that no letters will be allowed from the front for 30 or 90 days."[87] It was another hint that they were close to action.

After a few hours on the march, the men saw the effects of war. The debris of an army lay scattered alongside the road. The names "Bull Run" and "Manassas" passed up and down the column of sweating men. Some of the veterans viewed the devastation differently than did the majority of the Sharpshooters, who had not yet been in a battle. Nature was doing its best to cover the obscenity of war, but as Lieutenant Randall wrote in his journal:

> War has done its work thoroughly through this section. No buildings left, the brick chimney marking the spot where a dwelling once stood. Not a fence to be seen, dead horses lying along the road. Occasionally would see a shot or shell rusting on the ground.[88]

Willcox's division rested for an hour on the old battlefield, then resumed its march, crossing the Bull Run at Blackburn's Ford, where in 1861 the first shots of the Battle of Bull Run were fired. The column continued westward, following the line of the railroad to Bristoe Station, and camped for the night. The men could not help noticing that every bridge on the railroad was strongly guarded. The army depended on this line for its supplies, and its very lifeblood pumped over this iron artery.

On 29 April the division marched to Catlett's Station and halted to eat. The Sixtieth Ohio stayed there to garrison the town, and the rest of Willcox's force moved off to Warrenton Junction, where camp was set up. The march from Annapolis was over.

The next day, 30 April, the Third Division relieved all the troops detailed to guard Catlett's Station, and the various regimental commanders parceled out their men for picket duty, their business being to maintain a strong outpost against rebel raiders.[89]

On 1 May the Sharpshooters were mustered and paid. They also lost another officer at this juncture. First Lt. William Clark of Company B resigned his commission and departed the regiment. He had been an early recruiter and one of the first officers. Sick for quite some time, Clark was too ill to remain in the service.[90] Lieutenant Randall mentioned him briefly: "I sent my money home by Lieutenant Clark who was mustered out here and went to Michigan."[91] His next line was more incisive, though seemingly bland: "Preparing for our onward march to Richmond."[92] Preparations meant "to accumulate sixteen days' rations and a large supply of ammunition, and to hold ourselves in readiness to move any hour when orders should be received."[93] The ball was ready to begin, and the men knew it.

CHAPTER 6

The "Ping" of Flying Bullets

Into the Wilderness

Lt. Gen. Ulysses S. Grant planned to utilize all the Union armies in the 1864 campaign. While the Army of the Potomac (together with Burnside's independent Ninth Corps) attacked the Confederate Army of Northern Virginia, other Union armies would engage the remaining rebel forces. The Confederates would find it impossible to send aid to trouble spots because every rebel army would be threatened at once. With all military movements commencing concurrently, Grant hoped to overwhelm and destroy the Confederates.[1]

Grant accompanied the Army of the Potomac, which was actually commanded by Maj. Gen. George G. Meade. Grant stayed with the army rather than behind a desk in Washington because he despised the political machinations in the capital. And, owing to his position, Grant could facilitate coordination between Meade and Burnside until the Ninth Corps finally and formally became part of the Army of the Potomac.[2] Burnside (according to one of his officers), "then, as always, thoroughly patriotic, waived the matter of rank and continued in command of the corps."[3]

The spring campaign now began in earnest. The Army of the Potomac started crossing the Rapidan River on 4 May, preparatory to sidestepping Gen. Robert E. Lee's Army of Northern Vir-

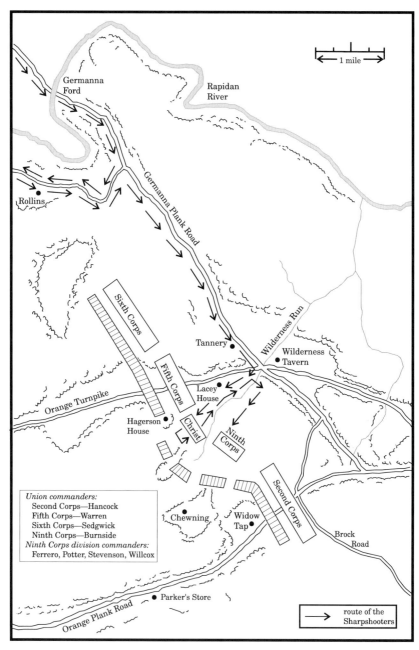

Battle of the Wilderness, 5-6 May 1864

ginia and getting between the rebels and the Confederate capital at Richmond. The Fifth and Sixth Corps tramped over pontoon bridges and were followed by the Second Corps. Rebel scouts quickly spied the advance, and Lee managed to halt the Federal army at a second-growth scrubby area called the Wilderness.

The Wilderness was no place to fight a battle. Amid the stunted trees and choppy ground were little rivulets and paths that seemingly led from one place to no place. Briars and creepers and bramble bushes ran riot in the low areas. Few roads pierced this thicket, and the ones that did were scarcely wide enough in places for a single wagon. Farms in this godforsaken land were isolated and scattered. The Battle of Chancellorsville had been fought through part of this territory just a year before, and it made the region even more frightening; it was a place of death, ghosts, and foreboding.

Grant hoped to push his way through this ominous woodland and force the rebels into battle in the open area beyond. The Confederates stymied his progress by moving quickly into the Wilderness. When he learned that the Army of Northern Virginia was maneuvering in force against him, Grant told Burnside, "Make forced marches until you reach this place. Start your troops now in the rear the moment they can be got off, and require them to make a night march."[4]

"The apple orchards around Warrenton were bright and sweet with bloom as we struck our tents," observed Lieutenant Colonel Cutcheon of the Twentieth Michigan.[5] Some men were ordered to stay behind to guard the depot, so the Second Brigade of the Third Division moved out with only three regiments: the Sharpshooters, the Twentieth Michigan, and the Fiftieth Pennsylvania. The Sixtieth Ohio had just come up from Annandale, and, together with the Seventy-ninth New York, would rejoin the brigade in a few days.

That day, 4 May (their last before entering the caldron), the Ninth Corps marched from Warrenton Junction, crossing the Rappahannock River at Rappahannock Station. "It is most fortunate that a veil is drawn between us and the future, and that we are not permitted to know what awaits us," wrote a Ninth Corps veteran.[6] The hour of reckoning approached; the Angel of Death awaited many of them just over the horizon.

A few miles before reaching Rappahannock Station, the division crossed a stream. Col. Frank Graves, commanding the

Eighth Michigan of the First Brigade, watched his men ford the
small tributary. Graves was a West Point graduate, a thorough
disciplinarian, and a gentleman of the old school. As in classical
drama, an event foreshadowed an unpleasant future. Graves
moved his horse a little downstream and attempted to cross a
mill dam. The horse slipped, dumping Graves into the muddy
water. His men hooted and laughed as the colonel, thoroughly
soaked and embarrassed, walked to the other shore.

The Eighth's surgeon commented wryly, "Colonel, if a Roman had suffered your mishap he would consider it as a fore-
warning of his downfall." Graves was too wet and uncomfortable
to reply to the doctor. The surgeon would ruefully recall his pro-
phetic epithet a few harrowing days later.[7]

The column continued on to Brandy Station, where it received orders to countermarch back to the bridge over the Rappahannock. With much grumbling and outright swearing, the men
trudged back to within a mile of the bridge, where they camped
for the night. They had covered 19 miles that day, 15 to Brandy
Station and 4 more backtracking. The Ninth Corps was strung
out for 40 miles. Willcox's Third Division was closest to the Army
of the Potomac, Potter's Second was back at Bealeton, and
Stevenson's First was at Brandy Station. Ferrero's Fourth, the
Colored Division, was more than a day's march away, at Manassas Junction.[8]

The next morning (5 May), the first sergeants roused the
men from their sleep before daylight. Fires soon dotted the landscape. Coffee was boiled, a meager breakfast consumed, equipment adjusted, and rolls called. Soon the corps resumed its march
and hurried to the junction with the Army of the Potomac. The
roads were hard and dry, and by 11:00 AM the Third Division had
reached the hills overlooking Germanna Ford on the Rapidan
River. For some time before they reached the river, the men in the
ranks could hear the booming of cannon.[9] It was the first time
many of them (including most of the Sharpshooters) had heard
the sound, but they needed no one to tell them what it was.

There was a halt; the men fell out to grab something to eat,
boil some coffee, and have a smoke. At noon the corps began
crossing the pontoon bridge at the ford.[10] The Rapidan River was
the turning point, the boundary line for the Sharpshooters. Their
monotonous (although, in retrospect, carefree) life was over. Now
began the days of excitement, tinged with terror and suffering.
Adjutant Buckbee noticed a difference in the rank and file as

they crossed the bridge. "When we started on this march," he related:

> there was much good natured chaffing, laughing, singing, etc., etc.; but by the time we struck the pontoon bridge . . . there was no noise came from the boys who had been so exuberant the night before; the only sound being an occasional low-voiced command from one of the file closers and the shuffling of many feet.[11]

The pontoon bridge stretched about 200 feet, its ends securely fastened to each shore. Officers had to dismount and lead their horses, and the men were told to march out of step as they traversed the swaying bridge.[12] Then it was a matter of "hurry up and wait." After the crossing, the Third Division halted, and the ubiquitous coffee boilers appeared. A half hour passed before the men received orders to hurry forward again. They continued on the Germanna Plank Road—a misnomer in that most of the planks had disappeared years before, either worn out or rotted.

A mile and half down the road, the division turned to its right and marched down a path hemmed in by trees and thickets to the "Rollins' Place," another mile and a half beyond. Colonel Hartranft's brigade took control of the area on the right once the division reached its destination; Colonel Christ's brigade deployed into the woods on the left.[13]

There were no troops on their right. The Third Division *was* the extreme right of the Union army. Its flank rested on the Rapidan River. Two regiments, one being the Sharpshooters, went out as pickets, while the balance of the division stacked arms and rested. Willcox's division had to guard the ford and the Germanna Plank Road from the west. General Grant wanted the rest of the Ninth Corps to cross the river as soon as it arrived and to connect with the Sixth Corps.[14]

The 109th New York Infantry relieved the Sharpshooters at dusk; they retired to a road at their rear.[15] The day's march and the excitement of being close to battle had spent the Sharpshooters. Officers filtered among their men, telling them to get some sleep. There would be fighting come the morrow. They had heard heavy artillery and musket fire all day off to the east. The noise of sporadic firing perked up the ears of the fitfully dozing men.

At about the time Willcox's division crossed the Rapidan River on 5 May, the Battle of the Wilderness began some four miles south. Essentially, two distinct battles raged in the forests of the Wilderness. Maj. Gen. Gouverneur K. Warren's Fifth Corps slugged it out against Confederate Lt. Gen. Richard S. Ewell's corps, and Maj. Gen. Winfield Scott Hancock's Second Corps went head to head with Lt. Gen. A. P. Hill's rebel corps.

Elements of Maj. Gen. John Sedgwick's Sixth Corps were thrown in to aid both sections of the army. Grant thought the Ninth Corps could tip the scales in his favor if Burnside could maneuver his corps into the gap between the Fifth and Second. One of the problems with the plan was the absence of a good road system in the area. Both Warren's Fifth and Hancock's Second were astride major roads that were roughly parallel but three miles apart. The tract between them was virtually pathless.

The gap that existed between the two Union corps, once their various brigades and regiments were spread across the landscape, was about a mile and a half. It was this hole that Grant wanted Burnside to plug and advance through.

The Sharpshooters slept little that night. At 2:00 AM under a bright, starry sky their division was roused, equipment readied, breakfast (such as it was) prepared and eaten. The men fell into formation and trudged off to the new day's battle just as a tinge of light scarred the horizon.[16]

When the column reached the Germanna Plank Road, it veered south. By this time Stevenson's First Division had already linked up with Hancock's corps on the Brock Road; Potter's Second Division, which had come up during the night, was just ahead of Willcox's command.[17]

Ferrero's Colored Division moved toward Germanna Ford, their 40-mile forced march a real test of endurance. No other Union division marched so far so fast; the "smoked Yankees" were becoming real soldiers. After reaching the Rapidan River, the sweaty and dusty Negroes set up their batteries and consolidated patrols to guard the ford.[18]

Marshall's Provisional Brigade (a temporary unit in the Ninth Corps made up of a dismounted cavalry unit and two heavy artillery regiments fresh from the forts around Washington) guarded the roads to the west of the Union army.

The day portended fair weather. Birds sang and a gray dawn lightened the sky as the Sharpshooters marched to the crossroads. The men heard no shots fired but observed a great deal. They passed an old tannery and the Greenwood Mine, and then they saw the wounded. The area around the Wilderness Tavern crossroads was a vast sea of anguish. Hundreds of men lay in large hospital tents or in the open. Humanity begged for assistance, but the column continued on.

Once the men passed the crossroads, they entered a large meadow at the southwestern angle of the two roads. It was here that Chief Division Surgeon Evan J. Bonine had set up the Third Division Hospital.[19] The Wilderness Run flowed through this meadow in a northeasterly direction on its way to the Rapidan, crossing the road some 250 yards west of the Wilderness Tavern. Lt. William Randall, detailed to the Hospital Corps, saw the efficacy of Bonine's choice:

> During a battle the Division Hospitals are established some distance in rear of the line of battle, near a stream or spring if possible. The Hospital tents are pitched and rude tables made for the surgeons to operate on. On these rough tables the surgeons saw off a leg or arm, probe a wound for a ball, cut out the broken bones, as the case may be.[20]

The Sharpshooters Meet the Enemy

As Potter's and Willcox's divisions filed onto the field, all was still quiet. Potter's men were on the east side of the run, and Willcox's on the west. The columns halted, and the men looked at the tree line ahead, about a third of a mile away; the sun had not yet cleared the tops of the trees to the east. Then the popping of gunfire erased the early morning reverie. It came from the south, where Hancock's corps was being savagely attacked by Longstreet's Confederates. Like a wave hitting the beach at an angle, crashing against the sand and rocks and getting louder and louder, the crackle of musketry increased as more men joined in the fray. The same cacophony then turned the heads of Willcox's men to their right, where Warren's Fifth Corps had started slugging it out with Ewell's rebels again.

Then the two Ninth Corps divisions moved out. Potter's men advanced along a road on the east side of Wilderness Run, which came out at the "Widow Tapp's place." Willcox took his regiments past the Lacey house onto the road that ran southwest, past the "Chewning Place" to Parker's Store. The road was hardly worthy of the name. After leaving the meadow, it meandered through a dense stand of pines. The going was difficult at best; the path was barely wide enough for a column of infantry, and was impassible to artillery or cavalry. Engineers moved to the front to chop down trees and clear brush to widen the road. In the meantime, the column halted.[21]

Much of the manpower in the Ninth Corps was new. For half the men in the corps, this was their first battle, and many of their officers were just as green. Worse, the rebels they faced were veterans who took chances.[22] When Willcox's men started up again, the going remained cautious.

The advance, with the Sharpshooters in the lead, continued until the Third Division reached a large clearing about a mile north of the Chewning farm. At the halt several officers consulted their watches; it was almost 7:00 AM.[23] Seven companies of Sharpshooters under Major Piper were ordered into the woods north of the clearing as skirmishers. They were to link up with Warren's corps on their right, but no one knew how far away that was. The three remaining companies, commanded by Colonel DeLand, were held in reserve to the skirmish line, ready to go when and where needed. The skirmishers advanced several hundred yards, but instead of joining with Warren's men, they ran into rebels building a log breastwork near the Hagerson clearing at 8:00.[24]

Adjutant Buckbee was with the skirmishers:

> We had been pushed forward gradually, small distances at a time, until we were up quite close—so close you could hear the "ping" of flying bullets, the patter of dropping twigs, leaves, etc. We had not up to this point commenced firing, but the men were told to take cover, move forward slowly, keeping alignment as much as possible on the center. It was really nothing but a heavy skirmish line and we were good at that business.[25]

The Indians of Company K carried some of the deadliest rifles in the regiment. By this time, after seven months of drill at Camp Douglas, the entire regiment was extremely well trained in the art of skirmishing, and the Indians (according to their officers) were the best skirmishers in the division.[26]

> They, on the very first day at the front, caught on to the great advantage our enemy employed over us in the color of uniform. Ours was blue, and could be seen at a long distance; while the "Johnny" (as we called them) could not be spotted at a comparatively short distance, even when lying in an open field.

This disadvantage to us was appreciated almost immediately that these Indians got in the field, and they would go out and find a dry spot of earth and roll in it until their uniform was the complete color of the ground before going out on the skirmish line; and if the day was wet, they would not hesitate to take mud and rub it over their clothes, for as soon as this dried a little they would have what they were after—the color of the earth. This custom was adopted by my whole Regiment; and it was often remarked that our Regiment could do the closest skirmishing at the least cost of any Regiment in the Division.[27]

Sgt. Thomas Ke-chi-ti-go, called "Big Tom" by the white Sharpshooters, further "ordered each brave to cover his breast and head with twigs and leaves to prevent contrast of color with their surroundings."[28]

Following Colonel DeLand's orders to move slowly over the ground and to take advantage of the cover offered by trees, bushes, fallen timber, and little hummocks of ground, the heavy skirmish line of Sharpshooters moved forward. Still, there was no firing from the Sharpshooters, although some rebel skirmishers were peppering them. With dry mouths and wet palms the riflemen groped their way forward—surely, they thought, into the heart of the rebel army.

Once the line reached what DeLand thought was an appropriate position, he sent the adjutant to the company commanders, telling them to have their men fire at will, "and to caution them not to attempt to fire too rapidly, and, on no account, to discharge their guns unless they saw something definite to fire at."[29] A general firing then erupted up and down the line; the Sharpshooters kept under cover as much as possible.

Here the Sharpshooters suffered the first casualty caused by hostile fire. A man was shot in the calf of his leg—only slightly, as it turned out. The shock of the hit and soldier's agitated state of mind at the time so affected him that "he threw his gun in the air and gave a whoop that made my hair stand on end," recalled Buckbee.[30] Half a dozen men ran to to help him off the field. One of the injured man's lieutenants included himself in this group of hopeful attendants. All vied for his acceptance, despite his telling them he could make it back to the aid station on his own. Major Piper then hollered down the line and the Good Samaritans quickly ran back to their positions, "for Piper not only had a manner of speaking which was very decisive and emphatic, but he could swear at a man forty rods away and there would be no uncertainty as to who he was talking to."[31] The wounded man hobbled to the rear on his own.

Over to the left, Potter's division had already run into stiff resistance in the woods to its front; Hartranft's brigade was detached from the Third Division to reinforce that side.[32] The three regiments of Christ's brigade still had to hold the gap between Potter's division and Warren's Fifth Corps. The Twentieth Michigan and Fiftieth Pennsylvania had formed a line of battle along the right of the open field, in the rear of the Sharpshooters, and were throwing together an abatis of branches and brush in their front when a rebel battery on a ridge to their south began dropping shells on them. While the Sharpshooters skirmished hotly with Ewell's rebels in the woods, Colonel Christ ordered the other two regiments to keep their formation and fall back to their left, leaving the Sharpshooters as the only link between Warren's men and Potter's division.[33]

Officers were expected to maintain a brave front when the enemy was close by, but even they had problems with the sound and the effects of battle invading all their senses. Enacting his responsibilities as the colonel's front man, Adjutant Buckbee admitted that "my heart was in my mouth all the time."[34] Probably more familiar with the rank and file than any other officer, Buckbee bantered with the men; as he passed up and down the line he would see a nervous grin and hear a familiar, "Hoop her up, Adj." Despite encouragement from others and a pretense on his part not to appear frightened, "I dared not look at my knees, for I could feel them shaking like a twig in the breeze and I was afraid that the others would notice it."[35]

Trouble continued brewing on the left. When Potter's division entered the meadow at the crossroads that morning, it followed a road to the east of the Wilderness Run. Potter's men ran into the flank of A. P. Hill's Confederates and drove them back for a while. That attack was terminated until Potter could make contact with Hancock's Second Corps, which was somewhere on his left. Then Hartranft's brigade was shifted over from the Third Division. Potter immediately charged the rebels again, but was still unable to link up with the Second Corps, due to the rough terrain and second-growth forest that hid both friend and foe.

Nonetheless, the attack was hard-pressed. Colonel Graves of the Eighth Michigan died in the advance, and the Second and Twenty-seventh Michigan suffered severe casualties in the for-

THE "PING" OF FLYING BULLETS

est.[36] Graves was a sick man when he led the Eighth Michigan in its charge. Falling back from a counterattack, the Eighth suffered heavy losses. One officer "saw men who saw Colonel Graves in the retreat, and he was then sitting in the rifle pits, where he had first stopped, and he was on the side sheltered from the enemy, and would not be likely to be struck [by a bullet]. Nothing more was seen or heard of him."[37] His body was never recovered.

At 3:00 in the afternoon Christ's small brigade left its position and moved off to reinforce Potter. Ordered to march immediately, the Twentieth Michigan, Fiftieth Pennsylvania, and the three reserve companies of the Sharpshooters withdrew back to the meadow, crossed Wilderness Run, and tramped down the route taken earlier by Potter's division and then Hartranft's brigade. So quickly were the men ordered to pull out that they had to leave their knapsacks behind.[38] At the time of the withdrawal the other seven companies of Sharpshooters were still in the woods in their skirmish line. They were ordered to withdraw "as quick & quietly as possible, so as not to let the rebels know of their leaving."[39]

Hardly had they begun to pull back than the Confederates attacked, driving the Michigan riflemen out of the woods. The rebel battle line moved so fast that it actually bypassed a few of the Sharpshooters. One group of Southerners from the Fourteenth North Carolina Infantry saw an Indian hiding behind a tree as they advanced. "We saw him and supposed he would surrender," wrote one of their officers. "As we moved on he shot our color bearer. Many turned and fired, riddling him with bullets. The Indians fought bravely in the wood. When driven into the open they did not again fire on us, but ran like deer. We captured not one of them."[40] What they did pick up, though, was quite interesting. "Among the captures were copies of the Bible in the Ojibwa language," remarked the Tarheel historian.[41]

The three-company reserve under Colonel DeLand "did not go to the support of the skirmishers, but continued to withdraw with the balance of the brigade," according to Lieutenant Colonel Cutcheon.[42] Attacked not only across their front, but also in the rear of their left flank, the skirmish line fell back quickly for about 300 yards, with the rebels coming up behind them, "yelling like a pack of fiends."[43]

Cpl. Charles Nash of Company I was standing behind Lt. Ira L. Evans when the skirmish line disintegrated. The seven companies rushed back in no order. They were "a howling mob" and "completely disorganized," recalled Nash. Lieutenant Evans stood in the middle of the trail, drew his sword from its scabbard, and cried out that he would "cut the first man in two, that tried to pass." Nash backed up the lieutenant. As the retreating men sheepishly slowed down and fell into ranks, a disgusted Evans turned to Nash and said, "Charley, look at that," at the same time pointing with his sword to Colonel DeLand on his horse taking shelter behind a tree. From that moment on, Nash lost all confidence in his colonel.[44]

Major Piper also pitched in to help halt the retreat at the edge of the woods and stopped the rebels from advancing any farther. "The regiment," wrote an officer, "was too much disorganized, however, to participate with the rest of the brigade in the remaining operations of the day."[45] Ever the professional, Piper pulled the men together and had them follow the rest of the brigade at a distance.

Back in the woods they had just left, several helpless Sharpshooters writhed in the underbrush. Levi Porter (Co. C) and Clark Carter (Co. I) were both wounded and abandoned in the rout. George Sawyer (Co. H) was down with a rebel bullet in his right side. Other wounded men fled for their lives or were helped along by their comrades.

Following Major Piper, they passed the flotsam and jetsam of battle: "overcoats, knapsacks, shirts, drawers, portfolios, Testaments, spiders [skillets], hatchets," even wounded and dead men "laid out in rows along the road."[46] This war—the real war—was so different from the gay march down Pennsylvania Avenue. Bullets hummed, men grumbled and cursed; the noise of battle battered the ears of the sweaty Sharpshooters. This was a place of confusion and chaos. Glory was nowhere.

After a short march the Sharpshooters came up behind Hartranft's brigade, which was pretty well chopped up after its fight with the rebels. Colonel Christ took his time forming the three regiments into a line of battle. The four right companies of the Sharpshooters were put in the second line supporting the First Brigade, and another company filed off to the left as skirmishers to keep an eye on that flank.[47] The other two regiments now formed in line of battle to the left of Hartranft. With Christ shouting, "Go in and give 'em hell," the little brigade plunged into the woods again.[48]

The attack commenced at 5:00 PM. Initially, it went well.[49] The brigade pushed back the rebel skirmishers and then ran into the main Confederate line. The Fiftieth Pennsylvania stumbled headlong into a rebel breastwork; in a few minutes 78 men fell to rebel bullets. The Twentieth Michigan was in a more protected sector and took fewer casualties.[50] The piece of land over which Christ's brigade advanced was a horror to behold; it had already been fought over two or three times, and the consequences were evident. Musketry fire had scythed off much of the undergrowth. Dead and wounded men, both blue and gray, could be seen scattered "pretty thickly" among the brush.[51]

John S. Vader (Co. C) and Henry Apted (Co. H) were both killed in the woodland. Cpl. James Jones (Co. G) was hit in the stomach with a rebel slug; in extreme agony, the 45-year-old from Niles would hang on for only a few hours before succumbing to his wound. John Rainbow (Co. H), a young volunteer from Coldwater, had his left shoulder smashed by an enemy bullet. Another Confederate shot fractured Cpl. Ezra Scott's left shoulder blade. First Sgt. Charles Allen (Co. K) took a bullet in the chest; he would die in less than two weeks from its effects.[52] George Sawyer (Co. H) was mortally wounded in the right side; left on the battlefield, he was captured by the rebels a few days later.[53] Clark Carter (Co. I), "wounded and left on the field May 6," was picked up by another regiment and eventually sent to Washington, DC, where he died in a hospital on 11 May.[54]

Dusk quickly concealed this macabre scene of desolation. The firing tapered off as darkness enveloped the thickets and meadows. General Willcox's men lay on their arms that night amid the dead and dying. Just in front of them, the woods burned out of control.[55]

The next day (7 May) was quiet compared to the two previous ones. Christ's brigade guarded the Parker's Store Road while the rest of the division followed Potter's division to another sector. A skirmish line crept forward early in the morning, but discovered the rebels had left their entrenchments during the night. The trenches dug by the Confederates the day before were invested by the skirmishers, and the rest of the brigade built breastworks. Those men not on the picket line or actively engaged in building defensive works brought in a number of wounded rebels and collected about 300 stands of small arms left on the field.[56]

As usual, the Sharpshooters were up front as skirmishers. They were on the extreme left of the line, forming a connection with the Second Corps. During the day the Seventy-ninth New York and Sixtieth Ohio rejoined the brigade.[57]

In the evening one of those nasty accidents that happen in every war occurred. The tenseness of the situation spooked a number of men. Around 10:00 a false alarm (plus the threat of a night attack by the Confederates) threw the Sixtieth Ohio into a panic. Unfortunately, the Buckeyes held a position just to the rear of DeLand's regiment. Firing into their backs, they killed two and wounded three Sharpshooters before realizing their mistake.[58] So ended the first fight of the Sharpshooters; the Wolverines had seen action, but their conduct was not as glorious as many of them had hoped.

All told, the Sharpshooters officially lost 25 men in the Wilderness: 11 were killed or died of wounds, 13 wounded, and one missing.[59] Cpl. Cyrus Hall (Co. G) had died in the confused fighting; shot in the stomach, he died in great pain. (Hall was the one who had brought Amos Farling to task for his vulgar comments about President Lincoln while the regiment marched through Washington a week before.) Levi Porter (Co. C), the one man officially listed as captured, died at the infamous Andersonville prison camp on 2 August 1864, the first of a long list of Sharpshooters to breathe his last foul breath in that blot on the Southern landscape.[60]

The March to Spotsylvania

On 8 May, having been ordered to withdraw to Wilderness Tavern, Willcox's division left its bivouac around 2:00 AM.[61] Before first light streaked across the eastern sky, the men were in position, "the last of the army to withdraw."[62] Behind Willcox were scattered U.S. cavalry outposts and rebel reconnaissance squads. The Ninth Corps moved slowly behind the rest of the Army of the Potomac as it shuffled its way south to the vicinity of Spotsylvania Court House, where the Army of Northern Virginia had retreated.

Colonel Christ's regiments fell out of ranks and set to boiling coffee and otherwise taking in their surroundings, while various parts of the army marched by. Some of the men sauntered over to gawk at Grant's and Burnside's staffs, which occupied a nearby grove. In the meantime, the Twentieth Michigan and Fiftieth Pennsylvania, with one section of Roemer's Thirty-fourth New

York battery, were detailed as rear guard for the corps.[63] Piles of ammunition were stacked close by (the wagons had been taken for the wounded). Details were sent out to destroy the abandoned munitions, much of which was thrown into Wilderness Run.[64]

Christ's brigade did not begin its march until 8:00 AM. A small rebel cavalry unit followed at a distance, "But did not press us at all," recalled Lieutenant Colonel Cutcheon.[65] After only traveling a mile, the column halted again; in a large clearing was another of the vast battlefield hospitals. As many wounded as possible were loaded into the available wagons; even then, hundreds had to be left behind. "Nothing else could be done," Cutcheon lamented.[66] Christ's men moved on. The oncoming rebels paroled the wounded back in the clearing.[67]

The brigade continued on past the old Chancellorsville battlefield. None of the Ninth Corps regiments had fought in that conflict (they were in Tennessee at the time), but the aftermath of even a year had not erased the scars that blotted the landscape:

> Fragments of guns, bayonets, haversacks, parts of uniforms, broken canteens, and everything of the kind were scattered promiscuously. The traces of shallow trenches, hastily thrown up, were still almost as plain as a year before. Trees were cut down by cannon shots and the branches of the big trees lopped off, and everywhere were the scars of bullets upon the tree trunks, which a year of growth had only partially obscured.[68]

"Skeletons of men and skeletons of horses bestrewed the ground," Cutcheon remarked. "Trees two feet thick cut down with shot and shell. Every twig and shrub and sapling shorn close with cannister [sic] and shrapnel and bullets."[69]

The brigade stopped again just a short march southwest of the ruins of the old Chancellor house at 11:00 AM, after "having moved very slowly indeed," according to Cutcheon.[70] Here the men rested until 2:00, while the rest of the army clogged the road ahead of them.

Potter's division left the line of march to guard the crossroads; Grant's supply route had to be protected. The immense wagon trains, made up of 4,000 ambulances, ammunition and quartermaster wagons, had to be guarded by a small army as they traversed the twisting Virginia byroads.[71] Ferrero's Fourth Division—the Colored Troops—would soon take over the brunt of this work.

Leaving Potter's division behind, Willcox's men took the road that led southwest from Chancellorsville to Aldrich's, a trek of about two miles. "[B]ut the road was so obstructed," wrote an officer, "and the march so difficult that it seemed much longer." [72] Halfway to Aldrich's, the Sharpshooters tramped past Stevenson's division, which was bivouacked on both sides of the road. [73] The men could hear heavy firing off to the south. [74]

CHAPTER 7

Our Losses Seemed in Vain

Marching to Spotsylvania

After leaving Chancellorsville, Colonel Christ halted his men for the night at Aldrich's. Just before dark the Michigan Cavalry Brigade—the First, Fifth, Sixth, and Seventh Michigan Cavalry Regiments—trotted in from the southwest and camped in an orchard close by. So many Michigan boys were in both camps that fraternizing went on late that night, as relatives and friends tried to find each other and talk over mutual events.[1]

At 4:00 the next morning (9 May), Christ's men were on the road again; they had not proceeded 100 yards when the cavalrymen "began to pour from the neighboring farm," cutting in front of Christ's brigade and delaying the footsoldiers for an hour.[2] When the road cleared, the Second Brigade, leading the Ninth Corps, continued its march toward the Fredericksburg and Spotsylvania Court House Road, about four miles distant.[3] The Sixtieth Ohio led the brigade, followed by the Twentieth Michigan, Fiftieth Pennsylvania, First Sharpshooters, and the Seventyninth New York.[4] At the intersection the brigade turned southwest toward Spotsylvania Court House.

Noise from battle could be heard off to the west during their march. Cannon and musketry fire announced that the Army of the Potomac was hitting the rebel lines a few miles away. The

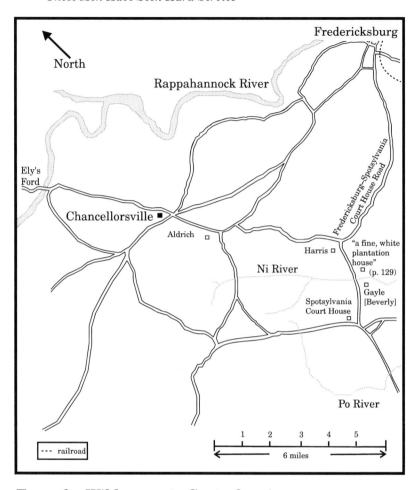

From the Wilderness to Spotsylvania

Fifth and Sixth Corps were trying to punch through the Confederate lines, while the Second Corps attempted to hit the rebel flank by crossing the Po River. In the next act of the play the Ninth Corps would batter the opposite flank.

Near 9:00 AM,[5] the vanguard of the brigade sighted the village of Spotsylvania Court House. The men were still a half mile from the Ni River crossing, and the village was another two miles beyond the river, but a high point on the road gave them a glimpse of the town. Spotsylvania sat on a broad ridge situated

128

between the Po and Ni Rivers. The hamlet itself was one of those out-of-the-way, nondescript habitations most travelers pass through on the way to somewhere else. Somewhat hidden by a stand of pine woods, the village consisted of about a dozen weather-beaten frame buildings, including a courthouse, a tavern, two small churches, and a few homes.[6]

A Lost Opportunity at the Ni River

From where the head of the column halted, the officers with field glasses could see the village just over two miles away "as the crow flies."[7] At the rise in the road where the Sixtieth Ohio stopped was the driveway to "a fine, large white plantation house," still occupied by its owners.[8]

General Willcox had orders to move his division north of the house about half a mile. He and his brigade commanders looked over the situation in their front and amended the orders. They could see no large body of enemy troops. The road dipped down to the Ni River, which was a half-mile ahead. There, at a bridge, was a small rebel picket. The road then rose to crest about another half mile beyond the bridge. On the crest they could see a Confederate cavalry outpost.

Willcox decided to advance his division and take the high ground; this would put the Ninth Corps closer to Spotsylvania than any other part of the Union army. A section of Capt. Adelbert B. Twitchell's Seventh Maine Battery galloped up, unlimbered, and positioned itself directly in front of the plantation house. Its target was the squad of cavalry a mile distant on the crest. A few shots drove the rebels away.[9]

As the enemy cavalrymen retreated, Willcox ordered Lt. Col. James N. McElroy's Sixtieth Ohio forward. A glance at his timepiece showed it to be a little after 9:00 AM.[10] Two companies of Buckeyes deployed to the left of the road as skirmishers; 50 men of the Twentieth Michigan filed off to the right of the road and advanced with them. The remainder of both regiments followed in column on the road, about 150 yards in the rear of the skirmish line, as a reserve.[11]

The rebel pickets at the bridge fled immediately, and the Union line crossed the stream with little resistance.[12] Gaining the opposite bank, the skirmishers kept after the fleeing rebels "almost double quick," with their reserve column trying to close the gap. Colonel Christ rode at the head of the Twentieth Michigan, just to the rear of the Sixtieth Ohio. Halfway to the crest from the bridge, Christ directed the Twentieth to take position in a somewhat sunken road leading to the Gayle house, which stood on a knoll about 200 yards to the left.

The Twentieth had a wide, open field in its front, some of it freshly plowed, "extending southward to a line of a sunken fence, bordering a road leading southeast to the Gayle [Beverly] place,[13] beyond which road was an old pasture, grown up with small sapling trees."[14] The Twentieth had a clear field of fire, "except near the road where the crest intervened."[15]

The entire Sixtieth Ohio, 295 strong, had already taken position on the crest and was trading shots with a Confederate force, a "regiment or small brigade" that was approaching from the courthouse.[16] The Sixtieth was a new regiment and probably should have been held in reserve, but it was up front and had not fought at the Wilderness, so Willcox ordered it to engage the enemy. This was actually "the first time the regiment was ever under fire."[17] There were many untrained men in the Sixtieth, some "never before having had arms in their hands";[18] but for an untried outfit, the men held on against an enfilading attack and even managed to perform a complicated maneuver under fire. Stopping the rebel charge on their front, the Buckeyes eventually drove back the attacking Confederates.

The enemy soon regrouped and advanced under cover of some woods, hitting the left flank of the Ohioans' battle line. Wheeling about, Lieutenant Colonel McElroy formed his men along the road that ran over the crest they were defending. A steady trickle of men, "both wounded and unhurt," melted from McElroy's line, continually weakening it.[19] If the enemy advanced again, McElroy informed Colonel Christ, he would not be able to hold the line. Christ told him to hang on "as long as possible." The rebels struck again, and McElroy saw what he believed were four regiments of dismounted cavalrymen descending on his small (and getting smaller) regiment. The Southerners almost enveloped the Buckeye line, hitting the front and right flank.

Two hundred yards in back of the crest, on the left of the road, DeLand formed his Sharpshooters for their advance. Colonel Christ had already sent one company of the veteran Twentieth Michigan to bolster the right flank of the Sixtieth Ohio; another company of only 24 men ran to the far left of the field to shore up that flank. They were told to hold until relieved by the

Sharpshooters. To their rear a dozen men from the Twentieth took over the house situated on a hillock just behind the line held by the Sixtieth Ohio and the four forward companies of the Twentieth (which now included the skirmishers sent out when the advance units crossed the river).[20]

Then, for seemingly no reason, there was a breathing space, one of those unexplained calms which mysteriously occur during a fight, when one or both sides maneuver for position or settle back to gather their wits. During this lull the Sharpshooters advanced in battle formation across the field on the left of the road. They filled the space along the fence line between the company of the Twentieth Michigan on the left and the Sixtieth Ohio on the right.

Men's minds contemplate strange ideas, even in the midst of battle. Adjutant Buckbee was going across the line and stepping over a ditch when one of his men, Charles Katzenstein of Company G, a pre-war peddler, spoke up, "Hadjutant, Hadjutant!! after the war will a soldier have to get a license to beddle [peddle]?" Buckbee laughed out loud at the incongruousness of the question. Here they were, under rebel fire, most of the Sharpshooters nervously thinking of home and heaven, and one man was calculating whether or not he would receive a free license to sell things after the war.[21] There was little time to think of any kind of answer to Katzenstein's question. No sooner did the Sharpshooters take their position than the rebel attack began in earnest.

Two brigades of Confederates proceeded at the double-quick on both sides of the road toward the Ninth Corps line. Their charge was too much for the Sixtieth Ohio. McElroy had already told Christ that the regiment could not hold on. The new attack caved in the Sixtieth, and the Sharpshooters—to the surprise of those in the rear watching the fight—lost no time in following the Buckeyes out of the melee.

Controversy forever marred this fight at the Ni River crossing. Colonel DeLand contended that the Buckeyes retreated before the main rebel line hit them, thus forfeiting the high ground along and to the right side of the road. The Confederates then moved on to the crest of the ridge, "from which a very severe raking fire was poured upon my whole line," he complained. In only a few minutes, the Sharpshooters sustained more than 30 casualties. Trying to counter the rebel fire, DeLand tried to move his left forward; in the process of doing so, the right wing of the regiment (which was taking the brunt of the enemy's flanking

fire) ran off the battlefield, leaving the wounded behind.[22] Seeing
their comrades retreating, the left wing quickly followed suit.

After some delay due to confusion and the mixing up of
companies, DeLand and Major Piper sorted out their men and
the Sharpshooters again advanced to the edge of the field. By
that time the fighting was over.[23]

When the Sharpshooters were driven from their line of battle, other regimental commanders saw the problem and promptly
moved ahead to plug the gap. The Fiftieth Pennsylvania double-
quicked to the right of the Sixtieth Ohio at the same time the
Sharpshooters fell back and, together with the bulk of the Twentieth Michigan, drove back the rebels and held the line.

The Seventy-ninth New York had moved up near the Beverly house, just behind the Sharpshooters. When DeLand's riflemen ran back, the Highlanders filled in the interval, assisted
after a while by the timely arrival of the Seventeenth Michigan
of the First Brigade.

The battle line was now occupied from the left by a company of the Twentieth Michigan, the Seventy-ninth New York,
the Seventeenth Michigan, the Fiftieth Pennsylvania, and the
rest of the Twentieth Michigan.[24] The combined Union firepower
forced the rebels back. The Confederates then broke off the fight
and retreated. When an embarrassed Colonel DeLand brought
his men back up to line, they took over the area held by the
Seventy-ninth New York.[25]

The Seventeenth Michigan in particular merited praise for
its quick action.[26] The regiment took over the line vacated by the
Sixtieth Ohio just as the rebel battle line came up the slope. "We
opened a well directed volley upon them," reported Col. Frederick
Swift, "doing great execution, and in spite of the frantic efforts of
their officers they broke and fled in the greatest disorder, leaving
many of their dead and wounded in our hands." [27] The Seventeenth also saved the dead and wounded of the Sixtieth Ohio
from falling into the hands of the Confederates. Incredibly, the
Seventeenth sustained no casualties at all.[28] The division also
bagged more than 50 Confederate prisoners.[29]

The Sharpshooters proffered a bag full of excuses for their
abject retreat. DeLand listed three reasons, all of which had
some basis in fact. When the Sixtieth Ohio vacated its position
on the crest, a gap opened through which the rebels advanced
while pouring a withering fire into the exposed Sharpshooters.
At the same time, the regiment sustained a frontal attack by an

extension of the Confederate line. Both Cutcheon of the Twentieth Michigan and McElroy of the Sixtieth Ohio alleged that this attack was difficult to contain.

Nonetheless, the Sharpshooters had a total of 444 officers and men that day, which constituted the largest regiment in the brigade. The smallest regiment in Christ's command was the Seventy-ninth New York. Destined for discharge in a couple of weeks, only 168 men and officers crossed the Ni that morning.[30] But it was the Seventy-ninth, with its small contingent, that plugged the breach made by the withdrawal of the Sharpshooters. At the same time the rebel line advanced on DeLand's men, the colonel tried to move his left companies to the front and then to the right of the regiment's line of battle. The rebels on the crest were firing down on the Wolverines; artillery fire was also creating havoc in the ranks, but it was Union artillery doing the damage.

Twitchell's Seventh Maine Battery fired from across the river at the charging Confederates, but some of their shots fell short, right into the midst of the Sharpshooters. "Most of their shells exploded over and in my lines," griped DeLand, "in several instances with fatal effect. This action of our batteries was inexcusable, as they were within plain sight and must have seen, if they had tried to see at all, that they were firing upon us."[31]

Those two reasons were still not sufficient to make the Sharpshooters leave their advanced position, according to their colonel. A flank fire, an attack on their front by overwhelming numbers, friendly and enemy artillery shells dropping into their ranks—these occurrences were only secondary to what DeLand considered the ultimate disgrace. Regardless of the problems already listed, "the men would not have flinched had they not been deceived by the acts and orders of one of the line officers, who gave the order to retreat without any authority for so doing."[32] Lieutenant Colonel Cutcheon of the Twentieth Michigan also knew the cause of the problem. "Cool-headed and steady officers are essential to cool-headed and steady men and regiments," he wrote about the conduct of the Sharpshooters that day, "and one panicky officer can bring disaster upon an entire command."[33]

Who was the officer? Only two men were named by DeLand in his after-action report, but he failed to give the particulars surrounding each officer's offense. On 26 May DeLand recommended that two of his second lieutenants, Guy Newbre (Co. A) and Albert P. Thomas (Co. C) be dismissed from the regiment "for having absented themselves from their commands on the field and for cowardice."[34] Exactly which one of these two men (if indeed it were either one) became frightened and confused enough to order the Sharpshooters off the field during the fight at the Ni River crossing may never be known.

There is another explanation. Almost two decades after the war, when John Robertson, Michigan's adjutant general, began gathering material as a tribute to the state's contribution to the war effort, he sent out questionaires to all the commanders of Michigan's Civil War regiments. The reminiscences, together with official reports and newspaper and encyclopedic references, were combined into a volume called *Michigan in the War*. Unfortunately, there were problems with the history. Feathers were ruffled, and reputations were at stake. A few years later, utilizing more information, Robertson came out with a revised (and in some respects a sanitized) edition of *Michigan in the War*.

Among the letters he received as a result of the first edition was one from George H. Murdoch of Berrien Springs, Michigan. Murdoch had served as captain of Company I during the early battles, and he vehemently disagreed with the official version of the Sharpshooters' actions at the Ni River crossing. The regiment "was never ever repulsed in the campaign," he declared. The Sharpshooters *did* retreat, though, a disgraceful and shameful occurrence, but it did so "at the command of Col DeLand." At first, the "regiment hesitated to comply," since the men were posted well. "But before obeying it delivered a volley and then fell back, and they had the satisfaction to know that the rebels had done the same thing on the receipt of our fire. They [the Sharpshooters] were not repulsed, [but they had] simply obeyed an order that was dictated by cowardice."[35] Captain Murdoch thus placed the onus squarely on the shoulders of Colonel DeLand.

An Official Censure

With the rebels driven from the immediate vicinity, the Third Division entrenched on the battleline. Part of General Stevenson's division came across the Ni River, and the line was extended on the right back to the river. The Twentieth Michigan went forward as a picket line and connected with that of the Fifth Corps to the north.

The next day, field orders were issued. General Willcox, commanding the division, congratulated those regiments which had participated in the 9 May fight, praising all the veteran regiments and giving the Sixtieth Ohio "honorable mention" for its conduct. "It is to be hoped," exclaimed Willcox, "that one other new regiment will soon regain the good name it won on the 6th instant, and came near losing yesterday."[36] Of course, the "other new regiment" was the Sharpshooters.

Colonel DeLand felt the chastisement was unmerited. "An implied censure was cast upon the regiment, which all felt to be unjust and the result of misapprehension."[37] It is interesting that DeLand used such a placating statement. From what source did the "misapprehension" spark? If the colonel were out to chastise an underling, such a statement would be uncharacteristic. Maybe, just maybe, Captain Murdoch was correct.

Lieutenant Colonel Cutcheon of the Twentieth Michigan later stated that the Sharpshooters were not lacking good men or good officers. Future events would erase the ignominy of the affair at the Ni River crossing. "Never again," related Cutcheon, "was there occasion for criticism of that gallant regiment."[38]

In the meantime, the men had entrenchments to dig and casualties to attend to. At least five of their comrades had died in the action (two immediately and three later) of wounds received there.[39] The number of wounded is more difficult to ascertain; casualty figures were later lumped together as from "Spotsylvania," which in fact was a series of engagements over a period of days.

Waiting for the Ball to Begin

The remainder of 9 May was spent fortifying the crest of the hill occupied by the Third Division. The regiments up on the line were so intermixed that no attempt was made until the evening of 11 May to separate them into their own brigades. The Eighth Michigan, the Fiftieth Pennsylvania, the Twentieth Michigan, and the Fifty-first Pennsylvania occupied the pits on the right side of the road in the order mentioned. The Fifty-first ran a skirmish line back along a ridge to the Ni River. The men of the Second Michigan were employed as pickets on the north side of the Ni River, where they linked up with the pickets of Potter's division to their right.

Alongside the left of the road was the Sixtieth Ohio. On their left was the Seventeenth Michigan, then came the Sharpshooters, the Twenty-seventh Michigan, the Seventy-ninth New York, and, on their left flank, the 109th New York. Colonel Hartranft, commander of the First Brigade, took command of the regiments on the right of the road, while Colonel Christ took over those on the left.[40]

The night of 9 May remained quiet; the men knew the rebels were close, so "the utmost vigilance was exercised to prevent a surprise."[41]

Grant, who had been keeping a close eye on the Confederate front, later regretted not being involved in Burnside's 9 May attack on Lee's right. Burnside, Grant later realized, "was not aware of the importance of the advantage he had gained." Although only "a few hundred yards" to the rebel rear, the Ninth Corps was ordered to attach itself to Wright's corps, a realignment that took Burnside farther from the rebel lines.[42] Sloppy staff work from general headquarters was to blame.

After leaving the Wilderness, General Lee's Army of Northern Virginia fortified the area around Spotsylvania Court House, blocking the Army of the Potomac's approach to the Confederate capital at Richmond. Trying to break the rebel positions were the Second, Fifth, Sixth, and Ninth Corps of the Union army. The four corps were strung out in that order, facing the Confederates.

On 10 May the Fifth and Sixth Corps assailed the Confederate left, but gave up the challenge about midday. Lee had chosen his defensive position well; he was on the high ground with both flanks near two rivers, the Po and the Ni. The right wing of Lee's army ran along the Ni River, more specifically, along the border of the high ground adjacent to the river. A mile and a half north of the Ninth Corps' position, the rebel line formed a salient, or point, with the enemy defenses angling to the southwest. The Fifth and Sixth Corps aligned themselves along the Confederate western front, the Ninth Corps opposed the eastern edge, and the Second Corps was stationed around the apex of the salient. It was around the salient—the "Mule Shoe"—that the most severe fighting raged on 10, 11, and 12 May. Men died by the score along both sides of the Confederate defenses.

The terrain and the trees in their front prevented most of the regiments in Willcox's division from learning anything at all about the rebels who opposed them. On the ridge between the Fifty-first Pennsylvania and the Twentieth Michigan stood a two-story house. Delapidated and deserted, it was one of the many Beverly houses in the vicinity. Some of the men from the Twentieth Michigan occupied it as a sniper position. From the second story they saw rebels about three-fourths of a mile away building breastworks, carrying rails and all sorts of material to strengthen their position. Some of the men in the house began taking pot shots at the working Confederates, stirring up a hornet's nest. Until this time a desultory fire had continued between the opposing pickets, but when fire erupted from the deserted house, more rebels joined in retaliation.[43]

The increased enemy fire may have caused the death of Gen. Thomas G. Stevenson, commander of the First Division. Stevenson and his staff had finished breakfast and were relaxing under a shade tree. Hit in the back of his head by a spent bullet fired by an anonymous skirmisher, Stevenson pitched forward, fatally wounded. He had earlier brought part of his division across the Ni River. At the time he was shot, he was sitting in the sunken road leading to the Gayle house, the same road the Twentieth Michigan had occupied the previous day.[44]

That same morning the Sharpshooters built strong earthworks, but they were continually harassed by rebel skirmishers. A number of men were hit by enemy fire until Colonel DeLand strengthened and extended his skirmish line. The rebel fire slackened after that.[45]

During the morning's skirmishing Adjutant Buckbee was wounded; for a moment he thought that the wound was mortal. Struck by a spent bullet just behind the ear, he fell unconscious. Sgt. Maj. Jim DeLand, with the assistance of drummer boy George Stone, pulled him over to a log. Stone at first thought the wound was deadly, since there was so much blood.[46] As Buckbee came to, one of the officers of the Twentieth Michigan passed by, saw the the adjutant's face streaked with dirt and blood and exclaimed, "Good Lord, where's he hurt?" Another man pointed to the back of his head, further throwing Buckbee into a panic. Sergeant Major DeLand, Buckbee's close friend, ran his fingers over Buckbee's scalp and reassuringly said, "Man alive! I don't believe you're hurt at all; I do not find any hole in your head; there is nothing but blood, and you know how a person's scalp will bleed from the least little cut."

Still suffering from shock, which manifested in general weakness and vomiting, Buckbee stumbled back to the division field hospital at the rear. After some rest, he would rejoin the regiment in a couple of days. Of the two men who helped him, Jim DeLand was only an enlisted man, but the two were fast friends. Well into the twentieth century they kept up their visits and correspondence with each other. The other helper was not a man at all. George Stone, the Orphan Train boy who had enlisted as a 13-year-old drummer under the protection of Capt. George N. Davis, was called the "Regimental Baby" by the Sharpshooters, but, as Buckbee testified, "he was the bravest child that man ever saw." Whenever a fight began, Stone always shucked his drum and under some pretense or other shouldered his way into the front rank where he could pick up a Springfield.[47]

Around 3:00 that afternoon orders filtered down from corps headquarters. The entire line had to be ready for a general advance by 5:30 PM. The Third Division would swing forward more or less on a right wheel, the Fifty-first Pennsylvania being the hinge.[48] A considerably large stand of pine woods covered the ground just in front of the Ninth Corps' position, and immediately beyond it (the corps staff believed) was a clearing reaching almost to Spotsylvania Court House. The corps was to swing right so as to allow the left of the line to break through the woods. The movement also was intended to feel out the Confederates and to determine their strength on this side of their defenses. If the rebels were weak in this section, then the corps was to advance and hopefully seize the area around the village. "In other words," related Lieutenant Colonel Cutcheon, "it was to be a reconnaissance or an assault, as circumstances should determine."[49]

Regimental commanders had two hours in which to ready their men for the attack. Soon after 5:00 the signal guns announced the intended movement.[50] A heavy skirmish line went over the breastworks, followed soon by another. After a space of a hundred yards, the regiments moved out in battle formation.[51]

No sooner had the men climbed over the breastworks than the Confederate artillery beyond the woods opened fire.[52] A rebel battery found the range, one of its rounds exploding directly in front of the Twentieth Michigan and severely wounding Cutcheon. Despite the cannonade, the Union line swung to the right as it was supposed to. The left of the Ninth Corps line inched forward and crossed the Fredericksburg Road. All told, the corps moved 500 yards closer to the main rebel line. The brigade on the far left of the corps took a position beyond the cover of the woods. The reconnaissance came to an abrupt end. New breastworks were constructed where the men were, and they rested on their muskets that night.[53]

The rebels inflicted more casualties on Christ's brigade during the advance. One of the wounded caused some suspicious glances, though. Second Lt. Albert P. Thomas of Company C showed up in the field hospital with a gunshot wound in his left foot. No one in the Sharpshooters had seen him receive the wound, and he was not with the regiment when wounded.[54]

The morning of 11 May started uneventfully, with only the skirmishers trying to kill each other. Toward the middle of the afternoon the whole Ninth Corps, excepting a line of skirmishers, was pulled from its position and regrouped back on the other side of the Ni River. A rain storm commenced during the maneuver, making the withdrawal even more miserable for the men involved. The corps formed a line of battle near the Third Division's field hospital, between the Beverly and the Harris houses. The left of the corps was just south of the Fredericksburg Road, the right almost on the river. Drenched by the rain, the soldiers nearest the river watched as engineers destroyed the bridge they had just crossed.[55]

Rumors of a grand assault swept through the corps. The Ninth Corps (so it was said) was going to shift to the north to support the Second Corps in its attack on the rebel salient. But orders were changed, and the common foot soldier could only curse the abominable weather and the inane commands. After loitering in the clearing east of the river for half a day, the First and Second divisions slogged back across the Ni after nightfall to the entrenchments formerly held by the Third Division. The same engineers who had destroyed the bridge now collected fence rails and laid them over the supports they had broken apart hours before.[56] Col. Elisha G. Marshall's Provisional Brigade moved to the left of the Fredericksburg Road. Made up of two big heavy artillery regiments (the Fourteenth New York and the Second Pennsylvania Provisional, which had just come from the defenses of Washington, DC) and a dismounted cavalry unit (the Twenty-fourth New York), Marshall's command remained there until 3:00 the next morning. Amazingly, although the Ninth Corps vacated the field for six hours, the Confederates did not advance into the abandoned positions.

Willcox's division remained east of the river that night. Before dawn the men were awakened, marched across the stream, and formed as a reserve to the rest of the corps. Much of the Ninth Corps was shuffled around. The men were moved about half a mile farther to the right, athwart the Second Corps lines. Along unfamiliar ground, Burnside's men now learned they had to attack the enemy entrenchments in their front.

Murder Most Glorious

At 6:00 AM on 12 May rebel artillery cut through the mist and fog of a dreary morning. The cannonade seemed to be directed at Capt. Jacob Roemer's four cannons near the Beverly house. Not until the heavy skies cleared a bit did Roemer's Thirty-fourth New York Battery reply, and it did so with a vengeance. The artillerymen would fire 552 rounds that day, silencing the rebel battery that had opened the ball, and later going to the support of the infantry in the general engagement that followed.[57]

Potter's division stepped out first. The Ninth Corps was ordered to maintain contact with the Second Corps on its immediate right, and Potter's men were the link. The First Division, now commanded by Maj. Gen. Thomas L. Crittenden after the fatal wounding of General Stevenson, supported Potter to the latter's left. Marshall's Provisional Brigade guarded the left of the corps by the Court House Road. Advancing steadily under overcast, drizzly skies, Potter's men proceeded over two lines of rifle pits and collared some prisoners.

The going was rough. The broken woods, swamps, knolls, and the intermittent rain helped squelch any and all coordinated movements between the two divisions. Still, they made contact with the main rebel battle line, and even managed to overrun part of it. No scouting parties had previously spied out the ground over which the attack was made, even though the Ninth Corps had moved into the area three days before. Now the fighting men paid the price for poor staff work.[58]

Willcox's division composed the left wing of the Union army, and its commander constantly worried about the status of his own left flank, even though Marshall's Provisional Brigade was there. To protect that sector he massed his own and other Ninth Corps batteries near the Court House Road. He detailed the Second Michigan Infantry to support Capt. Joseph B. Wright's Fourteenth

Massachusetts Battery, which was stationed on the road. Later, Willcox moved Wright's battery a half-mile to the right, on top of a low ridge astride the corps' battle line. The Second Michigan took a position in a shallow ravine on the right of the ridge. With no action forthcoming on the road during the morning hours, Willcox moved more guns closer to Wright's second position.[59]

During the morning the Sharpshooters' brigade bore no active role, except as a supporting column. At this time the Seventy-ninth New York left the Second Brigade to report to corps headquarters. There, those who had not reenlisted were detailed to guard prisoners on their way to Alexandria, Virginia. The balance of the regiment then proceeded to New York City, where they were dismissed from the army on 31 May. The first regiment to be mustered out of the Ninth Corps, the men of the Seventy-ninth had served their three years in the army. The rest of the brigade wistfully saw them off and remained in reserve until noon.[60]

Colonel Hartranft's brigade had crossed the Ni River earlier in the day, but his men were kept in the rear of the fighting. Just before noon Hartranft received orders to move his brigade to the right in support of Hancock's corps. Without taking time to call in his skirmishers (six companies of the Fifty-first Pennsylvania), Hartranft led his men out. He proceeded hardly half a mile when he was ordered to retrace his steps to the river. Returning to his former position, he learned that his skirmishers had been forced back in his absence. Hartranft deployed his regiments, preparatory to attacking the Confederates. At the same time Col. William Humphrey moved the Second Brigade into battle position.[61]

During the morning Colonel DeLand, as senior colonel in the brigade, had command of the Second Brigade. DeLand later wrote of his physical and mental condition at the time:

> Nothing of importance occurred until after I was relieved at my own request, and by order of General Willcox, being very much depressed and exhausted by sickness and labor. I received verbal permission from General Willcox to leave the field, but soon after, learning that a charge was to be made, I returned and assumed command of my own regiment.[62]

Colonel Humphrey commanded the Second Michigan Infantry. Mustered into the regiment at its inception in May 1861 as captain of Company D, Humphrey took over as colonel in April

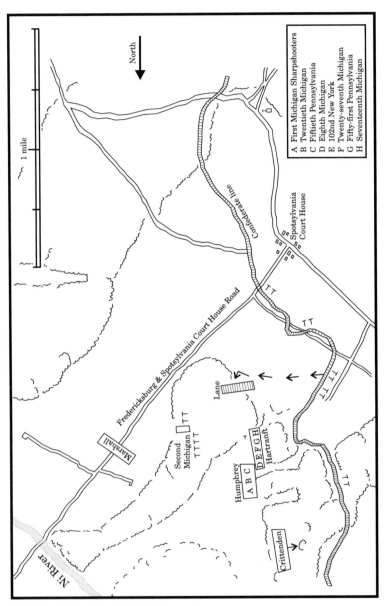

North

1 mile

A First Michigan Sharpshooters
B Twentieth Michigan
C Fiftieth Pennsylvania
D Eighth Michigan
E 102nd New York
F Twenty-seventh Michigan
G Fifty-first Pennsylvania
H Seventeenth Michigan

Confederate line

Spotsylvania
Court House

Fredericksburg & Spotsylvania Court House Road

Marshall

Lane

Second
Michigan

Humphrey

A B C

D E F G H

Hartranft

Crittenden

Ni River

Battle of Spotsylvania, 12 May 1864

1863. He was a known quantity in the Ninth Corps, thoroughly trustworthy and competent. DeLand's seniority as colonel dated from July 1863 when he was officially mustered. To say the least, General Willcox did not want him to command the brigade after the performance given by the Sharpshooters at the Wilderness and on 9 May at the Ni River crossing. Not able to relieve De-Land with a man of better rank in the Second Brigade, Willcox tapped Humphrey, whose regiment was in the First Brigade.

When Colonel Hartranft deployed his men, DeLand was relieved from his position, Humphrey was put in charge, and the Second Brigade took its place behind Hartranft's men, who began their advance against the enemy.[63]

There were only three regiments in the Second Brigade. From left to right they were the Fiftieth Pennsylvania, the Twentieth Michigan, and the First Sharpshooters. The Seventy-ninth New York had already marched off the line to be mustered out. The Sixtieth Ohio, temporarily detached from the brigade at 9:00 AM, was sent to Colonel Marshall's Provisional Brigade as skirmishers, to keep an eye on the left flank.[64] Major M. P. Avery, commanding the Sixtieth Ohio, deployed four of his companies, thus extending the Ninth Corps line from the left of the Provisional Brigade back to the Ni River. Avery took the rest of the regiment to the right, where it waited as a reserve unit behind the First Division.[65]

Each of the three regiments still in the Second Brigade had different terrain in their front. The Sharpshooters had to move through "a bushy, small growth of trees" that hid one part of the line from the other. On the left, in front of the Fiftieth Pennsylvania, a thick growth of mature pine forest chopped up their formation. In the middle, the Twentieth Michigan stared straight at the rebel line; open ground stretched between them and the enemy.[66]

Hartranft's brigade moved out immediately after 2:00 PM. The rain had let up, and his five regiments—Eighth Michigan, 109th New York, Twenty-seventh Michigan, Fifty-first Pennsylvania, and Seventeenth Michigan—angled left under a heavy artillery fire. They managed to proceed 200 yards.[67] Humphrey's brigade then joined the fray, his line advancing at 2:25 PM.[68]

Even before joining the assault, the Second Brigade had sustained casualties. Rebel artillery fire was falling quite regularly into their lines. One shell dropped into the ranks of the Twentieth Michigan, killing four men.[69]

After lying about without being able to punish the rebels, the Second Brigade was ready to swing into action. The three regiments, with remnants of whatever companies of the First Brigade cared to join them, charged to within 50 yards of the Confederate works. "With no cover the men were exposed to the enemy, to a murderous cross fire, and the loss bid fair to be a fearful record," wrote Colonel DeLand in his official report. "I ordered the men forward to the first line of the enemy's works."[70]

As the rebels retreated, the Sharpshooters occupied the deserted trenches. For a few moments the men rested, then they were ordered again to advance. The Sharpshooters worked their way into the scrubby woods in front of them. James and Sidney Haight of Company E, one of the many brother combinations, kept an eye on each other as they entered the timber. Jim was ahead with Sid close behind.

Suddenly, a rebel rose from behind a log with his musket leveled at Jim. Pulling up his own weapon, Jim reacted immediately. Both men fired at the same moment, but to those who saw the action, it sounded as if only one shot were discharged. Jim's weapon fell from his hands, and he twisted in pain, holding his left arm. "Sid," he called out, "I've been hit." Giving a quick look at his brother's wounded arm, Sid told Jim to go to the rear. Reluctantly, Sid left his brother, turned, and joined in the attack. As Sid stepped over the log behind which the rebel had hidden, he saw the man lying there, dead. The Confederate had been shot in the forehead, while his own bullet had hit the side of Jim's rifle and been deflected into the Sharpshooter's arm.[71]

Colonel Humphrey, mounted on a fine horse that afternoon, led by example, and his men followed him into the caldron. He remembered the advance vividly:

> The regiments went in with a vim that would have carried them over the enemy's works had the ground between us and the works been clear, as we had a right to suppose it was. I had no time to look over the ground, and in the mind of General Willcox, *to charge and at once* was the main thing. He did not know nor did any of our people, that the woods in front of our left sheltered counter-columns of attack, nor of the obstructions in front of the right. There had been no pickets on our front. The woods covered the movements of the enemy completely, and we went it blind.[72]

Poor staff work had hindered the Ninth Corps again.

The rebels were not content to sit defensively on this part of the line. While most of the Confederate units held their ground facing Willcox's charge, a brigade of North Carolinians led by Brig. Gen. James H. Lane moved out of their works and into the oak woods on their left. This movement put the rebels athwart Burnside's left flank. Forming his men in a five-regiment front, Lane intended to roll up the Union line.

Just after 2:00 PM, when Hartranft's brigade had commenced its assault, the Confederates moved out.[73] Lane's secondary objective was the Union battery beyond the woods, which was enfilading the rebel position. Primarily, though, he wanted to smash through Burnside's column.

Backed up by Humphrey's men, Hartranft moved his brigade into the dripping woods in line of battle. To their left Wright's Fourteenth Massachusetts Battery, planted on a low ridge, blasted the rebel salient directly in its front. With Wright to protect the left flank, Willcox sent in two sections of Twitchell's Seventh Maine and two sections of Rogers's Nineteenth New York Batteries. Rogers advanced his guns to a slight rise in front and to the right of Wright's position. The artillery gave a psychological edge to the Ninth Corps infantrymen as they moved forward through the intermittent drizzle. At least, they believed, their flank was protected.

Lane's North Carolinians kept moving forward, flanking the Union guns on the pine-covered knoll. Having already driven the blue-coated pickets from the woods, the rebels saw Rogers's guns out in the open only 100 yards away. The New Yorkers heard the rebel yell even before they saw the enemy and hurriedly turned their pieces on Lane's men, plowing their ranks with canister. The Massachusetts battery up on the ridge caught sight of the attacking rebels and fired clouds of iron at them. Lane's Thirty-seventh lost heavily, since it was in a direct path of fire from Rogers's guns.[74] Still the screaming Tarheels drove for the cannons, killing and wounding most of the artillerymen. For an instant, the awful guns stood silent, the sodden attackers almost on them, when the Second Michigan Infantry (which had been stationed earlier in a ravine to the right of the artillery position) poured a volley into the rebels. Without reloading, the Second jumped from the ravine and went for the guns. The Wolverines quickly reloaded the pieces; backed by the rifles of their comrades, they fired a salvo into the Confederates, who came within ten paces of the battery but no farther.[75]

The right wing of his column broken up by the artillery support and the hasty charge of the Second Michigan, Lane's brigade veered a little to its left and entered a wood. There it struck its primary objective, Colonel Hartranft's left flank. The first regiment the Southerners hit was the Seventeenth Michigan.

Hartranft moved his brigade forward against the rebel salient at about the same time Lane ordered his own men forward. Rebel artillery crashed against his front. The First Brigade entered a dense woods, following the sound of the rebel guns.

The noise was deafening. Struck on its left flank by a charging enemy, the Seventeenth Michigan folded. Lt. Col. Frederick Swift, the commander of the Seventeenth, was told by his adjutant, "We had better be getting out of this, the line to our left has given away, a rebel brigade has swept around to our rear, and the woods are full of them."[76] But the terrific noise, the heavy cover of second growth, and the sudden onslaught of Lane's Confederates stymied any quick action Swift could take. Out of the 225 men who followed their colors into that dank thicket, 23 were killed in the fighting, 73 wounded, and 93 listed as "missing." To add to the ignominy, the survivors of the "Stonewall" Regiment learned the rebels had also captured their colors.[77]

The next regiment in line, the Fifty-first Pennsylvania, went the way of the Seventeenth Michigan, losing both of its flags.[78] The Fiftieth Pennsylvania, the left regiment of Colonel Humphrey's line, moved forward into the same thickly wooded area. No sooner did the Pennsylvanians take their position than Lane's North Carolinians hit them in the left flank and rear. A wild hand-to-hand conflict raged in the wet woods. Bayonets and musket butts came into play on both sides. Sgt. James Levan of the Fiftieth Pennsylvania was as surprised as the rest of his regiment.

> The first thing I knew of our being surrounded was when I heard some one say, "Surrender[,] you Yank, it[']s all up with you." I looked up and saw a terrible big officer swinging his sword over my head. It was now every man for himself.[79]

A hundred men were captured, but a small group gathered around the colors and fought their way out of the maelstrom.[80] The rebels did not emerge from the fight unscathed, either. In the melee, amidst the smoke, the dripping pines, the undergrowth, the curses and yells, more than 200 of Lane's men were captured, including the colonel of the Thirty-seventh North Carolina.[81]

The next Union regiment to receive the brunt of the flank attack at least received some advance notice of the avalanche hurtling down on them. The Twentieth Michigan was advancing through a clearing when the North Carolinians fired at them from the woods where the two Pennsylvania regiments had been hit. There was so much noise of battle that Capt. Claudius Grant, on the far right flank of the Twentieth, could not make himself heard. He could see the rebels coming out of the woods, but most of his men did not know it. Grant frantically signaled "by motion of his hands, rather than by voice" to the Twentieth's commander, Major Barnes, finally getting his attention. Barnes then had his regiment face by the left flank and charge into the woods.[82]

Rebel fire still came at them from the salient, and the movement to their left created a gap in the Ninth Corps line. Furthermore, the attack in the woods nearly destroyed the Twentieth Michigan. Finding himself almost surrounded by the enemy, Barnes tried to find a way out of the firestorm. Hand-to-hand fighting was the norm. Men on both sides found themselves captured, set free by comrades, only to be recaptured soon after.[83] In no more than 30 minutes of fierce fighting, the Twentieth lost 130 officers and men in this seething hell.[84]

The Sharpshooters Make a Stand

The Sharpshooters had the good fortune to be on the far right of the brigade. Lane's attack spent itself in the woods; many of the rebels, having chopped up Hartranft's brigade and part of Humphrey's and now being pelted with Union cannon fire, retreated back to their own lines.

After they first moved into the stunted woods to the front, the Sharpshooters found an abandoned breastwork of fence rails and tree limbs about 50 yards from the rebel salient. Here they met up with the Twenty-seventh Michigan of Hartranft's brigade. Colonel DeLand ordered his men to find cover "amid the thick smoke of battle, the steady drizzling rain & in a dense thicket of pines."[85]

When the Twentieth Michigan was forced to leave the woods on their left, the Sharpshooters and the Twenty-seventh found themselves in a crossfire from the rebels on their left and

147

in their front. It was impossible to advance. Rebel cannon and infantry fire pinned them down. There were no friendly troops on their right, either. The 109th New York and Eighth Michigan had advanced with the rest of Hartranft's brigade; now they, too, were gone. Hit from three sides, the two Michigan regiments held their ground. Maj. Samuel Moody, commanding the Twenty-seventh, was shot in the hand and lost a finger. Borrowing a handkerchief from DeLand, he wrapped it around the wound and stayed on the field.[86]

The two commanders saw to their lines and anxiously wondered if any aid were on the way. Cannon fire blasted trees into slivers. Rebels worked their way close to the beleaguered outpost, and "the conflict became a series of furious and unrelenting single-handed combats," remembered DeLand.[87] Taunts and curses coursed through the trees along with the smoke and rain. "Surrender or I'll blow your brains out," yelled a rebel to one of the Sharpshooters. "I'll see you damned first," retorted the rifleman.[88]

Lt. George Fowler, "one of our best fighting officers," went down with a bullet through his left thigh.[89] Chunks of iron ripped through the dank air as the rebel batteries blasted the spindly pines. Musket balls rattled through the branches, every so often hitting a man with a dull thud.

Over the crash of musketry the rebels could hear war cries of the Ottawas and Chippewas, as they let the Confederates know "they were standing on dangerous ground." The Indian company held the left side fronting the woods, from which Lane's remaining men poured a murderous fire. The unerring aim from Company K kept the enemy at bay. They held their ground as their young lieutenant, "mild, calm" Garrett Graveraet, kept his watch on the firing line. One of his men ran to tell the lieutenant that his father, 1st Sgt. Henry Graveraet, had been shot in the head. The son ran to his father's body and saw that he was already dead.[90]

Casualties mounted in Company K. Cpls. Samuel Going and Benjamin Greensky were already dead. The Mash-kaw brothers, James and John, both died on the line. Big Tom Ke-chi-ti-go had his left arm broken by a shell fragment. Sgt. Louis Genereau was hit in the left leg. Daniel Mwa-ke-we-naw of Bear River went down with three wounds. Mark Pe-she-kee caught a bullet in his left shoulder; and Simon Keji-kowe sustained a severe wound in his left side. All told, the Indians lost at least 17 men in the fight.[91]

For an hour the two regiments stood alone against whatever the enemy could throw at them. Rebel artillery fire tore trees from the ground. Capt. John S. Vreeland of General Willcox's staff came, bringing a message from division headquarters, but a cannon ball cut him nearly in two before he could deliver it. In the heavy atmosphere the blood from the dead and wounded steamed. Men searched for their last cartridges, then looked to the dead for extra rounds. Others fixed their bayonets as the rebels made their second charge. Again, the enemy was driven back as much with steel as with lead.[92]

On his own volition, Major Piper hurriedly gathered a half-dozen men from the Twenty-seventh Michigan and ran back for more ammunition.[93] In a few minutes Piper returned with his squad; they quickly began distributing the cartridges. No sooner did he reach the lines than he was killed. Shot in the head, he died so close to the rebel line that his body could not be retrieved.[94]

After an hour of wild combat, orders reached DeLand and Moody to pull their men back. Going down his line with the word to retire, DeLand was hit by a piece of shell and knocked to the ground. As he slowly picked himself up, he was stunned by the impact of another shell. This time part of his coat was ripped away, and the wind was knocked out of him.[95] Fourteen-year-old George Stone, fighting on the line instead of seeking the safety of the rear, saw DeLand fall the second time and helped him to his feet. The colonel, still in a dazed state, ordered his men back from the ridge.[96]

As they fell back, some of the Sharpshooters cut through one of those small family graveyards which dotted the Southland. Private Farling with a sudden whoop literally flew into the air, adding some hilarity to the terror of the moment. Hit in the leg by a spent ball, the force of it lamed him, "but it did the boys so much good that afterwards I went by the name of 'twenty-feet in the air.'"[97] Gathering his wits, he soon rejoined his comrades where the regiment was reforming, about 200 yards to the rear in an open space.[98]

Even though General Willcox gave a "pat on the back" to those units who generally fought well and mentioned them favorably in his official reports, he did not even cite the Twenty-seventh Michigan or the Sharpshooters by name in their holding action. His comments on the two regiments were matter-of-fact:

The second line of both brigades, with little less in killed and wounded, pushed ahead and held their ground in the woods with obstinate pluck until their ammunition was exhausted, when, with fixed bayonets, they held on until ordered to withdraw to the edge of the woods, where their ammunition was replenished and a line of breast-works was hastily thrown up.[99]

That evening Colonel DeLand checked out the strength of the regiment by talking to his officers. One report caused some consternation. His brother, Sgt. Maj. Jim DeLand, while on an errand to procure more ammunition from division headquarters during the battle, noticed quite a few stragglers and headquarters personnel near the bridge. He spied about 20 Sharpshooters there. In company with them were two officers from the regiment—his cousin, Capt. Hooker A. DeLand, and Lt. Moses Powell. Worse, none of those near the Ni River bridge, except for a few aides and quartermaster personnel, had any business there.[100]

But that matter would have to wait. There were more pressing concerns. In the blessed darkness, lost men found their regiments, parties brought in the dead for identification, the injured had their wounds dressed and were sent to the rear. Whatever food could be found was consumed, but there was no time for real rest.[101]

During the night Second Lieutenant Graveraet sent word to Adjutant Buckbee. The young lieutenant sought permission to take out a detail of men and bury his father, 1st Sgt. Henry Graveraet, who had been killed in the fighting. Buckbee quickly gathered some men together to help the young lieutenant. After the interment, young Graveraet "very carefully marked the grave and the surrounding trees so that he could find it afterwards, telling me he expected to return and take up the body and bury it in Michigan."[102]

The day had been a hell for those who lived through it. The rebel attack was repulsed, but so was the Union assault. The drizzling rain added to the misery of the men that evening. All the regiments in the Second Brigade were bloodied. The Twentieth Michigan had lost 143 in killed, wounded, and missing; they had entered the fight that morning with 300 men.[103] Depressed at the carnage, Lieutenant Colonel Cutcheon wrote many years later that "our losses seemed in vain."[104]

There had been a telling effect on the rebels as well. This feeling was brought out the next day when the pickets in front of the Second Brigade brought in a captured Confederate officer. He told his captors:

> The lickin' you gave us yesterday evening was the badest we ever got. Our general told us we's gotter cary the hill & we'd skedadle all yer Yanks inter the Potomac in ten days. We reckoned there war only a few ov you, but twant no use.[105]

Colonel DeLand answered, "That's so, Mr. Reb., Twant."[106]

The battle of Spotsylvania marked a high point for the Sharpshooters. As bad as the contest turned out, and even though no immediate gains were made, the Sharpshooters ended the fight feeling better about themselves. They had taken horrendous casualties, but they had also proved a point, a point reiterated by Colonel Cutcheon in his official report of the battle. "On this occasion," he wrote, "they [the Sharpshooters] cancelled the unfortunate record they made on the 9th at Ny River."[107]

Colonel DeLand posted the remnants of his regiment, and entrenchments were dug during the night. In the morning he turned command of the Sharpshooters over to Capt. Levant C. Rhines of Company A, the senior line officer then present, and left the front for the Third Division hospital.[108] DeLand's wounds, though not necessarily noticeable, pained him terribly. Twice during the fighting he had gone down. The first time, pieces of a bursting shell hit him in the middle of his back on his spinal column and on his right shoulder. A few minutes later another shell exploded near him, stunning him and rendering him senseless for a short time.[109]

DeLand first checked into the division hospital, where the doctors decided to send him to Fredericksburg for further treatment. His shoulder injury was particularly painful, "causing permanent paralisis [sic] of muscle & nerve of right arm."[110] From Fredericksburg the colonel was transferred to a hospital in Washington, DC on 20 May. After a month, DeLand was sent to another hospital in Annapolis. Not until 10 July did he finally leave for the front, reporting back to his regiment on 16 July.[111]

A Storm of Controversy

Considerable contention developed over the colonel's absence. A controversial figure both back home in Jackson and in the army, DeLand had fueled arguments all his life. A newspaper editor in the pre-Civil War days of "give 'em hell" journalism, DeLand had friends and enemies, but precious few neutral onlookers. Taking a partisan stand on the issues of the day, he offended and chastised those who disagreed with him. Unfortunately, this type of chafing personality did not help him as colonel of the Sharpshooters. He alienated not only his superiors, like General Willcox, but also some of his subordinates as well.

When DeLand left the regiment on 13 May, the incessant character assassination continued unabated. Chaplain Heagle, not feeling too well himself at this juncture, assisted him. Unfortunately for the colonel, his wounds were not all that evident. There was no blood, and he was thought by some to be shirking. Human nature being what it is, we are willing to give the benefit of a doubt to those whom we admire, but not to those whom we detest. Authority figures rub some people the wrong way; and so it was with DeLand.

He was afflicted with diarrhea, but so were many of his men.[112] Diarrhea was one of the commonest ailments affecting the Union army. Most men simply withstood its effects, but the total consequence was too much for DeLand. He had complained of exhaustion and illness before the battle of 12 May. Now that it was over, he was ready to go to the rear for some help and rest.

Captain Rhines had little respect for Colonel DeLand. When and for what reason the two had had a falling out is shrouded by the cloak of time; whatever the cause, by 13 May Rhines did not have much regard for his commander. Writing a few days later, the captain related the incident of DeLand's leaving: "At present I am in command of the Regiment, Col DeLand having left in the hour of battle, and never returned; except to look over the brow of a hill, about thirty rods in the rear of the Regiment."[113]

The letter was printed in at least two Democratic newspapers back in Michigan. Reporting any miscue on the part of a political opponent was fair game then (as it is today). If the miscue had been made by a former Republican editor whose own editorials had drawn blood years before, then the volley went out with even more jaundiced glee. The editor of the Jackson *Eagle* said he knew the Sharpshooters:

had no confidence in their Colonel. They knew him to be an inso-
lent braggard [*sic*]. His position [in the regiment] was obtained not
because he possessed any merit, but in consequence of his doing
the dirty work of a political clique in this city.[114]

A few weeks later the editor of the *Eagle* again blasted De-
Land with a scathing article entitled "'Cowards'—Col. DeLand."

> A very respectable gentleman from this county recently visited the
> Holland settlement, in this State. While there, some wounded
> Sharpshooters came home, and declared that their Colonel was a
> coward and that he ran from . . . battle. A couple of wounded offi-
> cers who returned from the front a few weeks ago declared that
> DeLand was a coward, and that the Michigan soldiers in the Army
> of the Potomac were highly incensed at his conduct. A soldier
> writing to his relatives in this county reiterates the charge of
> cowardice.[115]

Joining in the fray, two Republican papers, the Jackson *Citizen* (DeLand's old weekly) and the Detroit *Advertiser and Tribune*,
defended the colonel. Give DeLand a chance to defend himself
against the charge, remonstrated the editor of the *Citizen*. "Well
known persons [in the regiment]," the editor continued, "write
home letters which emphatically contradict the rumors to his dis-
credit."[116] The *Advertiser and Tribune* repeated the same line,
emphasizing that the spurious charge was refuted by "the men of
the regiment."[117]

Sgt. Leverette N. Case in a letter to his hometown newspaper, the Jonesville *Weekly Independent*, denounced those who censured Colonel DeLand. "Men are too fond of assailing the private
and public character of their fellow man," he wrote. "They who
have tried to ruin the fighting character of our Regiment have
begun at its fountain head, but I say and vehemently re-assert
that *it can't be did*."[118]

The one other man quoted by either party as to the guilt or
innocence of the colonel was Chaplain Heagle, and he corrobo-
rated DeLand's testimony. "I was present at the time referred to,"
he reported, "which was no battle, but only some skirmishing. I
saw the Colonel with his regiment. He did not 'desert,' but medical authority induced him to go to the rear, and the next thing to
the hospital at Fredericksburg."[119]

The rumors became so general that DeLand was forced to
ask for a court-martial in order to exonerate his record. Not long

after he returned to the regiment in July, he requested and received a military commission to review the charge, "justifying his absence from his command." [120]

The commission cleared DeLand of all wrongdoing and returned him to duty, but he was not through with those who had libeled him. "I am going to prosecute the Eagle and the Patriot [the two Democratic papers in Jackson, Michigan]. Lying has got to stop in Jackson. They must back up *all* they say or back *square down*, or *fight*. The thing has gone too far for a joke." [121]

The Dead and Wounded

Only 250 Sharpshooters were left to draw rations a week after the bloodletting at Spotsylvania. [122] Losses in the Second Brigade were horrific. The Fiftieth Pennsylvania had suffered most severely. In all the fighting at Spotsylvania, that regiment had lost 241 men (25 killed or dead of wounds, 102 wounded, and 114 listed as missing or captured). [123] The Twentieth Michigan lost another 143: 20 killed, 104 wounded, and 19 declared missing at the end of the fighting. [124]

The Sharpshooters were no luckier; they had suffered 155 casualties. One officer and 33 men died, and another 6 officers and 111 enlisted men were wounded; 4 additional men were listed as missing. [125] Most of the injured were conveyed to Fredericksburg, and then to Washington. There were so many wounded that the final load was not sent off until 19 May. A few were so badly mangled that Dr. Whelan had to keep them at the aid station. [126] For such a small brigade, the loss was phenomenal. In addition, the Twenty-seventh Michigan (which had fought shoulder to shoulder with the Sharpshooters on 12 May) had 27 killed, 148 wounded, and 12 missing. [127]

The division hospital was jammed with wounded and dying men. Others lay on the battlefield. Some bodies were never recovered. Maj. John Piper, seen soon after he returned with a load of ammunition, was at first thought to have been captured, but no one ever brought back word of him. No body on the field was ever identified as his, and today he sleeps in a nameless grave somewhere in Virginia. [128]

The casualty list spanned the whole spectrum of the regiment. Sixteen-year-old Clark Fox, Jr. (Co. B) was killed in the battle, and his father was captured; the elder Fox would die in

Andersonville in August.[129] Twenty-three-year-old Cpl. Sylvester
Smith (Co. B) would never return to Spring Lake. Left mortally
wounded on the field, his body was never identified.[130] Henry
Kunce (Co. G), one of the veterans from the Third Michigan Cavalry, died among the dank pine trees as well.[131] Cpl. George S.
Williams (Co. F), who had served as a nurse in the smallpox ward
the previous winter at Camp Douglas, was killed in the action.[132]
Eighteen-year-old Charles Quance (Co. B), whose brother Stephen
had been severely wounded the day before, also was killed in the
fighting.[133] Thirty-year-old Lawrence Banks of Grand Haven had
been forced to parade around in a barrel at the Dearborn arsenal
as a punishment for drunkenness; now his lifeblood stained the
ground at Spotsylvania.[134]

Wives and loved ones throughout Michigan scanned casualty
reports in the local newspapers. Some received notices from officers of men in the bloodied regiments, telling of their husbands'
bravery; these were small consolation to women with young children and no man coming home.

The remains of 1st Sgt. Henry Graveraet (Co. K) never
came home. He rests in the national cemetery in Fredericksburg,
Virginia, although another stone commemorates him on Mackinac Island, Michigan. Quite a number of men lied about their age
when they enlisted in the army. Sergeant Graveraet listed his as
45, but he had shaved ten years from his life so he could take his
place in the ranks. At 57, he was the oldest man in the regiment
when he died on that drizzly 12 May.[135]

Another illustrious member lost to the regiment was Daniel
Mwa-ke-we-naw. Forty-one years old and over six feet tall, he
was a commanding presence, although only a private in the
ranks. He had played a significant role in enlisting Indians from
the Little Traverse Bay region; a crack shot, "his men say that in
the fight . . . he killed not less than thirty-two rebels, a number
of them officers." Wounded at least three times (in the face, hand,
and head) he was unable to keep loading and firing. Mwa-ke-we-
naw left the field and was transported to Fredericksburg with
the rest of the wounded. Surgeons dressed his injuries and amputated part of his hand, but infection (which totally baffled Civil
War surgeons) set in, and the warrior died in his nation's capital
the next month. His stature in his own community was such that
the officers of Company K prevailed upon Congressman John
Driggs of Saginaw, the father of 1st Lt. William Driggs of Company K, to have Mwa-ke-we-naw's body embalmed, "placed in a

handsome coffin," and sent to Michigan, where he was buried in East Saginaw.[136]

Sgt. Edmund P. Beadle (Co. H), younger brother of the lieutenant colonel, was shot in right side and sent to Lincoln Hospital in Washington, DC, to recover. Within a few weeks he was on his way home to Indiana. But he was still ailing and the wound was serious. Only 17 years old, he lingered in pain until the end of June, dying at his father's home in Rockville on the last day of the month.[137]

James Haight (Co. C), whose lucky shot had killed his assailant, made his way to the division hospital, but nothing was done for him there. His wound was painful, the doctors were busy with dozens of other cases, and he was lost in the shuffle. Receiving no help for his injured left arm, Haight did manage to get a drink of whiskey and milk, his only sustenance or anesthesia. Not until he reached Lincoln Hospital in Washington, DC, the same place where Sergeant Beadle lay, did he receive any medical assistance. He adamantly refused to have his arm amputated; the surgeon could do little more than probe the blackened limb for the bullet and pieces of bone. The arm healed, but the severe damage crippled it. Very reticent about his military career for the rest of his life, the 19-year-old farmer had to restart his civilian occupation with quite a handicap.[138]

After a man was shot on the line, generally he had his wound dressed or at least looked at by his regimental surgeon at the division aid station. The Third Division hospital was back across the Ni River, near the Beverly house. More than likely, he was then shuttled to Fredericksburg, where nearly every public and many private buildings were impressed as makeshift hospitals; 20,000 Federals and Confederates wounded at Wilderness and Spotsylvania had their wounds treated there. Those who died of complications, like Pvts. Garret Dumez, Co. F, and Edward Fisher, Co. I, were buried there in temporary plots, their bodies later transferred to permanent cemeteries.[139]

Others, although not wounded in battle, were still lost to the regiment. Capt. George N. Davis (Co. D) left the regiment on 12 May because of illness. For two months he slowly recovered in Washington hospitals. In August Davis went to Indianapolis as a hospital inspector. Subsequently, he wrote to DeLand, telling him he intended either to resign his commission or to obtain a transfer to the Veteran Reserve Corps. The transfer never worked out and Davis's chronic illness proved grounds enough for him to acquire a disability discharge on 26 November 1864.[140]

First Lt. Robert Hill (Co. I) left the regiment on 8 May. Ill from sunstroke, the 23-year-old spent his time convalescing in Washington, then was sent home to Kalamazoo. Hill never fully recovered from the effects of exhaustion and sunstroke; he procured a discharge for disability in December 1864.[141]

Some wounded men managed to get sent home to recover from the ill effects of their wounds. Capt. Edwin V. Andress, commander of Company K, had been wounded in the foot, albeit under suspicious circumstances. Within a week of the battle, the captain was back in Michigan. In an interview with a reporter from the Detroit *Free Press* he laid the canard to rest that the Indians would not fight. They "fought with the greatest courage," he stated in the strongest possible language. And to emphasize his remark, he told his audience that "a large number of them were killed or wounded." [142] It was reported that his "wound is not serious and he will soon recover," [143] but he never returned to active duty. The wound supporated and would not heal. After two months Andress received his honorable discharge due to physical disability caused by the injury.[144]

The folks back home hung on every word of the returning soldiers. After ascertaining the status of loved ones, they heard the "war stories"—a melange of fact, fiction, and hearsay they accepted as gospel from the lips of "one who was there." When Captain Andress and Sgt. Robert Farrell (Co. G) returned to Detroit less than a week after the slaughter at Spotsylvania, theirs was the first "live" report the Detroit papers related to their subscribers. The papers naively printed every word as fact, regardless if it were originally rumor or speculation. "Capt. Andress states that the rebels took their dead and made breastworks of them to fight behind. Such an instance of this is not recorded in the annals of warfare," related an astonished reporter to the Detroit *Advertiser and Tribune*.

A rebel prisoner told Sergeant Farrell that Colonel Graves of the Eighth Michigan Infantry had been murdered by the Confederates after he fell into their hands at the Wilderness. During the same battle, "the rebel sharpshooters killed numbers of our men from trees, shooting in a vertical direction." While having his wound treated at Fredericksburg, Andress said he witnessed an uprising by several thousand Confederate prisoners. "They were guarded by the Invalid Corps, whom the 'rebs' thought would not fight, undertook to take them prisoners and regain their liberty. The Invalid Corps killed 50 of them and wounded 125."[145]

Lieutenant Randall and the Ambulance Corps

Back on 26 April, 2nd Lt. William Randall of Company I was detailed to take charge of the Second Brigade ambulance train. Randall considered himself fortunate. He had "a splendid saddle horse to ride, carry a good wall tent, plenty of blankets, provisions, &c, &c."[146]

Willcox's division was allowed 50 ambulances; four more wagons carrying forage for the animals and extra gear to mend the wagons and the harness made up the train. In addition, there was a blacksmith forge, a blacksmith, and a wheelwright. Two stretcher bearers were assigned to each wagon.[147]

A veteran of the First Michigan Infantry (3 months), Randall was an educated, considerate, and religious young man. His journal entries are terse but filled with the thoughtfulness he had for others. During the fight in the Wilderness, Randall and his men carried dozens of wounded to the field hospital. He worked until 9:00 that first night, removing wounded from the front. Then he toiled through the dark, transporting them farther to the rear, out of reach of the enemy's shells. He hauled nine more seriously hurt men beyond the rebel guns that night but found two of them dead in the morning.[148]

Randall displayed his ambivalence toward battle in his diary entries. He saw the vast array of military might from his station in the rear of the fighting. "But amid this mighty magnificence of opposing armies, it is sad to contemplate the loss of life, the suffering of the wounded, the suffering of all."[149] The incessant work made him tired and overworked, and yet "I saw death and destruction all around me and thought nothing of it."[150]

During the day on 7 May there was no heavy firing on the Third Division's front. Randall had his men pick up whatever wounded they could reach, and with wagons loaded with mangled humanity they started to Warrenton Junction about 4:00 PM. The wagon train crossed the Rapidan River at Ely's Ford and went into camp at 10:00 PM. Near midnight orders reached him, telling him to recross the river and make haste to Spotsylvania. The wagons were hurriedly hitched up, and the detail made its way to the Chancellorsville crossroads. There Randall received new orders to move his train to Fredericksburg.

The agonies of the wounded sincerely disturbed the young lieutenant. The suffering injured men, many with their wounds yet undressed, had been loaded and unloaded three times already. They also had received no provisions, and were transported over roads that were rutted and "almost impossibly rough."[151] All during the night men died in the wagons, and every so often one of the conveyances pulled to the side while a still form was off-loaded and buried alongside the road in a nameless grave.

A detachment from the Twenty-fourth New York Cavalry, a dismounted unit from one of the new regiments, led the Third Division train. "As we neared Fredericksburg, it was rumored among them that the city was occupied by the enemy, and it was not safe to proceed." Indecision on the cavalrymen's part held up the wagons. Not believing the rumor for an instant, Wells B. Fox, surgeon of the Eighth Michigan Infantry, ordered his hospital guard (50 men of the veteran Fifty-first Pennsylvania Infantry) "to drive the cavalry off the pike and allow us to continue our journey." The Twenty-fourth was "skedaddled," the hospital attendants and surgeons seeing no more of them until they arrived safely in Fredericksburg.

Taking whatever they needed wherever they could find it, "because under such circumstances we were not very particular what we seized that would contribute to the comfort of our boys," the surgeons confiscated the mayor's house, a hotel, some churches and schools, and private homes for their maimed and anguished comrades.[152] The buildings, by and large, were in poor physical shape. Pvt. George Minnis of the Twentieth Michigan, one of the guards detailed to the ambulance train, commented:

> this city looks hard and there is not hardly a house but bears the marks which General Burnside gave them one year ago last fall [at the Battle of Fredericksburg]. The houses are rent with shot and s[h]ell so bad that their occupants did not see fit to live in them afterwards. But they make right-good hospitals for the thousands of our wounded.[153]

The sufferings of the wounded did not end at Fredericksburg. Laid on floors of whatever building was available, some of the injured waited agonizing days for a surgeon to examine their wounds. Aghast at the suffering, yet ordered back to the Wilderness, Randall knew the agonies of most of the shot and torn soldiers would not be alleviated "for several days before surgeons and supplies could be forwarded from Washington."[154]

Pvt. Samuel Gates of the Twenty-seventh Michigan left behind a sketch of the abominable conditions at Fredericksburg. His description assaults the senses; one can only wonder what emotional wounds were inflicted on the already physically wounded. "The situation of the wounded," wrote Gates in his diary:

> is most deplorable, there is said to be 30,000 wounded men in the city. Every home is a hospital and the stench from their wounds is almost suffocating, even on the streets. From 50 to 75 die daily. The bodies are taken out to the burial place in army wagons, 8 or 10 at a time wrapped in old overcoats, blankets or tent clothes [*sic*]. Trenches are dug, and the bodies laid side by side and the earth thrown over them. Many of them are unknown and their graves unmarked.[155]

The Third Division surgeons headed back to the front as soon as they could, leaving their wounded in the hands of the attendants. After depositing the men in his care, Lieutenant Randall took charge of 17 wagons under a flag of truce and retraced his path to the Wilderness. There he "met a squad of Confederate Cavalry beyond Chancellorsville. Made known to them our business and passed on."[156]

The many wounded left behind when Grant changed his base were captured by rebel cavalry. Not to be burdened by thousands of immobile prisoners, the Confederates paroled the lot. Randall's detachment loaded as many as could fit on the wagons. Searching the battlefield for additional casualties, Randall chanced upon two men, both of whom had been shot five days previously. "They were nearly dead," he wrote laconically. He filled all his ambulances that 10 May morning, and by evening he had them all in Fredericksburg.[157] Randall then took his wagons to the Third Division hospital near the Harris house on the east side of the Ni River. It was a spacious place, "one of those old Virginia homes surrounded by commodious porches so well appreciated in The South, with their slave quarters in the rear."[158]

Early on the foggy morning of 12 May Randall moved the Third Division ambulances across the river, near one of the batteries. During the rebel bombardment he and his men dodged shells while they carried out all the wounded they could gather.

The bodies of the dead were also removed for burial. Brought back to the ambulances, the corpses were arranged in rows. "Saw a Capt who was shot through the brain," recalled Randall. "Was laid with the dead. This man lived until night."[159] Nothing could have been done for the poor soul. In some cases, it was just a macabre waiting game.

After a quick nap, Randall had the ambulances loaded with the groaning cargo at 2:00 AM. After ten hours on the road, in springless wagons on rutted, potholed roads, the wounded fellows enduring an inferno of pain, the wagon train finally reached Fredericksburg.

The next day Randall rode back to the front with 15 Ninth Corps wagons under his command.[160] Returning early on the morning of 18 May to Fredericksburg with more carnage, he deposited his charges, then proceeded back to the Ninth Corps. On that same day a Union attack sputtered out near the Mule Shoe at Spotsylvania. Rebel artillery stopped the assault before the Federals approached within musket range. Soon after the attack ended, General Ewell's rebel corps "sidled" around the Union right wing to ascertain what the Union army was doing.[161] A section of Ewell's corps ran into Randall's detachment on its way back from Fredericksburg.

Earlier Randall had given his horse to an ambulance attendant to ride while he stretched out in one of the rearmost wagons to catch some sleep. He was dog-tired, but he woke in a trice when the attack came. The rebels hit the head of the column. Heavy firing at the front threw the rest of the drivers into a frenzy. What were the rebels doing this far behind the lines? Some ambulances overturned when their drivers tried to get them turned around. Eleven of the wagons rushed back to Fredericksburg "without orders," added an enraged Randall. During the excitement a baggage train ran into Randall's column, further adding to the panic. The drivers of the baggage wagons jumped from their horses and ran for the rear, leaving their horses and wagons on the darkened road. Union infantrymen quickly moved in from the woods, formed a line of battle parallel to the road, and pushed the Confederates back. Randall, the ranking officer in the ambulance train, waited for an hour on the road with the baggage wagons and a few ambulances, then started back to Fredericksburg, where he picked up the pieces of his command.[162] On the way back to the front he was struck with the enormity of the Union army's supply system.

The immensity of General Grant's attacking forces was rarely grasped by the front-line soldier. Whether in camp, on the march, or in battle, he saw only a small part of the army. Lieutenant Randall, roaming along the fringes of this mammoth enterprise, was awed by the sheer magnitude of Grant's entourage. The number of wagons and their draft animals was phenomenal. There were wagons for ambulances, baggage, forage, cannons— all of them pulled by four or six horses or mules.

> I will state that when I reached Bowling Green thousands of wagons were parked in the village & [wagon] trains [were] passing through the city from Bowling Green to Fredericksburg, a distance of 20 miles, the road was filled with wagons as close as they could drive. A baggage wagon with six mules attached is a ponderous machine.[163]

Despite this, only a small part of the army—his own regiment—remained uppermost in Randall's mind. Battles were fought. Men he knew well were killed or wounded, and he regretted playing no part in their fortunes. The attrition in the roll of Sharpshooter officers would soon call him back to the regiment to share in its destiny.

CHAPTER 8

It Is Now No Dishonor

Tough Marching through Virginia

With Colonel DeLand in a Washington hospital, Lieutenant Colonel Beadle transferred to the Veteran Reserve
Corps, and Major Piper dead, command of the Sharpshooters fell
on the shoulders of the senior captain of the regiment, Levant C.
Rhines.

Rhines was a no-nonsense lawyer accustomed to command,
a War Democrat, and an aspiring politician. Born in Batavia,
New York, in 1831, Rhines had come to Michigan in the westward flow of immigrants from that state. Graduating with highest honors from Spring Arbor College in 1853, he entered the law
offices of Walker and Russell in Jackson, Michigan. Admitted to
the bar in 1855, Rhines moved to Battle Creek where he put out
his own shingle. Within a year he was appointed prosecuting
attorney and then was elected to the same office for several
terms. When he joined the Sharpshooters late in 1862, he was
leaving a successful and lucrative practice. Rhines commanded
Company A until after Spotsylvania; then, as the ranking officer,
he took command of the regiment.[1]

The night of 12 May it rained again, as it had sporadically
throughout the day. The inclement weather thwarted General

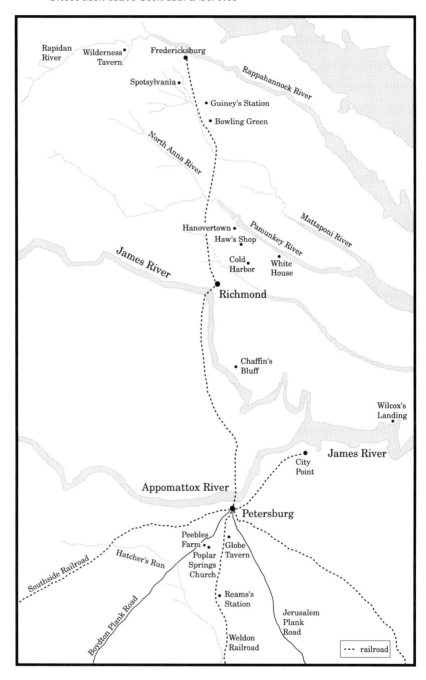

Virginia Campaign, 1864-1865

Grant's plans to sidle his army to the left around the Confederate force. Too much rain and the bottomless roads forced the Union commander to keep his lines relatively static. For about a week, the Sharpshooters and the Third Division rested (if that is what it could be called). Picket duty was constant, and the strain of skirmishing was telling on the men. Occupying rifle pits in the area they had taken on 9 May, they played a waiting game with the enemy.

The men of Willcox's division stayed there until the night of 17 May. The next morning they breakfasted at 3:00 and struck their tents, ready to spill out and move to their left. The rebels, not quite knowing what was happening and wanting to find out, attacked the Sixth Corps, which was to the right of Burnside's men. The Ninth Corps held its position, and at noon the men were ordered to put up their tents again.[2]

Early on the 19th, at about 3:00 AM, Burnside's corps finally moved from its entrenchments and marched southeastward to join the Sixth Corps, which had already trudged past Burnside's position. Toward evening, the rebels sallied out of their works and attacked some heavy artillery regiments near the Harris house. It turned out to be quite a sharp affair, and not until elements of the Second and Fifth Corps counterattacked did the rebels pull back.[3]

For the next day and a half the division stayed put. Late in the evening of 21 May the men were back on the road; they reached Guiney's Station early the next morning. After a short rest, the division marched out and made slow progress, plodding on until 4:30 in the afternoon. The next day, Monday, 23 May was another blur in the minds of the dog-tired soldiers. Willcox's men traveled from Bethel Church to Ox Ford on the North Anna River. Orders went out for Willcox's division to assault the Confederate lines the next morning, despite the fact that the rebels held the high ground on the south side of the river, their entrenchments bolstered by artillery. The Third Division regiments were deployed and rifle pits were dug. The Fiftieth Pennsylvania advanced under fire and took possession of an island in the river.[4]

Christ's brigade (with the Twentieth Michigan in the vanguard) made ready to lead the divisional assault against the Confederate positions, an attack few believed would end in success.[5] Lieutenant Randall reported a rumor that Willcox "offered to take this position if they would give him Mich[igan] troops."[6] After a reconnaissance of the enemy's emplacements, Burnside decided any chance of success was too remote, and "fortunately for us," recorded Colonel Cutcheon of the Twentieth Michigan, "the attack was abandoned."[7] Maj. Claudius B. Grant of the Twentieth was more emphatic: "Thank God Gen Burnside countermanded the order."[8]

The brigade did occupy its bank on the North Anna, and a lively exchange of fire was kept up all the time it stayed there. Casualties in the regiment kept mounting, although the Confederates did not go unscathed. The continual skirmishing resulted in the deaths of two Sharpshooters, Eugene R. Spencer (Co. I) and John Beck (Co. B); seven more were wounded, and five were captured while on picket.[9] Robert Finch (Co. B) sustained a particularly nasty wound; a rebel bullet fractured the right side of his skull. Surgeons removed pieces of bone, but Finch lost his right eye.[10]

While the Third Division skirmished at Ox Ford, strenuous fighting erupted both up- and downstream from their position. To their right the Fifth Corps, with Crittenden's division, forced a crossing; to their left the Second Corps and Potter's Ninth Corps division attacked Confederate entrenchments on the south side of the North Anna.

For two days (25 and 26 May) the Third Division traded shots with the rebels across the river but did not attack them. During the 26th the rain came down in torrents again.[11] Only Christ's brigade and a single battery remained at Ox Ford, skirmishing with the Confederates.[12] Early on 27 May the Sharpshooters moved out with the rest of the brigade. They would march 22 miles over roads turned dusty even after the storm of the previous day, not stopping until 1:00 AM the next morning. Taking an easterly route, they crossed the Pamunkey River over a pontoon bridge near Hanovertown before stopping for a few hours' rest.

"This was one of the hardest day's marching the regiment ever had," recalled the historian of the Twentieth Michigan.[13] The Sixtieth Ohio had more problems than most regiments on the march. Many of the Buckeyes had worn out their shoes and were now barefoot.[14] The sandy roads, the clouds of dust, the flies, and thirst plagued the Sharpshooters and their companions the entire 22 miles.

Totally fatigued, the Sharpshooters sleepwalked across the bridge, then advanced to a piece of high ground beyond the river. Skirmishers took their places, and those not so deployed "dropped in their tracks and went to sleep."[15] This particularly difficult march had resulted in stragglers galore. When Adjutant Buckbee called together his orderly sergeants to account for their respective companies, 1st Sgt. Edwin Conklin of Company F rammed his bayoneted rifle into the ground and disgruntedly reported, "Sir, Company 'F' present or accounted for—not a damn man here but myself."[16]

The Sharpshooters always pointed out that few of their numbers ever straggled; to do so was unusual, but so was this march. A number of them had grouped together while trying to keep up with the main body of the regiment. While recovering their strength along the side of the road, they saw a squad of Confederate cavalry approaching their resting place. The Sharpshooters hid, then jumped from their cover when the rebels came abreast of their position. Not only did they bag some prisoners, but the stragglers climbed atop the horses, four or five men to an animal, and marched their captives to the Sharpshooters' camp.[17]

In the hours before daylight most of the absentees made their way to the regiment; by dawn almost all the effectives were present.[18] After a few hours of treasured rest, the division again moved forward—but only for two miles—and bivouacked near Haw's Shop. Skirmishers took their places, and a scouting party of 100 men stepped out. Not finding any opposition, the brigade pulled back and made camp near Hanovertown.[19]

The men had been on campaign for a full month now. They were dirty and tired, many were sick, and they had endured horrendous battle casualties. Because they never stayed in one place very long, their mail could not catch up with them.[20] Ever since the beginning of May, when they had hurried to the Rapidan crossing, "it had been one continual march, intercepted occasionally by a quite strenuous battle, or slight skirmish."[21] The whole campaign was a succession of movements and short fights, either in battle order or on the skirmish line. Digging entrenchments and felling trees and the inevitable marching without end kept the men from any real rest. There was not a single day during which they had not received fire from the enemy. No one, it seemed, not even the officers, knew where they were. Richmond was on everyone's mind—at least, on the minds of those who could still think clearly. Richmond was the target; take it, they thought, and the war would end.

The Ambulance Train

At 4:00 on the afternoon of 25 May, Lieutenant Randall and his ambulances reached the Ninth Corps' position on the North Anna River. Only Burnside's men had not yet crossed it. The Second and Fifth Corps, after heavy fighting, had already forced their way over. On his way to the river Randall crossed paths with General Sheridan's Cavalry Corps. The horsemen were just returning from their raid on the outskirts of Richmond, which had thrown the Confederate capital into a tizzy. For more than an hour the cavalrymen passed Randall's wagons.[22]

The next day the skies opened up again and it rained hard, but the men moved across the North Anna and marched in another of Grant's sidelong maneuvers. The movement was tough on the men and animals. Randall's wagons were "loaded very heavy with sick." A couple of his horses fell from exhaustion and had to be replaced with the mounts ridden by Randall and his sergeant. After only a short distance, "more horses gave out & the [wagon] train was obliged to stop again."

Propitiously, General Burnside and his staff happened to pass by at this juncture. Asking Randall where his horse was, Burnside soon learned the state of affairs. Burnside then had General Willcox detail an officer and thirty men to help the wagons along. No horses were immediately available. The ones in harness "could drag the wagons along on the level but the men pushed the wagons up the hills." At midnight Randall's command crossed the Pamunkey River, still following the Third Division. He and his men had marched 32 miles that day. Writing in his journal that evening, an exhausted Randall recorded: "I am sick with dysentary [*sic*] but manage to do duty."[23]

Cold Harbor

After only five hours of rest, the division roused itself like some sort of half-sedated beast and continued its dreadful march to Cold Harbor. About 15 miles outside of Richmond, the men finally received orders to settle down for the night. The sound of musketry could be heard near evening.[24]

The entire Ninth Corps moved to the southwest on the morning of 30 May and crossed Totopotomy Creek under fire; the regiments filed to the left and right on the other side. Incessant skirmishing was the order of the day.[25] During the next day, still skirmishing, Christ's men stayed in support of Hartranft's brigade. That night a new line of entrenchments was thrown up only 200 yards from the rebel pickets.[26]

On 1 June at dusk, the Confederates fiercely attacked the First Division, which adjoined the right of the Third, viciously throwing Crittenden's men back. Bolstered by elements of the Third Division, the First was able to repulse the rebels and reoccupy their old lines.[27] The Sharpshooters lost two more men in the action. As the regiment advanced across a field in a supporting line, Pvt. John S. Urie, a 19-year-old from Scipio, Michigan, caught a ball in his left thigh, which took him out of the army, and Pvt. Amos Farling took a hit in his left hand, which kept him in a hospital for several weeks.[28]

Lieutenant Randall and his ambulance train, in the rear of Crittenden's division during the attack, watched the Ninth Corps batteries firing their shells at the rebels. Randall followed the men of the First Division with eight wagons as they marched from their lines that night.[29]

The next day Christ's brigade, closely followed by the enemy, moved from the Bethesda Church area on its way to Cold Harbor. As the rest of the division continued on its route, the Twentieth Michigan was detached to guard a crucial crossroads at its rear. The regiment had hardly arrived at its destination "when the rain came pouring down in torrents." At exactly the same time the Twentieth's pickets raced back with the rebels on their heels. The enemy attacked the Twentieth; had it not been for the timely arrival of Marshall's Provisional Brigade, the Twentieth would have been forced back. Willcox pulled his entire division together and advanced against the Confederates on the next day, 3 June.

Throughout that day the Second Brigade lay in support of Hartranft's men but bore no major role in the operations that took place. The First Brigade charged the enemy lines, but its ranks were enfiladed by rebel artillery fire. So close were the rebel lines that Hartranft could not deploy his artillery against them. There was also some confusion in moving the appropriate columns to jumping-off points against the Confederates. As a result, the attack was finally abandoned.

Then the Sharpshooters went to work. As the bulk of the division fell back, Company K came up. Taking cover amid the stands of pine trees in the area, the Indians carefully picked out their targets from among the rebel artillerymen. With casualties mounting, the Southerners decided to pull their artillery pieces out. But the Indians were well hidden and had found their range. When the Confederates tried to remove their guns, the Sharpshooters began picking off their horses. During the daylight hours, the rebels made every effort to withdraw their cannon, but horses went down with every try.

Under cover of darkness the enemy was finally able to pull its big guns back. Christ's brigade moved up and relieved Hartranft's. Heavy skirmishing continued all night, but by morning the rebels were gone. Union skirmishers reported that they "found 26 dead horses at one battery and 37 at another," mute testimony to the deadly accuracy of the Springfields in Company K.[30]

The Sharpshooters did not emerge unscathed. Three more men were lost. Lucius P. Spencer (Co. C) was hit in the left side; he would suffer for three weeks before dying from his wound. Two others received minor wounds.[31]

On 4 June the brigade moved out and relieved part of the Second Corps at Cold Harbor. For more than a week the Sharpshooters would hold a portion of the outer entrenchments there.[32] The name proved to be a misnomer. "I do not know why 'Harbor,'" confessed Adjutant Buckbee, "because I certainly saw no water there, not even enough to take a bath."[33] Besides the constant skirmishing, lack of water was the primary complaint. There was hardly a time the men could get enough to drink. "I do not remember of washing but once, and I think mother would have hardly known her youngest the morning we came out," wrote Pvt. Albert Keating (Co. B) to his parents.[34]

Capt. Asahel W. Nichols (Co. E) fell victim to sunstroke at Cold Harbor. The ambulance corps shunted him to Washington, DC. In late July, still not recovered, he traveled home to Lansing where he tried to rest up and recruit for the regiment.[35]

At Cold Harbor the Sharpshooters dug artillery redoubts and were themselves shelled by the enemy. "The Rebs amuse themselves every morning, noon, & night," wrote Buckbee to his mother, "by throwing shell for about ten minutes quite lively— and then—as if they thought they had given us a good *stirring up* they desist, and wait for the next regular hour."[36]

Old "One Eye"

Although stationed on the skirmish line in front of Cold Harbor, the regiment tried to recoup its strength. Skirmish warfare was the reason for the Sharpshooters, and no one did it better than the men of Company K. The Indians remained an enigma to the other men of the regiment. They generally kept to themselves. Some spoke English; most spoke two or three languages—French, English, and various Indian dialects. Many were crack shots. One older fellow was particularly good; the whites called him "One Eye." Before the war he had lost his right eye. That kind of handicap usually kept men out of the service, but (according to Buckbee) this man "could see further and shoot quicker and more accurately with his left eye than most men could if they had had a dozen eyes."[37]

A rebel rifleman had annoyed General Willcox's headquarters staff so persistently that orders came down asking for help in getting rid of the nuisance. Buckbee sent for old One Eye, and explained the situation to him. Asking no questions, nor making any comment, One Eye turned and walked over to division headquarters. Willcox's orderlies saw the Indian arrive. For half an hour One Eye sat on the ground, taking in the situation; he then rose and walked away, saying nothing to anyone. Near 3:00 the next afternoon, the pickets on the line reported a rebel sharpshooter in a tree being hit quite a way off to their right. They saw him fall through the branches and hit the ground. One Eye returned to camp that same evening and reported to Buckbee. Tersely, he said, "Me got 'im." Willcox had no more bullets flying through his tent.[38]

When Captain Rhines took command of the regiment at Spotsylvania, he was informed that his promotion to major was in the works, but he would not receive official confirmation until early June.[39] As regimental commander, Rhines had access to a number of maps that he and his adjutant constantly studied, but the maps available to the Union army were notoriously inaccurate. Cities, most hamlets, and railroads were to be found, but roads (except for main trunks) and streams (other than major rivers) were either absent or, worse yet, in the wrong place. That had been the root of the problem when Willcox's division approached the Ni River on its way to Spotsylvania back on 9 May. Willcox had missed the place he was to congregate his forces. He was actually closer to Spotsylvania than Burnside or Grant thought, but it was to no avail. The maps were believed, even though the local geography belied them.[40]

Mail and Fear

The incessant movement of the army caused the mail to back up somewhere in the rear. Some outfits had received correspondence from home, but others had had no news since crossing the Rapidan. "The boys are all very anxious to hear from friends," wrote Buckbee to his mother on 7 June; "it seems as if this Regiment has been slighted, for other Regiments get their Males [sic] as often as once in two weeks any way."[41]

Leaving Cold Harbor, the Third Division took up the march to the James River. One evening the Sharpshooters made their headquarters near the ruins of what once had been a considerably large house. The building's framework was long gone, no doubt as fuel for countless campfires; the only vestige of the home's earlier grandeur was a tall brick chimney.

Before darkness fell, word came in that a large mail consignment was in the rear. The news "caused considerable excitement," noted Buckbee, and a detail went to get the letters. No one in the regiment had received a letter from home in the month since crossing the Rapidan, and the bag of mail was eagerly awaited by all. A number of officers gathered around a rubber blanket and proceeded to sort the letters by company, but it was now so dark that the names on the envelopes could not be read. A couple of men hurriedly kindled a fire near the chimney.

No enemy gunfire had been noted since their arrival, even though skirmishers were out in front of the brigade as usual. The fire soon blazed up and shone on the chimney. The dancing light on the brickwork was an inviting target, and a Confederate field battery soon began shooting at it. One of the first shots hit the chimney, "scattering bricks like hail in every direction"[42] and startling the men.

As in all regiments, men speculated on their comrades. Some were deemed incapable of ever being fighting men, while others were thought to be potentially great leaders. One of those in the latter category was 1st Lt. Moses A. Powell of Company G. From Niles, Michigan, he was "one of the handsomest men I ever saw," remembered Buckbee:

standing 6′-1″ in his stocking feet; a large, handsome head, graced with a long, beautiful beard, and altogether a very prepossessing looking person. He was an ex-sheriff . . . , and I had been told tales of his nerve and courage, and of his having arrested[—]single-handed and unarmed[—]desperate characters.[43]

When the May campaign began, however, all sorts of rumors had made their way to regimental headquarters; one of them was that Powell managed to keep out of harm's way in every fight in which the Sharpshooters took part. Powell kept just close enough to the scene to say he had been there. Always present on the marches and during roll calls, he was never seen when bullets began to fly.

That night at the ruins, the crash of the rebel artillery shells and the destruction of the chimney were too much for Powell. "With a scream like a Comanche Indian he sprang in the air [and] made a dash for the rear," recalled the astonished Buck-bee.[44] Powell's nerves had reached the breaking point. He had become an officer from whom no leadership could be expected, and his days with the regiment were numbered.

Crossing the James

The constant skirmishing continued to eat away at the Sharpshooters' strength. During the last week Andrew K. Hart (Co. D) had been mortally wounded. Six more, including an officer, 1st Lt. Cyrenius Knight (Co. D), were also hurt, and ten were missing.[45]

On the evening of 12 June the Sharpshooters pulled back with the rest of the Ninth Corps and began their march toward White House Landing.[46] For a while the Confederates had absolutely no idea where the Union army was. Lt. Ira L. Evans took command of the rear guard; his men were all that stood between the rebels and the rest of the Army of the Potomac. Evans was convinced that he and his entourage would end up in Anderson-ville, so he kept up the pretense of having more men than he actually did for as long as possible. His ploy worked, for the rebels kept a safe distance from his detail. When he was told to abandon his position and rejoin his command, Evans and his men wasted no time. They "lit out" to catch up with the rest of the army.[47]

The Ninth Corps continued toward the James River via

Tunstall's Station and reached but did not cross the narrow, sluggish Chickahominy River, a distance of about 20 miles, before going into camp. It was hot that day, in the high 90s.

On 14 June the corps crossed Jones's Bridge on the Chickahominy, eventually reaching Wilcox's Landing on the James River in the late afternoon. The men had covered only 11 miles that day.[48] On the evening of the 15th the Ninth Corps crossed the James River over the longest pontoon bridge any of the men had even seen. "It was a mile wide where we crossed," one veteran wrote in his diary.[49] Actually, it was 2,100 feet long, but it must have looked like a mile to the footsore soldiers.

Lieutenant Randall

In the rear of the Ninth Corps, still in charge of the divisional ambulance train, Lieutenant Randall parked his wagons on the banks of the James River. On the thirteenth he had had the devil's own time trying to keep his vehicles together—the roads were jammed with army rigs, and the fields were packed with wagons in park. "[B]aggage and supply trains coming in from all directions and tending eastward, but whither no one knew or co'd tell."[50] Stop-and-go traffic, not knowing what lay ahead, and a snatch of sleep here and there had made up Randall's days since leaving Cold Harbor.[51]

Randall was an unabashed patriot; he believed the Union had to be preserved at all costs. Also a religious man, he easily tied the two sentiments together. Hearing a sermon preached by a Christian Commission representative on the evening of 15 June, he experienced one of those emotional impressions which gratefully intrude on daily mundane experiences. While raptly listening to the "splendid sermon," he noted a brilliant sunset bathe the minister in a golden light.[52] The scene etched itself in the young officer's memory; it filled his "soul with pure and lofty resolves. A desire to serve your country while a traitor stands in arms. A willingness to sacrifice all, even life if necessary for the good of all."[53]

These were not the words of an innocent adolescent. This war was a crusade for him. The Confederacy was undoubtedly wrong. "It would seem," he wrote while waiting on the banks of the James River, "that a just God in judgment was punishing them [the Southerners] for their great sin of inaugurating this terrible war."[54] The war had to be won. Randall believed that God *was* on the side of the Union.

Petersburg

At the time Randall was writing in his diary, the Sharp-shooters and their division, with the bulk of the Ninth Corps, were trudging toward Petersburg, the gateway to Richmond. Dust and grit coated every man. They figured they had marched 32 miles on 16 June.[55] Stragglers by the hundreds lined the route. At 8:00 AM on the 17th, Christ halted his brigade to make coffee and rest. After a two-hour break the Sharpshooters and their comrades marched to within four miles of Petersburg. The regiments were then drawn up in support of the First Brigade.[56] Even then, quite a few of those who had fallen out on the march still had not rejoined the brigade.

From City Point to the vicinity of Petersburg was a tough march. Staff officers galloped up and down the column, urging the tired men forward.[57] Hot, thirsty, tired, caked in dust, they plodded onward; when the pace became too grueling, many called it quits for a while. The column moved down the road to Old Prince George Court House, then on to a more direct route to Petersburg and the Confederate lines east of Harrison Creek, near the Shand house.

The Eighteenth Corps had cleared the area of the enemy from the Appomattox River to the Dunn house on 15 June. On the 16th the Second Corps took the high ground around the Hare house. By early afternoon the Ninth Corps had filed into the Petersburg lines, taking position to the left of the Second Corps.

The Shand house (around which the Third Division had gathered) was a large, two-story residence shaded by buttonwood and gum trees, with a peach orchard behind it. A narrow ravine, 15 feet deep, cut across the landscape for 50 feet in front of the house. Through the ravine a brook ran northward; another 50 yards west of the house was another stream. The two rivulets joined together about a 100 yards north of the house and flowed northward, parallel to the rebel lines, eventually into the Appomattox River.

In the forks of the two streams in front of the Shand house loomed the Confederate Redoubt No. 14. A rebel brigade backed by four guns held the position. A well-placed line of enemy entrenchments ran along the edge of the ravine east of the house; the rebels also had posted two more guns to enfilade the ravine.[58]

East of the Shand house was a wide plain. On it, Willcox's division first formed its line of battle. Christ's brigade lay in the rear of Hartranft's, but no charge was made that afternoon. By the time the First Brigade had formed the line of battle, it was 4:00 PM.[59] No orders came down for the attack. Instead, Christ's men went over to the right and took over the picket posts in front of the Second Corps.[60] Early on the 17th, Potter's division rushed the rebel emplacements near the Shand house. The 3:00 AM attack netted four cannons, five enemy flags, 600 prisoners, and 1,500 stands of small arms.[61]

Another line of rebel works lay beyond the Harrison Creek swamp. Replete with infantry emplacements and artillery redoubts, this next line (though not continuous) ran along the west slope of the Harrison Creek valley to the City Point Railroad line. It continued south a short way beyond a belt of woods.[62] The rebels had to hold this section of the line while another was being prepared behind it.

On the morning of 17 June General Willcox received orders to assault the rebel line in front of the Shand house. Hartranft's brigade was called back from its position on the right, but its course through the swamp and attendant thickets ate up quite a bit of time.[63] Willcox positioned his two brigades along the ravine that ran in front of the house.

Hartranft's men composed the first line of attack, with Christ's brigade in support. The First Brigade charged at the double-quick near 2:00 PM. An open field about a half-mile in length lay before the attackers.[64] Unfortunately, mere bravery does not win battles, and faulty staff work had pointed the men in the wrong direction. The brigade charged across a plowed field. The dryness of the past week, the attacking column, and the rebel bullets and cannon balls stirred up such a cloud of dust that the Confederate lines were obscured. The assaulting regiments swerved to their right and charged in a line almost parallel to the rebel front. Lt. Col. E. J. March, commanding the Second Michigan, remembered the attack as one against his own lines. His regiment lost 78 men in the charge.[65] The left end of the line, which brushed up against the Confederate entrenchments, was almost destroyed. Out of 1,890 men, Hartranft lost 840.[66]

During the attack Colonel Christ moved his regiments out of the ravine to the crest of the hill in front of him, but halted his men halfway to the rebel lines. The Sharpshooters were stationed on the far left of the brigade. Lying as they were in an open corn field with only small embankments for protection, the men suffered under a relentless sun. The Sharpshooters now showed their mettle. In order to take aim at the prostrate riflemen, the rebels had to rise about breast-high above their own earthworks.

Only four Sharpshooters were wounded by this fire, but the Confederates paid dearly. In the evening, when the enemy fire pits were captured, the Sharpshooters found them filled with dead and mortally wounded rebels. Only two of them, remembered Capt. George Murdoch (Co. I), had been shot so low as the shoulder, the rest having been hit in the head or neck.[67] "The poor fellows lay upon the ground with their eyes and noses carried away, their brains oozing from their skulls, and their mouths shot into horrible disfiguration, making a hideous spectacle."[68]

That day of 17 June was filled with chaotic charges and counterattacks by bone-weary soldiers being led by confused officers. As if the first charge by Willcox's division were not botched enough, Maj. Gen. James F. Ledlie, who now commanded the First Division, tried to take the same ground. By late afternoon some Ninth Corps batteries were finally in place near the Shand house. The corps' three white divisions were supposed to attack the rebel lines, but the men were not yet in line and the officers had a diffcult time getting them in place.

Ledlie's division, in place in the ravine and to the right of the Shand house, would lead the charge; Potter's division would go in right behind them, and Willcox's would follow.[69] So much for plans. Potter's troops were still not ready when Ledlie attacked in the early evening, so Willcox threw in whatever elements of his division he could find.[70]

Ledlie's men charged ahead with bayonets at the ready, not firing until they reached the Confederate lines. Military logic of that era dictated that if the men did not stop to fire, many more would get to the enemy lines faster. As the men of Ledlie's command, assisted by scattered units of the Third Division, double-timed across the field, they were raked by enemy cannon and musketry fire. They swarmed over the rebel ramparts. After a short but victorious fight, the Federals consolidated their gains and waited.

There was little light left now, and the rebels took up firing positions from a patch of woods just beyond their former fortifications.[71] General Willcox ordered Colonel Christ to move his brigade in support of Ledlie. Christ split his brigade, sending most of the men to bolster Ledlie's right flank.[72]

The Sharpshooters Attack the Salient Alone

When Ledlie's men charged the rebel works, the Sharpshooters (under Rhines's command) went forward as well. The 200 Sharpshooters were at the extreme left of the Union Ninth Corps; there were, as yet, no elements of the Fifth Corps on their left flank. When Ledlie's men attacked, the Sharpshooters did not actually join them. In fact, Ledlie's men had obliqued to the right, driving out the rebels, but the salient in front of the Sharpshooters was still held by the Confederates.[73]

Although they were the only Third Division troops on that part of the field, Major Rhines, apparently on his own volition, made the decision to attack the enemy. Just before the men formed up, Adjutant Buckbee asked Rhines why he was not going to wait for the balance of the brigade. Rhines's reply was laconic: "I know my business," he snapped. "Form the regiment." [74]

As Buckbee readied the men, his orderly, Pvt. James Walsh (the men called him "Adjutant's Walsh") brought him a pot of tea. Walsh should have stayed behind the lines, but he was devoted to the young adjutant. Since he was now up front, he decided to join in the attack.[75]

With bayonets fixed, the Sharpshooters set out "in as beautiful a line of battle as one seldom sees," noted Sgt. Leverette N. Case; at Rhines's order, they charged the rebel salient directly in their front, capturing it as the defenders ran off.[76]

At least two of the Sharpshooters had second thoughts regarding the charge. Lt. Moses Powell had last been seen in the ravine; no one noticed him during the charge or in the rebel entrenchments. The other was Cpl. Benjamin Youngs of Captain Murdoch's company. Chiding him constantly for being a shirker, Murdoch described Youngs as "a coward [who] kept to the rear from Wilderness to Petersburg where he was brought up under guard." [77] Realizing he had to keep a close eye on Youngs, the captain was not too surprised when the corporal refused to obey the order to join in the attack. Drawing his pistol, Murdoch threatened to shoot the young man on the spot. Only then did

Youngs take his place in the ranks. Murdoch would not lose sight of him for the rest of the evening.[78]

The sun had already set, but firing continued.[79] The Sharpshooters were by themselves. No Union soldiers were on their left, although the Fifth Corps was supposd to be there some place. Way off to the right were elements of Ledlie's division. Three hundred yards back was the ravine from which they had charged earlier that day; quite a few Union soldiers were still there. Some 300 yards in front of the Sharpshooters' position was heavy timber. A railroad track, the Norfolk & Petersburg line, ran through a deep cut just in front of the woods. To their immediate front was a little ravine filled with brush.[80]

The Sharpshooters set up a defensive perimeter. Some of the men grabbed whatever they could find to eat in their haversacks. Most set to work strengthening their earthworks.[81]

The rebels had not retreated too far. They moved up two cannons through the railroad cut and fired a few rounds at the Sharpshooters. Two companies formed the left flank—one was the Indian company, commanded by Lieutenant Graveraet. The Indians were sent out as skirmishers to deal with the artillerymen, "and as is always the case, soon silenced the rebel batteries," but not before Graveraet went down with a crippling arm wound from a piece of shell.[82]

While moving some of the Confederate wounded, Captain Murdoch noticed considerable movement in front of his position. Little could actually be seen on account of the darkness and the smoke in the air. The continual noise of battle faded in and out. Murdoch told his men to watch for any enemy activity.[83]

Ledlie's advance had almost broken the back of the Confederate defenses, but Brig. Gen. Matthew W. Ransom's brigade, part of Johnson's division, arrived in the nick of time for the rebels. Ransom immediately threw his five North Carolina regiments (the Twenty-fourth, Twenty-fifth, Thirty-fifth, Forty-ninth, and Fifty-sixth) into the breach. The conflict was surprising and bloody; 2,000 Federals were captured, and the fighting raged until 11:00 that night.[84] The Thirty-fifth North Carolina Infantry, made up of 28 officers and almost 500 men, charged the section held by the Sharpshooters.[85]

At 10:00 PM Major Rhines, Captain Gaffney of Company G, and Captain Murdoch were sitting together in the captured works, talking over the events of the evening, when a sentinel yelled, "Here they come!" As one, every man of the command was alert and staring into the semi-darkness. The rebels came at a run. Outnumbering the Sharpshooters, the 500 Southerners covered the distance so quickly that the Michigan riflemen could only fire two volleys into their ranks before the Confederates reached the trench line. The only cover offered was the dirt thrown up from the trench, but it was on the side opposite from the attack.[86]

For a few seconds the rebels confused the Sharpshooters. As they approached the works, they shouted, "We surrender, don't fire." Some of the Sharpshooters held their fire, others hurriedly reloaded their Springfields, and still others looked at their companions, wondering what to do. Major Rhines, undaunted, jumped atop the breastworks and cried, "If you surrender, throw down your arms." But the rebels had now reached the trench, and they in turn demanded the surrender of the bluecoats. Shoving their weapons into the faces of the panting rebels, the Sharpshooters fired their rifles. Sheets of flame ranged up and down the ridge of dirt between the two forces. So close were the two sides that the clothing of the men on both sides was burned from the musket fire. The flashes from the guns illuminated angry faces screaming obscenities. The Sharpshooters had the advantage, since the rebels had just completed a hard march and quite a run at the end of it. As the enemy came over the edge of the ditch, the Sharpshooters lunged at them with bayonets and clubbed them with empty rifles.[87]

One of the first rebels over the breastworks was a lieutenant; he ordered the Yankees within his hearing to surrender. Lt. Henry V. Hinckley ignored the Southerner's temerity, grabbed the enemy officer by his coat collar, and in no uncertain terms told the Confederate that he was a prisoner himself. The rebel, damning his luck, threw down his sword. Hinckley realized that he might be captured by the screaming North Carolinians; he gripped his prisoner tightly and jerked him along to the shelter of the ravine. Darkness and smoke screened his retreat.[88]

The rebels' numbers were greater and their momentum carried them; many leaped the embankment, but then found themselves on the horns of a dilemma (some literally). The two sides grappled in a vicious hand-to-hand fight. The Sharpshooters drove their bayonets into some of them; others, they forced to surrender. The Sharpshooters did not run. Training their weapons on the Confederates, they "commenced collering [*sic*] the Johnnies and hauling them over the works & sending them to the rear."[89]

Off to the left, the Indians had a doubly difficult job. The Tarheels came at them from both the front and the flank. The conflict resembled a scene out of the infernal regions as Graveraet's men fought off the enemy with bayonets and knives.

As the Southerners scurried over the breastworks and jumped into the ditch shielding the Sharpshooters, their color bearer called on his comrades to follow him. Shouting for all he was worth, the Confederate alighted directly in front of 18-year-old Pvt. Theodore Nash. Nash and most of his companions were on the other side of the trench. Totally undaunted, Nash held his ground, leaned down over the breastwork, put the point of his bayonet up to the rebel's chest, and ordered him to surrender and hand over the flag. Next to Nash was Benjamin Youngs, the recalcitrant soldier Captain Murdoch had threatened to shoot an hour earlier. The rebel proffered the flag, Nash's bayonet still perilously close to his chest. Murdoch witnessed the entire episode, being only a few steps from Nash. Murdoch ordered Youngs to jump into the trench and take the flag from the Confederate.[90]

Only minutes later Captain Murdoch was hit by a rebel bullet; it grazed the right side of his head, making a two-inch gash that took him out of the war zone for a few weeks.[91] James Walsh, Buckbee's orderly who had decided to stay with the regiment, took a bullet in his right leg; the doctors in the rear would have to amputate it.[92]

Col. John G. Jones, commander of the Thirty-fifth North Carolina, leaped the breastworks, sword in hand, urging his men onward. Pvts. John Buchanan and Moses Buckley (Co. A) jumped forward and bayoneted the rebel officer.[93]

Cpl. Will Styon of Murdoch's company sought out his commanding officer and told him he had been shot in the arm. Murdoch directed him to get to the rear. He never made it; his body was found the next morning with seven wounds.[94] A Confederate officer sprang at Major Rhines. In the brief encounter a bullet shattered the rebel's hand; he dropped his sword and was at the mercy of the Sharpshooters' commander. A rebel bullet then slammed into Rhines, and he fell with a mortal wound.[95]

The short but bloody engagement came to an end. Stiffened resistance had forced the rebels back, and the Sharpshooters hurriedly policed the area. Although short-lived, the fight had been devastating to the Sharpshooters; 50 men had been killed or wounded. Lieutenant Evans of Company E took charge of most of the prisoners (more than 80 at first count) and herded the lot back to the ravine; 30 men from Companies F and C went as guards.[96]

Lt. Joseph O. Bellair led back a smaller batch of rebels. He was accompanied by Benjamin Youngs, who was still clutching the captured flag of the Thirty-fifth North Carolina and now had a legitimate reason to leave the scene of carnage. Bellair and his squad located General Ledlie's headquarters, where they presented the flag to the commander of the First Division.[97]

Corpses from both sides were of necessity left where they had fallen. The place looked like a charnal house; dead and wounded littered the area. The smoky, dark atmosphere added a surreal quality to the battlefield.

Wounded Sharpshooters were either helped to the rear or made it on their own. Men from every company, but especially B and K, had gone down. Gilbert Morehouse (Co. C) had taken a rebel slug in his right thigh; so had Sgt. Immanuel Brown of the same company. Silas Pierce (Co. B) had been shot in the neck and left thigh. Victor Burk (Co. B) went down with a bullet wound that broke his left leg. Knudt Severson (Co. B) gingerly held what remained of his left hand, which had been shattered by an enemy ball. Michael Horrigan (Co. I) lay in a heap, hit in the head and left shoulder. John Andrew (Co. K) had taken a bullet in his right thigh, near the hip. A rebel bullet had torn through Samuel Kaquatch's right forearm. Joseph Fish (Co. F) tried to hold his left arm, which had been ripped by a chunk of lead.[98]

Major Rhines died later that night at the aid station. Captain Gaffney (Co. G) had been shot in the left shoulder; he died from the effects of his wound on 20 June. Gaffney still lingered under a cloud of disgrace. His actions with the married woman at Camp Douglas were never officially forgiven; dying a hero was probably the only way to expiate his offense.[99] Captain Murdoch had sustained a nasty head wound, and Lt. George Knight (Co. A) had been killed at the breastworks.[100] Lt. Charles Conn (Co. G) had a bullet in his left forearm.[101] And Lieutenant Graveraet's shell wound necessitated the amputation of his left arm; he died of complications on 1 July. Graveraet was interred in the Congressional Burying Yard in Washington, DC; through the efforts of Michigan congressman John Driggs, his body was later transferred to Mackinac Island where it now lies under a stone commemorating his and his father's ultimate sacrifice.[102]

All the uninjured Sharpshooters, with the exception of those sent to the back with the prisoners, manned their exposed position. There were only about 100 left. Adjutant Buckbee now commanded the regiment in the salient; there were no other officers on the line. Somewhat perplexed at the situation, Buckbee had no idea why the Sharpshooters were in their advanced position. Major Rhines had rebuffed him earlier when he asked the reason for the charge. Unsure of himself, Buckbee called over an old sergeant and asked him for some suggestions.

The "old sergeant" was Joseph Stevens of Company B. Although only 22 years old, Stevens had a good deal of experience and military know-how, and was one of the finest noncommissioned officers in the regiment. Originally in the Fourth Michigan Infantry, he had fought on the Peninsula in 1862, and had been captured and sent to Libby Prison in Richmond. Exchanged because of chronic illness, Stevens slowly recuperated in a Philadelphia hospital, was discharged, then went home to Hillsdale, Michigan. Chafing at the inactivity, he enlisted in the Sharpshooters after being home only one week. Stevens rose quickly to sergeant, and became a drillmaster in Company B.

That evening in the salient, Stevens had a rooster he had "liberated" from a farmhouse along the day's route tied to his belt; he was planning to have a good supper when time allowed. The dead bird was still dangling from his waist as he listened to Buckbee outline the problem. Stevens went along with the young officer. It would be best, he agreed, to hold this ground until they were relieved.[103]

Buckbee acted accordingly. He sent out skirmishers and looked to his flanks. Not an hour had passed since the Sharpshooters' first charge against the salient. That short but fierce fight had netted them quite a bag of prisoners. The night air reeked with powder smoke. Gunshots, cannon fire, and yells could be heard, although mostly from far away. The Sharpshooters did not have to be told that they held an isolated outpost.

The pickets soon came running back to the protection of the embankment. A rebel line, firing as it charged, poured out of the woods and descended directly on them. No sooner did Buckbee receive word of the frontal attack than he learned another column was coming in on his left and rear.[104] Believing—actually hoping—this latter force was the remnant of Christ's brigade from the ravine, Buckbee ran back to get a look. "My heart jumped to my throat," he wrote later, "for I thought that I recognized in the moonlight the 20th Michigan coming to our relief."[105] He proceeded cautiously. Then he saw their uniforms—rebels! Back he ran to his men, who were already firing at the Confederates coming at them. The enemy in front was the remainder of the Thirty-fifth North Carolina; those on the left and rear were from the Twenty-fourth North Carolina, of the same brigade. The 100 Sharpshooters parried the rebel onslaught for just a few minutes before caving in.

The wildest confusion raged. Every weapon was freely used in the melee. Sergeant Stevens remembered that "we met them with cold steel and had a fierce struggle until we were overpowered and obliged to surrender."[106] A Pennsylvania captain, lying wounded some distance away, was a helpless spectator to the brutal affair. Shot in the chest, he lay on the ground and observed "the most terrific hand to hand encounter he ever witnessed."[107] Those Sharpshooters who could get away took any exit available.

Color Sgt. George Caine, seeing the enemy avalanche, thought that the regimental flag was in mortal danger of being captured. Caine's mind was far from the peaceful parade ground in Michigan when the governor's wife had presented the banner to the regiment.[108] No worse calamity could befall a flag bearer; the heart and soul of the regiment were embodied in its flag. Capturing an enemy guidon was the supreme triumph; having one's own taken away was the ultimate tragedy. Caine, wanting to save the colors and himself, hurriedly rolled the state flag around the staff and buried it in the sand, hoping to rescue it some time later. He then ran from the rebels and made it safely to the ravine in the rear.[109] (The national colors already had been torn into strips and distributed among the men. Only a few stripes on the lower end still hung from the pole. It, too, was buried with the state flag.)[110]

Realizing his escape was cut off and death the reward for continuing the fight, Adjutant Buckbee shouted at his men to cease firing and to throw down their weapons. At the same time he yelled at the Confederates that he was surrendering. Buckbee threw away his sword and sword belt; he had no insignia of rank on his uniform and hoped to pass himself off as an enlisted man.[111] When captured, officers and enlisted men were sent to separate internment camps, and Buckbee meant to stay with his men. Unfortunately, several rebels had seen him toss his sword away; when they had him under guard, they made him retrieve it. Buckbee then presented it to Capt. Philip J. Johnson of the

Thirty-fifth North Carolina, whose regiment had been decimated by the Sharpshooters only minutes before. Johnson was the officer shot in the hand while fighting with Major Rhines. Buckbee made the best of a bad situation and helped to doctor Johnson's hand.[112]

The captured Sharpshooters were quickly divested of their weapons and accoutrements. As they were hustled away, the prisoners could only glance back at the crumpled heaps that were once their comrades. The bodies of at least 14 Sharpshooters had to be abandoned. Leroy M. Wilber (Co. A) had joined the regiment just three weeks before, at the North Anna River; 44-year-old Cpl. Edward F. Cox of the same company was one of the first enlistees in the regiment. Pardey T. Colvin (Co. E) had only recently been promoted to sergeant. Teenagers like Horace Martin (Co. I) and James Fullerton (Co. B) had died along with Cpl. Alonzo Campbell and David Graham (Co. G), who were in their forties.[113]

Led under guard, the captured Wolverines also noted the many casualties they had inflicted on the enemy. The survivors of the Thirty-fifth North Carolina had lost scores of their comrades to the Sharpshooters that night. About 500 Tarheels went into battle that evening, but fewer than 200 answered roll the next morning. Their colonel died in the fight with a bayonet wound in the throat;[114] of the two Sharpshooters who killed him, John Buchanan was killed in the first onslaught and Moses Buckley was captured in the second.[115]

The captors treated their Michigan charges with consideration. Buckbee was surprised; he expected worse treatment. He soon found out that "the men who did the fighting in the front were not the men who used abusive language or made insulting speeches to their prisoners."[116]

A company of the Fifty-sixth North Carolina, in need of better weapons, picked up the Springfields surrendered by the Indians of Company K. Impressed with the carvings of fish, snakes, and animals on the rifle stocks, the North Carolinians prized the uniquely carved rifles and carried them until the end of the war. Their original owners trudged sullenly into Petersburg; many would die during the next few months in rebel prison camps.[117]

As the prisoners passed through the yard of an old church, their guards informed them that the edifice was one of the oldest brick buildings in the country, the bricks having been brought over from England. But the Sharpshooters had other things on their minds; historical buildings meant nothing to them at that point in time.[118]

For three days they were confined in an old tobacco warehouse in the city. Then they boarded a train with hundreds of other captives taken at Petersburg; prisoner-of-war camps awaited all of them.[119] Because of the confusion in Petersburg, a few of the Sharpshooters did manage to escape. Some of the Indians set fire to their quarters. Their cries brought out the rebel sentries, who opened the doors and tried to extinguish the blaze; in the bedlam the prisoners ran off in all directions. At least one of them—Sgt. Louis Genereau of Company K—reached his own lines the next evening and told of the capture of the men in the salient.[120]

Because the Sharpshooters had advanced with Ledlie's men that night, chroniclers gave his division credit for anything accomplished. Writing in 1883, the army chief-of-staff Maj. Gen. Andrew A. Humphreys singled out Ledlie's division for capturing "a hundred prisoners and a stand of colors. . . . The attacking force was under a severe musketry fire on the right and left, the opposing batteries keeping up a quick and effective fire throughout."[121] Ledlie must have known of the Sharpshooters' success; Corporal Youngs had personally given him the flag of the Thirty-fifth North Carolina, and the parade of prisoners escorted by jubilant Sharpshooters must have been noticed by his headquarters staff. However, Ledlie left no record of it.

Ledlie's potential as a commander was woefully overrated. Why hadn't he sent reinforcements to the beleaguered left flank, where the regiment doggedly hung on? Ledlie's main line had troubles enough on the evening of 17 June. The Sharpshooters did not belong to Ledlie's division; perhaps he saw fit to take credit for their successes but could not be bothered with their problems.

That fight on 17 June was the one remembered longest by veterans of the First Michigan Sharpshooters. They had stood alone against the rebels and had inflicted tremendous casualties on the enemy—but they had also been bloodied beyond belief. The regiment that remained was a shadow of its former self. Out of about 200 who had entered the fight,[122] Buckbee had surrendered with 84 men, 31 more had been killed in the fight or later died of wounds, and 46 had been wounded.

Located about one and a half miles to the rear, the Third Division hospital lay just out of enemy cannon range. In the early morning hours "ambulances came passing in from the front."

George Warren, the hospital steward, was stunned by the carnage his regiment had suffered. "And here they are," he lamented, "stretched out upon the ground under every bush, arbor or tent. The poor shot-and-shell mangled objects of a sanguine [bloody] conflict." [123] More than 700 Sharpshooters had left Camp Douglas in March. On the morning of 18 June, only 61 answered roll call.[124]

Lt. Frank Whipple, who was returning from Michigan, reached Petersburg on 19 June. Startled by the reduced numbers in the regiment, he nonetheless recorded some positive tidings. "On all sides," he wrote home soon after his arrival, "I hear it spoken of in terms of highest praise. It is now no dishonor to be a member of this organization." [125] The shame of the affair at the Ni River had now been expiated; the Sharpshooters had paid in full for the debacle at Spotsylvania on 9 May.

More Fighting

At daylight on 18 June, skirmishers from Christ's brigade came back with word that the rebels had retreated during the night. Only four officers were still with the remnants of the Sharpshooters; the others were either dead, wounded, assigned to miscellaneous details, or unaccounted for. First Lieutenant Evans of Company E, as senior officer present, took command of the regiment.[126]

Colonel Christ advanced his brigade through the abandoned works. As the men cautiously moved forward, Color Sergeant Caine sought out the place where he had buried the flags the evening before. Hoping and praying the rebels had not located them, Caine feverishly dug in the same spot and found the banners. He rejoined the Sharpshooters on the line.[127] Others looked for friends among the bodies. Dr. Strong and Albert Keating sought in vain for their friend, Sgt. Joe Stevens; unbeknownst to them, Stevens was being "entertained" by his captors in Petersburg before being shunted off to a rebel prison.[128] The Sharpshooters removed the corpses of their compatriots for burial, and marked their graves. They left the rebels to be buried by others.

The blood contest on this new day was given to other regiments; the remaining Sharpshooters traded their rifles for shovels and dug earthworks for Roemer's battery at the edge of the belt of timber.[129]

Three Federal corps advanced on the new rebel line. The Fifth Corps moved on the Ninth Corps' left, while the Second Corps went up on Burnside's right. Christ's brigade entered the thick belt of pine timber, then moved through a field of grain sloping toward the railroad line and the new Confederate entrenchments. The Sixtieth Ohio protected the right flank as skirmishers.

The rest of the brigade charged the rebel line across a quarter-mile of open ground. Their target was a railroad cut, but it offered no sanctuary to those who got that far. The rebels managed to flank the attackers and poured on a murderous storm of lead and iron. Christ's men tore up the railroad bed while under horrific fire and made breastworks of the ties.[130] Among the hundreds of casualties was Maj. George C. Barnes of the Twentieth Michigan.[131]

Near 5:00 PM another charge was ordered; the objective was to advance on the rebels and to straighten out the Ninth Corps line.[132] Moving to within 150 yards of the Confederate trenches, the Second Brigade weathered a veritable tornado of enemy fire. Tin cups, bayonets, and bare hands dug whatever protection they could. Only nightfall stopped the awful slaughter. Sometime after midnight the brigade was relieved and sent to the rear.[133]

Col. Ralph Ely, commanding the Eighth Michigan Infantry in Hartranft's brigade, believed "the most severe firing of grape, cannister [sic] and musketry he ever experienced" had raked his lines that day. The Fifty-first Pennsylvania, another of Hartranft's regiments, lost its colors in the charge on the railroad; the men were terribly depressed at its loss. Ely had taken a flag from the dying color bearer of the Pennsylvania regiment, believing it to be the Eighth's standard, and had brought it back; the mistake was cleared up on closer examination.[134]

During the fighting a bullet had clipped Colonel Christ alongside the head, just behind his left ear, severely wounding him.[135] Col. William C. Raulston of the Twenty-fourth New York Cavalry then assumed command of the brigade; he too soon fell with a wound. Next in the line of succession, Lt. Col. George Travers of the Forty-sixth New York, stepped forward; he also went down. Finally, Lt. Col. Walter Newberry of the Twenty-fourth New York Cavalry, the senior oficer in the brigade, took charge until General Willcox appointed Col. William Humphrey of the Second Michigan commander. Willcox also transferred the Second to the brigade to augment its numbers.[136]

During the fighting on 17 and 18 June, the Third Division sustained 1,231 casualties; the overwhelming majority were wounded.[137] Confusion had mocked military order in most aspects of battle, and it was no different at the hospital. Two miles from the front lines, hundreds of walking wounded and dying men, many helped by musicians-turned-hospital attendants, funneled themselves to the division hospital. Dr. Whelan, chief surgeon for the Sharpshooters, was one of only six doctors in the hospital; he went four days and nights without adequate rest.[138] The wounded were treated and sent as soon as possible to City Point, where an immense hospital was spread out. There the sick and injured were either shipped to some medical facility up north or discharged, depending on the severity of the affliction.[139]

The Results from Two Days of Fighting

The morning following the fight at Petersburg dawned on a regiment with only four commissioned officers and just 61 men fit for field service. Second Lieutenant Whipple (Co. B), acting quartermaster of the Sharpshooters, at first could find only seven men belonging to his company.[140] First Lieutenant Evans commanded the regiment for several days, there being no higher grade officer present. Then division headquarters detailed Evans to serve with Willcox's staff for a few days, leaving 2nd Lt. Charles G. Conn in charge. He was assisted by Second Lieutenants Bellair and Hinckley.[141] Within a week, men returning from leave, from detached service, stragglers, and escaped prisoners brought the numbers up to six commissioned officers and 155 men.[142]

Other regiments in the brigade had also suffered terribly. The Fiftieth Pennsylvania was down to six officers and 150 men;[143] the Twentieth Michigan, having lost 13 killed and 44 wounded, had less than 100 men under arms.[144]

One of the Indians who had eluded the rebels after a day's captivity brought back word of those who were captured. Sergeant Case, Buckbee's friend and confidant, couched the news to Buckbee's sweetheart in reassuring terms. The escaped prisoner "says that Ed. is well and comparatively light hearted." What else could he say? To be taken captive at this point in the war was almost a death sentence; prisoners were no longer exchanged as easily as in the not-so-distant past. Buckbee and the men captured with him would probably never be seen again.[145]

Capt. Elmer Dicey of Company B fortuitously returned from sick leave and recruiting duty in Michigan to the front on 20 June.[146] Like Whipple, he was shocked. Some of the companies had no commissioned officers or even sergeants present. In some companies no one had any idea of company affairs or even knew the location of company records.

Dicey was now the highest grade officer present and hence in command. As a temporary measure, he consolidated the regiment into four companies, utilizing the remaining officers as best he could.[147] Since there were no captains other than himself present for duty, the four consolidated companies were put under control of the lieutenants. Companies A, F, and D (now the First Company) were in the charge of Joseph O. Bellair. Companies C, H, and E (the Second Company) had Ira Evans as commander. The Third Company (I and K) was commanded by Lieutenant Driggs until his disability discharge came through on 6 July; William Randall then took it over. The Fourth Company (B and G) was under Samuel Hudson.[148]

General Willcox's headquarters, eager to reward distinguished actions, issued General Orders No. 20 on 20 June. Benjamin Youngs was cited for capturing the flag of the Thirty-fifth North Carolina Infantry, and was promoted to sergeant for his "distinguished gallantry." Notice of Youngs's valor was sent to John Robertson, adjutant general of Michigan. No mention was made of Pvt. Theodore Nash,[149] and no one in particular took the trouble to seek Captain Murdoch's opinion. Murdoch reached his hometown of Niles, Michigan, during the first week of July. For the next few weeks, unaware of Youngs's accolades, he would recuperate before heading back to the regiment.[150]

Major Rhines's friends had his body embalmed and shipped home. His family had him interred in Spring Arbor, Michigan, where his "funeral was attended by a large number of sympathizing friends." His obituary mentioned the significant events of his life and the bloody fight on the evening of 17 June. "He lived but a few hours after, never for a moment regretting the sacrifice he was making for his country. His commission as Major did not reach the Regiment until after his death."[151]

Despite the horrendous casualties in the Ninth Corps, the eastern papers carried little notice of it. George Warren complained about the matter in a letter home:

I see the New York *Herald* is specially cautious of all favorable mention of the 9th army corps. And this, simply because it has not been of the old Army of the Potomac stripe of things. You know the 9th corps has been a sort of western "wide-awake" in this war on the whole, and Burnside feels at home wherever the Administration may happen to place him, no matter if in Ohio, Tennessee, or on the old grave pits of McClellan in Virginia, it is all the same to him. If there is a chance to fight he goes in with a will. For his bold and daring genius, he is of course hated and despised by traitors and cowards.[152]

The men in the Ninth Corps still backed Burnside; like Burnside, they also saw themselves as outsiders. They would soon find out how far beyond the pale they were. A Ninth Corps show was in the offing. Burnside would receive little help, and many of his men would pay the ultimate price.

CHAPTER 9

Contemptible Cowards
and Sneaks

An unfortunate order of business involving two of the regiment's officers had to be attended to now. The Sharpshooters had already had their share of miscreants, some of whom were currently serving sentences in various jails or prisons. Pvt. Charles Waubesis (Co. K) had killed a man while the Sharpshooters were at Camp Douglas; he was incarcerated in Illinois for life.[1] Scores of deserters had left the ranks since the early days at Camp Chandler in Kalamazoo. Some were still working off sentences in military camps for crimes they had committed. One such malefactor, Pvt. Edgar F. Davidson (Co. A), was building public works in Covington, Kentucky, and Pvt. Thomas Wood (Co. B) whiled away his time in the penitentiary at Columbus, Ohio.[2]

Infractions involving the regiment's officers were not all that rare, but most of them had occurred before the Sharpshooters entered the war zone. Captain Gaffney's carryings-on with an enlisted man's wife and Lieutenant Evans's bout with the bottle had taken place long before bullets and cannon balls were aimed at the regiment. Some of the offenses were disposed of quickly; others revolved around rumors. George Warren (always a source of gossip) complained, "a few of her officers have played the part in the regiment of the most contemptible cowards and sneaks."[3]

Those who had evaded their duty, while good men died, now had to pay the penalty.

At the end of June two courts-martial were held at Ninth Corps headquarters. Capt. Hooker A. DeLand (Co. F) and 1st Lt. Moses A. Powell (Co. G) were brought up on charges of cowardice. Both were accused of leaving their commands on three occasions in the previous month.

Powell's absences were noted at the North Anna River on 23 May, at the Cold Harbor entrenchments on 4 June, and during the big fight at Petersburg on 17 June.[4] Powell apparently had a phobia about warfare. Stories of his personal bravery as a law officer back in Niles, Michigan, had made the rounds when the regiment was being recruited.[5] His record as a noncommissioned officer in the Ninth Michigan Infantry, Colonel DeLand's old regiment, was unblemished, but the man literally quaked with fear at the front. As far as was known Powell was under enemy fire only once as a Sharpshooter—at the Wilderness. What he saw and endured there can only be conjectured; the records are silent on that point. Whatever happened had made him a quivering shell of a man, ready on the march, but nowhere to be seen during battle. Powell maintained "that it was a constitutional thing with him & he couldn't help it. That when shot & shell came around he could not stand it."

At Spotsylvania he was reported as absent sick. Surgeon Evan J. Bonine of the Second Michigan Infantry looked him over at the Third Division hospital. "He appeared somewhat debilitated," recalled the doctor, who then asked the Sharpshooters' surgeon, Arvin Whelan, to examine Powell. Although overworked from treating hundreds of men torn and suffering from the carnage at Spotsylvania, Dr. Whelan examined Powell and ascertained that the lieutenant "was suffering from very little fever & nervousness."

Whelan told Powell to return to the regiment on 16 May, but Powell came back for more treatment on the 24th, the day the Sharpshooters arrived at the North Anna River; again there was potential for action. After two days Powell left the hospital, but returned on 31 May. Dr. Whelan's description of the case was quite perceptive for that time, although he was unable to arrive at a cure. "I regarded this case as peculiar," he testified at the court-martial. "That mental excitement had as much to do with his disordered state as physical reason. . . . I interpreted it to arise from the action in front." The deduction was absolutely correct; Powell appeared at the hospital every time the Sharpshooters were going into a battle situation.

When unable or unwilling to see a surgeon for his problem, Powell simply headed for the rear. There he blended in with the rear echelon personnel—the orderlies, the cooks, the wounded and ill, and the usual stragglers and shirkers who could always be found there. Commissary Sgt. Milo E. Dyer, whose duties kept him in the rear, noticed Powell back there during the fights at Spotsylvania, the North Anna, and Cold Harbor. "He did not seem to have any particular business on hand," Dyer related to the court. "He laid back principally with the cook."

Powell participated in the various marches from battlefield to battlefield, but whenever "we went into position in breastworks[,] he was very seldom with the Co.," testified Second Lieutenant Conn from Powell's own company. Lieutenant Evans remembered seeing Powell "come up occasionally and then go back to the rear" when the regiment occupied entrenchments at Cold Harbor.

The straw that broke the camel's back was the fight at Petersburg on 17 June. Powell had accompanied the regiment to the ravine that day. That he was able to keep up with the men on that hot, dusty march showed he was physically capable, but his mental state must have been frail. Just as the Sharpshooters were ordered to make their initial assault as part of the Third Division advance, Powell was sitting near Conn and Evans. Conn remembered that Powell "was lying just in front of the company I commanded & we left him there." An officer was supposed to exude confidence, to disdain hardships, and to practice self-denial; in short, he was to be an inspiration to his men, the *beau ideal*. Powell's own company had to walk around him to get in position to charge the enemy.

Powell had fought in no engagement after the Wilderness (if indeed he had fought there) and was never under enemy fire from 12 May to 17 June, "unless once or twice under sharpshooter fire." Whatever terror infused Powell's mind, it was no defense for his actions (or nonactions) on the battlefield. The coterie of Ninth Corps officers on his court-martial board found him guilty of leaving his regiment at the North Anna River, at Cold Harbor, and at Petersburg. Because he was reported sick during the 12 May fight at Spotsylvania, he was not judged for that occurrence.

Powell's sentence was laden with humiliation. He was to be cashiered from the army, forfeiting any pay and allowances ever due or that would become due him; in the presence of the Sharpshooters his shoulder straps and buttons were to be cut from his uniform and his sword broken. Then he would be incarcerated for the remainder of his term of service. To add further ignominy, his sentence would be published in his hometown newspaper.

The editor of the Niles *Republican* gleefully proclaimed the story. Notwithstanding the tabloid's name, the editor was a rabid Democrat who had nothing but venom for Powell. Castigating the lieutenant for his preenlistment bombasity, the editor reminded his readers that Powell "is a fair specimen of an abolitionist—a miserable coward. Show us an abolitionist and a man who calls his neighbors copperheads and traitors, and we will show you a coward." He further informed the readers of Powell's desire to be appointed provost marshal of St. Joseph County, "just to make the copperheads hunt their holes." The editor condemned Powell as "a gentleman who has always been too lazy to work and he will find the Dry Tortugas a worse hole than any copperhead ever crawled into."[6]

The case against Capt. Hooker Ashton DeLand was quite different. DeLand had volunteered for service in the First Michigan Infantry in August 1861. By 1862 he was first sergeant of Company D and served in the campaigns of the Army of the Potomac until the Sharpshooters were formed in early 1863. Originally brought in as second lieutenant because of his wartime experience, he soon obtained the captaincy of Company F, although he was not yet 21 years old.[7] He was the youngest captain in the regiment, but there were some bad feelings because of his blood relationship to the colonel. Although various sources hinted at his fine record as an enlisted man, no one complimented his tenure as an officer in the Sharpshooters.

As with Powell, the testimony against DeLand began at the Battle of Spotsylvania on 12 May. Sgt. Maj. James S. DeLand, the colonel's brother, stated that he was sent to the rear before the regiment charged the rebels that day; on his return he saw Hooker "with another officer and about twenty men down by the bridge across the Ny." He never identified the other officer, but the 20 stragglers in question were all Sharpshooters.

Second Lt. Henry Hinckley delivered the most damning evidence to the board: "I know he was not in the battle," Hinckley stated conclusively. "He told me that he accompanied the Brigade as far as the edge of the woods before we made the charge in the afternoon and that he went no further." Hinckley asked Hooker DeLand a few days later why he did not participate in the battle and was told "that he thought it was too warm for him, that he did not want to get killed just then."

While at the North Anna on 23 May, Hooker again was not with his company. "I know that he was absent from his command and in the rear. When I went to the commissary for rations on the 24th I saw him there," related Hinckley. He further declared that Hooker:

> said to me that he did not calculate to go into any fight, that he had a mother and sister to support and that he was not going to get killed in this war, that he would resign if permitted, that sooner than get into a fight he would be dishonorably dismissed, or words to that effect.

Hinckley was so disgusted with Hooker DeLand's conduct that he said he would resign after this campaign rather than serve with officers who habitually sought the rear when bullets started to fly.

Hooker offered no proof that he participated in any engagement since crossing the Rapidan in early May. In the regiment's last two fights (4 June at Cold Harbor and 17 June at Petersburg), Hooker had been under arrest, so he was not expected to be with his men. The board found him guilty on two counts—absenting himself from his command at Spotsylvania on 12 May and at the North Anna on 23 May.

The court's judgment came on 6 July. In essence, Captain DeLand received the same sentence as Lieutenant Powell—buttons and shoulder straps to be cut off and his sword broken in the presence of his regiment, his sentence to be printed in his hometown newspaper, and confinement at hard labor at the Dry Tortugas, a fort in the Florida keys, until the expiration of his term of service. When the Jackson *Citizen* published the young officer's sentence, no editorializing accompanied the article out of deference to his cousin, Col. Charles DeLand.[8]

The distasteful ordeal of drumming Capt. Hooker A. DeLand and 1st Lt. Moses A. Powell out of the camp came two days after the court's decision. Since most of the brigade was needed on the front lines that day, only the Sharpshooters and the Twenty-fourth New York Cavalry (Dismounted) attended the painful exercise. The situation was embarrassing and sorrowful, especially for the Sharpshooters. Dress parade for the two regiments took place at 5:00 PM, Friday, 8 July.

Young DeLand and Powell entered the space between the two regiments under an armed guard. Their sentences were read aloud. Captain DeLand's sword was broken. Both officers then had their uniform buttons cut off. Maj. Claudius Grant of the Twentieth Michigan found the sentences just. "Capt D's motto," Grant wrote in his diary:

> was that "a live coward is worth more than a dead hero." For myself I prefer 6 ft of sod to lie under with my soul in the care of Him who gave it terrible as is the ordeal of battle. He seemed to brazen it out with a foolhardy manner. A disgrace to Mich. . . . Life at the expense of honor is worse than death.[9]

No sympathy came from Lieutenant Randall either. He had never liked Captain DeLand, and believed the latter achieved his rank only through his relationship to the colonel. The punishment, Randall thought, was just, though harsh. "This is a very severe sentence and shows that cowardice will not be tolerated or pass unnoticed in the army," he wrote in his journal.

As if to underscore the seriousness of the lesson, a rebel round shot found the distance, hitting two men of the Twenty-fourth during the activity, killing one man and mortally wounding the other.[10]

The fight to exonerate and free Hooker DeLand now began. Three days after his conviction for cowardice, a petition made the rounds in the Sharpshooters' camp; 68 officers and men appended their names to it. Seven officers, led by Captain Dicey, signed; even Second Lieutenant Bellair of DeLand's company wrote his name on the form. Conspicuous by its absence was Hinckley's name. The signers disagreed with the court's judgment, and asked President Lincoln to commute the young officer's prison sentence. Of the 61 enlisted men whose names appeared on the list, 19 represented Company F, which was probably every man left in the outfit; representatives from every other company signed as well. Sgt. Maj. James S. DeLand, Hooker's cousin, headed the names of the enlisted men.

A week after the petition reached the White House, the steamer *Keyport* left City Point, the vast supply base for the Army of the Potomac, located only six miles from Petersburg. On board in chains were Moses Powell and Hooker DeLand.[11] The two men were Sharpshooters no longer.

Col. Charles DeLand remained undaunted. He wrote a plaintive letter on 29 August to President Lincoln, pleading for a commutation of his younger cousin's sentence. The colonel tried to put Hooker DeLand's problem in perspective. There had been difficulties among the Sharpshooters while the colonel was in the hospital:

> & so far as [I] now can learn the Reg't became very much demoralized by quarrels & dissentions [*sic*] among the officers and straggling of the men. During these, charges were preferred against some, & several men were kept a long time in arrest. Two only of these officers have been brought to trial,—all the rest were returned to duty by order of the Divisional Commander.

Obviously, the only two "brought to trial" were Moses Powell and Hooker DeLand, but the colonel did not even mention Powell by name. His letter and entreaties pleaded for his cousin. He carefully stacked the deck for Hooker; the younger DeLand had a brother serving in the Fifteenth Massachusetts Infantry and another brother practicing law in Jackson, Michigan. In other words, he came from a good family, and that, implied the colonel, should mean something to the President.

Getting no reply from the White House, Colonel DeLand fired off another missive to the war department. This time he wrote specifically about his cousin. He mentioned the boy's age—he was only 21. The lad had entered the First Michigan Infantry as a private in 1861 and had earned the rank of first sergeant. He "has a sister partially dependent upon his support, . . . a brother in the service . . ., two cousins [also in the military, the colonel and sergeant major of the Sharpshooters] . . ., and . . . he is the first to bring disgrace upon the name." Then the colonel added some information that heretofore had not been inserted into the record. After mentioning that Hooker had been punished enough and citing his previous record, the colonel mentioned that his cousin's "faults were more the result of indiscretion than positive intention." Furthermore, "the testimony does not warrant the sentence, and that *some* of it, at least, was given under the influence of bitter personal hatred." Colonel DeLand obviously meant Hinckley.

Getting nowhere with the Bureau of Military Justice, the DeLand family now used its influence with state politicians to free Hooker from imprisonment at the Dry Tortugas. Gov. Austin Blair wrote a personal note to Lincoln, informing the latter that the unfortunate captain:

> expresses great sorrow for his conduct and desires to be allowed now to enlist in a Michigan regiment and thus serve out the remainder of his term. . . . His inexcusable misconduct grew out of a misunderstanding with the Colonel of his regiment & he left his command at Spotsylvania not from cowardice but from Anger.

Early in 1865 Blair wrote to John W. Longyear, Republican congressman from Lansing, asking him to use his influence with the president. Longyear evidently did, because Lincoln sent a note to the judge advocate general, Joseph Holt, asking for details of the DeLand case. A man not known for his mercy, Holt sent a laconic reply to Lincoln. After reviewing the case and any subsequent evidence, the judge felt that Captain DeLand's "punishment [was] entirely deserved."

All the chestnuts were not yet out of the fire. Colonel DeLand then contacted John F. Driggs, the Saginaw congressman whose son served as first lieutenant of Company K. Driggs wrote to Lincoln, stating the facts again, mentioning that the captain would enlist as a private and adding something new:

> He says that his crime was not from choice but from a *constitutional* weakness, but that he is now confident he has cultivated suficient [*sic*] moral courage to sustain him in facing the foes of his country.

Lincoln passed Driggs's letter on to Holt's office. An annoyed Holt replied that this was the third time he had been asked to examine the case. He found no merit in it and "if any mitigation is granted, it must be as an act of pure grace."

Even in the last month of the war, Hooker was begging his family to help him get out of his sentence. Colonel DeLand's mother penned an emotional appeal to her younger son James, who was recovering from a severe wound, pleading for help in the matter. "Hooker has written a letter to Charlie," she wrote:

begging him to try to get him away from where he is, [he] says he
will risk a year in the service or go to some other prison or be shot
rather than stay there longer than June—I feel sorry for him and
wish you could do something for him.[12]

Hooker served out his term of enlistment at the Dry Tortugas. What freed him was the end of the war. Asahel W. Nichols
wrote Congressman Driggs on 13 May 1865, asking for his help
in getting DeLand out of prison. Driggs passed the letter to Pres.
Andrew Johnson, who was most anxious to end the problems
associated with the hostilities. In one short, ungrammatical sentence the president terminated Hooker's confinement by executive order on 16 May 1865: "Hooker A DeLand is released his
sentence is remitted."

Young Hooker returned to Michigan after the war with a
cloud over his past. He was restless for the remainder of his life;
he moved around a lot in Michigan, then to Colorado, Canada,
and finally New York. When he approached middle age he tried
to obtain a pension from the government for his wartime service
in the First Michigan Infantry, but was denied. Whatever reason
he may have had for not following the Sharpshooters into battle,
he sincerely regretted it in his older years. If ever a man was
haunted by past deeds, that man was Hooker Ashton DeLand.

CHAPTER 10

Our Colors Were Still Flying

Consolidating the Regiment

The paucity of line officers forced the division commander, General Willcox, to recall some of the Sharpshooters' officers from detached service. Lt. William Randall, then in charge of the Third Division ambulance train, received orders on 23 June to return to his regiment. Randall took over Companies I and K, "numbering 30 muskets."[1] He evidently felt good coming back to the regiment. "I am leaving a splendid position in the Ambulance Corps where I have a good horse to ride, plenty of provisions, a good tent to sleep under and everything quite comfortable for a soldier." But he believed it was better to be part of the regiment. "The boys were glad to have me with them again."[2]

Capt. Elmer Dicey now commanded the regiment. The four consolidated companies were all under lieutenants; only two other junior officers (Lieutenants Hulin and Conn) were left in the regiment. For some reason Hinckley could be spared, and he took over the ambulance train. Captain Meigs and Lieutenant Whipple were in the Third Division hospital. Lt. Thomas Fowler was convalescing at City Point and would soon leave for home. Captain Davis was still sick in a Washington hospital. Captain Nichols and Lieutenant Hill were both on extended sick leave, and Captain Hall was back in Michigan trying to recruit a new company.

Captain Andress and Lts. Cyrenius Knight and George Fowler were home in Michigan recuperating from wounds. One hundred and fifty enlisted men manned the trenches.

In the rear echelon Dr. Arvin Whelan ran the division hospital "as active and successful as ever." The quartermaster, Milo Dyer, was again well after being hospitalized. And Chaplain Heagle, after two months of sickness in the hospitals of Washington and Annapolis, had recently returned to the regiment.[3]

Dividing the regiment into four companies helped somewhat, yet the everlasting paperwork was as difficult as ever. Working on the muster rolls for Companies I and K was as demanding a job as any Lieutenant Randall had had in the past. When Captain Murdoch left for Michigan to recuperate from his head wound, he took all the Company I papers with him. Randall now had to trace down the whereabouts of two companies of men since early May. Although he had 30 men under his command, he still had to account for about 120 others. Some were in various hospitals (either sick or recovering from wounds), some were dead, others were missing, and still others had been transferred out. Paperwork had to be completed on all of them.

On the Siege Line

On 20 June, two days after the fruitless assault near the railroad line, Willcox's division moved near the Hare house to relieve a Second Corps division. The assignment was short; at 2:00 AM on 24 June the division moved back more than a mile to the area it had occupied earlier.[4]

The Second Brigade took over the lines just north of the Baxter or Suffolk Road; the railroad bed was to its rear and Taylor's Creek was in front. About 180 yards in the front of the brigade was a two-gun rebel battery, dubbed the "Suffolk Road Battery" by the Federals but known as "Davidson's Battery" to the Confederates.[5]

The picket and main lines were within point-blank range of each other. No day passed without casualties in the brigade. Men burrowed trenches and dugouts into the earth, and habitually crouched when they moved around. Snipers on both sides had their sights on enemy territory, their fingers resting on triggers and firing at whatever moved. "We have to stoop down along the trench when we want to move," one of Hartranft's veterans wrote home. "If a man stands erect he is sure to get a poke in the eye or something else."[6]

Soon after the regiment had taken its position, Lieutenant Randall found himself pestered by a rebel marksman while looking over the enemy lines with his field glasses. The Confederate jumped up, fired quickly, and dropped down just as fast. After being on the receiving end of the rebel's rancor several times, Randall pinpointed the position, then told a dozen of his men to get their weapons ready; they waited until the Southerner showed himself. Randall immediately told his squad to fire. "Mr. Johnny collapsed very suddenly & did not show himself again," the lieutenant noted.[7]

Randall continued to survey the rebel lines with his field glasses. Looking at an area a mile to his right, he saw the Confederates fortifying a range of hills just outside Petersburg. He realized that his own position was almost untenable; the Sharpshooters were dug in on a knoll, an easy shot from enemy lines. "Cannot stir from our pits without being fired on," he penned in his journal.[8]

Sharpshooting by both sides continued unabated. Limping slightly from a bullet wound in the foot, 2nd Lt. Martin Wager of Company F returned from the Third Division hospital after recuperating a few days. On 25 June a rebel sniper caught Wager in his sights and fired a slug into his head. The young officer died before a surgeon could see him.[9]

In the Hospital

When a man was sent to the hospital, he had no idea if he would ever see his friends again. Some, like Pvt. Amos Farling, were lucky. Shot in the left hand on 1 June, Farling left the front for the field hospital, where he stayed for two days. He was then transferred to the division hospital at White House Landing. For four days he took in the sickening sights and sounds of thousands of wounded and sick men who "were sent North as fast as transportation could be procured for them."[10]

Farling's hospital experiences were not unique. After an examination by a doctor on his fifth day at White House Landing, Farling was taken to Carver Hospital in Washington. He liked the bill of fare at Carver. "This was a good place," he remembered. For two weeks he lived high on the hog, eating better than at any time since his enlistment. Once a day a doctor made rounds and medicine was doled out by the hospital steward. Each packet of medicine contained instructions and a patient's name. Ward masters received the medicine; they then passed it along to a nurse who gave it to the sick men at the appropriate time, "if it is not forgotten," added the impudent Farling.

He noticed that anywhere from two to ten men died each day. Their bodies were removed to a "dead house." Every two or three days the gravediggers picked up the corpses and buried them.

After three weeks at Carver, Farling was sent to Hadington Hospital in Philadelphia. He liked the civilians who crowded into the hospital each day, bringing paper, pens, stamps, books, fruits, tobacco, "and words of encouragement which did more good than all their good things." Farling's health took a turn for the worse. Afflicted with "lung fever, chronic diarrhea, and sore eyes," he suffered for five weeks, bedridden, eating little but receiving copious amounts of "Port wine, brandy and medicine enough to kill a dog." His constitution proved more rugged than the sickness, and he began to mend.

Farling stayed five days at a convalescent camp in Alexandria, Virginia, then was shipped out for City Point. He ended up in quarters with some drafted men going to the front. The next morning he awoke to find that his knapsack and its contents had been stolen. He reported the theft to the provost marshal; a squad searched the quarters and located all the stolen articles. Farling headed for his regiment the same day, no doubt with a poor perception of the new draftees. That afternoon he rejoined his comrades, who were sweltering in the trenches before Petersburg.[11]

Instead of wasting away in some hospital surrounded by strangers, a few men were lucky enough to be sent home to recover. Even that did not preclude harm coming to them. Tom Nelson (Co. K) was one of those sent home to Saginaw to recuperate. A few days before starting back to the regiment, Nelson, who was "lame and partly disabled," was good-naturedly speaking to a friend on a downtown sidewalk; both were violently accosted by a local tough "filled with the Copperhead venom against soldiers and their friends." Nelson was beaten severely in the face; his friend was so ferociously attacked that he hovered for a while between life and death. The attacker was fined $15 for drunken assault. Nelson returned to the regiment, but his battle wounds incapacited him from further action. He transferred to the Veteran Reserve Corps, from which he was discharged after the war.[12]

On the Front Line

During the last week of June, the Sharpshooters were ordered to advance their lines to a pine-covered knoll just in back of the pickets. Entrenching under fire was as hazardous as charging the enemy. On 26 June the bloodshed continued. Pvt. Charles Waterman (Co. I) was killed while working on the trenches. John Andrew (Co. K) was shot in the right thigh near the hip. Cpl. Asher Huff of the color guard was hit in the left knee. Jeremiah Tiner (Co. A) lost the little toe on his left foot after it had been smashed by a bullet, and Pvt. Frank Thayer of the same company was shot in his right hand.[13]

On 27 June Pvt. James Smith received a particularly nasty wound in his thigh. Unfortunately for the 40-year-old from Clyde, it proved to be fatal; he died on 2 July.[14]

Francis M. Perry (Co. B) was killed on 28 June.[15] The next day Sgt. Warren Sharp (Co. C) was shot in the leg; he suffered until 12 July, when he died from complications.[16] A rebel ball killed Pvt. Theodore Nash (Co. I) on 30 June; the bullet hit him in the chest while he was constructing entrenchments. His death affected a number of his superiors. "Young Nash was a fine looking boy and a splendid soldier," wrote Lieutenant Randall in his journal, "amiable in disposition, kind and obliging to his comrades, he was a favorite in the Company."[17] It was Nash who was primarily responsible for capturing the colors of the Thirty-fifth North Carolina Infantry on the night of 17 June; his friends buried him just in back of their lines.[18]

Most of the entrenching went on during the night hours. Breastworks, rifle pits, gun embrasures, covered ways, and the hundred duties of planning and executing such work were done in the dark. During the daylight hours men with sharp eyes and steady nerves stared through cuts in the trenches at the enemy across the field, waiting for a chance to bag someone.

On the Fourth of July Lieutenant Randall was trying to snatch some precious time for an afternoon nap near the breastworks when a rifle ball "scorched my ear warmly" and knocked off his hat. Grabbing a rifle, he angrily fired a few shots at the rebel breastworks, "which had the effect of making them keep low," he added.[19]

The next day Sgt. John Huston, one of the enlistees from Claybanks in Oceana County, was not as lucky. On the forward line a rebel marksman drew a bead on him and sent him to his Maker. His comrades buried him behind the lines.[20] Cpl. Ralph McClellan, "having always both in battle and out, conducted himself like a true soldier," took Huston's place as sergeant in Company B.[21]

Three Huston boys had left their home in Claybanks; only one returned after the war. Oceana County in northern Michigan was one of the more sparsely inhabited regions of the state; that made it even sadder when the 22-year-old Huston died in action. Peter Chichester had died at Spotsylvania; Oliver Perry had also succumbed to wounds suffered there. Perry's older brother, Francis Marion Perry, was killed 28 June by a rebel sniper. All had served in Company B; all were "intimate associates" in Claybanks before they enlisted to save the Union. All died far from the cool lake breezes of home.[22]

On the night of 8 July the Sharpshooters left the front lines and marched back about a mile for some time off. Before they pulled out another man was wounded. Pvt. Robert Bradley (Co. H) was struck in the head with a piece of shell.[23] One of the "old soldiers" in more ways than one, Bradley was 47 years old at Petersburg. He had previously served in two other Michigan regiments. He entered the Seventh Michigan Infantry in August 1861 but was dismissed on a surgeon's certificate of disability that same December. Two weeks later he joined the Thirteenth Michigan Infantry; he was discharged from that regiment a year later. After being at home for three months, he enlisted in the Sharpshooters in May 1863. This last wound, however, ended his wartime service. Leaving the regiment because of disability in September 1864, Bradley went home for good. His wound did not prove fatal, and he lived until 1893.[24]

Relief Organizations

"It is a heart-rending sight to see so many brave men cut down in the prime of life," related an Ypsilanti doctor who was visiting the front. While penning a letter home in early July, he watched wounded men being brought in from the rifle pits. Cannonading and picket fire serenaded the surgeon as he composed the letter. "I just went to the spring to get a pail of water," he wrote, "and looking at the headboards of sixteen men, I found that seven were from Mich." He had already assisted in two operations that morning. While writing the letter, an orderly called on him to help at another. "We are pleasantly situated in a copse of pine woods" was how he described the setting of the field hospital, yet he added, "all around us [are] the dead and dying." [25]

To help the sick and wounded soldiers, the Michigan branch of the U.S. Christian Commission sent a number of its delegates to the field hospitals and front lines outside of Petersburg. Its funds came from private (mostly church) collections throughout the state; the commission was never supported with state funds or staffed by state employees. The 57 delegates, mostly Protestant ministers and helpful laymen, visited every army in which Michigan units served. Each delegate served a minimum of six weeks, ministering to the physical and spiritual wants of Michigan's patriotic sons. [26]

Another private citizens' group looking after the welfare of the state's boys in blue was the Michigan Soldiers' Relief Association. Setting up collection depots in the state, the association procured anything a sick or well soldier could possibly want. Socks, shirts, fruits (dried or canned), pickles, jellies, newspapers, books, pens, writing paper, blankets, sheets—in short, whatever could be of use for "our wounded heroes"—found its way into the coffers of the organization. [27] In the first half of 1864 the association received $4,300 in contributions, much of it from small towns. Pontiac led the state with $514, Detroit put in $400, but little Coldwater came in third with $350. By the middle of 1864 the association had eight male and eight female agents in the field. [28]

Donations were solicited from local businessmen. In Coldwater a raffle for a saddle taken from Gen. John Hunt Morgan and a gun from a Confederate general in East Tennessee netted $57.75 for the association. Ice cream socials, sanitary fairs (which were similar to county fairs), and patriotic celebrations at local Fourth of July festivities brought in thousands of dollars for fathers, brothers, sons, and sweethearts at the front. [29]

One officer from the Third Division in a Washington, DC, hospital praised the efforts of all the associations from Michigan. "I do not know but the State is represented by other societies, at any rate they are all working in concert and doing an immense sight of good relieving suffering that would never be reached were it not for such organizations." In particular, he extolled the work of Mrs. E. A. Gridley of Hillsdale, an agent of the Soldiers' Aid Society. Her own health was poor, yet she visited sick and wounded Michigan boys in numerous hospitals, distributing little delicacies and giving all of them a kind word. The officer then admonished his readers:

> Those at home who think such duties pleasant and easy, a sort of romance, had better try it and they will soon see their bright visions vanishing, and find that they were only figments of the brain. The good those ladies are doing[,] who have left comfortable homes and voluntarily taken upon themselves such duties they can never know[;] for only those who receive their attention can properly value them.[30]

So many Michigan lads were attached to the Ninth Corps, principally Willcox's division, that delegates from the Christian Commission and the Soldiers' Relief Association regularly visited that sector. On the Fourth of July, representatives of both charitable groups visited the Third Division hospital; they brought boxes of maizena, farina, canned and dried fruit, gallons of wine, and three and a half tons of tomatoes, as well as vast quantities of hospital stores. "Never in a field hospital, has there been a better provision made for the sick than in ours," reported Chap. S. S. Hunting of the Twenty-seventh Michigan. Even the men on the Third Division line received tomatoes, lemons, and saurkraut.

An agent for the Christian Commission, E. C. Walker of Detroit, made an estimate of what was needed each week. The Michigan Soldiers' Relief Association also gauged the needs of the men at the front. By drawing from both groups, the Third Division hospital was kept well supplied with necessities not provided by the government.

"I bless these charitable organizations," Chaplain Hunting proclaimed to the people of Detroit. His colleague, Chap. Jonah Jones of the Twentieth Michigan, reiterated the grace. "Without these noble agencies," he said, "many hundreds of our men would have been in their graves, and a generous public, appreciating the success of their labors, will not fail to replenish their heartily taxed treasury."[31]

Despite these blessings, letters from both officers and enlisted men to the folks back home who were involved in patriotic fund-raising or collecting made clear that the Christian Commission was not the most effective of the charities. Berating the practices of that organization, the editor of the Coldwater *Union Sentinel* insisted that:

> The Sanitary Commission is the "good Samaritan." Soldiers *know* that sour krout [*sic*] and apple sauce will cure the scurvy—a chaplain was never known to do it. . . . Works, not professions, are now the test of patriotism and loyalty." [32]

The Michigan Soldier's Relief Association was a branch of the U.S. Sanitary Commission. At their state convention in 1863, Michigan Baptists passed a resolution asking "each church . . . to forward to the army at once a shipment of vegetables for winter use in our army hospitals through the Sanitary Commission." [33]

The Christian Commission, having been accused of distributing "a little jam to make the tracts go down," eventually confined itself to the religious work for which it had been founded. It bothered some people that an agent or minister of the commission carried a basket of goodies on one arm and distributed them with tracts from a basket on the other arm. In the summer of 1864 the commission's governing board decided to turn over whatever supplies it received to the Sanitary Commission. No one supporting the Union saw any problem with taking care of the physical needs of its fighting men. [34]

On the Front Line Again

Color Sergeant Caine (who had saved the state flag on the night of 17 June by burying it) was too sick to stay on the line and was relieved of duty. His replacement, 20-year-old Francis Urie of Scipio, received the distinction with an admonition "for the safe keeping [of the flag] and honor of which he will be held personally responsible." [35] Cpl. William Graves (Co. C), another recipient for honors, was rewarded with sergeant's stripes "for meritorious conduct both in field and in camp" on 13 July. [36]

The Sharpshooters stayed off the front lines and got some rest until 18 July—almost 11 days. Some of the men could not resist a bit of unwarranted playfulness. Intent on shocking their fellows, a few of the Sharpshooters tossed cartridges into campfires. The resulting "pop" and scattering of ashes did not amuse

Captain Dicey, the battalion commander. He ordered the first sergeants to inspect the cartridge boxes of their men daily. Anyone possessing less than the requisite number fell under the wrath of his company commander. A "habit equally pernicious and far more unsoldierly" also crept into the regiment. Disrespectful behavior, neglect of orders, "rude and ungentlemanly language" would not be tolerated. "Hereafter any soldier guilty of the above will be stringently dealt with," admonished the captain.[37]

Col. Charles DeLand returned to the regiment from his hospital confinement in Washington on 17 July.[38] On the next day, the regiment lost another officer. The Sharpshooters were marching back to their old haunts on the front line. As they moved forward they had to pass over an exposed section of ground; "the bullets rattled around us like hailstones," yet only 1st Lt. Thomas Fowler was injured. Fowler, one of the contingent from Jonesville in Hillsdale County was hit by a minié ball in the face, between the eye and the nose, the cheekbone turning it aside. The slug tore a path around Fowler's skull. A surgeon had to cut out the bullet from behind his ear.[39]

A short time after having taken over their segment of the trenches, another officer had a close call. The colonel's brother, Bvt. 2nd Lt. James S. DeLand, was hit in the left shoulder while placing pickets in front of the main line. The bullet left "a nice scar," he recalled, making light of the injury, "no bones broke."[40]

Defensive Works

The siege works devised by the engineers of the Army of the Potomac were those taught at West Point. Both sides, in fact, utilized the same techniques, although the Confederates held more high ground; they had planned their lines in preparation for the Union siege.

A heavy line of earthworks with redoubts for artillery detachments marked the strongest breastworks. About 150 yards in front of that line, on the Second Brigade's front, was a ravine with a small stream called Taylor's Creek flowing through it. The creek bank closer to the rebel line was steeper and more abrupt, and the Second Brigade occupied a position on that side. The ground then rose gently to the Confederate entrenchments. Al-

Photographs

Col. Charles V. DeLand, First Michigan Sharpshooters. The newspaperman from Jackson had many friends and enemies, but few neutral onlookers. Wounded at Spotsylvania and wounded and captured at the Battle of Peebles Farm, he was discharged on account of wounds in February 1865. Brevet Brigadier General. (Collection of John Buckbee.)

Lt. Col. William H. H. Beadle, First Michigan Sharpshooters. Resigned because of illness, then served in the Veterans Reserve Corps until the end of the war. Brevet Brigadier General. (Collection of John Buckbee.)

Maj. John Piper, First Michigan Sharpshooters. A stern taskmaster, he was killed at the Battle of Spotsylvania. (Collection of John Buckbee.)

Dr. Arvin F. Whelan, Surgeon, First
Michigan Sharpshooters. Chief Surgeon,
First Division, Ninth Corps. Brevet
Lieutenant Colonel. (Collection of John
Buckbee.)

Dr. George L. Cornell, Assistant Surgeon, First
Michigan Sharpshooters. Taken ill, he resigned
in December 1864. (Collection of John Buckbee.)

Dr. Jacob B. McNett, Assistant
Surgeon, First Michigan
Sharpshooters. Taken ill, he
resigned in April 1864.
(Collection of John Buckbee.)

First Lt. Ed Buckbee, Adjutant, First Michigan Sharpshooters. One of the youngest officers in the regiment, he became its last commander. His letters and reminiscences were providentially saved by his descendants. (Collection of John Buckbee.)

First Lt. David G. Palmer, Quartermaster, First Michigan Sharpshooters. Taken ill, he resigned in January 1865. (Collection of John Buckbee.)

Rev. David Heagle, Baptist Chaplain, First Michigan Sharpshooters. He was one of Colonel DeLand's staunchest supporters. He would be the last of the field and staff officers to die. (Collection of John Buckbee.)

Capt. Levant C. Rhines, Company A, First Michigan Sharpshooters. Promoted to major and commanding the regiment, he was killed in action in front of Petersburg on 17 June 1864. (Collection of John Buckbee.)

First Lt. George C. Knight, Company A, First Michigan Sharpshooters. Promoted captain, he was killed in action in front of Petersburg on 17 June 1864. (Collection of John Buckbee.)

Second Lt. Guy Newbre, Company A, First Michigan Sharpshooters. Wounded, discharged for disability. (Collection of John Buckbee.)

First Sgt. Michael Collins, Company A, First Michigan Sharpshooters, was captured near Petersburg on the night of 17 June 1864. (Collection of John Buckbee.)

Capt. Elmer Dicey, Company B, First Michigan Sharpshooters. Captured at the Crater, his health was broken while in prison. At repatriation he was discharged for disability. (Collection of John Buckbee.)

First Lt. William Clark, Company B, First Michigan Sharpshooters. Chronically ill, he was discharged for disability in May 1864. (Collection of John Buckbee.)

Second Lt. Frank Whipple, Company B, First Michigan Sharpshooters. A veteran of the First U.S. Sharpshooters, he was wounded at Spotsylvania on 12 May 1864. (Collection of John Buckbee.)

Sgt. Theodore Purdy, Company B, First Michigan Sharpshooters. Regimental Clerk. (Collection of John Buckbee.)

Sgt. Edwin O. Conklin, Company B, First Michigan Sharpshooters. He was Buckbee's best friend. Captured at the Crater, he died in the Danville, VA, prison. (Collection of John Buckbee.)

Sgt. George H. Saxton, Company B, First Michigan Sharpshooters. Promoted to quartermaster, then lieutenant, Company B. (Collection of John Buckbee.)

George W. Warren, Company B, hospital steward, First Michigan Sharpshooters, enlisted in the army because he had no more sons to give to his country. His letters home were filled with all sorts of "in house" gossip. (Collection of John Buckbee.)

Sgt. Joseph Stevens, Company B, First Michigan Sharpshooters. One of the "old soldiers" at the age of 21, Stevens was captured on 17 June 1864 in front of Petersburg. He later survived the sinking of the *Sultana*. (Collection of John Buckbee.)

Capt. Lucien Meigs, Company C, First Michigan Sharpshooters. Incapacitated by illness, he resigned in August 1864. (Collection of John Buckbee.)

First Lt. Thomas R. Fowler, Company C, First Michigan Sharpshooters. Wounded on 17 July 1864 in the face; promoted to captain; discharged for disability in October 1864. (Collection of John Buckbee.)

Second Lt. Albert P. Thomas, Company C, First Michigan Sharpshooters. Wounded at Spotsylvania under strange circumstances; he was discharged for disability in September 1864. (Collection of John Buckbee.)

Cpl. Leverette N. Case, Company C, First Michigan Sharpshooters. Another veteran, Case was promoted to sergeant major, lieutenant, and captain of Company H. The last promotion came because of his role in the assault on Petersburg, VA, on 2 April 1865. (Collection of John Buckbee.)

Pvt. Benjamin Caswell, Company C, First Michigan Sharpshooters, enlisted at age 36 in Hall's Independent Sharpshooters. (Dale Niesen Collection.)

Sgt. Maj. John W. Quackenbush, originally enlisted in Company C, First Michigan Sharpshooters. Twice demoted, he resigned to accept an officer's position in Hall's Independent Sharpshooters but was discharged as supernumerary in March 1865. (Collection of John Buckbee.)

Cpl. Mathew C. Sharp, Company C, First Michigan
Sharpshooters, died at Chicago on 17 October 1863
while the regiment was guarding Camp Douglas.
(State Archives of Michigan, Lansing.)

Sgt. Warren D. Sharp, Company C, First Michigan
Sharpshooters. Brother of Mathew Sharp, he died
of wounds received at the Battle of the Crater.
(State Archives of Michigan, Lansing.)

Pvt. Zena D. Ransom, Company C, First Michigan
Sharpshooters. Nephew of the Sharp brothers, he
lived through the war and later settled in Cross
Village, Michigan. (State Archives of Michigan,
Lansing.)

Cpl. Francis Urie, Company C, First
Michigan Sharpshooters, served in the
Color Guard and was captured at the
Battle of the Crater. (Collection of
Robert Coch.)

Pvt. John S. Urie, Company C, First
Michigan Sharpshooters. Brother of
Francis Urie, he was wounded in action
in June 1864. (Collection of Robert Coch.)

First Lt. Samuel E. Hudson, Company D., First
Michigan Sharpshooters, wounded, promoted
Captain, discharged for disability in December
1864. (Collection of John Buckbee.)

Capt. George N. Davis, Company
D, First Michigan Sharpshooters.
Slightly wounded in battle, he
later became U.S. Inspector of
Hospitals. He was discharged for
disability in November 1864.
(Collection of John Buckbee.)

Second Lt. Cyrenius B. Knight,
Company D, First Michigan Sharpshooters, in the Officer of the Day
uniform. Wounded at Petersburg,
he was discharged for disability in
October 1864. The bugle on his hat
denotes "sharpshooters." (State
Archives of Michigan, Lansing.)

Sgt. Goodwin S. Beaver, Company D, First Michigan Sharpshooters. Quartermaster Sgt. He died in Washington, DC, in June 1865. (Collection of John Buckbee.)

George W. Stone, Drummer Boy, Company D, First Michigan Sharpshooters. Second youngest member of the regiment, Stone continually elbowed his way into the front line and grabbed a musket whenever the Sharpshooters went into action. This photograph was "Taken after 2 years in Service." (State Archives of Michigan, Lansing.)

Capt. Asahel W. Nichols, Company E, First Michigan Sharpshooters. Promoted Major, he led the regiment in its last fight on 2 April 1865 in which he was wounded. Brevet Colonel. Committed suicide due to unrelenting pain from injury. (Collection of John Buckbee.)

First Lt. Ira L. Evans, Company E, First Michigan Sharpshooters. A veteran of the Second Michigan Infantry, he served as Provost Marshall in the winter of 1864–65, and was later promoted Captain. Never wounded in battle, he served well and was much admired by the men. He was brevetted Major at the end of the war. (Collection of John Buckbee.)

Second Lt. Henry V. Hinckley, Company E, First Michigan Sharpshooters. The brother-in-law of Captain Nichols, Hinckley was nevertheless the only original line officer to end the war at the same rank with which he was mustered. (Collection of John Buckbee.)

Sgt. Milo E. Dyer, Company E, First Michigan Sharpshooters. Commissary Sgt., later promoted First Lieutenant, Company F. (Collection of John Buckbee.)

Privates Sidney and James B. Haight, Company E, First Michigan Sharpshooters. Jim, 19, on the right, was wounded in the arm at the Battle of Spotsylvania and was mustered out of the service because of disability. Sid, 17, won the Medal of Honor for his bravery at the Battle of the Crater. (State Archives of Michigan, Lansing.)

Capt. Hooker A. DeLand, Company F, First Michigan Sharpshooters. A younger cousin of Col. Charles V. DeLand, he was cashiered and sentenced to the Dry Tortugas for cowardice. He spent the rest of his life vainly trying to rectify his record. (Collection of John Buckbee.)

First Lt. Joseph O. Bellair, Company F, First Michigan Sharpshooters, wounded and taken prisoner while aiding Colonel DeLand at the Battle of Peebles Farm. (Collection of John Buckbee.)

Second Lt. Martin Wager, Company F, First
Michigan Sharpshooters, killed near Petersburg
by a Confederate marksman on 25 June 1864.
(Collection of John Buckbee.)

Capt. Thomas H. Gaffney, Company G, First
Michigan Sharpshooters, ensnared in a scandal
while at Camp Douglas, died of wounds
received near Petersburg on 17 June 1864.
(Collection of John Buckbee.)

Cpl. George C. Dean, Company F, First
Michigan Sharpshooters.
(Collection of Dale Niesen.)

First Lt. Moses A. Powell, Company G, First Michigan Sharpshooters, court-martialed and sentenced to the Dry Tortugas for cowardice. (Collection of John Buckbee.)

Second Lt. Charles G. Conn, Company G, First Michigan Sharpshooters. For a short time he com-manded the remnant of the regiment after the fight on 17 June 1864. He was captured at the Crater. The bugle on his cap signifies "sharpshooter." Conn became famous and rich after the war because of the musical instrument company he founded. (Collection of John Buckbee.)

Sgt. George J. Davis, Company G, First Michigan Sharpshooters. After being wounded in June 1864, he transferred to the Veteran Reserve Corps. (Collection of Robert Coch.)

Capt. Andrew J. Hall, Company H, First Michigan Sharpshooters. He resigned from command in August 1864 and returned home to raise a company of "real" sharpshooters. He was forced to resign this latter position because of certain improprieties employed in forming the company. (Collection of John Buckbee.)

First Lt. George Fowler, Company H, First Michigan Sharpshooters. Called "One of our best fighting officers," he was shot in the leg at Spotsylvania. He was discharged on account of wounds. (Collection of John Buckbee.)

Second Lt. William Ruddock, Company H, First Michigan Sharpshooters. Wounded at Spotsylvania and in the Crater. Discharged because of wounds. (Collection of John Buckbee.)

Pvt. Edwin P. Beadle, Company H, First Michigan Sharpshooters. The 16-year-old brother of the Lieutenant Colonel, he died of wounds received at the Battle of Spotsylvania. (Collection of John Buckbee.)

Capt. George H. Murdoch, Company I, First Michigan Sharpshooters, was wounded on 17 June 1864 in front of Petersburg, VA. Brevet Major. (Collection of John Buckbee.)

First Lt. Robert Hill, Company I, First Michigan Sharpshooters. Hospitalized due to sunstroke, he was discharged for disability. (Collection of John Buckbee.)

Second Lt. William Randall, Company I, First Michigan Sharpshooters. He commanded the brigade ambulances and was later captured at the Crater. Promoted Captain. (Collection of John Buckbee.)

Cpl. Adam Walter, Company I, First Michigan Sharpshooters, enlisted in Company B, Hall's Independent Sharpshooters, in October 1864. (Collection of Dale Niesen.)

Pvt. Thomas Wightman, Company I, First Michigan Sharpshooters. He enlisted at age 43 from Marquette in August 1863. Note the corps badge on his cap and the non-regulation belt and blouse. His cap is now in the State Museum. (State Archives of Michigan, Lansing.)

Capt. Edwin V. Andress, Company K, First
Michigan Sharpshooters. Wounded at Spotsylvania on 12 May 1864, he was discharged
for disability. (Collection of John Buckbee.)

Second Lt. Garret Graveraet, Company K, First
Michigan Sharpshooters. Scion of a well-known
family from the Mackinac region, he was the only
Indian officer in the regiment. He died of wounds
received the night of 17 June 1864 in front of
Petersburg, VA. (Collection of John Buckbee.)

First Lt. William Driggs, Company
K, First Michigan Sharpshooters.
One of the veterans, his high-class
manners caused him to be called
"an English dude." He was discharged for disability. (Collection
of John Buckbee.)

Wounded Indian soldiers at Fredericksburg, VA, May 1864. One of the few photographs of Native Americans in the war, the men may be members of Company K. (Library of Congress, Washington, DC.)

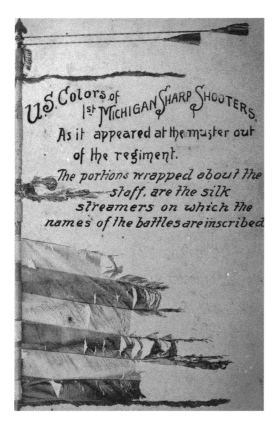

National Colors of the First Michigan Sharpshooters at the end of the Civil War. The state flag was captured by the enemy at the Battle of the Crater. This flag was torn into strips and handed to the men in the ranks in an earlier battle in front of Petersburg, VA. It was one of the very few flags in the Union Army to have ribbons on which were painted the names of the various engagements of the regiment. This was the first Union flag to wave over the city of Petersburg the morning of 3 April 1865. (Collection of John Buckbee.)

Capt. James S. DeLand, First Michigan Sharpshooters. The colonel's younger brother, he was grievously wounded in the regiment's last fight. (State Archives of Michigan, Lansing.)

First Lt. Levant W. Barnhart, Sixth Michigan Cavalry and one of Adj. Ed Buckbee's friends. The two of them paid an unannounced visit to Gen. George A. Custer. (State Archives of Michigan, Lansing.)

Capt. John Hardy, Second Michigan Infantry, spread the word of the Confederate attack on Fort Stedman the night of 25 March 1864. (State Archives of Michigan, Lansing.)

Col. Byron M. Cutcheon, Twentieth Michigan Infantry. He was the author of the history of his regiment, which fought alongside the Sharpshooters. (Byron Cutcheon, *The Story of the Twentieth Michigan Infantry*. Lansing, MI: Robert Smith Printing Co., 1904.)

Col. Claudius B. Grant, Twentieth Michigan Infantry. He served in all the forays of his regiment. His diary reflected a hard-bitten and competent officer. (Byron Cutcheon, *The Story of the Twentieth Michigan Infantry*. Lansing: Robert Smith Printing Co., 1904.)

Maj. George C. Barnes, Twentieth Michigan Infantry, died on 20 June 1864 of wounds received in front of Petersburg, VA, on 18 June 1864. (Byron Cutcheon, *The Story of the Twentieth Michigan Infantry*. Lansing, MI: Robert Smith Printing Co., 1904.)

Capt. Oliver Blood, Twentieth Michigan Infantry, killed in action at Peebles Farm 30 September 1864. (Byron Cutcheon, *The Story of the Twentieth Michigan Infantry*. Lansing, MI: Robert Smith Printing Co., 1904.)

Gen. John Hunt Morgan, Confederate cavalry leader. In the summer of 1863 Morgan led an abortive raid into Indiana. The Sharpshooters saw their first action against him. (State Archives of Michigan, Lansing.)

Capt. Clement A. Lounsberry, Twentieth Michigan Infantry. As AAAG, he accepted the surrender of the city of Petersburg on the morning of 3 April 1865. He would later chronicle the events of Custer's fight at the Little Big Horn. (State Archives of Michigan, Lansing.)

Capt. Philip J. Johnson, Thirty-fifth North Carolina Infantry, personally fought with the Sharpshooters' Maj. Levant Rhines at the Petersburg, VA, fight on 17 June 1864. (From Walter Clark, ed. *Histories of the Several Regiments and Battalions from North Carolina in the Great War, 1861–65*. 5 vols. Raleigh, NC: E. M. Uzzell, 1901.)

Lt. Col. John G. Jones, Thirty-fifth North Carolina Infantry, was killed in hand-to-hand fighting by two Sharpshooters on the night of 17 June 1864 in front of Petersburg, VA. (Walter Clark, ed., *Histories of the Several Regiments and Battalions from North Carolina in the Great War, 1861–65*. 5 vols. Raleigh, NC: E.M. Uzzell, 1901.)

Austin Blair, Michigan's Civil War governor. His military policies forestalled a plethora of regiments coming from the state; old regiments were encouraged to recruit after months and years in the field. (State Archives of Michigan, Lansing.)

Maj. Gen. John G. Parke—General Burnside's successor—and his staff at Ninth Corps Headquarters near Petersburg, VA, in late 1864. General Parke is seated at center, directly below the chimney. Lt. Col. P. M. Lydig is standing, second from right. Lydig and Lieutenant Colonel Cutcheon of the Twentieth Michigan Infantry walked between the lines after the Battle of the Crater to implement a truce. (State Archives of Michigan, Lansing.)

Brig. Gen. Orlando B. Willcox, Division Commander in the Ninth Corps. Colonel DeLand always believed that Willcox purposefully slighted the First Michigan Sharpshooters in his after-action reports. (State Archives of Michigan, Lansing.)

Soldiers from the Second Michigan Infantry raising their flag atop the customs house in Petersburg, VA, the morning of 3 April 1865. In the left background is the court house already festooned with at least three flags, including that of the First Michigan Sharpshooters. (*Harper's Weekly*, April 1865.)

Col. Charles V. DeLand and family at his home south of Jackson, MI, about 1900. The large boulder used as a podium during the 1890 regimental reunion is just out of the picture at left. (Charles V. DeLand, *DeLand's History of Jackson County, Michigan*. N.p.: B. F. Bowen, 1903.)

Zachariah Chandler, Detroit merchant and influential Republican senator from Michigan during the Civil War. He served on the infamous Joint Committee on the Conduct of the War. (Charles Richard Tuttle, comp., *General History of the State of Michigan with Biographical Sketches, Portrait Engravings, and Numerous Illustrations*. Detroit: R. D. S. Tyler & Co., 1873.)

Hon. John F. Driggs, Republican congressman from Saginaw whose son served as first lieutenant of Company K. (Charles Richard Tuttle, comp., *General History of the State of Michigan with Biographical Sketches, Portrait Engravings, and Numerous Illustrations*. Detroit: R. D. S. Tyler & Co., 1873.)

Maj. Gen. Ambrose Burnside, commander of the Ninth Corps. Admired by his own men, he and his corps were scorned by much of the Army of the Potomac. (State Archives of Michigan, Lansing.)

Front entrance to the Dearborn Armory. The Sharpshooters guarded these premises until their transfer to Camp Douglas in August 1863. (*Michigan History*, vol. 28, no. 4 [October–December 1944], p. 588.)

Petersburg Court House. On the morning of 3 April 1865 Adj. Ed Buckbee and the Color Guard of the First Michigan Sharpshooters knocked out a piece of the clock face and raised the first Union flag in the city. (Library of Congress, Washington, DC.)

Monument erected to the memory of the members of the First Michigan Sharpshooters on the grounds of the State Capitol, Lansing. (Collection of Chris Czopek.)

Government headstone of Pvt. John Waubenoo, Company K, First Michigan Sharpshooters. (Collection of Chris Czopek.)

most 50 feet in front of the second line were the pits for the pickets, which comprised the most advanced line. The main infantry breastworks followed the course of the creek along the far bank.[41] The rear sloped moderately back to the railroad bed.

The rank and file excavated "dugouts" in the slope, covering them with their shelter tents. Deep, wide ditches or "covered ways" ran from the main trench back to the dugouts; no one had to stand in the open in order to get from one place to another, except while going to and from the picket stations. The dirt, the mud, the heat, the scarcity of clean water, the abominable flies, and the rebel fire proved to be companions no one relished and all abhorred.

Details of men moved daily to brigade headquarters. Made up of levies from each regiment, the pioneers (as they were called) did all the excavating and construction at brigade and division headquarters. The Sharpshooters' contribution—Pvts. Aaron Knight (Co. C) and Lewis Fenton (Co. G)—bid adieu to their companions on 12 July and trod off to work for the generals.[42]

Picket duty was very hazardous. Men dug holes to the front of the main line, taking care to toss the red earth toward the enemy. They took their positions and were relieved from them only at night. These advanced posts were extremely important; the men in them were the eyes and ears of the army.

What seemed dangerous on the Ninth Corps line was not so on the Fifth Corps front, which was just to the Sharpshooters' left. The Fifth Corps seemingly had it easy. "There is no firing on their front," remarked Lieutenant Randall. "The pickets amuse themselves by watching each other and occasionally doing some tall bragging on both sides."[43] But the firing on Randall's own sector was continuous. It was so intense that Randall estimated a hatfull of minié balls could be picked up every fifteen minutes.[44]

At the same time Randall penned his thoughts into his journal, Chaplain Heagle sent off another dispatch to the Detroit *Advertiser and Tribune*. He listed 19 men killed and wounded since 22 June, another litany of misery for the anxious families back home. For some of those families, the newspapers carried the only word they would ever receive of a loved one's death. The inventory was as succinct as it was heartbreaking. Lt. Martin Wager, shot in the head, died 25 June; John Andrew, an Indian from Company K, shot in the thigh; Frank M. Perry, killed on 28 June; Theodore Nash, killed in the trenches on 30 June. Although it was only a list of names, a parent or friend reading the crabbed type would have an instant sinking feeling, and then read it again just to make sure. "Oh, how will Mother take this?" A letter from the chaplain or the boy's company commander might arrive in a few days. "He died peacefully," it would say. Many an aching heart in a Michigan home tried to remember a loved one as he was before this terrible war consumed him.

In front of Petersburg an enormous war machine inexorably ground up sons from across the country. The heat, the flying lead and shrieking iron, the fear and anger, and the omnipresent filth oppressed the men. There had been "no rain for several weeks," Chaplain Heagle closed, "and the air is perfectly filled with dust."[45]

Even amid the dirt and death and bitterness of war, Lieutenant Randall managed to find a touch of beauty. "It is a grand and beautiful sight," he opined, "at night on the picket line to watch the morter [*sic*] shells looking like a shooting star, moving in a perfect arc of a circle, and when nearing the horizon bursting, throwing a spray of sparks in all directions." In an afterthought he wrote that "Burnside is mining one of the enemy's forts." But that was not in their sector, and the Sharpshooters had their hands full where they were.[46]

Close calls became daily occurrences. On the night of 22 July the rebels suddenly opened with volley fire, at the same time throwing shells at the Second Brigade. Randall and three "of my boys" were in an advanced rifle pit when a shell hit the embankment in front of them, knocking off the sandbags and throwing dirt over them. The shell, its fuse still sputtering, rolled into the pit just to their left; a quick-witted Sharpshooter grabbed the cannonball and tossed it over the breastworks.[47]

Humphrey's brigade had occupied the trenches just behind Taylor's Creek for a month, from 24 June until the night of 25 July. The men lived in dugouts covered with their canvas shelter halves. (A dog tent was made up of two shelter halves that could be buttoned together; each man carried a shelter half.) Even with the rivulet nearby, water was at a premium. Precious little was available for bathing or washing their filthy clothes. The small amount they received had to be used for cooking or drinking.

To the rear of the Sharpshooters' line, just to the south of the Baxter Road, was an ice house. When the brigade had first occupied the area, Colonel Cutcheon of the Twentieth Michigan remembered that quite a few men put their lives in jeopardy by trying to get a piece of ice, and some had been killed in the process. It hardly merited the name "ice house," rather it was more of an ice well, with a small quantity of ice on the bottom covered with straw.[48] After the Sharpshooters fortified the area, they made good use of the ice. Procuring sugar and some lemons from the sutlers, they mixed up a batch of ice-cold lemonade; they were probably the only regiment on the line to have such an amenity in that hellhole.[49]

Not quite 200 yards in front of their position, the Sharpshooters stared at the Confederate gun emplacement they called the "Suffolk Road Battery."[50] One night part of the regiment worked straight through the dark hours, making sandbag embrasures for a pair of cannons. In the morning the rebels discovered the new gun emplacements and let fly with whatever artillery units they could bring to bear. During the latter days of July it seemed that most of the casualties were caused by cannon fire.[51]

A half mile behind the Sharpshooters was a battery of Union guns; the boys called them the "Petersburg Express." So many rounds were fired that there were bound to be mishaps. One day a shell burst just as it cleared the mouth of the gun. The men on the main line heard a "fierce howling" as a piece of the shell screamed through the air; a chunk of iron a foot long and three inches wide hit the breastworks just above the head of one of the Sharpshooters. Lieutenant Randall also made mention of a time when he was on picket. A shell from a U.S. battery in their rear exploded over the rebel breastworks, but a piece of it flew back to the Union lines and struck a Sharpshooter in the back. "Friendly fire" could be as dangerous as enemy fire.[52]

The Mined Fort

Colonel Humphrey moved his brigade out of the line during the daylight hours of 26 July. The men bivouacked in an open field shielded from rebel guns by a small belt of timber, near where the Sharpshooters had made their 17 June attack, but they did not tarry long.[53] The following day the Sharpshooters took over the extreme left of the Ninth Corps line, adjacent to the Fifth Corps. More digging consumed the next two days.

Another move had already been contemplated by the higher brass. The Sharpshooters joined the rest of the brigade at the Shand place on 29 July in the "Horseshoe," a bulge in the Union lines that was closer to the rebel entrenchments than any other point at Petersburg.[54] On a swell of ground fronting the Horseshoe—less than 125 yards away—loomed a Confederate fort known as Elliott's Salient. Four pieces of artillery and two South Carolina infantry battalions defended it. Throughout the month of July the soldiers who stared across the empty expanse of land toward Elliott's Salient referred to the rebel works as the "mined fort."[55]

The mined fort was the brainchild of Lt. Col. Henry Pleasants of the Forty-eighth Pennsylvania Infantry, one of the veteran outfits in Potter's division. A few days after his regiment had occupied the works directly in front of Elliott's Salient, Pleasants presented General Potter with the idea of running a tunnel to the rebel fort, filling it with gunpowder, and blowing it up.

Potter liked the proposal and sent Pleasants to Major General Burnside, who also endorsed it. Problems developed higher up, though. Major General Meade and his chief engineer, Maj. James C. Duane, saw no merit in the concept. No help would come from them. Pleasants had to find his own timbers to shore up the tunnel as he progressed. His men, anthracite coal miners from the Keystone State, also had to fashion their own mining tools. Figuring out how far to dig was another difficulty. Pleasants needed an instrument called a theodolite. There was one at Meade's headquarters, but Pleasants was not allowed to use it. Burnside had to send to Washington to get an outmoded version, but it worked.

Pleasants further had to rig up a system whereby his men would not smother in the mine from lack of oxygen. He did that by digging a ventilating chimney just behind his own picket line; a pipe ran the length of the mine and a fire drew out the bad air. Lastly, Pleasants had to dispose of the dirt from the mine without arousing the suspicions of the ever watchful rebels. Luckily, there was a ravine just behind his breastworks; his men cut bushes to hide the fresh piles of earth from the prying eyes of the enemy.

By 17 July the mine had hit a point directly below Elliott's Salient. The tunnel was 510 feet long. During the next week two galleries (one 38 feet long, the other 37) were dug at right angles to the mine shaft so as to completely undermine the rebel fort. Then, 8,000 pounds of gunpowder were stacked in the two galleries; sandbags wedged in the barrels of gunpowder so the force of the blast would be directed upward. Pleasants and his regiment had completed the job. Unfortunately, that was the only part of the entire operation to go according to plan.[56]

The rebels were not unaware that something was going on. It was common knowledge on the Ninth Corps front, and even the Petersburg newspaper carried a piece on the mine. The Confederates in Elliott's Salient sank a couple of countermines but did not succeed in locating the Union tunnel.

On 26 July General Burnside submitted an offensive plan that included the explosion of the mine. From this point on, everything went wrong for the Union forces. According to Burnside's plan, as soon as the salient was blown up, Gen. Edward Ferrero's Colored Division—Burnside's freshest outfit—would charge the demolished fort in a double column. The leading regiment on either side would break off and push along the rebel lines, taking the enemy entrenchments on both sides of the salient. The rest of the division would pass through the captured lines and aim straight ahead to Cemetery Hill, about 500 yards distant, and Petersburg itself. The First, Second, and Third Divisions of the Ninth Corps would follow the Colored Division into Petersburg.

General Meade refused to follow Burnside's plan; he feared Northern politicians would say that, if the attack failed, he had sacrificed the Colored Division. General Grant concurred with Meade. That being the case, Burnside now had only a day in which to make changes. All the preparations of the blacks had been for nought. The Colored Division had been training for this assault; the "smoked yankees" were ready. The three white divisions, conversely, had been exposed to horrendous killing for almost three months and their morale was low. Nonetheless, Burnside sat down to confer with the commanders of his white divisions on the afternoon of 29 July. The explosion was scheduled for the next morning. Unrealistically, Burnside had his three subordinates draw straws to see which division would charge the destroyed rebel works first.

Brig. Gen. James F. Ledlie picked the short straw—a most unfortunate choice. His First Division would be supported by the other two. Ledlie had only a few hours of daylight in which to inform his junior commanders of the place to attack, the ground to cover, and any subsequent actions they were to make.

Other preparations also had to be made. While the Ninth Corps took positions behind the mine entrance, other Union corps were set up as reinforcements on either side of them. Artillery emplacements, numbering more than 150 cannons and mortars, were readied. To draw as many Confederates as possible from the Petersburg lines, General Grant sent a mixed infantry/cavalry force to threaten the Richmond defenses north of the James River. That part of the plan worked admirably well. On the morning of 30 July, only 18,000 Confederates defended Petersburg. The Southerners, who were nervous about defending their capital, thought Grant's posturing in front of Richmond portended a major thrust.

The Mine Disaster

After sunset on the night of 29 July, Humphrey's Second Brigade moved into position near the old Shand house. A little after 10:00 PM the brigade reached General Warren's headquarters. In turn, each regiment learned of the coming day's scenario.

The Sharpshooters and their compatriots in the Third Division would rest in the rear of the breastworks until 1:00 AM. The men were to be awakened and provided with coffee and hardtack, then move into position near the front lines. At 3:00 AM the rebel fort would be blown up, the Ninth Corps would charge and carry the enemy's works, then advance into Petersburg, where they would eat a hearty breakfast.[57]

Few of the 15,000 soldiers of the Ninth Corps slept that night. Knowing that a desperate charge against a formidable foe awaited them before daylight did not predispose many men to peaceful rest. Spreading their blankets on the ground, many of them lost in thought, they looked up at the stars on that warm, clear night; some must have wondered if they would ever see them again. Others, like Colonel Cutcheon, disdained slumber; the last "probable moments of life seemed too short to be wasted in sleep."[58]

Lieutenant Randall's small company gathered about him that evening. In low voices they talked of the coming fight. Some of the boys gave him messages for family and friends in case they fell on the morrow.[59] Although the sounds were muffled, artillery units could be heard moving into position. All the Ninth Corps regiments took their places for the battle to come.

Slowly, the night faded away. At 1:00 AM the cooks brought up the hardtack and coffee. With little ado, the men filled their cups and sat in small groups, hardly speaking to one another. They awaited the inevitable order to fall in. Two o'clock passed, and then three o'clock. The Second Brigade finally received the order to form ranks and proceed to the covered way. Arranging their canteens and cups so as to make as little noise as possible, the brigade moved up.

Humphrey placed his men more or less into two columns. The right column was composed of the Sharpshooters in front, then the Second Michigan, and finally the Twentieth Michigan. On the left was the Forty-sixth New York with the Fiftieth Pennsylvania on their flank, and the Sixtieth Ohio and Twenty-fourth New York Cavalry (Dismounted) lined up behind them.[60] The other two white divisions, Potter's and Ledlie's, preceded Willcox's.

The covered way was jammed with soldiers. Willcox's men lay in a swale behind it; there was no room for them up front.[61] Ledlie's division waited to the left of the salient, Potter's to the right. Ferrero's Colored Division remained in the belt of woods a quarter-mile to the rear.[62] The regimental officers knew the mine was to be detonated at 3:30 AM, but the explosion did not materialize. The dark sky at the rear of the Ninth Corps turned gray, then streaks of red appeared. An hour passed. What was happening?

Unknown to anyone, the fuse to the four tons of gunpowder beneath Elliott's Salient had fizzled out at a splice. After an anxious hour's wait, Colonel Pleasants sent a sergeant and then a lieutenant into the tunnel to check things out. They respliced the fuse, lit it, and barreled out of the tunnel. Dawn had fully exposed the countryside.

At 4:45 AM, after a night of subdued excitement, tension, and dread, the mine exploded. Colonel Cutcheon jerked his head up:

> Suddenly, we felt the earth heave and tremble. We were in a position where we could see the explosion. A hillock of earth rose suddenly under the fort, then the earth opened and an immense column of earth shot into the air to the height of a hundred feet— From the center of this rose a column of white smoke. . . . Cannons, timber, men, great blocks of earth[,] all the *debris* of a fort, flew into the air and fell into the ruins, burying four companies of the 18th South Carolina.[63]

The falling wreckage filled the rebel trenches in front of the fort and covered much of the abatis in front of the salient. A great cloud of dust and smoke hid the blasted landscape for a few minutes; then Ledlie's division gingerly climbed over the breastworks and charged into the crater. As soon as the rebel fort blew up, the entire Union artillery line opened up "the most terrible

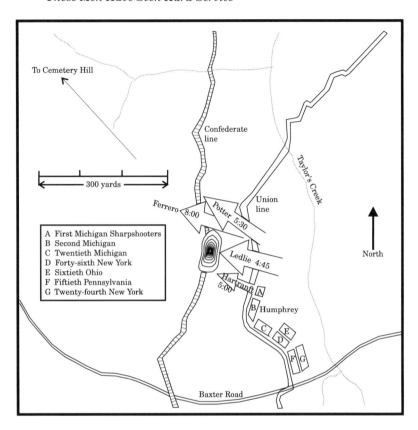

To Cemetery Hill

Confederate
line

300 yards

Taylor's Creek

Ferrero 8:00

Potter 5:30

Union
line

North

A First Michigan Sharpshooters
B Second Michigan
C Twentieth Michigan
D Forty-sixth New York
E Sixtieth Ohio
F Fiftieth Pennsylvania
G Twenty-fourth New York

Ledlie 4:45

Hartranft 5:00

A

B Humphrey

C

E

D

F G

Baxter Road

cannonade I ever heard," recalled Cutcheon. "It was awful."[64] Ledlie's men had no sooner gone over the breastworks than Hartranft's First Brigade charged the area to the left of the Crater.[65]

Soon a cheer was heard—a Yankee cheer—and all the men waiting knew the rebel line had been taken. Confederate prisoners, dazed from the explosion, were brought back under guard; the captured men said the whole Eighteenth South Carolina had been buried in the explosion. "We were all high with anticipation and felt confident that the city would be ours," recalled Maj. Claudius Grant of the Twentieth Michigan.[66]

Then came a long delay. No advance was made. Ledlie's men meandered through the Crater, an immense hole 170 feet long, 60 feet wide, and 30 feet deep. Piles of red clay (in some places huge blocks of it) littered the area surrounding the gashed landscape. There was no apparent effort to move the division up the crest to Cemetery Hill. The rebel lines on both sides of the Crater had been immediately abandoned by their defenders when the fort blew up. But the Union troops only invested the Crater and did not sweep into the trenches; the Confederates began reoccupying their breastworks on either side of the salient. Both enemy riflemen and artillerymen went into action.

A half-hour after the explosion, General Ledlie sought shelter in a bombproof ten rods behind the Union lines. He would be effectively out of the battle for its duration. At about 5:30 AM Potter's division charged the rebel emplacements over to the right. These Federals took 200 yards of rebel trenches north of the Crater, but the Confederate battery on their right ripped Potter's line to shreds, forcing many of those men to fall back to the comparative safety of the Crater.

Although Union troops crowded into and around the Crater and Union artillery pummeled the rebel lines, the Confederates on either side of the ruined fort poured a murderous hail of musketry into the area occupied by the two Ninth Corps divisions. Not only did rebel fire hit the men in the Crater, it effectively swept the 150 yards between the Crater and the Union lines.

The enemy battery on the Union right that had caused so many problems for Potter's men now inflicted numerous casualties on the Second Brigade, which was waiting for word to charge the rebel works. At least half a dozen men in the Twentieth Michigan were mangled by shell fragments. One young Sharpshooter was knocked unconscious when a musket ball struck him on the head. He lay as though dead for a few minutes, then roused himself, slowly picked himself up, and rejoined the regiment.[67]

The Second Brigade, seven regiments strong, had to wait until 8:12 AM before word came to advance. Ferrero's Colored Division had moved past Humphrey's men in columns of fours before 8:00. Full of enthusiasm, the Colored regiments could be seen moving out to the right of the Crater. They were to carry the rebel entrenchments on that side, while Willcox's division took the Confederate lines to the left of the Crater. Meanwhile, the enemy fire was terrible. Shelling and musketry made the men waiting in the trenches wonder if they would see another tomorrow.

Immediately after Ledlie's division charged the Crater, Hartranft's brigade of Willcox's division also went forward. Hartranft's men covered the ground in their front, hitting the rebel line left of the Crater, but Davidson's battery on their left raked them so savagely that they obliqued to their right into the destroyed rebel fort and the Crater, adding to the congestion already there.[68] Hartranft sent the Twenty-seventh Michigan to "clean out the rebels" on his left; after digging out one of the cannons in the rebel fort, he had it fired down his left flank, but he could not dislodge the Confederates there.[69] Only one brigade in the Ninth Corps—Humphrey's—had not yet made the charge.

Then the word came: "Forward!" Regimental commanders took the lead, expecting their men follow by example. The breastworks in front of the forward regiments were seven feet high, but that obstacle had already been conquered by the regiments preceding them. Officers had gouged out steps with their swords, and sandbags had been laid down to help the attackers over the forward trenches. Enlisted men stood ready to boost their comrades over.

Sword in hand, Colonel DeLand anxiously kept looking over the ground his men would have to cross. As he stepped up to mount the edge of the trench, a Confederate shell struck the berm in front of the breastworks, blasting DeLand with dirt and gravel and throwing him down. Captain Evans thought DeLand had been killed.[70] Helped up, yet stunned by the shock and the force of the stones, the colonel staggered to the rear, supported by Sergeant Case.[71] DeLand's side whiskers had been skinned off, as well as some of his scalp; he was dripping blood.[72] Capt. Elmer Dicey, the ranking line officer present, took command of the regiment.[73]

One of the first to scramble over the works was Color Sgt. Francis Urie, who held aloft the state flag, the regiment's only banner to enter the fray. What was left of the national colors were stored at regimental headquarters. The men farther back in the covered way saw the blue flag above them.

Officers shouted, and the men sprang forward as best they could, guiding to their right, toward the Crater. But not all men are heroes. One sergeant refused to advance, and Lieutenant Randall had to rough him up to make sure he accompanied the regiment.[74]

Behind and to the left of the Sharpshooters came the Second Michigan, keeping the guide right and adjoining them. Almost from the start, men became separated from their own regiments and units became intermixed. The ground was chopped up with debris from the explosion and rifle pits and entrenchments and abatis. Wounded men, on their own, and some assisted by their comrades, were trying to get back to the shelter of the Union lines. Cannon blasts and musketry cut holes in linear formations. Early as it was, the sun's heat promised a hot day.

As was the prevailing custom at that time of the war, few officers had any insignia of rank on them other than their swords. Colonel Cutcheon, his sword tied to his wrist by a handkerchief, followed the Second Michigan with his own regiment.

Rifle pits in front of their own lines slowed and fragmented the Union advance. To form any sort of cohesive line was impossible. Corpses littered the area; groups of men—Confederate prisoners, scared Federals, walking wounded—pressed back to the Union lines. The abatis in front of the enemy lines, as well as the secondary trenches running in front of and behind the main one, further confused the attacking forces. When the Union attackers reached the rebel lines, they found a bewildering labyrinth of dugouts, pits, trenches, and covered ways. Worse, "a tornado of bullets greeted us," recalled Cutcheon. "Many times I felt the breath of bullets on my face, and once it seemed to burn." [75]

Forcing the recalcitrant sergeant into the ranks had slowed Lieutenant Randall down a bit, and he ended up a few rods behind the regiment. He saw casualties up and down the line. In particular he noticed Pvt. Charles Carter (Co. K) fall before the Sharpshooters reached the rebel defenses. A Maryland Indian, Carter had joined the Sharpshooters during the campaign; he had hardly been with the regiment one month before dying under that blazing morning sun at Petersburg. [76]

Crossing the hundred odd yards of death, the Sharpshooters pulled apart the rebel abatis "under a heavy fire" and reached the left flank of the enemy fort, where they took cover with the Second Michigan immediately on their left. Rebels held these breastworks, and between them the two regiments took a score of prisoners. [77] Behind the Second Michigan and to their left was the Twentieth Michigan, which hit the rebel line and forced the surrender of 30 more Confederates.

Ordering the prisoners to come out of the breastworks, Colonel Cutcheon yelled at a rebel first lieutenant to hurry up. The Southerner held back; the irate Cutcheon raised his sword as if to strike the man. The reluctant rebel hurried out of the trench; just as he jumped, he was hit by a bullet from his own side. The wounded man begged to be taken to safety, but Cutcheon was not even able get his own wounded off the field at that time. He gave the rebel a drink of water and a rubber blanket to ward off the sun, which was burning its way through the haze of smoke and dust, and left the man. Cutcheon never saw him again.[78]

As soon as the Twentieth Michigan charged the enemy, the regiment to its left, the Forty-sixth New York Infantry, also climbed over the breastworks. On its left was the Fiftieth Pennsylvania. Not keeping its guide right, the Forty-sixth separated from the Twentieth. Believing it was on its own, the Forty-sixth hesitated in the face of a blast of canister and musket balls, then broke and ran back to the safety of the Union trenches, forcing the Fiftieth back with it. These two regiments, in turn, by stampeding through their reserves, the Sixtieth Ohio Infantry and Twenty-fourth New York Cavalry (Dismounted), forced them to retreat as well.

Much of the blame for the debacle at the Crater was later laid at the Forty-sixth New York's doorstep. The regiment was severely censured by both Colonel Humphrey and General Willcox. Except for their disgraceful retreat, Humphrey commented, "there is no doubt but the whole line would have been carried and the troops occupying it captured, and the achievement of the object for which we set out in the morning rendered more than probable."[79]

Confederate artillery and gunfire had forced the small Second Brigade toward the relative safety of the Crater. The Sharpshooters and the Second Michigan were now in the left of the destroyed rebel fort. Men from at least four Michigan regiments— the three from Humphrey's brigade and the Twenty-seventh from Hartranft's—were in this section of the fort. There were also two brass cannons and a countermine dug by the Confederates, which was about 30 feet deep. Lieutenant Randall looked into the pit and saw several dead rebels at the bottom of it.[80]

Men from various regiments helped man the cannons. Two Sharpshooters distinguished themselves that day as artillerymen, 1st Sgt. Charles H. DePuy (Co. H) and Pvt. Charles M. Thatcher (Co. B). DePuy was one of the "old soldiers." Although only 22 years old at Petersburg, he had earlier served in Battery D, First Illinois Light Artillery, from August 1861 to February 1863 when he was discharged for disability. Afflicted with "incipient consumption," he surely did not belong in the army, but after only a few months of convalescence he enlisted in the Sharpshooters. He had missed a good part of the present campaign by being confined to hospitals throughout May and June. But his experience as an artilleryman was put to good use when he reached the redoubt. Thatcher joined DePuy and some heavy artillerymen from the Fourteenth New York in manning the two cannons.[81]

The Twentieth Michigan, the left-most section of Union soldiers on the line, was initially outside of the fort. Cutcheon's regiment pushed the rebels back about 50 yards, then took cover from the battery firing from their left. The colors of the Sharpshooters, the Second Michigan, and the Twentieth Michigan flew over the enemy's works. No Union flags were on their left. So heavy was the Confederate fire in this part of the Crater that Color Sergeant Urie had trouble keeping the flag aloft. It was continually struck by enemy slugs.[82]

The Confederates had mustered enough strength by this time for a counterattack. For all practical purposes the Union assault had already shot its bolt, and the attack had hopelessly bogged down. No real advance beyond the Crater had taken place, although this was imperative. The rebel entrenchments on either side of the Crater had not been overrun, either.

The main problem was threefold. First, there were no division commanders on the spot in the Crater to get the men set up for a push to Cemetery Hill. Second, the rebel batteries on either side of the Crater could not be silenced. Third, time was quickly running out for those in the Crater itself. There were brigade commanders in the pit, but the men were so hopelessly intermixed that it was impossible to sort them out by brigade.

General Ledlie saw almost none of the battle. Still taking succor in a bombproof behind the Union lines, he found comfort in some medicinal brandy proffered by a surgeon of the Twenty-seventh Michigan. His only order, which became less viable as time passed by, was to charge the heights. Unbelievably, General Ferrero had joined him.

General Willcox, though not in a bombproof, was essentially ineffective as well. Willcox did watch the fighting, materially aiding his men when asked, but he did not go into the Crater. Colonel Hartranft sent word back to Willcox that he could hold his position if ammunition were supplied. Willcox had already prepared for such an exigency and had sent in 10,000 cartridges carried by the men of the Fifty-first Pennsylvania, Hartranft's old regiment, some of whom died in the crossing.

A wild yell informed the Union troops that the Confederates were mounting a charge. The Colored soldiers, who had taken the rebel lines to the right of the Crater and were trying to form in the open beyond the maze of rebel entrenchments, were hard hit and retreated back to the supposed shelter of the Crater. The white troops fared no better. Many hundreds had not left the Crater since entering it earlier that morning.

Colonel Cutcheon could not guess who broke first, the white or the black troops, "but it was the most fearful panic I ever saw or imagined."[83] Over and around the Second Brigade trampled the retreating soldiers. "It was fearful, sickening, *shameful, shameful,*" Cutcheon remembered. He shouted to his own regiment to pull back into the left of the rebel fort, there joining the remnants of the Second Brigade, where they helped repulse the rebel charge.

The attacking Confederates, two brigades of Virginians and Georgians, hit the line at the edge of the Crater with such vigor that not only the forward positions taken by the Ninth Corps were overrun, but much of the trench line to the Union right as well. In the attacking column was the Twelfth Virginia Infantry; its Company B was made up of local men who called themselves the Petersburg Grays. Fighting for their city, they probably had a bigger stake in the affair at the Crater than any other group of men on either side.[84]

Hundreds of Union soldiers surrendered in the onslaught. Many of Ferrero's men—the first black soldiers most of the rebels had ever seen—were killed outright. One Confederate remarked that his compatriots "seemed infuriated at the idea of having to fight negroes." During the initial ten minutes after the rebels had taken the line outside the Crater, "the whole floor of the trench was strewn with dead bodies of negroes, in some places in such numbers that it was difficult to make one's way along the trench without stepping upon them."[85]

Time crawled by. It was only 9:00 AM. The wounded and the unscathed lay in the dirt under a merciless sun. Men fell every second. Thirst began to plague the soldiers sealed in the Crater. Communications with the main Union line, which was only 150 yards away, were effectively broken. In what was left of the fort, the two remaining guns of the rebel battery, which were still serviced by DePuy, Thatcher, and a handful of brave infantrymen, belched their fury at the enemy. But there was no water to swab them out, and they became dangerous to load.[86]

If a man wanted to pull out at this juncture, he had to cross a gauntlet of angry lead and iron to reach safety. Rebel artillery pounded the spot, and mortars began finding the exact range; their shells dropped into the compact mass of men in and around the Crater.

Despite the cannon noise and musketry fire by both sides, the Union troops in the Crater paid close attention to the battery of mortars in their front. By watching closely and listening for the mortars' distinctive report, the men could see the shells reach their zenith and then try to dodge them as they descended. Lieutenant Randall saw one shell burst among 15 men in one corner of the redoubt. The explosion ripped them apart, and pieces of bodies and equipment further blasphemed the oppressive air in the Crater.[87]

Some men did actually manage to run back through the horrid storm to their own lines for water, taking along armfuls of canteens; then they made the trip back. Others made the two-way trip through the firestorm for more ammunition.

A line of bluecoats circled the inside edge of the Crater, digging their heels into the side of the pit and firing at the rebels. Men fell every second, almost all of them shot in the head; they slid down the wall, making a border of four or five dead men that hedged in those too scared or demoralized to fight back. Lieutenant Randall had to physically force some men to the edge of the redoubt. "Some would not fight & could not be drove to take a part in the action," he bitterly wrote.[88] Others tried to escape the inferno, but to leave they had to crawl over the lip of the Crater in full view of the rebels. Confederate artillery, mortars, and muskets took an ungodly toll on the Yankees trapped in the pit. If ever a hell had existed on earth, it flared there in all its horrible intensity.

At 1:30 PM Colonel Cutcheon found General Hartranft (who was not his commanding officer, but it did not matter; the command structure was so broken up). Cutcheon volunteered to run back to the main lines for water, ammunition, and help. The last resort would be a tunnel dug from the Union main line to the Crater, through which all manner of aid could go. In the meantime, men in the Crater were to dig from their side, "but the rebs got the range of that hole and plugged the bullets into it so thick and fast that no one could work on it."[89]

Racing frantically across the expanse and reaching his own lines, Cutcheon looked in vain for someone in authority to help the men in the Crater. Locating an aide-de-camp, he had him report the situation to General Burnside and beg him "for God's sake to silence their [the Confederates'] guns and mortars," because the Union guns were not firing at all.[90]

Willcox immediately dispatched requests to Col. Guy V. Henry, commander of a brigade in the Eighteenth Corps, and General Ferrero's Colored troops to begin digging three trenches toward the Crater—an unfeasible task, to be sure. The trenches would have to be more than 100 yards long, yet deep enough to conceal the workers. The construction would be under the most adverse conditions, but at this time no straw was too flimsy to be grasped.

Back in the Crater, hellfire continued unabated. Some men cowered in the redoubt to the left of the Crater. Others died or sustained wounds there. Some men ran back to their own lines, hoping beyond hope that they would not be struck as they raced the 150 yards to safety. Even now, the guns were far from silent. The sun was another enemy, further torturing those trapped in the Crater; the interior resembled a scene from an apocalyptic painting.

Eugene Taylor (Co. C) had been shot in the face, the bullet ripping through both cheeks. Lt. William Ruddock (Co. H) was much luckier. Hit in the chest by a spent slug, he sustained a severe contusion, but he was still alive. Forty-one-year-old Andrew J. Ellis of Ruddock's company was down with a broken right leg.

As always, the Indians were singled out for their composure under adversity. The officers had trouble forcing some men up to the breastworks to repel the Confederate attacks, but "the Indians showed great coolness. They would fire at a Johnny & then drop down. Would then peek over the works and try to see the effect of their shot."[91] Jacob Collins was down with a bullet in his left arm.[92] A number of the Indians who had been shot at the edge of the Crater lay dying near the bottom of the pit. One Ninth Corps officer watched them pull their blouses over their faces and chant their death song as they died a long way from the cool air and giant whispering pines of Michigan's north country.[93]

When Colonel Cutcheon returned to the main Union line, he saw the last Confederate charge on the fort. Blue-coated soldiers, at least those who could or would extricate themselves from the melee in the Crater, came tearing back to their own lines. After locating several of his own men, Cutcheon asked his few officers to gather the surviving remnant and form them under their colors, but the flag could not be located. Just then an enlisted man reached the regiment from the Crater. He told Cutcheon that the Twentieth Michigan's colors were still flying from the rebel fort.

It was about 3:00 in the afternoon. Cutcheon could see the flags of the three Michigan regiments of the Second Brigade still standing on the edge of the Crater, 150 yards away. The Sharpshooters' banner—the state colors given by Mrs. Austin Blair, which had been retreived from the sand of the 17 June fight— flew in the face of the onrushing rebels; Sergeant Urie kept it afloat till the very end. It and the standards of the two other Michigan regiments were captured with the men who were unable or unwilling to run back to their lines.[94]

A brigade of Virginians finally took the Crater and all those in it. During this last charge, the Sharpshooters held back and showed their character, giving the rebels a fight while allowing their comrades time to escape. Sergeant DePuy, the artilleryman, stuck by his guns to the last; the rebels captured him in the redoubt.

Some of the Sharpshooters, among them Pvts. Sidney Haight, Antoine Scott, and Charles Thatcher, covered the retreat as best they could before they pulled out. Scott (Co. K) was one of the last to leave the fort. Both Haight and Scott were conspicuous in their bravery and seemed to have charmed lives. During the fight both men were in front of the breastworks, ceaselessly firing at the enemy. When the last charge came they stood in the open and kept a brisk fire going. Only at the end, when all was falling apart, did they leave the fort, running the "gauntlet of shot and shell" to their own lines. Thatcher, Haight, Scott, and DePuy all were cited for the Medal of Honor for their exploits that day.[95]

Thatcher did not make it out of the Crater in time; he "continued to return the enemy's fire until he was captured."[96] The 18-year-old Haight was probably the very last Sharpshooter to leave the redoubt. As he fired his final shot, a rebel officer with sword upraised came at him, demanding his surrender. Haight lunged and rammed his bayonet into the Confederate. Not stopping to retrieve his weapon, Haight turned and bolted for the Union lines as fast as his legs could carry him. On his way across the shell-torn expanse of open ground he lost his cap and felt lead balls tear through the ends of his jacket. A bullet hit the heel of his shoe, ripping the sole back to within an inch of the toe; that sole flapped with every running step. The bullets spat around Haight until he dived into the Union trench out of breath, hatless, with a sole mostly pulled from his shoe, but safe and sound.[97]

The Sharpshooters' flag, shredded by minié balls, hung in the still, heavy air. When the Confederates overran the edge of the Crater held by the Sharpshooters, a rebel sergeant, J. W. Connell of the Twenty-second South Carolina Infantry, snatched the banner from Sergeant Urie and walked off with it.[98] The rebels took nineteen other Union flags that day, including the colors of the Second and Twentieth Michigan.

As the victorious Confederates sent their prisoners to the rear, Union artillery kept up a steady cannon fire, and the prisoners had to dodge their own shells. Lieutenant Randall helped Brig. Gen. William Bartlett of Ledlie's division to Petersburg. Bartlett had lost a leg during the fighting on the Peninsula in 1862; sometime during the day at the Crater Bartlett's wooden leg had been smashed. While hustling the prisoners out of the Crater, one rebel private noticed Bartlett's predicament and thought to add some levity to the situation. "General," he drawled, "you are a fraud. I thought that was a good leg when I shot it."[99] His attempt at humor fell on deaf ears.

Randall was stripped of his accoutrements—field glasses, pocketknife, money, and hat—and moved along with the hundreds of other captured men to about three miles behind the rebel lines. There the entire motley collection—officers and enlisted men, wounded and whole—encamped for the night.[100] On his way, the young lieutenant "had a chance to see the effect of our fire on the enemy. The ground was covered with their dead & wounded."[101]

So ended Randall's first battle as a Sharpshooter. He would have been proud to hear what his men said about him as they related the events of the fight to Captain Murdoch when the latter returned from convalescent leave. Murdoch was one to damn a man for less than expected behavior; he also praised men for doing well. Writing his wife soon after his return to the front, he mentioned that "Lieut Randall was taken prisoner on the 30th— He behaved very brave on that day."[102]

Cannonading and sniper fire continued until evening, but the results of the battle were clear to all on both sides. The Army of the Potomac had been whipped again. A great hole in the Confederate line had been shored up, and the Federals had not one more inch of ground to their credit.

The Ninth Corps, which bore the brunt of the fighting, lost 3,828 men and officers.[103] Willcox's division took 659 casualties, the Second Brigade accounting for 216; of that number, at least

168 were from the three Michigan regiments.[104] The Twentieth Michigan lost 47 of the 110 who went into the charge. The Second Michigan had losses of 59, 38 of whom had been captured. The Sharpshooters lost 62 men, most of them unaccounted for.[105] Only later could the list be amended, and it was found that quite a few of the missing were dead or wounded.

The Detritus of Battle

The field as seen from the Union lines was a red gash across the earth. The ground from the exploded mine gave a ragged look to the landscape. A great chunk of clay, as big as a room, had been thrown from the salient and now sat in front of the mined fort. Black and white corpses sacrilegiously carpeted the expanse between the lines. A few rebels—very few—were among them. Wounded men crying piteously for help and water could not be aided in any way. Rebel marksmen made the best of the situation by blasting away at every blue forage cap that showed itself in the Union lines. An unrelenting fire from the Union line answered the Confederates. Many of the less seriously injured crawled into the Union lines that evening. Even though it was a clear night, some soldiers put their own lives in peril by creeping over the breastworks to help the wounded come in.

On the morning of 31 July, the same fierce sun that had baked the soldiers in the Crater now had no mercy on the injured. Cries of "Water, water!" emanated from the wounded who were too far from Union lines to have been helped the night before. That morning Maj. P. M. Lydig of General Burnside's staff, accompanied by Colonel Cutcheon who was serving as divisional officer of the day, showed a flag of truce. In a short while the firing in the sector ceased, and the two officers marched to the Crater. Halfway there, they were met by a rebel officer and his attendant. Major Lydig presented a letter from General Burnside requesting a cease-fire so that the wounded could be gathered in and the dead buried. Confederate authorities refused to entertain the petition. The "rules of civilized warfare" prescribed that such a request emanate from the army commander, not a lowly corps commander. The staff work continued while more men died of their wounds on the open field.[106]

During the daylight hours of 31 July the rebels kept up a sporadic fire, at times desultory, at other times quite terrific.

Hundreds of dead and wounded comrades lay in plain sight, but it proved impossible to bring them in. The sun was merciless in its intensity, and the stench from unburied bodies and parts of bodies sickened veterans of many campaigns. The rebels did allow some water to be taken to the wounded, but no bodies, alive or dead, could be removed from the field.[107]

Rumors of a truce raced up and down the lines all day, but none came. Headquarters finally hammered one out; it went into effect for four hours—from 6:00 to 10:00 AM on 1 August. Ninth Corps surgeons and chaplains accompanied gravediggers and hospital attendants. Where a hundred men had lain wounded at battle's end, only a dozen still clung to life at this hour.

Rev. Henry E. Whipple, a Hillsdale College professor and father of Lt. Frank Whipple (Co. B), went with the Third Division burial detail. At the time he served with the U.S. Christian Commission. "I embraced the opportunity to survey more clearly the horrible scene," he wrote home a few days later. He was aghast at the butchery.

Blackened, bloated caricatures of men covered with flies exerted an unimaginable horror on the landscape.[108] The fortifications on both sides were filled with sightseeing soldiers—men who only minutes before had not dared show themselves to the enemy. Some rebel officers strolled over and spoke to their counterparts in the burial parties. High-ranking enemy officers, including Gens. A. P. Hill, Bushrod Johnson, and William Mahone, were seen looking out of the Confederate works.

A South Carolina captain, crude in the extreme, told Chaplain Jones of the Twentieth Michigan "with a savage satisfaction, 'At any rate we piled your damned niggers up for you.'"[109] The largest pile of bodies lay closest to the Crater itself. The rebels who had captured the Crater interred 54 black and 78 white Yankees; others were buried in the adjacent trenches.[110]

Major Claudius Grant of the Twentieth Michigan kept count of the number buried by his command. "We buried 180 negroes and 30 white men."[111] All told, about 400 men were interred on the field.[112] The bodies were laid out in rows, and shallow graves were dug. With no services, "coffinless and shroudless our gallant brothers were buried," intoned Reverend Whipple. While looking at a separate grave for three officers, Whipple spied a piece of paper protruding from the pocket of one of the men. He took it, then realized it may have been the man's last letter from home; it was postmarked Ionia, Michigan.

The bodies were covered with earth stained by their blood. Shortly after 9:00 the burial details began coming in, their ghoulish work finished. At 10:00 AM the picket gun signaled an end to the truce, and bullets from both sides started flying over the fresh graves.[113]

The Blame

As in all defeats, the blame had to be allotted. Too many things had gone wrong. Almost immediately General Meade instituted a court of inquiry made up of Gens. Winfield Scott Hancock, Romeyn B. Ayres, and Nelson A. Miles, all handpicked jurors. The men of the Ninth Corps received no justice from this packed court. What the generals decided surprised no one. The Battle of the Crater, they said, was a Ninth Corps fiasco, and "almost everybody connected with the Ninth Corps [was] at fault."[114]

There was another investigation, and the feared Joint Committee on the Conduct of the War, made up of Congressmen who demanded the war be a crusade against everything the Confederacy stood for, questioned every Ninth Corps general available for testimony. Even Meade and Grant sat before the committee. General Ledlie felt the sting of the committee first. Ledlie's sitting out the battle in a bombproof with John Barleycorn for companionship caused more than a few sets of eyebrows to arch. A devastating censure on Ledlie provoked his dismissal from the front a few months later. In the meantime, he had no actual command.

Six months after the "Mine Disaster," as the survivors dubbed it, Col. Byron Cutcheon wrote to Michigan's senator Zachariah Chandler, who was serving on the committee, asking for some sort of resolve:

> Allow me to say that the report of the Committee on the Conduct of the War on the "Mine Disaster" of July 30th 1864 meets the views of the troops in this Corps exactly. I participated in that charge, and have some very well defined view[s] in regard to it. I am most surprised that no one has been cashiered for it, for there is no doubt that "some one blundered."[115]

Colonel Cutcheon had correctly surmised the general feeling toward Ledlie. He would not be missed, commented Cutcheon. "It was an unfortunate day when he came to us."[116] Gratefully, the army would not be plagued with his presence any longer.

General Ferrero, the commander of the Fourth Division who had sat with Ledlie in the bombproof during the battle, must have had some high-ranking friends. Transferred to Bermuda Hundred east of Richmond, he retained division command. Generals Potter and Willcox received some blame, but they could live with that; neither was demoted or transferred.

Major General Burnside came in for most of the criticism. Meade had thwarted his every attempt, including the idea of digging a mine in the first place and then using the blacks as shock troops—and hindsight showed that Burnside was probably right in both instances. Despite this, the commander of the Ninth Corps received a heavy dose of opprobrium for the disaster. Why, the committee wanted to know, were the engineers not sent to the front lines to facilitate the first rush of troops over the ramparts? Why had no thoroughfare been cut through Union obstacles before the mine exploded?

Burnside was irate, and decided his country could do without him. When President Lincoln refused to accept his resignation, Burnside asked for a leave of absence, which was granted. He traveled back to New England where he sat out the rest of the war, no longer a potential scapegoat.

The Bitter Dregs of Defeat

At midnight on 1 August, the Second Brigade pulled out of the trenches. For two weeks Humphrey's men would be off the front line. New muster rolls were drawn up and the men received their pay. It was also a time for writing letters to loved ones. Some officers had the onerous duty of composing letters for those who could not—the dead, wounded, and captured. The casualty report stunned Colonel DeLand. Out of the 100 riflemen who had charged the Crater, the Sharpshooters had lost 62 men.[117]

DeLand had returned to his tent after his wounds were dressed. He resumed his duties after two days' rest, although severe headaches and fainting spells continued to plague him.[118] On 1 August he began the tough duty of penning letters to the parents of his missing officers:

> Mr. O. N. Conklin—I regret to inform you that your son Edwin is reported to be wounded and a prisoner. . . . he was a brave boy, and

I had recommended him for a promotion to a 1st Lieutenant. . . . Edwin was one of the pluckiest of the lost.[119]

Ed Conklin had known of the recommendation; his appointment as acting first lieutenant had come through on 7 July but was never officially confirmed.[120] Conklin was captured in the Crater and died insane on 30 November 1864 in the Danville prison pen in Virginia.[121]

Back in the days when the war was only a distant adventure, Conklin became Ed Buckbee's first recruit. Schoolmates and best friends, the two even dressed alike, as friends often do; so closely did they resemble each other that relatives of the two confused them from a distance. As first sergeant of Company F, Conklin had won the respect of his men by never showing fear or being intimidated by any of them, even though there were some trying men in his company, notably Mose Snay.

No word reached the regiment about Conklin's fate until the next spring. By that time Adjutant Buckbee had escaped from prison and was now in charge of the regiment. A man named Phillips from the Twentieth Michigan had been imprisoned with Conklin and brought back word of him.

A few mornings later, Mose Snay, the Detroit tough Conklin had subdued on the train trip in Indiana when the Sharpshooters were chasing Morgan's horse thieves, sauntered into the commander's tent. With no attempt to salute or make any motion of respect, Snay handed over a cup and said, "This cup was the one Sergeant Conklin always used when he measured out the sugar and coffee for the Company. I know that your folks knew his, and I thought perhaps you might want to send it to his mother." Buckbee knew Snay as a sordid character, "absolutely unprincipled," who never hesitated to use his fists. He was brave in battle, but a bully in camp. He had never showed this aspect of his temperament before. Buckbee made sure Conklin's mother received the cup.[122]

Cpl. Ed Shaw (Co. F) suffered his third war wound at the Crater. He had been hit twice at the North Anna River on 24 May, in the right arm and on the right side of his head. At the Crater he was again shot in the right arm.[123]

Pvt. Nelson Conklin (Co. C), officially listed as missing in action, never appeared on a list of prisoners. More than likely his body was one of those buried between the lines. Back in the Dearborn days Conklin had deserted the regiment; after two months a provost unit had found him and returned him to the arsenal. Conklin served a short stay in the guardhouse and went on to become a model soldier. While at Camp Douglas he had served as a nurse in the post hospital. Now he was officially one of the missing and probably occupied an unmarked grave in Virginia.[124]

William Dillabaugh (Co. I) also had his name appended to the missing in action list. No further word was ever received of him; it became evident that he, too, had died in the Crater. His bones lie in a nameless grave.[125] William B. Northrop's (Co. H) right leg had been fractured by an enemy bullet; the 40-year-old never fully recovered from the trauma and died on 15 August. The bullet that hit young Joseph Nichols (Co. E) had torn into his left shoulder and then traveled down into his chest; he died of complications.[126]

The Indians had taken a beating on 30 July. Survivors remembered that Charles Carter and Moses Williams had died in the fighting. Only Jacob Collins, whose arm had been smashed by a rebel ball, appeared on the wounded list. Six other Indians were missing, and only one of them ever turned up on any list of survivors. Gravely wounded Indians had been noticed by other men in "the horrid pit"; they had either died there or shortly thereafter.

DeLand himself had lasting effects from his injuries. At first judged superficial, the wounds caused by the shellburst resulted in years of headaches and fainting spells.[127]

At least 32 men were either missing or prisoners. Included in the total were Capt. Elmer Dicey (Co. B), who had led the regiment into the battle, and Lts. Charles G. Conn and William F. Randall. The regiment was a mere spectre of its former self. DeLand remained the only field officer on duty, and he had but four line officers present for duty. The regimental quartermaster was sick; the surgeon and chaplain were on detached duty with the division; and the sergeant major was out of action with a wound.

Listing every single man currently available, DeLand came up with a total of 155, but many were on detached duty in hospitals or recruiting stations or on temporary leave. Counting cooks, pioneers, musicians, and anyone on the front lines "for duty equipped," he came up with only 90 officers and men. Company K was down to just ten enlisted men, and he almost despaired of augmenting its numbers. Signing up white soldiers was difficult enough; enlisting Indians was almost impossible. Only a sergeant and a corporal were left to lead Company K.

What DeLand needed was a "good man who can speak indian [sic] and who has influence among them." What he did not have was a man qualified either to recruit more Indians or to lead a company of them. To this end he petitioned Michigan's adjutant general, John Robertson, for help. An order authorizing the recruitment of "1 or 2 cos. of Inds." was issued by Robertson's office, but very few Native Americans would make their way to the regiment.[128]

Pvt. Amos Farling, who like most of the Sharpshooters probably never gave a thought to any other than white people, found the Indians formidable fighters. Serving with them, forced to be with them on the firing line, and depending on them had given many white Sharpshooters a new appreciation for the Indians of the Old Northwest. "If the Indian is so willing to shed his blood in defense of the country which he can scarcely call his own, how much more readily should we take up arms and go forth to do service in a cause so near and dear to us," asked Farling rhetorically.[129]

Fittingly, 5 August was declared a national day of fasting and prayer; coming so soon after the Crater debacle, it signaled that all was not well with the nation or the army. Services appropriate to the occasion were conducted in regiments and brigades throughout the army.[130]

To the men in the ranks, the war was lasting forever and there was no relief in sight. The Battle of the Crater, handled as badly as it was, "came near putting an extinguisher upon us," one man in the Second Brigade said, speaking for all of his compatriots. "That was the gloomiest period in our history."[131]

CHAPTER 11

I Must Have More Help

Resignations

Capt. George Murdoch of Company I returned to the regiment on 8 August.[1] He had been wounded in the fight of 17 June, and had convalesced in Michigan. Murdoch came back to find a full-scale siege in action. He also learned that he was the senior (and only) captain with the regiment. Colonel DeLand was his sole superior. Almost immediately, command of the the Third Company was relegated to him. His second-in-command was 2nd Lt. James S. DeLand.[2] At the same time Lt. Frank Whipple took over the Second Company. The regiment was still consolidated into four companies.[3]

During the past three months the attrition in officers had gone from bad to worse. Besides the dead and wounded, resignations cut back the number of officers present for duty. The latest to resign was Capt. Lucien Meigs, who left on 9 August. Meigs had suffered from various maladies before the regiment crossed the Rapidan. Although wanting to participate in the campaign, he "is really unfit for service and has deeply mourned his physical inability to take part with his brave hearted boys in their hard struggle." As a hospital steward, George Warren knew enough about shirkers and malingerers to pronounce judgment on any slackers, and he genuinely felt sorry for Captain Meigs, who wanted to join his men on the line.[4]

Although he had been gone for some time, Capt. Andrew J. Hall finally tendered his resignation the week before Meigs. He was already back in Michigan in his home town of Coldwater, trying to raise an independent battalion of sharpshooters.[5]

The Third Division stayed in the trenches fronting the "Horse Shoe" (as the men of Humphrey's brigade called the Crater) until 7 August, when they pulled out and moved to the rear. There, the paymaster finally caught up with the Fiftieth Pennsylvania and paid each man six months' back wages.[6]

For one blessed week the Sharpshooters and their compatriots rested, although the cannons were never silent, nor the musketry stilled. "Blessed" was not what the men called the weather. "It is very hot," wrote Captain Murdoch to his wife on 10 August, "and we cant hardly do anything for flies."[7] Even though they were in a "safe" area a mile and half from the front lines, there were still casualties. It seemed there was really no safe area, not even at the hospital. On 5 August a piece of shell struck Dr. Whelan at the aid station, hitting him in the right thigh. The surgeon sustained a severe contusion but stayed on duty.[8]

There had been so many casualties in Willcox's division that each regiment had to send men to help out in the division hospital. Colonel DeLand was required to release six men from the front. Looking for ways to bend the order, he detailed only three fighting men: Pvts. Benjamin Bell (Co. C), Daniel Teachout (Co. E), and E. H. Nichols (Co. I). The other three were young musicians who generally found themselves doing the non-fighting chores of the regiment anyway—17-year-old Charles M. Stephens, 14-year-old William Duverney, and Watson B. Meks.[9]

To add to the problems at the hospital, Assistant Surgeon Asahel B. Strong had resigned his commission on 9 July, citing "disability" as the reason. His resignation left the regiment with only one surgeon, Dr. Whelan.[10]

Dr. C. J. Wirts of Hudson, Michigan, had accompanied the Sharpshooters to the front, hoping to be assigned as assistant surgeon, but the regimental strength remained so far below par that he was not appointed. Wirts did find work as a contract surgeon at City Point and eventually decided against becoming a regimental doctor. At that point Dr. Whelan became almost frantic. "I am able to give them [the Sharpshooters] but a small portion of my time, being the Senior Surg. of Brig. with all of its duties, do discharges, and one of the Operating Surgeons in Div. Hosp. necessarily keeps me laboring all the time." Fortunately, a new doctor joined the Sharpshooters during the first week of August. Thomas Eagleson, formerly a hospital steward with the Eighth Michigan Infantry, received his commission as assistant surgeon in the regiment in late July. Impressed by Eagleson's "professional ability exhibited in the field and at the operating table," Whelan wholeheartedly gave his endorsement of Eagleson to Governor Blair for consideration.[11]

"Sergeant" Youngs

When Captain Murdoch returned from from Michigan, one man did not appreciate his reappearance. Before and during the contest of 17 June, Murdoch had had trouble with Benjamin Youngs of his company. He regarded Youngs as a coward and a shirker. Murdoch had forced him to accompany the regiment under guard and then compelled him to join the charge that evening at gunpoint.

When the flag of the Thirty-fifth North Carolina was captured that night, Youngs had to be ordered to take it from the rebel color bearer. Pvt. Theodore Nash for all intents and purposes had forced the Confederate to give it up. Nash was later killed on the line at the end of June, and General Willcox had promoted Youngs to sergeant for bringing in the flag.

When Murdoch returned to the regiment and learned that Youngs had claimed the capture of the flag for himself, his rage knew no bounds. He quickly demoted Youngs, who then complained to Willcox. Called on the carpet, Murdoch refused to back down, and told Willcox his version of the event.

Murdoch continued to believe Youngs was a coward. Nash remained the real hero, "always cheerful and never complaining[,] always ready for any duty." That Youngs should claim the capture of the flag while making no mention of the part played by Nash seemed totally reprehensible to Murdoch. For as long as the captain commanded Youngs, the latter was never treated as a noncommissioned officer.[12]

Youngs was not the only man chastised. Six sergeants and corporals lost their stripes for lack of courage in the Crater. While most of the Sharpshooters stood up to the enemy in the "horrid pit," others cowered or ran off. Some of the weakhearted would later win back their stripes, but for the present all were "reduced to the ranks" after being found "guilty of shirking from duty, and leaving their commands in time of action.[13]

In the larger picture, General Grant decided to tighten the noose around Petersburg. The Union army had effectively blocked the eastern approaches to the city. Now Grant intended to sidle west and cut the lifeline from that sector. His target was the Weldon Railroad, which ran into Petersburg from the south. The Army of the Potomac would have to stretch west about two miles in order to straddle the railroad line and hold it.

Colonel DeLand Tries Again

During the regiment's last day in the rear, Colonel DeLand caught up on some lagging correspondence. One of his letters, fired off to Capt. Thomas Mathews, brigade A.A.A.G., proved to be another exercise in futility. Where, DeLand wanted to know, were the repeating rifles his regiment needed? He ran through the history of his requests for adequate sharpshooting weapons for his men. In April, "a requisition was made through proper Head Quarters." He did not even receive a reply.[14]

In June, Capt. Andrew J. Hall (Co. H) had personally traveled to Washington with another petition. Hall delivered the order and received an affirmative answer from the appropriate authorities. He was told that "the Rifles would be forwarded in a few days," but no weapons for the regiment ever showed up at City Point. DeLand deluged the ordnance officer at City Point with repeated requests, but discovered that he had been duped again.[15]

Now the colonel wanted to know if there were any possibility at all of his men obtaining the coveted armaments:

> The Regiment was enlisted and nearly all tested as Sharpshooters, but has been compelled to serve as Infantry for want of arms, and we are quite anxious to know whether any steps have been taken to supply us with the promised Rifles.[16]

On 13 August Major General Burnside made the last of his arrangements to depart the Ninth Corps. His leave of absence had come through, and command of the corps was turned over to

Brigadier General Willcox, the senior division commander. The next day, though, General Meade appointed John Grubb Parke, Burnside's former chief of staff, as Ninth Corps commander. Wilcox reverted to division commander.

As if to underscore the change in commanders, the Ninth Corps moved up to the front-line trenches on 14 August, taking the place of Warren's Fifth Corps, which filed off to the left to the area around the Weldon Railroad. Sniping, cannonading, dirt, flies, adrenalin rushes, and exhaustion again became part of the daily routine for the Sharpshooters.

The regiment lost another officer even before their "rest" ended. Lt. Ira Evans, always in the forefront of battle, received orders to report to the secretary of war, Edwin McM. Stanton. Told "to go to Michigan and take charge of bounty jumpers and drafted men and bring them to the front[,] and I don't want you to let any of them get away," Evans tried to beg off the detail, but he could not dissuade the secretary. "It will rest you," retorted Stanton.

For the balance of the year, Evans performed this duty, but he hated the work. "I did not find rest," he later wrote. "But there was none of them got away from me. . . . I had to ask to be relieved; I couldn't stand the work."[17]

The hot weather continued as the Sharpshooters took over their front-line assignment. Sharp skirmishing marked their arrival. No sooner did they take their new positions than they began to lose more men. Nineteen-year-old Pvt. Myron J. Fox (Co. I) narrowly missed being put permanently out of action; the day he reentered the trenches, a rebel minié ball skinned his right thigh.[18] On the very next day another 19-year-old, Pvt. Oscar McKeel (Co. C), had his skull grazed, resulting in a wound that kept him hospitalized until his discharge in May 1865.[19] Several days later Pvt. Noah Cain (Co. G) was shot in the stomach by a rebel marksman; he perished shortly after being carried to the aid station.[20]

The oppressive weather broke at 4:00 PM on 15 August, when a thunderstorm sent most of the skirmishers scurrying to their dugouts. The heavy rain washed out more than 100 feet of the works fronting the Twentieth Michigan, but the sniping continued. Repairs had to be made after dark.[21]

For a week the Sharpshooters manned the front line, dodging rebel hardware. And every night at exactly midnight the

Confederates shelled their position; the cannonade continued unabated until dawn.[22]

The Battle for the Weldon Railroad

Something big was happening to the left. All day on 18
August the sounds of battle drifted toward the Ninth Corps. Warren's Fifth Corps was trying to destroy the Weldon Railroad and
hold the area around it, but Lee's Confederates were giving Warren's men more than they bargained for.

On the night of 18 August most of the Ninth Corps moved
out of the trenches. The First Division (Ledlie's old outfit, now
commanded by Brig. Gen. Julius White) marched with Willcox.
Potter's division did not take part in the day's fighting; it was
stretched between the troops on the Weldon Railroad and the
breastworks near the Jerusalem Plank Road, trying to keep any
breach in the Union lines plugged.

Willcox's division rendezvoused near the Avery house.[23] With
only 78 men marching behind the colors, the Sharpshooters left
the trenches at 2:00 AM on the 19th. Since they were on the left
end of the line, they were the last to be relieved. Colonel DeLand
had felt ill that morning, so the regiment was led by the only two
officers still on their feet, Captain Murdoch and Lieutenant Hudson (Lieutenants Whipple and Bellair were still sick).[24] As soon as
they filed out, the Confederates in front of them opened up with a
terrific fire of shot and shell, prompting more than one man to
wonder if the rebels knew what they were planning.[25]

Cautiously moving out by a main road, the Third Division,
its flanks well covered in the wooded terrain, took its time
marching to the Globe Tavern on the Weldon Railroad. The tavern, also known as the "Yellow House," was a large colonial stop-
over where General Warren had established his headquarters.
The weather was terrible as usual, "very muddy and [it] rained
incessantly."[26] Willcox's men arrived at the tavern in the late
morning hours of 19 August. There was a big open field northeast
of the tavern known locally as the Dunlap farm; the division
bivouacked there. Coffee fires were coaxed into existence, rifles
were stacked, and stragglers drifted in. The rain kept falling,
now in torrents. Over in the Fiftieth Pennsylvania, the commissary sergeant distributed salt mackerel to the men. The Pennsylvanians accepted their fare with a soldier's fatalism. Tossing

their salted fish into water-filled holes to soak, the boys wondered how bad things could get.[27]

All of a sudden the crash of musketry erupted on their right and front. The long roll sounded and immediately the Ninth Corps veterans fell into formation. Federal cavalry skirmishers came back at a run. General White's First Division deployed to meet the rebel threat coming from the north. Willcox's men faced west, toward the woods on the left side of the tracks.[28] Hartranft's First Brigade took position to the right of Humphrey's Second Brigade, where it supported White's division. Not only small arms but also artillery fire crashed from the rebel lines. Some of the projectiles landed among the ambulance train, killing some horses and wrecking a few wagons. A New York surgeon died in the onslaught.[29] The rebel attack succeeded in throwing back much of Warren's corps in front of Parke's two divisions.

Pushing forward through the mangled brigades and regiments of Warren's Fifth Corps, Hartranft's men moved into the dripping woods on the right of the Second Brigade. When Hartranft's brigade entered the woods, it immediately came under heavy enemy fire.

The Eighth Michigan Infantry, on the left of Hartanft's line, was hit hard; its commander, Maj. Horatio Belcher was killed, and the regiment was forced back. It formed on the right of the Twentieth Michigan, the right regiment of Humphrey's brigade. Here, the Eighth stayed until Hartranft retired from the woods.[30]

Major Belcher was known as "one of the bravest men of the old 8th." Seemingly possessed of a charmed life, Belcher had survived a wound in the East Tennessee campaign the autumn before and a more serious one at Cold Harbor on 3 June. Brought to the aid station with five wounds received in the short fight in the woods, the major died that afternoon. His friends prepared the body and sent it home to Flint, Michigan, for burial.[31]

Humphrey's brigade had to do some considerable maneuvering in order to support Hartranft's brigade. Humphrey eventually filed his men about 500 yards to their left, toward the railroad line. The brigade then formed in two lines, with the Sharpshooters on the extreme left,[32] and was ordered to charge the rebels who were sheltered in their front. Their ostensible goal was to retake the line lost by General Crawford's division of the Fifth Corps. A gap had developed, and General Willcox now had to plug the hole.

Earlier, two Union brigades fighting in the dense woods, through which ran roads not charted on their poor maps, had been stunned by a Confederate attack that not only hit them in the flank, but rolled them up. More than 700 men of one Fifth Corps brigade were captured.

Humphrey's brigade now made ready to retake that same line. The hour was late; not much daylight remained. Humphrey advanced his men into the dark woods, toward the unsuspecting rebels. When in sight of the enemy line, the brigade charged with a yell, not even stopping to fire. "We came with so much determination and spirit," related one of the Sharpshooters, "and with so much suddenness upon the rebels their energies seemed paralyzed." [33]

Captain Murdoch's small command captured 12 Confederates.[34] The entire Second Brigade rounded up more than a hundred prisoners, together with a battle flag belonging to the Forty-seventh Virginia Infantry, which was captured by the Fiftieth Pennsylvania.[35] The rebels made only a feeble attempt to regain their position, and the brigade easily repelled them. Humphrey's command sustained only 54 casualties in the fighting. Of the total, there were 12 men killed, one officer and 38 men wounded, and 3 men missing.[36] Pvt. W. Samuel Chatfield of the Indian company was mortally wounded in the charge; he died the next day. A few other Sharpshooters received minor wounds.[37]

Accommodations for the brigade that evening caused quite a stir among the troops. The breastworks they captured were in a swampy area and were partially filled with water because of the incessant rain. Musket fire continued all night, so the men had to keep low in the trenches. The brigade waited out a long, wet, and muddy night with some trepidation. The warm rain kept them drenched as they expected an enemy attack.

Pickets crawled forward and tried to keep the rebels wary, during which an eerie incident befell the Fiftieth Pennsylvania. While out in front, with the rain falling and the lightning making movement seem everywhere, a Pennsylvanian mistook one of his own men for a rebel and fired, hitting him directly in the forehead. After the horrifying discovery, the picket carried the dead man's body back to his own lines and covered it with a gum blanket.

In the morning, while the men boiled coffee and munched on hardtack, the gum blanket was thrown off and the "dead" man sat up and asked for something to eat. The effect was startling.

The soldier had a bullet in his head, and the hole was quite obvious. His stunned comrades gave him a bit to eat and drink. Still groggy from the traumatic wound, he was led to the aid station. Not long after that, he died.[38]

During the early evening the Fifth Corps reestablished its line by connecting with the Second Brigade, which was to the left of the Ninth Corps. As to the rebels, at daylight pickets advanced and found the enemy had vacated the woods and could not be located in the open fields beyond.[39]

With the sector cleared of the enemy, Colonel Humphrey ordered the area policed and all small arms picked up. More than 500 weapons, almost all of which were from the Fifth Corps brigade captured by the rebels, were turned in. In one place dozens of rifles were still stacked, with accoutrements hanging from them. Quite a few shelter tents stood empty nearby. Even to the enlisted men, the previous scenario was plain. The Fifth Corps brigade had been taken completely by surprise, many of its men having taken refuge from the rain in their shelter tents. It was no wonder that the Confederates had bagged so many so quickly.[40]

At 10:00 AM the Second Brigade (after leveling the captured rebel works) pulled back from the line occupied the previous evening. The Sharpshooters remained up front as skirmishers until noon, when they were relieved by the Fiftieth Pensylvania.[41] The brigade then bivouacked in some open fields near the Globe Tavern.[42]

A little after noon the Confederates attacked the area around the Weldon Railroad again. Gen. William Mahone, who had lived in Petersburg before the war and consequently knew the region intimately, led the rebel onslaught. His division assaulted the breastworks formerly occupied by the Second Brigade. The pickets retreated before the rebels, but the brigade and its artillery held their fire until the Southerners reached the clearing. The Fiftieth Pennsylvania's skirmishers flew back to their own lines with the enemy on their heels.[43]

Ninth Corps batteries hit the charging Confederates with enough flying metal to stop their advance and then drive them back into the woods. The rebels did not press their attack.[44]

The affair remained essentially a Fifth Corps show, and Willcox's division pulled back to the right and rear of General Warren's men.[45] At this time Colonel DeLand joined his regiment (he had been ill when the Sharpshooters left the Petersburg front). Upon coming up, he reported to General White, who was commanding the First Division. White sent DeLand to set up a picket line connecting the two Ninth Corps divisions. DeLand relayed the orders to General Willcox, then moved his Sharpshooters up front. They were relieved the next morning.[46]

When Monday, 22 August, dawned, the Second Brigade moved up the right of the railroad in a reconnaissance in force about three-fourths of a mile to the Johnston house. No sooner did the men fall out of ranks and begin digging trenches and boiling coffee than they heard new orders for withdrawal. Amid grumblings and cursings, Humphrey's men shouldered arms and retraced their steps to the old bivouac. To add to the bleakness of the day, it started to rain hard again.[47]

The men stayed put the next day, but on Wednesday, 24 August, the brigade tramped a mile northeast of the Globe Tavern and helped construct a heavily fortified line near a new strong point in the Union defenses, Fort Howard. The Sharpshooters believed they would stay there a long time and were in the process of building a regular camp when frantic orders reached them to go to the aid of the Second Corps at Reams Station, which was about five miles to the south.

Even though the Union army had cut the Weldon Railroad, the Confederates still used it. The enemy stopped trains coming into Petersburg about a day's ride south of the Union position, off-loaded the goods onto horse-drawn wagons, and then drove west around the Union lines into Petersburg.

Maj. Gen. Winfield Scott Hancock's Second Corps went to work wrecking the railroad south of Warren's lines near the Globe Tavern. By the evening of 24 August the Second Corps had ripped up eight miles of track and was encamped at Reams Station, some five miles south of the Globe Tavern.

The Battle of Reams Station

Gen. Robert E. Lee sent 10,000 men to attack the Second Corps, roll it up, and retake possession of the Weldon Railroad. The rebels came perilously close to doing it. Hancock needed help, and fast!

At noon on 25 August Major General Willcox's division was told to proceed with all possible speed to aid Hancock. Willcox wanted to take his division directly south along the railroad line, but his orders were to proceed along the Jerusalem Plank Road to Shay's Tavern, where a road turned off to Reams Station. The route along the railroad was only five miles long, but the round-about way via Shay's Tavern stretched 12 miles. "Under a boiling sun" the division moved out quickly to the plank road near Fort Stevenson and then down the road to Shay's Tavern, where it passed part of Gen. Gershom Mott's division of the Fifth Corps, which was also on its way to help Hancock.[48]

Still a couple of miles from Reams Station, Willcox's column met a long parade of stragglers and deserters from the Fifth Corps, almost none of them wounded. Hancock sent word to Will-cox to detain these men, form them into regiments, then set up a line to cover the withdrawal of the Second Corps. Willcox was still trying to hammer out a defensive line using the shirkers when he received a peremptory order from Hancock to hurry his division to the battlefield. Almost at the double-quick, Willcox's men has-tened toward the crash of cannon and the rattle of musketry.

The light was fading. Willcox was still some distance from the fighting when he met the head of Hancock's corps coming off the field. The Second Corps had put up its poorest fight of the war this day. The Battle of Reams Station was a disaster, a black mark on the history of the corps. Hancock's lines had been broken, his breastworks taken, nine cannons captured, 610 men killed and wounded, and more than 2,100 captured, together with 12 colors and 3,000 stands of arms.

When Hancock met Willcox at the head of his division, Will-cox asked how the battle had progressed. "Licked like hell," was all the despondent head of the Second Corps could say. No other words needed to be uttered.[49]

Somehow or other Pvt. John Kedgnot was the only Sharp-shooter lost that day. Captured along with the thousands of Sec-ond Corps men, Kedgnot ended the war in a Confederate prison camp. His history with the regiment was interesting. He and his half-brother, William Duverney, were the first Indians to join the regiment, although they both served in Company B. Kedgnot de-serted in May 1863 and went his merry way until the provost marshal caught up with him in January 1864. Kedgnot served his punishment, returned to the Sharpshooters, and then accompa-nied the regiment into every action. Now the rebels had him and he would have to accept their hospitality for the duration of the war.[50]

Willcox's division covered the Second Corps' withdrawal un-til after midnight, when no more stragglers could be seen coming in. The division then followed Hancock's demoralized men, leaving rearguard duty to the cavalry. After a few miles, they made camp and rested until sunrise. Following the inevitable coffee boiling, the division "leisurely" made its way back to camp near the Aiken house. It remained there, about five or six miles from its former camp, until 29 September.[51] The men built fortifications between the Jerusalem Plank Road and the Aiken house. The entire brigade constructed abatis and breastworks, forts and redoubts. Particular attention was given to a rear line that would protect them from an attack on their left or rear. The lines here were not as close to one another as the ones near the Crater; consequently, there was not much firing and few casualties.

The weather continued to be hot, making life almost unbearable. Then it rained. It rained from the evening of 21 August until the 23rd, prompting one Ninth Corps wag to muse that "a little soaking, now and then, is more agreeable than otherwise, this hot weather, but not so the mud."[52]

Rest, Recuperation, and Consolidation

The Sharpshooters lost 24 men during the month of August; 11 were dead, 6 were hurt, and the others were either discharged or missing in action.[53] Taking stock of the regiment during this lull, Colonel DeLand wrote to Brig. Gen. Lorenzo Thomas, adjutant general of the U.S. Army, requesting the replacement of four officers already lost to the Sharpshooters. For the past month, he told Thomas, only three line officers had been present for duty and only two of those were currently with the regiment.

Capt. George N. Davis (Co. D) had not served with the regiment since 12 May; he was still in the hospital and showed no signs of improvement. Capt. Asahel Nichols (Co. E) had left the Sharpshooters on 25 May; he, too, was ill. First Lt. Robert F. Hill (Co. I) had gone down with sunstroke on 8 May, and had not yet fully recovered enough to return to the regiment. And 2nd Lt. Albert P. Thomas really exasperated the patience of the colonel; he "was wounded in the foot while [absent] from his Command." DeLand felt certain that Thomas had inflicted the wound himself in order to get away from the front. Nonetheless, DeLand needed more officers, and having these four removed from the rolls would help ensure replacements.[54]

In late July, before the Battle of the Crater, DeLand had

pleaded with Governor Blair (through Adjutant General Robertson) to replace officers through promotions within the regiment. He had asked that Capt. Elmer Dicey of Company B be elevated to lieutenant colonel, and Lts. Ira Evans, Frank Whipple, Joseph O. Bellair, and Charles G. Conn be promoted to captains. Further, he wanted 2nd Lts. Cyrenius B. Knight, William Randall, Henry V. Hinckley, Sgt. James DeLand, and 1st Sgts. Charles Lake and Edwin Conklin advanced to first lieutenants.[55]

"I hope for prompt action," DeLand reminded Robertson. "All the men recommended have been amply tried and merit is their chief commendation." He especially praised Second Lieutenant Conn: "His abilities and gallantry on the field has [sic] won for him the admiration and esteem of everyone in the Reg't."[56]

With the horrific casualty count produced by the unrelenting fighting in Virginia, a tightening of discipline ensued. To bring the matter to the attention of the men in the ranks, a lesson was made of one poor soul in Willcox's division. On Friday, 2 September, the division commander ordered his men out to witness the execution of a deserter. The soldiers marched to their assigned positions, and the brigade band, playing a doleful tune, preceded the prisoner, who was accompanied by a chaplain. The chaplain prayed a while with the condemned man. A guard then seated the prisoner on a coffin next to a freshly-dug grave, and an officer blindfolded him. At the command, "Fire!" the small guard carried out the sentence of the court, and the man pitched into his coffin, dead. Each regiment in the division then marched past the grave before heading back to camp.[57]

The overwhelming attrition caused by battle, disease, exhaustion, and the mustering-out of three-year regiments resulted in a reorganization of the Ninth Corps. On 1 September what was known as White's (formerly Ledlie's) division was written out of existence. One brigade went to Potter's division; the other was assigned to Willcox's. Then, on 13 September, the numbering of the divisions was altered. Willcox's division became the First, Potter's the Second, and Ferrero's the Third.[58]

In late November six new Pennsylvania regiments reported to Ninth Corps headquarters. They were formed into a provisional division under command of their fellow Pennsylvanian, Brig. Gen. John F. Hartranft. Two weeks later, Ferrero's Colored Division was assigned to the Twenty-fifth Corps, and Hartranft's provisional division became the Third Division of the Ninth Army Corps.[59]

Thousands of new recruits were being added to the depleted Army of the Potomac, and "old soldiers" were needed to provide some "stiffening." William Boston of the Twentieth Michigan wrote his aunt of the new commands from corps headquarters "ordering all detailed men to their Co[mpanies]. and filling their places with niggers[,] even to Co. cooks. [The blacks] get more curses than Copper[head]s here, but they are not to blame as I know of." The lowly ex-slaves, the contrabands, were the weak hens in the chicken yard; all who wanted, took advantage of them. Boston continued: "recruits and Convalescents keep pouring in every day, and the ranks are filling up fast."[60]

David Lane of the Seventeenth Michigan commented on the same activity. "This place has become a camp of instruction for recruits," he wrote. Then, tongue in cheek, he added, "The Fifty-fifth Massachusetts has received over two hundred 'Yankees' direct from Germany."[61]

With the transfer and addition of new and old regiments went new names and the switching around of old ones. Col. William Humphrey of the Second Michigan commanded the Second Brigade of Willcox's division until he mustered out on 30 September; General Hartranft then took temporary charge until 8 October. Then Lt. Col. Walter C. Newberry of the Twenty-fourth New York Cavalry (Dismounted) led the brigade for a week. Col. Byron M. Cutcheon of the Twentieth Michigan was put in command of the brigade at the behest of General Willcox, and held the post until 8 March 1865, when he mustered out. The final commander of the Second Brigade was Col. Ralph Ely of the Eighth Michigan; he retained charge until the end of the war.[62]

In early September all company commanders received a crisp order to "Arm and equip" all musicians in their commands. All able-bodied men were needed. Any and all noncombatants had to make a serious decision.[63]

Most of the former band members had already left the so-called Regimental Music Corps to serve in the ranks, receive their discharges, or become nurses in the Ninth Corps Hospital. Abner Thurber, former drum major, was now head nurse in Ward 13, Ninth Corps Hospital, at City Point.[64] Pvt. Charles M. Stephens (Co. A), a 17-year-old from Assyria, Michigan, accompanied by

14-year-old William Duverney of Grand Haven and Watson B. Meks (Co. H), had left the ranks at the end of July, when Colonel DeLand detailed them as hospital attendants.[65]

John W. Banta of Marshall, Michigan, Phillip Christman of Edwardsburgh, Michigan, and Albert Kubicek all transferred to the brigade band.[66] John Hamley, who was very ill during most of 1864 with chronic diarrhea, also managed to transfer to the band.[67] Benjamin Keyser left the regimental band after being detailed as a nurse in the Ninth Corps Hospital.[68] Charles Pickert had to leave the band because of ulcers on his legs; surgeons confined him to the general hospital at City Point as a patient.[69]

Thomas Jefferson Kessler had enlisted with his father in Elkhart, Indiana; his father died while the regiment guarded the Dearborn arsenal. When the band broke up, Kessler became the only band member to take his place in the ranks as a rifleman.[70] Jason Broderick, another of the volunteers from Edwardsburgh, had served as regimental bass drummer until he was detailed as ward master in the Ninth Corps Hospital.[71] William Crampton had left the ranks to play the cymbals in the regimental band. He had fallen ill in the spring of 1864 and languished in various hospitals for most of the year.[72]

On 10 September an impatient Colonel DeLand sent a pressing letter to Adjutant General John Robertson in Michigan. He had previously sent a list of new promotions to Robertson, and he now inquired on its progress. Having only three officers (including himself) on duty, he found the work load impossible to complete. "I *must* have more help," he pleaded. "Officers cannot stand such constant duty. Today not an officer in camp but myself & yesterday all of us were on duty."[73]

Less than a week later the regiment's numbers were augmented by returned convalescents, so that more than 200 men now filled the ranks.[74] Even recruits for Company K trickled in. Indian agent DeWitt C. Leach had signed up five Native Americans in Michigan's Upper Peninsula. Leach had accompanied the new enlistees to Detroit, where he told a reporter from the *Advertiser and Tribune* that the men—John Battice, 19; Amos Crane, 28; William Jackson, 26; George Ka-ba-ya-ce-ga, 30; and Robert Valentine, 23—"are all intelligent, and speak the English language." Leach added, they need "a close serveilance [*sic*] necessary to prevent their falling into the hands of strangers."[75] He need not have worried; each of the recruits had listed his occupation as

"Hunter."[76] These were men of the north woods, inured to hardship, with steady nerves and sharp eyes. They would quickly learn to become hunters of another kind. The Sharpshooters needed recruits such as these.

James S. DeLand finally received his first lieutenant's bar in late September. He took command of Company K; in two more months he would be captain of that company.[77]

There were promotions, long overdue in some cases, in the ranks as well. Richard Campbell and Clement Fessenden (Co. I) sewed corporal chevrons on their sleeves in September.[78] Cpl. Henry Call (Co. I), who received an arm wound at Spotsylvania, and Cpl. Antoine Scott (Co. K), repeatedly cited for bravery, became sergeants. Pvts. William B. Andrews (Co. I), John S. Sanders (Co. A), wounded in the arm at Spotsylvania, Wesley C. Williams (Co. F), and William Wick, who had sustained a wound at the Wilderness, received promotions to corporal. Unfortunately, at the same time, Sgt. John B. Calkins (Co. I), who had been absent since May, was reduced to the ranks.[79]

Good news came to the Federal army camped around Petersburg in early September. The light at the end of the tunnel could now be glimpsed. During the first week of the month Sherman's army marched into Atlanta, Georgia. It was an incalculable victory that infused a sense of worth into the war effort. In the middle of the month, General Sheridan routed a Confederate force in the Shenandoah Valley. A week later, he slammed into the rebels again.

The war might have an end after all, the men around Petersburg felt, but there was no victory here yet. In fact, most of September was spent somewhat peacefully, at least for the Second Brigade. There had been no major movements of troops, no large-scale fighting; instead, there was lots of digging and constructing trenches and forts. Chaplain Heagle figured that if the breastworks and abatis the brigade had built were put in a straight line, they would stretch two miles.[80]

The only break in routine was a sham battle on 15 September. On that day the Second and Third Brigades squared off for a mock engagement. "We charged each other," wrote a veteran of the Twentieth Michigan, "taking some prisoners on both sides and some of the boys got their fingers bruised a little."[81]

In the meantime, to keep the men busy and "up to snuff," every regiment drilled incessantly. "Barely enough men are left in the rifle pits to watch the enemy," related an enlisted man in the Seventeenth Michigan; "the rest are drilling—drilling in squads, by companies, battalions, brigades, and, twice a week, an entire division at a time."[82]

On 22 September came "Glorious news" of success in the Shenandoah. Cheers from thousands of throats informed the Confederates of a triumph of Union arms. But that victory was elsewhere, and the drilling continued.

One important logistical triumph, aside from all the defenses being built, was the military railroad line that ran from City Point to the trench lines around Petersburg. Northern ships ferried supplies by the ton to City Point on the James River. Only six miles from Petersburg, the goods were then loaded aboard trains and taken to the Union army's 20-mile siege line. Ammunition, food, cannons, fodder for horses and mules, weapons, tools, clothing—in short, all an army needed—was shunted over an unbelievably undulating line from City Point to the men in the breastworks. Running parallel to the siege lines, the railway kept the army supplied and returned with wounded and sick to the immense City Point hospital, which covered 200 acres and could take care of 10,000 sick and wounded men.[83]

Completed in early September, the railroad ran from City Point to Weldon Road.[84] More than a dozen locomotives, each pulling a score of cars, ran the line daily; every four hours another train off-loaded supplies along the line. The Confederates, though, had to keep tightening their belts, and General Grant had plans to make them cut another notch.[85]

On 27 September 1864 orders called for a grand review of the First Division of the Ninth Corps for Sunday, 2 October. There was much attendant moaning and groaning accompanying the command, but circumstances moved to cancel the pageant.[86]

The Battle of Peebles Farm

Lieutenant General Grant, still trying to cut all Southern lifelines to Petersburg, decided to take another sidestep around the city in late September. His strategy was a masterwork. He would attack the Richmond defenses in the north with elements of the Tenth and Eighteenth Corps. Simultaneously, the Fifth and Ninth Corps would strike at the Southside Railroad, which led into Petersburg. The Confederates would have to shift their forces north and south. The big show, though, was to be the southern one, near Petersburg. The rebels there were thin along the miles of trenches. They were hungry, too. Every yard of ground captured by the Federals meant the Southerners had to further spread out their men. Every rod of rail line taken meant less food and provisions for the rebel army.

Willcox's division was ordered to be ready to march on the morning of 29 September with four days' rations and 60 rounds of ammunition per man. Reveille sounded before daylight; at 4:00 AM the division commander started his men on a two-mile march to the Gurley house near Fort Davison, where Potter's Second Division waited. There the two divisions camped until the next day. The Fifth Corps was already in place near the Globe Tavern. All indications pointed to another confrontation with the rebels over to the left.[87]

The Tenth and Eighteenth Corps had opened the show the night of 28 September by making a concentrated attack on the Richmond defenses. As Lee maneuvered troops to meet that threat, the other segment of Grant's plan proceeded as scheduled.

Reveille again sounded early for the Sharpshooters on 30 September. Ready and in column at 6:00 AM, Willcox had to wait while the Fifth Corps and Potter's division preceded him. It was 10:00 AM before the First Division crossed the Weldon Railroad south of the Globe Tavern.

The Second Brigade saw Col. William Humphrey for the last time that morning. Humphrey had just mustered out and was leaving for City Point when his former brigade passed by. The old regiments remembered him from the days at Knoxville, Tennessee. The rest had served under him in most of the Virginia campaign. Many in the brigade had no idea he was leaving until this moment in front of the Gurley house.[88]

The man tapped to command the Second Brigade was Brig. Gen. John Hartranft. Always a fighter, this Pennsylvanian had the confidence of both his men and his superiors. Originally a political appointee, Hartranft had coloneled the Fifty-first Pennsylvania Infantry and had always been associated with the Ninth Corps. He was a known quantity. Even Colonel DeLand spoke admiringly of the man.

In the quest for a commander of the Second Brigade after the resignation of Humphrey, Colonel DeLand found he had been

passed over. It was originally decided to have Col. William Raulston of the Twenty-fourth New York Cavalry (Dismounted) take
the reins of command. Then, in a hierarchy where seniority often
counted more than ability, someone learned that DeLand was
senior to Raulston. Who decided that DeLand should *not* command the brigade? Only two men could have done so—Maj. Gen.
John G. Parke, Ninth Corps commander, and Brig. Gen. Orlando
B. Willcox, head of the First Division.

The evidence, which is circumstantial at best, points to
Willcox as the author of the canard. The tension between the
division commander and DeLand dated back to Morgan's inva-
sion of Indiana in the summer of 1863. Colonel DeLand had held
back his battalion until it was mustered into the Federal service,
with himself as colonel, even though Willcox was repeatedly blis-
tering the wires with telegrams urging him forward. Then there
was the business of the train trip back to Michigan that went
haywire, which DeLand had to explain to Willcox. Finally, there
was the official rebuke filed by Willcox citing the shameful retreat of the Sharpshooters at the Ni River crossing in early May.
Further, political enmity may have also played a role. Willcox
was an avowed Democrat, while DeLand was an obviously rabid
Republican.

But how could Willcox forestall DeLand taking over the
brigade? Willcox had just returned from a 17-day leave of absence on Thursday, 29 September. While he was gone, Hartranft
had commanded the division.[89] Upon Willcox's return, Hartranft
should have been sent back to his own command, the First Brigade; instead he took over the Second. The only explanation can
be that Willcox had no confidence in DeLand's ability. Hartranft
could not assign himself the command of the Second Brigade,
therefore someone (most likely Willcox) stopped DeLand from
taking over the brigade.[90]

The soldiers of the Fifth and Ninth Corps bided their time
for hours. Finally, at 9:00 AM the 20,000 Federals began filing out
in a westerly direction. Warren's men blocked the road for an
hour before the Ninth Corps was able to start out.[91]

On the morning of 30 September the three-year enlistments
of the Fiftieth Pennsylvania expired. Forty-six men and all but
three of the officers left the regiment. Then commanded by a
captain, the depleted unit marched with the brigade to Poplar
Springs Church.[92] Dense woods and tangled ravines gave way to

rutted roads, which in turn led to small openings euphemistically called farms. The Second Brigade under General Hartranft came in sight of Poplar Springs Church just after noon. The church, hardly recognizable as a house of worship due to its state of disrepair, would also give its name to the day's battle. About a quarter-mile ahead stood the Peebles farm. The Second Brigade turned north into Mr. Peebles's open fields. The Fifth Corps turned off before reaching Poplar Springs Church, and Potter's Second Division of the Ninth Corps went in on their left, between the Fifth Corps and Hartranft's brigade.

Quite a battle raged north and east of the Peebles house. An entire line of enemy breastworks was taken in a headlong charge. Col. Norvel E. Welch of the Sixteenth Michigan Infantry died leading his men into the rebel stronghold.

Hartranft's brigade was to anchor itself at the Clements house on its left and adjoin the Second Division on its right. In essence, Hartranft's command was the left flank of the army, and his job was to protect the left flank of Potter's division. After the Second Brigade tramped into the fields and faced westward, Colonel Cutcheon was detached with the Second and Twentieth Michigan. He led both regiments southwest a half-mile to the junction of Poplar Springs Road and Squirrel Level Road. He was told to hold the intersection and send small parties out along both roads to look for enemy videttes.[93]

As usual, the Army of the Potomac found itself stymied by poor reconnaissance. The maps for this portion of the front were again woefully inadequate. Distances were not marked with any degree of accuracy, and natural obstacles were depicted as being much smaller than they were.[94]

Hartranft called Cutcheon's unit back when nothing developed, and the brigade moved forward about a half-mile. It now formed a line of battle. The men stood a half-mile north of the Peebles farm, directly west of the Pegram house.

An almost impenetrable swamp lay directly in the path of the regiments on the left. A scouting party from the Second Michigan explored the swamp to learn if the brigade could proceed through it. After a short time the detachment returned, saying the men "could pass it, but with difficulty."[95]

During their wait for the scouting party to return, the men of the Second Brigade heard the roar of battle swinging to their end of the field. The Fifth Corps, off to the right, had its hands full. Potter's division, just to the left of the corps, was getting into

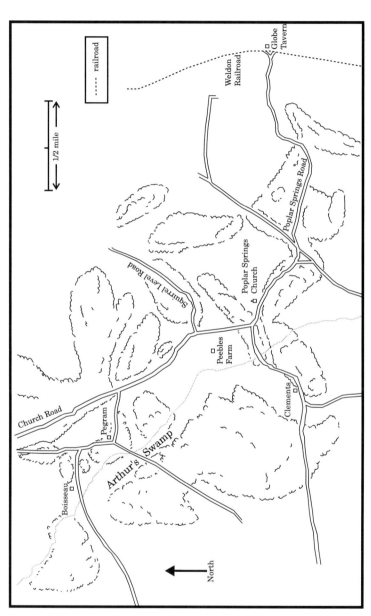

Peebles Farm Area, September/October 1864

the thick of things, and now artillery fire was hitting Willcox's division.[96]

Potter moved his division forward into some woods and came out on either side of the Boisseau house, another quarter-mile beyond Pegram's. The Second Brigade followed Potter, staying to his left. Skirmishers went ahead about 150 yards to a small crest. Then they saw it—the Boydton Plank Road, today's target—but that was as close as they would come to it. Only three-quarters of a mile away, the road was a main highway into Petersburg and the only primary road still in rebel hands. No sooner did the skirmishers of the Second Brigade see the road than they saw the Confederate battle lines advancing toward Potter's division. Hartranft's brigade was squeezed into a narrow front; only 200 yards separated the swamp on its left to the left flank of Potter's division. Consequently, Hartranft had to form his line of battle behind Potter's left, covering the latter's flank. Hartranft's right was now in front of the Boisseau house.[97]

The cacophony of firing from both artillery and musketry on the right of Hartranft quickly reached a crescendo, yet the Second Brigade was hardly involved. Soon, two of Potter's regiments, the Thirty-fifth and Thirty-sixth Massachusetts Infantry, dashed out of the woods into the line of the Second Brigade. Most of the retreating Bay Staters were rallied and put back into position, albeit with difficulty. While that was going on, Hartranft was ordered to fall back. Though he saw no reason to do so, Hartranft pulled his brigade out of line very slowly.[98]

The Second Brigade could tell by the noise that the rebels were now at its right rear. Then the brigade felt enemy fire on its front and right flank. Potter's division was badly cut up in the woods, and a disproportionate number were captured. Of the 1,600 casualties that afternoon in the Second Division, more than 1,200 were listed as missing.[99]

As the remnants of Potter's division fell back, Hartranft slowly kept pulling his brigade back. The men did not panic but stayed in "good order." They reached the road, halted, and turned to face the rebels. With Potter's division still retreating, Hartranft had no option but to order his brigade farther to the rear. For the first time, Hartranft realized that his left flank was having problems as well.

As Potter's men fell back in confusion, Willcox's right became exposed. At this same time, Confederate cavalry charged the skirmishers on the left of the division. One man in the Twentieth

Michigan felt his brigade had a poor choice to make: "to be cut to pieces, to no good purpose, to be captured or to fall back."[100]

Hartranft ordered the Second and Twentieth Michigan to face west toward the rebel cavalry that was bothering that side, thus placing those two regiments at a right angle to the main line. A gap developed between the Second Michigan and the Sixtieth Ohio, so Hartranft pulled the Sharpshooters from their position on the right flank and sent them to fill the hole on the left.

The Sharpshooters no sooner reached their new position than the men began taking hits. Colonel DeLand was one of the first to fall, with a bullet in his left thigh. Captain Bellair went down with what he feared was a mortal wound. He cautiously opened his blouse, and (somewhat relieved, though still hurt) found "a severe contusion in my side" from a piece of rebel shell. First Lt. Kirke Noyes (Co. K) fell with his third wound of the war.[101] The skirmishers already in front of the Sharpshooters found themselves caught in a deadly crossfire, and the rebels swarmed among them, capturing dozens. Vanorman Strout (Co. D) was one of the few to successfully escape the Confederate net.[102]

At this juncture the Twentieth Michigan ran to the edge of the swamp they had previously scouted, abandoning its wounded on the field.[103] Although slightly wounded himself, Pvt. Ben Hosmer (Co. B) ran over to the prostrate Colonel DeLand. Taking two handkerchiefs, he fashioned a tourniquet to staunch the flow of blood from DeLand's wound. The rebels picked up both men. Captain Bellair and First Lieutenant Noyes also fell into their clutches.[104]

Watching the Second Brigade retreat, which isolated the three Michigan regiments, a rebel cavalry detachment dashed out of its cover at the left of the Union line and charged the hapless bluecoats, hoping to cut them off.

The Twentieth Michigan, seeing its line of retreat totally eliminated, decided to cut its way through the brambles, vines, and ooze of the swamp. There they lost Capt. Oliver Blood and Adj. Jacob E. Siebert, both of whom were wounded and captured. Several others were shot down and 19 were nabbed in the "impassible jungle of the swamp."[105] The Twentieth was so badly scattered that some elements, after wandering the countryside all night, did not rejoin the regiment until the next morning.[106]

When the rebel cavalry charged, Captain Murdoch kept the Sharpshooters together as well as he could, and there was no rout. While looking for a place to make a stand, he saw Colonel Hartranft's guidon. When he reached the flag, Hartranft told him, "Captain, rally your men and commence firing."[107] Up to this time the regiment had fired no volleys; in fact, few of them had fired at all. Confederate infantry was over on the right flank, and enemy cavalry charged the left flank. The rebel yell and shouts of "'Surrender, you Yankee Sons of Bitches,' could be heard in every direction," but the regiment held its ground and threw two volleys into the advancing enemy. Captain Murdoch proudly maintained that as soon as the Confederate cavalry withdrew, the rest of the brigade formed on the Sharpshooters.[108]

After being pushed out of the Boisseau farm, the division formed in front of the Pegram house, with the Second Brigade on the left. The Twentieth Michigan established a fortified line that ran into the infamous swamp on their left.

The fight was barely over when darkness set in. Skirmishers took their positions 100 yards in advance. At midnight the brigade withdrew and adjoined the left of the First Division, near the Clements house. The men dug rifle pits and then hunkered down in them until a gray dawn heralded a new day.[109]

The Sharpshooters lost three officers and 21 men in the battle near the Peebles farm. Altogether, 18 officers and men were captured. One man, Anthony J. Thison (Co. A), was killed outright; another, Daniel H. Spicer (Co. I), died of wounds. Most of the others, including Colonel DeLand, Captain Bellair, and Lieutenant Noyes, were thought to be wounded. The wounded had to lie on the field all night in the cold rain.[110]

DeLand, after being hit in the leg, found himself a passive spectator to the rest of the battle. Half an hour after he went down, he saw the charge of the rebel cavalry on the Twentieth Michigan as it was trying to get through the swamp. Captain Blood of the Twentieth was wounded and captured in the swamp, and then taken to a log hut where little could be done for his injuries. He died that same night. Colonel DeLand was carried into the same shanty the next morning, and there he saw Blood's body. Because they were officers, DeLand, Bellair, and Noyes were shipped to Libby Prison in Richmond. Their wounds were further treated, and they were paroled in a week.[111] DeLand would not be able to thank Ben Hosmer for saving his life for 26 years.

Another captured Sharpshooter was Benjamin Youngs, the man who claimed to have captured the flag of the Thirty-fifth

North Carolina on 17 June. Paroled by the Confederates in October, Youngs returned home to Canada for his 30-day furlough. He never returned and was later classified as a deserter.[112]

Some of the other captured men were not as lucky. Six of them died in Southern prison camps; and another, Mason M. Sutherland (Co. E), died immediately after his repatriation.[113]

Siege Lines—More Entrenching

Rain fell during the first two days of October, but fighting continued at the Pegram farm. The Ninth Corps dug more trenches and fortified them both days; Hartranft's men feverishly worked on the defenses as the battle crept closer to them. Early on Sunday, 2 October, the Second Brigade, as part of a general advance by the entire corps, moved in line of battle to the Boisseau house. Although expecting fierce rebel resistance, the corps found little opposition. A permanent line was established there, and two new permanent forts, Fisher and Welch, were incorporated into their defenses.

At 3:00 PM Mott's division of the Second Corps passed to the rear of the Ninth Corps, formed battle lines, and charged a rebel fort 800 yards to the left of the Second Brigade. Willcox's division watched the spectacle, noting the charge "was not pushed with much spirit or persistence." Since it was only a reconnaissance, it "probably accomplished the object intended," rationalized Colonel Cutcheon of the Twentieth Michigan.[114]

The Second Brigade stayed in the area until 8 October, furnishing work parties for construction of the forts and cutting down many of the trees in front of their lines. Timber was needed for abatis, slashings, and breastworks. Pvt. Joel Haynes (Co. C) estimated that "we have got about fifty acres of woods cut down in front of us and they [*sic*] is no less then [*sic*] a thousand men chopping night and day."[115]

Haynes found plenty to complain about in the food department. After his watch in the rifle pits, he came back to camp to eat his breakfast. He found "it was hard Tack and coffee and some boiled pork that you could smell forty rods. . . . [W]e are going to have beans for dinner and tomorrow I guess we will draw soft bread[.] I tell you things are high here[.] [B]utter is ninety cents a pound[,] apples from five to ten cents apiece and poor at that."[116]

Water remained scarce. Haynes grumbled that "we cant get water enough to drink here and that is not fit to drink." But the defenses built by his corps could withstand any assault. "We are strongly fortified here[;] it would take a large force to drive us out[.]"[117] The new forts incorporated into the defensive lines— Fort Cummings near the Clements house, Fort Welch by the Pegram house, and Fort Fisher close by the Boisseau house—made the new line seem impregnable. The Second Brigade camped between the Pegram and Peeble houses.

On 8 October the First Division set out on a reconnaissance in force in light marching order. The men filed out west of the Clements house to try to get as close as possible to the Boydton Plank Road. The high brass wanted an idea of rebel strength in the area. A heavy skirmish line preceded the main body. It did not take too long to ascertain the enemy's position; after an exchange of shots, the division redeployed and marched back to camp in the dark.[118]

No sooner did the Second Brigade get back to its camp than a change in commanders took place. General Hartranft relinquished control of the brigade that same evening. The brigade then was temporarily commanded by Lt. Col. Walter C. Newberry of the Twenty-fourth New York Cavalry (Dismounted). There was no problem with Newberry being in command. The two rivals for the position—Colonels DeLand and Raulston—had both been captured on 30 September, and neither would return to the front. DeLand's injury would force his discharge from the service, and Raulston would be killed in a botched escape attempt from Danville Prison.

A Prodigal Returns

Captain Murdoch, who now commanded the Sharpshooters, was stymied by the appearance of one of the old recruits in the middle of October. Pvt. William H. Wilder rejoined the regiment after a hiatus of ten months. Wilder had been court-martialed in December 1863 for desertion while the regiment was still at Camp Douglas. Found guilty, he was sentenced to be:

confined at hard labor with Ball & Chain attached to his right leg during the balance of his term of enlistment, to forfeit all pay and allowance . . . and at the expiration of service to be dishonorably dismissed from service.[119]

Showing a pardon to his commanding officer, Wilder said he had been ordered to rejoin the Sharpshooters. Murdoch sent him to Lt. James DeLand who commanded Companies I and K. The chastised soldier served the remainder of his enlistment with his former bunkmates and was mustered out as a corporal with the rest of the Sharpshooters at the end of the war.[120]

Few new men entered the regiment at this juncture in the war. Actually, Captain Murdoch had to keep stripping soldiers from his command to serve in all sorts of capacities. On 20 October he detailed Pvt. Lewis H. Adams (Co. C) and Pvt. Lewis H. Fenton (Co. G) to serve as the Sharpshooters' contribution to the provost guard.[121]

Colonel Cutcheon of the Twentieth Michigan assumed command of the Second Brigade when the Twenty-fourth New York Cavalry (Dismounted) left the brigade on 16 October. The men of the Twenty-fourth New York jubilantly tramped to City Point to finally join the ranks of the cavalry. Their mounts and equipment were ready at last! Lieutenant Colonel Newberry's regiment became part of the Army of the Shenandoah's Second Division under Maj. Gen. George Crook.

The Peebles farm was home to the Second Brigade until 29 November. It was a pleasant area. Unfortunately for the men in the ranks, the relative quiet meant their officers had to find some means of keeping them occupied. Large, open fields constituted much of the farm, so brigade and regimental drills became a regular occurrence.

There were, of course, occasional forays into the real war. On the morning of 20 October the Sixtieth Ohio occupied the front line as a picket. Only a short time after taking over the entrenchments, a rebel force attacked the Buckeyes. So quietly and quickly did the Confederates overrun the line that they captured one officer and 54 enlisted men.[122]

The Battle of Hatcher's Run

Near 9:00 PM on 26 October orders came down that the brigade better be in marching order at 3:00 AM on the morrow, with four days' rations and 60 rounds of ammunition per man.

Captain Murdoch readied his 200 men and talked things over with his two present officers, Lt. James S. DeLand and Lt. Milo Dyer. Since Lieutenant Whipple was still sick, Sergeant Major Case would take over an officer's responsibilities on the march.[123] The new orders effectively canceled Captain Murdoch's inspection, which had been set for 27 October.[124] Just before pulling out, a slight switch in personnel occurred. Cpl. William B. Andrews took the place of Charles Renardin (Co. G) as the baggage guard. Renardin had recently become a sergeant, and he was needed in the ranks. Someone else now had to stay behind and guard the men's personal effects.[125]

The movement proved to be no surprise to the enemy. Two nights before the Ninth Corps left the line, the rebel pickets had called to their counterparts on the Second Brigade front and told them not to be so quiet, because they knew "we was going to move on the left."[126]

Before sunup on the Twenty-seventh the brigade was ready, and as soon as it was light enough to see, Cutcheon's brigade led the division to the left. The Forty-sixth New York stayed behind to guard the camp.

This time the target was Hatcher's Run. The Second and Fifth Corps took to the field early because they had farther to go. Near the Boydton Plank Road the Second Corps found itself "badly used" in a tussle with the Confederates.[127]

Cutcheon's Second Brigade picked its way through the woods for two miles. Chaplain Heagle accompanied the Sharpshooters as they advanced "over open fields and through the woods, up hill and down hill, on the level and on ground that was rough and rolling," before coming up against enemy breastworks and abatis on the east side of Hatcher's Run at 10:00 AM. All the time the brigade was moving for position against the rebels, it was under cannon fire. Confederate videttes, under cover of brush and trees, kept up a steady rifle fire. The Sharpshooters, "in proportion to the number of men present for duty," put more men "on the first line during this engagement than perhaps any other in our remembrance," the chaplain proudly reported.[128]

General Willcox, though, was content to learn the proximity

of the enemy, and his division did little fighting other than skirmishing. Consequently, few casualties were numbered in his command. The Second Brigade lost 30 men, including five from the Second Michigan who were captured.[129] Charles Walser (Co. D) was also nabbed by the rebels. In addition, there were five Sharpshooters hit in the reconnaissance. Charles Harris (Co. H) was the most seriously hurt, having been mortally wounded in the hip and back. The others received lesser hits.[130]

Shelters were dug for the night, and slashings were thrown in front of their position. That night a cold rain fell, and the men slept on their arms. The next morning at 11:00 AM the brigade tramped back to its camp at the Peebles farm, reaching it by evening.[131]

Something happened that night which puzzled the whole division for quite some time. Not long after dark, wild yelling was heard from the direction of the enemy lines. "The Johnnies cheered vociferously," reported Chaplain Heagle, "and this morning we could hear the lively *tooting* of their railroad engines." There were no rebel victories they knew about. "If we actually suffered defeat" at Hatcher's Run, mused the chaplain, "it is strange the army does not know of it."[132]

Captain Murdoch Examines the Rolls

Back in their old camping grounds, the Second Brigade reverted to incessant drilling by squads, companies, battalions, regiments, and brigade. To overcome the monotony, work details were appointed for the construction of various types of fortifications.

New recruits (mostly draftees and substitutes) joined the ranks of the Fiftieth Pennsylvania in October. A number of them received poor notice during the reconnaissance of 27 October. Capt. G. W. Brumm, commanding what remained of the regiment, had all those who exhibited defective soldierly qualities paraded on the drill ground when the Fiftieth returned to camp. Each maladjusted warrior had a placard hung on his back denoting his failure under fire. "I am a volunteer skirmisher in the rear," read one. "I skulked," read another. "So did I," reiterated a third. "I too," chimed in another. The old soldiers of the brigade read them all with derision and laughter.[133]

Over in the Twentieth Michigan Colonel Cutcheon wrote home to his wife, telling her the state of the regiment. The Twentieth was "in good health and spirits. We number about 175 muskets," he wrote. When the Twentieth had crossed the Rapidan, 353 voices had answered the roll call; at that rate there would be hardly a corporal's guard left whenever the war ended.[134]

On 11 October 1864 Captain Murdoch sat down to ascertain the status of the officer corps of the First Michigan Sharpshooters. Besides himself, only two commissioned officers were with the regiment. Col. Charles V. DeLand, now an exchanged prisoner of war, was on his way back to Jackson, Michigan, to convalesce from his wound. Surgeon Arvin Whelan had left the front on 26 September on sick leave; he was home in Hillsdale. Capt. George N. Davis, sick from May through August, had taken a position on a board examining hospitals around Indianapolis. Capt. Asahel Nichols was recruiting men in Michigan after his illness. Capt. Joseph O. Bellair, wounded, captured, and paroled with the colonel, was home on furlough. Lt. Thomas Fowler, wounded on 17 July, was still in a hospital in Annapolis. Lt. Samuel Hudson had languished in some hospital since late September.

Lt. Ira Evans was on recruiting duty in Michigan, principally collecting draftees and deserters. Lt. George Fowler, wounded at Spotsylvania, was also convalescing and recruiting in Michigan. Lt. Robert Hill, sick since May, was probably still in Michigan; his actual whereabouts were unknown. Lt. Guy Newbre, also proclaimed sick, was last heard from at City Point, but no one seemed to know what had happened to him. Lt. Albert P. Thomas, wounded 12 May, had reported to Camp Distribution at Harpers Ferry, West Virginia, for light duty, and then turned up at Annapolis. Lt. Cyrenius Knight, shot on 8 June, had been discharged in October for disability. Lt. William Ruddock, injured in the Battle of the Crater, was still on leave of absence. So many were gone (some for dubious reasons), and so few were left.[135]

Chaplain Heagle gave voice to the same question often asked by the rank and file: "Why are not more of our officers present with us?" It was a rhetorical question at best. Even Captain Murdoch could not fully hope to answer it.[136] Murdoch made inquiries on the absent officers but found little useful information forthcoming.

In November Murdoch requested the adjutant general's office of the Army of the Potomac to dismiss Capt. George N. Davis from the service. No official correspondence on Davis's situation had been communicated to the regiment since Davis had reached Indianapolis, stated Murdoch. Davis's duties in the Hoosier state "were to examine all enlisted Men in the Military Hospitals of Indiana and order such as were pronounced fit for duty to the field."[137] Unsaid in Murdoch's letter was the admonition that no one had examined or pronounced Davis fit or unfit. Murdoch wanted Davis either returned to the Sharpshooters or dismissed from the army. The adjutant general's office contacted Davis, and he received his discharge for disability before the end of the month.[138]

Trying to eliminate the chaff from the regiment, Murdoch pursued the problem of Lt. Albert P. Thomas. Learning that Thomas "had been drawing pay regularly from the Government, and now has a comfortable detail" at Camp Distribution in Harpers Ferry, Murdoch fired off an angry letter to the division A.A.A.G., Capt. Thomas Mathews, requesting that immediate action be taken against Thomas.[139] Murdoch stated unequivocally that Thomas had been absent from his command at the Wilderness and had seen no fighting at all at Spotsylvania. Furthermore, "he received his wounds while absent from his company and at the rear, and under circumstances which lead to the belief that he is also guilty of self mutilation."[140]

Murdoch then added Colonel DeLand's official report on the Battle of Spotsylvania, which cited both Thomas and Lt. Guy Newbre for "dishonorable conduct" and recommended they both be dismissed "from the service for having absented themselves from their commands on the field and for cowardice."[141] Murdoch asked that Lieutenant Thomas be ordered to the regiment for trial, but he was too late. Thomas had already requested a discharge for disability, which had been granted on 13 September, nearly two months previously.[142]

Desertion from the Hospital

A number of Sharpshooters pined away in hospitals, sick from wounds or the infections and debility following prolonged bouts with incipient illnesses. For some, the confinement led to depression so deep that they had to escape the hospital or lose their sanity. Instead of being released to return home and receive better care and food, the men responded listlessly to little treatment and the boredom of hospital routine. A few men decided that home was better, and it did not matter what the army thought about it.

Some appeared on muster lists as "absent wounded," which meant that no trace could be found of the man after he had been sent to a place for treatment. David Parkhurst (Co. A), wounded on June 24 in front of Petersburg, left the hospital to which he was assigned in October and returned home. Officially listed as a deserter, he later satisfied his inquisitors as to his whereabouts, and the charge of desertion was deleted from his record. He not only received an honorable discharge backdated to 29 August 1864, his comrades later elected him president of the First Michigan Sharpshooters Association.[143]

Parkhurst was not the only one to leave a hospital illegally. Jeremiah Tiner, at 47 one of the older men, had been wounded the same time as Parkhurst. By October he "deserted from hospital at Washington, D.C." No official ever received word from him again.[144] Wallace Betts (Co. C), wounded in the summer's battles and sent to a hospital, finally decided to go home on his own in September. He never reported to anyone in authority in the regiment again.[145]

There were too many absent men to trace down. Some would return, some would never be found. All Murdoch knew for sure was that there were too few on duty in front of Petersburg.

CHAPTER 12

Breastworks . . . Flankers . . . Bombproofs

Inspection

November 1864 began as had so many months before it—with an inspection. The first sergeants barked at the men to clean their weapons and themselves. Regimental inspection commenced at 9:00 AM on 5 November. To prolong the agony for the enlisted men, brigade inspection followed immediately thereafter. In fact, the inspection was a bit overdue. It replaced the one scheduled for 27 October, which had been canceled due to the excursion to Hatcher's Run.

Not only were the rifles, accoutrements, and clothing of the men inspected, but the camp streets had to be clean "and the interior of the tents arranged in as neat and tidy a manner as possible."[1]

The Election of 1864

Abraham Lincoln's opponent for the presidency in 1864 was none other than the vainglorious George B. McClellan. To the old veterans McClellan had given the army its soul, yet he was also the man who had failed to win the war with the best army on the planet. If the army were so invincible, why was it used so poorly? Lincoln wanted to push the war to its finality, a victory that would assure a united country. McClellan ran on a peace platform that seemingly would allow the Confederacy to exist as a separate entity. Why, many soldiers thought, are we fighting this war? Why have so many suffered and died? So the Confederacy could exist?

Wherever a hierarchy exists, there is generally a constant jockeying for power. Almost every organization—including the army—is prone to political conflict. As long as the men in the regiment abided by the Republican sentiment of their senior officers, all went well. Oftentimes, letter writers in the ranks complained via newspapers back home that their politics put them afoul of their superiors. Certain hometown weeklies—notably the Jackson *Eagle*, the Niles *Republican*, and the Detroit *Free Press*—pilloried Republican politics, politicians, and political military appointees. Colonel DeLand continually received vitriolic print.

On 29 October, just before the presidential and gubernatorial elections, the Niles *Republican* printed a letter from Cpl. Horace B. Seeley (Co. G), a hometown volunteer who had joined the Sharpshooters in June 1863. Seeley was no mere impressionable lad, but a 34-year-old veteran of all the regiment's battles.[2] Seeley was also a Democrat. His long letter, addressed to his "Fellow citizens of Niles City and Berrien County," called for an immediate end to the war.

The conflict may have had a noble purpose at first, Seeley wrote, and men had died for that exalted cause. "They fell trying to save the union, but not to liberate the nigger." Seeley expressed anger and shock over the unspeakable carnage produced by the fighting, and the ocean of graves that stretched from the Rapidan to Petersburg. "Fellow citizens," he pleaded, "how can you cast a vote to prolong manslaughter four years by reelecting Abraham Lincoln?" Vote for peace and Gen. George B. McClellan, he told them. "Bring back what few have survived this terrible campaign." Seeley then signed off with a request for a free paper: "Put on the wrapper [']Lincoln and Johnson,['] or it will not reach me, as there are no democratic papers or documents allowed in the army."[3] Seeley's letter soon caused quite a stir in the regiment.

The Presidential election took place on 8 November 1864. It provoked more than the usual politicking in the ranks. For some, the reputation of the Eighth Michigan Infantry was at stake. Col.

William Fenton, who had raised the Eighth and led it into battle for two years, was the Democratic opponent of Henry Crapo, the Republican candidate for governor of Michigan. Colonel Cutcheon predicted that "not a third of the Eighth Michigan would vote for Col. Fenton." Over in the Seventeenth Michigan, Willcox's "pet" regiment, Lt. Col. Frederick Swift "publicly pledged the vote of his regiment for 'Little Mac.' "[4]

When he was governor of Michigan, Austin Blair had campaigned early and vigorously for a law to enable the state's soldiers in the field to vote. "Surely," he declared to the legislature, "he who stands faithfully by his country in the shock of battle, may be safely trusted at the ballot box, though it should be carried to him at Vicksburg or Chattanooga." Michigan did pass a law allowing every absent citizen the right to vote—the only criterion was that he be in the military.[5]

Commissioners from the state canvassed all Michigan regiments, batteries, and detachments in and out of the war zones. Hospitals were combed, as were such disparate units as the 102nd U.S. Colored Troops (formerly the First Michigan Colored Infantry) and the Second Missouri Cavalry (also known as the Merrill Horse), which had three Michigan companies.

Joseph Warren of Detroit supervised the voting in the Second Brigade, First Division, Ninth Army Corps. The three Michigan regiments (the Second, Twentieth, and the Sharpshooters) all gave a substantial majority to Lincoln and Crapo. In the Second, the vote was 79 for Lincoln and 25 for McClellan. Lincoln received an impressive majority from the Twentieth, 135 to 53. The Sharpshooters cast 35 votes "for the diminutive figure with the big moustache and shoulder-straps" and 91 "for the ticket having on it the grand, honest face of Old Abe and Andy," reported Chaplain Heagle.[6]

"I never knew an election to pass off so quietly," related an enlisted man in the Seventeenth Michigan. "No drunken brawls, for whiskey could not be obtained. General Wilcox [*sic*] came over. . . . It had been confidently asserted that Wilcox [*sic*] would vote for McClellan, but he called for an 'Administration ticket' and deposited it in the ballot box."[7]

In all, Michigan's soldier vote totaled 9,402 for Lincoln and 2,942 for McClellan. Colonel Cutcheon had been correct; the Eighth Michigan failed to give even one-third of its votes to Colonel Fenton, Crapo getting 110 out of 164 cast. The "Stonewall Regiment"—the Seventeenth Michigan—went even farther, casting 148 votes for the Republican ticket and just 46 for the Democrats. Only four Michigan regiments—the First, Fourteenth, Fifteenth, and Sixteenth Infantry—gave McClellan a majority.[8] Cutcheon reported that "his division, with the gallant Willcox to lead them, vote and shoot the same way." As far as he was concerned, voting Democratic was equated with treason.[9]

As a whole, the Ninth Corps (and this included all regiments, not just the ones from the Wolverine State) gave Lincoln a resounding victory. General Parke reported 1,234 soldier votes for the president and 348 for McClellan.[10]

On election day, Cpl. Horace B. Seeley, letter writer and Democrat, was "reduced to the ranks." Captain Murdoch, still in command of the regiment, questioned Seeley about the authorship of the letter published in the Niles *Republican*. Seeley readily admitted his role. Murdoch, a Republican from Berrien Springs, a town only eight miles from Niles, threw the book at Seeley. Murdoch complained that the letter "contained an outrageous slander upon his brave comrades who have fallen and upon the living, remaining in the regiment,—a prayer for *ignominious* 'peace.'" He said Seeley lied when he asked "that a democratic paper be forwarded him in disguise in violations of rules and regulations which he assents to be in force." So, by giving voice to "gross falsehoods, for conduct prejudicial to good order and military discipline, and for expressing sentiments which totally unfit him to command any brave men," Seeley lost his stripes.[11]

The editor of the Niles *Republican* counterattacked with an editorial two weeks later. The election was long over. The Republicans had won handily, but the editor was not one to forgive and forget. Horace B. Seeley was a cut above most soldiers who sent letters to the paper. Others did so, "but each one would strictly forbid us publishing their letters as they said it would be almost sure to get them into trouble." The problem, exploded the editor, was that "no man can get promotion in the army unless he swallows the nigger policies of the administration and old wart Abe in the bargain."[12]

Return to the Petersburg Lines

Now that the election was history, more mundane matters involved the Sharpshooters. Dr. Whelan returned to the front after a few weeks of convalescence. As ranking surgeon, he again took command of the First Division field hospital. Occasionally, the U.S. Sanitary Commission representative made an appearance; on 7 November he distributed shirts to those sick and wounded men who had no extras. The dirty ones were collected by "the washerman, who is as indispensable as the cook."[13]

The field hospital at the Peebles farm was well laid out. There were tents for wards, hospital attendants, and officers. Even cooks and washermen had their own quarters. No sick or hurt man slept on the ground. At the very least each patient had a bed of poles covered with pine boughs, but straw ticks were more common. The wards were cleaned each day by a thorough sweeping, and evergreen trees, of which there were plenty in the surrounding country, decorated the grounds. They were planted on both sides of the road leading to the hospital. Ambulances entered the compound through an evergreen arch. A red shield denoting the First Division, Ninth Corps, hung below the boughs. An evergreen fence, made by driving stakes into the ground and entwining pine branches through them, surrounded the hospital. "This arrangement is all intended to please the eye of the sick and wounded, so as to take away the monotony and gloominess," recorded a member of the Twenty-seventh Michigan.[14]

A wild rumor swept through the Ninth Corps in early November. "We expect, too, General Burnside will be here, in a day or two, to take command of his old corps again," hoped an enlisted man in the Seventeenth Michigan:

> The event will be hailed by us with joy. Let others think of him as they may, he possesses the confidence of the Ninth Corps to an unlimited extent. The reverse is true of our present commander, General Parke.[15]

The rumor persisted, but it came to naught. The affable Burnside was out; like it or not, Parke retained command of the corps.

Another old face returned to the Sharpshooters on 4 November. Pvt. John Isaacs of the Indian company reached the regiment after a hiatus of 17 months. He and his brother William had enlisted in May 1863, but John deserted a month later. William served honorably in the regiment and was wounded in the fight of 17 June. John had some long explanations to make to quite a few people. Evidently he succeeded, for he served with the regiment until his discharge.[16]

On 29 November Willcox's division received orders to return back to the Petersburg trenches. At 10:00 AM the men started the ten-mile march from their pleasant camp, bidding farewell to the log huts and straight streets with wistful looks. After the exhausting and terribly bloody campaign of the summer, the Peebles farm, even given the incessant drills, inspections, and fortification building, had been far enough from the rebel lines to offer respite. Now it was back to the war zone.

Just three days prior to the move back to Petersburg, four more recruits joined the ranks. Three were assigned to Company E. William H. Senard, 19, and John Fishell, 27, had enlisted for three years; John A. Talbot, 18, had signed up for just one year. Another one-year enlistee, Frank Marquette, 35, who listed his occupation as "Hunter," entered Company K.[17]

The Second Brigade did some fancy marching on 29 November. From their quarters on the extreme left of the army, the men tramped to the extreme right, all the way to the Appomattox River facing Petersburg. There Willcox's men relieved Gibbon's division of the Second Corps. Arriving before dark, the various regiments were taken to their new shelters during the night. By the morning there were two Ninth Corps divisions in place on the front line.

On the river bank itself, where the picket line ran, the men of the Thirteenth Ohio Cavalry (Dismounted) made themselves at home. Another of the cavalry detachments used as infantry, the Thirteenth Ohio, joined the Second Brigade on 11 November. The regiment had formerly served in Hartranft's brigade. Disgruntled at being treated like common footsoldiers, the men of the Thirteenth stayed with the Second Brigade until they transferred to Sheridan's Cavalry Corps on 13 December. Until then, the 600 Buckeyes had to picket the line along the Appomattox River to Broadway Landing, a three-mile stretch.

The Forty-sixth New York garrisoned Battery V, which was on the right bank of Harrison's Creek, near the river. The Sharpshooters took over the breastworks from the river to Fort McGilvery, a large square fortification where the Page house had once stood. At least one Union battery occupied the fort. The Fiftieth Pennsylvania settled into Fort McGilvery, the Sixtieth Ohio

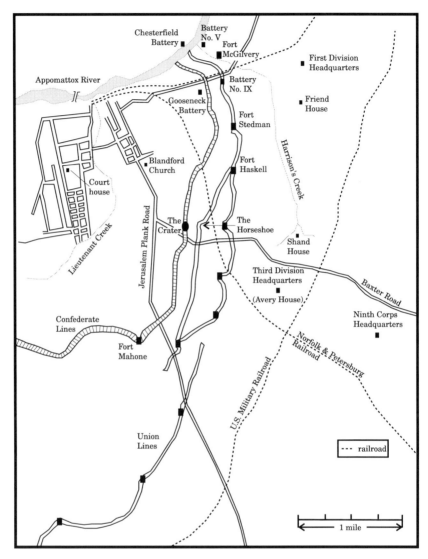

Siegeworks around Petersburg

guarded the breastworks from Fort McGilvery to Battery IX, and the Twentieth Michigan was in Battery IX, another enclosed fortification 100 feet square just north of the City Point Railroad.

Although it was a strong position, no artillery was stationed as yet in the fort.[18] The Second Michigan held the breastworks between Battery IX and Fort Stedman, where the Hare house had been.[19]

The regiments of the Second Brigade occupied these positions until the fighting ended in April. General Willcox set up his headquarters at the Friend house, while brigade headquarters were installed behind Fort McGilvery in a ravine. When the Thirteenth Ohio left the advanced lines on 13 December to join the cavalry corps, the Forty-sixth New York moved into the vacated position.[20]

Colonel Cutcheon came close to leaving the command post of the Second Brigade on 18 December. On that day he received his commission as colonel of the Twenty-seventh Michigan Infantry, a regiment in the First Brigade of Willcox's division; instead, he continued as commander of the Second Brigade. According to Cutcheon, the "change was made at the express and urgent desire of General Willcox, who apprehended the return of absent officers, senior to Colonel Cutcheon, in whose hands he did not wish to entrust the brigade."[21] There was also a tacit agreement between Willcox and Cutcheon that the Twenty-seventh Michigan would be transferred to the Second Brigade as soon as the division moved out of the trenches before Petersburg. The transfer never took place, because Petersburg fell as soon as the division moved out of the trenches and the war virtually ended.[22]

The Frontline Trenches

Unlike the camp at the Peebles farm, the lines here were very close to each other; only a couple hundred yards separated them. Rifle fire continued throughout the day, every day. Cannon and mortar barrages from both sides ripped through the air all too frequently.

The Second Brigade fronted three rebel batteries. The Chesterfield Battery was situated immediately across the river from Fort McGilvery. It was made up of heavy, English rifled cannons that could hit anything on the Union side from the river to Battery X next to Fort Stedman. Two rebel mortar batteries, the "Gooseneck" and the "Scab," were stationed in front of Fort Mc-Gilvery and lit the night skies with their pyrotechnics. These three Confederate emplacements caused untold labor in the Second Brigade; bombproofs, covered ways, and reinforced traverses had to be reconstructed and repaired after every cannonade.[23]

A bombproof was built by excavating a deep hole in the ground, covering it with logs, and then covering the logs with several feet of earth. One of the rebel officers in the Chesterfield Battery visited the Union emplacements that were within range of his battery after the close of the war. He was decidedly impressed "with the heavy traverse works, both on the picket line and the mail line, that were manifestly erected to protect against our enfilading fire."[24]

Usually, all men off duty (except skirmishers) found shelter in the bombproofs when the rebels opened fire with their artillery. The men in front of Fort McGilvery, namely the Fiftieth Pennsylvania and the Sharpshooters, had a healthy fear of the Chesterfield Battery on the opposite side of the Appomattox River.[25]

Bombproofs were not exactly bombproof. During one cannonade a Confederate shell dropped through the roof of a large shelter in the Fiftieth Pennsylvania's camp. At the time there were about 50 men inside taking refuge from the iron storm outside. The fierce "scramble to get out was exciting," understated the Fiftieth's historian. Fortunately, the shell did not explode, although several men were hurt in the panic to evacuate the quarters.[26]

The Sharpshooters and the Pennsylvanians shared the outpost duty in front of Fort McGilvery and continually worked to improve the picket line in their front.[27]

The Sharpshooters took a good look at their quarters as soon as they arrived and cursed their luck. What they had left behind were "regular little cities of the most comfortable log huts," recorded their chaplain. Here all the Second Corps provided them with were some bombproofs "and little holes excavated in the earth."[28] Picks and shovels were issued to the men and they set to work. They fashioned bombproofs, reinforced trenches, constructed traverses, and strengthened all manner of defenses.

Rarely did trenches run in straight lines; rather, they were dug in a zig-zag fashion. If the enemy captured a part of a line, it would be impossible simply to fire down its length. The trenches were dug deep enough so that a soldier walking in one would be well hidden from the Confederates. At the bottom of the trench on the side toward the rebels was a step or narrow ledge. Lookouts stood on this step to fire at the enemy. So as not to expose themselves, they first cut a small tunnel through the earth at the top of the breastwork. The marksman then slid his rifle barrel into the tunnel, squinted over the iron sights, and waited for someone on the other side to show himself.

The pickets on duty carefully surveyed the 400-yard gap between the two armies. One member of the Second Brigade wrote that the sentinel:

> looks across at the double row of palisades barring his advance to the ancient city, at the dull, red line of earthworks . . ., the fort[-] crowned knolls in the back ground, the thin fields of pine, the scattered dwellings of the suburbs, the "heights" with its solitary house, and the squares and circles of shrubbery standing amid the monuments of the old cemetery . . .[,] his eye closely scanning the red line of breastworks for some careless head to shoot at. . . . The solemn tones of the old Petersburg clock, as it tolls the hour of the night to the city and the adjacent country, only marks the time for the vidette to take his solitary advanced post.[29]

Because the rebel batteries fronted and flanked the Sharpshooters, "flankers" had to be built every 25 feet within the trenches. Flankers looked like small log cabins attached to the inside of the breastworks. Built of logs and filled with Virginia clay, they protected the defenders from mortar and cannon fire. Whenever the men found themselves caught in an enemy cannonade, they used the flankers for protection. At times it was tragicomical to see them dancing from one side of a flanker to the other, as they attempted to dodge shrapnel from the exploding mortar and cannon balls.

The breastwork itself was not just dirt piled up willy-nilly. Reinforced with logs, one atop the other, and strongly braced on the outside with logs covered with earth, it afforded the men good protection.

The Sharpshooters occupied the extreme right of the brigade, which itself was the extreme right of the Ninth Corps. On the right of the Sharpshooters was a deep ravine, and on the other side of the ravine was a high point of land occupied by Battery V.[30]

The men had their quarters, or "shebangs," just behind the breastworks. One officer said "they were made exactly as some of our pioneer farmers made their vegetable cellars."[31] After digging a hole in the ground, logs lined the sides and top; earth was then banked on three sides and the top. Room for a door was left in the rear. Almost none of the shelters had chimneys; the cooking was done in the ravine to the rear.

Rebel mortars and cannons kept up a continual fire from the batteries situated behind their own lines. Most of their shells went over the breastworks and bombproofs and down into the ravine where the cookhouses and stables were located, creating a deadly environment for the rear-echelon personnel.[32]

In front of the main line, on the bluff of the river bank, was the Second Brigade's picket line. It was a strong position, consisting of a reinforced breastwork with only a little ridge of dirt in front. Consequently, the pickets could fire along the level of the ground without showing themselves. Two zigzagging ditches connected the picket line to the main trench. The picket line always had a large complement of defenders.

The right of the picket line started on the river bank and ran to Fort Stedman, as did the main breastworks. The two lines joined together before reaching the fort and formed a "V"; the apex pointed toward the fort.[33]

Surveying his surroundings, Chaplain Heagle conceded that the new site "is prettier and more romantic than out at the left"; in fact, the boys could look directly into Petersburg from where they now were. But, he added, "the air is not so pleasant, being altogether too full of leaden missives for comfortable breathing."[34]

More than 30 years later the scene remained fresh in Lt. Leverette N. Case's memory. Writing of the Siege of Petersburg, he tried to put the reader in the correct state of mind: "Again you are wandering through covered dugways, steadily keeping hid behind huge breastworks, dodging around flankers or rushing into bombproofs to avoid the bursting shells."[35] For those who had lived through it, the experience was always just a thought away, regardless of the intervening years.

A New Commander

On 3 December Captain Nichols of Company E officially took command of the regiment and received his commission as major. (In fact, Nichols had actually commanded the Sharpshooters *de facto* since 12 November.)[36] The regiment was still understrength, with officers and men scattered over a dozen states, some at home, some sick or wounded in hospitals, some languishing in Southern prison pens, some dead and buried. Being understrength meant that the regiment could not have a new colonel or lieutenant colonel mustered. The highest rank in the regiment was that of major. Less than a week after Nichols's promotion, Captain Murdoch received a brevet appointment to major "for gallant services at the battle of Spotsylvania." The promotion was a total surprise to Murdoch, and also to Major Nichols who now commanded the Sharpshooters. The men in the ranks learned they now had two majors.

Murdoch, though, was about to leave the service. Not one to get along well with his superiors, he did have some problems with Colonel DeLand when the latter was in command of the regiment, and some questions of command may have come up with Nichols as well. For whatever reason, Murdoch resigned on 14 December.[37] To the men in the ranks, the political machinations of some of the officers must have seemed comical. Obviously, the officers felt differently.

The Toy Cannon Accident

A week after relocating, one of the Sharpshooters appropriated a toy cannon from somewhere or other. He and his messmates decided to fire salutes with it. Needing a quantity of black powder, they scoured their lines looking for unexploded cannon balls. A few boys of the Sixtieth Ohio joined them in their powder quest. After the scavenger hunt, the boys sat down in a rifle pit, pulled out the fuses, and dumped the powder onto a rubber blanket. They accumulated quite a pile in a short time. Six or eight of the men, including two from the Ohio regiment, worked undisturbed.

A heap of gunpowder lay between Henry Patterson (Co. B) and William Burns (Co. G) when the inevitable happened. Patterson's shell exploded in his hands and the flash ignited the pile of gunpowder in front of Burns. Burns's right leg, which was stretched out next to the gunpowder, was instantly charred. Tom McCall (Co. B) was seriously hurt in the foot by the blast. Both of the Ohio boys were injured (one of them critically) as well.

Other Sharpshooters came running because of the noise and smoke. Some thought a rebel shell had dropped into the pit. They quickly took Patterson to the hospital, but Dr. Whelan could do little for him; the burns were extensive, and he died a few hours later. Burns's badly seared right leg had to be amputated. He also suffered severe burns to his face, neck, and hands. Tom McCall's foot, although injured, did not keep him off the line for long.

The chaplain hoped "a lesson will be learned" through that sort of foolishness. The army hierarchy had always opposed such inane practices as playing with unexploded ordnance.[38] The lesson was made the more apparent when 20-year-old Private Patterson was buried the next day. One of the regiment's earliest recruits, he had enlisted in Grand Haven, Michigan, on 2 December 1862, almost two years before to the day. He now sleeps forever in Poplar Grove National Cemetery.[39]

Unfortunately, the tragedy did not impress itself too indelibly on some members of the regiment. Three months later Major Nichols was forced to issue an order forbidding the burning of gunpowder. "In future," he warned, "any enlisted man detected burning powder in any way except in the discharge of his duties will be severely punished. Neither will the men be allowed to extract powder from shell[s] that have not been exploded."[40]

Promotions

By late 1864 there were almost no desertions from the Sharpshooters' ranks. The core of men who had survived Camp Douglas, the rugged spring campaign, and the hellish summer battles knew each other well by now. Any thoughts of running away were long over, so the disappearance of a young Indian caused consternation.

In general, few Indians deserted, but this fellow was quite a "sport." When the regiment had stopped in Baltimore back in March, he had become involved with a girl. Whether she was the problem, no one ever found out, but the boy left the regiment in August. No trace or word of him could be found. The facts reached his family back home in Michigan. Three months later an old Indian walked into the Sharpshooters' camp and told the commanding officer that he was the father of the boy. He had paid his own railroad fare and had come to take his son's place in the ranks to maintain the family's honor. Ish-ka-buga-ma-ka signed the roll and entered Company K.[41]

The Year's Tally in Blood

As 1864 drew to a close, regimental and brigade clerks tallied their casualties for the past year, and the results were staggering. The Sharpshooters found themselves near the top of the list as far as all of Michigan's regiments were concerned. In their first year of active service the Sharpshooters had lost 106 men who died in action or from wounds incurred; another 40 had died of disease; and 227 had been wounded in action; another 158 were listed as "missing." On the plus side, 134 new recruits had joined the regiment during the year. Out of all of Michigan's 45 combat regiments the Sharpshooters ranked second in the number of battle deaths (the Twenty-seventh Michigan was first with 156) and fifth in total casualties; it was a sobering statistic.[42]

The old year ended amid a flurry of promotions and reductions in the regiment. Just after Thanksgiving Day in late November, Frank Tabasasch of La Croix was promoted to first sergeant of Company K. Simon Sanequaby and Thomas Smith became sergeants, and John Wau-be-noo, Peter Wells, and Charles Shaw took their places in the front rank as corporals.[43]
Capt. Ira L. Evans finally returned from provost duty in Michigan in late November, but he was immediately tapped for work at brigade headquarters. The First Consolidated Company would be his. Capt. Joseph O. Bellair, back from his furlough, took over the Second Company. James DeLand was appointed captain of Company K, and three sergeants were promoted to first lieutenancies: John Berridge to Company C, Lemuel R. Nichols to K, and Friend Soules to B; Henry Hulin advanced to sergeant major, taking John Berridge's place.
Two corporals, Hiram Fegles and Lewis Bryant, lost their stripes, "said men preferring to be cooks," the company clerk inscribed cryptically. Chief Musician Abner Thurber returned to the ranks of Company G, and Fifer John Jones of Company E took over the former's position. In other appointments Charley

Nash (Co. I), Alex Cahow (Co. C), Jason Soules (Co. A), and John Langland (Co. B) sewed on corporal's stripes. Sgt. Theodore Purdy (Co. B), absent since 30 June, was finally tracked down, "having lately been detailed in the Adjt. Gen. Office U.S." For not reporting back to the regiment Purdy "is hereby reduced to the ranks." By February Purdy was again in the regiment. His previous experience was really needed, however, and he became quartermaster sergeant before the regiment went home.[44]

Just to keep the men in tiptop condition and to reinforce discipline, Major Nichols held a regimental inspection and muster at 10:00 AM on 31 December. The Sharpshooters brushed their coats and trousers, cleaned their weapons, arranged their accoutrements, and stood another looking-at, the last of 1864.[45]

The very first regimental order for the new year issued a promotion. Cpl. Richard Campbell of Company I was appointed color sergeant. Campbell (who deserved the honor) replaced Sgt. Henry C. Call, whose wound from the past summer plagued him so much that he was discharged in the waning days of 1864.[46]

Since the capture of their state colors at the Battle of the Crater, the Sharpshooters had followed the national flag presented to them back at the Dearborn arsenal by the Albee family. The flag was not much to look at; the first seven stripes and the blue canton were missing. It had been torn up and the pieces given out to the men the night of 17 June when the regiment had decimated—and in turn was almost destroyed by—an attacking rebel column. Most regiments, both Union and Confederate, listed the names of their battles on their flags. Since there was so little of the national flag left, the Sharpshooters appended silk streamers to it, on which they recalled their martial exploits.[47] Few (if any) regiments in the entire army attached streamers to their flags. The Sharpshooters were unique in the Army of the Potomac.

Adjutant Buckbee Returns

In January one of the old officers reported back to the Sharpshooters. Returning from a 30-day furlough, Ed Buckbee had a hatfull of adventures to relate to his comrades. He had been captured on the night of 17 June with 80 men, and confined for a short time in a Petersburg tobacco warehouse. Separated from the rest of the captured Sharpshooters, he was put with other captured officers and sent to Camp Oglethorpe in Macon, Georgia. There, among 1,600 Union officers, he met Capt. James Morgan of the Seventeenth Michigan, an old school chum, who had been taken prisoner on 16 November 1863 in Tennessee.

Not long after he reached Macon, the rebels transferred 600 captives to Charleston, South Carolina; Buckbee and Morgan were part of the group. Buckbee escaped from a moving train but was soon recaptured and sent on to Charleston. From Charleston the prisoners traveled to Columbia, South Carolina. Buckbee and a couple of others escaped from the camp disguised as Confederates and managed to elude their pursuers for a few days before being picked up again.

The rebels then sent him to Camp Sorghum, four miles from Columbia. No wall surrounded the camp, and Buckbee and Morgan walked away from a work party one day. A providential thunderstorm aided their escape. Helped by slaves and a Southerner who ran a sort of underground railroad for refugees, Morgan and Buckbee made their way to the Edisto River. On 20 November 1864 they boarded the *U.S.S. St. Louis*, a gunboat patroling the North Edisto River, and experienced real freedom for the first time since their capture.[48]

After a visit home to relatives and friends in Ypsilanti and Chicago, Buckbee returned to the front. First he spent a day in Washington, DC, where he saw the sights and even got a close look at the president. He stayed a night at the Willard Hotel, and then took a steamer to City Point where he picked up the train to the trenches.

Arriving at his destination after dark, Buckbee departed the train and looked around for any familiar face among the dozens at the stop. All of a sudden, two horsemen rushed at him, almost running him down. One of the riders almost unseated himself by grabbing Buckbee by the collar and pulling him along. Then the assailants' laughter gave them away. Buckbee recognized his horse, John—John the Baptist—which one of the men was riding. Then the laughing highwaymen greeted him as only old friends can. Leverette Case and Jim DeLand, "two of my most intimate friends during my term in the service," had known Buckbee was scheduled to be on the train and had awaited his coming.

The last six months had wrought great changes in the men. When Buckbee trudged off to prison camp, Case was the regimental clerk and DeLand was sergeant major. Now Case was a first lieutenant and DeLand a captain, each in command of a company. More surprises greeted the adjutant as his friends hurried him to the regiment.[49]

Buckbee knew Col. Charles DeLand had been wounded and discharged. Likewise, he was aware of Lieutenant Colonel Beadle's sickness and consequent service in the Veteran Reserve Corps, with the rank of major, and his appointment to chairman of the board of examination for the VRC. He was also cognizant of the death of Maj. John Piper at Spotsylvania.

What he did not know was that no replacements above the rank of major had been made in the regiment. He learned that all the old captains, save the current commander of the Sharpshooters, were gone—killed, in prison camp, discharged, or on extended leave due to sickness or wounds. Buckbee was an easy fellow to get along with; rather than groping for promotion, he resumed his old duties as adjutant. His friendship with his comrades continued unabated with no rancor attached.[50]

Less than a week after Buckbee's return, General Willcox summoned him to division headquarters. Willcox questioned him about the 17 June battle; in particular, the general wanted to know from where and from whom the order had come to advance and attack the rebel defenses.

The only man who knew that was dead. Major Rhines had kept his own counsel that night. Even when Buckbee had asked Rhines what orders the latter had received, the major told him it was none of his business. Like a good soldier, Buckbee kept his mouth shut and accepted Rhines's explanation. Willcox evidently accepted Buckbee's rendering of the affair; he never questioned the young officer about it again.[51]

Buckbee returned to his unit at a time when death was not as frequent a visitor to the Second Brigade. Camaraderie between the warring outposts during the winter of 1864/65 was the norm. Some rifle fire and occasional cannonades disturbed the peace, but the winter months remained relatively quiet compared to the summer's activity.

The Union side of the Appomattox River had a high bank, astride which was the picket line. On the rebel side the ground was flat and lower than the banks held by the Second Brigade. The Confederate picket line was so weak that the Sharpshooters and the Sixtieth Ohio paid scant attention to it. As a consequence, "the men were quite chummy," Buckbee noticed.[52] Conversations between the pickets of both sides were common.

During the winter the river froze over a number of times, and the men of both sides often walked over. Some clandestine trading developed between the outposts; newspapers, tobacco, and coffee were the usual bill of fare. Once when the river iced over, one of the boys from Battery V crossed to the Confederate side. After a while, his business finished, he started to return. The rebel pickets, either out of caprice or whim, refused to allow him to recross. Quite a ruckus developed.

On the Union side of the river a number of heads poked over the breastworks to catch a view of the evolving melodrama. The prisoner, realizing the seriousness of his predicament, yelled to his comrades in the battery. They in turn called out to their commanding officer, who immediately stepped to the top of the battery walls. His voice carrying across the river, he ordered the rebels to send his man back at once or he "would blow their picket line off the earth damn quick."

Knowing what he said could be easily accomplished, the Confederates released the artilleryman. Dramatically, "the man came swaggering back across the ice to our side, turned, raised his hat, made an elaborate, mock bow to the Confederates and entered the fort."[53] War was not always hell and heroics.

One cold morning in January a rebel picket on duty on the other side of the Appomattox called out to Capt. William D. Bradford, who was commanding the Confederate battery directly across from Fort McGilvery. Peering for a while through his field glasses, Bradford saw men standing atop the Union breastworks. Looking to his right, he also noticed Confederates covering their works. Not being informed of any truce or armistice, Bradford ordered one gunner to "Give them a shot at high range." Immediately after the cannon was fired, the landscape was cleared of men both in blue and gray. For a long moment all was quiet; then every Union cannon that had the Chesterfield Battery in its range fired at it. For half an hour Bradford's Mississippians sustained their heaviest bombardment of the siege.

The next morning Captain Bradford learned that a truce had been in effect. The Federals had held their fire until the truce had been broken, and then sent every blast they could muster into the rebel battery. The Southern artillerymen spent several sleepless nights repairing the damage to their embrasures.[54]

Illness and Morale

Young George Stone, the regimental "baby," managed to go home on furlough in January. He had been sick for the last few months, and was emaciated and suffering from pneumonia when he reached Albion, Michigan. For four weeks he lay in bed. His original furlough of twenty days had to be extended three more times before he felt well enough to return to the siege lines in front of Petersburg. Even then he should have been confined to a hospital.

Martin Armstrong, who quartered in the same shebang as Stone, vividly recalled the young soldier's condition: "On his return to the Regiment," Armstrong remembered, Stone "never was able to do any duty until mustered out." Stone's friends approached Adjutant Buckbee, and asked his help in getting Stone a discharge; they did not believe the lad would live until spring. Stone, though, begged to stay on and was permitted to remain with the regiment.[55]

Stone was not the only sick Sharpshooter on the line. From November through March, 49 men were officially sent to the hospital for a variety of illnesses, and 9 others died. Diarrhea, pneumonia, and rheumatism were noted as the primary types of sickness; the severe living conditions were the main cause.[56] Despite the sickness, morale remained high in the Union camps during the winter, notwithstanding some desultory sniping and occasional cannonades, for the men in the ranks knew it was only a matter of time before the rebels would cave in. The Union army had plenty of food, clothing, and even such amenities as regular mail delivery.

Men returning to duty after furlough often brought back more than information from home. First Lt. Robert Farrell of Niles advertised in the local newspaper that he was willing to carry letters and packages back to the Petersburg trenches. Parents and wives hastily put a few needed items together for their loved ones at the front. When Lieutenant Farrell returned to the regiment he became the most popular man in the outfit.[57]

So many bundles arrived from home that an "unsoldierly" aspect appeared along the lines. Major Nichols did not like the look of his regiment. Company commanders were admonished to "take from the men all articles of citizen[']s dress. In future men returning from furlough will not be allowed to keep in their possession any citizen[']s clothing they may have brought from home."[58] In addition, to give the men a more uniform appearance, everyone in the regiment had to sew, not pin, a corps badge to the top of his hat or cap. Little red shields and not much else (no chevrons for corporals and sergeants and no shoulder straps for the officers) decorated their uniforms.[59]

Across the scarred landscape the rebels were faring poorly. While the enemy shivered in threadbare uniforms, and poor fare graced their tables, there seemed to be no shortage of anything in the Union entrenchments. Sgt. Mark Vining wrote the folks back home, informing them that their "soldier boys" were as well off as they could possibly be. "We have comfortable 'log' houses, built of pine, and pretty good rations," he told them.[60] Not enough food or clothing could be found for the Army of Northern Virginia, and the mail that came through told of Union armies moving at will through the South.

On 21 February rebel ears picked up a persistent cheering emanating from the Union lines. The deep bass of naval cannons could be heard on the Union right, while a hundred guns thundered from the rear of the Army of the Potomac. The demonstration celebrated Gen. William T. Sherman's victories in the Carolinas. Mile upon mile of blue-coated soldiers shouted their approval, while the Confederates must have wondered if they would ever have victories like the ones earlier in the war.[61]

In late January and early February both sides began shelling each other frequently. On 31 January "the rebs done us more damage this time than at any previous time we have been here," wrote a member of the Second Brigade. On the evening of 9 February a "heavy artillery duel" ripped through the cloudy skies.[62] Then, for almost two weeks, firing of all kinds tapered off to just about nothing on the First Division front.

At midnight on the beginning of 21 February, all the Ninth Corps batteries fired a "shotted salute" in recognition of Sherman's destruction of Columbia, South Carolina. For two hours, with suitable Confederate interjections, the "intensely exciting" presentation continued.[63] The next evening the Union lines erupted in a fiery tribute to George Washington in celebration of his birthday; the rebels tried to respond in kind.[64] On the evening of 24 February another salute, compliments of the U.S. artillery, was paid to the Union boys who had captured Wilmington, North Carolina.[65]

Prisoners Returning
and Some Never to Return

In early December a spate of letters reached the Sharpshooters from Annapolis, Maryland. Altogether, 187 Michigan soldiers had survived the horrors of rebel prison pens; they were gathered in Annapolis awaiting medical attention and furloughs home. Among them were 28 Sharpshooters who had been captured at Spotsylvania, Cold Harbor, and Petersburg. Unfortunately, just as many had died in rebel hands (most of them at Andersonville) before any hope of parole was tendered.

Among the living were 1st Sgt. Daniel Gore and H. Dorr Blakeman (Co. E), Zena D. Ransom (Co. C), and Marsh Hodges (Co. A). Quite a few of the Indians, most of them nabbed the night of 17 June, had also survived their prison ordeal, including Payson Wolfe, John B. Shomin, and Joseph Williams. Too many did not return. Men like Cpl. Alva Fordham (Co. D) and the colonel's orderly Dallas Jump (Co. E), and Joseph Gibson and the Indian doctor Jacko Pe-nais-now-o-quot (both of Co. K), had died in Andersonville.

Some of the men, like William Cassell (Co. I), were too sick to go anywhere except to a hospital. As soon as possible, though, every man received a new uniform, his back pay, and a 30-day furlough before returning to the regiment.[66]

As the old soldiers came back to the regiment during the winter, the whereabouts of certain missing members was cleared up. The soldiers told their stories of imprisonment and disease to a rapt audience.

Payson Wolfe, one of the Indians captured the night of 17 June, returned in late February. After his release, he had gone home on furlough to Northport, Michigan, to recuperate from the effects of his imprisonment. He told his family of the abominable conditions he and the other captured Sharpshooters had suffered in the prison camp:

> going sometimes 2 to 3 days and a number of times 4 days without eating at all. They were robbed of their blankets and overcoats & lived and slept in the open weather. . . . The water was sometimes 4 inches deep where they had to lie.
>
> He says that the men got so weak they could not keep their rations down and would vomit beans as soon as swallowed. . . . Often the boiled rice would be alive with full grown maggots.[67]

The Sharpshooters captured the night of 17 June had all arrived at Andersonville together. Charles D. Bibbins (Co. E) later remembered the reception given to the Indians by the "Raiders," a group of Union prisoners who preyed on the weaker inmates of the prison. The Indians:

> were great lovers of trinkets of all kinds, and those that were captured were well supplied with watches, chains, rings and ear-rings, which they refused to give up to their captors when first captured. . . . [The Raiders] proceeded to relieve them of their jewelry the second night after their arrival, but the Indians, back to back in a bunch, cut and slashed the "raiders" until they were obliged to quit the fight, with two killed and several wounded. They were not bothered after that, and the camp put an end to the raiders shortly afterward.[68]

Sgt. H. Dorr Blakeman (Co. E), also captured on 17 June, had a hand in stopping the depredations of the Raiders. He met up with a fellow townsman from Jackson who had been captured the year before. In turn, he was introduced to a number of men who planned to fight the Raiders. Described as "a thoroughly good fellow, and a sensible one," Blakeman was recognized as a dependable man in a tense situation. "It is a relief to see anyone who does not lose his head," commented Blakeman's friend.[69] In a week's time, and with the help of the Confederate authorities, the Raiders were arrested and tried. On 11 July, the worst six were executed by the prisoners themselves.

Thousands continued to die at Andersonville through neglect, starvation, inadequate medical facilities, and pure malice. By the time the Sharpshooters captured in front of Petersburg arrived at Andersonville, there were more than 25,000 already incarcerated there. In another month there would be 33,000.

There were no barracks to protect the prisoners from the intense Georgia sun; they had to provide their own shelter in the 27-acre sunbaked, treeless waste. A small creek flowed through the camp; it was both the source of drinking water and a sewer for the unfortunates kept there. The groans of the sick and dying, the stench, the filth and despair that filled every day and night drove many men insane.[70]

Rations were scanty at best; malnutrition, scurvy, dysentery, and diseases unknown yet rampant killed men by the score. In less than a year more than 13,000 Union soldiers died there,

48 of whom were Sharpshooters. Of the survivors, some were released in late November; some would not see freedom until the end of the war.

The Sharpshooters captured at the Battle of the Crater on 30 July were sent to a smaller prison camp at Danville, Virginia. Its total capacity was 2,400 men, but that did not lessen the sufferings of those kept there.[71] Confined in old tobacco warehouses, the men had no bed but "the soft side of a plank." In order to keep warm during the winter nights the men had to "spoon" in long rows.

Charles DePuy, who had helped man the cannon in the Crater until his capture, often thought of the difference between the way the rebel prisoners were treated at Camp Douglas the year before and the plight of the Sharpshooters at Danville. The Confederates at Camp Douglas "were well fed," he remembered, "had as comfortable barracks as we had, and plenty of fuel to keep them warm." Because of the prison fare at Danville, hardly more than "corn-cob and gruel," DePuy was a shadow of his former self when released in February 1865. "I weighed 150 pounds when captured, and eighty-five pounds when paroled."

DePuy's disgust knew no bounds when he passed some recently released Southerners:

> On our way to the flag of truce boat at Richmond, we met a detachment of rebels on their way from our lines. They were well-clothed—better than their comrades in the field, and better fed. What a different picture we made, starved and clothed in rags that barely concealed our bones![72]

As soon as a prisoner was repatriated, he received a hot bath and good food. Medical care was provided. Then the soldier, if not hospitalized, went home for his 30-day furlough. Oftentimes the leave was extended because of complications involving a wound or sickness.

After his furlough, Payson Wolfe brought with him three new recruits from Northport. John Jacko and John Kiniewaha-soipi (both 20 years old) and Aaron Sahgahnaquato (21) had all enlisted for one year. Kiniewahasoipi would die of disease on 5 March, just a couple of weeks after he reached the Petersburg lines; his bones still rest in Poplar Grove Cemetery. But that ultimate journey still lay in the future as the three eager young men and the 33-year-old veteran rode the train to Petersburg.[73]

On 22 February ten more enlistees reached the lines. Five of them were one-year recruits. Two went to Company A and three to Company H. The other five, all three-year enlistees, entered Company K.[74]

Hall's Independent Sharpshooters

Back in July 1864 Capt. Andrew J. Hall of Company H had disappeared from the regiment. On 20 July Colonel DeLand received a letter from Hall, who was then at City Point. DeLand sent Captain Dicey to learn what Hall was doing there, and discovered that Hall had been politicking on his own behalf. Hall had a letter from Michigan's governor, Austin Blair, addressed to Lt. Gen. Ulysses S. Grant, asking the latter to allow him to resign his commission in the Sharpshooters, "for the purpose of raising an independent Company of Sharpshooters."

In late July DeLand received a missive from Capt. Thomas Mathews, the acting assistant adjutant general for the Second Brigade, inquiring about Hall's status. DeLand wrote back, informing Mathews that Hall contemplated leaving the regiment in order to raise a "real" company of sharpshooters, as Hall had put it, this one "to be armed with heavy target rifles."[75]

Although DeLand needed all his officers, he was unable to impede Hall's determination. Hall resigned his commission on 1 August and returned to his hometown of Coldwater.[76] He obviously craved a more significant command; he began recruiting for a new organization—Hall's Independent Sharpshooters.

President Lincoln had issued a call for 500,000 men on 18 July to make up the deficiencies created by Grant's Overland Campaign. Furthermore, a draft was scheduled to go into effect after 5 September. Whereas drafted men had to serve one year, an enlistee could sign up for one, two, or three years.[77]

Recruiters were to comb the state for 15,760 men, Michigan's share of the new levy. The U.S. government offered a $100 bounty of to a one-year enlistee, $200 to a two-year volunteer, or $300 to a three-year man. The state tendered no bounty at all; "the appropriation made for that purpose is exhausted," lamented the governor. But towns, wards, and subdistricts were allowed to proffer bounties up to the $200 limit imposed by the legislature.[78]

Coldwater's town fathers devised a plan to up the ante. Every man whose name was on the roll of potential draftees would pay $30 to a special fund. The city also would levy a special tax to raise a municipal bounty of $100 for each soldier required from Coldwater. The two funds would then provide a bounty of $300 for each recruit. Those who wished to stay clear of the military had only to come up with $30, while those wishing to enlist would be able to leave a sizable nest egg with their families.[79]

There was another method of raising troops used by towns throughout the Union. Agents were sent to other states, where they offered whatever bounties their hometowns had available. Any new recruits from out of state were then credited to that town's quota, thus (hopefully) keeping the balance of their own men at home.

After Negroes were allowed into the Union ranks, agents signed up recently freed slaves from the Southern states then occupied by Northern soldiers. The Coldwater people thought about that idea, but more sensible heads prevailed. "The people of this county now understand that the quota of the county is to be filled at home. Those towns that take hold of the matter with energy and in season will succeed; those that do not, must endure the draft."[80]

Governor Blair encouraged men to enlist for the war's duration:

> This State has thus far raised no troops for a less term than three years. Both for the Government and the soldier the longest term is the best. Let us continue to adhere to this policy, which has given us a most honorable position in the service, and the reputation of the Michigan soldiery, which is now unsurpassed, will continue to grow.[81]

New regiments, and reorganized ones as well, only accepted men for three years or for the duration. Two old organizations, the Third and Fourth Infantry Regiments, were reorganized, and the Twenty-ninth Infantry was recruited and outfitted. The old Eleventh Michigan Infantry started to reorganize, and the Thirtieth Infantry (made up entirely of veterans to perform home guard duty) began receiving applicants. By the end of December 1864, Michigan had surpassed its quota, having enlisted 16,187 men. Of that number, 5,445 were veterans. Although Governor Blair had asked for three-year men, more than 6,000 had signed up for just one year. The governor admonished, "Those who enlist for a shorter term than three years will go into the regiments now in the field."[82]

Capt. Andrew J. Hall had secured authority from the governor to raise a battalion of sharpshooters as soon as he returned home from the front. Starting in late August, Hall gathered a corps of would-be officers, including John W. Quackenbush, who had been demoted twice in the First Michigan Sharpshooters, and began recruiting expert riflemen.

One hundred eight men joined the battalion. Hall formed them into two small companies; one was led by Capt. Allen E. Burnham, a Mexican War veteran, assisted by 1st Lt. Henry S. Fish and 2nd Lt. Edmund McWilliams. The other was officered by Capt. Nathaniel P. Watson, with First Lieutenant Quackenbush and 2nd Lt. William J. Thompson, who had also been a member of the First Sharpshooters.[83]

The men trained at Marshall, Michigan, until early November 1864. Even though this was a new organization, all the enlistees had signed up for one year of service. Most of them were older, married men who had not yet served in the army; they believed they could support their families for the one year they would be away from home with the government bounty. Only 17 of them were in their teens and 38 were past the age of 30; the average age was 28.

Captain Hall employed a novel method to procure officers for his battalion—he charged them for the privilege of commanding his two companies. First Lt. Fish paid the least amount, $150; 2nd Lt. Thompson, although he was a lower grade, laid out $180 for his commission. Hall got $200 from 2nd Lt. McWilliams, while the captaincies of Burnham and Watson cost each man $300. John W. Quackenbush paid a whopping $400 to sew his first lieutenant's bars on his shoulders. Hall told the officers that the money was "for expenses," but the six officers then had to recruit men to bring the battalion up to strength.

Lieutenant Fish managed to talk 11 men into joining Hall's Independent Sharpshooters, as the battalion came to be called. Not knowing what was expected of him, Fish then saw Governor Blair. The governor heard Fish's story and told him in no uncertain terms that officers were to be appointed—commissions were not to be sold. He informed Fish that Hall had absolutely no authority to sell positions in his battalion.

Military authorities received notice of the transaction and conducted an investigation; Hall did not hold up well under their scrutiny. The six investigating officers said Hall had incurred no debt in recruiting the battalion, therefore he should receive no money. Governor Blair did not believe that any of the officers, with the exception of Hall, were guilty of any crime. As a result, Hall returned the money; "if there was any error on the part of the officers here it was unintentional and . . . they acted in good faith," reported Capt. John H. Knight of the Eighteenth U.S. Infantry who headed the investigation. Hall was arrested and never accompanied his battalion to the seat of war.[84]

The two companies composing Hall's Independent Sharpshooters left their camp in Michigan on 10 November 1864. They arrived at City Point, Virginia, on 22 November, where they became part of the "defenses" of City Point, along with a hodgepodge of other small outfits: six companies of the Sixty-first Massachusetts Infantry, two companies of the First Maine Sharpshooters, and six companies of the Eighteenth New Hampshire Infantry.[85]

Guarding supplies while surrounded by the cornucopia of the Union was easy work. Unfortunately for the "fresh fish," the depleted regiment of Sharpshooters on the line near Fort McGilvery soon heard about this new independent unit from Michigan that was enjoying rear-echelon duty. Word quickly reached higher authority that the new sharpshooters were needed up front.

On 5 February 1865 the New England and Michigan defenders of City Point, together with the Fifteenth New York Engineers, about 1,900 men, entrained for the front. The whole group constituted a temporary brigade with orders to report to General Parke, commander of the Ninth Corps. The Fifteenth New York Engineers and Hall's Sharpshooters took up a position near Battery XXIV, fully five miles from the line guarded by the First Michigan Sharpshooters. For the next month Hall's Independent Sharpshooters manned the lines, but the rebel trenches were not too close in this sector and the position was relatively safe and quiet.

Things changed on 12 March. Hall's men bagged their equipment and trooped to the railroad. They were then transported to General Willcox's headquarters, where his staff informed them that they were now officially part of the First Michigan Sharpshooters. From this point on, Hall's independent battalion ceased to exist.[86]

Second Lt. William J. Thompson never made it back to his old regiment. He was discharged for disability on 30 December 1864.[87] The enlisted men and the remaining officers found themselves parceled out to the 9 white companies: 9 each to Companies A and B; First Lieutenant Fish took 8 men to C; Captain Watson led another 12 men to D; 11 men went to E; 14 to F; 9 to G; 9 more to H; and 14 became members of I.[88]

Two officers resigned from the service rather than be consolidated into the First Sharpshooters. Capt. Allen E. Burnham and 2nd Lt. Edmund McWilliams were both mustered out of the service on 15 March. A number of other officers and noncommissioned officers in the independent battalion found themselves discharged because they now had no command as supernumerary officials. The men who were excess baggage—1st Lt. John W. Quackenbush, Sgt. John Dauby, Sgt. Benjamin McLelland, and Sgt. John Wood—reported to Capt. Sylvester Keyser, assistant commissary of muster for the First Division, to be mustered out of the service.[89]

The influx of 97 officers and men to their ranks helped the morale of the Sharpshooters. Piecemealing them out to all the companies helped make the newcomers feel like part of the old regiment. Undoubtedly, the fresh fish were made to feel unequal to the task of becoming "real" soldiers by some of the old hands, whereas others joined in and welcomed them into the ranks. Other regiments along the line were also augmented with levies from home, both draftees and enlistees. In the meantime, the opposite was happening in the ranks of their enemies.

Cracks in the Rebel Wall

Chagrined with both news from home and from the farflung battlefields (all of it the reckoning of doomsayers) the Confederate army in Petersburg pondered its fate.

Back in the fall, notices from the Union army had gone out to the rebels, telling them that if they surrendered and brought their weapons with them, they would be given cash to take with them to a prisoner-of-war camp. As the winter dragged on and rebel morale sagged, Confederates began deserting in droves.

On New Year's Day the pickets in front of the Twentieth Michigan's position were startled by what at first looked like a charge by one man: "a Johnnie came in here last night," an enlisted man wrote in his diary; "he never stoped [*sic*] at the picket line but run to the main line and brought up in a bomb proof most scared to death."[90] A Confederate captain with 13 men surrendered to Willcox's division on 20 January.[91] On the night of 24 February, nine Confederates turned themselves in to the pickets fronting the Third Brigade, just to the left of the Sharpshooters' position. The next day five Southerners deserted their picket posts "in broad daylight." On the same night 14 men with a commissioned officer entered the Union lines in the same sector.[92]

The story repeated itself scores of times along the Union front. Hundreds of rebels, weapons in hand, abandoned the Army of Northern Virginia. They were heartily tired of a war for which they now had no stomach. They had fought the good fight, but enough was enough.[93]

On the Siege Line

At the end of February, when the weather turned "warm and pleasant," an order was sent to the men along the front. All those buried near the lines were to be dug up and reburied near the field hospital. Land had already been set aside for that purpose and fenced in. Hundreds of men had been interred just behind the lines since the investment of Petersburg. Others, like the ones killed during the Battle of the Crater, lay between the lines and would have to be taken care of later. In a letter home, one soldier in the Twentieth Michigan wrote:

> Graves are found everywhere where men have fallen, a board giving the name, regiment and day of death. Soldiers seldom molest these mounds, seeming to hold it a sacrilege to mar even by a footrack, the two-by-six feet of earth that will be his last earthly possession.[94]

As many as possible were disinterred, identified, and their remains moved "to a more loyal and congenial atmosphere."[95]

To keep up the morale of the men, Major Nichols ordered them to maintain a semblance of cleanliness, even though they lived in nothing more than holes in the ground. To facilitate that end, he charged Pvt. Horace B. Seeley of Company G, the acknowledged Democrat, to be the regimental barber. Nichols relieved Seeley of all guard and picket duty and had him "cut the hair & whiskers of such men as may be reported by the company commanders." Nichols wanted a showcase regiment. Long hair and untrimmed beards did not fit into his scheme of things; sloppy appearance was definitely unmilitary.[96]

When Adjutant Buckbee had returned to the regiment, he had moved into a shebang occupied by his friend Lieutenant Case. It was the only hut in the regiment with a fireplace.[97] The hearth was small, dug into the side of a hill, and was surmounted by a chimney made out of a barrel.[98] Each bombproof was home to eight or ten enlisted men, but the ones for officers, although the same size, were only tenanted by two or three.

Out in front of the main line was the forward trench. The men who occupied that line were totally cut off from communication with the main line. They were the eyes and ears of the regiment. All the Sharpshooters took their turn at this "extreme duty" for 24 hours at a stretch. After Hall's men joined them, the watches were not as frequent.

After being relieved in the predawn darkness, each man was allowed a big drink of whiskey, then he was off to his shebang where he could sleep until the next day. When the Indians came off duty, they received the same emolument. What "annoyed and mystified" the officers was that, by the third or fourth day of Company K's tour in the front trenches, "a lot of Indians would gather over in the ravine just in our rear, build a bonfire, and, to all appearances, have a regular old-fashioned drunk."

For months this recurring event proved to be a conundrum to the rest of the regiment. Enlisted men were not allowed to have whiskey. The officers had no such rule, but no officer ever complained of any liquor being stolen or missing.

Capt. Jim DeLand, who commanded Company K, finally solved the riddle of the repeated binges. He found that when his men came off "extreme duty," they filled their mouths with their ration of whiskey and, out of sight of their officers, spit it into their gun barrels. At their bombproofs they filled a canteen with the contents of their rifles until they had "enough for a good sized drunk."[99]

Even though officers were allowed to have spirits in camp, some who were too fond of John Barleycorn found whiskey difficult to procure at times. A certain officer in Willcox's division (one of those who daily needed a drink to clear the cobwebs from his mind) heard that Leverette Case had a supply. He decided to drop by Case's bombproof for a social chat and a libation. Case knew why the officer had happened by, but confined the small talk to war matters. Exasperated by the flow of conversation and the lack of flow of something else, the visiting officer finally asked Case point-blank for a drink.

"I'll make a bargain with you," quipped Case. "If you'll go to the top of that chimney and call 'CAPTAIN CASE' good and loud, I'll set up the drinks for the party." The other officer looked quizzically at Case, who then told him of his recent promotion to captain. "I want to hear how it will sound," smiled Case. They toasted Case's good fortune that evening.[100]

Two of the last recruits to reach the regiment reported on 28 February. George W. Morris (39), and Merritt F. Reed (30), both from Niles, were assigned to Company G, where they found some fellow townsmen.[101]

In March another of the old officers returned. Capt. Ira Evans came back from staff duty at brigade headquarters. After repeated personal requests to do so, he was glad to rejoin the Sharpshooters on the line.[102]

Adjutant Buckbee finally received word of his upcoming promotion that same month. Buckbee's advancement was different in that it originated within the regiment. Soon after the Sharpshooters had received word of Buckbee's repatriation in late 1864, a petition made the rounds. Capt. George Davis, who was commanding the regiment in place of Major Nichols, then detailed as inspector of hospitals, penned his name to the top of the list. Every line officer present signed the request, which was then sent to Michigan's governor, Henry Crapo.[103] The petitioners related how deserving Buckbee was of the field promotion, noting that he was "fully competent and deserving" of a higher rank than lieutenant. Realizing that Asahel Nichols was the only officer currently on staff who outranked Buckbee, the line officers hoped that whatever rank Nichols achieved, Buckbee would be just one grade below him.[104]

Another officer, albeit not presently on staff, also outranked Buckbee—Capt. Elmer Dicey. "Gov. Crapo refuses to commission me," Buckbee wrote on 28 March, because of Dicey, who was still "working for it" himself.[105]

On the same day that Buckbee penned his self-pitying letter, Lieutenant Colonel Nichols wrote the adjutant general of Michigan in defense of Buckbee. Nichols had seen Governor Crapo only a few weeks before, and had told him that Buckbee ranked all the present captains in the regiment before his capture on 17 June. The one exception was Captain Dicey. Nichols had heard that Dicey died as a prisoner of war. "His health was always poor," so Nichols thought the rumor was true; but Dicey had been paroled by the rebels and was currently recuperating in Michigan. In Buckbee's favor, Nichols said, he "has always been at *his post brave* and *competent*, and in my opinion will always be of more service to his country and Reg't." Dicey was "a good man—*true* and competent," but Dicey was ill, not yet exchanged, and in Michigan. Buckbee was with the regiment.[106]

The upshot of the whole matter resulted in Buckbee being promoted to major, while Nichols became lieutenant colonel, since the regiment was still too depleted for a new colonel.

While convalescing at home in Jackson, Michigan, Colonel DeLand had also sent in a list of recommended promotions to Brig. Gen. John Robertson. Considering the number of men then serving in the ranks (only 239) DeLand believed only first lieutenancies should be offered, not captaincies. To that end he suggested four promotions: 1st Sgt. Daniel Gore, 1st Sgt. Robert Farrell, 1st Sgt. Ralph McClellan, and Sgt. H. Dorr Blakeman. Gore had been serving as first lieutenant since early December and Blakeman since September; both were officially mustered as officers in February 1865 because of DeLand's recommendation.[107] Farrell received his promotion in December, but McClellan, for whatever reason, never received his.[108] Sgt. Frank Thayer of Company A received the final commission. He had been in the regiment since March 1863. Wounded in the hand at Petersburg in June 1864, Thayer at one time had tried for an officer's position in one of the newer regiments, but it never came through. In March he became first lieutenant of Company I.[109]

Lt. Henry V. Hinckley kept politicking for a higher rank for himself. His brother-in-law, Asahel Nichols, recommended him for a captaincy, but the effort was in vain. Colonel DeLand did not care for either Hinckley or Nichols, and he informed General Robertson in blunt language: "I deem it proper that no further promotion should be offered him at present." Hinckley was already a second lieutenant; under the aegis of Nichols, he refused to muster as a first lieutenant, hoping to attain a captain's bars instead. It never happened.[110]

CHAPTER 13

And Our Flag Was the First in the City

The Rebels Plan Their Last Offensive

A t the end of March 1865, the Ninth Corps still held the extreme right of the Union siege works in front of Petersburg. The Second Brigade of Willcox's First Division, under Lt. Col. Ralph Ely, occupied the trenches from the Appomattox River to Battery IX, located near the old City Point Railroad. Directly behind the brigade loomed Fort McGilvery, bristling with cannons. The Third Brigade, commanded by Col. Napoleon B. McLaughlen, defended the line from Battery IX to Fort Haskell, which was in a low area and subjected to continued fire from the rebel lines. Fort Haskell was a heavily fortified redoubt with four rifled cannons. To the front of Fort Haskell ran a sluggish stream, a lot of swampy ground, and some patchy woods. Col. Samuel Harriman's First Brigade occupied the works from Fort Haskell to Fort Morton, a formidable bastion situated on high ground.

It was about 1,000 yards from the river where the Sharpshooters made their winter quarters to Fort Stedman, which was just on the far side of Battery IX. Looking south from the Sharpshooters' position, Fort Stedman was the last point that could be seen on the Union line. It commanded the defenses in both directions.[1]

Gen. Robert E. Lee chafed at being confined to the Peters-burg defenses. His forte was the offensive, but since the previous May Lt. Gen. Grant had forced the rebel army to stay on the defensive. To stand still was to atrophy. The Union army contin-ued to thrust at various points along the line, and all Lee could do was parry.

During March, Lee had Gen. John B. Gordon, one of his corps commanders, devise a plan to punch a hole through the Federal lines, in the hope of ending the siege. Gordon's proposal, which was more hopeful than practical, was to attack Fort Sted-man.

In the predawn hours rebel detachments would clear the *chevaux-de-frise* (logs with sharpened stakes sticking from them) from the front of their own lines. Then, Union pickets would be captured quickly and quietly. Squads of Confederate axemen would assail whatever devices protected the Union lines. Three hundred men would then hurry through the Union lines and take the three redoubts believed to be in the rear of Fort Stedman. These redoubts contained cannons that could then be brought to bear on Fort Stedman. At the same time, the main rebel line would hit Fort Stedman and assail the trenches to the left and right of it. Thousands of Confederate soldiers were brought to the jumping-off point, and Lee promised thousands more if the breach were made.

Siege lines, of necessity, are quite complicated affairs, espe-cially if both armies have had time to improve on them. Military maps show clear lines of different colors, denoting each army generally parallel to the other. In reality, the lines were far more complex. Picket lines were fronted by *chevaux-de-frise*. Behind the picket lines ran the main trench, and in back of that was a maze of covered ways, redoubts, dead ends, and connecting trenches. Just such a labyrinth had confused the Federals at the Battle of the Crater in July 1864; now the Confederates were to have their turn.

Starting on the high river bank, quite some distance from the main Union line, was a heavy picket line. It differed from the main line in two particulars. First, a wide, deep trench with only a small elevation of dirt in front protected the pickets; the men sighted their weapons along the level of the ground itself. Quite a few men were always stationed in this advanced post. Two zigzag ditches connected the picket line with the main line, thus provid-ing cover for the men going to and coming from the "extreme duty" area. Second, no artillery occupied the advanced position. Cannons in the forts and in various batteries along the main line set up converging lines of fire and could easily protect the pickets. The picket line and main line were some distance apart, but they converged on enough of an angle so that they joined together just before reaching Fort Stedman.[2]

Nothing of note had transpired on the line for months, so there was no advance warning of the Confederate attack on Fort Stedman. Quietly leaving their lines at 4:00 AM on 25 March, Gordon's rebels stole across the field separating the two armies. Patchy fog shrouded the ground, further shielding the attackers. A few Union pickets fired at them, but the outposts were quickly taken. Gunshots were a normal occurrence up front, so no one in the Union lines was unduly alarmed. The axemen chopped through the Federal defenses, opening the way for hundreds of silent Southerners.

The brunt of the attack hit the area near Battery IX, to the right (or north) of Fort Stedman. Success was instant. Colonel McLaughlen, who was commanding the Fort Stedman line, was captured, as were hundreds of his men. Fort Stedman fell in the darkness. Rebel artillerymen commenced firing the captured cannons in the fort through the Federal trenches to the north and south of the fort. The Union force at Fort Haskell, 600 yards to the south, held its position and threw back the Confederate infantrymen. To the north, near Battery IX, the Federals formed a line of battle and held their position. In between, the rebels held three-fourths of a mile of Union entrenchments.

The Union Counterattack

The picket line, set up about a couple of dozen yards in front of the main line, was commanded by either a commissioned or noncommissioned officer. Each regiment was responsible for its own section, and the brigade also always had an officer patrolling the picket lines.

On the night of 25 March the picket officer in front of Fort Stedman was addressed by a Confederate who had crept silently to the Union line. The rebel said he wanted to desert and earn the bounty for turning in his weapon. He also told the officer that a clutch of his friends were a little way behind him, ready to come over, too.

The Confederate was told to send the other men across one at a time, and was assured there would be no shooting. The rebel soon reappeared, followed immediately by some 30 armed men, each of whom surrendered his weapon as he entered the picket trench. As the rebels crowded in, the picket officer thought of setting up a guard to escort the prisoners to the rear.

Then someone stuck a revolver in the officer's face and admonished him to keep quiet or his skull would have another hole in it, one that Mother Nature never intended. Looking around, he saw his pickets putting their hands up, rebel pistols trained on them. Moving down the trench, the rebels bagged all the Union pickets, one by one. Buckbee later learned that:

> The trench guards ahead of them were easy game as the troops approaching them carried their guns at "support" and in the darkness they could not tell what they were—relief, extra guard or what—until they themselves one by one, were added to the "mourners in the rear."[3]

The rebel vanguard crept around to the entrance of Fort Stedman and entered without firing a shot; 200 men—all belonging to the Fourteenth New York Heavy Artillery—were taken prisoner in the fort alone.[4]

One of the unsung heroes of that night was Capt. John C. Hardy of the Second Michigan Infantry. As staff officer of the day, Hardy's duties took him up and down the brigade lines. Immediately after the rebels had invested the picket line in front of Fort Stedman and hustled the captives away, Hardy sauntered unaware into their midst Something was wrong, thought Hardy. Even in the dark he knew, "he someway *felt*," that these men crowding in the silent trench were the enemy.

Saying nothing, he climbed out of the ditch and ran for the main line, realizing at the time that he was fair game for any Confederate who wished to shoot him. Captain Hardy, running "cross lots," reached his own lines and told the trench guards at the left of Fort Stedman to inform their officers of the attack. He then ran to brigade headquarters. In the meantime, the rebels took Fort Stedman and all of its men.[5]

The Second Brigade pickets, who were some distance from the attack, heard and saw nothing out of the ordinary until the enemy started firing Fort Stedman's cannons down their lines.[6]

Battery IX, an earthwork about one-half mile to the right of

Fort Stedman, was a strong point defended by two cannons and three Coehorn mortars. The Twentieth Michigan occupied the battery; the Second Michigan was stationed in the trench line just to the left of the position.

Near 4:00 AM Lt. Col. Ralph Ely, who was commanding the Second Brigade, learned of the attack from an officer of the Second Michigan (more than likely Captain Hardy). The rebels had broken the Union line between the Second and Third Brigades, then pushed down both lengths of the main line. The Fiftieth Pennsylvania, in reserve two miles in the rear, was told to hurry to the front. Not knowing exactly where the rebels or his own men were, Ely called up 50 men of the First Sharpshooters to act as skirmishers and moved toward Fort Stedman. The Sharpshooters, commanded by Capt. James DeLand, led the attack behind the Second Michigan's lines.

The rebels hit the Second Michigan along their trench line and a wagon road running parallel and to the rear of the Second's position. The Wolverines quickly took shelter in Battery IX. Capt. John C. Boughton of the Second Michigan formed a battle line at right angles to his breastworks and the wagon road, and checked the enemy's progress. It was still too dark to really see anything; the rebel attackers had no idea of the strength of their adversary on this line, so they held their position.

After surveying the situation, Colonel Ely ordered Lieutenant Bangs in Battery V to fire into Fort Stedman. Up until this point, Bangs had directed his fire across the river at the rebel artillery positions. Maj. Jacob Roemer in Fort McGilvery had had his big guns pouring their iron into Fort Stedman from the start, while the rebel gunners kept a steady stream of shells coming his way, too. Roemer sustained a hit while aiming one of his pieces and was severely injured, but he stayed in command of the fort until the action subsided.

When light came, the rebels to the right of Fort Stedman found themselves cut off from the fort. They would have to fully expose themselves to get to its shelter. The Second Brigade occupied its own forward positions, and also moved more men into the firing line facing the rebels.[7]

Three separate enemy assaults struck the rise where Battery IX was located. Rebel artillery bombarded the fortification, their Gooseneck, Chesterfield, and mortar batteries blasting the area. Two rebel brigades tried to move down the line and take the siege lines all the way to Fort McGilvery, hoping to eventually take that stronghold from the rear. Roemer, who was also commanding the artillery in Battery IX, found that he could not decline his pieces low enough to hit the advancing foe, so he had two guns removed from their positions and placed in the open on City Point Road to the right of the enclosure. The three attacks were repulsed handily. The Confederates did not expect such resistance. A captured Southern captain stated laconically that the attack was going well until they reached Battery IX, "where you'uns sort of discouraged us."[8]

The Sharpshooters Hold Their Line

Ed Buckbee and Leverette Case woke with a start that morning. "For God's sake, Major, wake up; Fort Stedman is firing on us," yelled the guard in front of the commanding officer's bombproof. Rolling over, still half asleep, Buckbee "had it on my tongue's end to tell the man he was drunk, when there was a crash, and an enormous amount of dirt came rattling down our fireplace."[9]

Now thoroughly awake, the half-dressed officers burst from their quarters. Orders precluded any officer from removing all of his clothing in case of an emergency; the wisdom of such discipline now became evident. In the darkness Buckbee and Case saw gun flashes from the vicinity of Fort Stedman and the sputtering fuses as the cannonballs flew down the inside of the Union lines. Buckbee's first thought was that the men in Fort Stedman were crazy.[10] Case ran off to rouse his company, and Buckbee ordered the adjutant to make sure every company commander was on the main line with his men. He then made his way to the picket line. There he found the regimental commander, Capt. Ira Evans, who assured Buckbee that the men with him were awake and ready for anything. Evans maintained that they would hold their position "against all hell," if need be.[11]

As officers and men hurried about in the darkness, Colonel Ely, the Second Brigade's commander, rushed up. Yes, he said, Fort Stedman was in enemy hands, which meant that the Second Brigade at least was cut off from the rest of the division. He informed Buckbee that the brigade had to look out for itself and hold its ground. Before he dashed off, Ely shouted to Buckbee:

> take your horse, and ride over to the bottom of that hill [where Fort Stedman was located] and see if the enemy have penetrated

the line. Take two companies and deploy them as skirmishers, and hold the enemy if there are any there, and report to me at once.[12]

With all available men under arms, Captain Evans called to Capt. Jim DeLand and told him to pull Companies I and K off the line.[13] Buckbee led them off to the left, while Evans remained in charge of the regiment and Captain Case commanded the picket line. Evans had his men maintain a continuous fire from their position, which they expected the rebels to attack. The fog was heavier near the river and the pickets had to squint into the haze.

Meanwhile, Buckbee led Captain DeLand and the two companies to the ravine in order to approach Fort Stedman from the rear. Nearing the stables, Buckbee met Cpl. Billy Buchanan, who had John the Baptist in tow. Mounting his horse, Buckbee conducted his men up the ravine until they came near Fort Stedman. He then deployed DeLand and the rest of the Sharpshooters behind an old railroad embankment.

On their way forward, the men cursed the darkness; all eyes were on the flashes of guns, both small and large, from the fort. One big Indian said aloud, "Me shoot-um damn Johnnie." Another let loose with, "Me kill-um much." Others kept up the elocutions, forecasting the doom of the audacious raiders. "It would have pleased you to hear their remarks," Buckbee proudly wrote his mother that evening.[14]

DeLand positioned his men along the railroad grade, and Buckbee safely piloted "Old John" back to the ravine, where he ran into a squad of Confederates. This small collection was one of several groups sent to attack Union emplacements behind Fort Stedman, but the rebels had become bewildered in the myriad trenches and roads in back of the fort.

At first, in the semidarkness, Buckbee thought them prisoners. If they had stayed quiet, he would have ridden into their midst; but some cried out, "See! See! Shoot that *cuss* on that horse—surrender, you damned yank." Swinging John the Baptist about, Buckbee spurred him back to Captain DeLand's position.[15]

> I have been under heavy fire a few times, but it did seem to me as though there were more bullets in the air to the square yard than ever I had experienced before. They sang over us and to the sides of us and all around us, but "Old John" applied himself to his work and made the dirt fly from his hoofs. He, evidently, however, appreciated the situation, for his ears were in one continual flap and quiver as balls would sing pretty close to him.[16]

Hollering, with his hat swinging in his free hand, Buckbee raced back to DeLand's position. As soon as he neared the line, the Indians "set up a yell that would have frightened old nick himself, and went straight at the Rebs on the run."[17]

The quick attack gobbled up the rebel party. The officer who proffered his sword to Captain DeLand asked, "Say, wait a minute—where is that Battery that I was told was up on the hill just beyond here? I lost my *barrins* entirely and in some way got away from my men."[18]

Buckbee left the prisoners with DeLand's men and hurried back to his own command. As he crossed a bit of high ground he saw, in slow motion, a rebel shell coming straight at him. It exploded just before it hit the ground directly in front of his mount. "Old John" stopped short in his tracks. Buckbee fell heavily and awkwardly out of his saddle; but he jumped up from the ground just as fast. With his hand on the saddle's pommel, he put his foot in the stirrup. Then everything went black. A chunk of iron from the exploding cannonball had ricocheted off the ground and struck Buckbee in his side, knocking the wind out of him and causing him to lose consciousness. The shrapnel "struck on the Testament cutting both coat & shirt a little."[19]

After his escape from Southern captivity, Buckbee had visited his mother during a short furlough. Before he returned to the regiment, his mother's domestic, whom he called fondly "Aunty," had given him a New Testament. That small book, which Buckbee carried in his blouse pocket, may have saved his life.

Buckbee was close to his own lines; a couple of his men ran to his aid and carried him into one of the cook shanties nearby and revived him. Realizing he was still whole, Buckbee hurried to the men in the front trenches. Through the late fog he "was surprised to see two or three rows of little sparks of fire along the surface of the ground." Actually, what he saw were the glowing coals in the men's pipes. They sat in drainage ditches, which were at right angles to the main line, and faced Fort Stedman. Calmly smoking their pipes, the Sharpshooters kept up a casual but steady fire toward the captured works and the open ground between both armies.[20]

Captain DeLand's men held their position along the railroad embankment and poured a hail of lead at the Confederates until the enemy either surrendered or withdrew.

Fort Stedman's elevation hindered the attacking Confederates. Union detachments on either side of the fort had a clear view of the enclosure, because of the height of the land on which it was perched. The rebels were bottled up in the fort and "in a road just back of the Fort, which was cut through the hill about shoulder high and opened down towards our [Second] Brigade."[21] When it became light, every soldier in the Second Brigade "had a plain shot at every man who stirred on the high ground in the little piece of woods just back of the Fort, or who, for self-protection, got down into this road, and thousands of them did this."[22]

The flank fire was so heavy that the harried rebels along the road dug out little holes to help conceal themselves from the flying lead.[23] The Fifty-sixth North Carolina formed the very left of the Confederate line. Some of its members still carried rifles captured from Company K's Indians the past summer;[24] these same rebels were now catching lead from Company K.

Brigadier General Hartranft, commanding the Third Division of the Ninth Corps, which was composed of six brand new Pennsylvania regiments that had not yet seen action, moved his men toward Fort Stedman. By 7:30 AM the rebels at the rear of the fort, who were taking a murderous flank fire from the Second Brigade, started to retreat. A galling fire from the picket line checked that thought.

The two Michigan regiments closest to the fort ("who made no disposition to get out of our way or let us alone," according to the commander of the Fifty-sixth North Carolina) captured 315 men, their officers, and a brass band that had followed their comrades into the Union lines.[25] Captain DeLand's two small companies captured four officers and 50 enlisted men.[26] Hartranft's division and the men already on the line made a sudden dash on the enemy in and around Fort Stedman between 8:00 and 9:00 AM and completely overran them.

The losses from the attack totaled 70 killed and 424 wounded on the Union side and another 523 captured. The rebels fared much worse. Their plan to punch a hole in the Union lines and wreak havoc, thereby prolonging or even winning the war, had come to naught. General Lee's last offensive of the war was an unmitigated disaster. About 1,500 rebels were killed or wounded, and another 1,949 were taken prisoner. The rebels lost seven flags, but the Federals lost not one flag or cannon.[27] Half of Ransom's brigade remained behind as prisoners. Included in the list of the captured were the colonel and many of the remaining men of the Thirty-fifth North Carolina, the regiment decimated by the Sharpshooters in the fight of 17 June 1864.[28]

Most of the Union losses centered on Fort Stedman and the lines to the left. This battle, mused Capt. Albert A. Day of the Twentieth Michigan, "compensated, in some degree, for the mortification of the disaster at the Crater."[29]

As bad as the fighting was to the right of Fort Stedman (in the Second Brigade lines), it was still lighter than what took place on the other side of the fort. The Second Brigade captured 333 Confederates and sustained only 51 casualties. The Second Michigan lost the most men—one killed, 8 wounded, 19 missing.[30] Only two Sharpshooters were wounded, and none were killed, although one of the wounded died on the operating table from the effects of chloroform.[31]

After the captured rebels had been sent to the rear and his men reoccupied their lines, Major Buckbee rode back to the brigade hospital to see if any of his men were hospitalized. Stretchers holding wounded men were grouped around the operating tent. Glancing at the faces of the hurt men, Buckbee saw none he recognized and turned to leave. His gaze rested for a moment on a cone of coagulated blood hanging like a stalactite from the bottom of one man's cot. Looking at the man's face, but not recollecting it, he again started to depart when the wounded soldier opened his eyes and smiled weakly at the major. Buckbee moved in closer and the man whispered, "We held them, anyway."

"What regiment?" asked Buckbee. Surprise now masked the pained face, and the soldier said, "Why! Your regiment. Don't you know me? I'm one of the new men." Bidding the lad to rest quietly, Buckbee quickly located the hospital steward, Al Keating. Moving the wounded boy ahead of the other men, Keating had the surgeon dress the Sharpshooter's wound. Although he had lost quite a bit of blood, the wound itself was not mortal; he rejoined the regiment before it was mustered out. It was the only fight he saw as a Sharpshooter.[32]

Buckbee returned to the regiment to check things out one last time, and then sat down to write a letter to his mother. He let her know that her youngest had come through unscathed. His boys had given the rebels more than "their fill and now I can see the bodies lying between their works and ours."[33] He wanted the war to end; and now he saw a solution. "I would be perfectly satisfied to have them try it over again," he wrote his sweetheart a few days later, "as we shall kill the whole lot at that rate."[34]

To be ready for any future predawn attack, all the men of the regiment, excepting those who had just come down from picket duty, were ordered to fall out at 4:00 AM each morning under arms. There was something in the offing—the men could feel it—and the Sharpshooters kept themselves ready for the inevitable.[35]

Lieutenant Colonel Nichols Returns

A day or two after the Fort Stedman fight, Asahel Nichols returned to the regiment. Nichols was the original captain of Company E and the only one of the ten charter captains still listed on the regimental roll. In May 1864 he had been sent to a Washington, DC, hospital due to exhaustion and sunstroke, and then furloughed home to Lansing in late July. He did some politicking while convalescing, trying to secure an appointment in the Twenty-ninth Michigan Infantry, which was then being organized, but orders enjoined him to report to the front in October 1864.[36]

Throughout the winter Nichols did not return to the regiment but was carried on the roll as "Absent on Special Duty." The special duty included inspecting hospitals, nothing to really tax a man physically. Then, out of the blue, he reported to the Sharpshooters with a lieutenant colonel's commission in hand.[37]

Major Buckbee, obviously surprised at the sudden appearance of Nichols, escorted him around the works and brought him up to date on the promotions and duties in the regiment. Nichols appreciated Buckbee's efforts and retained all of the current appointments, with one exception. The new commander did not care for the acting adjutant, Lt. Henry Hulin. Hulin was an early enlistee of Company E, Nichols's old command, having entered the regiment in December 1862. He had served in every campaign and battle in which the Sharpshooters participated; in December 1864 he had become sergeant major and in early March first lieutenant of Company G.[38] But Nichols preferred not to work with him.

Buckbee then brought in 1st Lt. Kirke Noyes. A thoroughly dependable soldier, Noyes had enlisted in Company D on the same day Hulin had signed his papers in Company E (27 December 1862), but Noyes had gone in as first sergeant of his company. He had been wounded three times, at Spotsylvania, the Crater, and the Peebles farm; he was captured at the last place and not paroled until the end of February.[39] At 34 Noyes was one of the older men, and entirely trustworthy and hard working. "He filled the bill of Adjutant in every way," remarked Buckbee, who knew the job better than any man in the regiment, "as he always did in any position in which he was placed."[40]

Grant Makes a Final Move

On the day of the Fort Stedman fight, President Lincoln paid General Grant a visit at City Point. Later in the day the president toured the scene of the morning's fighting. Actually, this was not a social call. Lincoln made the trip to confer with Grant, Sherman, and Admiral Porter. One more campaign was needed, Grant believed, and the Confederacy would be brought to its knees.

In Petersburg Lee began preparations to evacuate the city. His position was becoming too difficult to defend. With Sherman's Westerners moving up from North Carolina, it was only a matter of time before the Union armies would have the Army of Northern Virginia in a vise.

Fronting Lee along the Richmond–Petersburg lines were 125,000 Union soldiers. The Confederates had less than half that many men. The weak sector in the Southern lines was their right flank, where Grant tried a turning movement. On 29 March Gen. Philip Sheridan's Cavalry Corps sidestepped the rebels while two infantry corps (the Fifth and Second) left the siege lines in front of Petersburg to help him.

To answer this threat, the rebels stripped their already thinned lines of more men and transferred them to their right. Thunderstorms bogged down both armies on 30 March, although the Union elements pushed closer to the enemy lines. The next morning the rains abated and the rebel right flank, which was 13 miles southwest of Petersburg, was smashed by a series of Union hammer blows that culminated in an overwhelming Union victory the next day. On 1 April the enemy right flank collapsed. Grant ordered a series of feint attacks along his own right flank in front of Petersburg, thus keeping pressure on the rebel lines so they would not be able to pull units from one end of their line to reinforce the threatened sectors.

The rumor mill in the siege lines spread hearsay as usual. What with two full corps sidling to the left and then the cavalry corps passing in back of the Ninth Corps, plus standing orders for all men to sleep fully clothed in case of an offensive, every man in the army knew a big push was soon to come.[41]

The Boy General

While Grant conferred with President Lincoln at City Point, Capt. Levant W. Barnhart of the Sixth Michigan Cavalry rode up to Major Buckbee's shebang on the evening of 27 March. General Sheridan's Cavalry Corps was just then passing in the rear of the Ninth Corps,[42] returning from its victorious campaign in the Shenandoah Valley. The cavalry was resting a day before setting out again.

Hallooing for his old school chum, "Barney" called out to Buckbee and the two happily talked over each other's circumstances. Learning that Barnhart was on Maj. Gen. George Armstrong Custer's staff, Buckbee asked if it were possible for him to see and talk to the legendary cavalry leader. Barnhart told him to come along, but "it depended on the general's mood."[43] The two rode to Custer's tent, and Barnhart led the way in. The tent was a large one—larger than the average wall tent. Some saddles and blanket rolls lay piled in a corner; a round table with a scattering of correspondence stood in another corner.

Buckbee's eyes widened as he watched Custer pacing, back and forth, diagonally across the tent. Hands behind his back, his head bent "as in thought," the legend quickly stepped off his short march, then turned and repeated the procedure. When the two junior officers invaded his privacy, Custer looked up, acknowledged their salutes, but kept pacing, saying nothing. Barnhart looked at Buckbee, raised his eyebrows, and walked out; Buckbee followed. So ended Buckbee's interview with Custer. Barnhart had warned him that there was "no use to try to talk to him when he has one of his moods on." Buckbee was fatalistic about the meeting. Custer seemed taller, although he expected to see a tall man, "and his face seemed older and harder than I had expected to see it."

Custer was only 24 years old; Buckbee was just 21. Both were boys transformed into hardened warriors. Used to seeing pictures in *Harper's Weekly* and reading the glorious exploits of the boy general, Buckbee also expected to see the legend covered with gold braid. Disappointedly, he remarked "on this occasion there was not a piece of gilt about him."[44]

The Union push against the rebel lines southwest of Petersburg bogged down during the evening of 29 March and all through the next day. The Second and Fifth Corps kept moving to their left to join in the Federal advance. The rebels stripped their lines to reinforce the threatened sector and still tried to keep a modicum of pressure on the Union position up and down the outskirts of Petersburg.

Confederate artillery and musketry fire on the Ninth Corps front on 29 March kept the Federals awake. The cannonading and musketry commenced a little after 10:00 PM and continued for some two hours.[45] There was a halfhearted rebel charge against the Third Brigade, but (noted Sgt. Mark Vining of Company D) it "failed to accomplish anything except to drive in a few pickets." Still, the shelling that accompanied the charge was horrific. "I never saw so many shells in the air at one time as I did then," Vining admitted.[46]

The Sharpshooters moved into the main entrenchments and stayed there all night in case the artillery barrage preceded an infantry assault. Sgt. John Shipman (Co. I), one of the new men from Hall's Independent Sharpshooters, refused to turn out. The bombardment scared him unmercifully. He hid in his bombproof. An officer went looking for him and told him to get up on the line. Shipman refused and raised his rifle to strike him. Quickly grabbing the man's rifle, the officer called for a guard to march him to brigade headquarters, where he was put under arrest.[47]

The bombardment killed three men and wounded seven more in the regiment. Otherwise, nothing changed. "We are looking for busy times for a few days," Buckbee wrote his mother, "as Grant has sent the rest of the army off to the left, as Genl Sheridan, with his cavalry, and we are left to protect City Point. Genl Lee must be rather pressed, or he *never* would charge our works."[48] Of the ones who died in the barrage, two came from Camden in Hillsdale County, and both belonged to Company G: Robert Cummings was only 19 years old, and Cpl. Charles H. Fields was 28. An Indian, known only as Pe-to-zo-ourquitte, also died on 29 March. His friends buried him behind the lines.[49]

Two corporals who had been in the regiment since its early days caught the wrath of their commanding officer on 30 March. Emmet Bennett (Co. D) and John McCann (Co. G) both lost their stripes for "cowardly conduct" during the Fort Stedman fray. As retribution, both had to wear a placard bearing the contemptuous term "Coward" while being paraded in front of the entire regiment between the hours of 2:00 and 3:00 PM on 31 March.[50] Three old privates, John Clark and Alvin P. Earl (both of Co. D) and John Randall (Co. F) merited the same punishment a day later.[51]

The Last Charge

Colonel Ely summoned Lieutenant Colonel Nichols and the other regimental commanders to brigade hadquarters on the afternoon of 1 April. He told them to keep a close eye on the enemy in their front. The picket line had to be heavily reinforced. All the men were to have their haversacks filled so they could follow the rebels if the latter pulled out of their trenches.

Nichols thought the brigade was to attack and hold the rebel lines, and he ordered the regiment to prepare for battle. He called his officers together and laid out the plan. As far as Nichols was concerned, his regiment was supposed to take the enemy's works. (Only later did the Sharpshooters learn that they were to make "a strong demonstration to hold the enemy in their works."[52])

Over on the Union left, the Battle of Dinwiddie Court House proved to the Confederates that a major Union offensive had begun. On 1 April the Battle of Five Forks destroyed a rebel division and prompted General Lee to move from Petersburg. His right flank was now very vulnerable. While the Fifth and Second Corps assailed that sector, the thinly stretched Ninth Corps held the Union siege line from the Appomattox River to the Weldon Railroad, fully six miles of works.

General Parke readied his corps to attack the still formidable rebel entrenchments. Parke pulled together two divisions (Potter's and Hartranft's) and Harriman's brigade from Willcox's division; he decided to assault the line along Jerusalem Plank Road. Only the garrisons of various forts on the line and the bulk of Willcox's division, which was holding the line in front of City Point, stayed put.

To keep the enemy from massing troops to blunt Parke's attack, Willcox received orders to demonstrate on his right. Colonel Ely, commanding the Second Brigade, made plans to cause as much trouble as possible for the rebels on his front. He set the demonstration to begin at 4:00 AM.

Ely set up a two-column charge using four of his six regiments. The Second Michigan, supported by the Twentieth Michigan, would lead the left column. The Sharpshooters, backed by the Forty-sixth New York, headed the one on the right. The Fiftieth Pennsylvania and Sixtieth Ohio made up the reserve.[53] At 10:00 PM on the night of 1 April the cannons and mortars on the Ninth Corps front opened up on the rebels. Sgt. Mark Vining knew something "big" was going on. "There is a grand movement on hand," he wrote home. "A despatch [*sic*] just came in, that Sheridan has taken the South Side [Rail] Road, and the 'rebs' are evacuating Petersburgh. Heavy firing from gun-boats on the James River."[54]

Although rain had drenched everything during the last three days of March, none fell on 1 April, and the ground dried out quickly.[55] The scene in front of the Sharpshooters was not devoid of fortifications. Both sides utilized well-protected trenches about six and half feet deep, but fronting both sides were smaller trenches for pickets. In between the picket line and the main line were *chevaux-de-frise*; they were chest high, and their ends were usually tied or chained together so as to slow down any attacking force.

At 10:50 PM the Sharpshooters moved up to the front picket line. Rebel artillery fire caused the men to jump and dodge, so the force left the picket line and went to the rear, where coffee was prepared.[56] The cannonade continued until after midnight. Desultory musket fire broke the silence into the morning hours. Then, at 4:05 AM Lieutenant Colonel Nichols ordered his 300 men into the advanced picket emplacements.[57] Before they moved out, staff and line officers from other regiments came over to shake hands with some of the Sharpshooters. "I expected we were all *done for* sure," thought Buckbee.[58]

The regiment slowly and quietly filed into the picket entrenchments. Then Nichols ordered them onto the plain fronting the rebel lines. Dressing on the colors, the Sharpshooters filed out. Color Sgt. Richard Campbell gripped the staff in his hands, followed by the corporals in the color guard.[59] The double ranks tried to keep their order as they moved through their own abatis fronting their lines.

The only sound Buckbee recalled was the swish of the men's legs as they advanced through the tall weeds. When they reached the rebel picket line, the men were ordered in hushed tones to lie down and await further orders. A bright moon shone in a clear sky, giving the commanders in the rear a rare treat. They would be able to view a night attack. The Sharpshooters, of course, were concerned that the enemy could clearly see them coming.[60]

Captain Evans had the most hazardous job. He and his detail of 25 volunteers now moved ahead. Supplied with axes, they had to chop away the two lines of *chevaux-de-frise* in front of the rebel trench. There was no surprise in store for the Confederates; their pickets had known when the Sharpshooters left their breastworks. Most of them had fired a shot, and then retreated to their main line. Now all was quiet on the rebel side.[61]

Eyes and ears straining in the darkness, each man alone in his thoughts, the Sharpshooters all knew what lay ahead. They noticed that although there was considerable shooting off to their left, where the Second Michigan was supposed to be attacking, no shots came from their own front.

Fifty axemen had preceded the Second Michigan. They were to cut away the *chevaux-de-frise*, but a murderous volley of musketry dissuaded them. They ran back to their picket line and stayed there, keeping up a steady rate of fire, but advancing no farther.[62]

The Sharpshooters had their own problems. They all knew the layout of the Confederate works: a six-and-a-half-foot deep trench was protected by a double line of those pointed barriers.[63] All the officers took it for granted that the spiked logs were chained together. Every one of them, with the exception of Nichols, had at one time or another in the past few months ventured out in the early morning hours to spy out the rebel works, heart pounding, trying not to emit a sound. Evans's party had to break up the *chevaux-de-frise* to ensure that the men would not be unduly hung up in front of the rebel guns. However, no sound of chopping reached the Sharpshooters waiting in the weeds.

Captain Evans returned. In a soft voice he told Buckbee that the *chevaux-de-frise* were not locked together. He and his men had turned them at right angles to the rebel line, which was no farther than ten yards in front of the main group of Sharpshooters. Evans then ran to the left to tell Nichols.

Directly in front of the rebel line was a drainage ditch running parallel to the breastworks; the line of *chevaux-de-frise* guarded this ditch. In all the months they had been there, none of the Sharpshooters had noticed it. It was assumed that the *chevaux-de-frise* were directly in front of the main rebel line.

No sooner had Captain Evans reported the situation to Nichols than a Southern voice drawled across the darkness: "Aw! Come on, Yanks, we're getting tired waiting." So tense were the waiting Sharpshooters that some guffaws greeted the rebel's outburst; but all that was nipped in the bud. Lieutenant Colonel Nichols's shrill voice broke the silence: "Forward, all. On the run—go on, quick."

With a shout, the whole line rose and charged—right into the ditch fronting the rebel breastworks. Not suspecting the existence of the defile directly in their front, most fell headlong into the pit; those in the rear piled atop those who had preceded them. Hollers, grunts, and curses stabbed through the darkness. Here and there some men actually laughed at the absurdity of what had just transpired, but reality intervened at once. The rebel line opened with a volley. As the men tumbled into the ditch, "there was a deafening report and a flame of fire passed over our heads," recalled Buckbee. At first, some men thought a mine had blown up in their faces, but cooler heads kept shouting, "Forward, forward!" Captain Evans was one of the first to gather his wits. "Now is our chance," he yelled at the men around him, "go up and be damned quick about it."

If they were prompt, they could hit the rebels before they had a chance to reload. Frantically, the men grabbed handholds in the side of the ditch and hauled themselves upward. Reaching the top of the embankment, they tumbled into the rebel side of the breastworks.

Shouts of anger and pain rent the air. Some of the rebels had managed to reload and were shooting the Sharpshooters off the berm, but the Southerners were outgunned. The Sharpshooters fired into their midst and ran their bayonets into the moving shadows. Men died with curses on their lips and in their ears.

Above the din the sharp voice of Nichols exhorted his men onward. Sword upraised, he fell over the embankment with a bullet in his side. Capt. Jim DeLand, the fiercest warrior in his family, was one of the first out of the ravine screaming at the rebels. He, too, went down with a wound that shattered his left arm. Undaunted by the carnage, Captain Case led his men into the breastworks. Lieutenant Hulin, the man Nichols did not trust, fell with a wound, as did Lt. Friend Soules.

The ferocity of the attack broke any resolve the Confederates may have had. Some of the Southerners ran off; others threw down their weapons and threw up their hands, bawling, "I surrender!" Still others took refuge in their bombproofs. Rousting them out, the Sharpshooters sent them to the rear as prisoners. They captured 75 rebels in the attack, and an indeterminate number of their compatriots littered the entrenchment. Wounded Sharpshooters were also escorted back, leaving hardly more than 200 men to hold the position. But where was the reserve? The Sharpshooters possessed 200 yards of Confederate real estate, but for an hour no reinforcements would come up to help them hold it or to exploit it.[64]

The Confederate Fort Mahone, two miles to the left, fell to the Ninth Corps after a severe fight. A very strong point on the rebel lines, Fort Mahone (also known as Fort Damnation) was the main target for the corps. Learning of the success of the Sharpshooters, General Willcox rounded up three regiments and rushed them on the double-quick to help them.[65]

The Sharpshooters had held the rebel breastworks for more than an hour, when the pounding of feet to their rear attracted their notice. Their only reserve, the men of the Forty-sixth New York, were coming up to support them.[66] Even with that additional help, their position was as tenable as that of a man holding the tiger's tail. Musket fire from the enemy's secondary trenches pinned the two regiments down, and rebel cannon fire swept their location from another quarter.

Believing the galling fire would destroy the remnant of the Sharpshooters, the brigade commander sent one of his staff officers to get the men back before daylight really exposed them to the enemy. The aide had to run along the edge of the Appomattox River under cover of its banks to reach the bend in the rebel works that was held by the Sharpshooters. Hurriedly shouting orders to their riflemen, the officers made sure all the wounded had been gathered together, then, with the injured men in tow, the Sharpshooters and New Yorkers ran back to their own lines.[67]

After dodging the gauntlet of iron and lead, and once more safe behind their own breastworks, the exhausted Sharpshooters learned that the rest of the brigade had accomplished almost nothing. The regiment to their left (the Second Michigan) had advanced only a few yards, fired at the rebel entrenchments, but proceeded no farther. The Twentieth Michigan had never even left its entrenchments.[68]

Lieutenant Colonel Nichols had interpreted his orders differently than had the other regimental commanders. The Second Brigade was to make a "demonstration." Nichols had made it into an assault. His daring, though, was what the army needed. Unfortunately, two small regiments could not hold the line. The men felt that if the entire brigade had backed them in the "demonstration," the rebel lines on their front would have fallen. As it was, only the Sharpshooters, with some belated help from the Forty-sixth New York, had engaged the enemy.[69]

Buckbee was exhausted, but charged up. "We could have held the works if we had been so ordered," he asserted. "The Regiment fought splendidly."[70] Most individual praise he saved for Captain DeLand. "Jim done [sic] *nobly* and is acknowledge by *all* to be *the officer* of the Regiment."[71]

Captain Case and a squad of men had brought back Captain DeLand, who had caught a bullet in his left arm. Faint from loss of blood, DeLand was immediately taken to the hospital. There he learned the arm had to amputated, but DeLand absolutely refused. The surgeons found the bone shattered in the upper arm, near the shoulder, and extensive damage to the shoulder joint.

Little else could be done, but DeLand remained adamant. Sending for Dr. Arvin Whelan, who was then serving as surgeon-in-chief of the First Division, Case and Buckbee filled him in on the problem. Dr. Whelan tried to convince DeLand that the best way to save his life was to remove the arm, but one other option was available. The surgeon could try a resection. The section of shattered bone would be removed, so the two healthy ends could heal together. Hopefully, the two ends would fuse and nothing unfortunate would interfere with the process. Informed that the chance of success was only one in a thousand, DeLand said, "Go on, I'll take the chance for I am going back with two hands or not at all." The surgeons chloroformed him and resectioned the arm. They removed four inches of splintered bone but managed to save the limb. The operation was a partial success.

Two weeks later, DeLand still languished at City Point, where the worst cases were kept. His brother, Col. Charles V. DeLand, came down to see him and to report to their parents on the younger man's condition. The colonel was shocked at his brother's status. "The wound was large," he reported, "& there was extensive inflamation [sic], involving the neck. All the surgeons told me he could not get well, or if he did it would be almost a miracle." Nonetheless, he stayed at City Point, ministering to his brother until he was ready to travel home.[72] After it healed, Jim DeLand's left arm was noticeably shorter than his good one, and he never regained full use of it.[73]

Nichols had also received a severe injury that night. At first, most of his men thought he had suffered a mortal wound, and in a way it was; the bullet had injured Nichols's spinal column. The side effects would have a terrible consequence.[74]

Capt. John Berridge of Company C, who had been with the regiment since December 1862, was wounded and missing. Berridge was one of the original sergeants in Company D. In November 1864 he had become regimental sergeant major, and was promoted to first lieutenant of Company C in December 1864.

Since 7 March he had been company captain.[75] Two new lieuten-ants—19-year-old Henry Hulin of Jackson, who had been ser-geant major from December 1864 to March 1865, and Friend Soules, one of three brothers from Emmett who had enlisted in Company A—went down with wounds.[76] Soules's wounds were too serious for him to resume duty.

At least four enlisted men died in the action. Sgt. Flavius Dexter (Co. F), Cpl. Wallace Litchard (Co. D), and Pvt. Albert Smith (Co. G), all from Hall's Independent Sharpshooters, were killed.[77] George C. Marsh (Co. C), with the regiment since Febru-ary 1863, also died in the fray.[78] Major Buckbee listed another 23 men wounded and 14 missing. Sadly, he related that "probably a good part of the missing are killed or wounded."[79] Buckbee rec-ommended three men for further accolades to the brigade com-mander—Capts. James S. DeLand, Leverette N. Case, and Ira L. Evans—all for their bravery in what turned out to be the regi-ment's last fight with the enemy. "DeLand and Case sprang up the hill[,] calling upon the Men to follow and jumped over the enemys [*sic*] work into their midst." Evans, having "always and at all times shown himself an efficient officer and a brave man" and "having been constantly with the Regt," was recommended "for general good conduct," one of the finer military tributes an officer could pay another.[80]

The rebel prisoners rounded up by the Sharpshooters re-ceived "a good square breakfast" before being sent to brigade headquarters. The Sharpshooters learned how badly situated the Confederates were; the only food any of them carried in his hav-ersack was a little corn meal.[81]

Despite the casualties, General Willcox was pleased with what he had learned from the attacks. Because of the pressure on the entire rebel line, the enemy had found it impossible to send reinforcements to the main target—the area opposite Fort Sted-man, "where the real attack was completely successful.[82]

In his after-action report, Willcox noted that "a portion of Ely's Brigade actually carried some two hundred yards [of rebel works]. . . . Three regiments were withdrawn from other fronts, and double quicked to the point but before it could be reinforced, the enemy had recovered it." If indeed any reinforcements had rushed to the aid of the Sharpshooters, the Second Brigade marksmen never learned of it. Regardless of the bravery and dash shown by the Sharpshooters, the regiment was not even men-tioned by name in Willcox's report.[83]

Because of the ferocity and partial success of the engagement, the names of five men were submitted to Ninth Corps Headquarters. Recommended for Medals of Honor in the "demonstration" were Color Sgt. Richard Campbell and Sgt. William Wick (Co. D), both of whom "engaged in hand to hand conflict with the enemy." The other three were Cpls. Sidney Haight and Charles Thatcher (Co. E) and Pvt. Antoine Scott (Co. K), the last for "repeated gallantry."[84]

The last three had previously received medal citations for their conduct in the Crater. Unfortunately, no action took place with these later recommendations, and none of the five received any governmental congratulations or medals for their heroism in the "demonstration" of 2 April.[85]

The Rebels Leave Petersburg

During the daylight hours of 2 April, cannon fire was heard over to the left, beyond Petersburg. By that time all the men knew Sheridan's force had pummeled the Confederates there. At noon dark plumes of smoke rose from the city. The rebels had begun burning whatever baggage could not be carried away.

Petersburg was being evacuated by the Army of Northern Virginia. Flames licked buildings, flared into maelstroms, and then subsided into sooty smudges. Every so often explosions rocked the town as ammunition was destroyed.[86] Field glasses from a hundred different points along the Ninth Corps front focused on the city less than a mile away.[87] Intermittently, musketry fire rolled up and down the Union line, and then waned. So the day passed. Colonel Ely sent one of his aides into the front lines during the day to watch the movements of the enemy. A distant rumbling caused by wagons and artillery batteries moving out of the city was plainly heard by all. Rockets streaked across the night sky as the rebels signaled each other.[88]

At dark a great explosion rent the air. All heads turned toward the Old Gooseneck battery across the river, whose "monster shells" had so often crashed into the Second Brigade's defenses. Everything pointed to the rebels leaving Petersburg.[89] At 1:30 AM Ely sent word to the Sharpshooters and the Second Michigan to be ready to move out at a moment's notice.[90]

The Regiment's Final Advance

With Lieutenant Colonel Nichols in the division hospital, command of the Sharpshooters fell to Captain Evans (Ed Buckbee's commission as major was in transit, so he was still officially a lieutenant).

Between 4:00 and 5:00 on the afternoon of 2 April, Evans learned from Colonel Ely that the Sharpshooters had to assault the same ground again. Ely assured Evans that the rebels had evacuated most of their trench line. In turn, Evans told his men the same story, but they did not believe it. No one charging enemy emplacements ever believed them to be empty. The Sharpshooters were sure it was "a put up job" to get them to attack the breastworks again, and that ragged, hungry rebels with unerring aim occupied those earthworks,. Still, not a man stepped from his place when the regiment fell in at midnight. The men had already packed their knapsacks and stacked them before falling in.[91] To their left, the men of the Second Michigan readied themselves for the onslaught. Behind both regiments the Twentieth Michigan took its place as the reserve.[92]

Just before midnight, one of Colonel Ely's staff officers told Lt. H. Dorr Blakeman, the officer of the picket, to send out a noncommissioned officer to learn if the rebels were abandoning the lines in front of the brigade. Blakeman handed his revolver to Sgt. William Wixcey, who had heard the interchange between the officers, and told him to reconnoiter the ground in their front. Gingerly, Wixcey eased himself over the berm of the picket trench and began crawling along the ground. Straining eyes and ears for any sign of the enemy, all he "discovered was quiet—absolute quiet, in fact too much quiet—along the line." Wixcey hurried back with the news.[93]

The Sharpshooters waited more than an hour in the pitch blackness. Then Capt. Prescott Skinner of the Twentieth Michigan (one of Buckbee's old friends from Ypsilanti) approached Buckbee with a "shake—I've got some mighty good news." He had heard the rebels had left their works. Buckbee said he did not believe him, but Skinner told him the intelligence came from the highest authority. In fact, he said, the Sharpshooters would soon get the same message.[94]

Skinner was right. In a few minutes a staff officer from brigade headquarters brought the identical dispatch. Sensing, actually hoping, that it was true, Captain Evans conferred with

Buckbee. They called for the adjutant, Kirke Noyes, and ordered him to tell the men in the ranks the same report. Noticing no enthusiasm among their riflemen, the two officers asked Noyes about it when he returned. "They think it is a fake to encourage them," he replied. Even Buckbee felt the same way. Fortunately, clouds obscured the moon, unlike the previous night, and a low-lying misty fog shrouded much of the field.[95]

Just then, cheering was heard off to the left, the chorus becoming louder as it jumped from one regiment to another. At the same time Evans and Buckbee received orders to move their men out.

The Sharpshooters stepped forward at 3:10 AM.[96] Cpl. James Walton of Company I gripped the flagstaff in his hands and surveyed the landscape ahead.[97] Fires from the city made seeing what lay directly in front of them even more difficult. This trip over that clearing was infinitely more nerve-jangling than the one 24 hours earlier. Buckbee believed he walked among the bravest men in the army that morning, for the Sharpshooters knew the rebels were no fools. The enemy would hold their fire this time until the Sharpshooters stepped up from the little ravine in front of their works. They marched into the defile as silently as possible, but how quiet can more than 200 armed men be?

And then—Quickly! Hurry up, lads! Over the top, boys! Screaming like banshees, the whole crowd of blue-coated warriors jumped and rolled into the rebel breastworks. There were no rebels in the trench, at least no live ones—only the corpses of the Confederates killed by the Sharpshooters the previous day. Except for the dead, no Southerners could be found.

The First Union Regiment in Petersburg

Evans quickly reformed his men on the far side of the captured trench. Conferring with his officers, he told them they would probe the enemy lines as far as possible, even into Petersburg itself. Excitement lit up every man's face. The Sharpshooters cheered their success, letting the rest of the brigade back in their trenches know of the triumph.[98] As far as they knew, no Union regiment was close to them. They were alone, and no enemy confronted them.

Darkness still enveloped them, and they had to cover another mile of enemy territory before entering the Cockade City.

Earlier, Colonel Ely had told Evans and Capt. John C. Boughton, commander of the Second Michigan, that if possible they were to "cautiously" approach the town and hoist a Union flag on some prominent public building.

From where they stood, the Sharpshooters could see no friendly troops, nor did they have contact with any. The officers decided to forge into Petersburg regardless. God willing, they would be the first Union soldiers in the city. Scouts went out to find the road leading into Petersburg. Once it was located, the men moved out on the double-quick. Tired but elated, the command jogged down the dark, empty road.

Evans told Buckbee to send word down the column to stay closed up. They were hurrying in order to be the first Union regiment into the city. Shouts behind him told the commander the men were with him all the way. "Hustle, Adje., we can stand it as long as you can." The old familiar title was still used by the men for Buckbee, who was a favorite of the men in the ranks. Another called, "Go it, adje., we'll stick to your heels." The jests trailed off as the men kept running toward the city. Everyone saved his breath.

The column slowed as it crossed a small bridge over Lieutenant Creek, and then it entered the town proper. Rare it is that a man believes he is living a historic moment, but just such an instant embraced the Sharpshooters as they moved into Petersburg, their "way lighted by the glare from burning tobacco warehouses.[99] They were the first armed Union soldiers to move freely about the town in years. The object of ten months' killing was now theirs.

While searching the streets for a suitable building from which to flaunt their colors, the Sharpshooters met a small group of civilians. The three-man party carried what looked like a white tablecloth or bedsheet as a surrender standard. Their leader addressed the armed Federals, asking for the officer in charge. Captain Evans stepped forward and the spokesman, after a moment's indecision, said, "We come to surrender the city and hope private and public property will be respected."

Now there was absolutely no doubt that the Confederate army had left. The civilians—the mayor and a couple of councilmen—"asked for protection of the women and children and public property." Captain Evans decided to take the little group to a higher authority; he ordered Lieutenant Blakeman to keep the men spread out and to secure the immediate vicinity.[100]

Evans asked the surrendering party the location of the tallest building in the area. The mayor led him a couple of blocks to the Petersburg Courthouse. Then Evans and a squad of Sharpshooters accompanied the mayor and the two councilmen back down the road, keeping a lookout for Colonel Ely and his aides.[101]

The courthouse sat on a hill behind Sycamore Street, one of the main north–south streets in Petersburg. A set of stairs led to a landing, then another set of stairs led to the two-story Greek revival building. Six columns set off the front of the structure. Surmounting the edifice was a tower as high as the main structure, and on top of the tower stood a statue. A clock face covered the top front section of the tower just below the statue.

Posting guards on Sycamore Street, Buckbee took along the five members of the color guard. He decided against going in alone ("I remembered Ellsworth's fate").[102] He and the squad ran up the stairs to the courthouse. "We had quite a time with that Court House door, but soon got in," found the stairway to the right of the entrance, and mounted the steps. By the light of matches the men climbed to the clock tower. Then, ascending a ladder to a trap door, they reached a small room containing the clock mechanism. Squeezing into the area behind the clock, Buckbee borrowed Cpl. John Easey's Springfield, knocked out a piece of the clock face, took the regimental flag from Cpl. Walton, and stuck it through the hole. He then unrolled the flag and its streamers, securely lashing the staff to a beam inside. One man looked at his watch. It was only a few minutes past 4:00 AM. The earliest purple strands of morning outlined the eastern horizon.[103]

The First Michigan Sharpshooters was the first Union regiment to enter Petersburg and its flag was the first Union standard to fly over the city. "Ain't that *glorious?*" wrote an ecstatic Buckbee to his mother.[104]

Later, when it came time to tally the names of battles and honors on the silk streamers attached to the regiment's flag, the men included a final one that read, "THE FIRST FLAG IN PETERSBURG," a claim made official by the government. Twenty minutes later the Second Michigan hoisted its flag atop the customs house, a few blocks from the courthouse.[105]

While Buckbee and the color guard climbed the the tower and Captain Evans hustled the civil authorities back to the brigade commander, Captain Case took five men down the street, where they found a building darkened except for a light shining under a door. Laughter and the click of billiard balls sounded from inside. Pounding on the door, Case demanded admittance. Immediately, all noise inside the room stopped. The door opened and Case and his small party rushed in. To his amazement, Case found the room filled with Confederates. Seeing the armed men, one rebel stepped forward saying, "Well, I suppose we're in the hands of the provost guard." Then he took a closer look at Case and the other Sharpshooters and exclaimed, "Who the devil are you, anyway?" Informed that they were all prisoners of the Union army, the rebels meekly surrendered. Case marched the whole lot of them down to the courthouse.[106]

Buckbee and the color guard were outside the courthouse when Case returned. It was still too dark to see the flag on the tower. Buckbee marveled at the number of prisoners gathered in when Case arrived with his total. In addition, other squads were just coming back with more captured Confederates. Captain Evans also returned; he and his small squad had rounded up even more enemy stragglers. Some of the Sharpshooters were now sleeping on the darkened street. Evans did not awaken his men to get them to guard the rebels. "The boys are so worn out, I did not have the heart to make details for guarding prisoners," he told Buckbee.[107]

Evans also knew that there were too many mouths to feed with the food his men had. Besides, these prisoners were stragglers—men who had already given up. The chances of them rejoining the Confederate army were slim indeed. Buckbee and Evans saw the futility of holding and feeding the prisoners, so the rebels were told they were free to leave, to go anywhere they pleased. Not one stayed. "I doubt if any of them made any considerable effort to find their regiments," Buckbee added.[108]

Maj. Clement Lounsberry, acting assistant adjutant general of the Second Brigade, had met with Evans and the men with the tablecloth at the same time Buckbee was knocking a hole in face of the tower clock. The mayor of Petersburg, W. W. Townes, and his committee of two formally surrendered the Cockade City and asked for protection for its citizens and their property. Lounsberry waited until he knew Union flags were flying over the city and proper pickets and patrols had taken over. Then he gave his assurances in the name of Colonel Ely.[109]

When word reached General Willcox that the assault troops of the Second Brigade held Petersburg, the Third Brigade, which was still in its breastworks, formed line of battle and advanced into the city. *Chevaux-de-frise* were cut away, pioneers filled in trenches, and the artillery quickly followed the infantry.[110] As light greyed the morning sky, the high-spirited soldiers who tramped through the solemn streets of Petersburg saw the Sharpshooters' ragged flag atop the courthouse and jubilantly saluted it.

Buckbee wrote to his sweetheart that same day on a sheet of foolscap "I found lying on a table in a house here," that "the whole line took up with a cheer—and oh what a shout there was."[111]

Near 6:00 AM Colonel Ely and his staff entered the city. By that time the Twentieth Michigan had planted their flag on the courthouse tower as well, although some ten feet below that of the Sharpshooters. Near the Twentieth's flag flew the colors of the Sixtieth Ohio.[112]

When Ely arrived, even he became caught up in the headiness of the moment. Newly freed slaves surrounded him and his entourage, impeding his progress toward Sycamore Street. Then he saw the flags on the courthouse tower. Putting his spurs to his mount, he rode the animal up the steps of the building, then proudly turned back to his cheering men; the whole brigade filled the streets around the courthouse.[113]

The Second Brigade band, which included a number of former Sharpshooters, entered the city at daylight and played martial and popular airs from the courthouse, later moving to the customs house. Troops sang and cheered to the music and the ex-slaves joined in the uproar. At 8:00 AM the First Brigade band entered Petersburg, its score commingling with its sister brigade's band, "all adding merriment to the occasion."[114]

Guards took positions in front of stores, private dwellings, and public edifices to forestall civilians, recently emancipated slaves, and rampaging soldiers from breaking into and plundering the buildings and their contents. The Sharpshooters encountered no resistance and incurred no casualties.[115]

Grant's Petersburg Progress

While scouting around the vicinity of the courthouse, the Sharpshooters located the headquarters of the Petersburg *Express*, the last issue of which had appeared on 1 April. They found type, ink, and paper in the office. Men of all stripes, nationalities, and occupations could be found in almost every regiment.

Soldiers with journalistic proclivities stuck their heads into the *Express* office and decided to put out a newspaper, a paper with Union sentiments. Maj. R. C. Eden of the Thirty-seventh Wisconsin Infantry took on the job as editor. His two assistant editors were Capt. Charles McCreery of the Eighth Michigan and Chaplain Heagle of the Sharpshooters. J. W. Griffith of the Second Brigade Band became the foreman. His compositors included two of the band members, T. Marlatt and John Banta (the latter formerly a member of the Sharpshooters' band), Cpl. John Teasdale of the Eighth Michigan, and 1st Lt. Robert Farrell and Pvts. William H. H. Stewart and Palmer B. Bostwick of the Sharpshooters. One lone figure from the Sixth Corps, Pvt. S. Dalrymple of the Ninety-fifth Pennsylvania, drifted in to lend a hand.

Titling their creation *Grant's Petersburg Progress*, under the date 3 April 1865, the crew labored all morning. Hard news, editorials, and tongue-in-cheek reflections filled the columns. Repeating the story of the official surrender of the city by Mayor Townes and the "joyful tidings" of "the fast dying Confederacy," other pieces included "A Warning to Whiskey Drinkers," which was copied from a North Carolina paper, and "Fashionable Arrivals," which noted the appearance of "Gen. Grant and Staff and the Army of the Potomac, generally." [116]

More Flags

While prowling through the courthouse, a member of the Sharpshooters' color guard found a Union flag, an old-fashioned one with thirteen stars. An inscription noted that it had been presented to the Petersburg Grays, a local militia unit that was currently part of the Twelfth Virginia Infantry, one of the Confederate regiments retreating from the city. The organization had existed prior to the Civil War, and the flag had been presented to it by the ladies of the city back in 1850. When the rebellion broke out, the Petersburg Grays joined the Confederate army. Their flag, the old stars and stripes, actually had flown at the head of their column while on the march and in camp. After a while, though, the flag had been returned to Petersburg for safekeeping and stored in the courthouse. The Sharpshooter who found it gave it to Buckbee as a souvenir. [117]

Ninth Corps regiments filed into Petersburg during the morning hours of 3 April. Union "flags floated on every dome and pinnacle," remarked one staff officer.[118] The crowds that formed did not resemble anything sober or sedate. Officers on horseback smiled broadly as they led their regiments, brigades, or divisions through the city's streets. Thousands of soldiers, noisy and exuberant, marched through the town. General Willcox looked "happy and dignified" and was doubtless pleased that his division had entered the city first. A reporter from the New York *Herald* praised the usually taciturn commander. "General Orlando Willcox with his 1st Division of the 9th Army Corps has won imperishable honors. Many enough for one State." [119]

At 9:00 AM a Ninth Corps staff officer saw Generals Grant and Meade and their aides near the courthouse. Columns of men with bobbing banners swirled around Grant, who stopped for only a moment, then resumed the trail out of the Cockade City, "and that was all the attention [Grant] paid to Petersburg." [120]

Colonel Ely was left in charge of Petersburg, and he put everything in military order in a few hours. Food was distributed, private property protected, and paroles granted. Being a rebel city, the citizens as a whole did not feel too friendly toward their protectors. Pillaging, though, was minimal, and what did occur was the fault of a few citizens and some freedmen who were carried away with heady joy over their emancipation. Some of these problems may have been inadvertantly caused by the Twentieth Michigan. Adjacent to the courthouse was the Petersburg jail. When the Twentieth moved onto the grounds that morning, a number of them broke into the jail and set all the prisoners free, regardless of their crimes.[121]

During the day of 3 April the regimental quartermaster hitched up his teams and loaded all the men's personal and governmental baggage for transfer to Petersburg. Through some misunderstanding the baggage was unloaded at the courthouse instead of at the camp, which was some blocks away. Worse yet, no guard watched the bags and boxes. Citizens and soldiers alike stole whatever they pleased. One document that disappeared was the official commission for 1st Lt. Frank Thayer of Company I. He was in a quandary. No one believed he had been appointed an officer, since the orders were stolen along with the rest of his belongings. As quickly as possible he wrote to Michigan's adjutant general in Detroit, requesting a copy.[122]

CHAPTER 14

The Rebellion Is Crushed

The Chaffins

Colonel Ely's Second Brigade remained on provost duty
in Petersburg until the morning of Wednesday, 5 April,
when the command moved out via Cox Road to Sutherland Station on the South Side Railroad, about ten miles southwest of
Petersburg.[1] While most of the Army of the Potomac pursued the
main Confederate force, the Ninth Corps invested the countryside beyond Petersburg.

On Sunday, 9 April, the day Lee surrendered the remnant of
the Army of Northern Virginia to Grant, the Second Brigade
broke camp and marched to Ford's Station, about nine miles
farther west on the railroad line.[2] While there, Buckbee's commission, signed by Governor Crapo, finally caught up with him.
As the ranking officer in the regiment, Major Buckbee now took
command.[3]

Leaving camp, the Sharpshooters scouted out the countryside. They crossed Namozine Creek over a bridge and marched
about five miles to their destination, a large mansion. Captain
Evans led the regiment across some fields to the rear of the estate, while Major Buckbee and his orderly continued along the
road for another mile, where it turned and passed in front of the
residence.

Buckbee's orders were to proceed to the house and to thoroughly map the road, noting all bridges and habitations and byroads leading to the plantation. By the time he and his aide arrived at the house, Evans already had the men posted on the grounds and setting up camp. Buckbee had previously instructed Evans not to enter the house or to allow any of the men to go in or talk to the inhabitants.

The young commander dismounted his horse and walked up the front steps. As he did so he heard someone crying in the house. Knocking at the front door, he received no answer. He pushed the door open and walked inside, hat in hand, with his orderly at his heels.

To his immediate right was a drawing room. Two girls, both in their early twenties, sat in the middle of the floor trying to console each other. As Buckbee, who was uncomfortable with the situation, made his entrance, one of the girls suddenly jumped up and startled him with the exclamation, "Thank God, he is a gentleman."

Buckbee, who was hardly older than either girl, looked at them, his hat still in hand. His manner mollified them. One was a sassy little thing whose parents owned the plantation; the other was her cousin. The first one plaintively asked Buckbee if he could control "those men" in the yard. Assuring her that the situation was well in hand, he asked them what was agitating them so much. "My God," stated the girl, "that's a nigger Regiment." Perplexed by the statement, Buckbee looked out the window and saw the problem. Company K, the Indian contingent, was closest to the house. All the men in the regiment were dark. Exposure to the elements over the months had tanned all the whites, and the Indians were darker still.

Buckbee corrected the girl's misperception and assured the two that they had nothing to fear; no man, except himself and his orderly, had approached the house as yet, nor had anyone else tried to converse with them. Relieved, the girls asked if he could bring in some officers so they could "see a Yankee Officer at close range." Off went the the orderly to round up five officers—men with good singing voices, Buckbee ordered.

One of those summoned was Capt. Joseph O. Bellair, "one of the best performers on a piano I ever heard," related Buckbee, "and I have heard some good ones in my days." Bellair did not even look like an officer to the girls. Like all the men in the regiment, he was dirty, deeply tanned, his clothes were far from clean, and, like most front line officers, he had no identification of rank on him. He calmly put his old worn hat on a chair, sat down on the piano stool, and started playing, as the boys said, "to the Queen's taste." Spellbound, the girls listened, then begged him to continue when he stopped. The relationship was symbiotic. The men enjoyed the company of the girls in a peaceful setting; the girls, used to the finer things of life, needed the attention. The officers sang a medley of popular songs, both sentimental favorites and military tunes.

When they finished, one of the girls ran upstairs and came down leading an elderly woman, saying by way of introduction, "Gentlemen, I want to introduce you to my mother, Mrs. Chaffin." This was no inconsequential family; it numbered among the First Families of Virginia. Chaffin's Bluff on the James River had been named for them. Now reduced to more stringent circumstances, they apologized to the officers for not offering them to "take a snack," an expression the Northerners found amusing. "We literally have nothing to eat in the house."

The regiment camped that night in the Chaffin yard and the next day retraced its steps to the South Side Railroad. That afternoon Buckbee and his friend, Captain Case, each gathered a basket of food and delivered it to the Chaffins. For two weeks the brigade encamped on the railroad, and every few days Buckbee, Case, or both of them rode over to the Chaffin house, as much to deliver a basket of food as to see the girls.[4]

Lee Surrenders

All in all, these last days of the war were idyllic for the Sharpshooters. The brigade brass band entertained the men every day. Enamored of the area, Major Buckbee wrote his sweetheart Mollie of the beauty of the place. "I like this country first rate, and am thinking of buying a *large* plantation here about[.] Whew!!"[5]

Former Confederates, singly and in large groups, besieged the Second Brigade's camp for food. They came to surrender in droves and were admonished to move on. There was not enough food to keep doling out, for the Sharpshooters and the rest of the brigade carried their own rations. "Many a strong man I have seen cry because he had nothing for his family to eat," wrote one man of the Second Brigade.[6] Most of the hungry rebels trudged toward Petersburg, knowing the Union army kept mountains of provisions there.[7] Depressed by the abject poverty caused by the war, one Sharpshooter hoped "that our families at the North may never have to pass through such an ordeal as these people are subjected to."[8]

Surrounded by Union forces, the Confederates had surrendered on Sunday, 9 April, at a small crossroads called Appomattox Court House. It was a somber occasion there, but a more riotous affair erupted behind the Union lines. On Monday afternoon the Sharpshooters heard cheering off to the west. They looked at each other quizzically. Half an hour later a lone horseman galloped out of the woods to their front, swinging his hat and shouting. As he hastened past the veterans of the Second Brigade, he cried out the news of Lee's surrender.

Pandemonium broke loose. "Then there was one wild cry of joy, cheering, shouting, dancing, and many crying for joy," recalled Amos Farling of Company G. "Our work was finished," he continued. The war was over.[9] It was only a matter of time before the other rebel army, under Gen. Joseph Johnston, would give up the ghost in North Carolina. Sherman's Westerners should defeat them soon. Immediately thereafter, they hoped, all the men would be going home.

Drill and Promotions

Until all Confederates surrendered or were defeated in the field, the men had to keep sharp. As such, Major Buckbee issued a new schedule:

Reveille (Roll Call)	Sunrise
Sick Call	7:00 AM
1st Sgt's Call (Morning Report)	7:30 AM
Police Call	8:00 AM
Company Drill	9:00 AM
Recall	11:00 AM
Drill	1:30 PM
Recall	3:00 PM
1st Sgt's Call (Orders)	4:00 PM
Dress Parade	5:00 PM
Tattoo (Evening Roll Call)	8:00 PM
Taps (When All Lights—	
Except in Officers' Quarters	
Will be Extinguished.)	9:00 PM

Some problems had cropped up since the fall of Petersburg. The men felt the war was all but over, yet the officers had their orders. They were to "do all in their power to perfect their commands in Drill as in Action" in order to eliminate problems noticed by the commanders. Buckbee told his officers that "it is of vital importance that the men be able to Manouver [*sic*] without becoming confused, or loosing [*sic*] their place in the ranks."[10]

In the meantime new promotions were noted and old faces returned to the regiment. Cpl. Winfield Shanahan finally received his commission as second lieutenant from the governor's office on 10 April. The 20-year-old from Cassopolis had been with the regiment since March 1863, and had been waiting for months for the promotion. He was assigned to command Company K.[11] A few days later Lt. Daniel Gore returned to take over Company A, and Lieutenant Fish moved over to take charge of Company B.[12]

The Assassination

Early one dark morning, one of General Willcox's aides hurriedly made the rounds from one regimental commander to another. Awakening Major Buckbee, the staff officer excitedly told him, "You're to double your guards, every one of them, immediately, and no man is allowed to leave your camp from this time forward until further orders, not even for meals." The messenger then galloped off into the night. No other information came forth. Knowing something important had either recently happened or was about to happen, Buckbee issued the appropriate orders.[13]

A few hours later Dan Robbins, the commissary sergeant, straggled into camp, crying and blubbering so loudly that the guards thought him drunk. Finally, one of them asked what the problem was. Robbins blurted out, "Lincoln is dead." Someone told him to go to bed and sleep it off. Coming as it did from an emotional man, the news had little credence. Within the hour, though, other sources confirmed it.[14] Some men, like Robbins, cried aloud; others wept quietly. Some, recalled Private Farling, "rejoiced[,] but made no remarks."[15] There were still rabid Democrats in the ranks, but now Father Abraham belonged to the ages, and the camp was quieter than usual that day.

In the camp of the Seventeenth Michigan one "reptile" with definite Democratic leanings was too vocal. "I'm glad of it," he crowed. "If I had been there, I would have helped to do it." Quickly subdued by others in the regiment, the "reptile" was hustled over to a tree with a rope around his neck. Saved by an officer, the tactless soldier was put under guard, both to save him and to teach him a lesson.[16]

Sherman Finishes the Job

On 18 April, a few hundred miles south in North Carolina, General Sherman met with one of the last rebel holdouts, Gen. Joseph Johnston. The two agreed to an armistice. Except for a few diehards, the war was now over. Celebrations swept the camps of the Army of the Potomac in Virginia. Still, some called for vengeance. In a vitriolic letter to his parents from Washington, DC, the next day, Col. Charles V. DeLand, mouthing the sentiments of an Old Testament prophet, announced:

> The Rebellion is crushed, the traitors *will be punished*, the Nation saved and purified. Slavery, treason & the Democratic party all died, & were cursed and eternally damned with that fatal shot at that fatal hour when Lincoln was made from a man into martyr.[17]

A Triumphant Return to Alexandria

The Sharpshooters never again saw a picket line or served as skirmishers. On 20 April the men of the Second Brigade gathered their gear and moved back to Petersburg and City Point.[18] They marched alone; the rest of the division and the corps did not accompany them. The men's feet fairly flew, remembered Buckbee.

> In Julia Ward Howe's "Battle Hymn of the Republic," she uses the expression "Be jubilant, my feet." Well, my boys' feet were so jubilant there was no necessity of repeating the usual command while on a march "Close up," for everybody actually trod on the heels of the men in front of them.[19]

Early on 23 April the brigade boarded transports for Alexandria, Virginia.[20] Only a year had passed since the Sharpshooters had left Annapolis for the front. The Wilderness, Spotsylvania, North Anna River, Cold Harbor, the attack on Petersburg, the Crater, Weldon Railroad, Peebles farm, Hatcher's Run, Fort Stedman, the final attack on Petersburg, the raising of the colors on the courthouse—all now hid behind a veiled mist called the past.

Of the original 39 commissioned officers who had marched with the regiment through Washington, DC, only six—Major Buckbee, Captain Evans, Captain Bellair, Lieutenant Hinckley, Surgeon Whelan, and Chaplain Heagle—now returned with it. When the regiment left Annapolis on 23 April 1864, 963 officers and men had crossed over to Virginia's bloody soil, and another 198 officers and men had joined the regiment since then. Now just over 300 returned to the nation's capital.[21]

Arriving at Alexandria on 24 April, the brigade proceeded to march through the city and encamp a couple of miles beyond the town near Fort Lyon, one of the many defensive points encircling the District of Columbia.

Ragtag, bobtailed, and lousey, the brigade's regiments unfurled their colors for the march through Alexandria. Headed by the brass band, with the Sharpshooters in the lead, "we were a *tough* looking lot I tell you," Major Buckbee wrote home.[22] As the brigade entered the town, a tremendous crowd awaited them. The men were totally unprepared for the accolades that followed. Marching down the main thoroughfare to a joyous welcome— they were the first soldiers of the victorious Army of the Potomac to return—the elated riflemen heard the heartwarming expressions of the citizenry as they trod the streets: "Oh my!" said one admiringly, "Just look at them." A companion commented, "These men have seen hard service."[23]

Cheers greeted the Sharpshooters and their comrades in arms. Flags and handkerchiefs fluttered in the crowd. To Major Buckbee it seemed "as though every man, woman and child wanted to get a good look at close quarters at the brown, dirty soldiers." These were the first returning fighting men, and the crowd's enthusiastic joy knew no bounds.

Every man had bouquets of flowers stuck in his hat, pockets, accoutrements, and rifle. The parade dissolved into an indistinguishable mass of humanity with smiling, happy faces and unbounded happiness. Ladies insisted on carrying the weapons of the soldiers. They adorned John the Baptist, Buckbee's mount, with flowers. They tied ribbons to his mane, tail, saddlebags, bridle, and saddle. The conquering heroes had come home. It was a glorious day for the Second Brigade.[24]

For the Twentieth Michigan it was sort of a homecoming. On the day of their arrival in Washington, DC, back on 4 September 1862, the regiment had camped in the same area. History has an odd way of treating its performers. Almost three years later the bronzed and calloused veterans of the Twentieth returned to their starting point. Men older and wiser than their years looked at the same ground they had strolled over as wide-eyed boys only three years before—or was it centuries ago?[25]

The brigade camped near Fort Lyon for four days. On 28 April Colonel Ely had his men again break camp and march across the Potomac River on the Long Bridge, and pass through Washington and Georgetown. Filing through Tenallytown, they set up their camp on its outskirts.[26]

Conn and Randall Return from Prison

On 5 May Capts. Charles G. Conn and William Randall returned from furlough following their release from Confederate prisons. Both had been captured at the Crater, and now they brought their fellow riflemen up-to-date on their whereabouts.[27]

Separated from the enlisted men after their capture, the commissioned officers had been transported to Danville, Virginia, and then to Columbia, South Carolina. While in transit, Conn had escaped in North Carolina with another officer, but both had been picked up the next day. Buckbee had actually seen Conn in the Richland County jail after his own abortive escape:

> I was standing listlessly at our cell door watching a number of these prisoners, who were coming down from the floor above on their way to the yard, where they were allowed to spend a time for a little fresh air and exercise, when I suddenly saw a face that I *knew*, and called as loud as I could[,] "CONN", "CONN".
>
> Sure enough, it was my old comrade and chum, Charles G. Conn. . . . He turned, pushed his way through the crowd of prisoners, threw aside the guards and we clasped hands through the grating. The confederates, however, hustled him away before I could learn how he came to be there, or how long he had been a prisoner of war.[28]

Conn was incarcerated for the next few months in Columbia with Dicey and Randall. The three made another attempt at escape. When Sherman's army moved through the Carolinas after its famous March to the Sea, the rebels decided to move their prisoners to "safer quarters." Just before the captives were ordered out, the three Sharpshooters had themselves buried under some dirt and rubbish, hoping to escape and join Sherman's men. Their plans went for naught; some guards, prowling about for plunder, discovered the ruse. Crestfallen, Conn, Dicey, and Randall were forced to rejoin their unfortunate comrades en route to a more secure prison.[29]

As more men returned from furloughs after their release from Southern prisons, the regiment's numbers swelled to more than 400 present for duty. First Sgt. Michael A. Collins (one of Company A's earliest recruits), who had been captured with Buckbee the night of 17 June, received his commission as first lieutenant at the end of May. He was given Company H to command.[30]

Two returning Sharpshooters must have caused more than a few tongues to wag. Pvt. James Harper (Co. A) had deserted from Camp Douglas on 23 October 1863; he returned in December 1864. Harper's court-martial finally convened on 20 April 1865; a lenient board sentenced him "to make good the time lost by desertion—1 yr, 1 mo, 12 days with loss of pay for that time."

Pvt. Louis Bennett (Co. K), who had absconded with Harper, received the same sentence, with the admission from the court that "the prisoner is a . . . Chippeway, and at the time of his desertion was unacquainted with the rules and customs of the U.S. Service." In actuality, nothing happened to either man. The war was over. Bygones were bygones. To expedite paperwork and all its attendant problems, both Harper and Bennett were formally mustered out with the rest of the regiment.[31]

More comments were probably made over 21-year-old John Fuller of Detroit, who reported to the Sharpshooters in late April. A one-year enlistee, Fuller was the last recruit for the regiment. While most of the men were awaiting orders to go home, here was a fresh fish. Fuller's appearance must have caused more than a few of the old soldiers to "learn" him how to become a soldier.[32]

Tenallytown and the Last Grand Review

The men liked Tenallytown. Amos Farling recalled having "a very fine time while at this place."[33] More regiments, brigades, and divisions invested the District of Columbia during the next few weeks, until 150,000 soldiers surrounded the capital. Even Sherman's Western troops were there.

Secretary of War Edwin McM. Stanton urged President Johnson to order one last grand review of the armies of the United States before they mustered out. Here were the victorious legions of America. Here was a last chance to look over the veterans of battles the likes of which had never before been experienced by any generation of Americans.

A reviewing pavilion—emblazoned with the names of Union victories and bedecked with bunting and flowers and flags and evergreen branches—was constructed in front of the White House. The president, his generals, and his cabinet would give a final salute from this pavilion to those armies which had brought an end to a terrible war, but a war that nonetheless had ensured the integrity of the United States.[34]

Ushered in by a pleasant morning, 23 May portended to be a fine spring day. The Army of the Potomac had been cleaning itself up for days. Hair and beards were trimmed, brass polished, clothes brushed. For the last time regiments that had fought side by side in hundreds of engagements would march to the drum. Flags and bunting hung from homes and buildings along the route. Bands tuned up one more time. At 9:00 AM the signal gun inaugurated the parade, and the Grand Review was on.

Gen. Phil Sheridan's Cavalry Corps formed the vanguard, its hooves clattering along Pennsylvania Avenue to the jingle of metal sabres and the blaring of bugles. The darling of the cavalry, Gen. George Armstrong Custer, resplendent as always, was idolized by the crowds. Behind the cavalry came the provost marshal general's brigade, followed closely by the engineers. The three infantry corps then stepped up the avenue; only the Sixth Corps was absent from the festivities.[35]

The three Ninth Corps divisions, preceded by their commander, Maj. Gen. John G. Parke, came next. Leading the Second Brigade in Willcox's First Division was the First Michigan Sharpshooters. How many voices had been stilled since a year before, when the regiment had marched past Willard's Hotel?

The Fifth Corps followed, and the Second Corps finished the parade. The soldiers filed by—tens of thousands of infantrymen, cavalrymen, artillerymen, engineers, and their officers. Ambulances, bands, cannons. As they passed the reviewing stand, the corps commanders joined the president and Grant. Parke went in first, followed at long intervals by Gen. Charles Griffin, commander of the Fifth, and Gen. Andrew Humphreys, commander of the Second.

The last soldier paraded by in the late afternoon. The cheers faded, the enthusiasm dimmed. Tomorrow, the Westerners of Sherman's army would troop by the same stand, but for now the military panoply was over, just like the war.

The Second Brigade tramped back to Tenallytown. As ideal as their camp may have been, the men were edgy. The war was over. The citizen-soldiers wanted to go home. The men had enlisted to put down the rebellion. Well, it was put down. It was time to get on with normal pursuits.

Marking Time

On 25 May, two days after their grand review, the men of the First Division were entertained by all sorts of Michigan dignitaries. Governor Crapo, Lieutenant Governor Grosvenor, Congressman Gregg, General Willcox, Colonel Poe—formerly of the Second Michigan and lately chief engineer of Sherman's army— and Lt. Col. Joseph Dickerson of the Tenth Michigan Infantry addressed the Michigan soldiers. The most burning question concerned mustering out. When, the soldiers wanted to know, were they going home? [36]

The Twentieth Michigan left first. Together with the Seventeenth Michigan and 109th New York, all of whose enlistments would expire by 1 October 1865, they departed on 1 June for home and family. They were envied by those still left.[37]

The rest of the First Division regiments stayed at Tenallytown. Men with little to do often find mischief to fill the time. Amos Farling and the first sergeant of Company G watched orderlies, messengers, and staff officers trot past their camp continually. Farling had little respect for authority and had repeatedly thwarted officers and their demands during his term of service.

One day, to relieve the monotony, the two Sharpshooters fired some rocks at a Captain Barry (one of General Hartranft's aides), causing the man's horse to buck and throw the officer. Farling and his friend quickly made themselves scarce. The next morning the regiment was ordered out, "and then our officers selected the roughs from the good ones." Whether they liked it or not, the men were still in the army, and someone had to pay for the transgression.[38]

On another occasion, Farling and some of his friends went foraging—an activity that was strictly forbidden. Eluding some guards, they robbed a potato patch and filled their haversacks. Almost intercepted on their way back to camp, Farling managed to outrun the guard, but his two companions were caught and lost their freedom for four days and their potatoes for good. When he reached his own regiment, Farling was accosted by a guard he knew, who demanded that Farling give him the countersign, which he did not know. Farling instead stepped up and said, "Potatoes for your breakfast." The guard passed him.[39]

To keep the men in line, a myriad of inspections were held. Regimental inspections came often, usually with words of admonition from Major Buckbee. On 15 June all the men had to "appear in heavy marching order," making sure that "great care . . . be paid to the condition of the company streets and quarters."[40]

On 1 July Buckbee, after receiving numerous recommendations from company commanders, promoted Sgt. William Wixcey to color sergeant. Wixcey was told that he "will be held responsible for the drill and good appearance of the 'Color Guard.' " Five corporals, each from a separate company, joined him as members of the guard: Franklin W. Wright (Co. A), Peter Stevens (Co. B), Eston Hoag (Co. I), Augustus T. Call (Co. H), and Charles Shaw (Co. K). All the men had been with the regiment since the beginning and could recite from first-hand knowledge every adventure experienced by the Sharpshooters. All were young men who had aged tremendously in the last year. Wixcey was the oldest of the group at 23; all the corporals were under 21.[41]

Complaints from civilian property owners reached regimental headquarters on a daily basis. Soldiers from Colonel Ely's brigade were blamed for "lurking about the residences of inhabitants in adjacent vicinities[,] destroying Fruit trees[,] shrubbery[,] and carrying off and trampling down yards[,] vegetables[,] and uselessly destroying property."[42] Regimental officers tried to crack down on chronic absences, but they may as well have tried to stop the sun from rising in the morning.

On 7 July division headquarters informed the commander of the Sharpshooters that six of his men had been caught in the act of stealing. Chagrined, Major Buckbee could only reply that "it was hoped that the men had too much regard for the reputation of the Regt. and their own good name to be guilty of such meanness."[43] Nonetheless, the depredations continued. Two corporals, Augustus Call (Co. D) and John D. Hunt (Co. C), lost their stripes for "committing theft." Call had only recently made corporal; he lost his rank and his position in the color guard.[44] Cpl. William Lindsley, one of Hall's Independent Sharpshooters, took Call's place near the colors.[45] Even Sgt. Antoine Scott, who had been repeatedly honored for bravery in action, was "reduced to the ranks" while the regiment marked time at Tennallytown.[46] He quickly managed to work himself up to corporal again.[47]

In all, from the end of the war until the Sharpshooters mustered out in August, 22 men found themselves "reduced to the ranks" for various infractions. Keeping the soldiers in line proved to be the most taxing problem for the officers. Philo R. Smith (Co. H) lost his stripes "for disobedience of orders and cowardly conduct." Sgt. Norman Engle of the same company was "reduced" for continual "Absence without leave."[48] Horace B. Seeley, who had lost his stripes in November for writing a letter to the Niles *Republican* castigating the Republican politics in the army, had worked his way up to first sergeant of Company G; he lost his stripes again on 20 April "for having overstaid [*sic*] time granted in furlough."[49]

The last men to forfeit their rank were Cpls. Ono S. Cass and Marshall Adams, both of Company E. They did not think they would be missed from battalion drill one hot day in July, while the rest of the regiment marched through various formations. Buckbee saw the matter in a different light.[50]

In early July division headquarters contacted Buckbee, asking him what he wanted done with Sgt. John Shipman. Shipman had refused to take his place on the line during a bombardment on the night of 29 March. He had also raised his weapon to strike his company commander when ordered out of his bombproof. Since that time he had been under arrest; now the higher-ups wanted specific charges filed. Buckbee told the A.A.G. to release Shipman. "His Co[mpany] Officer thinks that the man has been sufficiently punished by his confinement as he was very much excited at the time." A chastened Sergeant Shipman returned to the regiment on 6 July.[51]

Near mutinies affected many of the regiments still in the District of Columbia by late July, and the Sharpshooters proved to be no exception. Major Buckbee sympathized with the plight of the men, but his rank required certain responsibilities on his part. "I am worried a good deal now by my regiment," he wrote his sweetheart in late July:

The boys think they ought to be discharged and sent home, or else paid, and *I* think so too. But then we can not put up with mutinous conduct. The general, commanding the Division, has issued an order requiring us to hold an extra "roll call[''] during the night, as the soldiers are in the habit of pillaging, about here. The men are determined that they won[']t get up at night, for anybody. One regiment in the Division got to gether in a body and went down to their Colonel[']s tent and told him flatly that they would not attend any "roll call" after "Taps." And they did not.

My regt thought *they* could do the same thing, but I heard them coming and just as they halted in front of my tent, I threw up the flaps of the tent, and stepping out asked for the spokesman. It took them by surprise, and when they looked about, no one wanted to speak first. I talked *very* quietly for a moment and then told them to go back to their tents, and come at "roll call." And they *did*.

But it has cost me trouble, and I have two companies under arrest.[52]

The work of mustering out the remaining regiments proceeded rapidly, although some regiments, like the Sharpshooters, found the process all too slow. The Eighth Michigan finally left on 25 July.[53] Hardly had the near-mutiny been quelled by Major Buckbee when the Sharpshooters received word that they, too, would soon be going home.

On 28 July 1865 the First Michigan Sharpshooters assembled at the Delaney House to be mustered out of the service of the United States.

Pvt. Jason Broderick and his brother Dennis of Company G probably never realized their good fortune. Of the 69 groups of family members to enlist in the regiment, they were the only intact set left. Jason had enlisted in in June 1863. Dennis entered two months later.[54] Of the other 68, in some cases no one was left to be discharged.

Both John and James Mash-kaw of Co. K died at Spotsylvania. Charley Nash of Co. I was mustered out, but his brother Theodore was killed at Petersburg. The Woodward brothers died of disease, Hiram at Chicago in January 1864 and Myron six months later at City Point, Virginia. Lott Willett of Co. I stood in line, but his brother William was captured at the Battle of Peebles Farm and died in Salisbury Prison. The two Sutherland brothers, Charles and Mason, were captured at the Peebles farm, too. Charles died at Salisbury. Mason was repatriated but died from the effects of his imprisonment three months later. Horace Martin of Co. I was killed the night of 17 June 1864. His brother Ira was captured in the Crater, was later exchanged, but, like Mason Sutherland, died from the ravages of disease and maltreatment. Both Fullerton brothers of Company B died in battle, Elias at Spotsylvania and James in front of Petersburg. Among the officers, neither of the Graveraets, father or son, was present. The DeLand family had no representatives in the ranks, either. Charles had already been mustered out due to wounds; James was still recuperating from his wound; and Hooker had recently been released from the Dry Tortugas.[55]

The war had taken its toll. Of the more than 1,300 men who could proudly call themselves members of the First Michigan Sharpshooters, just over 400 would be going home together.

One who arrived in Jackson, Michigan, just one week before the regiment was Hooker A. DeLand. Released by order of President Johnson, the young DeLand immediately returned to his hometown to visit friends and family. He "will probably receive his back pay and allowances," intoned the editor of the Jackson *Eagle*. "Although the captain may have been indiscreet in the use of language to his superiors, he has given abundant evidence of his bravery on many battle fields." Neither the editor nor Hooker DeLand could know of the long travails that still awaited the cashiered officer.[56]

Home

On 30 July, near 7:00 PM, the steamer *Morning Star* docked at Detroit. "The regiment arrived home," read the notice of its homecoming, and an enthusiastic crowd awaited the gallant warriors. Lt. Col. Edward J. Buckbee led his complement of 23 commissioned officers and 386 enlisted men off the ship and into a spirited throng of well-wishers.[57] A sumptuous dinner awaited the conquering heroes.

The next day the Sharpshooters boarded a train for Jackson. There they again waited until the overworked clerks completed the necessary paperwork. Finally, on 7 August 1865, each man received the pay due him, and the regiment officially disbanded with very little fanfare.[58]

CHAPTER 15

There Is To Be a Roll Call

Pensions

The end of the war did not mean that the regiment ceased its existence. As the men scattered to their homes to take up the normal pursuits of mankind—work, marriage, church, family—middle age slowly overtook them. Despite this, thousands of times their collective memories must have zoomed them back to the bone-chilling cold at Camp Douglas, the wet woods of Spotsylvania, the dusty marches in Virginia, and the mud and stench of the Petersburg trenches.

Some reminisced with men of other units at Grand Army of the Republic (G.A.R.) meetings. Others mentioned odds and ends of their experiences to their wives and children, who probably had little or no idea of what it was really like to belong to a fraternity of warriors. At times in their daily pursuits, a thought from nowhere may have intruded into their consciousness. Some had psychological injuries that totally baffled the old soldiers and the medical community of the time. Others had more vivid reminders of their service; empty sleeves and scars from gunshot wounds reminded them and everyone else on a daily basis of what toll the war had taken.

The United States government spent millions of dollars a year on pensions for the former Union soldiers and their dependents. If ever anyone needed a constant reminder of the war, it came in the mail with the monthly payment. The amount of money one received depended on what kind of wound or sickness had befallen the soldier during the Civil War.

For Col. Charles DeLand, whose injuries included a gunshot wound in the left thigh and shell wounds to his head, back, and face, that meant $30 a month. His brother Jim, whose left arm was totally useless, obtained $20. Marcus Otto of Company K, whose right arm had been amputated above the elbow, received $24 every month from the government. For "lesser" injuries, the pension dropped. John Rainbow had been shot in the left shoulder at the Wilderness; his pension amounted to $4 a month.[1]

Widows and mothers with no sons to support them obtained hardly enough to keep body and soul together. Chic-ah-milgun Mash-kaw, whose sons were both killed at Spotsylvania, received $8 a month from a grateful government. And Sophia Graveraet, who lost her son and her husband, was given $15 per month until her own death in the 1890s.[2]

The First Reunion

The old Sharpshooters noticed the annual reunions that other units held and wrote to old friends, asking if such an event were feasible for the members of the regiment.

In the early summer of 1886 H. Dorr Blakeman of Jackson sent out invitations to as many Sharpshooters as he had addresses for. Blakeman enlisted in the regiment in November 1862 as a sergeant. Captured the night of 17 June 1864 in front of Petersburg and later released, he was commissioned a first lieutenant in February 1865. Now treasurer of Jackson County, his invitations to the reunion went out on county stationery:

Jackson, June 22, 1886.

Comrade:
    There is to be a roll call of all the First Michigan Sharpshooters upon the second day of the State Fair in Jackson[,] September 14th. Now, you can and must be present. Railroad fare will be one-half rate and you will never regret the expense. During the G.A.R. encampment held here in April last ten or twelve of the old regiment were together and we enjoyed ourselves; we did and no mistake.

Almost every Michigan regiment holds reunions except our own, and there is no reason why we should not except that we do not. We do not care much for the fair, and less for the fare, but let us take advantage of the half fare and get together once more.

Will you come? If not, why not? Please answer at once giving the address of any of the regiment that you know that I may give him an invite, and at the same time you drop him a postal card giving him the joyful news and urging him to be present in Jackson on the *second day* of the *State Fair, rain or shine.*

Ever and fraternally yours,
Dorr Blakeman, of Co. E.

P.S. Why not bring your wife?
Dorr.[3]

Men slowly contacted each other, and 21 years after their muster-out more than 80 of the former riflemen joined for a day of stories, back-clapping, and wide grins. The first annual reunion took place in Jackson, Michigan—the scene of their last gathering in 1865. Meeting at the Emmet Rifles Armory at 2:30 on the afternoon of Tuesday, 14 September 1886, men from all over Michigan, and from Illinois, Dakota Territory, Nebraska, and Kansas greeted each other, introduced their wives, and sat down to an afternoon and evening of conviviality.[4]

They set up the First Michigan Sharpshooters Veterans Association, with Col. Charles V. DeLand as president, Lt. Col. Ed Buckbee as first vice-president, Lt. Frank Whipple as second vice-president, George Saxton as secretary, and H. Dorr Blakeman as treasurer. The men passed a resolution adopting Mrs. Dell Clark, the colonel's daughter, who had been born in camp while the regiment guarded the Dearborn arsenal in 1863, as "Daughter of the Regiment." Immediately after the roll call and the election of officers, the Sharpshooters, at the invitation of Warden Hatch, trooped off to inspect the state prison at the north edge of town.

In the evening the boys and their wives assembled again at the armory. James O'Donnell, formerly of the First Michigan Infantry and editor of the Jackson *Citizen*, and currently the local congressman, greeted the Sharpshooters in the name of the city. Rev. Washington Gardner, county historian and future congressman, then congratulated the assembly and praised the regiment in "an eloquent address, reiterating its wartime history."

After the meeting the comrades gathered around a campfire to swap tales and relive old times. They also set a date a year in the future for the next reunion.[5]

Annual meetings followed in Lansing, Grand Rapids, and Battle Creek. When they gathered in Battle Creek in the fall of 1889, "about 70" were in attendance.[6] The old comrades "ate their dinner at the Williams House; after which, headed by drums and fife, they marched to the G.A.R. Hall. They appear to be enjoying the occasion immensely."[7]

It was a rather raucous event. The Sharpshooters:

> are shaking hands with one another in the most cordial way, while once in a while one will hear a whoop that will make him think some one is going to make "a charge." —But they aint; these "Old Vets" never go out to see a friend and then have it charged; they pay the case. This is a great day with them, and many a comrade has shook hands with messmates of twenty-five years ago. While the old boys are enjoying to-day, just think of the hardships they endured during the war, and see to it that they have plenty of leeway, as many of them will never meet again.[8]

One important item of business had to be concluded before the meeting adjourned—a new slate of officers for the association had to be elected. Frank Whipple of Port Huron (first lieutenant, Co. B) was elected president. Mark Vining from Ypsilanti (sergeant, Co. D) became first vice-president. Andrew S. Reed (Co. I), then living in Grand Ledge, was made second vice-president. H. Dorr Blakeman became secretary, and Truman Gee of Dundee (Co. C) was elected treasurer. For orator the men picked a lawyer, Benjamin F. Smith (Co. H) of Hastings, Nebraska. Smith had lost a hand in the fight on 17 June 1864. George W. Stone, the former drummer boy, rounded out the slate of officers as historian.[9]

Colonel DeLand's Reunion

The 1890 reunion was planned for Jackson; this time Colonel DeLand would host the festivities. DeLand had retired from the newspaper business in Saginaw and moved to a brick residence called "Pleasantview" just south of Jackson, where he was a gentleman farmer. He still retained the position of political gadfly. Old habits died hard.[10]

The colonel's brick home in Summit Township became a beehive of activity. Buses provided transportation free of charge from the G.A.R. hall in town for the four miles south to Pleasantview.

DeLand had chosen an auspicious date for the gathering—
30 September 1890—26 years since his regiment had fought at
Peebles' farm (the local paper dubbed it "the bloody assault on
Ft. Pegram"). Sharpshooters and their wives departed the trains
at the depot, found carriages waiting for them, and were taken to
the G.A.R. hall where omnibuses escorted them to DeLand's
home. Those who arrived early glad-handed each other and
whooped it up while looking over DeLand's acreage.

The colonel had prepared a lavish reunion. Four large tables,
set for 134 veterans, their wives, and some guests groaned under
a bountiful noon meal of pork and beans, salads, sandwiches,
doughnuts, cakes, fruits, coffee, tea, and milk. A couple of dozen
young ladies headed by Mrs. DeLand "kept the platter supplied to
the end of the repast." Old jokes and lively reminiscences passed
from table to table until 2:00 PM, when the formal meeting began.

The association president Frank Whipple, who had been
wounded at bloody Spotsylvania on 12 May 1864, called the boys
together. They seated themselves on chairs arranged in circles
around a large boulder that served as a speaker's stand.

Whipple introduced Austin Blair, the former governor of the
state, who acknowledged the salute of the boys in attendance and
strode to the boulder.[11] He "warmed up the hearts of his hearers
by his eloquent portrayal of the stirring days when they were
soldiering in dead earnest."

Warm applause hailed his speech, and the boys asked Blair
to take their sincere greetings and thanks to his invalid wife "for
the affectionate interest she had always expressed and exhibited
towards the regiment." She had presented the state flag to the
Sharpshooters when they were at Dearborn. That flag had flown
on the berm of the Crater, where it had been shredded by lead
and iron, on 30 July 1864, until the rebels overran the position.
Charles DePuy, Charles Thatcher, and Sidney Haight had won
the Medal of Honor there for extreme bravery.

The Hon. Roswell G. Horr, U.S. Congressman from Saginaw,
then jumped atop the rock. His talk was interrupted frequently
with applause and laughter. Jesting about his own military record
in the "home guards," Horr told of his long friendship "with your
old colonel, and if he was only half as good a fighter in war as he
was in politics, he must have been a good one." It was no "wonder
that his old regiment had won such imperishable renown."

Another of DeLand's friends, Congressman James O'Donnell, followed Horr and reviewed the regiment's war record, its

participation in 26 battles, the deaths of 157 officers and men in the last year of the war, the raising of the Stars and Stripes in Petersburg, and its hard-earned membership in the top 300 fighting regiments in the Union Army. He then spoke of current matters. He explained the subject of pensions, something of supreme interest to his listeners. In the present year, he told them, $167 million would go out to veterans and their dependents. He said it was money well distributed. "The soldier was not a subject of charity but a preferred creditor, and the government was honestly and earnestly trying to pay the veteran just what it honestly owed him."

It was a day for speechmaking, and the other dignitaries duly took their place on the boulder and serenaded the Sharpshooters with appropriate remarks. Gen. William H. Withington of Jackson, the first colonel of the Seventeenth Michigan Infantry, who was breveted brigadier general for leading a glorious charge at South Mountain in 1862, gave a short address. Two more speakers followed Withington.

Capt. Kirke W. Noyes of Paw Paw then stepped to the front and asked Colonel DeLand to join him. Relating a number of interesting stories about the colonel, Noyes ended his reminiscing of the old days by presenting "our old friend, the colonel" with a gold-handled cane on which was inscribed:

Presented to C.V. DeLand, Col. 1st Mich. S. S.
by survivors of his regiment, Sept. 30, 1890.

Momentarily dazed by the presentation, DeLand, who was "rarely at a loss for words," was hardly able to tender his most heartfelt appreciation. Holding the cane and pulling himself together, he surveyed his Sharpshooters as a father would his family. "He told the boys how sincerely he would prize that gift above all others in his life."

Standing on the boulder, clutching his cane, Colonel DeLand looked over the remnant of his old regiment with eyes that alternately viewed two worlds—one in the present and another a quarter-century earlier. The lump in his throat slowly dissolved and his eloquence returned as he recalled the shared experiences of the men before him. He remembered the confusion of the new recruits at Camp Chandler; marking time at the arsenal in Dearborn; chasing Morgan's horse thieves out of Indiana; guarding rebel prisoners at Camp Douglas; joining the Ninth Corps at

Annapolis; and the mind-searing battle scenes. He paid particular attention to three battlefields—Spotsylvania, Petersburg, and Peebles farm.

Rather than reiterate the regiment's past glories, DeLand slowly and purposefully ticked off a litany of the dead: John S. Vader, Henry Apted. . . . Men and boys who gave their lives for their country . . . James Jones, Levi Porter. . . . Men and boys who languished in hospitals and on bloody fields . . . John M. Benedict, Benjamin F. Hinckley. . . . Men and boys buried in manicured military cemeteries or in unknown graves in forgotten patches of Virginia woods . . . Levi Lewin, John W. Reed, Thomas Wright. . . . Men and boys who died instantly when rebel shells or bullets ploughed wicked roads through muscle and bone . . . George Arnold, Jonah Dabasequam, John Piper. . . . Men and boys who starved to death in some obscene rebel prison . . . Elisha Fowler, Clark Fox, Sr., Peter South. . . .

As each name fell from his lips, a collective nod shuddered through his audience. Eyes misted over as the Sharpshooters remembered their youth, and their friends and comrades who never saw the end of the war. They were young again, and full of life. They stood shoulder to shoulder again with the men whose names echoed through the years.

DeLand continued his recitation of the regiment's fallen: Garrett Graveraet, John H. Hanken, David Graham. . . . Every so often he stopped and related an incident about one of the lads they had all known so well . . . Henry Kunce, Sylvester Smith. . . . Scores of men and boys . . . Moses Williams, William Northrop, Charles Harris. . . . Each man in the audience was now alone in his thoughts . . . Flavius Dexter, George Marshall, Thomas Gaffney. . . . The list continued until the colonel had named all those who were on the other shore. Now silence reigned. A few men cleared their throats, while others fumbled for handkerchiefs. Some stared straight ahead into a vortex dimmed by time and experience, seeing nothing of the present for a few moments.

DeLand began speaking again. He eulogized his friend Arvin Whelan, the chief surgeon who had only recently died, "the man most loved, best respected and most deeply mourned of any officer of the regiment, but who had gone before to meet us as we shall come one by one into the great hospital of eternal peace."

Finally, DeLand reminded the audience of the day's anniversary. Twenty-six years before, the Sharpshooters had fought at the Peebles' farm, where he took a bullet in the leg just as the

Confederates charged them. Although wounded himself, Pvt. Ben Hosmer had refused to leave the colonel's side. Taking a couple of handkerchiefs, Hosmer fashioned a tourniquet, staunched the flow of blood, and saved DeLand's life. Both had been picked up by the rebels and Hosmer had accompanied DeLand into Libby Prison in Richmond. Having lost all touch with Hosmer until this day, DeLand picked him from the assemblage and delivered the most profound thanks to him for his act of charity.

After a few more speeches by association officers, the meeting broke up. The aging veterans took leave of their colonel. Each man was presented with "a large signed photograph" of Colonel DeLand, a souvenir of the reunion, before leaving. Returning to Jackson, the boys met again at the county courthouse as guests of H. Dorr Blakeman. For several hours the men swapped stories; when the breakup came, they told each other they would make all efforts to get to Detroit at the annual G.A.R. encampment, and their next reunion, the following year.

In 1891, 81 members attended the gathering in Detroit.[12] One of those in attendance was Thomas Ke-chi-ti-go of Company K. "I was glad to see all our boys. . . . I did not know some of them they were so old and gray," he wrote in a letter to Ed Buckbee. Age did not seem to harbor a grudge against Big Tom. "I am pretty well, 'big Indian me.' I can kick six feet high yet. I do not feel old at all. I am just as good a man to day as I was 31 yrs ago."[13]

Not all the men had fared as well as Ke-chi-ti-go. A year later only 44 Sharpshooters attended the meeting in Lansing.[14] The reunions continued on into the new century, but the members slowly dropped out to join their comrades on the "other side."

Their Monument on the Capitol Lawn

A special call gathered the Sharpshooters together in 1915. On Tuesday, 14 December, the monument honoring the First Michigan Sharpshooters was dedicated on the grounds of the state capitol.[15] For some time now the Sharpshooters Association had been soliciting funds for the statue. A committee headed by George W. Stone (and including Charles G. Conn, George N. Davis, Charles W. Lake, George W. Hartley, and Robert Finch) had completed the necessary paperwork, collected the needed funds, and made the idea a reality. The editor of the Lansing *State Journal* sent a reporter to cover the festivities:

SURVIVORS OF FAMOUS REGIMENT SEE MONUMENT
TO ITS MEMORY UNVEILED

Michigan Sharpshooters' Services in Civil War Are Recounted
By Lansing Veterans During Ceremonies

Surviving members of the First Michigan Sharpshooters gathered in Lansing today for the unveiling of the monument on the capitol lawn erected in memory of this organization that served with distinction during the Civil war.

Mrs. DeLand Clark, of Jackson, known as "the daughter of the regiment," unveiled the monument and simple exercises, in which only the members of the organization and the Charles T. Foster post, G.A.R., of Lansing, participated, were held in the senate chamber. Mrs. Clark is a daughter of Colonel C. V DeLand, who headed the regiment, when it was mustered in for service. She was born in the army camp at Dearborn, Mich.

The monument was built by popular subscription among the survivors of the regiment. General George W. Stone, of Lansing, past commander of the state G.A.R., was chairman of the committee. The monument was designed by Frank D. Black, of Grand Rapids, and those who saw it today for the first time expressed themselves as being well pleased with the work.

Among the prominent members of the organization, who attended the unveiling ceremony today was Colonel J. E. Buckbee, of Minneapolis. Colonel Buckbee at the age of 22 years led the First Michigan Sharpshooters into Petersburg and planted the stars and stripes on the courthouse. Colonel George N. Davis, of Grand Rapids, a member of the regiment, and now a member of the board of control of the Michigan Soldiers' home, also was present.

General Stone, of Lansing, made formal presentation of the monument and the speech of acceptance was made by Colonel Buckbee.[16]

The Last Reunions

At the thirty-fourth meeting of the surviving Sharpshooters on 20 June 1917, only one officer, "noble old" Captain James S. DeLand showed up. "[H]e looked fine," noted George Stone, "his health is splendid except some Rheumatism."[17] The gathering was notably short of enlisted men as well.[18]

Two themes were consistent in all the reunions—age and patriotism. "His heart is loyal, and heroic," Stone wrote in a testimonial to his friend Ed Buckbee, who was recuperating from an operation and could not attend the 1917 event, "and so is ours, but our bodies are weak but we love him and old glory—God bless them both and protect them." [19]

The reunions continued until at least 1919. On 27 August of that year, 18 "old comrades" met in Battle Creek to talk over events that took place more than a half century ago. George Stone, the unofficial historian of the regiment, reckoned that at least 63 Sharpshooters were still alive out of the 1,320 who had served in the unit. The Angel of Death was hovering near by. No officer attended the reunion of 1919; letters from absent members were read to those in attendance. In the previous year eight more comrades had left this vale of tears, including Sgt. Joseph Stevens (Co. B), who had died only the week before in Buffalo, New York. [20]

CHAPTER 16

Our Old Comrades Have Gone

A Captured Flag Goes Home

The Sharpshooters barely noticed that Dame Time had passed not only them, but all of their generation. Their sojourn in the sun was now in the yesterdays of their youth. To be sure, they were so busy they hardly even noticed. The years swept by. The ailing South meant little to them. That part of their lives happened long ago. Politics, national and international affairs, the attitudes of the day, marriages, mortgages, children, pensions, and jobs—those were the real concerns.

Their generation had subdued the frontier, and a few of them actually had a hand in it. Amos Farling, whose antics in the ranks had kept him one step from a court-martial during his tenure as a Sharpshooter, joined the Twenty-seventh U.S. Infantry after the war and went west to fight Indians. Finding himself in dire economic straits when he left the army, Farling authored a 43-page book in 1874 that chronicled his experiences in the Sharpshooters and in the Twenty-seventh Infantry. *Life in the Army* was filled with disjointed vignettes from both tours of duty. Roughly half the book referred to the Civil War, and some of the tales resided on the "tall story" side of belief. As short as it was, his book was the only published reminiscence of any Sharpshooter's experience.

Lt. Col. William H. H. Beadle resigned from the Sharpshooters in June 1864. He transferred to the Veteran Reserve Corps and dropped one grade. He served in the defenses of Washington, DC, commanding a brigade of the corps in and about the capital city. In January 1865 Beadle was promoted to lieutenant colonel for "gallant services" during the rebel raid on Washington in July 1864. Brevet promotions to colonel and brigadier general followed at the end of the war. For a year after Appomattox he served with the Freedmen's Bureau in Virginia and North Carolina.

Mustering out of the service in January 1866, Beadle returned to Michigan where he earned his LL.B. from the University of Michigan in 1867. He practiced law in Evansville, Indiana, and Boscobel, Wisconsin, before moving to Dakota Territory in 1869. There he became surveyor general of the territory. He involved himself in educational affairs and served as superintendent of public instruction for six years, and then as president and professor of history at Madison State Normal School from 1889 to 1905. He died while visiting his daughter in San Francisco on 13 November 1905. His family brought his body back to Riverside Cemetery in Albion, Michigan, where it was interred next to his wife's.[1]

Gen. Orlando Bolivar Willcox, although not a member of the regiment, played a very significant role in its history. At the end of the war President Johnson appointed him assessor of internal revenue at Detroit, his hometown. In 1866 he reentered the army as colonel of the Twenty-ninth U.S. Infantry. Three years later he transferred to the Twelfth U.S. Infantry in California, with which he served until 1878. During the next four years he commanded the Department of Arizona when the Apache Wars brought havoc to that region.

Willcox retired in 1887 after his appointment as brigadier general and settled in Washington, DC, where he became governor of the National Soldiers Home. Congress voted him the Medal of Honor in 1895 for "most distinguished gallantry" at the First Battle of Bull Run. He moved to Coburg, Ontario, in 1905, where he died two years later. Burial was in Arlington National Cemetery.[2]

John Anderson, the "smallest private, and a tail under that" in Company E, left the Sharpshooters while they guarded prisoners at Camp Douglas. Accepting a commission as second lieutenant in the Fifty-seventh Massachusetts Infantry, another Ninth Corps regiment, he served with it for the remainder of the war.

Following the Civil War he served in the Eighteenth U.S. Infantry for 25 years. He wrote a history of the Fifty-seventh Massachusetts, taught American history, and was commandant of the military department at the Massachusetts Agricultural College in Amherst.

"I have had a pretty good time all my life. 'The world, the flesh and the devil' have all been mighty nice to me," he wrote to Ira Evans after the turn of the century. In a more pensive mood, he stated, "I always pray, 'From battle, murder and sudden death good Lord deliver me.'" Anderson, the teacher and warrior, lived on well into the twentieth century.[3]

Clement Lounsberry, the staff officer who accepted the formal surrender of the city of Petersburg, led his regiment, the Twentieth Michigan Infantry, in the grand review. At age 22 he was the youngest man to advance in grade from private to colonel in any Michigan regiment. He, too, traveled west after the war, to Dakota Territory and founded the Bismark *Tribune*. On 5 July 1876 Lounsberry composed the kind of story that happens only once in a journalist's lifetime. Fully aware that he was the first newspaperman to learn the details of the Seventh Cavalry's defeat, he hurriedly cleared the lines for a shattering dispatch. For 22 hours the telegraph clicked the news of George Armstrong Custer's death at the Little Big Horn. The 50,000-word article electrified the nation. Lounsberry outlived most of compatriots and died on 3 October 1926. He was buried in Arlington National Cemetery.[4]

Mostly, though, the Sharpshooters lived their lives in and around Michigan. Their only contact with the demise of the western frontier was the newspapers.

Thirty-three years after the War of the Rebellion, another conflict flared and died like lightning. Boys whose fathers had worn the blue or gray flocked to the colors of one nation to teach the Spanish a lesson, and they conquered more land than the United States knew what to do with. The war with Spain was a coming-out party for the reunited country. The United States lost no battles. Its navy was a superb example of readiness and planning. Most importantly, it seemed that the terrible wounds of the Civil War were healed at last. The country had risen as one against a common enemy.

During the Spanish–American War, Northern and Southern regiments learned the rudiments of drill together. In one of the camps, the sons of the Sharpshooters learned that an outfit called the Petersburg Grays was drilling with them. As boys, these Michigan lads had heard of their fathers raising the Stars and Stripes over the Petersburg Courthouse. They had attended reunions with the old men and had heard some of the stories (at times many versions of the same one) until they had them memorized. They also knew about the old flag appropriated by their fathers from the Petersburg Courthouse during the last week of the war. Here, at last, was a link to the other side of the saga.

The flag of the Petersburg Grays—"not much more than a rag," commented Ed Buckbee who brought it back to Michigan as a war trophy—consisted of a blue field and not much else. Hardly anything of the thirteen red and white stripes existed. An inscription impressed with gold letters on the blue swatch read:

> Presented to the
> Petersburg L. I. Grays
> By the ladies of
> Petersburg, Va.,
> Feb. 22, 1850.

For a decade before the Civil War the Petersburg Grays had unfurled the flag and followed it in all of their parades and meetings. At the outbreak of the war, the unit marched to Norfolk where the Grays became Company B of the Twelfth Virginia Infantry. Incongruously, their banner flew on the march and in camp until the regiment received its true Confederate colors. The captain of the Grays sent the flag back to Petersburg, where one of the Sharpshooters in the color guard found it the morning of 3 April 1865. As spoils of war, the flag was given to Ed Buckbee, who took it back to Michigan. He presented it to state authorities who placed it in the state archives.[5]

After learning of their sons' meeting with the modern Petersburg Grays, the Sharpshooters decided to send their war trophy back to Virginia as a good will gesture. George W. Stone, former drummer and the most active of the regiment involved in veterans' affairs, worked to have a resolution passed in the Michigan legislature authorizing the return of the flag. Stone picked Buckbee and Henry J. Stephens, who had been captured the night of 17 June 1864 with Buckbee, to accompany him on the journey. Charles G. Conn, who had been captured at the Crater, was also chosen, but a series of crossed signals prevented his going.[6]

As the three old riflemen rode the train to Petersburg during the last days of August 1899, they must have ventured a few thoughts on their probable welcome to the Cockade City. The last time they had seen the town, a war of attrition was grinding down the rebel army. What the three Sharpshooters experienced on their second arrival eclipsed all reverie.

As the train pulled into the Petersburg depot a delegation of prominent citizens, mostly ex-Confederates, headed by the mayor warmly greeted Stone, Buckbee, and Stephens. Shaking hands all around, the three Northerners found themselves escorted to a hotel, where their every wish was granted. The next few days passed in a frenzied series of speeches, parades, and feasts, punctuated throughout with "the unbounded southern hospitality which was showered upon them."[7] For their entire stay, the three men from Michigan were not left unattended for a minute.

Henry J. Stephens reflected on his last stay in Petersburg to his hosts. On 17 June 1864, the survivors of the Thirty-fifth North Carolina Infantry had escorted him into the city, "but he did not come in a carriage as he did today," he mused. He thought the courthouse had been turned around since his last sojourn, having seen it only once before being taken to a camp near the river that warm June night of 1864. On this occasion "he was most righteous glad to be here. This had been one of the most pleasant days of his life. He did not anticipate such a reception as he had had today."[8]

On their first night the Sharpshooters presented the flag to its original owners. Local citizens jammed the hall to witness the ceremony. After 49 years only five of the charter members of the Petersburg Grays still survived, and just three could attend the meeting. One of those who did was a Dr. Claiborne, who had served under both the United States and Confederate flags. What the assemblage heard from him was an outpouring of patriotism. "I look upon it," Dr. Claiborne said of the returned banner:

as the ensign of a great, united nation, promising to all peoples liberty and happiness, and wherever it waves, from the dome of the capitol at home, or the storm rocked top mast abroad upon the sea, may it ever be the love and pride of the American heart. . . . But I say this, comrade, without one feeling of disloyalty to that other flag which we furled at Appomattox, but which we buried in our hearts, as we tore it from its standards, and which we loved more than we loved life.[9]

"When you go back north," intoned one of the ex-Confederates, "tell the people there is no question of our loyalty to the old flag." All three Sharpshooters were genuinely moved by the sincere patriotic display from their old enemies.[10]

When the men of the A. P. Hill Camp learned that Buckbee had been a prisoner of war, they asked him to recall his stay in the sunny South. A raconteur of the best sort, Buckbee entertained his hosts with a humorous rendition of his incarceration and escapes from their hospitality.[11]

During their stay, the Sharpshooters toured the siege lines left from the old war. A committee of former Confederate officers accompanied them as guides. For two days both parties recalled the food, the insects, the heat, the incessant bombardments, and their personal involvements in the fight for Petersburg. The old warriors explored remnants of the rebel forts and Union redoubts, "but none of these places was more interesting to me than the spot on which I stood the 17th of June, 1864, when I was taken prisoner," reminisced Buckbee.[12] All three men had stood in the exact location light years before, when the world was a less complicated but more terrifying place.

Thirty-five years zipped by in a moment. A twenty-year-old, Adjutant Buckbee saw his world crumble about him as he surrendered the remnant of his regiment to the onrushing rebels. Henry Stephens of Company A was a bewildered 18-year-old who thought his life was over as he and his pards were hurriedly searched by the enemy soldiers before being hustled off to Petersburg and then to the dreaded Andersonville. Fifteen-year-old George W. Stone, having tossed aside his drum for a musket when the shooting started, was already in the rear guarding a batch of Southern prisoners when Buckbee and Stephens were being led off.

Peering through older and wiser eyes, the three comrades surveyed the scene of their youth. There was nothing here that they wished to relive. Nostalgia, tempered with truth, grabbed them for a moment; but all three knew what they had left behind. They had no desire to relive some mysterious past event or even to see their old friends. Their youth had been spent in those trenches, and that was the elusive will o' the wisp they sought. They and their Confederate hosts had grown up fast, too fast. War was not for children. These middle-aged men poking about the relics of the past had pursued a great adventure, and they had survived it. They were pragmatic men now, and war had made them so. They had revisited their old haunts. With that, they took their departure from Petersburg. They had relived a moment of their youth. Now they had to get on with the present.

Colonel DeLand Crosses to the Other Shore

Charles V. DeLand maintained his prewar reputation as a political gadfly and newspaperman. Although he was the most able to construct a regimental history, given his primary vocation as a journalist, DeLand wrote relatively little on the role of the First Sharpshooters in the Civil War other than a few letters to Adj. Gen. John Robertson. What he did write was either to enhance the reputation of the regiment or to condemn those who denigrated it. The name of Orlando B. Willcox always headed the latter category.

On 18 January 1866 Colonel DeLand sent to Robertson a list of 33 engagements, skirmishes and battles, in which the Sharpshooters had participated. Appended to the record was a damning indictment of Gen. O. B. Willcox:

> The officers & men of the regiment generally feel that they have never received, at the hands of their Divisional General, Gen. O. B. Wilcox [sic], the attention, commendation and credit its services and sacrifices entitled it too [sic], but all are confident that a fair accounting of its history in the field, though comparatively brief, will establish its reputation and acknowledge its services second to none of its companions, despite the neglect of its Commanding Generals, & the unjust prejudices these neglects have engendered in the minds of a portion of the Army & the people of the State.[13]

DeLand was not a misanthrope. He certainly did despise Willcox, but he also singled out other generals for accolades. A prime example was Brig. Gen. Alpheus Williams, one of Detroit's favorite sons who had commanded a division in the Twelfth, later the Twentieth, Corps throughout the war. When the war ended, the unassuming but steady and caring Williams was back home in Detroit two days before the public realized it. DeLand editorialized in the Saginaw *Enterprise*:

> General Williams has served with great honor to himself and the State, all the while in the front where he commanded brigades, divisions, and corps with equal ability. This is the second visit he

has made to his home in four years, and he now comes unheralded and without puffery, very unlike an other Detroit General.[14]

And Williams was a Democrat, too.

When DeLand heard of Gen. John Hartranft's nomination for state auditor for Pennsylvania, he wrote another glowing tribute in his newspaper:

> With Gen. H. we are personally acquainted, and pronounce that nomination one eminently fit to be made. Methodical, thorough and practical in business, courteous, and gentlemanly in intercourse, an enlightened and intelligent politician, he will wear the honors of office well. He rose in the army from a subordinate position to a Brevet-Major-Generalcy, and is known all over the country as "the hero of Fort steadman [*sic*]." He is a man peculiarly deserving of the public confidence and support.[15]

DeLand had lost much because of the war. He spent a considerable amount of his private fortune to finance the regiment in its early days, and he sustained a series of wounds that caused him untold pain in his later years. His reputation was not significantly enhanced because of the conflict—a fact that must have distressed him immeasurably. His ego and ambition could not keep up with the pace of post-war America. He did not have the "steam" that had driven him before the war.

After the leg wound that disabled him at the Peebles farm in late 1864, DeLand recovered in Washington, DC, and Jackson, Michigan. His troubles began immediately thereafter. All of his equipment was gathered and Marsena Patrick, the provost marshal general, "sent my horses to Washington on a Govt steamer[;] my luggage was put in an old canal boat in tow with a lot of condemned guns & then foundered & was cut loose in Chesapeake bay, and all my property, swords, pistols &c were lost."[16] When he moved to Saginaw in June 1865 to take over the *Daily Enterprise*, DeLand lost even more pertinent paraphernalia. "My discharge, commission & all other Military papers were accidentally lost in Moving, the trunk having been wet & papers mildewed & rotted." Only his pocket diaries survived.[17]

After only two years at the helm of the *Enterprise*, the first daily newspaper in the Saginaw Valley, ill health forced DeLand to resign. But journalism still drove him, and he founded and operated the Saginaw *Daily Republican* through the 1870s. While running the newspaper, DeLand managed to serve as controller of the city of East Saginaw, chief engineer of the city, marshal and supervisor, and he dabbled in real estate and insurance. In 1872 he was elected to the state senate from Saginaw County. The *Daily Republican* merged into the Saginaw *Morning Herald* in 1878; DeLand controlled the *Herald* until 1883. In 1882 DeLand returned to Jackson and settled on Pleasantview Farm.[18]

DeLand kept notice of the political situations and managed to make his thoughts heard. A local publication described him as "Being a man of radical views, and exemplifying at all times the 'courage of his convictions,' he has often encountered strong antagonisms, but none accuse him of intentional injustice, much less with anything like dishonesty or deceit."[19] At the time DeLand was in a running feud with the Progressive governor of Michigan, Hazen Pingree.

At a banquet of the Lincoln Club on 12 February 1898, DeLand showed that he had lost none of his bite. He reviewed Michigan's role in the Civil War and then lamented that Michigan trailed the other states in the list of veterans elected to high public office. Only General Russell A. Alger of the Michigan Cavalry Brigade and Captain Julius C. Burrows of the Seventeenth Michigan Infantry fit the bill.

DeLand lashed out at the governor, and, "using some very harsh language . . . said that Mr. Pingree was a 'boy private' from another state, and spent most his time during enlistment in the hands of the rebels as a prisoner of war." Calling the governor a "boodle egotist and a demagogue," DeLand said:

> We are not grateful that we have among us one who has the unbearable ignorance and egotism to style himself a "second Lincoln. . . ." Those of us who knew Lincoln, who labored with him in the gigantic struggle against slavery and the rebellion, will refuse to acknowledge any "second" in such an egotist and pigamy [*sic*] as this man Pingree. . . . He has talked great things, but has accomplished practically nothing. A few local reforms brought about with the cooperation of all the best class of citizens has been the foundation of all his claims for reforms. Practically he has everywhere increased the burdens of the taxpayers in both city and state. The tax levy this year is many thousands of dollars higher than ever before.[20]

The speech was vintage DeLand and showed that he had lost none of his form. But the years had taken their toll physically, and the venerable curmudgeon did not need to be told that he had crested the ridge of human mortality quite some time ago.

DeLand's new history of Jackson County was scheduled for completion in 1903. He had assembled the stories of his hometown's past, utilizing the abundant resources from his former newspaper, *The Citizen*, but that spring his health took a downturn. Suffering a stroke that resulted in partial paralysis, the 77-year-old warhorse still managed to finish his book, entertain visitors, and keep in touch with old cronies. In early September, though, his condition worsened and he became bedridden. DeLand sank fast; he knew the end was near.[21]

In control of his thoughts until his last breath, DeLand said his goodbyes to family and friends, and then dictated his plans for his last earthly journey. He died quietly at his home, the scene of the 1890 reunion, on Monday, 21 September 1903, at 1:30 in the morning surrounded by his family.

The local paper, which he had founded more than a half-century before, duly reported the old editor's demise with the usual hyperbole and pathos reserved for the great and near-great of the time. His politics and his military valor of necessity came up in the ensuing eulogies. Representatives from the local G.A.R. post, the Masons, and the First Michigan Sharpshooters Association attended the final rites to pay their last respects.

The funeral, conducted by Rev. Bastian Smits of the Congregational Church, took place at the Jackson home of DeLand's oldest daughter. Floral tributes bedecked the residence. The largest was a three-foot wreath symbolizing the Ninth Corps emblem; it had been sent on behalf of the regimental association by its current president, David Parkhurst of Battle Creek.

Among the old Sharpshooters attending the funeral were John Easey of Bedford Center, one of the first enlistees of Company D; Capt. Joseph O. Bellair of Grand Rapids, who had been captured with the colonel at the Battle of Peebles Farm; Henry J. Stephens of Company D, one of the color guard to raise the first Union flag in Petersburg; and Oscar Soules of Penfield, another member of Company D who had been captured in the Crater.

His old comrades took a final look at their colonel, his body wrapped in the flag of his country, his coffin festooned with flowers, flags, and tributes from friends and functionaries, soldiers, politicians, and journalists. Reverend Smits slowly intoned a chapter from the Bible and closed the home service with a prayer. Family and friends then filed out of the house while six pallbearers, comrades from the local G.A.R. post, shouldered the coffin to the waiting hearse. A caravan of horse-drawn vehicles then followed the mortal remains of one of Jackson's most prominent sons to Mt. Evergreen Cemetery, a few blocks away. The cortege passed the former park, now a residential neighborhood, where DeLand had helped bring to life the Republican Party fifty years before. The mourners continued down the streets the old editor had trodden as a boy, a young man, and a mature citizen. They entered the graveyard. There, on a small hill just inside the gate, the pallbearers set the coffin near an open grave.

A few short prayers were said after the arrival of the procession, and "the veteran was lowered to his long resting place, amid the flowers of peace and the banner of the republic embracing the inanimate clay." [22]

DeLand epitomized the political soldier. He blew his own horn, to be sure, and he castigated those who sat on the back burner and those who differed with him on the issues of the day. He made so many enemies that his writings and speeches were filled with as much defensive posturing as they were with offensive vitriol. His life moved from one confrontation to another. He certainly worked hard and was competent in the various roles he played, but his intransigence on most issues combined with his general abrasiveness kept him from the pinnacles of success he so often sought.

During his lifetime he was a force to be reckoned with, but today the name of Charles V. DeLand—and his deeds, his ambitions, his services—are not recognized by more than a handful of citizens of Jackson.

The Last Reveille

As they departed Colonel DeLand's funeral, the veterans of the old regiment must have talked about the comrades who were gone. Dozens of the old boys had already passed to their reward. Dr. Arvin Whelan, chief regimental surgeon, had mustered out of the army as surgeon-in-chief of the Third Division, Ninth Corps. While in the service he had been wounded three times. Dr. Whelan enjoyed the universal respect of the regiment. He was not one of those "sawbones" who elicited terror from his charges; rather, he was undoubtedly the most loved and respected officer in the regiment. Returning to his wife and children in Hillsdale, he became active in both politics and the medical field. An ardent Republican, he served as country treasurer and mayor of Hillsdale. In 1883 and 1884 his peers elected him president of the state medical society. He was active in the G.A.R. and the Masonic order, all the while plying his profession as general practitioner and medical lecturer at Hillsdale College. He died in 1890 in Hillsdale at the age of 59.[23]

Most of the Sharpshooters received scant attention from the press when they passed from this world into the next. They lived out their lives of quiet desperation after they had served their country in her greatest need; many times their deaths occasioned only brief notice.

When John Clark of Company D died on 21 February 1906 in Lincoln, Vermont, the article noted that he "is survived by a widow."[24] Henry Decker of Company E had an even more succinct notice. His obituary listed the time and place of his death and nothing more. He died in Jackson, Michigan, on 5 May 1907.[25]

Lott Willett of Company I died in 1909. He was buried in Pine Grove Cemetery in Ingham County near Lansing.[26]

Asahel Nichols, who had commanded the regiment in its last fight at Petersburg, received the award of brevet colonel for his courageous leadership. Unfortunately, the bullet that tore into his side left him a wreck of a man; he suffered unspeakable pain for months. He seemed to recover, though, and soon after the Sharpshooters left Tenallytown, Nichols picked up a clerkship at the treasury department in Washington, DC. A relapse, probably caused by an infection from his wound, forced him to return to his home in Lansing in early January 1866, in hopes of some relief, but severe head pains made every waking moment a living hell. Prostrated by the incessant nightmare of headaches, "he believed he should become insane." The delirium caused by the continued agony manifested itself in nightly hallucinations in which he still fought the Confederates. The physical anguish so dulled his mental capacity that he shot himself in the head to rid himself of the excruciating pain. He died on the morning of 19 January 1866; he was only 28 years old. His family buried him in Lansing.[27]

Nichols's brother-in-law, Henry V. Hinckley, mustered out with the regiment as second lieutenant. It was the same rank with which he had mustered in, although he had been recommended for higher office by both Colonel DeLand and Major

Nichols. At one time he, like Lt. William Randall, commanded the brigade ambulance corps. He returned to Lansing after the war. Like a macabre melodrama, his life proceeded to a frightful end on 31 March 1868. Suffering from some mental illness, Hinckley "often complained that he had not seen a well hour since a shell had burst close to his head." For a year before his death, he was unable to work due to his agitated state of mind. During that time he lived with his sister, the widow of Asahel Nichols. On the day before he died, Hinckley finally agreed to go to the Kalamazoo Insane Asylum. He then sought out a friend and asked for the gun Nichols had used to kill himself. Rebuffed, Hinckley bought a cheap pistol and had it loaded. That evening at 10:00 in his room at his sister's house, the veteran of the Twentieth Michigan Infantry and the First Michigan Sharpshooters put an end to the terrors he feared in this life by firing a bullet into his head. He died the next day. The distress this second suicide caused his family can only be imagined. War and its attendant horrors reached far beyond the fighting zone and 1865.[28]

Vanorman Strout of Company D died in Port Huron in 1887. Only 16 when he enlisted in the Sharpshooters, he had fought in all the regiment's battles and was discharged as a sergeant. At his funeral one of his officers touted him as "an ideal soldier, prompt in performance of every duty, fearless in battle, in camp cheerful and lighthearted." One of the largest funerals ever held in Port Huron marked his passing after he died of consumption at the age of 43.[29]

Thomas B. Tallady of Company C died at his home in Kalamazoo "from the effects of a gunshot wound in the shoulder" in 1890.[30]

John B. Shomin was the fifth man of Company K to be buried in Lakeview Cemetery in Harbor Springs; he died on 10 September 1913. There he joined his comrades Augustus Boushaw, who had died on 23 March 1887; Antoine Tabyant, 22 May 1894; John Shomin, 3 July 1895; and Cpl. Leon O-tash-qua-bon-o who had crossed to the other shore, at age 61, on 3 April 1902.[31]

Marvin Maloney of Company B passed away on 13 June 1892 at age 52 from "a complication of diseases, resulting from disease contracted while in the service." He died near Nokesville, Virginia, leaving a widow. "He was a quiet, unobtrusive man," read his obituary.[32]

Edwin Andress, the first captain of Company K, had been wounded when a musket ball tore through his right foot on 9

May during the crossing of the Ni River. He suffered for years from the effects of the wound; it kept supporating and a medical board recommended his dismissal from the service. He married an Englishwoman in Detroit in 1874 and fathered four children. As a result of his wartime exposure, he developed a lung ailment. Moving west did not improve his health; he died of consumption on 10 October 1884 in Onyx, California.[33]

Antoine Scott of Company K was cited by his superiors at least twice for extreme bravery, but never received a Medal of Honor. Only 37 years old when he died in 1878, he probably never learned that he even qualified for one. Unfortunately, medals were not then awarded posthumously.[34]

Charles Thatcher, also cited twice for bravery—at the Crater and at the regiment's last charge on 2 April 1865—received his Medal of Honor on 31 July 1896, thirty-two years and one day after qualifying for it. After the war he moved to Kalkaska, Michigan, where he worked as a laborer. He died there at age 53 from pleurisy, on 13 December 1900. A very worn government headstone marks his grave today.[35]

Charles H. DePuy of Company H received the Medal of Honor on 30 July 1896. Like Thatcher, he had to wait 32 years after he had earned it in the maelstrom of the Crater. Captured with a score of Sharpshooters, DePuy was confined at Danville until February 1865, when he was released. Mustered out due to poor health, he moved to Kalkaska, Michigan. Thatcher and Depuy continued their friendship into civilian life. They often went fishing together, and they belonged to the same G.A.R. post. One of the last of the Sharpshooters, DePuy died of pneumonia at age 92 on 5 January 1935. He was buried in Kalkaska.[36]

Allen Stephens, one of the old soldiers (he was 44 when he enlisted in Co. G in August 1863), died on 12 March 1889 at the Northwestern Branch of the National Military Home. Earlier he had served in the 193rd New York Infantry, a six-month regiment. His enlistment in the Sharpshooters was cut short when a medical board ordered him discharged because of disability in December 1864. Old veterans moved into a military home when their funds ran out and no family member could or would take them in. It was the last resort for many men who were aged, infirm, and poor and had nowhere else to go.

William Duverney, the youngest enlistee in the regiment at age 13, died on 25 August 1893 while an inmate at the same institution as Stephens.[37]

On 8 October 1915 Charles E. Judson died at the Michigan Soldiers' Home, "where he was a resident." Judson, another of the young men who left his youth on the battlefield, was only 16 when he mustered into Company H in September 1863.[38]

Charles Wirts, an assistant surgeon from Hudson, Michigan, had joined the Sharpshooters in early 1864 in Annapolis, Maryland. Forced to decline his commission in July because of ill health, he returned home. He died in February 1884 at his home in Reading, Michigan.[39]

Louis Muskoguon of Company K of Charlevoix, Michigan, was captured the night of 17 June 1864 in front of Petersburg. Sent to Andersonville, he managed to survive in that bottomless pit of misery, but the end of the war did not stop his sufferings. With 2,400 other ex-prisoners, Muskoguon boarded the ill-fated *Sultana* for the trip up the Mississippi River in late April 1865. On the night of 27 April 1865 the ship suddenly blew up, and more than 1,800 men died, either from the explosion or from drowning in the cold waters of the Mississippi. It proved to be the worst maritime disaster in American history. Muskoguon survived the blast and returned home to Northport in July. He had endured battles, marches, imprisonment, and shipwreck. "He seems to have lived through almost every thing," his minister penned in his diary after listening to Muskoguon's army tales. "It is wonderful that he is alive." No doubt, his military experiences took their toll. Muskoguon later moved to Hayes Township in Charlevoix County, Michigan, where he died in the early 1890s.[40]

Lucien Meigs, captain of Company C, had resigned from the regiment because of chronic illness in August 1864. He returned to Hillsdale, recovered much of his health, and went on to hold many local governmental positions, always representing the Republican Party. Meigs died on 3 August 1891.[41]

Robert Bradley, a patriot of the first stripe, succumbed to age and its infirmities on 12 June 1893 in Owosso. At age 44 in 1861, he had enlisted in the Seventh Michigan Infantry but was mustered out a year later because of disability. In 1862 he reenlisted in the Thirteenth Michigan Infantry. Again, a year later he was mustered out for disability. In 1863 he joined Company H of the Sharpshooters. On 8 July 1864 in front of Petersburg pieces of a rebel shell hit him on the left side and on his head. Two months later he was discharged for the third time. He was 76 at the time of his death.[42]

William H. Buchanan of Company A lost two brothers in the war. Arthur died of wounds received at Spotsylvania and John succumbed to injuries at Petersburg on the night of 17 June 1864. William, the oldest of the three, was mustered out with the regiment at Delaney House and moved back home. He died in Abscota, Michigan, on 9 August 1886.[43]

In the years yet to come the Sharpshooters heard of each other at the annual reunions or from short notices in newspapers. "Did you hear that he died last year?" "You don't say." "That's right, somewhere out West." And slowly the old boys gathered for the last bivouac.

Lt. Cyrenius B. Knight of Company D, like quite a number of other Sharpshooters, journeyed to California after the war. He died in Los Angeles the day after Christmas in 1900. His family brought his body home for burial in Newton, Michigan.[44]

Leverette N. Case received a brevet appointment to major for conspicuous bravery at Petersburg on 2 April 1865. For a while he served as secretary of the Detroit Board of Waterworks. He, too, traveled out West, eventually settling at Elsinore, California. There the bosom friend and confidant of Ed Buckbee died of cancer.[45]

Albert C. Keating of Hillsdale had enlisted in the Sharpshooters as a rifleman but became a hospital steward. After the war he studied, became a doctor, and moved to California, settling in San Bernardino. At various times he served as president of the board of health, U.S. Government pension examiner, and surgeon for the Southern Pacific Railroad Company. Touted as "man of genial personality," Dr. Keating died at age 63 in the soldiers' home in California on 7 November 1906.[46]

Another of the Sharpshooters to move to California was Benjamin Youngs, the young Canadian who was awarded the Medal of Honor for allegedly capturing the flag of the Thirty-fifth North Carolina on the night of 17 June 1864. Constantly chided by his commanding officer for not deserving credit for the deed, Youngs left the regiment in the time-dishonored way—he deserted. After being captured by the enemy at Peebles Farm on 30 September 1864 and then paroled a week later, Youngs was allowed to return home to Brookdale, Ontario. He never came back to the army, and the authorities appended the charge of desertion to his record. In the 1890s he moved to New York, and then to California after the turn of the century. Since Congress had already voted him the Medal of Honor, it was only up to him to accept it. Finally, in May 1913 he received it. "It is a beauty," he declared, "and I am proud of it."

Major George Murdoch, who remained convinced of Youngs's dishonorable conduct, wrote the state adjutant general in 1881 giving his rendition of the capture of the Thirty-fifth North Carolina's flag on that night in June. "I am prepared to furnish testimony bearing on that issue if desired," he affirmed. That he despised the duplicitous Youngs was evident. Murdoch further averred that Youngs "was a deserter from a New York regiment." Nevertheless, Murdoch's correspondence remained buried in the adjutant general's files, and Youngs received the medal. Further, Youngs's apology that "I was too young at the time to consider discharge papers of much importance" earned him an honorable discharge by special act of Congress in 1925.[47]

Murdoch's own military service had come between stints as county clerk for Berrien County, Michigan. No sooner did he leave the regiment than he was reelected to the post in 1864. The next year he was elected village clerk of Berrien Springs. In 1876 he bought and edited the Berrien County *Journal*, a weekly newspaper "independent in politics, with Democratic proclivities."

Murdoch was no fan of Charles DeLand, and complained bitterly to the state adjutant general, John Robertson, about the first edition of *Michigan in the War*. "The reference in the history of the 1st Michigan Sharpshooters to Col DeLand will not be endured by the members of that regiment nor by any official reports of his making." Sensing that Robertson must have relied almost entirely on DeLand's recollections, a peeved Murdoch retorted, "Why Col DeLand should get such a record in your book and the record of the other officers ignored is suspect to me." The history of the Sharpshooters in the second edition of *Michigan in the War* was significantly different.

Murdoch died in 1904 at the age of 75. He was buried in Berrien Springs Cemetery.[48]

David G. Palmer, by trade a wagonmaker, left the Sharpshooters in January 1865. Having served as regimental quartermaster during his tenure in the regiment, Palmer returned to Jackson County, Michigan, and entered the grocery trade. In later years he served one term as Jackson chief of police and four terms as justice of the peace.[49]

Wright D. Smith died in Dowagiac, Michigan, on 14 June 1904. He had been one of the Company G men taken prisoner in the Crater on that hot July day in 1864. Three months later, Melvin Dalrymple, also of Company G, breathed his last and was buried in Marcellus, Michigan.[50]

After the war Col. Byron M. Cutcheon of the Twentieth Michigan Infantry was awarded the brevet of brigadier general of volunteers for repeated gallantry in action. He returned to Ypsilanti where he studied law, passed the bar, and practiced in his hometown, Ionia, and Manistee. Following a term as president of the Michigan Soldiers' Home, he served as an elected member of the University of Michigan's Board of Regents. Cutcheon was a member of Congress from 1883 until 1891, and paid close attention to military affairs. He coauthored a standard history of Michigan and wrote a chronicle of his own regiment, the Twentieth Michigan Infantry. He died in Ypsilanti on 12 April 1908.[51]

John D. Hanken, at age 44 one of the older enlistees of Company H, died in Coldwater, Michigan on 22 January 1888. His son had died of wounds from the 17 June 1864 fight in front of Petersburg.[52]

Zena D. Ransom of Company C, whose two uncles had died in the service, settled in Cross Village after the war. In the 1880s he became interested in the local veterans' organization (one of the smallest in the state with only 30 members), George Washington Post, G.A.R., No. 106, in which he served as junior vice-commander. Sgt. Frank Tabasasch of Company K held the post of officer of the guard. Today they both sleep under government headstones in the Cross Village Cemetery. Two of their compatriots, Joseph Ach-Au-Nach and the inimitable Payson Wolfe, rest nearby.[53]

Cpl. Edmund E. Shaw, who was only 18 when he enlisted in Company F, had been wounded at Spotsylvania, the North Anna River, and in the Crater, yet he lived to see 83 birthdays. When he died on 18 September 1927 he still occupied his own home outside Grand Rapids. He was survived by two sons. Following services at St. James Church, Shaw was buried in Mt. Calvary Cemetery.[54]

The Snay brothers, Richard and Moses, seemingly dropped from sight after the war. Richard reappeared in 1868, when he was convicted of passing counterfeit money. Sentenced to a two-year term in Jackson Prison, he served his time. He later married a notorious madame in Bay City, Michigan, and then again faded from recorded history.[55]

Stanley W. Turner of Company C spent a comparatively short time in the regiment. He came as a 20-year-old veteran of the Eighteenth Michigan Infantry, and joined the Sharpshooters on 26 May 1864, while they were still at the North Anna River. After fighting in June and July in front of Petersburg, he was captured at the Crater. He spent the rest of the war in a prison camp. Turner died in Detroit in 1905.[56]

Andrew Bailey of Company C died at his home in Reading, Michigan, in 1906. The local G.A.R. post officiated at his interment in the local cemetery. Later that the same year, on 10 November, Edward F. Rodgers of Company D, one of the survivors from Andersonville, died in Northport.[57]

Another of the veterans who had cast his lot with the Sharpshooters, 1st Lt. George Fowler, had also previously served with Colonel DeLand's old regiment, the Ninth Michigan Infantry. Fowler, of Company H, died in Lansing on 17 January 1907.[58]

William B. McNeil of Company G joined the regiment when he was 45 years old. He never saw any fighting, having been discharged from Camp Douglas at about the same time the Sharpshooters left for Annapolis. He died on 17 May 1887 and was buried in Moody, Michigan.[59]

Sidney Haight returned to Hillsdale after the war. He didn't receive the Medal of Honor for his heroic behavior in the Crater until the 1890s. He died in 1918 at 71 years of age. His brother James, whose arm had been permanently crippled at Spotsylvania, followed him to the grand reveille in 1919.[60]

George W. Stone, the "baby" of the regiment, never fully recovered from his wartime experiences. Stone was so sick at his muster out that his compatriots wondered if he would die before the regiment reached home. For the next four years he was so ill that he "was not able to do any labor whatever." During much of that time he lived with Captain George N. Davis in Albion, Michigan.

Soon after getting well, Stone married Kittie Rice in 1869. They had one son. For three years (1870 to 1873) they lived in Virginia; again he was "not able to do any manual labor, but attempted to supervise some business and was compelled to give it up." For the next ten years Stone lived in Lapeer, Michigan, doing "lighter work in a grocery store" and selling agricultural implements. Friends in Lansing procured a desk job for him in the state capital in 1883. For some time Stone was auditor general of Michigan, while George N. Davis was warden of Jackson Prison. Both Davis and Stone later managed the Michigan Soldiers' Home in Grand Rapids.[61]

Stone had no peer when it came to knowing the history of the regiment. Unfortunately, he never wrote a history of the unit, although he was recognized by the old survivors as the historian of the Sharpshooters. "He has done more," maintained Ed Buckbee, "to keep the members of the old Regiment in touch with each other than all the other survivors combined."[62]

Stone was the quintessential G.A.R. man. Not only active in Sharpshooter circles, Stone also served in both state and national offices. As such, he must have been one of the few acknowledged Democrats to do so. During the administration of President Cleveland, he was appointed postmaster. On 11 November 1921, as Comrade Stone and his fellow members of the Charles F. Fisher Post, G.A.R., were getting in line to march in an Armistice Day parade in Lansing, he suddenly died of a heart attack. He probably could not have chosen a more apropos setting. He was seventy years old.[63]

William Driggs, first lieutenant of Company K, mustered out of the Sharpshooters in July 1864 on account of deafness. After the close of hostilities he reenlisted in the army, entering as a second lieutenant in February 1866. Within one month he rose to first lieutenant and served at that rank until he left the service in January 1871. His deafness grew progressively worse; in 1904 a doctor reported that Driggs was totally deaf in his left ear and one had to speak in "a very loud voice" in order to be heard in Driggs's right ear. By that time the veteran of the Sixth and Seventh Michigan Cavalry regiments and the First Michigan Sharpshooters had what the doctor termed a very anxious look; in appearance the poor man was very thin and worn. Driggs died in Evart, Michigan, on 12 December 1914.[64]

Charles Gerard Conn, who had started out as the second lieutenant of Company G, returned home as a captain after the war to Elkhart, Indiana. His name became indelibly wedded to his hometown's primary industrial effort; music went from being an avocation to the central part of his life. As a result of a fight in which his lip was so lacerated that he found it impossible to play the cornet, he invented and patented a rubber-rimmed mouth-piece for the instrument.[65] The business expanded, and he founded his musical instrument company in 1876.

The factory became the largest musical instrument manu-facturer in the world. Conn also entered the world of music pub-lishing.[66] Way ahead of his time, Conn instituted a profit-sharing plan for his employees.[67] He eventually held 50 patents and was responsible for numerous industry innovations. In fact, he engen-dered so many improvements in musical instruments that one of his flyers announced that Conn cornets were so well made that "ere long the Conn cornets will play themselves."[68]

Conn organized and became colonel of the First Regiment of Artillery in the Indiana Legion, later the Indiana National Guard. He published a newspaper in Elkhart; as a Democrat he served as mayor of Elkhart and state legislator. In 1892 he was elected to Congress, and bought and operated the Washington *Times* in the nation's capital during his term of office.[69]

In 1915 he sold his interest in his million-dollar company and moved to California. He died in Los Angeles on 5 January 1931 at age 86. In sixteen years he had lost almost all of his money and died penniless. The Elkhart Masonic Lodge, which he helped found, paid for his funeral; he was buried in his hometown cemetery. He was the last survivor of the 56 charter members of the Elmer Post, G.A.R., in Elkhart. Six years after his death the Chamber of Commerce and employees of his musical instrument company, which bears his name to this day, put up a stone to honor the "founder of the band musical instrument industry."[70]

Sgt. Joe Stevens of Company B, a "soldier's soldier," on whom Adj. Buckbee leaned when the regiment found itself cut off from the rest of the army the night of 17 June 1864, spent the rest of the war in Andersonville. There he met some of his old compatriots from the Fourth Michigan Infantry. He helped put an end to the depredations of the "raiders" in the prison camp.

At the war's end he and hundreds of other former prisoners boarded the ill-fated *Sultana* for passage north on the Missis-sippi River. The overloaded steamer blew up, and more than 1,800 men died. Stevens was saved by a friend who was floating on a bale of hay. He recovered in a Memphis hospital and was mustered out of the army at Camp Chase, Ohio. He engaged in the "live stock commission business, under the firm name of Dunning & Stevens" in East Buffalo, New York, at which he made a very comfortable living. He died in Buffalo on 15 August 1919 at the age of 78.[71]

Henry John Stephens was also captured the night of 17 June 1864. The rebels cooped him up for five months at Andersonville and for two months at Savannah and Millen. His health shattered, he returned home and tried his hand at farming. He had studied to be an agriculturalist before the war cut short his education. No longer having the physical stamina for such work, he obtained a position in the state auditor general's office, where he worked with another Sharpshooter, George W. Stone.

In 1901 he began a real-estate, fire insurance, and pension business, and eventually turned the enterprise over to his son. Governor Chase Osborn appointed him county agent for the State Board of Charities and Corrections in 1912. As a loyal veteran, he joined the local G.A.R., Farragut Post No. 32, in Battle Creek, and twice served as its commander. His brother Charles and comrades John Easey and William O. Holmes also belonged to the same post.

Stephens, with George Stone and Ed Buckbee, returned the captured flag to Petersburg in 1899. He married Jenny Mercer; the two had one son, Charles M., born in 1890. He died in 1922 and was buried in Oak Hill Cemetery, Battle Creek.[72]

James Walsh, or "Adjutant's Walsh," returned to Ypsilanti after his right leg was amputated as a result of the fight on 17 June 1864. To Adjutant Buckbee's chagrin, Walsh made himself a ward of Buckbee's mother, who continued to treat the Irishman as a hero for years. She gave him clothes and meals and let him and his wife live in a small cabin on her property.

When Ed Buckbee returned home and married, Walsh lived off his good graces. The disabled veteran constantly bedeviled Buckbee, who always felt guilty over the loss of Walsh's leg. After all, Walsh had lost it because he went out of his way to bring some tea to the adjutant the evening of the charge, and then stayed to take part in it. Walsh continually pawned his artificial leg for whiskey money; Buckbee inevitably bought the limb back.

Just before Buckbee left the Detroit area he succeeded in having Walsh appointed keeper at a lighthouse on the flats north of the city. Hearing that his old orderly did well at his job, Buckbee "did not doubt, for his best hold was 'cleaning up' and polishing brass."[73]

Otis F. Kimball of Company A, descended from men who had served in the Revolution and the War of 1812, had his right arm amputated as a result of a wound incurred at Spotsylvania. Hospitalized until December 1864, Kimball received his discharge and returned home to the Battle Creek area. Despite his disability he farmed 160 acres in Newton, Michigan, and raised a family. One of his daughters attended Northwestern University.[74]

James Speed DeLand, wounded in the arm in the Sharpshooters' last charge on the morning of 2 April 1865, recovered from the resection that resulted in his left arm being four inches shorter than his right. His country awarded him the brevet rank of major for his "gallant conduct" in the assault, but the arm was a useless appendage for the remainder of his life.

Jim followed his older brother to East Saginaw after the war, where he entered the grocery business. After a year he returned to his home in Jackson, where he again entered the employ of the *Citizen*. For the next decade he worked as a journalist; then he turned to farming. In 1867 he married Mary Elizabeth Parker, and three children resulted from the union. His free time was taken up with the G.A.R. and the Masonic Lodge. His later years were not kind to him.

Unable to care for himself, DeLand lived with his son. In his eighties, he was a "helpless" individual, "having to be dressed and undressed and put to bed, being unable to stand on his feet, afflicted with rheumatism so that he could only get around with the aid of a wheel chair." His daughter Gertrude took him into her Detroit home, where she cared for him until his death on 13 January 1926 at age 89. They buried him in the family plot just down from his brother's grave at Mt. Evergreen Cemetery in Jackson.[75]

Thomas Ke-chi-ti-go, the powerful and resourceful sergeant of Company K, returned to Michigan after his discharge, where he joined the army of axemen who cut down the state's forests. He became a "river hog," known for his ability to ride logs during the spring drives down the Au Sable River in northern Michigan. Wearing spiked boots and freely using a pike pole, he and men like him kept the logs floating down to the sawmills.

Despite his physical prowess, it was the inner man his contemporaries remembered. In his eulogy, the editor of the Crawford County *Avalanche* wrote of him: "Deprived in early life of parental influence, thrown entirely upon his own resources, without any chance of improvement, his whole life spent in the coarsest of surroundings, it is doubtful if anyone of any race would have developed better manhood." Few men receive a more fitting tribute to their lives. He died on 24 April 1916 in Grayling, Michigan, at age 80. His burial at Elmwood Cemetery was "attended by nearly every soldier whose health would permit." [76]

Benjamin F. Smith of Coldwater, who served in Company H, lost his right hand because of the 17 June fight. Before the war he was a shoemaker by trade; he had few other skills and was illiterate. After mustering out he went to live with his sister's family. She turned his life around. A "very superior woman," married to a successful attorney, she encouraged him to develop his mind.

Swallowing his pride, Smith attended school with little boys and girls. He persisted and worked hard. In time he became a lawyer, and a good one. His business occasionally took him to Washington, DC, from his home in Nebraska. He always said "that next to his sister he owed everything to the bullet that shattered his hand." [77]

John F. Rainbow, also from Coldwater, spent four months in the hospital after being wounded in the left shoulder at the Wilderness. He returned to the regiment and eventually was promoted to first sergeant of Company H. After the war he lived in Iowa for five years. Securing a homestead in Kalkaska County, Michigan, Rainbow moved there in 1873. He involved himself in the lumber business, operating a sawmill and running a broom handle factory. Always a Republican, he served as sheriff of Kalkaska County for four years and subsequently was elected for a number of terms as register of deeds for the county.[78]

Another of the Sharpshooters to settle in the Kalkaska area was Capt. Allen E. Burnham, the Mexican War veteran who had come in with Hall's two additional companies. Discharged in March 1865, Burnham moved to Kalkaska County where he was elected the first treasurer of Cold Spring Township. Afterward he served as superintendent of schools and justice of the peace.[79]

Hooker A. DeLand's post-war physical problems could fill volumes.[80] Released from Dry Tortugas by executive order, DeLand returned to Jackson, Michigan, where he married in 1868. He moved to Grand Rapids and then to Fort Collins, Colorado, where he worked as a teamster. By 1879 he and his wife had divorced; their union produced one daughter who stayed with her mother. DeLand suffered from a series of maladies that he attributed to his time in the service, but because he had been cashiered from the Sharpshooters, the U.S. Pension Bureau turned down his numerous claims for aid.

DeLand then took another tack. He claimed his physical ailments were the result of service with the First Michigan Infantry in which he had served as a sergeant from 1861 to 1863. Contending that "intermittent fever," which continued to prostrate him, as well as his troublesome left knee, were cause enough for a pension, he continually dunned the bureau for relief. Testimony from former soldiers with whom he had served in the First Michigan Infantry, local physicians, neighbors, and fellow workers failed to sway the U.S. government, which turned down every single request.

He continually suffered from "General disability caused by loss of teeth that I am unable to digest my food and my whole system is thrown into disorder—also my left knee which was put out of joint a[t the Battle of] Fredericksburg affects me severely." He listed heart trouble and stomach problems; of the latter, "he has an attack about every ten days and is not able to work for two or three days" [after the attack].

Joseph O. Bellair, DeLand's first lieutenant in Company F, sent in a noteworthy affidavit in 1894. In it, he listed the physical problems attendant on DeLand during the latter's service with the Sharpshooters as "pains in his stomach and in region of the heart resembling heart disease, and was also troubled with a hacking cough." Bellair then tried to explain the reason for DeLand's incarceration at Dry Tortugas, injecting some material not included in DeLand's wartime court-martial:

> On account of some unpleasantness with Lieut. [Henry] Hinckley of Company E 1'-Mich. S.S. he, Hinckley, had charges preferred against DeLand, to Col. Nichols, who was a brother-in-law of Hinckley's, for cowardice. The origin of the trouble was a love affair. Capt. [Hooker] DeLand and Hinckley, both courting a young lady residing in Chicago, Ills.—and she favored DeLand, causing a jealousy. In the spring of 1864, DeLand was Court-Martialed, and a request was made that I should be a witness to explain the difficulty, which was refused, and he was found guilty and sentenced to Dry Tortugas below Florida for 2 years. A statement of facts of the case was forwarded to President Lincoln, also a Petition signed by members

of the Regiment, and he was pardoned by the President in March 1865. I know that DeLand was a brave soldier, and have no reason to believe otherwise.

In 1897 DeLand tried again, and again he met with rebuff. He further petitioned the bureau in 1901, 1904, and 1905 to no avail. He then moved to Seneca Falls, New York, where his daughter and a niece lived. His family decided to try again for a pension in 1926. The bureau rejected this application as it had the others. Hooker DeLand, the government maintained, was ineligible for a pension because he was dishonorably discharged from his last contract of service.

The family did not give up hope. Contacting Senator William Vane of New York, DeLand's relatives explained the situation again. By then, the tough, cocky soldier was barely a shell of his former self. Eighty-four years old, he was "practically blind from catarach [*sic*]—has to be dressed and undressed—has chronic diarrhoea unable to control bowels—bedding & trousers constantly soiled—has paralysis agitans worse on the right side, cannot take fluids without attendance—very deaf—this person is practically helpless," intoned his physician. Senator Vane took DeLand's case, exclaiming, "I am led to believe that a serious injustice has been done to Captain DeLand."

The Civil War had ended generations ago. It was now time to heal the old wounds. By an Act of Congress approved on 3 May 1928, DeLand was granted a pension of $50 per month. He and his family thought the ordeal, the shame, the finger-pointing were finally over. They were wrong.

Hooker Ashton DeLand breathed his last on 5 April 1931 in Seneca Falls and was buried in Restvale Cemetery. He was the last of the original officers of the Sharpshooters to die. Following the funeral, his family submitted a bill for expenses to the pension bureau, but the government disavowed any payment for the interment. The bureau maintained that DeLand's original sentence had not been modified. He had not been granted any sort of remission for his actions during the Civil War; only a pension had been given. Hooker DeLand, the government stated, was still not entitled to a veteran's farewell. His grave is still unmarked.

Joseph O. Bellair, who left the service as a captain, moved to Grand Rapids and became a pension attorney. He came under particular scrutiny in 1897 by a special examiner from the pension bureau who berated him for his unscrupulous practices: "I have to state that the reputation of Joseph O. Bellair, in Pension matters is unreliable. He is a disbarred Pension Atty. considered a good . . . man—but not all right in pension matters." Bellair's willingness to help old comrades was his undoing. Bellair died on 30 October 1916 and was buried in Oak Hill Cemetery in Grand Rapids.[81]

First Lt. Frank Whipple moved to Port Huron after the war. He married Abbie J. Riddle in 1869 and had four children. In Port Huron he studied for the bar and became a lawyer in 1871. He was appointed to a circuit judgeship by Governor Hazen Pingree, and was later elected to the same post. Active in civic affairs, Whipple played a large role in the Red Ribbon Movement (a temperance revival of the 1870s), and was elected president of the Port Huron club of 2,500 members. To the day of his death he wore a charm on his watch chain depicting the motto of the movement: "Dare To Do Right." Like most of the Sharpshooters, Whipple also became active in veterans' affairs, and served as commander of the William Sanborn Post, G.A.R., in Port Huron. In the summer of 1901, at age 63, he died of stomach cancer.

The paeans from the press expressed the esteem with which Judge Whipple was held in the community. With his death, read his obituary, "Port Huron loses one of its best citizens, as good a judge as ever occupied the bench, and an honest man." His death created a void difficult to fill.[82]

Julian Edward Buckbee mustered out of the Sharpshooters as commander of the regiment and a brevet lieutenant colonel at age 22. He penned his memoirs in 1916. They were based on a series of lectures he had delivered in 1911, aided by magic lantern slides. Amusing, somber, emotional, though totally without rancor, he titled his shows, "The Story I Tell My Children." His later reminiscences were not for publication but "for my children, and their children, and for their children's children." Luckily for posterity, Buckbee also collected likenesses of most of the regiment's officers. These, too, he passed to his descendants.

After the war Buckbee had returned to Chicago where he married Mary Church, the "Mollie" of his letters. He petitioned the secretary of war for an appointment as lieutenant in the U.S. Cavalry. Both of Michigan's senators and five representatives sent in their recommendations. When a commission for second lieutenant in the regular army came his way, Buckbee refused it. An old schoolmate, Prescott M. Skinner of the Twentieth Michigan, accepted it in his stead. Buckbee did serve in the Detroit Light Guard until 1869.

He became a land agent for the Chicago and Northwestern Railroad and kept in touch with his old comrades, notably Jim DeLand and George Stone. He also maintained a close friendship with Capt. P. J. Johnson of the Thirty-fifth North Carolina, who had captured him on 17 June 1864. During the Chicago World's Fair of 1893 Buckbee and his wife entertained the Johnsons at their home near Chicago. Johnson still retained Buckbee's sword and asked if he wanted it back. The old Sharpshooter told Johnson to keep it and give it to his own son. Johnson reciprocated by giving Buckbee "an elegant, gold-headed cane." [83]

In 1899 Buckbee headed the delegation to return the flag of the Petersburg Grays. The old adjutant died in April 1920 and was buried in Rose Hill Cemetery in Chicago, where some of the Sharpshooters who had died while at Camp Douglas in 1863 and 1864 were interred. Chaplain Heagle officiated at the service. [84]

Dr. David Heagle, the regimental chaplain, married upon his muster-out, and progressed to an illustrious career in the Baptist Church. Although practicing his first calling as a minister of the gospel, he also became known in ecclesiastical circles as a lecturer, author, and teacher.

Heagle's speech on "Solomon's Temple and Jerusalem" became a feature at the St. Louis World's Fair. The author of many theological texts, Heagle taught in a series of colleges, culminating his career as a founder and teacher at the Northern Baptist Theological Seminary in Chicago. One admirer's eulogy portrayed him as "a veritable theological encyclopedia, a vigorous thinker, an acknowledged scholar, a forceful speaker, and an effective teacher." He continually encouraged others to do better: "He was a man of strong convictions and warm feelings. He was intensely devoted to the institutions he served and was tenderly attached to his many students and followed their careers with deep interest." Heagle followed his God, his conscience, and his country. Nothing else can be asked of any man.

Heagle died in Chicago on 13 February 1922, leaving behind two daughters and several grandchildren. His funeral resonated with tributes from fellow ministers and teachers and former students. [85]

Ira L. Evans settled down in Jackson, Michigan, after being mustered out with the brevet rank of major for bravery during the 2 April 1865 assault on Petersburg, Virginia. He served as a sheriff's deputy, prison guard, and county coroner. Although never wounded in battle, Evans suffered from a number of ailments but refused hospitalization during the war, and "there were years of massive struggle with the federal Government Pension Dept. from which he succeeded in wresting $17 a month in 1903."[86]

One of the bravest, most respected officers of the regiment, Evans received mail from former Sharpshooters testifying to his dignity and the honor with which they regarded him. Charley Nash wrote: "You were about the only one in the whole shooting match, that I ever cared anything about."[87]

He started a tradition by working at the state prison in Jackson, where, his great-granddaughter said, "one by one, each generation of my family worked: Ira, Charles his son, and my dad—who was 'Night Captain.' I almost got a job there in the hospital but decided to break tradition & opted out."[88]

As county coroner Evans "showed considerable emotionality over the cases which appeared before him."[89] He may at this time have been manifesting signs of delayed stress syndrome, that malady which affects those who have withstood tremendous trauma, such as the carnage in which he participated during the Civil War.

In the late 1880s Evans fell down a flight of stairs and broke his hip; he walked with a cane the rest of his life. On 6 July 1911, Ira L. Evans passed away in Kalamazoo. He was the last of 12 brothers and sisters to die. He was buried in Mt. Evergreen Cemetery in Jackson.

In a letter to Ira Evans in 1905, John Anderson had reminisced about the early days of the Sharpshooters when the regiment guarded rebel prisoners at Camp Douglas. In closing his missive, Anderson, a proud old soldier who was looking back on a life of accomplishment, signed off with a wish for a positive future. "Please accept my best wishes," he wrote, "for all the good things of life, finally, a long way off, a peaceful death and a glorious resurrection in that distant land where so many of our old comrades have gone and are waiting for us."[90]

In December 1946 the last of the Sharpshooters bade farewell to his earthly existence. Cyrus Perrigo of Millington, Michigan, joined his comrades "in that distant land." Back in September 1863, when the regiment was stationed at Fort Dearborn, the 18-year-old farmer from Tuscola County had signed his enlistment papers. In the summer of 1938 Perrigo, late of Company I, then living in Vassar, Michigan, attended the last reunion of the Union and Confederate armies, which was held in Gettysburg, Pennsylvania. No other Sharpshooter attended the affair.[91]

An era ended when Perrigo, 101 years of age, sighed his final breath on the morning of 9 December 1946. Two days later his family buried his earthly form in Newton Cemetery in the southern part of Tuscola County, Michigan, where he joined those of his parents and his brothers. Next to his is the stone honoring the memory of his brother Simeon, who died on the ramparts of Jonesboro while carrying the flag of the Tenth Michigan Infantry.[92]

Cyrus Perrigo was the last of the Sharpshooters and one of the last survivors of the Civil War. With his passing in 1946 no one was left who could absolutely recall the participation of the First Michigan Sharpshooters in the War of the Rebellion. Their lips were stilled, and for the most part so was their memory.

They sleep today in a hundred different cemeteries. They were young men who were ripped to shreds in the midst of battle. Mature men who succumbed to wounds. Boys who languished in hospitals and could not throw off the curse of a disease. Men who died in the filth and noise of a Confederate prison camp. Old men who came home to die in bed a score and more years after the great adventure. They sleep amid strangers in Arlington, Andersonville, and Brooklyn, and with friends and relatives in Jackson, Hillsdale, Battle Creek, and Harbor Springs.

The First Michigan Sharpshooters existed no longer. The organization took its place in history, that ethereal land which does not intrigue future generations very much. Their sons and daughters had heard stories of Camp Douglas and Spotsylvania and the siege of Petersburg, but the stories had little relevance to their own lives.

As the members of the next generation took their place, they saw their grandpas as old men, and they could not imagine them as the young men they were when the great adventure took place. An old greybeard who slurred his words or shuffled as he walked could not be transformed and transported back to the days of youthfulness by grandchildren to whom the words "rebels," "Union," and even "Sharpshooter" meant almost nothing.

And after grandpa died and was laid to rest in the town cemetery, with maybe some official attendance by the dwindling fellows of the local Grand Army of the Republic post, a government stone with strange initials was put at the head of the plot.

Decoration Day became Memorial Day, but few of the veteran's descendants hardly realized they had a relative who had fought in battles too terrible for modern minds to even comprehend. In another generation the same stone would become even more of an enigma. Only infrequently did the old soldier's descendants visit the grave any longer, or even seem to care about what the Civil War was ever about.

The soldier's remaining family died or moved away until no one but passing strangers ever took the time to pay any notice at all to the man whose remains rested beneath a hard-to-read and listing stone with the strange initials and words, "1st Mich. S.S." It would take "a fair accounting" to set forth the record of the 1,300 men who once called themselves the First Michigan Sharpshooters.

Appendix A
Battle Casualties
in the First Michigan Sharpshooters
★ ★ ★ ★ ✯

This compilation is made up of lists of casualties found in newspapers, letters, and official documents. Even still, it is not complete. It is arranged in chronological order and by company.

6–7 MAY 1864—BATTLE OF THE WILDERNESS

Killed in Action:

John S. Vader..................................Co. C
Henry Apted ....Co. H

Died of Wounds:

Warren Jackson ....Co. D—Died at Alexandria, VA 4 June 1864. Buried Alexandria National Cemetery.
Cyrus Hall ....Co. G—Gunshot wound, abdomen. Died 7 May 1864.
Cpl. James Jones...........................Co. G—Gunshot wound, stomach. Died 7 May 1864.
George Sawyer ....Co. H—Shot right side.
Cpl. David S. George......................Co. I—Died at Washington, DC 16 May 1864.
Clark S. Carter..............................Co. I—Wounded and left on field 6 May 1864. Died at Washington, DC, 11 May 1864.
1st Sgt. Charles Allen....................Co. K—Breast, left side. Died at Fredericksburg, VA, 18 May 1864.

Wounded:

Jason H. Soules ....Co. A—Neck, left side.
William Burroughs ....Co. C—Left foot, slight.
Ichabod Eugene Skinner ....Co. C—Left side.
Charles Lashbrooks........................Co. D
Cpl. Ezra S. Scott ....Co. D—Shoulder blade, fractured.
William Wick..................................Co. D
Mark Shell......................................Co. F—Knee.
2nd Lt. Charles G. Conn.................Co. G—Slight flesh wound
Joseph Barney................................Co. G
Sylvester Berry ....Co. G

John E. Rainbow .... Co. H—Left shoulder.
James Baskerville .... Co. I
William Dillabaugh .... Co. I—leg.

Captured or Missing:
Levi Porter .... Co. C—Died at Andersonville, 2
August 1864.

9 MAY 1864—BATTLE OF SPOTSYLVANIA (Ni River)

Killed in Action:
Cpl. John M. Benedict .... Co. D—Shot in spine.
Cpl. Levi M. Lewin .... Co. G

Died of Wounds:
Arthur Buchanan .... Co. A—Gunshot, entered between
vertebra and scapula. Died of
wounds in Harewood Hospital.
Buried in Arlington National
Cemetery.
Benjamin F. Hinckley .... Co. A—Flesh wound, left arm. Died
in Washington, DC, of wounds. Bur-
ied in Arlington National Cemetery.
John Livingston .... Co. A—Gunshot, right foot, ampu-
tated. Died of wounds 17 June 1864.
Oliver E. Perry .... Co. B—Head, occipital protuberance.
Died of wounds at Armory Square
Hospital, Washington, DC, on 18
May 1864. Buried in Arlington
National Cemetery.
Andrew K. Hart .... Co. D—Right temple. Died of wounds
7 June 1864 at Cold Harbor, VA.
John W. Reed .... Co. D—Flesh wound, left hip. Died of
wounds in Washington, DC, on 31
May 1864.
Thomas C. Wright .... Co. D—Died in Washington, DC, of
wounds—gangrene and chronic diar-
rhea—on 18 September 1864. Buried
in Arlington National Cemetery.

Wounded (9, 10 May):
Adj Edward J. Buckbee .... Head, slight.
Otis Kimball .... Co. A—Right humerus fractured, am-
putated middle third.
Cpl. Archibald M. Miller .... Co. A—Leg, left shoulder, contusion.
Cpl. John S. Sanders .... Co. A—Gunshot, left hand.

Sgt. Samuel Patterson .... Co. B—Gunshot, right gluteal region.
Stephen Quance .... Co. B—Gunshot, forehead and left temple.
Silas B. Beckwith .... Co. C—Gunshot, foot.
Cpl. John D. Hunt .... Co. C—Gunshot, face. 9 May.
Sgt. Frank Palmer .... Co. C—Gunshot, left leg, flesh wound.
2d Lt. Porter Thomas .... Co. C—Gunshot, left foot, toe. Wounded while straggling from his command.
John Arehart .... Co. D—Head.
Jay H. Brewer .... Co. D—Cheek and left shoulder.
Oliver Byington............................. Co. D—Gunshot, left arm, contusion, slight.
Sgt. John Easey.............................. Co. D—Hip, flesh.
Daniel McLoud............................... Co. D—Right breast, contusion.
John Reynolds .... Co. D—Head.
William Woods .... Co. D—Left foot.
Cpl. Jacob Barnhart....................... Co. E—Second finger of left hand.
Cpl. Melvin Phelps........................ Co. E—Gunshot, scalp wound.
Florian Fountain .... Co. F—Gunshot, left hand, flesh.
Edmond E. Shaw............................ Co. F—Head, slight.
David Ash .... Co. G—Right breast and arm.
Edward Carey .... Co. G—Arm and breast.
1st Sgt. Robert Farrell .... Co. G—Gunshot, left forearm, flesh.
Cpl. Barney Craton .... Co. H—Forehead, over right eye.
Cpl. Jeremiah O'Leary.................... Co. H—Scalp.
William J. Thompson .... Co. H—Gunshot, scalp wound above left ear.
Cpl. Henry C. Call.......................... Co. I—Gunshot, right forearm, flesh.
Henry C. Smith .... Co. I—Left hip, superficial.
William H. Sturgis .... Co. I—Right arm.
Capt. Edwin V. Andress .... Co. K—Right foot, slight. 9 May.
George Stoneman........................... Co. K—Gunshot, 2nd and middle fingers amputated.

12 MAY 1864—BATTLE OF SPOTSYLVANIA

Killed in Action:

Major John Piper
Irving R. Dell.................................. Co. A
Lawrence Banks .... Co. B
Peter S. Chichester .... Co. B
Clark Fox, Jr................................... Co. B
Elias Fullerton .... Co. B
Sylvester M. Osborn .... Co. B

Charles Quance .... Co. B
Frank Wagoner .... Co. B
Noah Dick .... Co. D
Charles D. Jackson .... Co. D
Sgt. Richard H. Freeligh .... Co. F
George W. Moore .... Co. F
Cpl. George S. Williams .... Co. F
Henry Kunce .... Co. G
Albert Shedd .... Co. G
George Arnold .... Co. H
Samuel Taylor .... Co. H
Cpl. Albert A. Johnson .... Co. I
Jonah Dabasequam .... Co. K
John E-tar-ivegezhik .... Co. K
Cpl. Samuel Going .... Co. K
1st Sgt. Henry G. Graveraet .... Co. K
Cpl. Benjamin Greensky .... Co. K
Thaddeus Lamourandiex .... Co. K
James Mash-kaw .... Co. K
John Mash-kaw .... Co. K

Died of Wounds:

William Davis .... Co. A—Left thigh. Died 12 July 1864.
John Livingston .... Co. A—Right foot amputated. Died
at Carver Hospital on 17 June 1864.
Reuben Evey .... Co. B—Leg, severe. Died at Lincoln
Hospital, Washington, DC, on 6 June
1864. Buried in Arlington National
Cemetery.
Cpl. Sylvester Smith .... Co. B—Mortally wounded and left on
the field.
Webster Tozer .... Co. B—Shoulder, severe. Died at
Washington, DC, on 13 June 1864.
Alexander Wallace .... Co. B—Left wrist. Died at Annapolis
Junction on 23 June 1864.
Thomas Holmes .... Co. D—Gunshot, left side, severe.
Died 6 June 1864.
Cpl. Perry D. Griswold .... Co. E—Died 12 May 1864.
John R. Seram .... Co. E—Died 25 May 1864 at Wash-
ington, DC. Buried in Arlington
National Cemetery.
Garret DuMez .... Co. F—Gunshot, right arm. Died at
Fredericksburg ,VA.
Sgt. Edmund Beadle .... Co. H—Died at Rockville, IN, on 30
June 1864.
William Austin .... Co. I—Died at Washington, DC.

Appendix A

Edward Fisher .... Co. I—Died at Washington, DC, on
13 May 1864.
Cpl. John S. Welch.......................... Co. I—Died 13 May 1864.
David L. George .... Co. K—Head. Died from exhaustion
and hemorrhage. Buried in Ar-
lington National Cemetery.
Daniel Mwa-ke-wenah.................... Co. K—Right arm, face, and left
hand. Died 5 June 1864. Buried in
Brady Hill Cemetery, Saginaw, MI.

Wounded:

Col. Charles V. DeLand.................. Shell, head and back.
Elias Farwell .... Co. A—Gunshot, left ear and neck.
Samuel Harper................................ Co. A—Gunshot, right forearm,
fracture. Amputated middle third.
John H. DeLong .... Co. B—Gunshot, neck, not serious.
Robert Finch................................... Co. B
Clark Fox, Sr.................................. Co. B—Wounded, captured and sent
to Andersonville.
Cpl. Benjamin F. Hosmer .... Co. B—Gunshot, right shoulder,
severe.
William Wells .... Co. B—Gunshot, head, scalp wound.
2nd Lt. Frank Whipple .... Co. B
Lewis H. Adams .... Co. C—Left side.
Randolph Betts .... Co. C—Left knee. Captured. Died at
Andersonville on 14 August 1864.
Levi J. Foulk .... Co. C—Gunshot, right foot,
contusion.
Thomas B. Tallady .... Co. C—Left shoulder.
Will Wagner.................................... Co. C—Right hand, thumb.
Amos Hamley.................................. Co. D—Left shoulder.
1st Sgt. Kirke W. Noyes .... Co. D
James B. Haight............................. Co. E—Gunshot, left forearm.
1st Sgt. John S. Paul .... Co. E—Gunshot, left hand, second
and third fingers.
John Wise .... Co. E—Gunshot, left leg and forearm.
Charles W. Mathews .... Co. F—Left leg.
John Winman .... Co. F—Left hand, one finger off.
John Knoll .... Co. G—Right thigh, severe.
1st Lt. George Fowler .... Co. H
Joseph Vallequette......................... Co. H—Gunshot, head.
John Fitzgerald .... Co. I—Right forearm, badly.
Lott W. Willett .... Co. I—Left foot, slightly.
Clark Wright .... Co. I—Gunshot, left hand.
Sgt. Louis Genereau .... Co. K—Gunshot, left leg, flesh.
Thomas Ke-chi-ti-go .... Co. K—Shell, left forearm, fracture.

Simon Keji-kowe .... Co. K—Gunshot, left side, severe.
George W. Mogage .... Co. K—Left hand, amputated third finger.
Mark Pe-she-kee .... Co. K—Gunshot, shoulder.
Joseph Shaw-au-ase .... Co. K—Left hand, index finger.
Joseph Shaw-au-os-sang .... Co. K—Gunshot, left leg.

Captured or Missing:

Clark Fox, Sr .... Co. B—Died at Andersonville on 27 August 1864.
Randolph Betts .... Co. C—Died at Andersonville on 14 August 1864.
John W. Lathrop .... Co. C—Released 20 November 1864.
Patrick Mulligan .... Co. F—Died at Andersonville on 30 March 1865.

14 MAY 1864

Wounded:

Robert Cummings .... Co. C—Gunshot, right hand, second finger.

18 MAY 1864

Wounded:

Edward Misisaius .... Co. K—Right hand, flesh.

24 MAY 1864

Wounded:

Edmond Shaw .... Co. F—Gunshot, right shoulder and head, contusion.

25 MAY 1864—NORTH ANNA RIVER

Killed in Action:

John Beck .... Co. B
Eugene R. Spencer .... Co. I

Died of Wounds:

Joseph Tripp .... Co. A—Right leg fractured, amputated upper third. Died of wounds. Buried in Arlington National Cemetery.

Wounded:

Dan Fisher .... Co. A—Gunshot, left elbow, flesh.

Robert Finch .... Co. B—Gunshot, head, skull fractured. Pieces of bone removed; lost right eye.

Hiram Upham .... Co. F—Gunshot, scalp wound.

26 MAY 1864

Wounded:

Augustus Call .... Co. H—Gunshot, right side, ball penetrated posterior of lung, lodging in left side. Ball extracted.

Captured or Missing:

William O. Hill .... Co. A—Missing while on picket. Died at Andersonville on 24 October 1864.

William Vickery .... Co. A—Missing while on picket. Died at Andersonville on 28 August 1864.

Eugenio K. Tompkins .... Co. A—Missing while on picket. Reported dead by returned prisoners.

Marshall Hodges .... Co. A—Missing while on picket. Returned 2 December 1864.

1 JUNE 1864

Wounded:

John S. Urie .... Co. C—Left thigh, flesh.

Amos Farling .... Co. G—Left hand, flesh.

3 JUNE 1864

Died of Wounds:

Lucius P. Spencer .... Co. C—Gunshot, left side, penetrating chest. Died of wounds at David's Island, NY, on 28 July 1864.

Wounded:

Absolum W. Stoner .... Co. C—Gunshot, right foot, big toe.

Michael Wayaubemind .... Co. K—Gunshot, back, contusion.

5 JUNE 1864

Died of Wounds:

Andrew K. Hart .... Co. D—Gunshot, right leg, severe. Died of wounds 7 June 1864.

7 JUNE 1864

Captured or Missing:

James Norton .... Co. F

8 JUNE 1864

Wounded:

2nd Lt. Cyrenius B. Knight .... Co. D—Gunshot, right leg, calf, flesh.

9 JUNE 1864

Wounded:

John Hanover .... Co. G

10 JUNE 1864

Wounded:

Edgar M. Hovey .... Co. G—Left hand, little finger.

12 JUNE 1864

Captured or Missing:

Charles D. Bibbins .... Co. E—Missing at Cold Harbor. Returned.

John Riley .... Co. E—Missing at Cold Harbor. Returned in December 1864.

Cpl. Winfield S. Shanahan .... Co. E—Missing at Cold Harbor. Returned on 2 December 1964.

13 JUNE 1864

Wounded:

Sgt. George J. Davis .... Co. G—Gunshot, left hand, severe.

14 JUNE 1864

Captured or Missing:

William O. Clemans .... Co. C—Straggled on road to Petersburg. Died at Andersonville on 26 July 1864.

Jocko Pe-nais-now-o-quot .... Co. K—Died at Andersonville.

15 JUNE 1864

Wounded:

Sgt. John Berridge .... Co. D

16 JUNE 1864

Wounded:

Isaac B. Willitts .... Co. D—Gunshot, left foot, second toe amputated.

17 JUNE 1864—BATTLE AT PETERSBURG

Killed in Action:

Major Levant C. Rhines .... Buried in Spring Arbor, Michigan.
Cpl. Edward F. Cox .... Co. A
Capt. George C. Knight .... Co. A
Leroy M. Wilber .... Co. A—Buried in Petersburg National Cemetery.
James Fullerton .... Co. B
John B. Gilbert .... Co. C—Buried in Petersburg National Cemetery.
James H. Benjamin .... Co. D
Levi H. Waite .... Co. D
Sgt. Pardey T. Colvin .... Co. E
Cpl. Alonzo Campbell .... Co. G
David Graham .... Co. G
1st Sgt. Frederick Dawson .... Co. H—Buried in Poplar Grove National Cemetery.
Sgt. Clinton S. Trim .... Co. H
Horace Martin .... Co. I
Cpl. William Styon .... Co. I

Died of Wounds:

John Buchanan .... Co. A—Died of wounds on 17 June 1864. Buried in Petersburg National Cemetery.
Michael Gleason .... Co. A—Died of wounds on 30 June 1864. Buried in National Cemetery, Brooklyn NY.
George Hough .... Co. A—Captured. Died of wounds while captured.
Victor Burk .... Co. B—Left leg. Died of wounds in Philadelphia, PA, on 30 July 1864. Buried in National Cemetery, Philadelphia, PA.

Roland Mills .... Co. C—Died of wounds on 17 June 1864.

Gilbert Morehouse .... Co. C—Gunshot, right thigh, upper third fractured. Died of wounds on 29 August 1864.

Thomas Durning .... Co. F—Gunshot, left side. Died of wounds on 24 June 1864. Buried in Arlington National Cemetery.

John Keedle .... Co. F—Shell, fracture of skull.

Capt. Thomas Gaffney .... Co. G—Gunshot, left shoulder. Died of wounds in Washington, DC, on 20 June 1864.

Joseph Wilson .... Co. G—Gunshot, head. Died some-time after 23 June 1864.

Michael Fillinger .... Co. H—Shell, back, contusion of lumbar vertebra. Died of wounds 18 June 1864.

John H. Hanken .... Co. H—Gunshot, right shoulder. Died of wounds at Washington, DC, on 24 July 1864. Buried in Arlington National Cemetery.

Oliver Ar-pe-targe-zhik .... Co. K—Died of wounds at Washington, DC, on 9 July 1864. Buried in Arlington National Cemetery.

2nd Lt. Garret Graveraet .... Co. K—Shell, left forearm fractured. Died of wounds in Washington, DC, on 10 July 1864. Buried at Mackinac Island, MI.

Wounded:

Sgt. Willard A. Slate .... Co. A—Shell, right arm above elbow.

Cpl. Charles Collins .... Co. B—Gunshot, right thigh, flesh.

Silas Pierce .... Co. B—Gunshot, neck and left thigh.

Knudt Severson .... Co. B—Left hand, amputated.

Cpl. Frank E. Steward .... Co. B—Gunshot, left thigh.

Cpl. William W. Walker .... Co. B—Left foot.

Sgt. Immanuel Brown .... Co. C—Gunshot, right thigh.

1st Lt. Thomas Fowler .... Co. C

Eugene Hall .... Co. C—Gunshot, right hip.

Cpl. Amos Hoffman .... Co. C—Gunshot, left thigh.

William P. Dean .... Co. D—Gunshot, left ankle, flesh.

Edward Dumphrey .... Co. D—Gunshot, left elbow, flesh.

John Fry .... Co. D—Shell, right gluteal, contusion.

Luke D. Hatch .... Co. E—Gunshot, left forearm.

Hammond L. Rolfe .... Co. E—Gunshot, left lower leg, flesh.

Joseph Fish .... Co. F—Left arm, amputated.

2nd Lt. Charles G. Conn .... Co. G—Left forearm, slightly.
William H. Curliss .... Co. G—Above ankle.
Thomas Dunning .... Co. G
Edgar M. Hovey .... Co. G
Benjamin F. Smith .... Co. H—Gunshot, right hand and wrist, joint.
James Walsh .... Co. H—Gunshot, right leg fractured, amputated.
Michael Horrigan .... Co. I—Gunshot, head and left shoulder.
Capt. George H. Murdoch .... Co. I—Head.
John Andrew .... Co. K—Gunshot, right thigh, near hip, flesh.
Charles Chatfield .... Co. K—Gunshot, back, contusion.
Luther Dutton .... Co. K—Gunshot, right thigh, flesh.
William Isaacs .... Co. K
Samuel Kaquatch .... Co. K—Gunshot, right forearm.
John She-go-ge .... Co. K—Gunshot, right hand, flesh.
Michael Wayaubemind .... Co. K

Captured and Missing:

Adjutant Edward J. Buckbee .... Escaped.
Cpl. John Beebe .... Co. A—Died at Andersonville on 20 September 1864.
James B. Brown .... Co. A—Reported dead by returned prisoners.
Moses Buckley .... Co. A—Died on steamer *Spaulding* on 4 March 1865 while returning from prisoner-of-war camp. Buried in Annapolis.
1st Sgt. Michael Collins .... Co. A—Returned.
Henry J. Stephens .... Co. A—Returned.
Andrew H. Face .... Co. B—Returned.
Cyrus Face .... Co. B—Died at Andersonville on 9 September 1864.
Coland Stafford .... Co. B—Returned in December 1864.
Sgt. Joseph Stevens .... Co. B—Returned.
Vernon W. Thorpe .... Co. B—Returned.
Nathan R. Tompkins .... Co. B—Died at Danville, VA, on 24 August 1864.
Charles Keeber .... Co. C—Returned on 2 December 1864.
Zena Ransom .... Co. C—Returned on 2 December 1864.
Alva Fordham .... Co. D—Died at Andersonville on 13 October 1864.
Cpl. James H. Peek .... Co. D—Died at Andersonville on 30 August 1864.

James Sanders ....Co. D—Returned on 2 December 1864.

Nelson A. Storey.............................Co. D—Died on transport *Baltic* on 26 November 1964 while returning from prisoner-of-war camp.

Otis Sylvester.................................Co. D—Died at Andersonville.

Sgt. Horatio Dorr Blakeman ....Co. E—Returned on 2 December 1864.

C. Cook..Co. E

Frank Cook.....................................Co. E—Sent to Andersonville.

Willis S. Coon ....Co. E—Died at Andersonville on 10 September 1864.

William Dingman............................Co. E—Returned on 2 December 1864.

1st Sgt. Daniel C. Gore ....Co. E—Returned on 2 December 1864.

Joseph Hall.....................................Co. E—Died at Andersonville on 18 October 1864.

Dallas P. Jump ....Co. E—Died at Andersonville on 1 September 1864.

Samuel Milligan.............................Co. E—Returned on 2 December 1864.

James Noyes...................................Co. E—Died at Andersonville on 16 October 1864.

William Petrie ....Co. E

Wilson Ryan ....Co. E—Died at Andersonville on 1 September 1864.

Hartwell S. Seeley..........................Co. E

James Sharkey...............................Co. E—Returned.

William Stubbs..............................Co. E—Returned on 2 December 1864.

Sidney Washburne ....Co. E—Died at Andersonville on 9 August 1864.

Daniel A. Wells ....Co. E

Charles Wibert ....Co. E—Returned.

Cpl. Edwin T. Wiley.......................Co. E—Died at Andersonville on 24 August 1864.

Cpl. James Dennis ....Co. F—Returned on 2 December 1864.

Dexter Etheridge ....Co. F—Returned on 2 December 1864.

Benjamin Freeman ....Co. F—Died at Andersonville on 26 October 1864.

Jacob Gohl ....Co. F—Died at Andersonville.

John McGraw ....Co. F—Died at Andersonville on 18 November 1864.

Appendix A

Royal G. Platt .... Co. F—Returned.
Sgt. Alexander Donnelly .... Co. G—Died at Andersonville.
Solon Shepard .... Co. G—Died at Andersonville.
Wright D. Smith .... Co. G—Returned.
Nathan Cahon .... Co. H—Died at Andersonville on 26 August 1864.
Joseph A. Conklin .... Co. H—Returned.
Thomas Crossman .... Co. H—Returned on 2 December 1864.
Oscar Dennis .... Co. H—Died at Andersonville on 18 August 1864.
William Durfey .... Co. H—Died at Andersonville on 3 September 1864.
David Earley .... Co. H—Returned.
Byron S. Edmonds .... Co. H—Died at Andersonville on 9 September 1864.
John Kelly .... Co. H—Returned.
Cpl. Hugh Kennedy .... Co. H—Returned on 2 December 1864.
Thomas McLane .... Co. H—Died at Andersonville on 30 August 1864.
Jeremiah O'Leary .... Co. H—Died at Andersonville on 9 November 1864.
Miles Osterhout .... Co. H—Returned.
Cpl. William H. Ross .... Co. H
George W. Sackett .... Co. H—Died at Andersonville.
Cpl. David S. Seybert .... Co. H—Died at Andersonville on 29 June 1864.
Benjamin Vanordstrand .... Co. H—Returned.
Harrison Weidman .... Co. H—Died at Andersonville on 9 August 1864.
William Cassell .... Co. I—Returned on 2 December 1864.
Isaac Huff .... Co. I
David McFarland .... Co. I—Returned.
Sgt. Henry H. Miller .... Co. I—Returned.
Charles Sutherland .... Co. I—Died at Andersonville on 6 September 1864.
Amos Ash-ke-bug-ne-kay .... Co. K—Returned.
Daniel Ashman .... Co. K—Died at Andersonville.
Joseph L. Gibson .... Co. K—Died at Andersonville on 3 September 1864.
James H. Hamblin .... Co. K—Died at Andersonville on 21 October 1864.
Michael Jondrau .... Co. K—Died at Andersonville on 5 January 1865.
Louis Marks .... Co. K—Returned.
William Mixinasaw .... Co. K—Died at Andersonville on 26 October 1864.

Louis Muskoguon .... Co. K—Returned.
Jacko Pe-nais-now-o-quot .... Co. K—Died at Andersonville.
Adam Saw-be-come .... Co. K—Died at Andersonville on 26 October 1864.
Cpl. John B. Shomin .... Co. K—Returned on 2 December 1864.
Peter South .... Co. K—Died at Andersonville on 19 December 1864.
Joseph Williams .... Co. K—Returned on 2 December 1864.
Payson Wolfe .... Co. K—Returned on 2 December 1864.

18 JUNE 1864

Died of Wounds:

Halvah Brady .... Co. B—Died of wounds on the passage from the field to the general hospital.

Wounded:

James Harper .... Co. A—Shell, right forearm.
John R. Randall .... Co. F

19 JUNE 1864

Wounded:

John Wallace .... Co. G—Gunshot, through left foot.

20 JUNE 1864

Wounded:

William H. Crandall .... Co. A
2nd Lt. Martin Wager .... Co. F—Gunshot, fourth and fifth toes.
John Shomin .... Co. K—Gunshot, left elbow.

22 JUNE 1864

Died of Wounds:

Gilbert Morehouse .... Co. C—Thigh, serious. Died of wounds 29 August 1864. Buried at City Point, VA.

Wounded:

David P. Parkhurst .... Co. A.—Gunshot, right thumb.
Kearny Brown .... Co. B.—Gunshot, right foot fractured, metacarpal bone.
James S. Ramsey .... Co. I—Gunshot, right leg, flesh.

23 JUNE 1864

Wounded:

Jedidiah Grey .... Co. C—Gunshot, small of back.

24 JUNE 1864

Wounded:

Milton Calkins .... Co. A.—Gunshot, left hand, fracture of second metacarpal bone, index finger amputated.

Jeremiah Tiner............................... Co. A—Gunshot, little toe of left foot amputated.

25 JUNE 1864

Killed in Action:

2nd Lt. Martin Wager .... Co. F—Gunshot, left side of head.

26 JUNE 1864

Killed in Action:

Charles Waterman.......................... Co. I—Buried near Petersburg.

Wounded:

Frank Thayer .... Co. A—Right hand.

Cpl. Asher Huff .... Co. I (Color Guard)—Gunshot, left knee, flesh.

John Andrew .... Co. K—Right thigh, near hip, flesh.

27 JUNE 1864

Died of Wounds:

James B. Smith .... Co. H—Gunshot, entered thigh above and posterior to femur, passed downward and inward. Died of wounds on 2 July 1864.

28 JUNE 1864

Killed in Action:

Francis Marion Perry .... Co. B

29 JUNE 1864

Died of Wounds:

Sgt. Warren Sharp .... Co. C—Gunshot, left leg. Died of wounds 12 July 1864.

Wounded:
Stephen Teeter ....Co. G—Leg.

30 JUNE 1864

Killed in Action:
Theodore Nash ....Co. I—Buried near Petersburg.

8 JULY 1864

Wounded:
Robert Bradley ....Co. H—Shell, head, contusion, left side.

11 JULY 1864

Wounded:
Sgt. Maj. James S. DeLand.............Shoulder

17 JULY 1864

Wounded:
1st Lt. Thomas R. Fowler ....Co. C—Gunshot, entered left cheek, fractured molar bone, passing downward and backward, exit behind mastoid muscle, broken jaw.

19 JULY 1864

Wounded:
Alvin P. Earl ....Co. D

20 JULY 1864

Wounded:
Charles Herbert ....Co. K

25 JULY 1864

Wounded:
Albert Quance ....Co. B—Shell, left thigh.

30 JULY 1864—BATTLE OF THE CRATER

Killed in Action:

Cpl. Henry R. Horton...................... Co. B
Sgt. Alonzo B. Walls .... Co. C
Charles Carter .... Co. K
Moses Williams .... Co. K

Died of Wounds:

Joseph Nichols .... Co. E—Gunshot, left shoulder, passing downward. Died of wounds at Portsmouth Grove, RI. Buried in National Cemetery, Brooklyn, NY.

William B. Northrop .... Co. H—Gunshot, right leg fractured. Died of wounds on 15 August 1864. Buried in National Cemetery, Brooklyn, NY.

John Pa-ke-mabo-ga .... Co. K

Wounded:

Col. Charles V. DeLand................... Shell, head and face.
Sgt. Lloyd G. Walker .... Co. B—Shell, right hand, phalange of index finger.
Eugene Taylor .... Co. C—Gunshot, both cheeks, severe.
Sgt. Kirke W. Noyes .... Co. D—Gunshot, right foot, contusion.
Edmond E. Shaw............................. Co. F—Shell, right arm, flesh.
2nd Lt. William Ruddock............... Co. H—Breast, contusion.
Andrew J. Ellis .... Co. H—Gunshot, right leg, fracture.
Jacob Collins .... Co. K—Left arm fractured.

Captured or Missing in Action:

Oscar Soules................................... Co. A—Confined at Danville, VA, until 1 February 1865.
Albertus Andrus............................. Co. B—Returned.
1st Sgt. Edwin O. Conklin .... Co. B—Died at Danville, VA, on 30 November 1864.
Capt. Elmer C. Dicey .... Co. B—Returned.
William Gott................................... Co. B
Charles M. Thatcher...................... Co. B—Returned.
John Vandenburg........................... Co. B—Died at Danville, VA.
David Blanchard............................ Co. C
Nelson Conklin .... Co. C
Stanley W. Turner .... Co. C—Returned 13 June 1865.
Francis Urie .... Co. C—Returned.
Lafayette Weston .... Co. C—Returned and died at Annapolis, MD, on 8 November 1864.
Sgt. William H. Bates .... Co. D—Returned.

Charles R. Bonfoey ....Co. D—Returned.
Cpl. Samuel G. Ellis.......................Co. D—Died at Danville, VA, on 11
November 1864.
Elisha Fowler ....Co. D—Died 23 October 1864 on
transport returning from prisoner of
war camp. Buried at Annapolis, MD.
2nd Lt. William H. Randall ....Co. D—Returned.
Cpl. Edward F. Rodgers ....Co. D—Returned.
Richard Snay.................................Co. F—Returned.
Frederick Williams ....Co. F
2nd Lt. Charles G. Conn ....Co. G—Returned.
1st Sgt. Charles A. DePuy ....Co. H—Returned.
Walter Brown ....Co. I—Died at Salisbury, NC, on 2
November 1864.
George Colberth ....Co. I—Died 19 October 1864 on
steamer *New York* while returning
from prisoner of war camp.
William Dillabaugh........................Co. I
John H. Fairbanks ....Co. I
Ira A. Martin ....Co. I—Returned in December 1864.
Died at Annapolis MD on 13 January 1865.
A. Chibadice ....Co. K
Amable Kitcherbalist......................Co. K
Louis Muskoguon...........................Co. K
Jackson Nar-we-ge-she-qua-bey ....Co. K
John Wa-be-sis ....Co. K

5 AUGUST 1864

Wounded:
Surgeon Arvin F. Whelan................Shell, right thigh, contusion.

14 AUGUST 1864

Wounded:
Myron J. Fox...................................Co. I—Gunshot, right thigh grazed.

15 AUGUST 1864

Oscar McKeel ....Co. C—Gunshot, head grazed.

17 AUGUST 1864

Died of Wounds:
Noah Cain......................................Co. G—Gunshot, abdomen. Died in
field hospital.

19 AUGUST 1864—BATTLE OF REAMS STATION

Killed in Action:
W. Samuel Chatfield .... Co. K

24 AUGUST 1864

Wounded:
Albert Quance .... Co. B

26 AUGUST 1864

Captured or Missing in Action:
John Kedgnot .... Co. B—Returned.

30 SEPTEMBER 1864—BATTLE OF PEEBLES FARM

Killed in Action:
Anthony J. Thison .... Co. A

Died of Wounds:
Daniel H. Spicer .... Co. I—Died of wounds on 11 October 1864 at Alexandria VA.

Wounded:
Col. Charles V. DeLand .... Gunshot, leg.
Cpl. Benjamin F. Hosmer .... Co. B
Cpl. John W. Potter .... Co. C—Gunshot, left foot fractured.
Capt. Joseph O. Bellair .... Co. F
Simon Keji-kowe .... Co. K
1st Lt. Kirke Noyes .... Co. K
Solomon Otto .... Co. K
Jacob Prestawin .... Co. K

Captured or Missing in Action:
Col. Charles V. DeLand .... Returned.
George Demarest .... Co. B—Died at Salisbury, NC, on 8 February 1865.
Cpl. Benjamin F. Hosmer .... Co. B
Augustus H. Ferris .... Co. C—Died at Salisbury, NC, on 5 January 1865.
John Sanders .... Co. D—Returned.
John Saunders .... Co. D—Died at Salisbury, NC.
William Shaw .... Co. E—Returned.
Charles Sutherland .... Co. E—Died at Salisbury, NC, on 20 January 1865.
Mason M. Sutherland .... Co. E—Returned. Died at Annapolis, MD, on 17 March 1865.

Capt. Joseph O. Bellair .... Co. F—Returned.
Thomas H. Blake .... Co. F—Returned.
Amasa A. Coon .... Co. F—Returned.
George Lewis .... Co. G—Returned.
James Rhinehold .... Co. H—Died at Andersonville.
Joseph Vallequette .... Co. H—Returned.
1st Sgt. William Willett .... Co. I—Died at Salisbury on 10
January 1865.
Benjamin Youngs .... Co. I—Paroled 8 October 1864.
1st Lt. Kirke Noyes .... Co. K—Returned.

27 OCTOBER 1864—BATTLE OF HATCHER'S RUN

Died of Wounds:
Charles Harris .... Co. H—Gunshot, back and hip. Ball
entered thorax. Died of wounds on
12 November 1864.

Wounded:
Robert Fletcher .... Co. A—Gunshot, head, flesh (right
eye).
John McGivern .... Co. E—Gunshot, left hand, contusion.
John H. Thomas .... Co. I—Left leg, contusion.
Louis Shomin .... Co. K—Left leg.

Captured or Missing:
Charles Walser .... Co. D—Returned to regiment on 10
May 1865.

5 DECEMBER 1864

Wounded:
Thomas D. McCall .... Co. B—Accident. Shell, right leg,
flesh.
William H. Burns .... Co. G—Accident. Shell, right leg,
knee joint,leg amputated.

14 DECEMBER 1864

Wounded:
Cpl. Charles H. Fields .... Co. C—Gunshot, head, flesh.

6 FEBRUARY 1865

Wounded:
Alonzo Parks .... Co. A

8 FEBRUARY 1865

Wounded:

George Lewis.................................... Co. G

11 FEBRUARY 1865

Wounded:

Morris N. Graves............................. C—Gunshot, left shoulder, flesh.

20 FEBRUARY 1865

Died of Wounds:

Petros A-won-o-quot .... Co. K—Shell, right femur fractured. Died the same day.

13 MARCH 1865

Wounded:

Joseph LaLonde .... Co. G—Gunshot, third toe, right foot.

17 MARCH 1865

Wounded:

James Peacock .... Co. B—Gunshot, ball passing into cavity of abdomen.

29 MARCH 1865

Killed in Action:

Robert Cummings........................... Co. C—Buried in Petersburg National Cemetery.
Cpl. Charles H. Fields .... Co. C

Wounded:

Fred Falker..................................... Co. B—Gunshot, left eye.
Thomas Wesaw............................... Co. K—Gunshot, face, severe.

2 APRIL 1865—ASSAULT ON PETERSBURG

Killed in Action:

George C. Marsh .... Co. C
Wallace Litchard............................. Co. D
Flavius J. Dexter............................. Co. F
Albert Smith................................... Co. G

Died of Wounds:

Porter Fales ....Co. A—Right hand, fracture. Amputated three fingers. Died of wounds 18 May 1865.

Jessie Davidson...............................Co. E—Died of wounds at Washington, DC, on 10 April 1865. Buried in Arlington National Cemetery.

Wounded:

Lt. Col. Asahel Nichols ....Gunshot, left side, ball removed.
1st Lt. Friend D. Soules..................Co. B—Shell, left leg.
Wesley M. Sage ....Co. C—Shell, head.
Andrew J. Sawyer ....Co. C—Shell, scalp.
George W. Fry ....Co. D—Wounded, inferior maxillary, part of maxillary carried away.
W. Daniel Watson ....Co. D—Shell, right thigh.
Sgt. Alvin Jones...............................Co. E—Contusion, head.
Cpl. William Mitchell......................Co. E—Shell, right thigh.
1st Lt. Henry H. Hulin ....Co. G—Shell, head and face.
Cpl. Cephas Parker.........................Co. G—Shell, right thigh.
William Price...................................Co. H—Shell, left thigh.
Sgt. Richard Campbell....................Co. I—Shell, left shoulder joint.
Capt. James S. DeLand ....Co. K—Left arm.
Jacob Greensky ....Co. K—Shell, left thigh.
Cornelius Hall ....Co. K—Shell, right arm.
Freeman Sutton ....Co. K—Shell, left thigh.

Appendix B
Sharpshooters Who Were
Discharged for Disability
★ ★ ★ ★ ★

Thomas C. Allyn .... Co. D—5 September 1863
Capt. Edwin V. Andress .... Co. K—26 July 1864
James Austin .... Co. I—5 November 1863
Henry P. Bannon .... Co. D—May 1865
Henry S. Barnes .... Co. E—16 September 1863
Cpl. Jacob Barnhart .... Co. E—14 October 1864
Myron Beach .... Co. I—31 December 1863
Silas Beckwith .... Co. C—August 1864
Sylvester Berry .... Co. G—27 September 1864
Robert F. Bradley .... Co. H—5 September 1864
Immanuel Brown .... Co. C—6 May 1865
Rollin O. Brownell .... Co. C—2 July 1863
Ripka Bukema .... Co. B—2 September 1863
William Burroughs .... Co. C—15 December 1864
Oliver Byington .... Co. D
Seneca Canfield .... Co. I—10 June 1864
Absolom Cargill .... Co. A
Joseph H. Conway .... Co. I—July 1864
Erastus M. Cool .... Co. F—8 October 1864
Melvin Dalrymple .... Co. G—20 March 1865
Capt. George N. Davis .... Co. D—26 November 1864
Gilbert Davis .... Co. A—18 September 1864
Harvey Davis .... Co. A—13 September 1864
Samuel Davis .... Co. G—March 1864
Henry Drawbolt .... Co. H—21 January 1865
1st Lt. William J. Driggs .... Co. K—6 July 1864
Judson Eldred .... Co. C—4 September 1863
Harvey M. Evans .... Co. G—5 November 1863
Cornelius Filkins .... Co. D—4 September 1863
Robert Finch .... Co. B—3 October 1864
Joseph Fish .... Co. F—29 December 1864
Joseph Fisher .... Co. A—20 June 1864
Thomas Fisher .... Co. I—17 December 1864
Florian Fountain .... Co. F—27 March 1865
1st Lt. George Fowler .... Co. H—27 December 1864
Capt. Thomas R. Fowler .... Co. C—17 October 1864
George W. Fry .... Co. D—29 June 1865

Henry C. Gates .... Co. E—28 September 1864
Obediah Gleason .... Co. D
John T. Green .... Co. D—17 January 1865
James B. Haight.............................. Co. E—23 February 1865
Amos Hamley .... Co. D—6 June 1865
John Hanover .... Co. G—10 December 1864
Samuel Harper................................ Co. A—7 January 1865
1st Lt. Robert F. Hill .... Co. I—10 December 1864
Amos Hoffman .... Co. C—3 March 1865
William R. Howland........................ Co. D—31 January 1865
Charles A. Hudson .... Co. B
Capt. Samuel E. Hudson .... Co. D—31 December 1864
Luther Huntsley .... Co. F—2 August 1864
John H. Kerth................................ Co. A—21 September 1864
1st Sgt. Joseph H. Kilbourn .... Co. E—22 March 1864
Otis Kimball .... Co. A—7 January 1865
Ira King .... Co. D—31 January 1865
William S. Knapp............................ Co. E—19 December 1863
1st Lt. Cyrenius B. Knight .... Co. D—22 October 1864
Frederick Lafleur............................ Co. G—17 September 1864
Charles W. Lake .... Co. C—7 January 1865
Charles Lashbrooks .... Co. D—2 June 1865
George T. Lowrey............................ Co. G—21 March 1864
Thomas McLaughlin........................ Co. H—22 March 1864
William B. McNeil........................... Co. G—March 1864
Capt. Lucien Meigs .... Co. C—9 August 1864
Cpl. Archibald M. Miller................. Co. A—14 November 1864
James S. Minott .... Co. F—15 October 1864
George H. Morse .... Co. I—28 January 1865
2nd Lt. Guy Newbre .... Co. A—22 October 1864
Lt. Col. Asahel W. Nichols.............. 2 June 1865
Marcus Otto................................... Co. K—18 August 1864
1st Sgt. John S. Paul .... Co. E—8 September 1864
Charles Porsley .... Co. K—17 December 1864
Cpl. John W. Potter .... Co. C—5 May 1865
Albert Quance .... Co. B—20 January 1865
Robert B. Ready .... Co. G—29 December 1864
Hammond L. Rolfe .... Co. E—10 April 1865
Joseph M. Rounds .... Co. C—4 March 1864
2nd Lt. William Ruddock................ Co. H—25 November 1864
Henry Runkle................................. Co. E—29 November 1864
James Scoby .... Co. C—16 June 1863
Ezra Scott .... Co. D—17 December 1864
Knudt Severson.............................. Co. B—15 April 1865
Joseph Shaw-au-os-ang .... Co. K—17 January 1865

Appendix B

Mark Shell...Co. F—17 December 1864
Benjamin F. Smith ....Co. H—2 April 1865
1st Lt. Friend D. Soules...................Co. B—15 May 1865
Horton M. Squires ....Co. D—24 May 1865
Allen Stephens ....Co. G—29 December 1864
Caleb Stiles ....Co. E—22 March 1864
Asst. Surgeon Asahel B. Strong .....9 July 1864
Joseph Ta-ohe-de-niw ....Co. K—18 August 1864
2nd Lt. Albert P. Thomas................Co. C—13 September 1864
Oscar E. Thompson ....Co. E—22 March 1864
2nd Lt. William J. Thompson ....Co. H—30 December 1864
John Unrah ....Co. G—25 May 1865
James Walsh....................................Co. H—December 1864
George W. Warren ....Co. B—10 September 1864
James V. Watson..............................Co. K—20 June 1864
Evon B. Webster..............................Co. A—8 October 1864
1st Lt. Francis Whipple ....Co. B—13 September 1864
Lott W. Willett ....Co. I—23 February 1865
Isaac B. Willitts..............................Co. D—2 June 1865

410

Appendix C
Sharpshooters Who Transferred to Other Regiments
★ ★ ★ ★ ★

John Anderson	Co. E—Fifty-seventh Massachusetts Infantry
Francis W. Drake	Co. E—Seventh Michigan Infantry
Judson Kitchen	Co. A—Second Missouri Infantry
Robert McKay	Co. A—Cavalry
Sgt. Henry Miller	Co. I—United States Colored Troops
Charles M. Wheeler	Co. E—Ninth Indiana Infantry

Appendix D
Sharpshooters Who
Enlisted in Veteran Reserve Corps
★ ★ ★ ★ ★

Lt. Col. William H. H. Beadle .... 13 June 1864
Albert E. Bennett .... Co. D—1 May 1864
Zenas Brott .... Co. D—Co. E, Twenty-first VRC,
                                  24 January 1865
George R. Counterman .... Co. D—Co. A, Second Regt.
John H. Countryman .... Co. G—Thirty-sixth Co., Second
                                  Battalion, 17 April 1865
George W. Crisler .... Co. A—Fourth Co., Second Battalion,
                                  February 1865
Daniel Cross .... Co. C—15 January 1864
Sgt. George J. Davis .... Co. G—118th Co., Second Battalion
Abram Dubois .... Co. D—Fifty-first Co., Second Battal-
                                  ion, 18 January 1865
Thomas Dunning .... Co. G—Co. E, Seventh Regt.
Elias Farwell .... Co. A—Co. F, Second Regt.
John Fitzgerald .... Co. I—7 April 1865
George W. Hartley .... Co. G
Luke D. Hatch .... Co. E—Thirty-eighth Co., Second
                                  Battalion, 2 March 1865
Edgar M. Hovey .... Co. G—Co. D, Eleventh Regt., 11
                                  March 1865
Martin Huizenga .... Co. B—Co. H, Twelfth Regt.
Albert Kubicek .... Co. G—Eighth Co., Second Battalion,
                                  August 1864
Isaac Loree .... Co. F
Lewis Matthews .... Co. G—Fifth Co., Second Battalion
James Maule .... Co. B—Co. F, Twenty-fourth Regt., 3
                                  December 1864
Michael Navel .... Co. C—10 March 1865
Thomas Nelson .... Co. K—16 September 1864
William Parker .... Co. B—Co. E, Twelfth Regt., Novem-
                                  ber 1864
James Reid .... Co. H—15 January 1864
Horton M. Squires .... Co. D
Eugene A. Taylor .... Co. C—Co. C, Eleventh Regt., 1 May
                                  1865
Charles Van Brocklin .... Co. A—10 August 1864
Oliver Wells .... Co. E—Fourth Co., Second Battalion
Frederick Williams .... Co. F
Clark Wright .... Co. I—7 April 1865

Appendix E
Sharpshooters Who Died
as Prisoners of War
★ ★ ★ ★ ★

The first date is date of capture; the second is date of death.

Daniel Ashman.................................Co. K—17/6/64 Andersonville
Cpl. John Beebe..............................Co. A—17/6/64 Andersonville 20/9/64
Randolph Betts ....Co. C—12/5/64 Andersonville14/ 8/64
James B. Brown ....Co. A—17/6/64 "Reported Dead"
Walter Brown ....Co. I —30/7/64 Salisbury 2/11/64
Nathan Cahon.................................Co. H—17/6/64 Andersonville 26/8/64
William O. Clemans.......................Co. C—14/6/64 Andersonville 25/7/64
1st Sgt. Edwin O. Conklin ....Co. B—30/7/64 Danville 30/11/64
Willis S. Coon ....Co. E—17/6/64 Andersonville 10/9/64
George Demarest ....Co. B—30/9/64 Salisbury 8/2/65
Oscar C. Dennis.............................Co. H—17/6/64 Andersonville 18/8/64
Sgt. Alexander Donnelly................Co. G—17/6/64 Andersonville ?/?/65
William C. Durfey ....Co. H—17/6/64 Andersonville 3/9/64
Byron S. Edmonds.........................Co. H—17/6/64 Andersonville 9/9/64
Samuel G. Ellis..............................Co. D—30/7/64 Danville 11/11/64
Cyrus Face.....................................Co. B—17/6/64 Andersonville 9/9/64
Augustus H. Ferris.........................Co. C—30/9/64 Salisbury 5/1/65
Cpl. Alva Fordham ....Co. D—17/6/64 Andersonville
                                                          13/10/64
Elisha Fowler ....Co. D—30/7/64   19/10/64
Clark Fox, Sr..................................Co. B—12/5/64 Andersonville 27/8/64
Benjamin Freeman ....Co. F—17/6/64 Andersonville
                                                          26/10/64
Joseph Gibson ....Co. K—17/6/64 Andersonville 3/9/64
Henry Giley ....Co. A—Andersonvill 1/9/64
Jacob Gohl ....Co. F—17/6/64 Andersonville ?/?/65
Joseph H. Hall................................Co. E—17/6/64 Andersonville
                                                          18/10/64
James M. Hamblin.........................Co. K—17/6/64 Andersonville
                                                          21/10/64
William O. Hill ....Co. A—26/5/64 Andersonville
                                                          24/10/64
George Hough.................................Co. A—17/6/64   ?/?/64
Michael Jondrau ....Co. K—17/6/64 Andersonville 5/1/65
Dallas P. Jump ....Co. E—17/6/64 Andersonville 1/9/64
John M. McGraw.............................Co. F—17/6/64 Andersonville
                                                          18/11/64

Thomas McLane...............................Co. H—17/6/64 Andersonville 30/8/64
William Mixinasaw..........................Co. K—17/6/64 Andersonville 26/10/64
Patrick Mulligan.............................Co. F—12/5/64 Andersonville 3/30/65
James Noyes...................................Co. E—17/6/64 Andersonville 16/10/64
Jeremiah O'Leary............................Co. H—17/6/64 Andersonville 9/11/64
Cpl. James H. Peek.........................Co. D—17/6/64 Andersonville 30/8/64
Jacko Pe-nais-now-o-quot...............Co. K—14/6/64 Andersonville ?
Charles Porcelay.............................Co. I — Salisbury 2/11/64
Levi Porter.....................................Co. C—6/5/64 Andersonville 2/8/64
James Rhinehold............................Co. H—30/9/64 Andersonville ?
Wilson Ryan...................................Co. E—17/6/64 Andersonville 1/9/64
George Sackett...............................Co. H—17/6/64 Andersonville ?
John Saunders................................Co. D—30/9/64 Salisbury 2/1/65
Adam Saw-be-come.........................Co. K—17/6/64 Andersonville 26/10/64
Cpl. David Seybert.........................Co. H—17/6/64 Andersonville 29/6/64
Solon Shepard................................Co. G—17/6/64 Andersonville ?/?/65
A. Sockum......................................Co. K— Andersonville 26/10/64
Peter South....................................Co. K—17/6/64 Andersonville 19/12/64
Charles Sutherland.........................Co. E—30/9/64 Salisbury 20/1/65
Charles Sutherland.........................Co. I— 17/6/64 Andersonville 6/9/64
Otis Sylvester.................................Co. D—17/6/64 Andersonville ?
Eugenio K. Tompkins.....................Co. A—26/6/64 "Reported Dead"
Nathan R. Tompkins.......................Co. B—17/6/64 Andersonville 24/8/64
John Vandenburg............................Co. B—30/7/64 Danville ?
William Vickery.............................Co. A—26/5/64 Andersonville 28/8/64
John Wade......................................Co. F— Andersonville 24/8/64
Sidney Washburne..........................Co. E—17/6/64 Andersonville 9/8/64
Harrison Weidman..........................Co. H—17/6/64 Andersonville 9/8/64
Lafayette Weston............................Co. C—30/7/64 Andersonville 8/11/64
Cpl. Edwin T. Wiley........................Co. E—17/6/64 Andersonville 24/8/64
1st Sgt. William Willett..................Co. I— 30/9/64 Salisbury 10/1/65

Appendix F
Sharpshooters Who Died of Disease
★ ★ ★ ★ ★

Charles A-Gaer-Go..........................Co. K—Alexandria, VA, 10 January 1865.

Jefferson S. Bagley..........................Co. B—St. Mary's Hospital, Detroit, MI, 29 August 1863.

Albert C. Baker ....Co. C—Camp Douglas, IL, 21 February 1864.

Alvin H. Barber..............................Co. C—Chicago, IL, typhoid fever, 16 October 1863, buried in Rose Hill Cemetery.

Willard Barnes ....Co. C—City Point, VA, typhoid fever 19 August 1864.

Q.M. Sgt. Goodwin S. Beaver ....Carver Hospital, Washington, DC, chronic diarrhea, 28 June 1865, buried in Arlington National Cemetery.

John A. Benner...............................Co. A—Washington, DC, typhoid pneumonia, 5 June 1865, buried in Arlington National Cemetery.

Samuel Bennett ....Co. H—Chicago, IL, buried in Rose Hill Cemetery.

Edgar W. Bray ....Co. G—Chicago, IL, 16 September 1863.

Nathan P. Bristol ....Co. H—10 April 1865, buried in Poplar Grove National Cemetery.

William Brott ....Co. D—Washington, DC, chronic diarrhea, 2 August 1864.

Moses Buckley................................Co. A—On steamer *Spaulding* returning from prisoner-of-war camp, 4 March 1865, buried at Annapolis.

Jeremiah Burcher ....Co. H—First Division Hospital, 13 June 1865, buried in Arlington National Cemetery.

Sgt. Peter Burns.............................Co. K—Chronic dysentery, 14 September 1864.

Milton Calkins ....Co. A—Battle Creek, MI, 17 October 1864.

Hiram Call......................................Co. F—Camp Douglas, IL, measles, 16 October 1863.

Mark H. Child ....Co. E—Annapolis, MD, 28 April 1864.

Barney Craton...............................Co. I—Alexandria, VA, 10 April 1864, buried in Alexandria National Cemetery.

Joseph Crawford ....Co. C—Annapolis, MD, pneumonia, 31 March 1864.

Nicholas Crilley ....Co. C—August 1864.

William Cummings........................Co. C—Alexandria, VA, 3 July 1864, buried in Alexandria National Cemetery.

E. S. Cunningham..........................Co. B—5 July 1864, buried in Arlington National Cememtery.

John David ....Co. K—Annapolis, MD, 4 May 1864, buried at Annapolis.

Edgar D. Davidson.........................Co. A—Camp Douglas, IL, 23 June 1864.

Alfred Davis ....Co. C—On hospital boat, 15 October 1864.

Simon Davis ....Co. G—17 August 1864, buried in Brooklyn National Cemetery.

A. Eckles.......................................Co. D—7 March 1864, buried in Camp Nelson, KY.

James H. Edmons ....Co. D—18 July 1864, buried in Brooklyn National Cemetery.

Silas D. Fegles ....Co. A—Annapolis, MD, typhoid pneumonia, 23 April 1864, buried at Annapolis.

John Fisher ....Co. A—Kalamazoo, MI, 28 January 1863.

Samuel N. Fitch ....Co. A—13 August 1864, buried in Petersburg National Cemetery.

Apollos Fordham............................Co. D—Dearborn, MI, 21 August 1863.

C. B. Fowler ....Co. D—19 October 1864, buried in Hampton National Cemetery, VA.

Charles Fox ....Co. B—Annapolis MD, typhoid pneumonia, 28 March 1864.

William W. Frost ....Co. G—June 1865.

Isaac Gorringer ....Co. ?—Buried in Rose Hill Cemetery.

David E. Grant...............................Co. G—Chicago, IL, 9 February 1864.

William Grant ....Co. ?—Buried in Rose Hill Cemetery.

Austin Harmon ....Co. I—Chicago, IL, 23 December 1863.

John Harvey...................................Co. G—Chicago, IL, 3 December 1863.

George H. Haulterbaum.................Co. H—Chicago, IL, typhoid pneumonia, 3 January 1864.

William Hawley .... Co. D—Chicago, IL, 26 February 1864.

Joseph Heogler .... Co. K—24 October 1864, buried in Elmwood Cemetery, Detroit, MI.

Henry A. Howe .... Co. I—Camp Douglas, IL, 24 November 1863.

Sgt. John Huss .... Co. H—17 July 1864, buried in Poplar Grove National Cemetery.

Cpl. Henry H. Jackson .... Co. G—Chicago, IL, 3 October 1863.

John Johnson .... Co. I—Willett's Point, NY, 31 October 1864, buried in Brooklyn National Cemetery.

Frank S. Joslyn .... Co. G—Petersburg, VA, 28 July 1864.

Joseph Kadah .... Co. K—St. Mary's Hospital, Detroit, MI, 23 October 1864.

Eugene Kerknickerbocker .... Co. A—Detroit, MI, 8 March 1863.

Henry Kessler .... Co. G—Elkhart, IN, 3 July 1863.

John Kiniewahasoipi .... Co. K—Petersburg, VA, 5 March 1865, buried in Poplar Grove National Cemetery.

Eliphalet Knapp .... Co. F—Washington, DC, 6 June 1864, buried in Arlington National Cemetery.

Samuel B. Knight .... Co. D—Newton, MI, May 1865.

James N. Laraway .... Co. C—City Point, VA, typhoid fever, 12 August 1864, buried in Alexandria National Cemetery.

Russel F. Lawrence .... Co. C—Alexandria, VA, chronic diarrhea, 2 December 1864.

Asher W. LeBarron .... Co. E—Chicago, IL, 25 January 1864, buried in Rose Hill Cemetery.

Adoniram Lewis .... Co. D—31 July 1864, buried in Hampton National Cemetery.

William L. Marcey .... Co. I—Washington, DC, 1 June 1864.

Ira A. Martin .... Co. I—Annapolis, MD, 13 January 1865, buried at Annapolis.

Samuel McArthur .... Co. G—Chicago, IL, 26 November 1863.

Michael McCoy .... Co. F—Camp Douglas, IL, 13 November 1863, buried in Rose Hill Cemetery.

John McIntosh .... Co. D—Chicago, IL, 25 March 1864, buried in Rose Hill Cemetery.

Isaac Middleton .... Co. F—Typhoid malarial fever, 13 July 1865.

Appendix F

Thomas Mixonauby .... Co. K—Detroit, MI, 12 March 1865.

Cpl. Cornelius Montgomery .... Co. E—Chicago, IL, relapse from measles, 20 January 1864, buried in Rose Hill Cemetery.

Joseph Nar-qua-quot .... Co. K—Chicago, IL, 11 December 1863.

Cpl. Charles Nichols .... Co. H—Camp Douglas, IL, "fits," 20 January 1864.

Marion A. Northrop .... Co. H—Camp Douglas, IL, pneumonia, 17 April 1864.

John A. Northrup .... Co. D—Camp Douglas, IL, 12 February 1864.

Jerome B. Paddock .... Co. G—Died en route to hospital, 6 July 1864.

Pe-to-zo-ourquitte .... Co. K—29 March 1865, buried at Petersburg.

Odoniram J. Pettengill .... Co. D—6 October 1864.

Hiram Pierce .... Co. C—Reading, MI, chronic diarrhea, 7 September 1864.

Sgt. James A. Preston .... Co. A—Annapolis, MD, 21 August 1864.

Calvin Refner .... Co. H—Pneumonia, 30 March 1864.

C. Rhinholdt .... Co. H—15 March 1865, buried in Loudon Park National Cemetery, Baltimore, MD.

Mathew C. Sharp .... Co. C—Chicago, IL, pneumonia, 16 October 1863.

James Signs .... Co. B—Camp Douglas, IL, 29 March 1864.

George Simonson .... Co. B—Chicago, IL, 10 September 1863.

Frederick Smith .... Co. F—Annapolis, MD, 23 March 1864, buried at Annapolis.

Peter Smith .... Co. H—Chicago, IL, 26 September 1863, buried in Rose Hill Cemetery.

Lucius P. Spencer .... Co. C—David's Island, NY, 24 July 1864, buried in Cypress Hill National Cemetery, Brooklyn, NY.

Seaton Spencer .... Co. A—Died 31 May 1864, chronic diarrhea, buried in Arlington National Cemetery.

Daniel H. Spicer .... Co. I—Alexandria, VA, 11 October 1864, buried in Alexandria National Cemetery.

James G. Stanbaugh .... Co. C—Dearborn, MI, 5 July 1863.

Emanuel J. Stiffler...........................Co. F—Washington, DC, inflammation of the brain, 13 January 1865.

Nelson A. Storey..............................Co. D—Died on steamer *Baltic* on way back from prisoner-of-war camp at Hilton Head, SC, 26 November 1864.

Mason Sutherland ....Co. E—Annapolis, MD, 17 March 1865, buried at Annapolis.

William B. Tafts ....Co. B—Camp Douglas, IL, 26 September 1863, buried in Rose Hill Cemetery.

Cpl. Stephen Teeter ....Co. G—Died in the field, 10 September 1864, buried in Cypress Hill National Cemetery.

Thomas Waubanoo...........................Co. K—Isabella, MI, 7 January 1864.

William W. Whitbeck........................Co. F—Camp Douglas, IL, 10 February 1864, buried in Rose Hill Cemetery.

Charles Whiteface...........................Co. K—Camp Douglas, IL, 14 February 1864.

William Wiseman............................Co. G—Chicago, IL, 10 April 1864, buried in Rose Hill Cemetery.

Hiram Woodward ....Co. A—Chicago, IL, typhoid fever, 24 January 1864.

Myron Woodward ....Co. A—City Point, VA, typhoid fever, 30 June 1864.

Appendix G
Other Deaths
★ ★ ★ ★ ★

William E. Holmes .... Co. H—Angola, IN, murdered while at home on furlough, 23 September 1863.

Samuel Kaquatch .... Co. K—Philadelphia, PA, killed by railroad car, 2 August 1864, buried in National Cemetery at Philadelphia.

Samuel H. Patterson .... Co. B—Near Petersburg, VA, killed by accidental explosion of a shell, 5 December 1864, buried in Poplar Grove National Cemetery.

Sash-ko-bon-quot .... Co. K—Camp Douglas, IL, accidentally killed, 27 December 1863.

Abel Shaw .... Co. F—Dearborn, MI, died of wounds received while on guard duty, 5 June 1863.

Henry Smith .... Co. H—Camp Douglas, IL, suicide, 25 September 1863.

Charles A. Vliet .... Co. C—Camp Douglas, IL, accidentally killed on the railroad, 8 February 1864.

Appendix H
Roster of First Regiment
Michigan Sharpshooters
✷ ✷ ✷ ✷ ✷

FIELD AND STAFF

Colonel—Charles V. DeLand
Lt. Col.—William H. H. Beadle
Major—John Piper
Surgeon—Arvin T. Whelan
Assistant Surgeons—George L. Cornell
Jacob McNett
Charles J. Wirts
Asahel B. Strong
Thomas Eagleson
Adjutant—Edward J. Buckbee
Quartermaster—David G. Palmer
Chaplain—David A. Heagle

COMPANY A

CAPTAIN—Levant C. Rhines
1st Lt—George C. Knight
2nd Lt—Guy Newbre

Ashalter, Joseph L.
Bailey, Charles
Bailey, John
Beebe, John
Benner, John (Hall's—A)
Bierce, Alonzo (Hall's—A)
Bowen, Amos W.
Bradley, Merrick
Branard, Corlan E. (Hall's—A)
Branyan, William R. (Hall's—A)
Britton, Alonzo H. (Hall's—A)
Brooks, Benjamin C. (Hall's—A)
Brown, James B.
Buchanan, Arthur
Buchanan, John

Buchanan, William H.
Buckley, Moses
Calkins, Ambrose
Calkins, Milton
Campbell, Samuel H.
Cargill, Absolom
Carr, Arnott W.
Carr, Harvey (Hall's—A)
Carr, Simeon D.
Carter, William
Chapin, William A.
Chase, Benjamin
Clarence, Robert
Claus, Henry
Collins, Michael
Conklin, Joseph A.
Conley, George E.
Cox, Edward F.
Crandall, William
Crawford, John S. (Hall's—A)
Crisler, George W.

Culver, Walter S. (Hall's—A)
Curtis, William R.
Darling, Lambert
Davidson, Curtis A.
Davidson, Edgar D.
Davis, Gilbert
Davis, Harvey
Davis, Joseph
Davis, Samuel
Davis, William
Dell, Irving R.
Detro, John R.
Dixon, Robert
Doyle, Henry (Hall's—A)
Dutcher, John A.
Eaton, John B. (Hall's—A)
Eaton, Levi M.
Edmonds, Daniel
Engle, Miles
Fales, Porter (Hall's—A)
Farwell, Elias
Fegles, Hiram P.
Fegles, Silas D.
Fisher, Daniel
Fisher, John
Fisher, Joseph
Fisher, Joseph
Fitch, Samuel N.
Flagg, Clark
Fletcher, Robert
Forbes, William G.
Frasier, Luman
Freeman, Edgar O.
Giley, Henry
Gleason, Michael B.
Harper, Harvey
Harper, James H.
Harper, John
Harper, Samuel
Hill, William O.
Himes, Andrew P.
Hinckley, Benjamin F.
Hodges, Marshall
Hough, George
Hummel, William
Jacobs, Albert W.

Jeffreys, Nathaniel
Jones, John W.
Kelly, Patrick
Kent, Darius A.
Kerknickerbocker, Eugene
Kerth, John H.
Kimball, Otis
Kitchen, Judson
Lapham, Squire
Livingston, John
McKay, Robert
McMahon, Alexander
Miller, Archibald M.
Murry, Martin W.
Newman, James V.
Parkhurst, David
Parks, Alonzo
Pierce, Almeron
Preston, James A.
Reed, Truman D.
Sanders, John S.
Sheely, Osborn (Hall's—A)
Shields, Frank
Slate, Willard A.
Soules, Friend D.
Soules, Jason H.
Soules, Oscar P.
Spencer, Seaton
Stephens, Charles M.
Stephens, Henry J.
Taylor, Edward S.
Thayer, Frank
Thison, Anthony J.
Tiner, Jeremiah
Tompkins, Eugenio K.
Trego, Benjamin J. (Hall's—A)
Tripp, Joseph W.
Underwood, Henry
Van Brocklin, Charles
Vandusen, John W.
Vickery, William
Webster, Evon B.
Westfall, Joseph
Wilber, Leroy M.
Willetts, James
Winslow, Willard

Woodward, Hiram
Woodward, Myron
Wright, Franklin W.

COMPANY B

CAPTAIN Elmer C. Dicey
1st Lieutenant William Clark
2nd Lieutenant Francis Whipple

Allen, Nathan S.
Andrus, Albertus
Bagley, Jefferson S.
Banks, Lawrence
Barnes, George W.
Beck, John
Boylin, Charles
Brady, Halvah A.
Brown, Kearny
Bryant, William
Bukema, Ripka
Burk, Victor
Burton, Henry
Byrnes, Edward C.
Byrnes, Mathon D.
Canah, James
Carbonnor, John
Chichester, Peter S.
Coleman, John
Collins, Charles F.
Conklin, Edwin O.
Cunningham, E.S.
Davis, Cortland
Davis, Walter P.
DeLong, John H.
Demarest, George
Demarest, Peter
Divine, John
Duverney, William
Evey, Reuben
Face, Andrew H.
Face, Cyrus
Falker, Fred
Finch, Robert
Fox, Charles
Fox, Clark, Jr.

Fox, Clark, Sr.
Fuller, Henry
Fullerton, Elias
Fullerton, James
Garmire, Albert (Hall's—A)
Gauntlett, William (Hall's—A)
Gill, Edwin
Gott, William
Greenman, Frank
Hale, Daniel (Hall's—A)
Harris, Isaac (Hall's—A)
Hedglen, Joshua C. (Hall's—A)
Herthwick, August
Hoag, Socrates (Hall's—A)
Hopkins, Orlon (Hall's—A)
Horton, Henry R.
Hosmer, Benjamin F.
House, Amasa G.
Hudson, Charles A.
Huizenga, Martin
Huston, John
Hutchinson, Plunkett (Hall's—A)
Jorgonson, Peter
Keating, Albert C.
Kedgnot, John
Langland, John
Louthe, Edward
Lukens, John
Maloney, Marvin
Maule, James
McCall, Thomas D.
McClellan, Ralph
McQueen, William
O'Brien, John
Oleson, Rasmus
Osborn, Sylvester M.
Parker, William
Patterson, Samuel Henry
Peacock, James
Perkins, Lyman P.
Perry, Francis M.
Perry, Oliver E.
Phillips, Chester R.
Pierce, Silas
Purdy, Theodore V.
Quance, Albert

Quance, Charles
Quance, Stephen
Raymond, Benjamin F.
Read, Albert D.
Reeves, Emmet (Hall's—B)
Robbins, Daniel S.
Sanford, David P.
Saxton, George H.
Severson, Knudt
Signs, James
Simonson, George
Sly, William W.
Smith, Sylvester
Snyder, Harrison
Stafford, Charles
Stafford, Coland
Stevens, Joseph
Stevens, Peter
Steward, Francis E.
Stocker, Irwin
Sweet, John H.
Tafts, William B.
Taylor, Augustus E.
Taylor, William H.
Thatcher, Charles M.
Thorpe, Vernon W.
Tompkins, Nathan R.
Tozer, Webster E.
Trombly, Richard
Vandenburg, John
Vaughan, Alfonzo
Wagoner, Frank
Walker, Lloyd G.
Walker, William W.
Wallace, Alexander
Waring, James O.
Warren, George W.
Waters, John H.
Wells, William W.
Wood, Thomas H.

COMPANY C

CAPTAIN—Lucien Meigs
1st Lt—Thomas R. Fowler
2nd Lt—Albert P. Thomas

Abbott, Almon C.
Abbott, Ira
Abbott, Lemon
Adams, James S.
Adams, Lewis H.
Adams, William
Anderson, John
Austin, Enos (Hall's—B)
Bailey, Andrew
Baker, Albert C.
Baker, Tobias
Barber, Alvin H.
Barber, Eliphalet
Barnes, Willard
Beard, Spencer
Beckwith, Silas B.
Bell, Franklin
Bell, John W.
Betts, Randolph
Betts, Wallace
Blanchard, David
Bolton, Enos
Brown, Benjamin
Brown, Immanuel
Brownell, Rollin O.
Burgess, Henry L.
Burroughs, William
Cady, William
Cahow, Alexander G.
Case, Leverette N.
Caswell, Benjamin (Hall's—B)
Clemans, William O.
Conklin, Nelson
Cook, Albert H.
Crandall, George
Crawford, Joseph
Crilley, Nicholas
Cross, Daniel
Cummings, Robert
Cummings, William W.
Davis, Alfred
Davis, George
Draper, Philetus
Eldred, Judson
Ellis, Burton J.
Evans, John D.

Ferris, Augustus H.
Fields, Charles H.
Fish, Henry S. (Hall's—B)
Foulk, Levi J.
Fouls, Darius
Fox, Joel
Gee, Truman
Gilbert, John B.
Graves, Morris N.
Graves, William J.
Grey, Jedidiah
Grey (Guy), William H.
Hall, Eugene T.
Hatch, Thomas D.
Haynes, Joel B.
Haywood, John M.
Hoffman, Amos
Hughes, William C.
Hunt, John D.
Irish, Cyrenius F. (Hall's—B)
Keeber, Charles
Knight, Aaron
Lake, Charles W.
Laraway, James N.
Lathrop, John W.
Lawrence, Russel F.
Lenhart, George D.
Marsh, George C.
McClellan, Robert
McConnell, James
McKeel, Oscar
Mills, Roland
Monteath, George E.
Morehouse, Gilbert
Morey, John
Navel (Naral), Michael
Nichols, Charles E.
Nichols, Lemuel R.
Palmer, Franklin
Parks, John W.
Pierce, Hiram
Porter, Levi
Potter, John W.
Powers, Elihu M.
Priest, Job
Quackenbush, John W.

Ransom, Augustus
Ransom, Zena D.
Raymond, William C.
Roberts, Pliletus V.
Rodgers, Nathaniel
Rounds, Joseph M.
Sage, Wesley M.
Sawyer, Andrew J.
Schauppner, Christopher
Scoby, James
Sharp, Lewis
Sharp, Mathew C.
Sharp, Warren
Shaw, Spencer L. (Hall's—B)
Skinner, Ichabod Eugene
Smith, Alonzo B.
Spencer, John H.
Spencer, Lucius P.
Stafford, Samuel
Stanbaugh, James G.
Standard, Oliver N.
Stoner, Absolum W.
Strong, Charles
Tallady, Thomas
Tanner, George
Taylor, Eugene A.
Turner, Stanley W.
Urie, Francis
Urie, John S.
Vader, John S.
VanSickle, Volney (Hall's—B)
Vliet, Charles A.
Wagner, William
Walls, Alonzo B.
Weaver, Francis
Wendhausen, Frederick (Hall's—B)
Weston, Lafayette
Williams, John
Young, Edward

COMPANY D

CAPTAIN George N. Davis
1st Lt—Samuel E. Hudson
2nd Lt—Cyrenius B. Knight

Adams, John
Allyn, Thomas C.
Arehart, John
Armstrong, Martin R.
Backus, John D. (Hall's—B)
Bannon, Henry P.
Barker, Joseph H. (Hall's—A)
Bates, Gilbert
Bates, William H.
Beaver, Goodwin S.
Benedict, John M.
Benjamin, James H.
Bennett, Albert E.
Bennett, Emmet M.
Berridge, John
Black, Jacob
Bonfoey, Charles R.
Brace, James H.
Bradley, Lyman H.
Brewer, Jay H.
Briggs, Charles D.
Briggs, Peleg A.
Brott, William H.
Brott, Zenas
Bryant, Lewis
Byington, Oliver
Calhoun, Charles
Chatfield, Stephen H.
Clark, John
Counterman, George R.
Dean, William P.
Dick, Noah
Doty, William S (Hall's—A)
Draper, Olney W. (Hall's—A)
Dubois, Abram
Dumphrey, Edward
Earl, Alvin P.
Easey, John
Eckles, A.
Edmons, James H.
Ellis, Samuel G.
Filkins, Cornelius
Fordham, Alva
Fordham, Apollos
Fordham, William C.
Fowler, C.B.

Fowler, Elisha
Fry, George W.
Fry, John
George, Elnathan (Hall's—A)
George, Warren
Gleason, Obediah
Goff, Stillman
Grant, David E.
Green, John T.
Hamley, Amos
Hart, Andrew K.
Hassell, Benjamin (Hall's—A)
Hawley, William
Holmes, Thomas
Holmes, William O.
Howland, William R.
Ireland, William A.
Jackson, Charles D.
Jackson, Warren
King, Ira
Knight, Samuel B.
Lashbrooks, Charles
Lewis, Adoniram
Lewis, Thomas
Litchard, Wallace (Hall's—A)
McIntosh, John (Justin)
McLoud, Daniel M.
Meacham, David R.
Messacar, John
Miller, George
Miller, James H. (Hall's—A)
Northrop, John A.
Noyes, Kirke W.
O'Dwyer, Martin
Peek, James H.
Pettengill, Odoniram J.
Preston, Parkenson W. (Hall's—A)
Quigley, James
Reed, Henry
Reed, John W.
Reynolds, John
Richardson, James
Roach, Charles
Rodgers, Edward F.
Root, Luther D.
Ross, Charles

Sanders, James
Sanders, John
Saunders, John
Schall, Peter (Hall's—A)
Scott, Ezra
Shekell, John (Hall's—B)
Smith, John
Spooner, John
Squires, Horton M.
Steppleford, William
Stone, George W.
Storey, Nelson A.
Strout, Vanorman
Sylvester, Otis
Thayer, George
Tift, Jerome B. (Hall's—A)
Vangilder, Barnabas (Hall's—A)
Vangilder, Henry (Hall's—A)
Vining, Mark
Waite, Levi H.
Walser, Charles
Watson, Nathaniel P. (Hall's—A)
Watson, W. Daniel
Webster, Myron
Wick, William
Wildey, George M.
Willitts, Isaac B.
Woods, William
Wright, Thomas C.
Young, Charles H.
Young, Henry
Young, John C.

COMPANY E

Captain—Asahel W. Nichols
1st Lt—Ira L. Evans
2nd Lt—Henry V. Hinckley

Adams, Marshal M.
Anderson, Charles
Anderson, John
Barber, Warren
Barnes, Harry C.
Barnes, Henry S.
Barnhart, Jacob

Barris, John
Bartlett, Robert S.
Bennett, Amasa (Hall's—B)
Bennett, Theron (Hall's—B)
Betts, Edward L. (Hall's—B)
Bibbins, Charles D.
Blakeman, Horatio D.
Cass, Ono S.
Chance, Othniel
Child, Mark H.
Colvin, Pardey T.
Conner, Andrew S.
Cook, C.
Cook, Francis
Coon, James
Coon, Lewis
Coon, Willis S.
Cooper, William H.
Daley, Joseph
Daniels, Paul
Davidson, Jessie (Hall's—B)
Decker, Henry
Deming, Lafayette P.
Dingman, William
Disbrow, James (Hall's—B)
Drake, Francis W.
Dyer, Milo E.
Emmons, Henry H. (Hall's—B)
Emmons, William (Hall's—B)
Ferman, Jacob (Hall's—B)
Fishell, John
Folsom, William
Foote, John
Fox, Charles E. (Hall's—B)
Gates, Henry C.
Gore, Daniel C.
Graham, John
Griswold, Perry D.
Hagerman, Peter
Haight, James B.
Haight, Sidney
Hall, Joseph H.
Hatch, Luke D.
Holcomb, Justin (Hall's—B)
Holt, Darius
Hoye, Oliver J.

427

Hulin, Henry H.
Jones, Alvin
Jones, John
Jones, Nelson
Jump, Dallas P.
Kilbourn, Joseph H.
Knapp, William S.
LeBarron, Asher W.
Lilhart, Morris H.
Lunger, George M.
Mahan, John
McGivern, John
Meade, Henry
Milligan, Samuel
Mitchell, William H.
Montgomery, Cornelius
Nichols, Alexander
Nichols, Joseph
Noyes, James
Odell, Isaac
Patterson, Peter
Paul, John S.
Petrie, William
Phelps, Melvin
Potter, Byron E.
Quimby, Isaac W.
Rickley, Anthony (Hall's—B)
Riley, John
Rolfe, Hammond L.
Rood, Lemuel
Runkle, Henry
Ryan, Wilson
St. Amour, Leander P.
Seeley, Hartwell S.
Senard, William
Seram, John R.
Shanahan, Winfield S.
Sharkey, James
Shaw, William
Smith, Alonzo
Stiles, Caleb
Stockwell, Henry C.
Stone, Harrison
Stubbs, William H.
Sutherland, Charles
Sutherland, Mason M.

Talbot, John A.
Teachout, Daniel
Tebo, George
Terwilliger, Edward
Thompson, Oscar E.
Trowbridge, Edwin R.
Tuthill, Francis H.
Van Dusen, William H.
Washburne, Sidney
Waters, Benjamin F.
Wells, Daniel A.
Wells, Oliver
Wheeler, Charles M.
Wibert, Charles
Wiley, Edwin T.
Wixcey, William T.
Wyant, George
Yerrington, William
Young,Charles

COMPANY F

CAPTAIN—Hooker A. DeLand
1st Lt—Joseph O. Bellair
2nd Lt—Martin Wager

Barber, Sidney
Barrett, William H.
Blair, David H.
Blake, Thomas H.
Boucher, Paul
Brown, Hiram
Caine, George A.
Call, Hiram A.
Cameron, James
Cool, Erastus M.
Coon, Amasa A.
Dailey, Charles
Dean, George C.
DeLand, James S.
Dennis, James
Dexter, Flavius J. (Hall's—A)
Dickson, Robert
DuMez, Garret
Dumford, John
Durning, Thomas

Dutton, Birney
Eaton, Spencer G.
Etheridge, Dexter
Fagan, Henry
Fish, Joseph
Fountain, Florian
Freeligh, Richard H.
Freeman, Benjamin
Fye, Henry
Gibbs, Myron W.
Gill, Edward H.
Gohl, Jacob
Grover, Nathan
Hall, Nicholas
Hero, William
Hodgeman, George
Huntsley, Luther
Ingram, George W. (Hall's—A)
Ingram, Orrin (Hall's—A)
Ivens, Nelson J. (Hall's—A)
Johnesse, Charles
Johnson, Jeremiah
Johnson, Richard
Keedle, John
Keopfgen, Phillip
Kilbourn, Benjamin
Kirkland, John W. (Hall's—A)
Kitchen, Nelson
Knapp, Eliphalet
Knickerbocker, George
Knorr, Albert H. (Hall's—A)
Laird, Joseph
Lee, James
Lester, Abner
Lewis, Frank
Little, William
Loree, Isaac
Machemer, Perry (Hall's—A)
Manehan, Daniel
Mark, John
Mathews, Charles W.
McBride, Neil
McCoy, Michael
McCullouch, Samuel
McGraw, John M.
McLelland, Frank (Hall's—A)

Middleton, Isaac (Hall's—A)
Miller, John C.
Minott, James S.
Moore, George W.(Wilson G.)
Morrissey, John
Mulligan, Patrick
Murray, Michael
Noble, Albert D. (Hall's—A)
Norton, James
Payfer, Charles B.
Percival, George A.
Pierson, William (Hall's—A)
Platt, Royal G.
Pride, Ezra (Hall's—A)
Randall, John R.
Robbins, Edward P. (Hall's—A)
Ross, Josiah
Ross, William J.
Rugar, Daniel H.
Ryan, Michael
Sage, Willard
Saunders, William
Shafer, Oliver (Hall's—A)
Shaw, Abel
Shaw, Edmond E.
Shell, Mark
Sidney, George
Sinclair, Samuel
Smith, Frederick
Snay, Moses
Snay, Richard
Stevens, William
Stewart, Charles A.
Stewart, William H.H.
Stiffler, Emanuel J.
Stowell, Charles E.
Thayer, Samuel
Tuttle, Stephen
Underhill, David
Upham, Hiram
Wade, John
Wells, Martin H.
Whipple, Alson W.
Whitbeck, William W.
White, James A.
Willetts, William

429

Williams, Frederick
Williams, George S.
Williams, John
Williams, Wesley C.
Wilson, Oren B.
Winman, John

COMPANY G

Captain—Thomas H. Gaffney
1st Lt—Moses A. Powell
2nd Lt—Charles G. Conn

Ash, David
Banta, John W.
Barney, Joseph
Beardsley, Howard A.
Bergen, William
Berry, Sylvester
Bostwick, Palmer
Bray, Edgar W.
Brayman, Nelson E.
Broderick, Dennis
Broderick, Jason
Burns, William
Bush, Benjamin F.
Cain, Noah
Campbell, Alonzo
Carey, Edward
Ceisea, Joseph
Christman, Phillip
Countryman, John H.
Crampton, William H.
Curliss, William H.
Dalrymple, Israel R.
Dalrymple, Melvin
Davidson, Jarius M.
Davis, George J.
Davis, Samuel
Davis, Simon E.
Donnelly, Alexander
Donnelly, Daniel
Druillard, Charles H.
Dunning, Thomas
Evans, Harvey M.
Farling, Amos

Farrell, Robert
Feeley, James
Fenton, Lewis H.
Frost, William W.
Graham, David
Grant, David E.
Hall, Cyrus W.
Hamley, John
Hanover, John
Hartley, George W.
Harvey, John
Hasson, Hugh B.
Hemstable, Charles
Hovey, Edgar M.
Jackson, George W.
Jackson, Henry H.
Jeffrey, John H.
Johnson, Charles E.
Jones, James
Joslyn, Frank S.
Katzenstein, Charles D.
Kessler, Henry
Kessler, Thomas J.
Keyser, Benjamin
Knoll, Charles A.
Knoll, John
Kretzer, Henri
Kubicek, Albert
Kunce, Henry
Lafleur, Frederick
Lagarde, John
Lagarde, Joseph
LaLonde, Joseph
Lambert, Charles W.
Lewin, Levi M.
Lewis, George
Limebeck, Harvey W.
Lorveig, Felix
Lowrey, George T.
Mahew, Caleb
Matthews, Lewis
McArthur, Samuel
McCann, John
McNeil, William B.
Miller, Monmouth (Hall's—A)
Morris, Abram

Morris, George W.
Mortsolf, John W.
Motley, Daniel F. (Hall's—A)
Murray, Lafayette
Norris, Abram
Paddock, Jerome B.
Parker, Alvin M.
Parker, Cephas C. (Hall's—B)
Pickert, Charles
Potter, Manford A.
Purdy, Alexander (Hall's—A)
Purdy, George R. (Hall's—A)
Purdy, Harrison O. (Hall's—A)
Purdy, Orange (Hall's—A)
Ready, Robert B.
Reed, Merritt F.
Renardin, Charles
Robe, William A.
Sanford, Rossiter R.
Scram, John R.
Seeley, Horace B.
Sheckles, Albert
Shedd, Albert
Shepard, Solon
Smith, Albert (Hall's—A)
Smith, Charles C.
Smith, Wright D.
Stephens, Allen
Teeter, Stephen
Thayer, Alvah
Thorp, Albert
Thurber, Abner
Tift, Roswell D. (Hall's—A)
Unrah, John
Wallace, John
Wilder, William H.
Wilson, Joseph
Wiseman, William

COMPANY H

CAPTAIN—Andrew J. Hall
1st Lt—George Fowler
2nd Lt—William Ruddock
Apted, Henry
Arnold, George

Baker, John
Balbirnie, Joseph
Barnes, James L.
Beadle, Edmund P.
Bennett, Samuel
Bennett, William F.
Betzer, Jacob
Bradley, Robert F.
Bragdon, Charles
Bristol, Nathan P.
Budden, Charles E.
Burcher, Jeremiah
Burgess, Joseph
Cahon, Nathan J.
Cain, Alexander
Call, Augustus T.
Carpenter, Loren
Chanbotte, Louis
Cleavland, Henry B.
Cole, Orrin M.
Collum, William H.
Conklin, Daniel H.
Conklin, Joseph A.
Conklin, Stephen H.
Conkrite, Daniel S.
Connell, Isaac C.
Cornell, Reuben
Craig, Henry
Crossman, Thomas
Curley, Edward
Darling, William W.
Davidson, Harvey (Hall's—B)
Dawson, Frederick
Dennis, Oscar C.
DePuy, Charles H.
Dewain, John
Doucette, Simeon
Drawbolt, Henry
Dummont, Andrew
Durfey, William
Eagle, Francis A.
Earley, David
Earley, Thomas
Edmonds, Byron S.
Ellis, Andrew J.
Engle, Norman M. (Hall's B)

431

Fillinger, Michael
Freer, Albert (Hall's—B)
Fry, Charles H. (Hall's—B)
Fuller, Orville
Hanken, John D.
Hanken, John H.
Harper, Hannibal
Harrington, Joseph
Harris, Charles
Harris, Christopher
Haulterbaum, George H.
Helmer, George H.
Hollenbeck, George (Hall's—B)
Holmes, William E.
Huss, John
Judson, Charles E.
Kelly, John
Kennedy, Henry
Kennedy, Hugh
Ketchum, Erastus
Knapp, George
Lindsley, James
Lindsley, William, Jr. (Hall's—B)
Lucas, Alexander
McLane, James
McLane, Thomas
McLaughlin, Thomas
Meks, Watson B.
Miller, Jerome
Miller, John
Nichols, Charles W.
Northrop, Marion A.
Northrop, William B.
O'Leary, Jeremiah
Osterhout, Milo
Price, Cyrus (Hall's—B)
Price, William (Hall's—B)
Priest, Lewis
Rainbow, John E.
Refner, Calvin
Reid, James
Reid, Thomas
Reid, William
Rhinehold, James
Rhines, Christopher
Rhinholdt, C.

Ross, William H.
Sackett, George W.
Sackett, Jacob
Salsbury, Joseph
Sawyer, George W.
Sayers, H.
Schwark, Hendrick
Seybert, David
Shekell, Alonzo C. (Hall's—B)
Smith, Benjamin F.
Smith, Henry
Smith, James B.
Smith, Peter
Smith, Philo R.
Styan, William
Taylor, Samuel
Taylor, William
Thacker, Robert A.
Thompson, William J.
Trim, Clinton S.
Trudy, Henry
Valentine, Charles
Vallequette, Joseph
Vanordstrand, Benjamin
Wade, John
Walsh, James
Weeks, Watson B.
Weidman, Harrison
West, Andrew
Wheeler, John Q.
Winkleblack, James A.
Wood, O. Henry

COMPANY I

CAPTAIN—George H. Murdoch
1st Lt—Robert F. Hill
2nd Lt—William H. Randall

Andrews, William B.
Austin, James
Austin, William A.
Baskerville, James
Beach, Myron W.
Bedford, William
Bell, Stephen

Bickford, Charles D.
Blackman, George
Bliss, Joseph (Hall's—B)
Bouffard, Louis P.
Brennan, James
Brown, Walter
Bruce, William
Calkins, Caleb W. (Hall's—B)
Calkins, John B.
Call, Henry C.
Campbell, Richard
Canfield, Seneca
Carter, Clark S.
Cassell, William
Chrouch, James E.
Clark, William
Cobb, Chester
Colberth, George
Conway, Joseph H.
Cooper, Franklin O.
Cotian, George
Craton, Barney
Cunningham, George
Davis, Andrew J.
Devan, William
Dibble, George
Dillabaugh, William
Fairbanks, John H.
Fessenden, Clement
Fisher, Edward
Fisher, Thomas
Fitzgerald, John
Fox, Myron J.
Frederick, John
Fuller, John
George, David S.
Harmon, Austin
Hazel, Douglas
Hoag, Eston
Horrigan, Michael
Howe, Henry A.
Huff, Asher
Huff, Isaac
Hunt, James
Johnson, Albert A.
Johnson, Andrew

Johnson, George W. (Hall's—A)
Johnson, Henry D. (Hall's—A)
Johnson, John
Kelsey, Albert M.
Lamb, Isaac J. (Hall's—B)
Lemay, Louis
Long, Benjamin F.
Marcey, William L.
Marshall, George
Martin, Horace
Martin, Ira A.
Marvin, Lemuel
McFarland, David
McFarland, John
McIntyre, Herman P.
Miller, Adolphus
Miller, Henry H.
Monroe, Freeman
Morgan, John A.
Morse, George H.
Muntjoy, George W.
Nash, Charles
Nash, Theodore
Nichols, Eli H.
Noise, George
Palmer, Enos
Perrigo, Cyrus
Pitts, John R.
Porcelay, Charles
Ramsey, James S.
Reed, Andrew S.
Reed, Charles
Reed, Loren A.
Reed, William M.
Richardson, George
Sherer, Jeremiah (Hall's—B)
Shipman, John (Hall's—B)
Sloat, John
Smith, Charles H.
Smith, Edward
Smith, Henry C.
Spencer, Eugene R.
Spicer, Daniel H.
Stebbins, William H. (Hall's—B)
Stevenson, Lemuel
Sturgis, William H.

Styon, William
Sutherland, Charles
Thomas, John H.
Walker, Josiah (Hall's—A)
Walker, Sylvester
Walter, Adam (Hall's—B)
Walter, Israel (Hall's—B)
Walton, James M.
Waterman, Charles
Welch, John S.
Wendell, Theodore
Wickham, Joseph (Hall's—A)
Wickham, Stephen (Halls'—A)
Wightman, Thomas
Willett, Lott W.
Willett, William
Wilson, Riley (Hall's—A)
Winard, Andrew
Wood, John
Woolsey, Wallace
Wright, Clark
Young, Cornelius, Jr.
Youngs, Benjamin F.

COMPANY K

CAPTAIN—Edwin V. Andress
1st Lt—William J. Driggs
2nd Lt—Garrett A. Graveraet

Ach-Au-Nach, Joseph
A-Gaer-Go, Charles
Allen, Charles
Anderson, Peter
Andrew, John
Arno-woge-zice, James
Ar-pe-targe-zhik, Oliver
Ashe-ke-bug, George
Ash-ke-bug-ne-kay, Amos
Ashman, Daniel
A-won-o-quot, Petros
Battice, John
Bennett, Louis
Bensus, John
Boushaw, Augustus
Burns, Peter

Ca-be-coung, William
Carter, Charles
Chamberlain, Amos
Chatfield, Charles
Chatfield, W. Samuel
Chibadice, A.
Church, Albert
Collins, Jacob
Collins, John
Collins, William
Corbin, George
Crane, Amos
Dabasequam, Jonah
David, John
Dutton, Luther
E-tar-ivegezhik, John
Genereau, Louis
George, David
Gibson, Joseph
Going, Samuel
Graveraet, Henry G.
Greensky, Benjamin C.
Greensky, Jacob
Gruet, Peter
Hall, Cornelius
Hamblin, James M.
Hannins, Joseph
Heogler, Joseph
Herbert, Charles
Isaacs, John
Isaacs, William
Ish-ka-buga-ma-ka
Jacko, John
Jackson, Andrew
Jackson, William
Johns, David
Johns, William
Jondrau, Michael
Ka-ba-o-sa, Louis
Ka-ba-ya-ce-ga, George
Kadah, Joseph
Ka-ka-hee, Joseph
Kaquatch, Samuel
Kar-ga-yar-sang, Solomon
Ke-chi-ti-go, Thomas
Keeses, John

Keji-kowe, Simon
Kewaconda, Benjamin
Kiniewahasoipi, John
Kitcherbalist, Amable
Lamourandiex, Thaddeus
Lidger, Daniel
Light, Josiah
Marks, Louis
Marquette, Frank
Mash-kaw, James
Mash-kaw, John
Miller, Thomas
Misisaius, Edward
Mixinasaw, William
Mixonauby, Thomas
Mogage, George W.
Moses, Thomas
Muskoguon, Louis
Mwa-ke-wenah, Daniel
Nar-quam, Thompson
Nar-qua-quot, Joseph
Nar-we-ge-she-qua-bey, Jackson
Nelson, Thomas
Ne-so-got, Jospeh
Nevarre, William
Newton, William
Olwayquonske, James
Oshburn, James R.
O-tash-qua-bon-o, Leon
Otto, Marcus
Otto, Solomon
Pa-ke-mabo-ga, John
Pemas-se-gay, Daniel
Pe-nais-now-o-quot, Jacko
Pe-she-kee, Mark
Pe-to-zo-ourquitte
Pisherbay, Albert
Porsley, Charles
Prestawin, Jacob
Quar-bo-way, James
Rubberdee, John
Sahgahnahquato, Aaron
Sanequaby, Simon
Sash-ko-ban-quot
Saw-be-come, Adam
Scott, Antoine

Seymour, Joseph
Shabema, Charles
Shaw, Charles
Shaw-au-ase, Joseph
Shaw-au-os-sang, Joseph
She-go-ge, John
Shomin, John
Shomin, John B.
Shomin, Louis
Smith, Thomas
Sockum, A.
South, Peter
Stoneman, George
Sutton, Freeman
Tabyant, Antoine
Tabasasch, Francis
Ta-ohe-de-niw, Joseph
Valentine, Robert
Wa-be-sis, John
Wassagezic, Henry
Watson, James V.
Waubanoo, Thomas
Wau-be-noo, John
Waubesis, Charles
Way-ge-she-going, William
Wayaubemind, Michael
We-ash-kid-ba, Noah
Wells, Peter
Wesaw, Thomas
Wesler (Wesley), John
Whiteface, Charles
Williams, James
Williams, Joseph
Williams, Moses
Williams, Samuel
Wolfe, Payson

NO COMPANY GIVEN

Bevin, Peter
Champing, Louis
Cornwall, Daniel
Durfey, Charles
Echler, Andrew
Foote, Charles
Frank, William

Gerrington, William
Gorringer, Isaac
Grant, William
Haley, Patrick
Hoyt, William
Hully, William
Ibbotson, Wallace
Judson, Michel
Kemp, Chester
Kennedy, Frederick A.

Lee, W. J.
Lewis, William
McCormick, —
Morris, William P.
Noyes, Oliver
Platts, Richard S.
Segard, Joseph
Warren, William P.
Wheadon, William

Notes

✫ ✫ ✫ ✫ ✫

Introduction

1. Charles V. DeLand, *DeLand's History of Jackson County, Michigan* (n.p.: B. F. Bowen, 1903), 389 (hereafter cited as *DeLand's Jackson County*).
2. Detroit *Advertiser and Tribune*, 21 July 1865, 4.
3. Charles V. DeLand to Brig. Gen. John Roberston, Folder no. 8: "Letters and Telegrams—1861–1881," Records of Michigan Military Establishment, *Regimental Service Records, First Michigan Sharpshooters*, Michigan State Archives, Lansing, MI (hereafter cited as *1st MSS Records*).
4. Ibid.
5. Ibid., Charles V. DeLand to Brig. Gen. John Robertson, East Saginaw, 18 January 1866, Folder no. 6: "List of Engagements and Skirmishes."
6. William F. Fox, *Regimental Losses in the American Civil War, 1861–1865*, 4th ed. (Albany, NY: Albany Publishing Co., 1898), 379. Every Michigan regiment in Brig. Gen. Orlando B. Willcox's division of the Ninth Army Corps (First Sharpshooters, Second, Eighth, Seventeenth, Twentieth, and Twenty-seventh Infantry) were all part of Fox's "Fighting 300."

Chapter 1

1. Col. Charles V. DeLand to Brig Gen. L. Thomas, Headquarters, First Michigan Sharpshooters, 5 September 1864, *Regimental Letter and Order Book, 1st Michigan Sharpshooters*, Record Group 94, Records of the Adjutant General's Office, National Archives, Washington, DC (hereafter cited as *Letter and Order Book*); Folder no. 9, "History," *1st MSS Records*. This regimental "History" was written by Colonel DeLand long after the war; Jackson *Eagle*, 10 January 1864, 3.
2. Folder no. 9, "History," *1st MSS Records*.
3. Jackson *Weekly Citizen*, 3 December 1862, 3.
4. *Michigan Biographies*, vol. 1 (Lansing: Michigan Historical Commission, 1924), 233; *History of Saginaw County, Michigan; Together with Sketches of Its Cities, Villages and Townships, Educational, Religious, Civil, Military, and Political History: Portraits of Prominent Persons, Biographies of Representative Citizens* (Chicago: Charles C. Chapman & Co., 1881), 465 (hereafter cited as *History of*

Saginaw County); *DeLand's Jackson County*, 333; *Portraits and Biographies of Jackson County, Michigan* (Chicago: Chapman Bros., 1890), 219.

5. Elizabeth Read Brown, "Michigan Pioneer Newspapers, A Sketch," *Michigan History*, vol. 41, no. 4 (December 1957), 424–425.

6. Early on, DeLand maintained a pro-temperance stand that so infuriated the local whiskey faction that his office was burned out on 4 July 1851. Back in business in just six weeks, DeLand showed his enemies that he was not a man to back off. See *DeLand's Jackson County*, 289.

7. In his own words, DeLand became "an early advocate of the affiliation of all the opposition to the further spread of human slavery and the policy of the South" (ibid., 439).

8. Ibid., 347.

9. Ibid., 172.

10. Ibid., 439

11. *History of Saginaw County*, 465.

12. Jackson *Weekly Citizen*, 10 October 1861, 3.

13. John Robertson, comp. rev. ed., *Michigan in the War* (Lansing: W. S. George & Co., 1882), 293.

14. Jackson *Weekly Citizen*, 14 May 1862, 4.

15. Charles V. DeLand to Parents, Near Nashville, 28 March 1862. DeLand–Crary Family Papers, Box 1: Civil War Correspondence, 1862–1865. Bentley Historical Library, University of Michigan, Ann Arbor, MI (hereafter cited as DeLand–Crary Papers).

16. Jackson *Weekly Citizen*, 16 July 1862, 1.

17. Ibid., 11 June 1862, 1.

18. Robertson, *Michigan in the War*, 298.

19. Jackson *Eagle*, 25 October 1862, 1.

20. Charles V. DeLand to J. W. Houghton, Jackson, Michigan, 23 November 1886, Clarke–DeLand Family Papers, 1830–1919, Michigan Historical Collections, Bentley Historical Library, University of Michigan, Ann Arbor, MI (hereafter cited as Clarke–DeLand Papers).

21. *Portraits and Biographies of Jackson County*, 219.

22. Chandler may have prodded the commissary general of prisoners, Col. William Hoffman, either to hurry up DeLand's exchange or to periodically check on his status as a prisoner. A portion of a letter from Hoffman to the senator (which was reprinted in the *Citizen*) stated that a "list of exchanged officers has been made up, and I am happy to assure you that your friend, Capt. C. V. DeLand is one of the number." Jackson *Weekly Citizen*, 3 December 1862, 3.

23. Charles V. DeLand, Combined Military Service File, National Archives, Washington, DC.

24. E. B. Long and Barbara Long, *The Civil War Day by Day: An Almanac 1861–1865* (Garden City, NY: Doubleday & Co., 1971), 236.

Casualty figures are found on 162, 167, 168, 172, 173, 180, 184, 188, 190, 195, 202, 207, 208, 216, 220, 224, 227, 230, 231, 232, 233, 234, 235.

25. Robertson, *Michigan in the War*, 26, 38, 39. Michigan's population stood at 749,113 in 1860, making her the eighth most populous Free State. Included in that number were 6,799 free Negroes and 7,755 Indians. See Long, *The Civil War Day by Day*, 701; and Laurence M. Hauptman, *Between Two Fires: American Indians in the Civil War* (New York: The Free Press, 1995), 127.

26. Robertson, *Michigan in the War*, 31. These were the Seventeenth through the Twenty-third Michigan Infantry regiments.

27. Ibid. The Eighteenth Michigan Infantry rendezvoused at Hillsdale; the Nineteenth at Dowagiac; the Twentieth at Jackson; the Twenty-first at Ionia; the Twenty-second at Pontiac; and the Twenty-third at East Saginaw.

28. Ibid., 33.

29. Ibid., 31.

30. Perry F. Powers, *A History of Northern Michigan and Its People*, vol. 1 (Chicago: The Lewis Publishing Co., 1912), 231.

31. The best sources on the Civil War bounty system and draft from the Northern perspective are Eugene C. Murdock's two books, *One Million Men: The Civil War Draft in the North* (Westport, CT: Greenwood Press, 1971 [Reprinted 1980 with permission of the State Historical Society of Wisconsin]) (hereafter cited as Murdock, *One Million Men*), 4, and *Patriotism Limited 1862–1865: The Civil War Draft and the Bounty System* (Kent, OH: Kent State University Press, 1967) (hereafter cited as Murdock, *Patriotism Limited*).

32. George N. Fuller, ed., *Messages of the Governors of Michigan*, vol. 2 (Lansing, MI: Michigan Historical Commission, 1926), 468, 501–507.

33. Murdock, *One Million Men*, 173–176.

34. Charles Lanman, *The Red Book of Michigan: A Civil, Military and Biographical History* (Detroit: E. B. Smith & Co., 1871), 165; Robertson, *Michigan in the War*, 37. In addition, hundreds of Michigan men served in regiments with no Michigan appellation. Two full companies of Michigan lads composed the "Merrill Horse" of the Second Missouri Cavalry, and another was currently recruiting in Battle Creek. Eight companies of Michigan recruits served in Illinois regiments: the Forty-second Illinois had three companies; the Forty-fourth had two more; the Thirty-seventh had one; the Sixty-sixth (also known as the Western Sharpshooters) contained one; an all-Irish company from Detroit made up Company A of the Twenty-third Illinois. Company K of the First New York Cavalry (the "Lincoln Cavalry") was raised in Grand Rapids. And Company C, Seventieth New York Infantry, hailed from Paw Paw in Van Buren County. The Forty-seventh Ohio Infantry contained one

company of men from Adrian. Four companies of riflemen from the state joined the U.S. Sharpshooters, three in the First Regiment, and one in the Second. Hundreds more joined the Regular Army. There were 104 men from Michigan in the Second U.S. Infantry; 242 joined the Eleventh U.S.; and almost the entire Nineteenth U.S. Infantry came from Michigan. See Robertson, *Michigan in the War*, 742–745.

35. Fuller, *Messages of the Governors of Michigan*, vol. 2, 467.
36. Jean Joy L. Fenimore, "Austin Blair: Civil War Governor, 1861–1862," *Michigan History*, vol. 49, no. 3, September 1965, 211–212. Two of the prominent Democrats appointed by Governor Blair were fellow townsman, Michael Shoemaker as colonel of the Thirteenth Michigan Infantry, and William M. Fenton of Flint as colonel of the Eighth Michigan Infantry.

    Other than the First Michigan Sharpshooters, there were 30 infantry regiments, 11 cavalry regiments, a Colored regiment, a regiment of engineers and mechanics, and 14 six–gun batteries raised in the state during the Civil War.

    There were actually more than 45 full regiments. The original First Infantry served only three months. Returning home after the First Battle of Bull Run, it was organized into a three-year outfit. The Third, Fourth, and Eleventh Infantry regiments served their three year enlistments and in turn were reorganized into new regiments, keeping their original numerical designations.

    The artillery batteries never fought as a unit but were recruited and organized into 14 separate batteries. The state adjutant general's office also officially recognized that 4,635 men from Michigan either served in regiments from other states, the Regular Army, or in the navy. A total of 90,747 served in Michigan regiments; all were filled to the maximum number, 20 having more than 1,800 recruits each during the war. Of the 20, there were 4 with more than 3,000 men each: the First Engineers and Mechanics, the artillery batteries, and the First and Eighth Cavalry regiments. The largest infantry regiment was the Fifteenth, with 2,371 officers and men. Governor Blair's policy of continually recruiting instead of constantly forming new regiments proved beneficial for the men in the ranks and for the army as well. See Robertson, *Michigan in the War*, 68–69.

37. *DeLand's Jackson County*, 275.
38. Fuller, *Messages of the Governors of Michigan*, vol. 2, 471.
39. In 1861 three companies from Michigan were raised for service in the First Regiment U.S. Sharpshooters, a select group chosen especially for their marksmanship. Colonel Berdan (an expert shot himself) organized two full regiments of sharpshooters composed of men from a number of states. One more company from Michigan was part of the Second Regiment United States Sharpshoot-

ers. Elite units, the men wore green uniforms, and many used heavy target rifles that were accurate at 500 yards. Utilized primarily as skirmishers in the Army of the Potomac, these marksmen became famous to friend and foe alike. See Wiley Sword, *Sharpshooter: Hiram Berdan, His Famous Sharpshooters and their Sharps Rifles* (Lincoln, RI: Andrew Mowbray Inc., 1988).

40. "History," Folder no. 9, *1st MSS Records*.

41. Jackson *Eagle*, 22 November 1862, 2; Lansing *State Republican*, 30 November 1862, 2; Robertson, *Michigan in the War*, 37.

42. John Piper to Adj. Gen. John Robertson, Camp Douglas, Chicago, Illinois, 14 October 1863, Folder no. 9: "History," *1st MSS Records*.

43. Levant C. Rhines to Adj. Gen. John Robertson, Camp Douglas, Chicago, Illinois, 14 October 1863, Folder no. 8: "Letters and Telegrams: 1861–1881," *1st MSS Records*.

44. Battle Creek *Journal*, 14 November 1862, 3.

45. Ibid., 12 December 1862, 2.

46. Washington Gardner, *History of Calhoun County Michigan: A Narrative Account of Its Historical Progress, Its People, and Its Principal Interests*, vol. 1 (Chicago: Lewis Publishing Co., 1913), 541.

47. Asahel H. Nichols to Adj. Gen. John Robertson, Lansing, Michigan, 29 October 1862, Folder no. 8: "Letters and Telegrams: 1861–1881," *1st MSS Records*.

48. Jackson *Weekly Citizen*, 3 December 1862, 3.

49. Michigan Adjutant General's Office, *Record of Service of Michigan Volunteers in the Civil War 1861–1865: First Regiment Michigan Sharpshooters*, vol. 44 (Kalamazoo, MI: Ihling Bos. & Everard, 1905), 33 (hereafter cited as *Record of Service, 1st MSS*).

50. John Allen to Adj. Gen. John Robertson, Lansing, Michigan, 19 February 1863, Folder no. 3: "Recommendations, Promotions, Appointments," *1st MSS Records*; *Record of Service, 1st MSS*, 45. Nichols had married Hinckley's sister, Sarah, in 1860. See *Ingham County Families* [Working Papers of Hammell Collection], MSS., vol. M–O, Library of Michigan, Lansing, MI.

51. Charles V. DeLand to D. R. Mann, Kalamazoo, Michigan, 23 January 1863, *Letter and Order Book*.

52. Ibid.

53. Charles V. DeLand to Brig. Gen. L. Thomas, Headquarters, First Michigan Sharpshooters, 5 September 1864, *Letter and Order Book*; *History of Saginaw County*, 465.

54. Hillsdale *Standard*, 23 December 1862, 3.

55. Ibid., 2 December 1862, 3; *History of Hillsdale County, Michigan, With Illustrations and Biographical Sketches of Some of Its Prominent Men and Pioneers* (Philadelphia: Everts & Abbott, 1879), 69.

56. *Portrait and Biographical Album of Hillsdale County, Michigan* (Chicago: Chapman Bros., 1888), 220–221.

57. *History of Branch County, Michigan, With Illustrations and Bio-*

graphical Sketches of Some of Its Prominent Men and Pioneers (Philadelphia: Everts & Abbott, 1879), 78–79.

58. Record of Henry V. Cleavland, Records of the Michigan Department of Correction (General), Series I, State Archives of Michigan, Lansing, MI; Jackson *Eagle*, 24 October 1863, 3.

59. *Record of Service, 1st MSS*, 29; Leo C. Little, *Historic Grand Haven and Ottawa County* (Grand Haven, MI: n.p., 1931), 306.

60. Hillsdale *Standard*, 2 December 1862, 3.

61. Ibid., 29 July 1862, 2.

62. Ibid.

63. Port Huron *Weekly Times*, 2 August 1901, 5. Whipple was born at Grafton, Vermont in 1838. His father, a teacher, immigrated to Hillsdale, Michigan, in 1856. Young Whipple clerked in a drug store, saving his earnings for law school. When the war came, he joined the First U.S. Sharpshooters instead. Like many young officers, he was ambitious and adventurous. Both qualities served him well in the Sharpshooters and later in life.

64. William H. Randall, Reminiscences, Michigan Historical Collections, Bentley Historical Library, University of Michigan, Ann Arbor, MI (hereafter cited as Randall Reminiscences). These reminiscences, written some time after the Civil War, were based on a diary Randall kept during the war. Much of the beginning is a long, undated essay detailing his service in the First Michigan Infantry, his illness, and his enlistment in the First Michigan Sharpshooters. The rest is dated. Unless a date is cited, the material from the Reminiscences comes from the essay section.

65. Ibid.; *Record of Service, 1st MSS*, 73.

66. Michigan Adjutant General's Office, *Record of Service of Michigan Volunteers in the Civil War 1861–1865: First Regiment Michigan Infantry*, vol. 1 (Kalamazoo: Ihling Bros. & Everard, 1905), 35; Jackson *Weekly Citizen*, 1 April 1863, 3; Jackson *Eagle*, 28 March 1863, 3.

67. Joseph O. Bellair to Gov. Austin Blair, Ninth Corps Headquarters, 10 March 1865, Folder no. 3: "Recommendations, Promotions, Appointments," *1st MSS Records*.

68. Memoirs of Julian Edward Buckbee, Private collection of John Buckbee. These memoirs were written after the turn of the century for a series of lectures that Buckbee gave. His real name was Julian Edward Buckbee. He did not care for his first name, so he juxtaposed his given names on his enlistment papers. Throughout the war all his friends called him Ed. He reverted to his real name after the war. The memoirs are not dated, and different versions exist, so the pages are not consistently numbered (hereafter cited as Buckbee Memoirs). Record of Richard Snay, Records of the Department of Correction (General), Series I, State Archives of Michigan, Lansing, MI.

69. Buckbee was the fourth and youngest child of Walter A. Buckbee and Amanda Weed. They left Vermont for Michigan in 1837 and settled in Ypsilanti, where the elder Buckbee continued his law practice. He died in 1850. The oldest daughter, Sarah, married H. M. Cheever, a lawyer from Detroit. Walter, the second child, moved to Chicago and became a clerk for Jansen, McClurg & Co., booksellers. The third child, Mary, married the "Jansen" of Jansen, McClurg & Co. One of Buckbee's first cousins was Stephen A. Weed, a captain of artillery in the Army of the Potomac. In June 1863 Weed would sew on the star of a brigadier general; in July he would meet his destiny on a rock-strewn hill called Little Round Top near the town of Gettysburg, Pennsylvania. See Buckbee Memoirs; Ezra J. Warner, *Generals in Blue, Lives of the Union Commanders* (Baton Rouge: Louisiana State University, 1964), 547–548; *History of Washtenaw County, Michigan* (Chicago: Charles C. Chapman & Co., 1881), 1195–1196.

70. Buckbee Memoirs.

71. Ibid.; Austin Blair to Edward J. Buckbee, Jackson, Michigan, 18 November 1862, Buckbee Papers, John Buckbee Collection (hereafter cited as Buckbee Papers). These papers include the correspondence to and from Julian Edward Buckbee both during and after the Civil War.

72. Buckbee Memoirs.

73. Ibid.

74. Ibid.

75. *Record of Service, 1st MSS*, 9; William H. H. Beadle to Brig. Gen. John Robertson, Albion, Michigan, 15 April 1867, Folder no. 9: "History," *1st MSS Records*; Allen Johnson and Dumas Malone, eds., *Dictionary of American Biography*, vol. 2 (New York: Charles Scribner's Sons, 1930), 86 (hereafter cited as Johnson and Malone, *DAB*).

   Colonel DeLand had little to say about Beadle in his postwar writings; when he did, it was not complimentary. DeLand, always one to exaggerate when the exploits of his regiment or himself were called into question, put Beadle in a negative light as late as 1885, when he wrote of the formation of the Sharpshooters: "Governor [Blair] then commissioned one Beadle as Lieut Colonel, & he was immediately mustered & drew pay from the U.S. while doing little or no duty," while DeLand himself was "in command all the time & so recognized by the military authorities of the State and the United States." Furthermore, DeLand "never received any pay or compensation" for his services from 6 January until 7 July 1863. See Deposition of Charles V. DeLand, Jackson, MI, January 1885, Miscellanea [3], Clarke–DeLand Papers.

76. Robertson, *Michigan in the War*, 742.

77. Lorenzo A. Barker, *Military History (Michigan Boys): Company "D"*

66th Illinois, Birge's Western Sharpshooters in the Civil War, 1861–1865 (Reed City, MI: n.p., 1905), 10, 49.

78. Battle Creek *Journal*, 15 May 1863, 2.
79. Elon G. Reynolds, ed., *Compendium of History and Biography of Hillsdale County, Michigan* (Chicago: A. W. Bowen & Co., n.d.), 339–340.
80. Hillsdale *Standard*, 23 December 1863, 3.
81. Charles R. Tuttle, comp., *General History of the State of Michigan* (Detroit: R. D. S. Tyler & Co., 1873), 505–506.
82. Battalion Order No. 1, Camp Chandler, Michigan, 5 January 1863, *Letter and Order Book*.
83. Detroit *Advertiser and Tribune*, 12 January 1863, 3. This was a copy of General Order No. 1 issued by the state adjutant general's office; Detroit *Free Press*, 7 January 1863, 1.
84. *Detroit Advertiser and Tribune*, 6 February 1863, 1. This was General Order No. 5 from the state adjutant general's office.
85. Starting 8 March 1863 the state of Michigan gave $50 to all new recruits. Local governments received the official nod to raise and bestow extra bounties. The U.S. government also offered a $100 bounty, but only $25 was doled out at enlistment. The recruit collected the remainder at his muster in. See Robertson, *Michigan in the War*, 41; Charles V. DeLand to Brig. Gen. L. Thomas, Headquarters, First Michigan Sharpshooters, 5 September 1864, *Letter and Order Book*.
86. Charles V. DeLand to Col. John R. Smith, Kalamazoo, Michigan, 20 January 1863, 23 March 1863, *Letter and Order Book*.
87. Charles V. DeLand to Brig. Gen. L. Thomas, Headquarters First Michigan Sharpshooters, 5 September 1864, *Letter and Order Book*; Detroit *Advertiser and Tribune*, 16 March 1863, 1. The newspaper article was a copy of General Order No. 9 from the state adjutant general's office, detailing the payment of bounties; Murdock, *Patriotism Limited*, 19.
88. Men, aged 20 to 45, were liable for the draft. Also, substitutes were men *not* liable to the draft. The latter category included noncitizens (foreigners and Indians), men between the ages of 18 to 20, men who had already served two years in the army or navy, and men from the rebel states seeking protection in the Union. See Murdock, *Patriotism Limited*, 9; Murdock, *One Million Men*, 179.
89. Charles V. DeLand to Lt. William Clark, Camp Chandler, Kalamazoo, Michigan, 13 February 1863, *Letter and Order Book*.
90. Detroit *Advertiser and Tribune*, 8 April 1863, 2. Some of the Sharpshooters tried to seek redress from the court system. None had received the bounty money promised them by their hometowns. Although Adjutant General Robertson handed a certificate of discharge to John H. Sweet, Daniel S. Robbins, Henry Burton, and Peter Demarest (all of Company B), Colonel DeLand refused to

abide by the decision. In a trial held in Detroit in the middle of March, DeLand stated that, since his regiment had never been in the service of the state of Michigan, the discharges issued by the state adjutant general were invalid and null. Sweet had initiated the proceedings, hoping to be released from the regiment. Sweet withdrew his petition and all four men returned to the regiment. See Hillsdale *Standard*, 24 March 1863, 3; 31 March 1863, 3.

91. Battalion Order No. 1, Camp Chandler, Michigan, 5 January 1863, *Letter and Order Book*. Frank Plogart spent $100 recruiting men with Andrew J. Hall; then he learned that another individual was promised the first lieutenancy in the company when it was raised. Disgusted, Plogart began recruiting men for the Twenty-eighth Michigan Infantry, in which unit he did obtain a commission. See Frank Plogart to Gov. Austin Blair, Coldwater, Michigan, 10 July 1863, Folder no. 8: "Letters and Telegrams—1861–1881," *1st MSS Records*.

92. The number was accrued through the lists of names in both the *Letter and Order Book* and *Record of Service, 1st MSS*.

93. Charles V. DeLand to Lt. Col. John R. Smith, Camp Chandler, Michigan, 12 February 1863, *Letter and Order Book*.

94. Folder no. 9, "History," *1st MSS Records*.

95. Ibid.

96. Charles V. DeLand to Col. John R. Smith, Camp Chandler, Michigan, 21 January 1863, 26 February 1863, 4 March 1863, *Letter and Order Book*.

97. Ibid., Charles V, DeLand to Lt. Col. John R. Smith, Camp Chandler, Michigan, 8 February 1863; Charles V. DeLand to E. Pringle, Camp Chandler, Michigan, 12 February 1863; Charles V. DeLand to Lt. H. Smith, Camp Chandler, Michigan, 12 February 1863.

98. Ibid., Charles V. DeLand to Col. Cameron [65th Illinois Inf.], Camp Chandler, Michigan, 30 January 1863. At times the situation would reverse itself, as when Robert C. Cooley (a deserter from the First U.S. Sharpshooters) enlisted in DeLand's regiment at Niles, picking up the $100 bounty offered there. See ibid., Charles V. DeLand to Lt. Col. John R. Smith, Camp Chandler, Michigan, 27 February 1863.

99. Ibid., Charles V. DeLand to Wesley Cross, Camp Chandler, Michigan, 6 March 1863.

100. Hillsdale *Standard*, 2 December 1862, 2.

101. Special Orders Nos. 1 and 2, 14 March 1863, Camp Chandler, Michigan, *Letter and Order Book*.

102. *Record of Service, 1st MSS*, 31, 52.

103. George W. Stone, Compiled Military Service Record, National Archives, Washington, DC; *The National Tribune*, 1 June 1911, 2.

104. *Record of Service, 1st MSS*, 65.

105. Ibid., 95.

106. Ibid., 15, 59.
107. Ibid., 61, 73.
108. Gardner, *History of Calhoun County*, vol. 2, 713, 1176.
109. Chester D. Berry, *Loss of the Sultana and Reminiscences of Survivors* (Lansing, MI: Darius D. Thorp, Printer and Binder, 1892), 335.
110. *Record of Service, 1st MSS*, 19.
111. Detroit *Advertiser and Tribune*, 23 July 1863, 1.
112. Detroit *Free Press*, 8 May 1861, 1.
113. Johnson and Malone, *DAB*, vol. 4, 433.
114. Detroit *Free Press*, 8 May 1861, 1; Detroit *Daily Advertiser*, 24 May 1861, 1.
115. Detroit *Daily Tribune*, 28 May 1861, 1.
116. Bay City *Times*, 21 January 1978, 3–A.
117. Frank B. Woodward, *Father Abraham's Children* (Detroit: Wayne State University Press, 1961), 252. The quote came from the Detroit *Free Press*, 14 May 1861.
118. Detroit *Advertiser and Tribune*, 1 July 1863, 4.
119. L. M. Hartwick and W. H. Tuller, *Oceana County—Pioneers and Businessmen of To-day* (Pentwater, MI: Pentwater News Steam Print, 1890), 48. A modern interpretation by Laurence Hauptman lists the reasons the Michigan Indians would want to enlist. Among the possibilities was one that no white man had: The Native Americans in the state wanted to stay in Michigan and not be forcibly sent by the U.S. Government to so-called Indian territories west of the Mississippi River. Their joining the army would possibly forestall any action and perhaps give them some advantage when a (hopefully) new treaty would be drawn up. See Hauptman, *Between Two Fires*.

Chapter 2

1. Battalion Order No. 2, Camp Chandler, Kalamazoo, Michigan, 14 January 1863, *Letter and Order Book*.
2. Ibid., Battalion Order No. 3, Camp Chandler, Kalamazoo, Michigan, 15 January 1863.
3. Ibid.
4. Ibid.
5. Ibid., Battalion Order No. 9, Camp Chandler, Kalamazoo, Michigan, 21 January 1863.
6. Ibid.
7. Ibid.
8. Ibid., Battalion Order No. 10, Camp Chandler, Kalamazoo, Michigan, 22 January 1863.
9. The three regiments were the Sixth, Thirteenth, and Twenty-fifth Michigan Infantry regiments.

10. Battalion Order No. 12, Camp Chandler, Kalamazoo, Michigan, 24 January 1863, *Letter and Order Book*.

11. "Annual Returns of Alterations and Casualties for the War Ending Dec 31 '63," Office of the Adjutant General of the United States, Muster Rolls, Returns, Regimental Papers, Record Group 94, Michigan 1st Sharpshooters, Box 1947, National Archives, Washington, DC (hereafter cited as "Regimental Papers, 1st MSS"). Foote was not released until 14 November 1865. See Record of Charles Foote, Department of Corrections (General), Series 1, State Archives of Michigan, Lansing, MI.

12. Battalion Order No. 13, Camp Chandler, Kalamazoo, Michigan, 25 January 1863, *Letter and Order Book*.

13. Ibid., Battalion Order No. 9, Camp Chandler, Kalamazoo, Michigan, 21 January 1863.

14. Ibid., Battalion Order No. 37, Camp Chandler, Kalamazoo, Michigan, 19 February 1863.

15. Ibid., Battalion Order No. 38, Camp Chandler, Kalamazoo, Michigan, 20 February 1863.

16. Ibid.

17. Ibid.

18. Ibid., Battalion Order No. 38, Camp Chandler, Kalamazoo, Michigan, 20 February 1863.

19. Ibid., Battalion Order No. 39, Camp Chandler, Kalamazoo, Michigan, 21 February 1863.

20. Ibid., Battalion Order No. 44, Camp Chandler, Kalamazoo, Michigan, 26 February 1863. Lapses of good judgment also affected the colonel at times. Many of DeLand's choices for positions of authority were notoriously poor. His selection for acting regimental sergeant major was Samuel Stafford of Kalamazoo. Stafford no sooner advanced to the post than he deserted the regiment; 19-year-old Michael Collins quickly received the vacancy. See ibid., Battalion Order No. 21, 3 February 1863, Camp Chandler, Kalamazoo, Michigan, and Battalion Order No. 37, 19 February 1863, Camp Chandler, Kalamazoo, Michigan.

21. "Dr. David Heagle," *The Watchman–Examiner*, 2 March 1922, vol. 10, no. 4, 279; "Dr. David Heagle," *The Baptist*, 4 March 1922, vol. 3, no. 5., n.p.

22. Battalion Order No. 12, Camp Chandler, Kalamazoo, Michigan, 24 January 1863, *Letter and Order Book*.

23. Capt. George N. Davis now took charge over both his and Captain Meigs's detachments. Capt. Asahel Nichols managed both his and Capt. Andrew Hall's recruits, and Capt. Samuel Hudson's command included both his own and those of Capts. Elmer Dicey, George Murdoch, Joseph Bellair, and Fitch. Colonel DeLand consolidated Lt. William Clark's detachment with the hospital personnel and the extra duty men, which included the quartermaster's

men, orderlies, and clerks. See ibid., Battalion Order No. 21, Camp Chandler, Kalamazoo, Michigan, 3 February 1863.

24. Ibid.

25. Ibid., Battalion Order No. 4, Camp Chandler, Kalamazoo, Michigan, 16 January 1863.

26. Wayne County and all of southwestern Michigan would vote the Democratic Party ticket in 1864. See Lawrence M. Sommers, ed., *Atlas of Michigan* (Grand Rapids, MI: Michigan State University Press, 1977), 128–129.

27. George W. Stark, *City of Destiny: The Story of Detroit* (Detroit: Arnold–Powers, Inc., 1943) (hereafter cited as Stark, *City of Destiny*), 382–384.

28. The word "colored" was used interchangeably with "Negro" during the Civil War. In fact, the U.S. government used the former term when African Americans were enlisted, e.g. 102nd Colored Troops. Ibid., 388–389; *A Thrilling Narrative from the Lips of the Sufferers of the Late Detroit Riot, March 6, 1863, with the Hair Breadth Escapes of Men, Women and Children, and Destruction of Colored Men's Property, not less than $15,000* (Detroit: n.p., 1863) [Reprint: Royal Oak, MI: Russell's Book Store, n.d.]; John C. Schneider, "Detroit and the Problem of Disorder: The Riot of 1863," *Michigan History*, vol. 58, no. 1 (Spring 1974), 4–24.

29. The newspapers actually reported that 55,000 Enfields and 10,000 Springfields were stored in the arsenal. See Detroit *Advertiser and Tribune*, 11 February 1863, 1.

30. Battalion Order No. 44, Camp Chandler, Kalamazoo, Michigan, 26 February 1863, *Letter and Order Book*.

31. Ibid., Battalion Order No. 45, Camp Chandler, Kalamazoo, Michigan, 27 February 1863.

32. Folder no. 2: "List of Deserters," *1st MSS Records*.

33. Ibid., Folder no. 9: "History."

34. Detroit *Advertiser and Tribune*, 24 April 1863, 2.

35. Battalion Order No. 2, Dearborn, Michigan, 25 April 1863, *Letter and Order Book*.

36. Ibid.

37. Detroit *Advertiser and Tribune*, 30 April 1863, 1.

38. Ibid.

39. Special Order No. 1, Dearborn, Michigan, 27 April 1863, *Letter and Order Book*.

40. Detroit *Advertiser and Tribune*, 4 May 1863, 3.

41. Special Order No. 1, Dearborn, Michigan, 27 April 1863, *Letter and Order Book*. The military law referred to was General Order No. 38, Department of the Ohio, issued by Major General Ambrose Burnside on 13 April 1863.

42. Ibid.

43. Some companies needed more men to bring them to maximum

strength, and this required that both staff and field officers establish recruitment offices. Lt. Col. William H. H. Beadle and Maj. John Piper put in their time. Capts. Andrew J. Hall, Thomas Gaffney, Levant Rhines, Asahel W. Nichols, George Davis, Hooker A. DeLand, and Elmer Dicey individually scoured the state for more men. See Special Order No. 17, Dearborn, Michigan, 18 May 1863, *Letter and Order Book*.

44. Ibid., Special Order No. 18, Dearborn, Michigan, 19 May 1863.

45. Ibid., Special Order No. 2, Dearborn, Michigan, 1 May 1863; Robertson, *Michigan in the War*, 823.

46. Ibid., Special Order No. 27, Dearborn, Michigan, 16 June 1863; Detroit *Advertiser and Tribune*, 25 June 1863, 3.

47. Special Order No. 36, Dearborn, Michigan, 1 July 1863, *Letter and Order Book*. In addition to civilians trying their hand at earning shoulder straps, various privates and noncommissioned officers vied for openings in the regiment's officer's corps. Scattered to various parts of the state, some brought in one or two recruits, others none. Pvt. Charles Smith used recruiting service as the occasion to desert. No wonder a testy DeLand dictated a letter to Col. J. R. Smith, Michigan's Military Commandant.

   DeLand actually had no idea as to how many officers he had in his regiment at the end of May 1863. He asked that certain men be mustered as officers, yet a number of those were refused; others were mustered without his consent. "It seems a matter of simple justice," he wrote, "that the commanding officer of a regiment should know who his officers are, *officially*, from some quarter, but I am denied that privilege. . . . In future will you do me the favor to either require my consent or to notify me when an officer is mustered into the Regiment." See ibid., Special Order No. 35, Dearborn, Michigan, 30 June 1863 and Charles V. DeLand to Col. J. Smith, Dearborn, Michigan, 28 May 1863; *Record of Service, 1st MSS*, 82.

48. Bay City *Times*, 21 January 1978, 3–C; *Record of Service, 1st MSS*, 20; C. D. Bibbins, "The Indian Sharpshooters," *The National Tribune*, 16 October 1917, 7.

49. Payson Wolfe and his wife, Mary Jane Smith, would have 13 children. See The Leelanau Township Historical Writers Group, *A History of Leelanau Township* (Chelsea, MI: Book Crafters, Inc., 1982), 28.

50. Ibid., 46.

51. Ibid., 60.

52. Special Order No. 27, Dearborn, Michigan, 1 June 1863, *Letter and Order Book*.

53. William J. Driggs, Military Pension Record, National Archives, Washington, DC.

54. Special Order No. 27, Dearborn, Michigan, 1 June 1863, *Letter and Order Book*; Detroit *Advertiser and Tribune*, 16 March 1863, 1.

55. Special Order No. 34, Dearborn, Michigan, 23 June 1863, *Letter and Order Book*.
56. Even though many of Michigan's Indians were moved west of the Mississippi River before the Civil War in accordance with the U.S. government's Indian Removal policy, there were still thousands of them living in the state. Clusters could be found throughout the Upper Peninsula, near the Straits of Mackinac, around Little Traverse and Grand Traverse Bays, and in Oceana, Saginaw, and Isabella Counties. In 1860 there were 1,300 Native Americans living in Oceana County out of a total population of 1,816. See Hartwick and Tuller, *Oceana County*, 59, 426.
57. Ibid., 45.
58. Detroit *Advertiser and Tribune*, 23 May 1863, 1.
59. *Record of Service, 1st MSS*, 64; Dr. M. L. Leach, *A History of the Grand Traverse Region* (Traverse City, MI: Grand Traverse Herald, 1883) (hereafter cited as Leach, *The Grand Traverse Region*), 82; Special Order No. 53, Dearborn, Michigan, 31 July 1863, *Letter and Order Book*.
60. Minnie Dubbs Millbrook, "Indian Sharpshooters," in *Twice Told Tales of Michigan and Her Soldiers in the Civil War*, ed. Minnie Dubbs Millbrook (Lansing, MI: Michigan Civil War Observance Commission, 1966), 46.
61. *Record of Service, 1st MSS*, 39; Grand Traverse *Herald*, 12 August 1864, 3.
62. *The Traverse Region, Historical and Descriptive, with Illustrations of Scenery and Portraits and Biographical Sketches of Some of Its Prominent Men and Pioneers* (Chicago: H. R. Page & Co., 1884), 136; *Record of Service, 1st MSS*, 41.
63. Henry G. Graveraet was the "son of a German soldier of the Revolution." His wife, Sophia Bailly, whose father was a French fur trader and whose mother was the daughter of an Indian chief, was adopted by Madame LaFramboise, a famous fur trader of the Great Lakes. Sophia received a very good education in Canada and taught school at St. Ignace, Michigan, for 15 years. Just prior to the Civil War the Graveraets moved to Little Traverse. Garrett Graveraet was obviously groomed by his parents for better things than fur trading. Although the young man was well educated in the arts, he had the tenacity of his warrior ancestors on both sides of his family. See John C. Wright, "Indian Legends of Northern Michigan," *Michigan History Magazine*, vol. 2, no. 1 (January 1918), 81, 87, 88.
64. *The Traverse Region*, 136; *Record of Service, 1st MSS*, 87.
65. Detroit *Advertiser and Tribune*, 7 May 1863, 3; 19 May 1863, 1; 20 May 1863, 3; 29 May 1863, 3.
66. Ibid., 28 May 1863, 2.
67. Bibbins, "The Indian Sharpshooters," 7.
68. Ibid.

69. *Detroit Advertiser and Tribune*, 4 June 1863, 3.
70. Battalion Order No. 2, U.S. Arsenal, Dearbornville, 25 April 1863, *Letter and Record Book*.
71. Detroit *Advertiser and Tribune*, 28 May 1863, 3.
72. Battalion Order No. 12, Dearborn, Michigan, 5 May 1863, *Letter and Order Book*.
73. Ibid., Battalion Order No. 14, Dearborn, Michigan, 7 May 1863.
74. Ibid.
75. Ibid.
76. Ibid.; *Record of Service, 1st MSS*, 81.
77. Battalion Order No. 7, Dearborn, Michigan, 30 April 1863, *Letter and Order Book*.
78. Ibid., Battalion Order No. 15, Dearborn, Michigan, 8 May 1863. Pvt. Merrick Bradley left the camp and his guard post. Not only was his name penned to the black list, it stayed on the roll for 60 days, with one month's pay deducted for good measure.

    Charged with desertion, Pvt. Francis Weaver received five days' hard labor with one month's pay forfeited. Within a month he deserted for good.

    Pvts. Joseph Westfall and Christopher Schauppner, two of the older recruits, secured passes to attend church services one May Sabbath. The record is not clear if they actually participated in Sunday worship, but the next time they appeared in camp, both were as drunk as lords. Their names went on the black list.

    Pvt. Charles Bailey paid a fine of $5 and received fifteen days's hard labor with ball and chain—for sleeping on guard duty.

    Pvt. William Little left his guard post and the camp and refused to return. Arrested while drunk, he was forcibly returned to the arsenal. He slept in the guardhouse the next five nights, his days occupied with hard labor projects.

    Pvt. William O. Clemans abandoned his guard post to buy a "bottle of gin." His punishment was the same penalty as Little's.

    Pvt. Lawrence Banks appeared in front of the court-martial board again in late May. For leaving camp and "putting on a toot," Banks lost one month's pay and ended up in the guardhouse for five days on bread and water, "except one hour in the forenoon & one hour in the afternoon when he shall be drilled in the manual of arms." Banks served his sentence, although his weakness for the bottle continued to plague him. Few, if any, remembered such failings long after the war, for a little less than a year later he died for his country in some pine woods in Virginia.

    Pvt. Job Priest refused to report back when his furlough expired, and a party had to be sent out to seize him. Forced to return, Priest found he had to reimburse the United States for the expenses incurred in his arrest: $8.00.

    Pvt. William Hero, more enterprising than most others, left

camp with a forged pass. After being returned under armed guard, Hero spent three days at hard labor. See ibid., Battalion Order No. 16, Dearborn, Michigan, 9 May 1863; Battalion Order No. 24, Dearborn, Michigan, 17 May 1863; Battalion Order No. 43, Dearborn, Michigan, 4 June 1863; Battalion Order No. 44, Dearborn, Michigan, 6 June 1863; Battalion Order No. 37, Dearborn, Michigan, 29 May 1863; Battalion Order No. 30, Dearborn, Michigan, 23 May 1863; Battalion Order No. 34, Dearborn, Michigan, 26 May 1863; *Record of Service, 1st MSS*, 95, 7.

79. Ibid., Battalion Order No. 59, Dearborn, Michigan, 21 June 1863.

80. Ibid., Battalion Order No. 34, Dearborn, Michigan, 26 May 1863; *Record of Service, 1st MSS*, 76, 100.

81. Battalion Order No. 47, Dearborn, Michigan, 9 June 1863, *Letter and Order Book*.

82. Until the end of May 1863 the Sharpshooters drilled without weapons. Generally, the officer of the day marched a guard detail to the quartermaster, who issued the requisite number of muskets and accoutrements. At the end of their duty the squad returned the weapons and leathers to the quartermaster's office. See Battalion Order No. 50, Dearborn, Michigan, 12 June 1863, *Letter and Order Book*.

83. *Detroit Advertiser and Tribune*, 12 May 1863, 1.

84. Ibid., 13 May 1863, 1.

85. *Record of Service, 1st MSS*, 79.

86. Battalion Order No. 18, Dearborn, Michigan, 11 May 1863, *Letter and Order Book*.

87. Another accidental shooting took place on 1 June. As 2nd Lt. Cyrenius B. Knight took out his pistol to clean it, the weapon discharged, and the contents hit Sgt. Jacob Black in the wrist. The wound turned out to be more painful than serious, but resulted in Colonel DeLand issuing orders forbidding anyone to carry a loaded weapon on the arsenal grounds, excepting the officer of the day and the officer of the guard. See Detroit *Advertiser and Tribune*, 2 June 1863, 3.

88. Battalion Order No. 24, Dearborn, Michigan, 17 May 1863, *Letter and Order Book*.

89. Ibid., Battalion Order No. 17, Dearborn, Michigan, 11 May 1863.

90. *Record of Service, 1st MSS*, 72; *Descriptive Rolls—Civil War, First Michigan Sharpshooters*, vol. 44, State Archives of Michigan, Lansing, Michigan, 24. Hereafter cited as *Descriptive Rolls*.

91. Battalion Orders 33 and 34, Dearborn, Michigan, 26 May 1863, *Letter and Order Book*.

92. *Descriptive Rolls*, 6. Keeping his men in line occupied most of DeLand's time. Likewise, outside influences had to be kept at a minimum. Itinerant vendors caused some problems. It irritated DeLand to such a degree that he issued an order forbidding the presence of

strangers in camp without a personal authorization from him. He was adamant: "All persons found in camp peddling jewelry or other 'notions,' or dealing in clothing, liquors, or other peddlar's wares will be immediately arrested."

To further annoy DeLand, the commander of the arsenal, Charles Wilkins of the Regular Army, told the colonel to keep his men from visiting the small number of regulars stationed at the Arsenal Yard. The regulars kept a few animals, and to augment their meager army pay they sold butter and milk to the Sharpshooters. But Wilkins tired of Michigan recruits going in and out of quarters ostensibly to buy fresh dairy products. He told DeLand that the regulars would bring the milk and butter to the Sharpshooters' quarters, thereby keeping them from interfering in his business. See Battalion Order No. 24, 17 May 1863, and Battalion Order No. 28, 21 May 1863, *Letter and Order Book*.

93. *Detroit Advertiser and Tribune*, 5 May 1863, 1.
94. Ibid., 28 May 1863, 94.
95. Ibid.
96. Ibid., 4 June 1863, 3.
97. Ibid., 29 June 1863, 3.
98. Ibid., 5 June 1863, 3; Battle Creek *Journal*, 12 June 1863, 2.
99. Brig. Gen. Edward Canby to Austin Blair, Washington, DC, 26 May 1863, Folder no. 8, "Letters and Telegrams—1861–1881," *1st MSS Records*.
100. Battalion Order No. 30, Dearborn, Michigan, 23 May 1863, *Letter and Order Book*.
101. Ibid.
102. Ibid., Battalion Order No. 35, Dearborn, Michigan, 27 May 1863.
103. Detroit *Advertiser and Tribune*, 5 June 1863, 1.
104. Folder no. 9: "George A. Caine," "History," *1st MSS Records*; *Record of Service, 1st MSS*, 17.
105. Charles V. DeLand to Brig. Gen. L. Thomas, Headquarters, First Michigan Sharpshooters, 5 September 1863, *Letter and Order Book*.
106. Ibid.
107. Ibid., Battalion Order No. 53, Dearborn, Michigan, 15 June 1863.
108. Detroit *Advertiser and Tribune*, 17 June 1863, 1.
109. Ibid.
110. Buckbee Memoirs.
111. Ibid.
112. Detroit *Advertiser and Tribune*, 17 June 1863, 1.
113. Ibid.
114. Ibid.
115. Deposition of Charles V. DeLand, January 1885, Jackson, Michigan, File E: Miscellanea, Clarke–DeLand Papers. Beadle had high-placed benefactors, as did DeLand. He received his commission from Governor Blair probably through the intercession of Dr.

Henry Tappan, president of the University of Michigan. Beadle had been a student there before the war. In May 1863, Tappan presided over Beadle's marriage. See May Beadle Frink, "The Hoosier," *South Dakota Historical Collections*, vol. 3 (1906), 88.

116. Battalion Order No. 63, Dearborn, Michigan, 25 June 1863, *Letter and Order Book*.
117. *Portraits and Biographies of Jackson County*, 220.
118. Battle Creek *Journal*, 3 July 1863, 2.
119. Battalion Order No. 71, Dearborn, Michigan, 3 July 1863, *Letter and Order Book*; Detroit *Free Press*, 7 July 1863, 3.
120. Battalion Order No. 71, Dearborn, Michigan, 3 July 1863, *Letter and Order Book*.
121. Ibid., Battalion Order No. 73, Dearborn, Michigan, 4 July 1863.
122. Detroit *Advertiser and Tribune*, 17 June 1863, 1.
123. Ed. J. Buckbee to "Friend Mollie," Dearborn, Michigan, 20 June 1863, Buckbee Papers.

Chapter 3

1. Robertson, *Michigan in the War*, 452.
2. Ibid., 451–453; Edison H. Thomas, *John Hunt Morgan and His Raiders* (Lexington, KY: University Press of Kentucky, 1975), 77.
3. Brig. Gen. Orlando B. Willcox to Adj. Gen. John Robertson, Indianapolis, Indiana, 5 July 1863, Folder no. 7: "Telegraphic Dispatches Relative to Movement of Sharpshooters—July 1863," *1st MSS Records*.
4. Ibid., Brig. Gen. Orlando B. Willcox to Adj. Gen. John Robertson, Indianapolis, Indiana, 6 July 1863, Folder no. 7: "Telegraphic Dispatches Relative to Movement of Sharpshooters."
5. Ibid., Brig. Gen. Orlando B. Willcox to A. A. Gen. Morley, Indianapolis, Indiana, 6 July 1863, Folder no. 7: "Telegraphic Dispatches Relative to Movement of Sharpshooters—July 1863;" Detroit *Advertiser and Tribune*, 8 July 1863, 1.
6. *1st MSS Records*, Brig. Gen. Orlando B. Willcox to A. A. Gen. Morley, Indianapolis, Indiana, 6 July 1863, Folder no. 7: "Telegraphic Dispatches Relative to Movement of Sharpshooters."
7. Charles V. DeLand, Compiled Military Service File, National Archives, Washington, DC.
8. Battalion Order No. 75, Dearborn, Michigan, 7 July 1863, and Special Order No. 40, 6 July 1863, *Letter and Order Book*.
9. Detroit *Free Press*, 7 July 1863, 1.
10. Jackson *Weekly Citizen*, 15 July 1863, 3.
11. Buckbee Memoirs.
12. Ibid.
13. Ibid.

14. North Vernon, Indiana was a crossroads for two rail lines, the Madison, Indianapolis and Peru and the Ohio and Mississippi.
15. Buckbee Memoirs.
16. Ibid.; Robertson, *Michigan in the War*, 544.
17. Detroit *Free Press*, 16 July 1863, 1.
18. Detroit *Advertiser and Tribune*, 23 July 1863, 1.
19. "General Morgan Invades the North," ed. Henry Steele Commager, *The Blue and the Gray*, vol. 2 (New York: Bobbs–Merrill, 1973), 95; Detroit *Free Press*, 16 July 1863, 1.
20. Robertson, *Michigan in the War*, 544.
21. Buckbee Memoirs.
22. Ibid.
23. Ibid.
24. Ibid. Morgan kept a telegrapher, George A. Ellsworth, on his staff. Ellsworth's role involved sowing false leads and learning the whereabouts of Union detachments. Cutting into a telegraph wire, the rebel informed Union listeners that Morgan had twice the men he actually had. Learning where Union troops lay in wait, he informed Morgan, and the confrontations were generally avoided. See George Dallas Mosgrove, "Following Morgan's Plume through Indiana and Ohio," *Southern Historical Society Papers*, vol. 35, 1907 (hereafter cited as Mosgrove, "Following Morgan's Plume"), 113.
25. Buckbee Memoirs.
26. Robertson, *Michigan in the War*, 544.
27. Mosgrove, "Following Morgan's Plume," 115.
28. Detroit *Advertiser and Tribune*, 23 July 1863, 1.
29. Ibid.
30. Buckbee Memoirs.
31. Detroit *Advertiser and Tribune*, 23 July 1863, 1.
32. Jackson *Weekly Citizen*, 29 July 1863, 2.
33. Charles V. DeLand to Capt. James Ekin, Chicago, Illinois, 1 November 1863, *Letter and Order Book*.
34. Ibid.
35. Detroit *Free Press*, 24 July 1863, 2.
36. Grand Rapids *Eagle*, 27 July 1863, 2.
37. Jackson *Weekly Citizen*, 29 July 1863, 2; Grand Rapids *Eagle*, 27 July 1863, 2.
38. Charles V. DeLand to Capt. James Ekin, AQM USA, Chicago, Illinois, 1 November 1863, *Letter and Order Book*.
39. Detroit *Free Press*, 8 July 1863, 1.
40. Marshall *Democratic Expounder*, 28 May 1863, 2.
41. Detroit *Free Press*, 27 May 1863, 3; 8 July 1863, 1; Detroit *Advertiser and Tribune*, 10 July 1863, 3.
42. Detroit *Advertiser and Tribune*, 21 July 1863, 3.
43. Special Order No. 54, Dearborn, Michigan, 3 August 1863, *Letter and Order Book*. DeLand thought Cooper was the man to raise at

least another company of Indians. He recommended Cooper to Adj. Gen. John Robertson as a recruiter and potential officer. Acknowledged as the first white settler at Little Traverse (where he had lived since coming from New York in 1851), Cooper ran a store there, trading with the Indians and fishermen. He knew the people in that region of the state well, but even he would be unable to raise enough men for another full company. See Charles V. DeLand to Gen. Robertson, Dearborn, Michigan, 26 July 1863, Folder no. 8: "Letters and Telegrams—1861–1881," *1st MSS Records*; Leach, *The Grand Traverse Region*, 80–81.

44. Detroit *Advertiser and Tribune*, 14 July 1863, 1.
45. Special Order No. 44, "On the March," 21 July 1863, *Letter and Order Book*.
46. Detroit *Free Press*, 22 July 1863, 1.
47. Special Order No. 45, Dearborn, Michigan, 22 July 1863, *Letter and Order Book*.
48. Ibid., Battalion Order No. 84, Dearborn, Michigan, 25 July 1863.
49. Detroit *Advertiser and Tribune*, 22 July 1863, 3.
50. Special Order No. 56, Dearborn, Michigan, 3 August 1863, *Letter and Order Book*. Three others, besides Powers and Bolton, left the regiment in Indiana. When the regiment detrained at Indianapolis on 9 July, Michael Ryan (Co. F) decided he had enough of soldiering and never came back. John Barris (Co. E) was last seen at Vernon on 15 July; and John W. Bell (Co. C) left his company at Sidney, Ohio on 19 July. None of the three was apprehended. See *Record of Service, 1st MSS*, 76, 8, 10.
51. Battalion Order No. 92, Dearborn, Michigan, 2 August 1863, *Letter and Order Book*.
52. Ibid., Charles V. DeLand to Capt. Jas. McMillan, Dearborn, Michigan, 31 July 1863.
53. Ibid., Special Order No. 46, Detroit Arsenal, 23 July 1863.
54. Ibid., Special Order No. 59, Dearborn, Michigan, 5 August 1863.
55. Ibid., Charles V. DeLand to Col. J. R. Smith, Dearborn, Michigan, 5 August 1863.
56. Ibid., Battalion Order No. 102, Dearborn, Michigan, 12 August 1863.
57. A number of the absent men were just that—absent. After a few days most came back. They saw no reason to stay at the arsenal; they were far from a war zone and wondered why their officers should get so agitated because of a few men overstaying their leaves. Nonetheless, the officers did become upset and quite a few noncommissioned officers lost their stripes for not obeying regimental regulations.

Sgt. Lafayette Murray (Co. G) left camp in violation of orders, was ordered back, but refused to obey. He even tried to get others to join him. Murray was "reduced to the ranks" and the word "deserter" was entered after his name on the regimental books. The regiment never saw him again after 4 August 1863.

Cpl. Benjamin Raymond lost his rank by disobeying an order, but he stuck with his bunkmates for the duration. Cpl. Rasmus Oleson (Co. B) disappeared from camp in early August, never returning. Two days later Cpl. Harvey Limebeck (Co. G) found himself "reduced to the ranks" after he was judged "guilty of gross neglect of duty & conduct prejudicial to good order & military discipline." A day later Sgt. Daniel Manehan (Co. F), who had disappeared from the arsenal camp, was declared "unfit and incompetent," and was sentenced to be reduced to the ranks, but he never came back to learn of the board's decision. See ibid., Battalion Order No. 97, Dearborn, Michigan, 7 August 1863; Battalion Order No. 99, Dearborn, Michigan, 9 August 1863; Battalion Order No. 101, Dearborn, Michigan, 11 August 1863; Battalion Order No. 102, Dearborn, Michigan, 12 August 1863; *Record of Service, 1st MSS*, 64, 73.

58. *Record of Service, 1st MSS*, 23; Provost Marshall, 3rd Dist. Mich. to Capt. S. F. Brown, n.p., 3 July 1863, "Regimental Papers, 1st MSS."
59. Charles V. DeLand to Brig. Gen. J. M. Ripley, Dearborn, Michigan, 6 August 1863, *Letter and Order Book*.
60. The Leelanau Township Historical Writers Group, *History of Leelanau Twp.*, 61.
61. *Record of Service, 1st MSS*, 100.
62. Ibid., 69 and vol. 10, 87.
63. Charles V. DeLand to Brig. Gen. L. Thomas, Headquarters, First Michigan Sharpshooters, 5 September 1864, *Letter and Order Book*.
64. Ibid., Special Order No. 57, Dearborn, Michigan, 4 August 1863.
65. Detroit *Advertiser and Tribune*, 14 August 1863, 3.
66. Battalion Order No. 105, Dearborn, Michigan, 15 August 1863, *Letter and Order Book*.
67. Ibid., Battalion Order No. 105, Dearborn, Michigan, 15 August 1863.
68. Detroit *Advertiser and Tribune*, 17 August 1863, 1.
69. Ibid., 11 August 1863, 3.

Chapter 4

1. Marshall *Democratic Expounder*, 20 August 1863, 2.
2. Battalion Order No. 106, Dearborn, Michigan, 16 August 1863, *Letter and Order Book*.
3. Ibid.
4. Ibid., Battalion Order No. 108, Dearborn, Michigan, 16 August 1863. No mention of drunkenness on the march in Indiana found its way into the official regimental correspondence. The mystery of whoever was involved cannot now be solved.

5. Detroit *Advertiser and Tribune*, 18 August 1863, 3.
6. Marshall *Democratic Expounder*, 20 August 1863, 2.
7. Buckbee Memoirs.
8. Joseph L. Eisendrath, Jr., "Chicago's Camp Douglas, 1861–1865," *Journal of the Illinois State Historical Society*, vol. 53, no. 1 (Spring 1960) (hereafter cited as Eisendrath, "Chicago's Camp Douglas."), 38; E. B. Long, "Camp Douglas: 'Hellish Den?'" *Chicago History: The Magazine of the Chicago Historical Society*, vol. 1, no. 2 (Fall 1970) (hereafter cited as Long, "A Hellish Den?"), 84.
9. Eisendrath, "Chicago's Camp Douglas," 41.
10. Ibid., 42.
11. Ibid., 42–43.
12. Ibid., 53.
13. Battalion Order No. 107, Camp Douglas, Illinois, 21 August 1863, *Letter and Order Book*.
14. Ibid., 39–40.
15. Buckbee Memoirs.
16. Buckbee Papers.
17. Randall Reminiscences, 13 April 1864; *Confederate Soldiers, Sailors and Civilians Who Died as Prisoners of War at Camp Douglas, Chicago, Ill. 1862–1865* (Kalamazoo, MI: Edgar Gray Publications, n.d.), n.p.
18. Marshall *Democratic Expounder*, 20 August 1863, 2.
19. Detroit *Advertiser and Tribune*, 18 August 1863, 3.
20. Marshall *Democratic Expounder*, 20 August 1863, 2.
21. Detroit *Advertiser and Tribune*, 22 August 1863, 3.
22. Eisendrath, "Chicago's Camp Douglas," 47.
23. Detroit *Advertiser and Tribune*, 22 August 1863, 3.
24. Letter of T. A. Nettles, *Confederate Veteran*, vol. 16, no. 7 (July 1908), 349.
25. Marshall *Democratic Expounder*, 3 September 1863, 2.
26. Charles V. DeLand to Mary DeLand, Camp Douglas, Illinois, 19 August 1863, Clarke–DeLand Papers.
27. Detroit *Advertiser and Tribune*, 22 August 1863, 3.
28. Marshall *Democratic Expounder*, 3 September 1863, 2.
29. Amos Farling, *Life in the Army, Containing Historical and Biographical Sketches, Incidents, Adventures and Narratives of the Late War* (Buchanan, MI: Amos Farling, 1874), 7. Farling was the only Sharpshooter to actually publish his war experiences. It is a very small book—only 43 pages, 30 of which were devoted to life in the Sharpshooters, the rest being his adventures in the West after the war.
30. Detroit *Advertiser and Tribune*, 3 September 1863, 3.
31. Charles V. DeLand to Gov. Henry Crapo, Jackson, Michigan, 18 January 1865, Clarke–DeLand Papers.
32. Detroit *Advertiser and Tribune*, 3 September 1863, 3.

33. Ibid., 28 September 1863, 3.
34. Ibid., 1 October 1863, 1.
35. *DeLand's Jackson County*, 396; Detroit *Advertiser and Tribune*, 25 September 1863, 3; Niles *Republican*, 5 September 1863, 3.
36. Eisendrath, "Chicago's Camp Douglas," 47.
37. Ibid., 54–55; Long, "A Hellish Den?" 91.
38. Long, "A Hellish Den?" 91–92.
39. Randall Reminiscences, 13 April 1864.
40. Long, "A Hellish Den?" 92; Detroit *Advertiser and Tribune*, 3 November 1863, 4.
41. Hillsdale *Standard*, 10 November 1863, 1; T. M. Page, "The Prisoner of War," *Confederate Veteran*, vol. 8, no. 1 (January 1900), 63.
42. Bruce Catton, *A Stillness at Appomattox* (New York: Doubleday & Co., Inc., 1953), 162; Buckbee Memoirs.
43. Constantine *Weekly Mercury and* St. Joseph County *Advertiser*, 5 May 1864, 2.
44. Catton, *Stillness at Appomattox*, 162.
45. Detroit *Advertiser and Tribune*, 5 November 1863, 1.
46. Ibid., 1 December 1863, 3.
47. Detroit *Free Press*, 28 October 1863, 1.
48. Detroit *Advertiser and Tribune*, 3 November 1863, 4.
49. Hillsdale *Standard*, 15 September 1863, 2.
50. Randall Reminiscences.
51. Marshall *Democratic Expounder*, 3 September 1863, 2.
52. Detroit *Advertiser and Tribune*, 22 September 1863, 4. A rebel prisoner related the following tale of how one Confederate escaped from Camp Douglas: "a Kentucky gentleman called on Gen. [*sic*] DeLand with two boxes. They contained cigars, and the Colonel was asked to smoke one box and send the other to the son of the visitor. On examining, the Colonel found one box contained prime Havanas, and the other a much inferior domestic smoke. . . . he wisely smiled and kept the first and sent the other to the son of a Solomon—for the son found a greenback bill inside each wrapper of the lower layer of 'stogies,' and bribed a guard to let him out of prison with one of them." See T. M. Page, "The Prisoner of War," 64.
53. Long, "A Hellish Den?" 89.
54. Detroit *Advertiser and Tribune*, 22 September 1863, 4.
55. Ibid., 14 October 1863, 4.
56. Hillsdale *Standard*, 10 November 1863, 1.
57. Ibid.
58. Detroit *Advertiser and Tribune*, 3 November 1863, 4.
59. Farling, *Life in the Army*, 7–8; Eisendrath, "Chicago's Camp Douglas," 56.
60. Marshall *Democratic Expounder*, 17 December 1863, 1; Randall Reminiscences, 13 April 1864. DeLand examined the tunnel and came up with a plan to foil any future diggings. He had the floors

in all the rebel barracks nearest the fence removed. Furthermore, sand was strewn beneath the floors of all the other buildings. Consequently, no fresh earth from a tunnel could be thrown beneath a structure without it being noticed immediately. See Detroit *Advertiser and Tribune*, 18 December 1863, 3.

61. Ibid., 14 November 1863, 1; 30 November 1863, 1.
62. Battalion Order No. 116, Camp Douglas, Illinois, 22 October 1863, *Letter and Order Book*.
63. Ibid., Battalion Order No. 91, Dearborn, Michigan, 31 July 1863.
64. Hillsdale *Standard*, 10 November 1863, 1.
65. Buckbee Memoirs.
66. Detroit *Advertiser and Tribune*, 22 September 1863, 4.
67. Battalion Order No. 122, Camp Douglas, Illinois, 20 November 1863, *Letter and Order Book*.
68. Farling, *Life in the Army*, 9.
69. *Record of Service, 1st MSS*, 82; Farling, *Life in the Army*, 8; *Annual Report of the Adjutant General of the State of Michigan for the Year 1863* (Lansing, Michigan: John A. Kerr & Co., 1864), 426.
70. Besides deserting, other outward manifestations of the tedium oppressing the Sharpshooters were fist fights and drunkenness. Cpl. William Van Dusen (Co. E) lost his stripes for "disorderly & unsoldierly conduct," an army euphemism for fighting. See Regimental Order No. 128, Camp Douglas, Illinois, 17 December 1863, *Letter and Order Book*. Primarily for running the guard and drunkenness, men were reduced to the ranks, fined, or punished in some novel way, although the most common punishments for such transgressions were to be tied up by the thumbs or extra guard duty.

    No sooner had the Sharpshooters taken over Camp Douglas than Sgt. William H. Curliss (Co. G) lost his stripes for "conduct prejudicial to good order." One day later Sgt. W. J. Lee and Cpl. Henry H. Hulin (Co. E) were both demoted to privates for "insubordinate & mutinous conduct." They were berated during dress parade and humiliated in front of the entire regiment.

    Cpl. William Buchanan (Co. A) left camp without permission and got drunk to boot. He lost his rank and was incarcerated to mull over his infraction. Not being enlightened by what happened to Buchanan, Cpls. Alexander Wallace and David Sanford (Co. B) pulled the same stunt a week and a half later and met with the same punishment.

    On 15 October Cpl. Joseph Segard ran off and was never seen again by the regiment. Cpl. Robert F. Bradley, another of the old soldiers of Company H who served with both the Seventh and Thirteenth Michigan Infantries before joining the Sharpshooters, was reduced to the ranks for being intoxicated in camp. Sgt. John A. Dutcher (Co. A) was brought up on charges of "repeated disobedience of orders," and joined the ranks of the privates. Cpl. Benjamin F. Smith (Co. H) was demoted "for conduct prejudicial to good order" on 9 December.

In fact, 9 December was a big sentencing day for courts-martial held back on 22 October, and the court cleared up quite a bit of unfinished business that day. Pvts. Robert Clarence, Milton Calkins, Oscar McKeel, and Levi Porter were judged guilty of being absent from the command without permission, and all had to forfeit one month's pay. Pvt. Abner Lester (Co. F) had the charge of desertion stricken from the books, but he was "guilty of so much" that he had to forfeit three months' pay and was confined to hard labor for six months. Lester ran off at the first opportunity, being officially listed as a deserter on 2 March 1864. See Charles V. DeLand to Gov. Henry Crapo, Jackson, MI, 18 January 1865, Correspondence 1861–1865, Clarke–DeLand Papers; Battalion Order No. 111, Camp Douglas, Illinois, 11 September 1863, *Letter and Order Book*; ibid., Battalion Order No. 109, Camp Douglas, Illinois, 12 September 1863; ibid., Battalion Order No. 113, Camp Douglas. Illinois, 3 October 1863; ibid., Battalion Order No. 114, Camp Douglas, Chicago, 12 October 1863; ibid., Battalion Order No. 115, Camp Douglas, Illinois, 15 October 1863; ibid., Battalion Order No. 120, Camp Douglas, Illinois, 7 November 1863; ibid., Battalion Order No. 121, Camp Douglas, Illinois, 19 November 1863; ibid., Battalion Order No. 125, Camp Douglas, Illinois, 9 December 1863; ibid., Regimental Order No. 126, Camp Douglas, Illinois, 9 December 1863; *Record of Service, 1st MSS*, 13, 56.

71. Marshall *Democratic Expounder*, 3 September 1863, 2.
72. Detroit *Advertiser and Tribune*, 5 September 1863, 3.
73. *Record of Service, 1st MSS*, 12.
74. Hillsdale *Standard*, 2 February 1864, 3.
75. Regimental Order No. 2, Camp Douglas, Illinois, 1 February 1864, *Letter and Order Book*.
76. East Saginaw *Courier*, 27 January 1864, 4; "Regimental Papers, 1st MSS;" *Record of Service, 1st MSS*, 77.
77. Charles V. DeLand to Lt. Col. W. H. H. Beadle, Camp Douglas, Illinois, 30 January 1864, *Letter and Order Book*.
78. Ibid.
79. *Record of Service, 1st MSS*, 33; Ira Lester Evans Papers, Collection of Emily Evans Walsh.
80. *Letter and Order Book*, Charles V. DeLand to Lt. Col. W. H. H. Beadle, Camp Douglas, Illinois, 30 January 1864.
81. Special Order No. 1, Camp Douglas, Illinois, 1 January 1864, *Letter and Order Book*; Niles *Republican*, 12 September 1863, 3.
82. Compiled Military Record of Thomas H. Gaffney, National Archives, Washington, DC; Niles *Republican*, 6 February 1864, 2.
83. *DeLand's Jackson County*, 288–289; George B. Catlin, "Adventures in Journalism: Detroit Newspapers Since 1850," *Michigan History*,

vol. 29, no. 3 (July–Sept., 1945), 346–347, 348. The editor of the Lansing *Republican* castigated Storey and the Chicago *Times*, calling the latter "the worst newspaper in the Northern states. While his name smells rank all through the State of Michigan, and the pestiferous influence he exerted will be felt in our State for years." See Lansing *Republican*, 7 March 1866, 2.

84. Charles Moore, *History of Michigan*, vol. 1 (Chicago: The Lewis Publishing Co., 1915), 415.

85. Mildred Throne, ed., *The Civil War Diary of Cyrus F. Boyd, Fifteenth Iowa Infantry, 1861–1863* (Millwood, NY: Kraus Reprint Co., 1977), 102, 108; Wood Gray, *The Hidden Civil War: The Story of the Copperheads* (New York: n.p., 1942), 98–99.

86. Marshall *Democratic Expounder*, 3 September 1863, 2.

87. Jackson *Eagle*, 29 August 1863, 2.

88. Ibid., 24 October 1863, 3.

89. *History of Washtenaw County*, 234, 761–762.

90. Charles V. DeLand to Gov. Henry Crapo, Jackson, Michigan, 18 January 1865, Correspondence 1861–1865, Clarke–DeLand Papers.

91. Ibid.

92. Ibid.

93. *History of Washtenaw County*, 762.

94. Henry B. Cleavland, Department of Corrections, (General), Series 1, State Archives of Michigan, Lansing, Michigan.

95. Ibid.; *History of Washtenaw County*, 762. For another Sharpshooter there was no reprieve. Sgt. Charles Waubesis, an Indian from Pentwater, committed a murder while the regiment was stationed at Camp Douglas. He would serve a life sentence in an Illinois prison. "Annual Returns of Alterations and Casualties for the Year ending Dec. 31, 1863," "Regimental Papers, 1st MSS."

96. Ibid.

97. Ibid.

98. Detroit *Advertiser and Tribune*, 18 December 1863, 3.

99. Dee Brown, *The Galvanized Yankees* (Urbana, IL: University of Illinois Press, 1963). This is a very good popular account of the Galvanized Yankees.

100. Hillsdale *Standard*, 10 November 1863, 1.

101. Randall Reminiscences, 1 January 1864; Marshall *Democratic Expounder*, 7 January 1864, 2.

102. Randall Reminiscences, 1 January 1864.

103. Ibid.; Marshall *Democratic Expounder*, 7 January 1864, 2.

104. Buckbee Memoirs.

105. Ibid.

106. Ibid.

107. Ibid.

108. Ibid.

109. Charles V. DeLand to Brig. Gen. L. Thomas, Headquarters, First

Michigan Sharpshooters, 5 September 1864, *Letter and Order Book*.

110. Ibid., Battalion Order No. 97, Dearborn, Michigan, 7 August 1863; Regimental Order No. 3, Camp Douglas, Illinois, 4 February 1864.

111. Ibid.

112. Charles G. Conn, Military Pension Record, National Archives, Washington, DC.

113. Battalion Order No. 104, Dearborn, Michigan, 14 August 1863, *Letter and Order Book*.

114. Randall's Reminiscences, "Introduction."

115. Charles V. DeLand to Adj. Gen. L. Thomas, Annapolis, Maryland, 10 April 1864, *Letter and Order Book*.

116. Ibid., Regimental Order No. 13, Near Annapolis, Maryland, 9 April 1864.

117. Hillsdale *Standard*, 2 February 1864, 3.

118. Jonesville *Weekly Independent*, 21 January 1864, 3; *Record of Service, 1st MSS*, 96.

119. Detroit *Advertiser and Tribune*, 25 March 1863, 1.

120. Regimental Order No. 8, Camp Douglas, Illinois, 8 March 1864, *Letter and Order Book*.

121. Three Rivers *Western Chronicle*, 9 September 1863, 3.

122. "The Family Tree," Box No. 2, DeLand–Crary Papers.

123. James S. DeLand, Military Pension Record, National Archives, Washington, DC.

124. *Biographical History of Northern Michigan* (n.p.: B. F. Bowen and Co., 1905), 527.

125. *Record of Service, 1st MSS*, 42.

126. *Detroit Advertiser and Tribune*, 27 January 1864, 4.

127. Randall Reminiscences, 13 April 1864.

128. Buckbee Memoirs.

129. Randall Reminiscences, 13 April 1864.

130. Ibid.

131. Lansing *State Republican*, 20 January 1864, 2.

132. Detroit *Advertiser and Tribune*, 27 January 1864, 4.

133. Ibid.

134. Jonesville *Weekly Independent*, 11 February 1864, 2.

135. Ibid.; *Record of Service, 1st MSS*, 23.

136. Jonesville *Weekly Independent*, 11 February 1864, 2.

137. Detroit *Advertiser and Tribune*, 22 December 1863, 3.

138. At least four of the current members of the regiment had served previously in Sharpshooter units. Maj. John Piper transferred from the Western Sharpshooters, the Sixty-sixth Illinois Infantry, as captain of Company D. Second Lt. Frank Whipple (Co. B) had enlisted in the First U.S. Sharpshooters in 1862, and served for a while as commissary sergeant before joining the regiment early in 1863. Pvt. William Bruce (Co. I), originally a member of the Second U.S. Sharpshooters, was discharged for disability in January 1863. He

joined the First Michigan Sharpshooters in August 1863. Sgt. Henry Miller (Co. I), like Lt. Whipple, served in the First U.S. Sharpshooters. Those members of the regiment with experience in sharpshooting matters must have initiated the others into the intricacies of the game. See *Record of Service, 1st MSS*, 70, 97, 15; *Descriptive Rolls*, 70.

139. Detroit *Advertiser and Tribune*, 17 February 1864, 4.
140. The First U.S. Sharpshooters recruited three companies (C, I, and K) from Michigan in 1861 and early 1862. Severe testing of marksmanship kept the caliber of men high. Another recruitment effort made the same demands on its enlistees, and its members were mustered in as Company B of the Second U.S. Sharpshooters in October 1862. See Robertson, *Michigan in the War*, 744.
141. Regimental Order No. 4, Camp Douglas, Illinois, 4 February 1864, *Letter and Order Book*.
142. Detroit *Advertiser and Tribune*, 17 February 1864, 4.
143. Ibid.
144. Ibid.
145. Detroit *Free Press*, 15 March 1864, 1.
146. Detroit *Advertiser and Tribune*, 8 March 1864, 1.
147. Special Orders No. 110, War Dept, Adj. Gen. Office, Washington, DC, 8 March 1864, *War of the Rebellion: A Compilation of the Official Records of the Union and Confederate Armies* (Washington, DC: Government Printing Office, 1880–1901) (hereafter cited as *OR*; all references are to Series 1), Vol. 33, 657.
148. Detroit *Advertiser and Tribune*, 17 February 1864, 4.
149. Buckbee Memoirs.

Chapter 5

1. Detroit *Advertiser and Tribune*, 21 March 1864, 4.
2. Randall Reminiscences, 21 March 1864.
3. Detroit *Advertiser and Tribune*, 21 March 1864, 4.
4. Augustus Woodbury, *Major General Ambrose E. Burnside and the Nith Army Corps* (Providence, RI: Sidney S. Rider & Brother, 1867) (hereafter cited as Woodbury, *Burnside and the Ninth Corps*), 366–367.
5. Ibid., 365.
6. Edward Steere, *The Wilderness Campaign* (New York: Bonanza Books, 1960) (hereafter cited at Steere, *Wilderness Campaign*), 23.
7. Byron Cutcheon, *The Story of the Twentieth Michigan Infantry* (Lansing, MI: Robert Smith Printing Co., 1904) (hereafter cited as Cutcheon, *20th Michigan*), 102.
8. Detroit *Advertiser and Tribune*, 28 March 1864, 4.
9. Ibid.

10. *Descriptive Rolls*, 46.
11. Ibid., 12; *Record of Service, 1st MSS*, 16.
12. Randall Remniscences.
13. Detroit *Advertiser and Tribune*, 8 April 1864, 1; 16 April 1864, 4.
14. Detroit *Advertiser and Tribune*, 16 April 1864, 4; 11 June 1864, 4; *Descriptive List*, 3, 6; *Record of Service, 1st MSS*, 35.
15. Quackenbush later left the Sharpshooters, garnering a promotion in another outfit, but a surprise awaited him. The new command would be incorporated into his old regiment. Whatever proceedings were initiated against Quackenbush (as well as their outcome) are lost in history. See Regimental Order No. 10, Annapolis, Maryland, 1 April 1864; Regimental Order No. 15, Annapolis, Maryland, 12 April 1864, *Letter and Order Book*.
16. Ibid., Regimental Order No. 10, Annapolis, Maryland, 1 April 1864; Regimental Order No. 15, Annapolis, Maryland, 12 April 1864.
17. Hillsdale *Standard*, 26 April 1864, 2.
18. Ibid.
19. Special Order No. 6, Annapolis, Maryland, 5 April 1864, *Letter and Order Book*.
20. Ibid., Special Order No. 9, Annapolis, Maryland, 13 April 1864.
21. Ibid., Special Order No. 10, Annapolis, Maryland, 14 April 1864.
22. Ibid., Special Order No. 11, Annapolis, Maryland, 15 April 1864.
23. Ibid., Special Order No. 12, Annapolis, Maryland, 17 April 1864.
24. Ibid., Special Order No. 13, Annapolis, Maryland, 17 April 1864.
25. Ibid., Special Order No. 14, Annapolis, Maryland, 22 April 1864.
26. Ibid., Special Orders Nos. 14 and 15, Annapolis, Maryland, 22 April 1864.
27. Ibid., Special Order No. 8, Annapolis, Maryland, 9 April 1864; Special Order No. 15, Annapolis, Maryland, 22 April 1864.
28. Arvin F. Whelan to Hon. A. Blair, Camp Douglas, Chicago, Illinois, 14 January 1864, Accession 59–14–A, Lot #1, Box 130, "Records of the Michigan Military Establishment," File 3, State Archives of Michigan, Lansing, MI.
29. Charles V. DeLand to Capt. O .C. Bosbyshell, AAAG, Ninth Corps, Annapolis, Maryland, 27 March 1864, *Letter and Order Book*; *Record of Service, 1st MSS*, 86.
30. Charles V. DeLand to Brig. Gen. John Robertson, A.G. of Michigan, Annapolis, Maryland, 21 April 1864, *Letter and Order Book*; Ibid., Ninth Corps Special Order No. 49, Sec. 11, Annapolis, Maryland, 19 April 1864.
31. Charles V. DeLand to Capt. O. C. Bosbyshell, Annapolis, Maryland, 27 March 1864, *Letter and Order Book*; ibid., Regimental Order No. 15, Annapolis, Maryland, 12 April 1864; ibid., Regimental Order No. 16, Annapolis, Maryland, 15 April 1864.
32. Farling, *Life in the Army*, 9.
33. Buckbee Memoirs.

34. Regimental Order No. 13, Annapolis, Maryland, 9 April 1864, *Letter and Order Book*.
35. Randall Reminiscences, 13 April 1864.
36. Hillsdale *Standard*, 26 April 1864, 2.
37. Ibid., 26 April 1864, 2.
38. Special Order No. 14, Annapolis, Maryland, 22 April 1864, *Letter and Order Book*.
39. *Battles and Leaders of the Civil War*, vol. 4: *The Way to Appomattox* (New York: Thomas Yoseloff, 1956) (hereafter cited as *Battles and Leaders*, vol. 4), 181.
40. Constantine *Weekly Mercury and* St. Joseph County *Advertiser*, 5 May 1864, 2.
41. Ibid., 5 May 1864, 2.
42. Johnson and Malone, *DAB*, 243.
43. Cutcheon, *20th Michigan*, 98; Frederick H. Dyer, *A Compendium of the War of the Rebellion*, vol. 3 (New York: Thomas Yoseloff, 1959) (hereafter cited as Dyer, *Compendium*, vol. 3), 1448.
44. Dyer, *Compendium*, vol. 3, 1590–1591.
45. Ibid., 1524–1525.
46. Cutcheon, *20th Michigan*, 172.
47. Ibid., 173.
48. Robertson, *Michigan in the War*, 190–195; Cutcheon, *20th Michigan*, 173.
49. Robertson, *Michigan in the War*, 399–403.
50. Byron M. Cutcheon, "The Twentieth Michigan Regiment in the Assault on Petersburg, July, 1864," *Michigan Pioneer and Historical Collections*, vol. 30 (Lansing, MI: Wynkoop Hallenbeck Crawford Co., 1906) (hereafter cited as Cutcheon, "Assault on Petersburg"), 127.
51. Robertson, *Michigan in the War*. 281–288.
52. Ibid., 470–472.
53. Wells B. Fox, *What I Remember of the Great Rebellion* (Lansing, MI: Darius D. Thorp, 1892) (hereafter cited as Fox, *What I Remember*), 27.
54. Dyer, *Compendium*, vol. 3, 1435.
55. William Boston to Rosa W. Brown, Annapolis, 10 April 1864, Letters of William Boston—Civil War Letters—1863–1865, Michigan Historical Collections, Bentley Library, University of Michigan, Ann Arbor, Michigan (hereafter cited as Boston Letters).
56. Charles V. DeLand to Brig. Gen. Ramsay, Annapolis, Maryland, 19 April 1864, *Letter and Order Book*.
57. Randall Reminiscences, 22 April 1864.
58. Detroit *Advertiser and Tribune*, 29 April 1864, 4.
59. Cutcheon, *20th Michigan*, 98.
60. Detroit *Advertiser and Tribune*, 2 May 1864, 4; Randall Reminiscences, 13 April 1864.

61. Cutcheon, *20th Michigan*, 99.
62. Ibid., 99; Constantine *Weekly Mercury and* St. Joseph County *Advertiser*, 5 May 1864, 2.
63. Farling, *Life in the Army*, 9.
64. Cutcheon, *20th Michigan*, 99.
65. Detroit *Advertiser and Tribune*, 2 May 1864, 4.
66. Randall Reminiscences, 22 April 1864.
67. Constantine *Weekly Mercury and* St. Joseph County *Advertiser*, 5 May 1864, 2; Cutcheon, *20th Michigan*, 99.
68. Woodbury, *Burnside and the Ninth Corps*, 368. Even the poet Walt Whitman noticed the Indians of Company K. He was waiting along the parade route to welcome his brother, an officer in Potter's division, which followed Willcox's. See Walt Whitman, *The Correspondence, Vol. I: 1842–1867*, ed. by Edwin Haviland Miller (New York: New York University Press, 1961), 212.
69. Randall Reminiscences, 22 April 1864.
70. Buckbee Memoirs.
71. Farling, *Life in the Army*, 10.
72. Buckbee Memoirs.
73. Fox, *What I Remember*, 52.
74. Cutcheon, *20th Michigan*, 99–100; Detroit *Advertiser and Tribune*, 2 May 1864, 4.
75. Constantine *Weekly Mercury and* St. Joseph County *Advertiser*, 5 May 1864, 2.
76. Farling, *Life in the Army*, 10–11.
77. Cutcheon, *20th Michigan*, 100.
78. Constantine *Weekly Mercury and* St. Joseph County *Advertiser*, 5 May 1864, 2.
79. Ibid., 28 April 1864, 2.
80. Cutcheon, *20th Michigan*, 100.
81. Randall Reminiscences, 27 April 1864.
82. Cutcheon, *20th Michigan*, 100.
83. Samuel K. Gates, "Diary," 27 April 1864, Bentley Historical Library, Michigan Historical Collections, University of Michigan, Ann Arbor.
84. Detroit *Advertiser and Tribune*, 3 May 1864, 4.
85. Constantine *Weekly Mercury and* St. Joseph County *Advertiser*, 5 May 1864, 2.
86. Ibid.
87. Detroit *Advertiser and Tribune*, 3 May 1864, 4.
88. Randall Reminiscences, 28 April 1864.
89. Cutcheon, *20th Michigan*, 101.
90. Hillsdale *Standard*, 24 May 1864, 3.
91. Randall Reminiscences, 1 May 1864.
92. Ibid.
93. Cutcheon, *20th Michigan*, 101.

Chapter 6

1. While the Army of the Potomac moved against the Army of Northern Virginia, General Sherman's army in the West would attack the rebels fortifying Atlanta, Georgia. Gen. Franz Sigel would roam the Shenandoah Valley, tying up rebel forces there. Gen. George Crook proceeded against the Virginia and Tennessee Railroad to wreck Confederate communications in western Virginia. And Gen. Benjamin Butler was to threaten Richmond, Virginia, from his base at Fortress Monroe, east of the rebel capital. See U. S. Grant, *Personal Memoirs of U. S. Grant*, vol. 2 (New York: Charles L. Webster & Co., 1886), 124–137.
2. William D. Matter, *If It Takes All Summer: The Battle of Spotsylvania* (Chapel Hill, NC: University of North Carolina Press, 1988), 5. The Ninth Corps finally became part of the Army of the Potomac on 24 May 1864.
3. Cutcheon, *20th Michigan*, 102.
4. Horace Porter, *Campaigning with Grant* (New York: Bonanza Books, 1961) (hereafter cited as Porter, *Campaigning with Grant*.), 44.
5. Cutcheon, *20th Michigan*, 102.
6. Ibid.
7. Fox, *What I Remember*, 53–55.
8. Steere, *Wilderness Campaign*, 58.
9. Hillsdale *Standard*, 19 July 1864, 1.
10. Lewis Crater, *History of the Fiftieth Regiment, Pennsylvania Veteran Volunteers, 1861–1865* (Reading, PA: Coleman Printing House, 1884) (hereafter cited as Crater, *50th Pennsylvania*.), 51.
11. Buckbee Memoirs.
12. Ibid.
13. Cutcheon, *20th Michigan*, 103.
14. Steere, *Wilderness Campaign*, 120.
15. *OR*, 36–1, 244, 975.
16. Ibid., 36–1, 243, 972; Charles V. DeLand, Washington, DC, 26 May 1864, *Letter and Order Book*; Cutcheon, *20th Michigan*, 105.
17. Cutcheon, *20th Michigan*, 105.
18. Ibid.
19. Fox, *What I Remember*, 54.
20. Randall Reminiscences, 6 May 1864.
21. Cutcheon, *20th Michigan*, 106; *OR*, 36–1, 242, 965.
22. Steere, *Wilderness Campaign*, 315.
23. *OR*, 36–1, 243, 972.
24. Cutcheon, *20th Michigan*, 106.
25. Buckbee Memoirs.
26. DeLand, *Jackson County*, 50; Buckbee Memoirs.
27. Buckbee Memoirs.

28. George W. Campbell, "Old Choctaw," *The National Tribune*, 11 September 1913, 7. Thomas Ke-chi-ti-go's named was spelled various ways in the official documents. In *Record of Service, 1st MSS*, which is a compilation of all the Sharpshooters, he is listed as "Thomas K. Chetego." In the dialect he spoke, there was the habit of dropping the first syllable, so he was commonly called "Chitigo," which could be remembered haphazardly as "Choctaw" a half-century later.
29. Ibid.
30. Ibid.
31. Ibid.
32. Cutcheon, *20th Michigan*, 107.
33. *OR*, 36–1, 242, 965.
34. Buckbee Memoirs.
35. Ibid.
36. Cutcheon, *20th Michigan*, 107.
37. Detroit *Free Press*, 8 June 1864, 1.
38. Randall Reminiscences, 6 May 1864.
39. *OR*, 36–1, 242, 966; *OR*, 36–1, 243, 972.
40. Maj. W. A. Smith, *The Anson Guards* (Charlotte, NC: Stone Publishing Co., 1914), 235. One of the Tarheels picked up a bag with beautiful bead work, obviously dropped by someone of Company K. But even he lost the prize; he sent it home and it was taken by a Union bummer when Sherman made his famous march through the South.
41. Walter Clark, comp., *Histories of the Several Regiments and Battalions from North Carolina in the Great War, 1861–1865*, vol. 2 (Goldsboro, NC: State of North Carolina, 1901) (hereafter cited as Clark, *North Carolina in the War*), 46.
42. *OR*, 36–1, 242, 966.
43. Ibid., 36–1, 243, 972; William Bradford Irwin, "Journal of William Bradford Irwin, 1862–1865" (hereafter cited as Irwin Journal), 6 May 1864, Irwin Family Collection, Michigan Historical Collections, Bentley Historical Library, University of Michigan, Ann Arbor.
44. Charles Nash to Ira Evans, Cripple Creek, Colorado, 4 June 1896, Ira L. Evans Papers, Collection of David J. C. Evans.
45. *OR*, 36–1, 242, 966.
46. Cutcheon, *20th Michigan*, 107; Irwin Journal, 6 May 1864.
47. *OR*, 36–1, 242, 966; *OR*, 36–1, 243, 972.
48. Cutcheon, *20th Michigan*, 107.
49. *OR*, 36–1, 243, 972.
50. Cutcheon, *20th Michigan*, 107.
51. Ibid., 109.
52. Fox, *What I Remember*, 56; *Record of Service, 1st MSS*, 5, 50, 91.
53. Detroit *Advertiser and Tribune*, 20 May 1864, 4.
54. "Regimental Papers, 1st MSS."

55. Cutcheon, *20th Michigan*, 109.
56. *OR*, 36–1, 244, 976.
57. Ibid., 36–1, 242, 967.
58. Ibid., 36–1, 243, 973; Charles V. DeLand, Washington, DC, 26 May 1864, *Letter and Order Book*.
59. See Appendix I for list of casualties. Officially, the casualties consisted of 7 men killed or died of wounds, 17 wounded, and one missing. See Folder no. 9: "Casualties and Alterations," *1st MSS Records*. The *Official Records* listed the casualties for the Sharpshooters a little differently: Killed—4 enlisted men, Wounded—23 enlisted men, Missing—2 enlisted men. See *O.R.*, 36–1, 132.
60. *Record of Service, 1st MSS*, 70.
61. Cutcheon, *20th Michigan*, 110; DeLand said it was 3:00 AM. See *OR*, 36–1, 243, 973.
62. Cutcheon, *20th Michigan*, 110.
63. Ibid., 110; *OR*, 36–1, 242, 967.
64. Cutcheon, *20th Michigan*, 110.
65. *OR*, 36–1, 242, 967.
66. Cutcheon, *20th Michigan*, 110.
67. Ibid.
68. Ibid., 111.
69. Ypsilanti *Commercial*, 4 November 1864, 3.
70. Cutcheon, *20th Michigan*, 111.
71. Ibid.
72. Ibid.
73. Matter, *If It Takes All Summer*, 74–75.
74. Cutcheon, *20th Michigan*, 111.

Chapter 7

1. Cutcheon, *20th Michigan*, 111–112.
2. Ibid., 112.
3. This road, the main thorofare between Fredericksburg and Spotsylvania Court House, went by a variety of names: the Fredericksburg Road, the Court House Road, the Spotsylvania Court House Road, and the Fredericksburg and Spotsylvania Court House Road.
4. Ibid.; *OR*, 36–1, 242, 967.
5. *OR*, 36–1, 242, 967; Cutcheon changed the time to 10:00 AM, see Cutcheon, *20th Michigan*, 112; but Lieutenant Colonel Avery of the Sixtieth Ohio remembered crossing the Ni River at 9:00 AM, see *OR*, 36–1, 245, 979.
6. Cutcheon, *20th Michigan*, 113.
7. Ibid.
8. Ibid.
9. Ibid., 114.

10. *OR*, 36–1, 245, 979.
11. Cutcheon, *20th Michigan*, 114; *OR*, 36–1, 242, 967.
12. *OR*, 36–1, 245, 979.
13. There were a number of Gayles and Beverlys living in the area, and different maps show one or the other name for the same house.
14. Cutcheon, *20th Michigan*, 114.
15. Ibid.
16. Ibid.
17. *OR*, 36–1, 245, 979.
18. Ibid.
19. Cutcheon, *20th Michigan*, 114.
20. Ibid., 114–115.
21. Buckbee Memoirs.
22. Robertson, *Michigan in the War*, 380.
23. *OR*, 36–1, 243, 973.
24. Ibid., 36–1, 242, 968; Cutcheon, *20th Michigan*, 115–116.
25. Ibid.
26. Robertson, *Michigan in the War*, 381.
27. Ibid., 380.
28. Ibid., 381.
29. Woodbury, *Burnside and the Ninth Corps*, 376–377.
30. Just behind the Sharpshooters in numbers was the Twentieth Michigan with 347 present for duty, followed by the Fiftieth Pennsylvania with 316, and the Sixtieth Ohio with 295. See *OR*, 36–2, Ninth Corps Circular, 9 May 1864, 585.
31. *OR*, 36–1, 243, 973; Charles V. DeLand, "In Hospital," Washington DC, 26 May 1864, *Letter and Order Book*.
32. Ibid.
33. Cutcheon, *20th Michigan*, 117.
34. *OR*, 36–1, 243, 973; Charles V. DeLand, "In Hospital," Washington, DC, 26 May 1864, *Letter and Order Book*.
35. George H. Murdoch to Gen. John Robertson, Berrien Springs, Michigan, 5 September 1881, Folder no. 8, "Letters and Telegrams— 1861–1881, *1st MSS Records*.
36. Cutcheon, *20th Michigan*, 117.
37. *OR*, 36–1, 243, 973.
38. Cutcheon, *20th Michigan*, 117.
39. See Appendix I for casualties at Spotsylvania.
40. Cutcheon, *20th Michigan*, 119.
41. Ibid., 119.
42. Grant, *Personal Memoirs*, 225.
43. Cutcheon, *20th Michigan*, 120.
44. Matter, *If It Takes All Summer*, 139; Cutcheon, *20th Michigan*, 120.
45. *OR*, 36–1, 243, 973.
46. George Stone to Walter Buckbee, Battle Creek, Michigan, 5 January 1920, Buckbee Papers.

47. Buckbee Memoirs; Affidavit of Ed. J. Buckbee, Detroit, Michigan, 4 November 1865, Folder 9, *1st MSS Records*.

48. *OR*, 36–1, 242, 969; Cutcheon, *20th Michigan*, 120.

49. Cutcheon, *20th Michigan*, 120.

50. *OR*, 36–1, 240, 962; 240, 977.

51. Ibid.

52. Cutcheon, *20th Michigan*, 120.

53. Ibid., 121.

54. Folder no. 1: "List of Officers and Residences," 1st MSS Records.

55. Matter, *If It Takes All Summer*, 174.

56. Ibid.

57. *OR*, 36–2, 247, 984–985.

58. Matter, *If It Takes All Summer*, 223–224.

59. Ibid. The Second Michigan Infantry was pulled from the Second Brigade in the morning and sent across the Ni River to support Captain Wright's Fourteenth Massachusetts Battery on the Court House Road near the battle line of 9 May. Later in the day, the Second was ordered to protect Capt. Edward W. Rogers's Nineteenth New York Battery farther to the right. See Cutcheon, *20th Michigan*, 122.

60. Cutcheon, *20th Michigan*, 122.

61. Ibid., 121–122.

62. *OR*, 36–1, 243, 973–974.

63. Cutcheon, *20th Michigan*, 122.

64. *OR*, 36–1, 242, 969.

65. Ibid., 36–1, 245, 979–980.

66. *OR*, 36–1, 242, 969.

67. Ibid.

68. Cutcheon, *20th Michigan*, 122.

69. Ibid., 124.

70. *OR*, 36–1, 243, 974.

71. Floyd B. Haight, "Shot for Shot," Minnie Dubbs Millbrook, ed., *Twice Told Tales of Michigan and Her Soldiers in the Civil War* (Lansing, MI: Michigan Civil War Centennial Observance Commission, 1966), 77–78.

72. Cutcheon, *20th Michigan*, 122.

73. Matter, *If It Takes All Summer*, 239.

74. J. H. Lane, "History of Lane's North Carolina Brigade," *Southern Historical Society Papers*, vol. 9, no. 4 (April 1881), 149.

75. Ibid.; *OR*, 36–1, 242, 969–970; *OR*, 36–1, 234, 944.

76. Lt. Col. F. W. Swift, "My Experiences as a Prisoner of War," War Paper No. 3, *Michigan Commandery, Military Order of the Loyal Legion of the United States* (Detroit, MI: Wm. S. Ostler, Printer, 1888), 4.

77. Robertson, *Michigan in the War*, 381; Lane, "The History of Lane's North Carolina Brigade," 151.

78. Matter, *If It Takes All Summer*, 240.
79. Crater, *50th Pennsylvania*, 56–57.
80. *OR*, 36–1, 242, 969–970.
81. Lane, "History of Lane's North Carolina Brigade," 152–153.
82. Cutcheon, *20th Michigan*, 124.
83. *OR*, 36–1, 242, 970.
84. Ypsilanti *Commercial*, 4 November 1864, 3.
85. "History," Folder no. 9, *1st MSS Records*.
86. Ibid. Major Moody formerly captained a steamboat on Lake Superior. Wounded again in a fight at Bethesda Church, Virginia, on 3 June 1864, Moody had his right arm amputated. He died from the effects of the operation and was buried in Washington, DC. See Detroit *Advertiser and Tribune*, 18 June 1864, 4; 25 June 1864, 1.
87. "History," Folder no.9, *1st MSS Records*.
88. Ibid.
89. Jackson *Citizen*, 25 May 1864, 2.
90. Ibid.; Hauptman, *Between Two Fires*, 138.
91. Fox, *What I Remember*, 76, 77, 82, 83; *Record of Service, 1st MSS*, 40, 41, 61.
92. Ibid.
93. Jackson *Citizen*, 25 May 1864, 2.
94. Hillsdale *Standard*, 26 July 1864, 1; Jackson *Citizen*, 25 May 1864, 2.
95. Jackson *Citizen*, 25 May 1864, 3.
96. "History," Folder no. 9, *1st MSS Records*.
97. Farling, *Life in the Army*, 13.
98. *OR*, 36–1, 243, 974; Charles V. DeLand, "In Hospital, Washington, D.C.," 26 May 1864, *Letter and Order Book*.
99. *OR*, 36–1, 234, 944.
100. "Proceedings of a General Court Martial Held near Petersburg, Virginia, June 28, 1864," Records of the Judge Advocate General's Office, Court Martial Case Files, No. NN 2032, Record Group 153, Captain Hooker A. DeLand, National Archives, Washington, DC.
101. "History," Folder no. 9, *1st MSS Records*.
102. Buckbee Memoirs.
103. Cutcheon, *20th Michigan*, 124.
104. Ibid.
105. Folder no. 9: "History," *1st MSS Records*.
106. Ibid.
107. *OR*, 36–1, 242, 970.
108. Ibid., 36–1, 243, 974.
109. Charles V. DeLand, Compiled Military Service File, National Archives, Washington, DC.
110. Charles V. DeLand to Adj. Gen. John Robertson, East Saginaw, Michigan, 19 November 1865, Folder no. 5: "Report of Wounds and Vacancies," *1st MSS Records*.

111. Charles V. DeLand, Compiled Military Service File, National Archives, Washington, DC.
112. Ibid.
113. Jackson *Eagle*, 16 July 1864, 2; Marshall *Democratic Expounder*, 28 July 1864, 2.
114. Jackson *Eagle*, 16 July 1864, 2.
115. Ibid.
116. Jackson *Citizen*, 20 July 1864, 2.
117. Detroit *Advertiser and Tribune*, 12 August 1864, 1.
118. Jonesville *Weekly Independent*, 4 August 1864, 3.
119. Detroit *Advertiser and Tribune*, 3 August 1864, 4.
120. "Special Orders No. 41, Headquarters, 3rd Division, 9th A. Corps, Before Petersburg, Va., July 21st 1864," Charles V. DeLand, Compiled Military Service File, National Archives, Washington DC.
121. Charles V. DeLand to "Friend James," nd., np, DeLand–Crary Papers.
122. Jackson *Citizen*, 25 May 1864, 2.
123. Crater, *50th Pennsylvania*, 54–62.
124. Cutcheon, *20th Michigan*, 124.
125. "Casualties and Alteration," 26 October 1864, Folder no. 9: "History," *1st MSS Records*.
126. Jackson *Citizen*, 25 May 1864, 2.
127. Robertson, *Michigan in the War*, 472. Officially, the casualties for Willcox's division for the battles around Spotsylvania:

	Killed		Christ's Brigade Wounded		Missing	
	Officers	Men	Officers	Men	Officers	Men
1st SS	1	37	6	115	0	3
20th MI	4	13	3	105	0	19
79th NY	3	3	1	12	0	0
60th OH	0	22	4	55	0	8
50th PA	0	23	4	105	3	110
			Hartranft's Brigade			
2nd MI	1	1	1	9	0	0
8th MI	0	9	4	44	0	0
17th MI	2	20	1	33	7	89
27th MI	0	30	4	152	0	9
109th NY	1	24	3	83	0	29
51st PA	1	7	3	88	2	30

See: *OR*, 36–1, 149.

128. "Regimental Papers, 1st MSS." Although no Sharpshooter was able to identify Major Piper's body, one Southerner did. Capt. W. T. Nicholson of the Thirty-seventh North Carolina noticed "a very

fine water-proof coat" on a dead Union officer after the fighting. Pulling the coat off the dead man he carried it to the rear. Once there, Nicholson opened the coat and discovered the diary of Major Piper in it. Nicholson kept the coat but gave the diary to a friend, who used it till the war's end. See W. D. Alexander, "Grant Outgeneraled," *Confederate Veteran*, vol. 31, no. 6 (June 1923), 212.

129. *Record of Service, 1st MSS*, 37.

130. "Regimental Papers, 1st MSS."

131. *Descriptive Rolls*, 54.

132. Ibid., 50; *Record of Service, 1st MSS*, 98.

133. *Record of Service, 1st MSS*, 72.

134. Ibid., 7.

135. Tombstone inscription, St. Anne Cemetery, Mackinac Island, Michigan; *Descriptive Rolls*, 76.

136. Detroit *Advertiser and Tribune*, 23 June 1864, 4; Saginaw *Weekly Enterprise*, 30 June 1864, 2. The old accounts lead to some confusion as to where Mwa-ke-we-naw was buried. One newspaper said he was to be sent to his relatives in Bear River (now Petoskey, Michigan). Other notices stated the body was to be either temporarily or permanently buried in the City Cemetery (now Brady Hill Cemetery) in Saginaw. See Saginaw *Weekly Enterprise*, 30 June 1864, 2; Detroit *Advertiser and Tribune*, 4 August 1864, 4; *Record of Service, 1st MSS*, 64. Today, Mwa-ke-we-naw's government headstone can be found in Brady Hill Cemetery in Saginaw.

137. Detroit *Advertiser and Tribune*, 30 July 1864, 1.

138. Haight, "Shot for Shot," 78. James Haight's grandson, who recalled the incident, wrote, "I well remember that my grandfather, when questioned about the Confederate soldier found dead behind the log, would walk away to avoid having to admit he had ever shot a man. He was a staunch admirer of Lincoln and the ideas for which he stood but the war to him was a sad experience," 79.

139. Detroit *Advertiser and Tribune*, 3 June 1864, 4.

140. Charles V. DeLand to Capt. Thomas Mathews, AAAG, 16 September 1864, *Letter and Order Book*; *Record of Service, 1st MSS*, 26.

141. Charles V. DeLand to Capt. Thomas Mathews, AAAG, 16 September 1864, *Letter and Order Book*; *Record of Service, 1st MSS*, 45.

142. Detroit *Free Press*, 31 May 1864, 1.

143. Detroit *Advertiser and Tribune*, 19 May 1864, 1.

144. Edwin V. Andress, Pension Record, National Archives, Washington, DC. The hospital steward George Warren saw most of the wounded Sharpshooters when they were treated in the division hospital. A gossipy sort of man, Warren did not care for a number of the officers, but he certainly loved the regiment. A regular correspondent with his hometown newspaper (the Hillsdale *Standard*), he duly reported all that fell to him. Captain Andress received no accolades from Warren when the latter referred to the officer's "

'foot' wound obtained some doubtful way or other." See Hillsdale *Standard*, 26 July 1864, 1.

145. Detroit *Advertiser and Tribune*, 19 May 1864, 1.
146. Randall Reminiscences, 5 May 1864.
147. Ibid.
148. Ibid., 6 May 1864. The original First Michigan Infantry was enlisted for three months. When the boys returned home, the regiment was reconstituted as a three-year regiment.
149. Ibid., 5 May 1864.
150. Ibid., 6 May 1864.
151. Ibid., 7 May 1864.
152. Fox, *What I Remember*, 64–66.
153. George Minnis to Mother, Fredericksburg, Virginia, 19 May 1864, Larry Massie Collection, Regional History Collections, Western Michigan University, Kalamazoo, MI.
154. Randall Reminiscences, 7 May 1864.
155. Gates Diary, 17 May 1864.
156. Randall Reminiscences, 7 May 1864.
157. Ibid.
158. Fox, *What I Remember*, 67–68.
159. Randall Reminiscences, 12 May 1864.
160. Ibid., 14 May 1864.
161. E. M. Law, "From the Wilderness to Cold Harbor," *Battles and Leaders of the Civil War*, vol. 4, 134.
162. Randall Reminiscences, 18 May 1864.
163. Ibid., 23 May 1864.

Chapter 8

1. Jackson *Eagle*, 23 July 1864, 4; Marshall *Democratic Expounder*, 7 July 1864, 2.
2. Claudius Buchanan Grant, Diary and Correspondence, 18 May 1864, Michigan Historical Collections, Bentley Library, University of Michigan, Ann Arbor, Michigan (hereafter cited as Grant Papers). Grant was an officer in the Twentieth Michigan Infantry.
3. Cutcheon, *20th Michigan*, 126.
4. *OR*, 36–1, 242, 971; Cutcheon, *20th Michigan*, 127.
5. *OR*, 36–1, 242, 971.
6. Randall Reminiscences, 25 May 1864.
7. *OR*, 36–1, 234, 945; Cutcheon, *20th Michigan*, 127.
8. Grant Papers, 24 May 1864.
9. "Casualties and Alterations," File no. 9: "History," 26 October 1864, *1st MSS Records*. See Appendix A for a full list of casualties.
10. *Record of Service, 1st MSS*, 35.
11. Randall Reminiscences, 26 May 1864.

12. Crater, *50th Pennsylvania*, 62.
13. Cutcheon, *20th Michigan*, 127.
14. *OR*, 36–1, 245, 980.
15. Buckbee Memoirs.
16. Ibid.
17. Ibid.
18. Ibid.
19. Cutcheon, *20th Michigan*, 127.
20. Randall Reminiscences, 29 May 1864.
21. Buckbee Memoirs.
22. Randall Reminiscences, 25 May 1864.
23. Ibid., 27 May 1864.
24. Ibid., 29 May 1864.
25. Cutcheon, *20th Michigan*, 127.
26. Ibid., 128.
27. *OR*, 36–1, 242, 971.
28. *Record of Service, 1st MSS*, 91; Fox, *What I Remember*, 87; Farling, *Life in the Army*, 13.
29. Randall Reminiscences, 1 June 1864.
30. George W. Campbell, "Old Choctaw," *The National Tribune*, 11 September 1913, 7.
31. See Appendix A for list of casualties.
32. *OR*, 36–1, 242, 971; Lansing *State Republican*, 29 June 1864, 1; "Casualties and Alterations," Folder no. 9: "History," 26 October 1964, *1st MSS Records*.
33. Buckbee Memoirs.
34. Hillsdale *Standard*, 28 June 1864, 2.
35. Lansing *State Republican*, 27 July 1864, 3.
36. Edward J. Buckbee to his mother, In the Field, 7 June 1864, Buckbee Papers.
37. Ibid.
38. Ibid.
39. *Record of Service, 1st MSS*, 74.
40. The army's incessant movement as it tried to sidle around the Confederates delayed much of the paperwork that the various components of the vast military machine of the Union had to complete. Officers became sick or wounded, and some were killed in action or captured. Official correspondence was lost or delayed somewhere behind the lines. As a result, much of the day-to-day affairs of the Sharpshooters was never recorded. Except for one short report, the official record is silent on their activities from the beginning of May until the end of July. It was during this period that the regiment fought most of its battles and sustained most of its casualties.
41. Edward J. Buckbee to his mother, In the Field, 7 June 1864, Buckbee Papers.
42. Buckbee Memoirs.

43. Ibid.
44. Ibid.
45. "Casualties and Alterations," Folder no. 9: "History," 26 October 1864, *1st MSS Records*. See Appendix A for list of casualties.
46. Capt. Elmer C. Dicey to Adj. Gen. John Robertson, Petersburg, Virginia, 5 July 1864, *Letter and Order Book*; Cutcheon, *20th Michigan*, 130.
47. Evans Papers.
48. Cutcheon, *20th Michigan*, 131.
49. Ibid.
50. Hillsdale *Standard*, 26 July 1864, 1.
51. Randall Renminiscences, 16 June 1864.
52. Ibid.
53. Ibid.
54. Ibid.
55. Hillsdale *Standard*, 5 July 1864, 2.
56. Cutcheon, *20th Michigan*, 131.
57. Buckbee Memoirs.
58. W. F. Beyer and O. F. Keydel, eds., *Deeds of Valor* (Detroit: Perrien–Keydel Co., 1905), 366.
59. Crater, *50th Pennsylvania*, 65.
60. Cutcheon, *20th Michigan*, 132.
61. Ibid.
62. Ibid.
63. Ibid., 133.
64. Hillsdale *Standard*, 5 July 1864, 2.
65. Ibid.
66. *OR*, 40–1, 195, 571; Cutcheon, *20th Michigan*, 133; Hillsdale *Standard*, 5 July 1864, 2.
67. George H. Murdoch, "Before Petersburg," Battle Creek *Daily Morning Call*, 30 May 1886, n.p., Kimball House Historical Society Archives, Battle Creek, MI (hereafter cited as Murdoch, "Before Petersburg").
68. Farling, *Life in the Army*, 19.
69. *OR*, 40–1, 176, 532.
70. Ibid., 40–1, 195, 572.
71. Ibid., 40–1, 176, 533.
72. Ibid., 40–1, 195, 572.
73. Murdoch, "Before Petersburg."
74. Buckbee Memoirs.
75. Ibid.
76. Leverette N. Case to Mollie Church, near Petersburgh, 19 June 1864, Buckbee Papers.
77. George Murdoch to Adj. Gen. John Robertson, Berrien Springs, Michigan, 8 August 1881, *1st MSS Records*.
78. Ibid.

79. Maj. Gen. Andrew A. Humphreys, Meade's Chief of Staff, believed the capture of the enemy entrenchments took place after sunset, "as I witnessed the contest from a near point of view, and the attack had not succeeded up to the time of my leaving the Ninth Corps, which was after dark." He added, that since Burnside and Warren were close by, "we cannot suppose that either would have failed to throw forward more troops at once when they learnt the intrenchment [sic] was carried. The line was probably retaken before either knew it had been captured." See A. A. Humphreys, *The Virginia Campaigns of '64 and '65* (New York: Charles Scribner's Sons, 1883), 219.
80. Murdoch, "Before Petersburg."
81. Detroit *Advertiser and Tribune*, 4 July 1864, 4.
82. Ibid.; Fox, *What I Remember*, 108.
83. Lansing *State Republican*, 6 July 1864, 2.
84. Clark, *North Carolina in the War*, vol. 2, 621–622; G. T. Beauregard, "Four Days of Battle at Petersburg," *Battles and Leaders of the Civil War*, vol. 4, 542.
85. Clark, *North Carolina in the War*, vol. 2, 622.
86. Lansing *State Republican*, 6 July 1864, 2; Detroit *Advertiser and Tribune*, 29 June 1864, 4; Murdoch, "Before Petersburg."
87. Leverette N. Case to Mollie Church, near Petersburg, 19 June 1864, Buckbee Papers; Lansing *State Republican*, 6 July 1864, 2; Detroit *Advertiser and Tribune*, 29 June 1864, 4.
88. Lansing *State Republican*, 6 July 1864, 2.
89. Randall Reminiscences, 17 June 1864.
90. George Murdoch to Adj. Gen. John Robertson, Berrien Springs, Michigan, 8 August 1881, Folder no. 8: "Letters and Telegrams— 1861–1881, *1st MSS Records*; Minnie Dubbs Millbrook, *A Study in Valor—Michigan Medal of Honor Winners in the Civil War* (Lansing, MI: Michigan Civil War Centennial Observance Committee, 1966), 14. Lt. Joseph Bellair also saw the scene from a short distance.
91. "Statement by George H. Murdoch," n.d., n.p., Folder no. 9: "History," *1st MSS Records*.
92. Buckbee Memoirs.
93. Murdoch, "Before Petersburg." Murdoch stated that Arthur Buchanan stabbed the Confederate colonel, but Arthur had died at Spotsylvania; Buckbee Memoirs. Buckbee also agreed that Colonel Jones was bayoneted; but the Confederates reported that Jones (whose body was not recovered), was shot three times in the charge, see Clark, *North Carolina Troops in the War*, vol. 2, 622.
94. Murdoch, "Before Petersburg."
95. Clark, *North Carolina in the War*, vol. 2, 622.
96. Detroit *Advertiser and Tribune*, 29 June 1864, 4; Hillsdale *Standard*, 28 June 1864, 2.

97. Millbrook, *A Study in Valor*, 14.
98. Fox, *What I Remember*, 105, 107. See also Appendix A for a full list of casualties.
99. Ibid., 108; Compiled Military Record of Thomas A. Gaffney, National Archives, Washington, DC.
100. Forty years after the 17 June fight, Andrew Knight, a sergeant in the Twentieth Michigan and brother of Lt. George Knight, sought information as to the whereabouts of his brother's sword, which had been presented to him by the citizens of Battle Creek and which was never found after that night. He wrote to *Confederate Veteran*, and his inquiry was answered by Capt. Philip J. Johnson of the Thirty-fifth North Carolina. The Tarheels had to pull back immediately after the fight, "and our dead were in the enemy's hands, so I think it is likely that some one of his own army got Lieutenant Knight's sword." See "Sword of Lieut. Knight, a Federal," *Confederate Veteran*, vol. 11, no. 1 (January 1903), 25.
101. Fox, *What I Remember*, 110.
102. Ibid., 108; Detroit *Advertiser and Tribune*, 4 August 1864, 4; Grand Traverse *Herald*, 29 July 1864, 3; and 12 August 1864, 3.
103. Berry, *Loss of the Sultana*, 335–337; Buckbee Memoirs.
104. Leverette N. Case to Mollie Church, Near Petersburg, 19 June 1864, Buckbee Papers.
105. Buckbee Memoirs.
106. Berry, *Loss of the Sultana*, 335.
107. Detroit *Advertiser and Tribune*, 4 July 1864, 4.
108. Hillsdale *Standard*, 28 June 1864, 2.
109. Affidavit from George A. Caine, Folder no. 9: "History," *1st MSS Records*.
110. Charles V. DeLand to Adj. Gen. John Robertson, Before Petersburg, Va., 5 August 1864, *Letter and Order Book*; Hillsdale *Standard*, 28 June 1864, 2; Randall Reminiscences, 17 June 1864; *OR*, 40–1, 203, 585; Buckbee Papers; Reminiscences of Ira Evans, Evans Papers.
111. In late November 1864 an order came down from the secretary of war. Although adhered to by line officers throughout the army for months, the government finally relaxed its rules regarding badges of rank. General Order No. 286 permitted officers to forgo any ornamentation on overcoats or hats. Sashes and epaulettes were no longer required; shoulder straps were no longer necessary. Enemy sharpshooters habitually tried to pick off officers. Starting with Grant's Overland Campaign, many officers eschewed rank identification for the rest of the war. It took the war department many months to catch up to reality. See General Order No. 286, War Department, Washington, DC, 22 November 1864, Buckbee Papers.
112. Buckbee Memoirs. Buckbee mentioned that, as a token of appreciation, Captain Johnson allowed him the next day (under guard, of course) to go to the Appomattox River and take a bath, his first

since crossing the Rapidan River in early May.

113. *Record of Service, 1st MSS*, 97, 24, 22, 60, 39, 18, 40. See Appendix for list of casualties.

114. Clark, *North Carolina in the War*, vol. 2, 622; Buckbee Memoirs.

115. Murdoch, "Before Petersburg."

116. Buckbee Memoirs.

117. Clark, *North Carolina in the War*, vol. 3, 361–362.

118. Buckbee Memoirs.

119. Ibid.

120. Pamela J. Dobson, ed., *The Tree that Never Dies: Oral History of the Michigan Indians* (Grand Rapids, MI: Grand Rapids Public Library, 1978), 129.

121. Humphreys, *The Virginia Campaigns of '64 and '65*, 219.

122. Murdoch, "Before Petersburg."

123. Hillsdale *Standard*, 26 July 1864, 1.

124. Proceedings of a General Court Martial, Near Petersburg, Virginia, June–July, 1864, Registers of the Records of the Proceedings of the U.S. Army, General Courts-Martial, 1809–1890, roll 5, vols. 11 and 12, NN 2032, Captain Hooker A. DeLand and 1st Lieutenant Moses A. Powell, 1st Michigan Sharpshooters, National Archives, Washington, DC (hereafter cited as Court Martial Records—Hooker A. DeLand and Moses A. Powell), Testimony of Lt. Charles G. Conn.

125. Hillsdale *Standard*, 28 June 1864, 2.

126. Evans Papers.

127. Hillsdale *Standard*, 28 June 1864, 2; *Record of Service, 1st MSS*, 17.

128. Hillsdale *Standard*, 26 July 1864, 1.

129. *OR*, 40–1, 203, 585.

130. Hillsdale *Standard*, 5 July 1864, 2.

131. *OR*, 40–1, 203, 585.

132. Hillsdale *Standard*, 5 July 1864, 2.

133. *OR*, 40–1, 203, 585.

134. Detroit *Advertiser and Tribune*, 14 July 1864, 4.

135. Crater, *50th Pennsylvania*, 66.

136. *OR*, 40–1, 203, 585. Humphrey was a known entity to the veterans of Willcox's division. He joined the Second Michigan in April 1861 as captain of Company D. In February 1863 the governor commissioned him colonel of the regiment. A brigade commander in the East Tennessee campaign, the men had great faith in his leadership. Back in early June Maj. Claudius Grant of the Twentieth Michigan watched a debacle develop in the Second Brigade and blamed the brigade command. "Our Brig. Hd Qrs were probably drunk as usual," he wrote contemptuously in his diary, "and none seemed to know how [the skirmish] was going. . . . It is a burning shame to put men under such whisky bloats. Would that Col Humphrey was in command." See Grant Papers, Diary, 7 June 1864.

137. *OR*, 40–1, 195, 573; Of that number only 129 were listed as miss-

ing. Total casualties for the Ninth Corps for the two days was 2,903, broken down as follows: Killed—377, wounded—1957, missing—569. See *Report of the Committee on the Conduct of the War on the Attack on Petersburg on the 30th Day of July, 1864* (Washington, DC: Government Printing Office, 1865) (hereafter cited as *Attack on Petersburg*), 159.

138. Hillsdale *Standard*, 5 July 1864, 2.
139. Fox, *What I Remember*, 133.
140. Hillsdale *Standard*, 28 June 1864, 2.
141. Court Martial Records—Hooker A. DeLand and Moses A. Powell, Testimony of Lt. Charles G. Conn. Answering testimony, Conn stated the numbers fit for service on the three consecutive dates after the 17 June fight: "On the 18th 61, on the 19th over 70 and on the 20th over 100."
142. Detroit *Advertiser and Tribune*, 29 June 1864, 4.
143. Leverette N. Case to Mollie Church, Near Petersburg, Va., 19 June 1864, Buckbee Papers.
144. Crater, *50th Pennsylvania*, 66–67.
145. Cutcheon, *20th Michigan*, 135.
146. Elmer Dicey to Adj. Gen. John Robertson, Before Petersburg, VA, 5 July 1864, *Letter and Order Book*.
147. Ibid.
148. Ibid., Regimental Order No. 19, Before Petersburg, VA, 30 June 1864.
149. Copy of General Orders No. 20, Headquarters 3rd Division, 9th Army Corps, Near Petersburg, 20 June 1864, Folder no. 3: "Recommendations, Promotions, Appointments," *1st MSS Records*; Detroit *Free Press*, 29 June 1864, 1.
150. Niles *Republican*, 2 July 1864, 3.
151. Jackson *Citizen*, 6 July 1864, 3.
152. Hillsdale *Standard*, 19 July 1864, 1.

Chapter 9

1. *Record of Service, 1st MSS*, 95.
2. Special Order No. 189, 27 May 1864, and Special Order No. 421, 5 August 1865, War Department, Adjutant General's Office, Washingon, DC, Folder No. 4: "Removals of Desertions, Discharges, Etc.," *1st MSS Records*.
3. Hillsdale *Standard*, 26 July 1864, 1. One officer in particular he cited was Capt. Edwin V. Andress of Company K who suffered "a 'foot' wound obtained some doubtful way or other at Spotsylvania."
4. Unless otherwise noted, all particulars regarding the courts-martial of Capt. Hooker A. DeLand and 1st Lt. Moses A. Powell are from Court Martial Records—Hooker A. DeLand and Moses A. Powell.

5. Buckbee Memoirs.
6. Niles *Republican*, 23 July 1864, 3.
7. *Record of Service of Michigan Volunteers in the Civil War 1861–1865: 1st Regiment Michigan Infantry* (Kalamazoo, MI: Ihling Bros. & Everard, n.d.), 35; DeLand, *Jackson County*, 395.
8. Jackson *Citizen*, 20 July 1864, 3.
9. Grant Papers, Diary, 8 July 1864.
10. Randall Reminiscences, 10 July 1863.
11. Detroit *Free Press*, 22 July 1864, 1.
12. Mary G. DeLand to James S. DeLand, Jackson, Michigan, 13 April 1865, DeLand–Crary Papers.

Chapter 10

1. Randall Reminiscences, 23 June 1864.
2. Ibid.
3. Detroit *Advertiser and Tribune*, 3 August 1864, 4; Lansing *State Republican*, 27 July 1864, 3.
4. Randall Reminiscences, 25 June 1864.
5. Cutcheon, *20th Michigan*, 136–137.
6. Detroit *Advertiser and Tribune*, 14 July 1864, 4.
7. Randall Reminiscences, 25 June 1864.
8. Ibid.
9. Ibid., 26 June 1864; Fox, *What I Remember*, 123.
10. Farling, *Life in the Army*, 13.
11. Ibid., 13–15.
12. Saginaw *Weekly Enterprise*, 28 July 1864, 3; *Record of Service, 1st MSS*, 65.
13. Fox, *What I Remember*, 123.
14. Ibid., 124.
15. *Record of Service, 1st MSS*, 69.
16. Fox, *What I Remember*, 125.
17. Randall Reminiscences, 30 June 1864.
18. Ibid.
19. Ibid., 4 July 1864.
20. Quarterly Returns, "Regimental Papers, 1st MSS."
21. Regimental Order No. 26, Before Petersburg, Va., 6 July 1864, *Letter and Order Book*.
22. Hartwick and Tuller, *Oceana County*, 53, 239.
23. Fox, *What I Remember*, 127.
24. *Record of Service, 1st MSS*, 13.
25. Ypsilanti *Commercial*, 22 July 1864, 1.
26. Robertson, *Michigan in the War*, 128–130.
27. Ibid., 127–128; Coldwater *Union Sentinel*, 27 May 1864, 3; 3 June 1864, 3.

28. Coldwater *Union Sentinel*, 19 August 1864, 2.

29. Ibid., 27 May 1864, 3; 17 June 1864, 3; 24 June 1864, 3; 15 July 1864, 3.

30. Hillsdale *Standard*, 5 July 1864, 2.

31. Port Huron *Press*, 27 July 1864, 3; *Detroit Advertiser and Tribune*, 14 July 1864, 4.

32. Coldwater *Union Sentinel*, 8 July 1864, 3.

33. Judson Leroy Day II, *The Baptists of Michigan and the Civil War* (Lansing, Michigan: Michigan Civil War Observance Commission, 1965), 11.

34. Coldwater *Union Sentinel*, 26 August 1864, 3.

35. Regimental Order No. 22, Before Petersburg, 11 July 1864, *Letter and Order Book*. It seems the national colors (what was left of them) was put away at this time. The Sharpshooters would follow their state flag until the next battle.

36. Regimental Order No. 27, Before Petersburg, 13 July 1864, *Letter and Order Book*.

37. Ibid., Regimental Order No. 25, Before Petersburg, Va., 12 July 1864.

38. Randall Reminiscences, 10 July 1864.

39. Jonesville *Weekly Independent*, 4 August 1864, 3; Buckbee Papers.

40. James S. DeLand to Adj. Gen. John Robertson, East Saginaw, Michigan, 20 November 1865, Folder no. 9: "History," *1st MSS Records*.

41. Cutcheon, *20th Michigan*, 137.

42. Regimental Order No. 24, Before Petersburg, 12 July 1864, *Letter and Record Book*.

43. Randall Reminiscences, 9 July 1864.

44. Ibid., 24 July 1864.

45. Detroit *Advertiser and Tribune*, 18 July 1864, 1.

46. Randall Reminiscences, 9 July 1864.

47. Ibid., 22 July 1864.

48. Cutcheon, *20th Michigan*, 137.

49. Randall Reminiscences, 24 July 1864.

50. The Confederates called this position "Davidson's Battery." See Cutcheon, "Assault on Petersburg," 129.

51. Randall Reminiscences, 24 July 1864.

52. Ibid.

53. Cutcheon, "Assault on Petersburg," 129.

54. Cutcheon, *20th Michigan*, 138; Randall Reminiscences, 27 July 1864.

55. Cutcheon, *20th Michigan*, 138.

56. William H. Powell, "The Battle of the Petersburg Crater," *Battles and Leaders of the Civil War*, vol. 4), 545–549.

57. Ypsilanti *Commercial*, 12 August 1864, 2.

58. Ibid.

59. Randall Reminiscences, "Incidents of the Battle."
60. *OR*, 40–1, 204, 586.
61. *Attack on Petersburg*, 206.
62. Cutcheon, "Assault on Petersburg," 131.
63. Ypsilanti *Commercial*, 12 August 1864, 2.
64. Ibid.
65. *OR*, 40–1, 195, 574.
66. Claudius Grant to his wife, Before Petersburg, Virginia, 1 August 1864, Grant Papers.
67. Randall Reminiscences, "Incidents of the Battle."
68. Cutcheon, "Assault on Petersburg," 134.
69. *OR*, 40–1, 195, 574–575.
70. Reminiscences of Ira Evans, Evans Papers.
71. Newspaper article, *Post and Tribune* (no city given), 20 August 1881, Folder E: "Miscellanea," Clarke–DeLand Papers.
72. Charles V. DeLand, Compiled Military Service File, National Archives, Washington, DC; Charles V. DeLand to "Friend James," n.p., n.d., Box 1: "Civil War Correspondence, 1862–1865," DeLand–Crary Papers.
73. Randall Reminiscences, "Incidents of the Battle;" Report of Charles V. DeLand, 3 August 1864, *Letter and Order Book*.
74. Randall Reminiscences, "Incidents of the Battle."
75. Ypsilanti *Commercial*, 12 August 1864, 2.
76. Randall Reminiscences, "Incidents of the Battle."
77. Ibid.
78. Ypsilanti *Commercial*, 12 August 1864, 2.
79. *OR, 40–1, 204, 586.*
80. Randall Reminiscences, "Incidents of Battle."
81. *Record of Service, 1st MSS*, 28; Millbrook, *A Study in Valor*, 44.
82. Randall Reminiscences, "Incidents of Battle."
83. Ypsilanti *Commercial*, 12 August 1864, 2.
84. "The Petersburg Grays," *Southern Historical Society Papers*, vol. 36 (1908), 360.
85. George S. Bernard, "The Battle of the Crater," *Southern Historical Society Society Papers*, vol. 18 (1890), 15.
86. Ypsilanti *Commercial*, 12 August 1864, 2; Randall Reminiscences, 27 July 1864.
87. Randall Reminiscences, "Incidents of the Battle."
88. Ibid.
89. Bernard, "The Battle of the Crater," 18.
90. Ypsilanti *Commercial*, 12 August 1864, 2.
91. Randall Reminiscences, "Incidents of the Battle."
92. Fox, *What I Remember*, 138.
93. Bernard, "The Battle of the Crater," 18.
94. Ypsilanti *Commercial*, 12 August 1864, 2.
95. Maj. Asahel W. Nichols to Capt. Thomas Mathews, AAAG, 28 De-

cember 1864, "Regimental Papers, 1st MSS"; Millbrook, *A Study in Valor*, 45; *The Medal of Honor of the United States Army* (n.p.: Dept. of the Army Public Information Div., 1948), 167.

96. Millbrook, *A Study in Valor*, 45.
97. Floyd Haight to Raymond Herek, Allen Park, MI, 8 November 1986, Author's Collection.
98. Clark, *North Carolina in the War*, vol. 2, 624.
99. John C. Featherston, "Graphic Account of Battle of Crater," *Southern Historical Society Papers*, vol. 33, 1905, 365.
100. Randall Reminiscences, "Incidents of the Battle."
101. Ibid.
102. George Murdoch to his wife, Petersburg, Virginia, 10 August 1864, Berrien County Historical Association, Berrien Springs, Michigan.
103. *Attack on Petersburg*, 159. A further breakdown showed the following: Killed—52 officers, 376 men; wounded—105 officers, 1556 men; missing—87 officers, 1652 men.
104. *OR*, 40–1, 247.
105. Ibid.; Ypsilanti *True Democrat*, 12 August 1864, 2.
106. Featherston, "Graphic Account of Battle of Crater," 367; Cutcheon, *20th Michigan*, 147.
107. Hillsdale *Standard*, 23 August 1864, 2.
108. Ibid.; Arlan K. Gilbert to Raymond Herek, Hillsdale, MI, 6 August 1992, Author's Collection.
109. Detroit *Advertiser and Tribune*, 8 August 1864, 4.
110. Featherston, "Graphic Account of Battle of Crater," 369.
111. Grant Papers, Diary, 1 August 1864.
112. Cutcheon, *20th Michigan*, 147.
113. Hillsdale *Standard*, 23 August 1864, 2.
114. Cutcheon, *20th Michigan*, 145.
115. Byron M. Cutcheon to Zachariah Chandler, Near Petersburgh Va, 13 February 1865, Papers of Zachariah Chandler 1855–1899, Library of Congress, Washington DC. Container No. #3: January 11, 1864–February 12, 1865, Clarke Historical Library, Central Michigan University, Mt. Pleasant, MI.
116. Cutcheon, *20th Michigan*, 145.
117. Ypsilanti *True Democrat*, 12 August 1864, 2.
118. Leverette Case, affidavits, 21 December 1881, 27 December 1881: Charles V. DeLand, Compiled Military Service File, National Archives, Washington DC.
119. Ypsilanti *True Democrat*, 12 August 1864, 2.
120. Regimental Order No. 20, Petersburg, Virginia, 7 July 1864, *Letter and Order Book*.
121. *Record of Service, 1st MSS*, 22.
122. Buckbee Memoirs.
123. Edmond Shaw to George Stone, Grand Rapids, Michigan, October 1903, Folder no. 9: "History," *1st MSS Records*.

124. *Descriptive Rolls*, 21; *Record of Service, 1st MSS*, 22.
125. *Record of Service. 1st MSS*, 29.
126. Ibid., 66; Fox, *What I Remember*, 136.
127. Charles V. DeLand, Compiled Military Service File, National Archives, Washington, DC.
128. Charles V. DeLand to Brig. Gen. John Robertson, Before Petersburg, Virginia, 5 August 1864, *Letter and Order Book*; "Regimental Papers, 1st MSS."
129. Farling, *Life in the Army*, 16.
130. Cutcheon, *20th Michigan*, 147.
131. Detroit *Advertiser and Tribune*, 27 October 1864, 4.

Chapter 11

1. George Murdoch to his Wife, Petersburg, Virginia, 10 August 1864, Berrien County Historical Association, Berrien Springs, Michigan
2. Regimental Order No. 21, Petersburg, Virginia, 10 July 1864, *Letter and Order Book.*
3. Ibid., Battalion Order No. 28, Petersburg, Virginia, 10 August 1864.
4. Hillsdale *Standard*, 26 July 1864, 1.
5. Folder no. 1: "List of Officers and Residences," *1st MSS Records*; Michigan Adjutant General's Office, *Annual Report of the Adjutant General of the State of Michigan, For the Year 1864* (Lansing, MI: John A. Kerr & Co., 1865), 32.
6. Crater, *50th Pennsylvania*, 70.
7. George Murdoch to his Wife, Petersburg, Virginia, 10 August 1864, Berrien County Historical Association, Berrien Springs, Michigan.
8. Fox, *What I Remember*, 141.
9. Charles V. DeLand to Capt. Thomas Mathews, Before Petersburg, 28 July 1864, *Letter and Order Book.*
10. Ibid., Statement by Charles V. DeLand, Before Petersburg, 8 August 1864.
11. *Record of Service, 1st MSS,* 32; Folder no. 1: "List of Officers and Residences," *1st MSS Records;* ibid., Arvin F. Whelan to Gov. Austin Blair, Near Petersburg, Virginia, 22 July 1864, Folder no. 3: "Recommendations, Promotions, Appointments."
12. George Murdoch to Adj. Gen. John Robertson, Berrien Springs, Michigan, 8 August 1881, Folder no. 8: "Letters and Telegrams—1861–1881," *1st MSS Records.*
13. Battalion Order No. 28, Before Petersburg, Virginia, 10 August 1864, *Letter and Order Book.* The demoted noncommissioned officers were Sgt. Andrew P. Himes (Co. A), Sgt. Simon E. Davis (Co. G), Sgt. John S. Paul (Co. E), Cpl. Vanorman Strout (Co. D), Cpl. William B. Hughes (Co. C), and Cpl. J. W. Quackenbush (Co. C).

14. Ibid., Charles V. DeLand to Capt. Thomas Mathews, Petersburg, Virginia, 13 August 1864.
15. Ibid.
16. Ibid.
17. "Reminiscences of Ira Evans," Evans Papers.
18. Fox, *What I Remember*, 141.
19. Ibid.; *Record of Service, 1st MSS*, 59.
20. Fox, *What I Remember*, 142.
21. William Boston, Diary, 15 August 1864, Michigan Historical Collections, Bentley Historical Library, University of Michigan, Ann Arbor, Michigan. Boston was a member of the Twentieth Michigan Infantry.
22. Detroit *Advertiser and Tribune*, 27 October 1864, 4.
23. Cutcheon, *20th Michigan*, 148.
24. Detroit *Advertiser and Tribune*, 5 September 1864, 4.
25. *OR*, 42–1, 218, 596.
26. Detroit *Advertiser and Tribune*, 13 September 1864, 4.
27. Crater, *50th Pennsylvania*, 70.
28. Cutcheon, *20th Michigan,* 149.
29. Fox, *What I Remember*, 144.
30. Cutcheon, *20th Michigan*, 149.
31. Fox, *What I Remember*, 149.
32. Detroit *Advertiser and Tribune*, 5 September 1864, 4.
33. Ibid.
34. *OR*, 42–1, 218, 597.
35. Crater, *50th Pennsylvania*, 71.
36. *OR*, 42–1, 217, 596.
37. Ibid., 42–1, 218, 597; Detroit *Advertiser and Tribune*, 5 September 1864, 4.
38. Crater, *50th Pennsylvania*, 71.
39. Cutcheon, *20th Michigan*, 150.
40. *OR*, 42–1, 217, 596; Cutcheon, *20th Michigan*, 150.
41. *OR*, 42–1, 218, 597; Crater, *50th Pennsylvania*, 71.
42. Cutcheon, *20th Michigan*, 150.
43. Crater, *50th Pennsylvania*, 71.
44. *OR*, 42–1, 219, 597.
45. Ibid., 21–1, 217, 596.
46. Ibid., 42–1, 218, 597.
47. Cutcheon, *20th Michigan*, 151.
48. Detroit *Advertiser and Tribune*, 13 September 1864, 4.
49. Cutcheon, *20th Michigan*, 151.
50. *Descriptive List, 14; Record of Service, 1st MSS*, 52.
51. Detroit *Advertiser and Tribune*, 5 September 1864, 4.
52. David Lane, *A Soldier's Diary, 1861–1865—The Story of a Volunteer* (n.p., 1905), 192.
53. The dead were Noah Cain and W. Samuel Chatfield (both of whom

were killed in action); Gilbert Morehouse, Roland Mills, Thomas Dunning, and William Northrup all died of wounds. Samuel Fitch, Willard Barnes, Nicholas Crilley, James Laraway, and A. J. Lewis succumbed to disease. Discharged for disability were Capt. Lucien Meigs, Silas Beckwith, Oliver Byington, and Luther Huntsley. Missing were William O. Clemans, Willis Coon, and John Kedgnot. Wounded during the month were Oscar McKeel, George C. Marsh, Simon E. Davis, Myron J. Fox, Sgt. John Unrah, and Silas Pierce, the last of whom had his knee cut open with an axe while "slashing" in front of the breastworks. See Detroit *Advertiser and Tribune*, 13 September 1864, 4.

54. Charles V. DeLand to Brig. Gen. L. Thomas, Head Quarters 1st Michigan Sharpshooters, 30 August 1864, *Letter and Order Book*. For a while rumors persisted that the Seventeenth Michigan would be split up, and "our recruits are to be transferred to the First Michigan Sharpshooters, both officers and men, while the old members are to be retained . . . as provost guards." Instead, both old and new members the Seventeenth found themselves detailed as division engineers for the reminder of the siege of Petersburg. See Lane, *A Soldier's Diary*, 262.

55. Charles V. DeLand to Brig. Gen. John Robertson, Before Petersburg, 25 July 1864, *Letter and Order Book*.

56. Ibid.

57. Irwin Journal, 2 September 1864.

58. Cutcheon, *20th Michigan*, 153.

59. Ibid.

60. William Boston to Emma W. Wood, Before Petersburg, 18 September 1864, Boston Letters.

61. Lane, *A Soldier's Diary*, 203.

62. Cutcheon, *20th Michigan*, 153–154. To realize how much recruiting for the Union army was done overseas, especially in the German states, see Murdock, *One Million Men*, 317–324.

63. Regimental Order No. 31, Before Petersburg, 16 September 1864, *Letter and Order Book*.

64. Ibid., Charles V. DeLand to Brig. Gen. L. Thomas, Petersburg, Virginia, 5 September 1864; *Record of Service, 1st MSS*, 89.

65. Charles V. DeLand to Capt. Thomas Mathews, Before Petersburg, 28 July 1864, *Letter and Order Book; Record of Service, 1st MSS*, 31, 85.

66. Charles V. DeLand to Brig. Gen. L. Thomas, Before Petersburg, 5 September 1864, *Letter and Order Book*.

67. Ibid.

68. Ibid.

69. Ibid.

70. Ibid.

71. Ibid.

72. Ibid. Three other bandsmen had already left the regiment. Samuel Davis of Buchanan, Michigan, and George T. Lowrey, another musician from Edwardsburgh, played in the band until their respective discharges for chronic illness came through (about the time the regiment left Camp Douglas). A month later, in April 1864, William B. McNeil of Adamsville, Michigan, the last of the former bandsmen to be accounted for, was discharged for disability. See ibid.

73. Charles V. DeLand to Gen. John Robertson, Headquarters, 1st Michigan Sharpshooters, 10 September 1864, Folder no. 8: "Letters and Telegrams—1861–1881," *1st MSS Records.*

74. Detroit *Advertiser and Tribune*, 27 September 1864, 4.

75. Ibid., 24 August 1864, 1.

76. Descriptive List, 75, 76, 81.

77. *Record of Service, 1st MSS*, 28.

78. Regimental Order No. 32, Before Petersburg, 19 September 1864, *Letter and Order Book.*

79. Ibid., Regimental Order No. 29, Before Petersburg, 1 September 1864.

80. Detroit *Advertiser and Tribune*, 27 September 1864, 4.

81. Irwin Journal, 16 September 1864.

82. Ibid.

83. Catton, *A Stillness at Appomattox*, 359.

84. Lane, *A Soldier's Diary,*

85. Horace Porter, "Five Forks and the Pursuit of Lee," *Battles and Leaders of the Civil War*, vol. 4, 708; Catton, *A Stillness at Appomattox*, 359–360; Roy Meredith and Arthur Meredith, *Mr. Lincoln's Military Railroads* (New York: W. W. Norton & Co., 1979), 178–184; *Lansing Republican*, 15 February 1865, 1.

86. Regimental Order No. 34, Before Petersburg, 27 September 1864, *Letter and Order Book.*

87. Cutcheon, *20th Michigan*, 154; Richard J. Sommers, *Richmond Redeemed: The Siege at Petersburg* (Garden City, NY: Doubleday & Co., 1981), 183.

88. Ibid., 154–155. Humphrey was missed already. If he had not mustered out, he would have commanded the First Division of the Eighteenth Corps. Even though a brigadier general was needed for the position, General Grant had proposed Humphrey's name for the post. See Sommers, *Richmond Redeemed*, 155.

89. Sommers, *Richmond Redeemed*, 232.

90. Ibid.; Dr. Richard J. Sommers to Raymond J. Herek, Carlisle Military Barracks, PA, 22 March 1986, Author's Collection.

91. Sommers, *Richmond Redeemed*, 238, 240–241.

92. Crater, *50th Pennsylvania*, 73.

93. Cutcheon, *20th Michigan*, 155.

94. Sommers, *Richmond Redeemed*, 238.

95. Cutcheon, *20th Michigan*, 155.

96. Ibid.
97. *OR*, 42–1, 198, 565.
98. Ibid. One of Hartranft's problems was that he could not see the ebb and flow of the battle in front of him. A sorghum field blocked his view. See Sommers, *Richmond Redeemed*, 284.
99. Cutcheon, *20th Michigan*, 156.
100. Detroit *Advertiser and Tribune*, 27 October 1864, 4.
101. Joseph O. Bellair to Gov. Henry Crapo, 1st Division Headquarters, Ninth Army Corps, 10 March 1865, Folder no. 3: "Recommendations, Promotions, Appointments," *1st MSS Records; Record of Service, 1st MSS*, 66.
102. Obituary, Vanorman Strout, *The National Tribune*, 2 June 1887, 4.
103. Robertson, *Michigan in the War*, 408.
104. Jackson *Daily Citizen*, 1 October 1890, 7; *Record of Service, 1st MSS*, 66.
105. Cutcheon, *20th Michigan*, 156.
106. Ibid.
107. George Murdoch to Adj. Gen. John Robertson, Berrien Springs, Michigan, 5 September 1881, Folder no. 8: "Letters and Telegrams—1861–1881," *1st MSS Records*.
108. Ibid. The obvious reference that Murdoch made when he said the other regiments formed on the Sharpshooters was that his regiment was the only steady one in the brigade at that juncture.
109. *OR*, 42–1, 198, 565.
110. *Record of Service, 1st MSS*, 89, 84. See Appendix for list of casualties.
111. Charles V. DeLand to Adj. Gen. John Robertson, East Saginaw, Michigan, 14 August 1881, Folder no. 8: "Letters and Telegrams—1861–1881," *1st MSS Records*.
112. *Record of Service, 1st MSS*, 100.
113. For a full list of casualties, see Appendix.
114. Cutcheon, *20th Michigan*, 157.
115. Joel Haynes letter, Near Petersburg, 6 October 1864, Gerald Weaver Collection, Regional History Collections, Western Michigan University, Kalamazoo, MI.
116. Ibid.
117. Ibid.
118. Cutcheon, *20th Michigan*, 157.
119. George Murdoch to Capt. Mathews, Near Petersburg, 24 October 1864, *Letter and Order Book; Record of Service, 1st MSS*, 97.
120. Ibid.
121. Special Order No. 20, 20 October 1864, Letter and Order Book.
122. OR, *42–1, 597*.
123. Detroit *Advertiser and Tribune*, 10 November 1864, 1.
124. Regimental Order No. 41, Before Petersburg, 24 October 1864, *Letter and Order Book*.

125. Special Order No. 21, Headquarters, 1st Michigan Sharpshooters, 26 October 1864, *Letter and Order Book.*
126. William Boston to Emma Wood, Before Petersburg, 28 October 1864, Boston Letters.
127. Cutcheon, *20th Michigan*, 159; Detroit *Advertiser and Tribune*, 10 November 1864, 1.
128. Detroit *Advertiser and Tribune*, 10 November 1864, 1.
129. *OR*, 42–1, 199, 570.
130. Detroit *Advertiser and Tribune*, 10 November 1864, 1; *Record of Service, 1st MSS*, 43; *Descriptive Rolls*, 34. See Appendix for list of casualties.
131. Ibid.
132. Ibid. William Boston of the Twentieth Michigan opined that the rebels "may have heard good news to them." See Boston Diary, 10 October 1864.
133. Crater, *50th Pennsylvania*, 75.
134. Ypsilanti *Commercial*, 4 November 1864, 3.
135. George H. Murdoch to Capt. Bertolette, A.A.A.G., Before Petersburg, 11 October 1864, *Letter and Order Book.*
136. Detroit *Advertiser and Tribune*, 10 November 1864, 1.
137. George H. Murdoch to Brig. Gen. Seth Williams, Adjutant General, Head Quarters, 1st Mch. S.S., 17 November 1864, *Letter and Order Book.*
138. Ibid.; *Record of Service, 1st MSS*, 26.
139. George H. Murdoch to Capt. Thomas Mathews, A.A.A.G., Before Petersburg, Virginia, 24 October 1864, *Letter and Order Book.*
140. Ibid.
141. Ibid.
142. Ibid.; *Record of Service, 1st MSS*, 89.
143. *Descriptive List*, 8.
144. Ibid., 9.
145. Ibid., 20.

Chapter 12

1. Regimental Order No. 45, Before Petersburg, 5 November 1864, and Regimental Order No. 41, Before Petersburg, 24 October 1864, *Letter and Order Book.*
2. *Record of Service, 1st MSS*, 78.
3. Niles *Republican*, 29 October 1864, 2.
4. Detroit *Advertiser and Tribune*, 15 November 1864, 4. Austin Blair chose not to run for another term as governor of Michigan; he wanted to run for the Senate.
5. Fuller, *Messages of the Governors of Michigan*, vol. 2, 484.
6. Detroit *Advertiser and Tribune*, 13 December 1864, 4.

7. Lane, *A Soldier's Diary*, 223.
8. Robertson, *Michigan in the War*, 79–84.
9. Detroit *Advertiser and Tribune*, 15 November 1864, 4.
10. *OR*, 42–3, 578.
11. Regimental Order No. 27, 8 November 1864, *Letter and Order Book*.
12. Niles *Republican*, 26 November 1864, 3.
13. Detroit *Advertiser and Tribune*, 17 November 1864, 4.
14. Ibid.
15. Lane, *A Soldier's Diary*, 228–229.
16. *Descriptive List*, 75; *Record of Service, 1st MSS*, 49.
17. Regimental Order No. 53, Before Petersburg, 26 November 1864, *Letter and Order Book*; *Descriptive List*, 78.
18. Buckbee Memoirs.
19. Cutcheon, *20th Michigan*, 160–161. Originally, the dispositions were to have been a bit different. The Thirteenth Ohio Cavalry was to occupy the line from the extreme right to Battery V *and* garrison the battery. The Sharpshooters had the line from Battery V to Fort McGilvery. The Fiftieth Pennsylvania would garrison Fort McGilvery. The Forty-sixth New York took the line between Fort McGilvery and Battery IX. The Twentieth Michigan garrisoned Battery IX. The Second Michigan occupied the breastworks from Battery IX "to the angle of the works between Batteries Nos. 9 and 10." The Sixtieth Ohio would be held in reserve behind Fort McGilvery. See *OR*, 42–3, General Order No. 34, Second Brigade, First Division, Ninth Army Corps, 30 November 1864, 757.
20. Cutcheon, *20th Michigan*, 161.
21. Ibid.
22. Ibid., 162.
23. Robertson, *Michigan in the War*, 409.
24. Leverette N. Case, "Personal Recollections of the Siege of Petersburg by a Confederate Officer," *Michigan M.O.L.L.U.S.*, vol. 2, 161.
25. Crater, *50th Pennsylvania*, 77.
26. Ibid., 78.
27. Ibid.
28. Detroit *Advertiser and Tribune*, 13 December 1864, 4.
29. Lansing *Republican*, 15 February 1865, 1.
30. Buckbee Memoirs.
31. Ibid.
32. Ibid.
33. Ibid.
34. Detroit *Advertiser and Tribune*, 13 December 1864, 4.
35. Case, "Personal Recollections of a Confederate Officer," 166.
36. Detroit *Advertiser and Tribune*, 13 December 1864, 4.
37. *Record of Service, 1st MSS*, 64; Detroit *Advertiser and Tribune*, 16 December 1864, 4.

38. Detroit *Advertiser and Tribune*, 16 December 1864, 4.
39. *Record of Service, 1st MSS*, 68.
40. Regimental Order No. 11, Head Quarters, 1st Mich. Sharp Shooters, 1 March 1865, *Letter and Order Book*.
41. Buckbee Memoirs.
42. Detroit *Advertiser and Tribune*, 7 November 1865, 4. The casualty report amassed by Michigan's adjutant general's office for 1864 showed the following:

    5th Mich. Inf.: 103 killed or died of wounds, 375 wounded
    8th Mich. Inf.: 86 killed or died of wounds, 287 wounded
    20th Mich. Inf.: 90 killed or died of wounds, 344 wounded
    27th Mich. Inf.: 156 killed or died of wounds. 511 wounded

43. Regimental Order No. 52, Before Petersburg, 26 November 1864, and Regimental Order No. 55, Before Petersburg, 6 December 1864, *Letter and Order Book*.
44. Ibid., Regimental Order No. 54, Before Petersburg, 3 December 1864; Regimental Order No. 55, Before Petersburg, 6 December 1864; Regimental Order No. 57, Before Petersburg, 8 December 1864; Regimental Order No. 58, Before Petersburg, 14 December 1864; Regimental Order No. 60, Before Petersburg, 20 December 1864.
45. Ibid., Regimental Order No. 62, Before Petersburg, 30 December 1864.
46. Ibid., Regimental Order No. 1, Before Petersburg, 1 January 1865.
47. Buckbee Memoirs.
48. Ibid. Captain James Morgan married his sweetheart soon after his return to Michigan. "In consideration of his long captivity and exposure, and from the probability of a course of sickness, which has usually followed a Southern prison life, the Governor kindly transferred him to the 30th [Michigan Infantry] regiment, which was to remain in the State." Morgan commanded a company of the new regiment at Wyandotte. He died suddenly on 31 May 1865. See Robertson, *Michigan in the War*, 892; Ypsilanti *Commercial*, 10 June 1865, 3.
49. Buckbee Memoirs.
50. Ibid.
51. Ibid.
52. Ibid.
53. Ibid.
54. Case, "Personal Recollections of a Confederate Officer," 162.
55. George W. Stone, Pension File, National Archives, Washington, DC.
56. Fox, *What I Remember*, 208–229.
57. Niles *Republican*, 4 February 1865, 3.

58. Regimental Order No. 8, Before Petersburg, 22 February 1865, *Letter and Order Book*.
59. Ibid., Regimental Order No. 11, Before Petersburg, 1 March 1865.
60. Ypsilanti *Commercial*, 17 March 1865, 2.
61. Clinton *Republican*, 3 March 1865, 2.
62. Boston Diary, 29 January 1865, 31 January 1865, 9 February 1865.
63. Lane, *A Soldier's Diary*, 249–250; Boston Diary, 21 February 1865.
64. Boston Diary, 22 February 1865.
65. Ibid., 24 February 1865.
66. Detroit *Advertiser and Tribune*, 9 November 1864, 4; ibid., 8 December 1864, 4; ibid., 14 December 1864, 4; ibid., 30 December 1864, 4. A complete list of returned Sharpshooters from the above sources is as follows:

Marshall Hodges—Co. A	Daniel C. Gore—Co. E
Coland Stafford—Co. B	Dexter Etheridge—Co. F
Charles Keeber—Co. C	Patrick Mulligan—Co. F
Zena D. Ransom—Co. C	Josiah Ross—Co. F
John W. Lathrop—Co. C	James Dennis—Co. F
Augustus Ransom—Co. C	Hugh Kennedy—Co. H
James Sanders—Co. D	Thomas Crossman—Co. H
Stillman G. Goff—Co. D	William Cassell—Co. I
H. Dorr Blakeman—Co. E	Ira Martin—Co. I
William Dingman—Co. E	Payson Wolfe—Co. K
William H. Stubbs—Co. E	John B. Shomin—Co. K
Winfield S. Shanahan—Co. E	Joseph Williams—Co. K
John Riley—Co. E	William Newton—Co. K
Samuel Milligan—Co. E	Louis Marks—Co. K

67. The Leelanau Township Historical Writers Group, *A History of Leelanau Township*, 62.
68. C. D. Bibbins, "The Indian Sharpshooters," *The National Tribune*, 16 October 1917, 7.
69. John L. Ransom, *John Ransom's Andersonville Diary* (Middlebury, VT: Paul S. Eriksson, Publisher, 1986), 93, 101.
70. Blakeman's friend also commented on the Indians a number of times, but it is unknown if he meant the Sharpshooters or not. In one case he mentioned a group of Indians getting together to thwart the designs of the Raiders. On another occasion, he wrote, "Some of them [the Indians] here are despisable cowards." There were Indians from some of the Minnesota regiments at Andersonville. Indians also served in some Wisconsin units, though they were not segregated into specific companies as was done in the First Michigan Sharpshooters. See ibid., 98, 103.
71. William B. Hesseltine, *Civil War Prisons: A Study in War Psychology* (New York: Frederick Ungar Pub. Co., 1958), 169.

72. Charles H. DePuy, "Union and Rebel Prisons Compared," *The National Tribune*, 5 July 1883, 3.
73. *Record of Service, 1st MSS*, 49, 53, 77; Grand Traverse *Herald*, 10 February 1865, 3.
74. The recruits for Company A were Miles Engle, 33, and Benjamin Chase, 47; for Company H—John Baker, 28, Christopher Harris, 22, and John Miller, 22; for Company K—Joseph Hannins, 25, Thomas Moses, 18, Daniel Lidger, 28, David Johns, 19, and William Johns, 20. See Regimental Order No. 8, Before Petersburg, 22 February 1865, *Letter and Order Book*.
75. Ibid., Charles V. DeLand to Capt. Thomas Mathews, A.A.A.G., Before Petersburg, 26 July 1864, and Elmer C. Dicey to Capt. Thomas Mathews, A.A.A.G., Before Petersburg, 26 July 1864.
76. *Record of Service, 1st MSS*, 42.
77. Robertson, *Michigan in the War*, 50. Some men still tried to forestall going into the army. The Sharpshooters must have guffawed when they read the following in the Jackson *Citizen*: "We learn that Nile M. Western, of Concord, who was drafted a few days since, broke off his teeth with a pair of forceps, came to town, and claimed exemption; but imagine his surprise when Surgeon Shank informed him 'he would pass.' Thereupon he procured a substitute." See Jackson *Citizen*, 22 June 1864, 3.
78. Robertson, *Michigan in the War*, 50–51; Murdock, *Patriotism Limited*, 19.
79. Coldwater *Union Sentinel*, 6 August 1864, 3. Men eligible for the draft donated a sum to be paid volunteers. The collected money was commonly called "draft insurance." See Murdock, *One Million Men*, 170–174.
80. *Coldwater Union Sentinel*, 12 August 1864, 3.
81. Robertson, *Michigan in the War*, 50–51.
82. Ibid., 51–59.
83. Captain Burnham was quite a catch. In August 1847 he enlisted in the First Michigan Infantry for service in the Mexican War. He was the only Mexican War veteran to serve in the Sharpshooters. See *The Traverse Region*, 318–319.
84. Capt. John H. Knight to Capt. N. P. Watson, Detroit, Michigan, 1 December 1864, and Brigade Inspector Stephen Clinton to Brig. Gen. H.W. Bonham[?], City Point, Virginia, 3 January 1865, "Regimental Papers, 1st MSS".
85. *OR*, 42–3, Pt. 3, 1114.
86. Ibid., 46–1, 72.
87. *Record of Service, 1st MSS*, 89.
88. Regimental Order No. 25, Before Petersburg, Virginia, 31 March 1865, *Letter and Order Book*.
89. Ibid.; Robertson, *Michigan in the War*, 787, 886.
90. Boston Diary, 2 January 1865.

91. Clinton *Republican*, 3 March 1865, 2.
92. George L. Kilmer, "Gordon's Attack on Fort Stedman," *Battles and Leaders of the Civil War*, vol. 4 (New York: Thomas Yoseloff, 1956) (hereafter cited as Kilmer, "Gordon's Attack"), 580; Lane, *A Soldier's Diary*, 250.
93. All was not perfect in the Union lines, either. Bounty jumpers were being made to see the error of their ways. Since all governmental agencies were offering cash payments, the inducement to enlist was more palatable. The problem was complicated by the fact that some men enlisted two, three, or more times. Once they received their bounty money they were off to another locality for more cash. An enlisted man in the Second Michigan Infantry wrote home telling his folks about the problem bounty jumpers were causing in the army. When caught, their penalty was severe. Usually they paid for their folly at the end of a rope. "One of these scenes is to come off on Friday next, to witness which, as many of the Division as can be spared from the lines, are ordered to assemble." Desertion was something to encourage in the enemy. In your own ranks, it was reprehensible. See Clinton *Republican*, 3 March 1865, 2.
94. Lansing *Republican*, 15 February 1865, 1.
95. Ibid., 3 March 1865, 2; Boston Diary, 26 February 1865; Lane, *A Soldier's Diary*, 250.
96. Regimental Order No. 9, Before Petersburg, 27 February 1865, *Letter and Order Book*.
97. Buckbee Memoirs.
98. Ibid.
99. Ibid.
100. Ibid.
101. Regimental Order No. 18, Before Petersburg, 15 March 1865, *Letter and Order Book*.
102. Evans Papers, "Reminiscences."
103. Petition to Governor Henry Crapo, Folder no. 3: "Recommendations, Promotions, Appointments," *1st MSS Records*. The officers who signed the petition were Capt. George N. Davis, Capt. Joseph O. Bellair, Capt. James S. DeLand, 1st Lt. Leverette N. Case, 1st Lt. H. D. Blakeman, 1st Lt. Milo Dyer, and 1st Lt. Robert Farrell.
104. Ibid.
105. Ed J. Buckbee, Headquarters, 1st Michigan Sharpshooters, 28 March 1865, Buckbee Papers.
106. Asahel Nichols to Brig. Gen. John Robertson, Headquarters, 1st Michigan Sharpshooters, 28 March 1865, Folder no. 3: "Recommendations, Promotions, Appointments," *1st MSS Records*.
107. Ibid., Charles V. DeLand to Brig. Gen. John Robertson, Jackson, Michigan, 7 January 1865; *Record of Service, 1st MSS*, 12, 40.
108. *Record of Service. 1st MSS*, 34.
109. Ibid., 88–89; Sgt. Frank Thayer to Gov. Austin Blair, Before Peters-

burg, Va., 24 July 1864, Folder no. 8, "Letters and Telegrams—1861–1881," *1st MSS Records*.

110. Charles V. DeLand to Brig. Gen. John Robertson, Jackson, Michigan, 7 January 1865, Folder no. 3: "Recommendations, Promotions, Appointments," *1st MSS Records*.

Chapter 13

1. Kilmer, "Gordon's Attack," 579–580.
2. Buckbee Memoirs.
3. Ibid.
4. Kilmer, "Gordon's Attack," 583; John F. Hartranft, "The Recapture of Fort Stedman," *Battles and Leaders of the Civil War*, vol. 4 (hereafter cited as Hartranft, "The Recapture of Fort Stedman"), 589.
5. Buckbee Memoirs; *OR*, 46–1, 139, 327–328.
6. Buckbee Memoirs.
7. *OR*, 46–1, 137, 325–326.
8. Kilmer, "Gordon's Attack," 582–583.
9. Buckbee Memoirs.
10. Ed. J. Buckbee, Headquarters, 1st Michigan Sharpshooters, 28 March 1865, Buckbee Papers.
11. Buckbee Memoirs.
12. Ed. J. Buckbee to Mollie Church, Headquarters, 1st Michigan Sharpshooters, 28 March 1865, Buckbee Papers.
13. Ibid., Ed. J. Buckbee to his mother, Headquarters, 1st Michigan Sharpshooters, 25 March 1865; *OR*, 46–1, 138, 327.
14. Ed. J. Buckbee to his mother, Headquarters, 1st Michigan Sharpshooters, 25 March 1865, Buckbee Papers.
15. Ibid., Ed. J. Buckbee to Mollie Church, Headquarters, 1st Michigan Sharpshooters, 28 March 1865.
16. Buckbee Memoirs.
17. Ed. J. Buckbee to Mollie Church, Headquarters, 1st Michigan Sharpshooters, 28 March 1865, Buckbee Papers.
18. Buckbee Memoirs.
19. Ed. J. Buckbee to his mother, Headquarters, 1st Michigan Sharpshooters, 25 March 1865, Buckbee Papers.
20. Buckbee Memoirs.
21. Ibid.
22. Ibid.
23. Ibid.
24. Clark, *North Carolina in the War*, vol. 3, 390–391.
25. Cutcheon, *20th Michigan*, 164; Clark, *North Carolina in the War*, vol. 3, 391.
26. *OR*, 46–1, 138, 327.

27. Kilmer, "Gordon's Attack," 583; Hartranft, "The Recapture of Fort Stedman," 589; *OR*, 46–1, 136, 324.
28. Clark, *North Carolina in the War*, vol. 2, 625.
29. Cutcheon, *20th Michigan*, 164.
30. *OR*, 46–1, 138, 326–327.
31. Buckbee Memoirs.
32. Ibid.
33. Ed. J. Buckbee to his mother, Headquarters, 1st Michigan Sharpshooters, 25 March 1865, Buckbee Papers.
34. Ibid., Ed. J. Buckbee to Mollie Church, Headquarters, 1st Michigan Sharpshooters, 28 March 1865.
35. Regimental Order No. 21, Before Petersburg, 27 March 1865, *Letter and Order Book*.
36. Lansing *State Republican*, 27 July 1864, 3; 12 October 1864, 3; Charles V. DeLand to Capt. Thomas Mathews, A.A.A.G., Headquarters, 1st Michigan Sharpshooters, 16 September 1864, *Letter and Order Book*.
37. Buckbee Memoirs.
38. *Record of Service, 1st MSS*, 48.
39. Ibid., 66.
40. Buckbee Memoirs.
41. Ibid.
42. Ed. J. Buckbee to Mollie Church, Headquarters, 1st Michigan Sharpshooters, 28 March 1865, Buckbee Papers.
43. Ibid.
44. Ibid.
45. Maj. Gen. Orlando B. Willcox, Headquarters, First Division, Ninth Army Corps, 15 May 1865, Folder no. 9: "History," *1st MSS Records*.
46. Ypsilanti *Commercial*, 14 April 1865, 2.
47. Ed. J. Buckbee to R. A. Hutchins, A.A.G., Headquarters, 1st Michigan Sharpshooters, 2 July 1865, *Letter and Order Book*.
48. Ed. J. Buckbee to his mother, Headquarters, 1st Michigan Sharpshooters, 30 March 1865, Buckbee Papers.
49. *Record of Service, 1st MSS*, 25, 35, 69.
50. Regimental Order No. 23, Before Petersburg, 30 March 1865, *Letter and Order Book*.
51. Ibid., Regimental Order No. 26, Before Petersburg, 1 April 1865.
52. Buckbee Memoirs.
53. *OR*, 46–1, 159, 1047.
54. Ypsilanti *Commercial*, 14 April 1865, 2.
55. Ibid.
56. Ed. J. Buckbee to Charles V. DeLand, Petersburg, Virginia, 2 April 1865, DeLand–Crary Papers.
57. Ibid.; *OR*, 46–1, 159, 1047.
58. Ed. J. Buckbee to his mother, Headquarters, 1st Michigan Sharpshooters, 11 April 1865, Buckbee Papers.

59. Millbrook, *A Study in Valor*, 47.
60. Robertson, *Michigan in the War*, 549.
61. "Reminiscences," Evans Papers; Buckbee Memoirs.
62. Robertson, *Michigan in the War*, 410.
63. Ed. J. Buckbee to Charles V. DeLand, Petersburg, Virginia, 2 April 1865, DeLand–Crary Papers.
64. Buckbee Memoirs; Ed. J. Buckbee to his mother, Headquarters, 1st Michigan Sharpshooters, 11 April 1865, Buckbee Papers; ibid., Ed. J. Buckbee to Mollie Church, Headquarters, 1st Michigan Sharpshooters, 12 April 1865.
65. Robertson, *Michigan in the War*, 548.
66. Ed. J. Buckbee to Charles V. DeLand, Petersburg, Virginia, 2 April 1865, DeLand–Crary Papers.
67. Photograph Album, Buckbee Papers.
68. Cutcheon, *20th Michigan*, 166.
69. Buckbee Memoirs.
70. Ed. J. Buckbee to Charles V. DeLand, Petersburg, Virginia, 2 April 1865, DeLand–Crary Papers.
71. Ibid.
72. Ibid., Charles V. DeLand to his parents, n.p., 18 April 1865.
73. Buckbee Memoirs.
74. Asahel W. Nichols, Washington, DC, 13 November 1865, Folder no. 5: "Report of Wounds and Vacancies," *1st MSS Records*.
75. *Record of Service, 1st MSS*, 11.
76. Ibid., 48, 83.
77. Ibid., 29, 57, 82.
78. Ibid., 60.
79. Ed. J. Buckbee to Charles V. DeLand, Petersburg, Virginia, 2 April 1865, DeLand–Crary Papers. See Appendix for list of casualties.
80. Ed. J. Buckbee to Maj. C. A. Lounsberry, A.A.A.G., Headquarters, 1st Michigan Sharpshooters, 24 April 1865, Buckbee Papers.
81. Buckbee Memoirs.
82. Robertson, *Michigan in the War*, 548.
83. Report of Maj. Gen. O. B. Willcox, Headquarters, First Division, Ninth Army Corps, Washington, DC, 15 May 1865, Folder no. 9: "History," *1st MSS Records*.
84. Millbrook, *A Study in Valor*, 47.
85. Antoine Scott, the only Indian in the regiment who was ever nominated for the award, never received a medal for any of his heroism during the war. He died at Pentwater, Michigan, in December 1878. Sidney Haight received his medal in 1896. Scott probably never even knew he qualified for the honor. See Millbrook, *A Study in Valor*, 47.
86. Cutcheon, *20th Michigan*, 166.
87. Lansing *State Republican*, 26 April 1865, 2.
88. Cutcheon, *20th Michigan*, 166.

89. Ibid.
90. *OR*, 46–1, 159, 1047.
91. William Wixcey, "The First Flag in Petersburg," *The National Tribune*, 4 July 1907, 6.
92. Buckbee Memoirs.
93. Wixcey, "The First Flag in Petersburg," 6.
94. Ibid.
95. Ibid.; Robertson, *Michigan in the War*, 550.
96. *OR*, 46–1, 159, 1047.
97. *The National Tribune*, 10 February 1887, 3; 28 April 1887, 3.
98. William Bradford Irwin to his mother, 12 miles from Petersburg Va, 6 April 1865. Maxine Irwin White, comp., *Dear Father, Mother and Sister* (n.p., 1971).
99. Wixcey, "The First Flag in Petersburg."
100. "Reminiscences," Evans Papers.
101. Ibid.
102. Ed. J. Buckbee to Mollie Church, In Petersburg, Virginia, 3 April 1865, Buckbee Papers. Buckbee here alluded to the demise of Col. Elmer Ellsworth. In 1861 in Alexandria, Virginia, Ellsworth tore a rebel flag from a hotel roof, and on his way down the stairs of the building was killed by the hotel proprietor.
103. Ibid., George Stone to Ed J. Buckbee, Undated letter. Stone also mentioned that William Wixcey and Henry J. Stephens were two of the color guard. Colonel Ely, who was not present when the flag was raised on the courthouse, mentioned the occurrence as happening at 4:28 AM, see *OR*, 46–1, 159, 1047.
104. Ed. J. Buckbee to his mother, Headquarters, 1st Michigan Sharpshooters, 11 April 1865, Buckbee Papers.
105. *OR*, 46–1, 159, 1047; Wixcey, "The First Flag in Petersburg"; Buckbee Memoirs.
106. Buckbee Memoirs.
107. Ibid.
108. Ibid.
109. Cutcheon, *20th Michigan*, 166; *OR*, 46–1, 159, 1048.
110. Lansing *State Republican*, 26 April 1865, 2.
111. Ed. J. Buckbee to Mollie Church, In Petersburg, Virginia, 3 April 1865, Buckbee Papers.
112. William Bradford Irwin to his Mother, Petersburg, Virginia, 3 April 1865; White, *Dear Father, Mother and Sister*.
113. *OR*, 46–1, 159, 1047.
114. *Grant's Petersburg Progress*, 3 April 1865, facsimile reprint of a newspaper put together primarily by Second Brigade soldiers, including a number of Sharpshooters.
115. "Report to Headquarters," 4 April 1865, *Letter and Order Book*.
116. *Grant's Petersburg Progress*, 3 April 1865, facsimile reprint.
117. Undated newspaper clipping, Buckbee papers.

118. Lansing *State Republican*, 26 April 1865, 2.
119. Telegram to Gen. John Robertson, New York, 3 April 1865, 10:30 AM, Folder no. 8: "Letters and Telegrams—1861–81," *1st MSS Records*.
120. Lansing *State Republican*, 26 April 1865, 2.
121. Cutcheon, *20th Michigan*, 167.
122. Frank Thayer to Adj. Gen. John Robertson, Camp 1st Michigan Sharpshooters, 12 April 1865, Folder no. 8: "Letters and Telegrams—1861–81, *1st MSS Records*.

Chapter 14

1. Cutcheon, *20th Michigan*, 167; Lansing *State Republican*, 26 April 1865, 2.
2. Cutcheon, *20th Michigan*, 167.
3. Petition from Officers of 1st Michigan Sharpshooters to Gov. Crapo, n.d., Folder no. 3: "Recommendations, Promotions, Appointments," *1st MSS Records*.
4. Buckbee Memoirs.
5. Ed. J. Buckbee to Mollie Church, Headquarters, 1st Michigan Sharpshooters, 20 April 1865, Buckbee Papers.
6. Lansing *State Republican*, 26 April 1865, 2.
7. Buckbee Memoirs.
8. Lansing *State Republican*, 26 April 1865, 2.
9. Farling, *Life in the Army*, 22.
10. Regimental Order No. 29, 14 April 1865, *Letter and Order Book*.
11. Ibid., Regimental Order No. 27, 10 April 1865.
12. Ibid., Regimental Order No. 28, 14 April 1865.
13. Buckbee Memoirs.
14. Ibid.
15. Farling, *Life in the Army*, 20.
16. Lane, *A Soldier's Diary*, 262.
17. Charles V. DeLand to his parents, Armory Square Hospital, 19 April 1865, DeLand–Crary Papers.
18. Cutcheon, *20th Michigan*, 167.
19. Buckbee Memoirs.
20. Cutcheon, *20th Michigan*, 167.
21. Lanman, *The Red Book of Michigan*, 165; Detroit *Advertiser and Tribune*. 31 July 1865, 1.
22. Ed. J. Buckbee to Mollie Church, Near Alexandria, Virginia, 24 April 1865, Buckbee Papers.
23. Ibid.
24. Buckbee Memoirs.
25. Cutcheon, *20th Michigan*, 167.
26. Ibid.; Buckbee Memoirs.
27. Regimental Order No. 36, 5 May 1865, *Letter and Order Book*;

William H. Randall to Adj. Gen. John Robertson, Ypsilanti, Michigan, 19 November 1865, Folder no. 9: "History," *1st MSS Records*.

28. Buckbee Memoirs.
29. "Hon. Charles G. Conn," *Pictorial and Biographical Memoirs of Elkhart and St. Joseph Counties, Indiana* (Chicago: Goodspeed Brothers, Publishers, 1893), 27.
30. Regimental Order No. 42, 30 May 1864, *Letter and Order Book*.
31. Regimental Order No. 35, Near Georgetown D.C., 3 May 1865, *Letter and Order Book*; *Descriptive List*, 7; *Record of Service, 1st MSS*, 10, 43.
32. Regimental Order No. 33, 20 April 1865, *Letter and Order Book*; *Record of Service, 1st MSS*, 38.
33. Farling, *My Life in the Army*, 22.
34. Margaret Leech, *Reveille in Washington: 1860–1865* (New York: Harper and Bros., 1941), 414.
35. Ibid., 415.
36. Boston Diary, 25 May 1865.
37. Cutcheon, *20th Michigan*, 167; *OR*, 46–3, 1238.
38. Farling, *My Life in the Army*, 23.
39. Ibid., 22–23.
40. Regimental Order No. 47, 12 June 1865, *Letter and Order Book*.
41. Ibid., Regimental Order No. 52, 1 July 1865.
42. Ibid., Regimental Order No. 43, Headquarters, 1st Michigan Sharpshooters, 31 May 1865.
43. Ibid., Headquarters, 1st Michigan Sharpshooters, 7 July 1865.
44. Ibid., Regimental Orders No. 53, 7 July 1865; *Record of Service, 1st MSS*, 48.
45. Regimental Orders No. 54, 9 July 1865, *Letter and Order Book*.
46. Ibid., Regimental Orders No. 36, 5 May 1865.
47. Ibid., Regimental Order No. 53, 7 June 1865.
48. Ibid., Regimental Order No. 31, 17 April 1865.
49. Ibid., Regimental Order No. 33, 20 April 1865.
50. Ibid., Regimental Order No. 57, 16 July 1865.
51. Ibid., R. A. Hutchins to Ed. J. Buckbee, 1 July 1865; Buckbee to Hutchins, 2 July 1865; Hutchins to Buckbee, 6 July 1865.
52. Ed. J. Buckbee to Mollie Church, Headquarters, Second Brigade, 21 July 1865, Buckbee Papers.
53. Fox, *What I Remember*, 202.
54. Five more family sets came into the Sharpshooters with Hall's volunteers. Only two of those were still in the ranks: Henry and William Emmons of Coldwater and Charles and John Knoll of Weesaw. See *Record of Service*, 33, 54.
55. Ibid., 14, 61, 64, 99, 98, 87, 60, 38–39, 39, 41, 27–28.
56. Jackson *Eagle*, 29 July 1865, 3.
57. Detroit *Advertiser and Tribune*, 31 July 1865, 1.
58. Ibid.

Chapter 15

1. *List of Pensioners on the Roll: January 1, 1885*, vol. 4 (Baltimore: Genealogical Pub. Co., 1970), 369, 310, 308, 317.
2. Ibid., 279.
3. H. Dorr Blakeman to Ira Evans, Jackson MI, 22 June 1886, Evans Papers.
4. Jackson *Daily Citizen*, 14 September 1886, 1.
5. Ibid., 15 September 1886, 5.
6. Battle Creek *Daily Moon*, 1 October 1889, 7.
7. Ibid.
8. Ibid.
9. Ibid., 1 October 1889, 8.
10. All the information on the reunion of 1890 was found in Jackson *Daily Citizen*, 1 October 1890, 7.
11. Austin Blair, with whom Charles DeLand had quarreled intermittently since the war, had ceased to be an object of scorn to the old colonel. In fact, DeLand now maintained a lofty opinion of Michigan's Civil War governor. Blair "was a noble example of personal and official rectitude and honesty both in opinion, principal and action," wrote DeLand in his history of his hometown shortly before his death. DeLand had no apologies to make in his text, and he clearly saw the stature of his one-time adversary. Blair's "motto was 'to see the right is to do it.' No citizen of the city or state has left a prouder monument than the reputation of Austin Blair." See *DeLand's Jackson County*, 275.
12. File E: Miscellanea [3], Clarke–DeLand Papers.
13. Thomas Chittigo to Ed. J. Buckbee, Pinconning MI, 19 June 1892. Buckbee Papers.
14. Lansing *State Republican*, 14 September 1892, 1.
15. On 1 April 1915 the state legislature permitted the First Michigan Sharpshooters Association to erect a monument to the regiment on the state capitol lawn. The monument was designed and built by Frank D. Black, a Grand Rapids monument dealer. Black "never copied monuments on the grounds that it would be immoral." See Fay L. Hendry, *Outdoor Sculpture in Lansing* (Okemos, MI: Iota Press, n.d.), 21, 133.
16. *Lansing State Republican*, 14 December 1915, 1.
17. George W. Stone to Ed. J. Buckbee, Lansing MI, 21 June 1917. Buckbee Papers.
18. Ibid.
19. Ibid.
20. Ibid., George W. Stone to Ed. J. Buckbee, Battle Creek MI, 2 September 1919.

Chapter 16

1. William H. H. Beadle to Brig. Gen. John Robertson, Albion, Michigan, 15 April 1867, Folder no. 9, *1st MSS Records*; May Beadle Frink, "The Hoosier," *South Dakota Historical Collections.* vol. 3 (1906), 87–88; Johnson and Malone, *DAB* vol. 2, 86–87; *University of Michigan—Catalogue of Graduates, Non-Graduates, Officers, and Members of the Faculties 1937–1921* (Ann Arbor: University of Michigan, 1923), 61.

2. Warner, *Generals in Blue*, 559; Johnson and Malone, *DAB* vol. 20, 243; *Detroit Free Press*, 11 May 1907, 1.

3. John Anderson to Ira Evans, New Haven, Connecticut, 3 November 1906; John Anderson to Ira Evans, Amherst, Massachusetts, 11 April 1905, Evans Papers.

4. E. R. Rolfsrud, *Lanterns Over the Prairies* (Bainerd, MN: Lakeland Press, n.d.), 50, 56, found in Lounsberry Papers, Accession Box 77, State Archives of Michigan, Lansing, MI.

5. Undated Chicago *Evening Post* [1899?], Buckbee Papers.

6. Ibid.; undated letter, George W. Stone to Ed Buckbee; C. G. Conn to George W. Stone, New York City, 5 September 1899, Buckbee Papers.

7. Undated Chicago *Evening Press* [1899?], Buckbee Papers.

8. Battle Creek *Daily Journal*, 13 September 1899, 3.

9. Ibid.

10. Lansing *State Republican*, 12 September 1899, 1.

11. Ibid.

12. Undated Chicago *Evening Post* [1899?], Buckbee Papers.

13. Charles V. DeLand, East Saginaw MI, 18 January 1866, Folder no. 6: "List of Engagements and Skirmishes," *1st MSS Records.*

14. Saginaw *Weekly Enterprise*, 10 August 1865, 2.

15. Ibid., 14 September 1865, 2.

16. Charles V. DeLand to J. W. Houghton, 23 November 1886, Jackson, MI, Correspondence—1885–1890, Clarke–DeLand Papers.

17. Charles V. DeLand, Complete Military Service File, National Archives, Washington, DC.

18. *DeLand's Jackson County*, 440, 441; *History of Saginaw County*, 334, 464, 465; *Portraits and Biographies of Jackson County*, 220–221.

19. *Portraits and Biographies of Jackson County*, 221.

20. Bay City *Times-Press*, 12 February 1898, 1. An editorial in the Bay City paper followed DeLand's attack on Pingree. "When comrades Pingree and DeLand are criticising each other's war record with derogatory innuendoes, they would do well to recall the story of the Irishman. An alleged wag thought to have a little fun with him and asked if he was at the battle of Bull Run. 'Yes, sor, I was!' answered Pat. 'Well, did you run?' was the next question. 'Indeed I

did,' said the Irishman, 'the fellows that didn't run are there yet.' Gov. Pingree and Col. DeLand doubtless rendered brave and efficient service in the union army and it is not seemly for them to be publicly assailing each other with insinuations that are born of political animosities and have no other foundation." See Bay City *Times-Press*, 15 February 1898, 2.

21. Jackson *Daily Citizen*, 21 September 1903, 1; 22 September 1903, 7; 23 September 1903, 6. All the information concerning DeLand's death and funeral come from these three issues.

22. Ibid.

23. *History of Hillsdale County*, 118; Elon G. Reynolds, ed., *Compendium of History and Biography of Hillsdale County, Michigan* (Chicago: A. W. Bowen & Co., n.d.), 340.

24. Obituary, John Clark, *The National Tribune*, 8 March 1906, 7.

25. Ibid., Obituary, Henry Decker, 2 July 1908, 6.

26. *Ingham County Families*, [Working Papers of Hammell Collection], MSS., vol. M–O, Library of Michigan, Lansing, MI, no pagination.

27. Lansing *State Republican*, 24 January 1866, 3.

28. Ibid., 2 April 1868, 8.

29. Obituary, Vanorman Strout, *The National Tribune*, 2 June 1887, 4.

30. Obituary, Thomas R. Talladay, ibid., 17 April 1890, 6.

31. *Lakeview Cemetery Records Book*, Harbor Springs, MI.

32. Obituary, Marvin Maloney, *The National Tribune*, 7 July 1892, 6.

33. Edwin V. Andress, Complete Military Pension Record, National Archives, Washington, DC.

34. Millbrook, *A Study in Valor*, 48–49.

35. Ibid., 50; *Kalkaska Township Cemetery Records Book*, Kalkaska, MI, 65.

36. Sue Imogene Silliman, *Michigan Military Records* (Baltimore: Genealogical Publishing Co., 1969), 184–185; *The Medal of Honor*, 166; Charles H. DePuy, Burial Record, "Records—Evergreen Cemetery, Kalkaska Township, Kalkaska County, Michigan."

37. *Descriptive Rolls*, 13, 57; *Record of Service, 1st MSS*, 85. If the Sharpshooters were any indication, there must have been an almost endless list of old soldiers who were residents of old soldiers' homes across the country. A look through the *Descriptive Rolls* lists the following old Sharpshooters living, and dying, in the institutions:

John Harper, Co. A, d. 26 Dec 1907, Michigan Soldiers' Home
Friend Soules, Co. A, d. 15 Feb 1917, Michigan Soldiers' Home
George Barnes, Co. A, d. 17 March 1910, Michigan Soldiers' Home
William Duverney, Co. B, d. 25 Aug 1893, NW Branch Nat'l Mil. Home
David P. Sanford, Co. B, d. 4 May 1911, Michigan Soldiers' Home
John Anderson, Co. C, d. 9 Apr 1889, NW Branch Nat'l Mil. Home

Daniel Cross, Co. C, d. 16 Dec 1918, Michigan Soldiers' Home
John Parks, Co. C, d. 24 Sept 1914, Michigan Soldiers' Home
William Bates, Co. C, d. 21 Aug 1893, Michigan Soldiers' Home
Elnathan George, Co. D, d. 27 Nov 1912, Michigan Soldiers' Home
James Sanders, Co. D, d. 27 Sept 1903, Soldiers' Home, Dayton,
   OH
John Sanders, Co. D, d. 19 July 1916, Michigan Soldiers' Home
Oliver Wells, Co. E, d. 25 March 1912, Michigan Soldiers' Home
Charles Wibert, Co. E, d. 14 May 1918, Michigan Soldiers' Home
John Hamley, Co. G, d. 17 March 1904, Soldiers' Home, Danville,
   IL
John McCann, Co. G, d. 25 Sept 1893, NW Branch Nat'l Mil. Home
Abram Norris, Co. G, d. 24 Dec 1888, Central Branch, Nat'l Mil.
   Home
Allen Stephens, Co. G, d. 12 March 1889, NW Branch Nat'l Mil.
   Home
Isaac Connell, Co. H, d. 7 November 1911, Michigan Soldiers'
   Home
Charles Judson, Co. H, d. 8 Oct 1915, Michigan Soldiers' Home

See *Descriptive Rolls*, 7, 9, 12, 13, 16, 19, 21, 24, 28, 30, 33, 41, 53, 55, 57, 60, 62.

38. Francis Hull, "Michigan Veterans' Obituaries, 1898–1939," vol. 2 (Manuscript), Grand Rapids Public Library, Grand Rapids, MI, 98.
39. *Descriptive Rolls*, 1–2.
40. Jerry O. Potter, *The Sultana Tragedy* (Gretna, LA: Pelican Publishing Co., 1992), 236; Bryan Lee Dilts, comp., *1890 Michigan Census Index of Civil War Veterans or Their Widows* (Salt Lake City: Index Publishing, 1985); The Leelanau Township Historical Writers Group, *A History of Leelanau Township*, 62.
41. *Portrait and Biographical Album of Hillsdale County*, 220–221.
42. *Descriptive Rolls*, 59; *Record of Service, 1st MSS*, 13.
43. *Record of Service, 1st MSS*, 15.
44. Photograph Album, Buckbee Papers; *Descriptive Rolls*, 27; *Record of Service, 1st MSS*, 54.
45. Ed J. Buckbee to James DeLand, 31 January 1917, Houston TX, Buckbee Papers.
46. *The National Tribune*, 13 December 1906, 5.
47. Millbrook, *A Study in Valor*, 14, 17; George Murdoch to Adj. Gen. John Robertson, 8 August 1881 [Battle Creek, Michigan], Folder no. 8: "Letters and Telegrams—1861–1881," *1st MSS Records*.
48. *History of Berrien and Van Buren Counties, Michigan* (Philadelphia: D. W. Ensign & Co., 1880), 140, 149, 283; *Cemetery Records—Berrien County, Michigan* (St. Joseph-Benton Harbor, Michigan: Algonquin Chapter, Daughters of the American Revolution, 1930), 211.

49. *DeLand's Jackson County*, 265.
50. *Descriptive Rolls*, 57, 52; *Record of Service, 1st MSS*, 83, 25.
51. *The City of Grand Rapids and Kent County, Michigan* (Logansport, IN: A. W. Bowen & Co., 1900), 128–131; *University of Michigan— Catalogue of Graduates*, 61.
52. *First Annual Reunion of the First Mich. Sharpshooters* (n.p., n.d.); *Record of Service, 1st MSS*, 42–43.
53. *The Traverse Region*, 143.
54. Hull, "Michigan Veterans' Obituaries," vol. 3, 57.
55. Record of Richard Snay, Records of the Department of Correction (General), Series I, State Archives of Michigan, Lansing, MI; Richard Snay may died in the Detroit House of Correction while serving a sentence for beating his wife, see Bay City *Daily Morning Call*, 4 March 1884, 3.
56. *Descriptive Rolls*, 26.
57. Ibid., 19, 32.
58. Ibid., 58.
59. *Record of Service, 1st MSS*, 59.
60. Reading *Hustler*, 25 September 1918, 4.
61. George W. Stone, Complete Pension Record, National Archives, Washington, DC; Frederick C. Martindale, comp., *Michigan Official Directory and Legislative Manual for the Years 1913–1914* (Lansing, MI: Wynkoop Hallenbeck Crawford Co., 1913), 842.
62. Buckbee Memoirs.
63. Hull, "Michigan Veterans' Obituaries," vol. 2, 187 .
64. William Driggs, Complete Pension Record, National Archives, Washington, DC; *History of Saginaw County*, 374.
65. Margaret Downie Banks and James W. Jordan, "C. G. Conn: The Man (1844–1931) and his Company (1874–1915)," *Journal of the American Musical Instrument Society* (1988), 65.
66. "C. G. Conn—His 'Truth' Was a Personal Promotion," The Elkhart *Truth*, 20 October 1989, 2.
67. "Hon. Charles G. Conn." *Pictorial and Biographical Memoirs of Elkhart and St. Joseph Counties, Indiana* (Chicago: Goodspeed Brothers, Publishers, 1893), 28.
68. Banks and Jordan, "C. G. Conn," 94, 112.
69. Ibid., 69–77, 85, 86.
70. Ibid., 62.
71. George Stone to E. J. Buckbee, Battle Creek, MI, 2 September 1919, Buckbee Papers; Berry, *Loss of the Sultana*, 338–343.
72. Gardner, *History of Calhoun County*, vol. 2, 346, 713; Battle Creek *Enquirer and News*, 1914, Kimball House Historical Society Archives, Battle Creek, MI.
73. Buckbee Memoirs.
74. Gardner, *History of Calhoun County*, vol. 2, 1167, 1176.
75. James S. DeLand, Complete Military Pension Record, National Ar-

chives, Washington, DC; *Portraits and Biographies of Jackson County*, 127, 128.

76. Bay City *Times*, 21 January 1978, 3–A; Crawford *Avalanche*, 27 April 1916, 7.
77. Buckbee Memoirs.
78. *Biographical History of Northern Michigan*, 527–528.
79. *The Traverse Region*, 318–319.
80. Hooker A. DeLand, Complete Military Pension File, National Archives, Washington, DC. All the information on his postwar activities comes from this source.
81. Special Examiner George C. Anderson to Department of the Interior, Bureau of Pensions, Grand Rapids, Mich., 31 December 1897, Hooker A. DeLand Pension Record, National Archives, Washington, DC.
82. *The National Tribune*, 15 August 1901, 6; *Port Huron Weekly Times*, 2 August 1901, 5.
83. Philip Jefferson Johnson died in Lenoir, North Carolina, on 21 March 1907. See *Confederate Veteran*, vol. 16, no. 2 (February 1908), 87.
84. Buckbee Memoirs; Buckbee to E. M. Stanton, Washington, DC, 21 May 1866; George W. Wilcox to Buckbee, Detroit MI, 9 March 1869; George Stone to Buckbee, Lansing, MI, 11 September 1899; David Heagle to Cheever Buckbee, Chicago, IL, 23 April 1920, Buckbee Papers.
85. "Dr. David Heagle," *The Watchman–Examiner*, 2 March 1922, 279; "Rev. David Heagle," *The Baptist*, 4 March 1922, n.p.
86. Emily Evans Walsh to Raymond J. Herek, Howell, MI, 15 May 1990, Author's Collection.
87. Charley Nash to Ira Evans, Omaha, NB, 4 June 1896, Evans Papers.
88. Emily Evans Walsh to Raymond J. Herek, Howell, MI, 19 October 1991, Author's Collection.
89. Case File No. 12517: Ira L. Evans, Michigan Asylum for the Insane, Kalamazoo, MI, Evans Papers.
90. Ibid., John Anderson to Ira Evans, Amherst, MA, 11 April 1905.
91. Paul L. Roy, *The Last Reunion of the Blue and Gray* (Gettysburg, PA: The Bookmart, 1950), 65. This volume lists all the veterans who attended the last reunion.
92. Cyrus Perrigo, Certificate of Death, Tuscola County Death Records, vol. 46, p. 512, Caro, MI.

Bibliography

Newspapers

(All are Michigan newspapers unless otherwise noted.)

Battle Creek *Journal*
Battle Creek *Morning Call*
Bay City *Morning Call*
Bay City *Times*
Bay City *Times–Press*
Bay City *Tribune*
Clinton *Republican*
Coldwater *Union Sentinel*
Constantine *Weekly Mercury* and
   St. Joseph County *Advertiser*
Crawford (Grayling) *Avalanche*
Detroit *Advertiser*
Detroit *Advertiser and Tribune*
Detroit *Free Press*
Detroit *Tribune*
East Saginaw *Courier*
Elkhart *Truth* (Indiana)
Grand Rapids *Eagle*
Grand Traverse *Herald*

Grant's Petersburg Progress
   (Virginia) [facsimile]
Hillsdale *Standard*
Jackson *Citizen*
Jackson *Eagle*
Jonesville *Independent*
Lansing *State Journal*
Lansing *State Republican*
Marshall *Democratic Expounder*
National Tribune (Washington, DC)
Niles *Republican*
Port Huron *Press*
Port Huron *Weekly Times*
Reading *Hustler*
Saginaw *Enterprise*
Three Rivers *Reporter*
Three Rivers *Western Chronicle*
Ypsilanti *Commercial*
Ypsilanti *True Democrat*

Unit Histories

Barker, Lorenzo A. *Military History (Michigan Boys), Company "D" 66th Illinois, Birge's Western Sharpshooters in the Civil War, 1861–1865.* Reed City, MI: n.p., 1905.

Bennett, Charles W. *Historical Sketches of the Ninth Michigan Infantry.* Coldwater, MI: Daily Courier Print, 1913.

Clark, Walter, comp. *Histories of the Several Regiments and Battalions from North Carolina in the Great War, 1861–1865*, 3 vols. Goldsboro, NC: State of North Carolina, 1901.

Crater, Lewis. *History of the Fiftieth Regiment, Pennsylvania Veteran Volunteers, 1861–1865.* Reading, PA: Coleman Printing House, 1884.

Cutcheon, Byron, comp. *The Story of the Twentieth Michigan Infantry.* Lansing, MI: Robert Smith Printing Co., 1904.

Duke, Basil W. *Morgan's Cavalry*. New York: Neale Publishing Co., 1906.

Lane, J. H. "History of Lane's North Carolina Brigade." *Southern Historical Society Papers*, vol. 9, no. 4 (April 1881), 145–156.

"The Petersburg Grays." *Southern Historical Society Papers*, vol. 36 (1908), 360–362.

Smith, A. W. *The Anson Guards* (14th NC Inf.). Charlotte, NC: Stone Publishing Co., 1914.

Thomas, Edison H. *John Hunt Morgan and His Raiders*. Lexington, KY: University Press of Kentucky, 1975.

Published Reminiscences

Alexander, W. D. "Grant Outgeneraled." *Confederate Veteran*, vol. 31, no. 6, (June 1923), 211–212.

Beauregard, P. G. T. "Four Days of Battle at Petersburg." *Battles and Leaders of the Civil War*, vol 4: *The Way to Appomattox*. 540–544.

Bernard, George S. "The Battle of the Crater." *Southern Historical Society Papers*, vol. 18 (1890), 3–38.

Bibbins, C. D. "The Indian Sharpshooters." *National Tribune*, 16 October 1917, 7.

Campbell, George W. "Old Choctaw." *National Tribune*, 11 September 1913, 7.

Case, Leverette N. "Personal Recollections of the Siege of Petersburg by a Confederate Officer." *Michigan Commandery Military Order of the Loyal Legion of the United States*, vol. 2 (1897), 153–166.

The Confederate Soldier in the Civil War: The Campaigns, Battles, Sieges, Charges and Skirmishes. N.p.: The Fairfax Press, n.d.

Cutcheon, Byron M. "The Twentieth Michigan Regiment in the Assault on Petersburg, July, 1864." *Michigan Pioneer and Historical Collections*, vol. 30 (1906), 127–139.

Featherston, John C. "Graphic Account of Battle of Crater." *Southern Historical Society Papers*, vol. 33 (1905), 358–374.

Frink, May Beadle. "The Hoosier." *South Dakota Historical Collections*, vol. 3 (1906), 87–88.

Farling, Amos. *Life in the Army, Containing Historical and Biographical Sketches, Incidents, Adventures and Narratives of the Late War*. Buchanan, MI: Amos Farling, 1874.

Grant, Ulysses S. *Personal Memoirs of U. S. Grant*, 2 vols. New York: Charles L. Webster & Co., 1886.

Hartranft, John F. "The Recapture of Fort Stedman." *Battles and Leaders of the Civil War*, vol. 4: *The Way to Appomattox*. 584–589.

Kilmer, George L. "Gordon's Attack at Fort Stedman." *Battles and Leaders of the Civil War*, vol. 4: *The Way to Appomattox*. 579–583.

Lane, David. *A Soldier's Diary: The Story of a Volunteer*. N.p., 1905.

Law, E. M. "From the Wilderness to Cold Harbor." *Battles and Leaders of the Civil War*, vol. 4: *The Way to Appomattox*. 118–144.

Mosgrove, George Dallas. "Following Morgan's Plume through Indiana and Ohio." *Southern Historical Society Papers*, vol. 35 (1907), 110–120.

Nettles, T. A. "Letter." *Confederate Veteran*, vol. 16, no. 7 (July 1908), 349–350.

Page, T. M. "The Prisoner of War." *Confederate Veteran*, vol. 8, no. 1 (January 1900), 62–64.

Porter, Horace. *Campaigning with Grant*. New York: Bonanza, 1961.

_____. "Five Forks and the Pursuit of Lee." *Battles and Leaders of the Civil War*, vol. 4: *The Way to Appomattox*. 708–722.

Powell, William H. "The Battle of the Petersburg Crater." *Battles and Leaders of the Civil War*, vol. 4: *The Way to Appomattox*. 545–560.

Ransom, John L. *John Ransom's Andersonville Diary*. Middlebury, VT: Paul S. Eriksson, Publisher, 1986.

Swift, Frederick W. "My Experiences as a Prisoner of War." War Paper No. 3: *Michigan Commandery Military Order of the Loyal Legion of the United States*. Detroit: William S. Ostler, 1888.

A Thrilling Narrative from the Lips of the Sufferers of the Late Detroit Riot, March 6, 1863, with the Hair Breadth Escapes of Men, Women and Children, and Destruction of Colored Men's Property, Not Less than $15,000. Detroit, MI: n.p., 1863. (Reprint by Russell's Book Store, Royal Oak, MI, n.d.)

Throne, Mildred, ed. *The Civil War Diary of Cyrus F. Boyd, Fifteenth Iowa Infantry, 1861–1863*. Millwood, NY: Kraus Reprint Co., 1977.

Walton, J. M. "Letter." *The National Tribune*, 10 February 1887, 3.

War of the Rebellion: A Compilation of the Official Records of the Union and Confederate Armies. 69 vols. Washington, DC: The Government Printing Office, 1890–1901.

White, Maxine Irwin, comp. *Dear Father, Mother and Sister*. N.p.: 1971.

Whitman, Walt. *The Correspondence*: Vol. I: *1842–1867*. Ed. by Edwin Haviland Miller. New York: New York University Press, 1961.

Wightman, Thomas. "Letter." *The National Tribune*, 28 April 1887, 3.

Wixcey, William T. "First Flag in Petersburg." *The National Tribune*, 4 July 1907, 6.

Secondary Sources

Applegate, Tom S. "A History of the Press in Michigan." *Michigan Pioneer and Historical Collections*, vol. 6 (1884), 62–98.

Bailey, Ronald H., and the Editors of *Time–Life* Books. *The Civil War—Foreward to Richmond: McClellan's Peninsular Campaign*. Alexandria, VA: *Time–Life* Books, 1983.

Banks, Margaret Downie, and Jordan, James W. "C. G. Conn: The Man

(1844–1931) and His Company (1874–1915)." *Journal of the American Musical Instrument Society* (1988), 61–113.

Berry, Chester D. *Loss of Sultana and Reminiscences of Survivors.* Lansing, MI: Darius D. Thorp, Printer and Binder, 1892.

Beyer, W. F., and Keydel, O. F. Eds. *Deeds of Valor: How America's Heroes Won the Congressional Medal of Honor*, vol. 1. Detroit: Perrien–Keydel Co., 1905.

Biographical History of Northern Michigan. N.p.: B. F. Bowen & Co., 1905.

Brown, Dee. *The Galvanized Yankees.* Urbana, IL: University of Illinois Press, 1963.

Brown, Elizabeth Read. "Michigan's Pioneer Newspapers, A Sketch." *Michigan History*, vol. 41, no. 4 (December 1957), 413–425.

Catlin, George B. "Adventures in Journalism: Detroit Newspapers since 1850." *Michigan History*, vol. 29, no. 3 (July, August, September 1945), 343–376.

Catton, Bruce. *A Stillness at Appomattox.* New York: Doubleday & Co., 1953.

The City of Grand Rapids and Kent County, Michigan. Logansport, IN: A. W. Bowen & Co., 1900.

Commager, Henry Steele. Ed. *The Blue and the Gray*, vol. 2. New York: Bobbs–Merrill Co., 1973.

Day, Judson Leroy, II. *The Baptists of Michigan and the Civil War.* Lansing, MI: Michigan Civil War Centennial Observance Commission, 1965.

"Death of Orrin S. Case." *Michigan Pioneer and Historical Collections.* Vol. 6 (1884). 297.

DeLand, Charles V., comp. *DeLand's History of Jackson County, Michigan.* N.p.: B. F. Bowen & Co., 1903.

Deming, Brian. *Jackson: An Illustrated History.* N.p.: Windsor Publications, 1984.

Dobson, Pamela J., ed. *The Tree That Never Dies: Oral History of the Michigan Indians.* Grand Rapids, MI: Grand Rapids Public Library, 1978.

Eisendrath, Joseph L., Jr. "Chicago's Camp Douglas, 1861–1865." *Journal of the Illinois State Historical Society*, vol. 53, no. 1 (Spring 1960), 37–63.

Fenimore, Jean Joy L. "Austin Blair: Civil War Governor, 1861–1862." *Michigan History*, vol. 49, no. 3 (September 1965), 193–227.

_____. "Austin Blair: Civil War Governor, 1863–1864." *Michigan History*, vol. 49, no. 4 (December 1965), 344–369.

Fox, Wells B. *What I Remember of the Great Rebellion.* Lansing: Darius D. Thorp, 1892.

Gardner, Washington. *History of Calhoun County, Michigan: A Narrative Account of Its Historical Progress, Its People, and Its Principal Interests.* 2 vols. Chicago: Lewis Publishing Co., 1913

Bibliography

Gray, Wood. *The Hidden Civil War: The Story of the Copperheads.* New York: The Viking Press, 1942.

Hartwick, L. M., and Tuller, W. H. *Oceana County—Pioneers and Business Men of To-Day.* Pentwater, MI: Pentwater News Steam Print, 1890.

Hauptman, Laurence N. *Between Two Fires: American Indians in the Civil War.* New York: The Free Press, 1995.

"Heagle, Dr. David." *The Watchman–Examiner,* vol. 10, no. 4 (2 March 1922), 279.

"Heagle, Rev. David." *The Baptist,* vol. 3, no. 5 (4 March 1922).

Hendry, Fay L. *Outdoor Sculpture in Lansing.* Okemos, MI: Iota Press, n.d.

Hesseltine, William Best. *Civil War Prisons: A Study in War Psychology.* New York: Frederick Ungar Publishing Co., 1958.

History of Berrien and Van Buren Counties, Michigan. Philadelphia: D. W. Ensign & Co., 1880.

History of Branch County, Michigan, With Illustrations and Biographical Sketches of Some of Its Prominent Men and Pioneers. Philadelphia: Everts & Abbott, 1879.

History of Cass County, Michigan. Chicago: Waterman, Watkins & Co., 1882.

History of Hillsdale County, Michigan, With Illustrations and Biographical Sketches of Some of Its Prominent Men and Pioneers. Philadelphia: Everts & Abbott, 1879.

History of Jackson County, Michigan. Chicago: Inter-State Publishing Co., 1881.

History of Saginaw County Michigan; Together With Sketches of Its Cities, Villages and Townships, Educational, Religious, Civil, Military, and Political History: Portraits of Prominent Persons, Biographies of Representative Citizens. Chicago: Chas. C. Chapman & Co., 1881.

History of Shiawassee and Clinton Counties, Michigan, With Illustrations and Biographical Sketches of Their Prominent Men and Pioneers. Philadelphia: D. W. Ensign & Co., 1880.

History of Washtenaw County, Michigan. Chicago: Charles C. Chapman & Co., 1881

Humphreys, Andrew A. *Campaigns of the Civil War.* Vol. 12: *The Virginia Campaign of '64 and '65.* New York: Charles Scribner's Sons, 1883.

Jackson, Donald Dale. "It Took Trains to Put Street Kids on the Right Track Out of the Slums." *Smithsonian* (August 1986), 94–103.

Johnson, Robert Underwood, and Buel, Clarence Clough. Eds. *Battles and Leaders of the Civil War.* Vol. 4: *The Way to Appomattox.* New York: Thomas Yoseloff, 1956.

Lanman, Charles. *The Red Book of Michigan: A Civil, Military and Biographical History.* Detroit: E. B. Smith & Co., 1871.

Leach, Dr. M. L. *A History of the Grand Traverse Region*. Traverse City, MI: Grand Traverse Herald, 1883.

Leech, Margaret. *Reveille in Washington, 1860–1865*. New York: Harper & Bros., 1941.

Leelanau Township Historical Writers Group. *A History of Leelanau Township*. Chelsea, MI: Book Crafters, Inc., 1982.

Little, Leo C. *Historic Grand Haven and Ottawa County*. Grand Haven, MI: n.p., 1931.

Long, E. B. "Camp Douglas: A Hellish Den?" *Chicago History: The Magazine of the Chicago Historical Society*, vol. 1, no. 2 (Fall 1970), 82–95.

Matter, William D. *If It Takes All Summer: The Battle of Spotsylvania*. Chapel Hill, NC: University of North Carolina Press, 1988.

May, George S. *Michigan Civil War Monuments*. Lansing, MI: Michigan Civil War Centennial Observance Commission, 1965.

Medal of Honor of the United States Army. N.p.: Department of the Army Public Information Division, 1948.

Meredith, Roy, and Meredith, Arthur. *Mr. Lincoln's Military Railroads*. New York: W. W. Norton & Co., 1979.

Michigan Biographies. Vol. 1: "Charles V. DeLand," 233. Lansing, MI: Michigan Historical Commission, 1924.

Millbrook, Minnie Dubbs. *A Study in Valor—Michigan Medal of Honor Winners in the Civil War*. Lansing: Michigan Civil War Centennial Observance Commission, 1966.

_____, ed. *Twice Told Tales of Michigan and Her Soldiers in the Civil War*. Lansing, MI: Michigan Civil War Centennial Observance Commission, 1966.

Moore, Charles. "The Days of Fife and Drum." *Michigan Pioneer and Historical Collections*, vol. 28 (1900), 437–453.

_____. *History of Michigan*. Vol. 1: "Michigan in the War of Secession," 411–440. Chicago: The Lewis Publishing Co., 1915.

Murdock, Eugene C. *One Million Men: The Civil War Draft in the North*. Westport, CT: Greenwood Press, 1971. (Reprinted in 1980 with permission of The State Historical Society of Wisconsin.)

_____. *Patriotism Limited 1862–1865: The Civil War Draft and the Bounty System*. Kent, OH: Kent State University Press, 1967.

Pictorial and Biographical Memoirs of Elkhart and St. Joseph Counties, Indiana. Chicago: Goodspeed Brothers, Publishers, 1893.

Portrait and Biographical Album of Hillsdale County, Michigan. Chicago: Chapman Bros., 1888.

Portraits and Biographies of Jackson County, Michigan. Chicago: Chapman Bros., 1890.

Potter, Jerry O. *The Sultana Tragedy*. Gretna, LA: Pelican Publishing Co., 1992.

Powers, Perry F. *A History of Northern Michigan and Its People*. 3 vols. Chicago: The Lewis Publishing Co., 1912.

Report of the Michigan Andersonville Monument Commission on Erection of Monument at Andersonville, Georgia. Lansing, MI: Robert Smith Printing Co., 1905.

Reynolds, Elon G. *Compendium of History and Biography of Hillsdale County, Michigan.* Chicago: A. W. Bowen & Co., n.d.

Richardson, John. Comp. *Michigan in the War* (Revised Edition). Lansing, MI: W. S. George & Co., 1882.

Rolfsrud, E. R. *Lanterns over the Prairies.* Brainerd, MN: Lakeland Press, n.d.

Roy, Paul L. *The Last Reunion of the Blue and Gray.* Gettysburg, PA: The Bookmart, 1950.

Schneider, John C. "Detroit and the Problem of Disorder: The Riot of 1863." *Michigan History*, vol. 58, no. 1 (Spring 1974), 4–24.

Shoemaker, Michael. "Jackson County." *Michigan Pioneer and Historical Collections*, vol. 2 (1880), 272–356.

Silliman, Sue Imogene. *Michigan Military Records.* Baltimore: Genealogical Publishing Co., 1969.

Small Arms Used by Michigan Troops in the Civil War. Lansing, MI: Michigan Civil War Centennial Observance Committee, 1966.

Sommers, Lawrence M. *Atlas of Michigan.* Grand Rapids, MI: Michigan State University Press, 1977.

Sommers, Richard J. *Richmond Redeemed: The Siege at Petersburg.* Garden City, NY: Doubleday & Co., 1981.

Stark, George W. *City of Destiny: The Story of Detroit.* Detroit: Arnold–Powers, Inc., 1943.

Steere, Edward. *The Wilderness Campaign.* New York: Bonanza Books, 1960.

Sword, Wiley. *Sharpshooter: Hiram Berdan, His Famous Sharpshooters and Their Sharps Rifles.* Lincoln, RI: Andrew Mowbray, Inc., 1988.

"Talladay [sic], Thomas R." Obituary. *The National Tribune.* 17 April 1890, 6.

The Traverse Region, Historical and Descriptive, with Illustrations of Scenery and Portraits and Biographical Sketches of Some of Its Prominent Men and Pioneers. Chicago: H. R. Page & Co., 1884.

Tuttle, Charles R., comp. *General History of the State of Michigan.* Detroit: R. D. S. Tyler & Co., 1873.

Warner, Ezra J. *Generals in Blue: Lives of the Union Commanders.* Baton Rouge: Louisiana State University Press, 1964.

Woodbury, Augustus. *Major General Ambrose Burnside and the Ninth Army Corps.* Providence, RI: Sidney S. Rider & Brother, 1867.

Woodward, Frank B. *Father Abraham's Children.* Detroit: Wayne State University Press, 1961.

Wright, John C. "Indian Legends of Northern Michigan." *Michigan History*, vol. 2, no. 1 (January 1918), 81–88.

Manuscript Materials

Andress, Edwin V. Military Pension File. National Archives. Washington, DC.

Boston, William. Papers. Bentley Historical Library. Michigan Historical Collections. University of Michigan. Ann Arbor.

Buckbee, Julian Edward. Memoirs and Papers. Personal Collection of John W. Buckbee.

Chandler, Zachariah. Papers—1855–1899. Library of Congress. Washington, DC. Container No. 3: January 11, 1864–February 12, 1866. Microfilm. Clarke Historical Library. Central Michigan University. Mt. Pleasant.

Clarke–DeLand Family. Papers—1830–1919. Bentley Historical Library. Michigan Historical Collections. University of Michigan. Ann Arbor.

Cleavland, Henry B. Prison Record. Records of Department of Correction (General). Series 1. State Archives of Michigan. Lansing.

Conn, Charles G. Military Pension File. National Archives. Washington, DC.

DeLand–Crary Family. Papers—1842–1913. Bentley Historical Library. Michigan Historical Collections. University of Michigan. Ann Arbor.

DeLand, Charles. Compiled Military Service File. National Archives. Washington, DC.

DeLand, Hooker A. Military Pension File. National Archives. Washington, DC.

_____. Proceedings of a General Court Martial Held near Petersburg, Virginia, June 28, 1864. Records of the Judge Advocate General's Office. Court Martial Case Files. No. NN 2032. Record Group No. 153. National Archives. Washington, DC.

DeLand, James S. Military Pension File. National Archives. Washington, DC.

Descriptive Rolls—Civil War. Vol. 44: 1st Michigan Sharpshooters. State Archives of Michigan. Lansing.

Driggs, William J. Military Pension File. National Archives. Washington, DC.

Evans, Ira L. Papers. Private Collections of David J. C. Evans and Emily Evans Walsh.

Foote, Charles. Prison Record. Records of Department of Correction (General). Series 1. State Archives of Michigan. Lansing.

Gaffney, Thomas H. Compiled Military Service File. National Archives. Washington, DC.

Gates, Samuel K. Diary. Bentley Historical Library. Michigan Historical Collections. University of Michigan. Ann Arbor.

Irwin, William Bradford. Journal. Irwin Family Collection. Bentley Historical Library. Michigan Historical Collections. University of Michigan. Ann Arbor.

Lounsberry, Clement A. Papers. State Archives of Michigan. Lansing.

Grant, Claudius Buchanan. Papers. Bentley Historical Library. Michigan Historical Collections. University of Michigan. Ann Arbor.

Haynes, Joel. Letter. Gerald Weaver Collection. Regional History Collections. Western Michigan University. Kalamazoo.

Ingham County Families. Working Papers of Hammell Collection. Library of Michigan. Lansing.

Minnis, George. Letters. Larry Massie Collection. Regional History Collections. Western Michigan University. Kalamazoo.

Murdoch, George. Letter. Berrien County Historical Association. Berrien Springs, MI.

Office of the Adjutant General of the United States. Muster Rolls, Returns, Regimental Papers. Record Group No. 94. Michigan 1st Sharpshooters. Box 1947. National Archives. Washington, DC.

Office of the Adjutant General of the United States. Regimental Record Books. Record Group No. 94. 1st Michigan Sharpshooters. National Archives. Washington, DC.

Perrigo, Cyrus. Death Certificate. Death Records, Liber 46, p. 512. Tuscola County Clerk's Office. Caro, MI.

Powell, Moses A. Proceedings of a General Court Martial held near Petersburg, Virginia, June 30, 1864. Records of the Judge Advocate General's Office. Court Martial Case Files. No. NN 2032. Record Group No. 153. National Archives. Washington, DC.

Randall, William H. Reminiscences. Bentley Historical Library. Michigan Historical Collections. University of Michigan. Ann Arbor.

Records of the Michigan Military Establishment. Regimental Service Records. 1st Michigan Sharpshooters. Lot 1. Box 130. State Archives of Michigan. Lansing.

Snay, Richard. Prison Record. Records of Department of Correction (General). Series 1. State Archives of Michigan. Lansing.

Stone, George W. Military Pension File. National Archives. Washington, DC.

Reports, Lists, Studies

Algonquin Chapter, Daughters of the American Revolution. *Cemetery Records—Berrien County, Michigan.* St. Joseph–Benton Harbor, MI: n.p., 1930.

Civil War Centennial Observance Committee. Graves Registration Committee. List of Graves of Civil War Veterans in the State of Michigan. N.p., n.d.

Confederate Soldiers, Sailors and Civilians Who Died as Prisoners of War at Camp Douglas, Chicago, Ill. 1862–1865. Kalamazoo, MI: Edgar Gray Publications, n.d.

Dilts, Bryan Lee. Comp. *1890 Michigan Census Index of Civil War Vet-*

erans or Their Widows. Salt Lake City, UT: Index Publishing, 1985.

Dornbusch, C. E. Comp. *Regimental Publications and Personal Narratives of the Civil War: A Checklist.* 2 vols. New York: The New York Public Library, 1961.

Dyer, Frederick H. *A Compendium of the War of the Rebellion*, vol. 3. New York: Thomas Yoseloff, 1959.

Ellis, Helen H. Comp. *Michigan in the Civil War: A Guide to the Material in Detroit Newspapers 1861–1866.* Lansing, MI: Michigan Civil War Centennial Observance Commission, 1965.

First Annual Reunion of the First Mich. Sharpshooters. Brochure in Library of Michigan, Lansing. N.p., n.d.

Fox, William F. *Regimental Losses in the American Civil War, 1861–1865.* 4th Ed. Albany, NY: Albany Publishing Co., 1898.

Fuller, George N. Ed. *Messages of the Governors of Michigan.* Vol. 2. Lansing, MI: Michigan Historical Commission, 1926.

Hull, Francis. Comp. "Michigan Veterans' Obituaries, 1898–1939." Vols. 2–3. Unpublished listing in Grand Rapids Public Museum, Grand Rapids, MI.

Johnson, Allen, and Malone, Dumas. Eds. *Dictionary of American Biography*. Vols. 4, 20. New York: Charles Scribner's Sons, 1930.

"Kalkaska Twp. Cemetery Records Book." Kalkaska, MI.

"Lakeview Cemetery Records Book." Harbor Springs, MI.

List of Pensioners on the Roll, January 1, 1885. Baltimore: Genealogical Publishing Co., 1970.

Long, E. B., with Long, Barbara. *The Civil War Day by Day—An Almanac 1861–1865.* Garden City, NY: Doubleday & Co., 1971.

Martindale, Frederick C. Comp. *Michigan Oficial Directory and Legislative Manual for the Years 1913–1914.* Lansing, MI: Wynkoop Hallenbeck Crawford Co., 1913.

May, George. Ed. *Michigan's Civil War History: An Annotated Bibliography.* Detroit: Wayne State University Press, 1961.

Michigan Adjutant General's Office. *Annual Report of the Adjutant General of the State of Michigan for the Year 1863.* Lansing, MI: John A. Kerr & Co., 1864.

_____. *Annual Report of the Adjutant General of the State of Michigan for the Year 1864.* Lansing, MI: John A. Kerr & Co., 1865.

_____. *Annual Report of the Adjutant General of the State of Michigan for the Years 1865–6*, 3 vols. Lansing, MI: John A. Kerr, 1866.

_____. *Record of Service of Michigan Volunteers in the Civil War 1861–1865—Vol. 1: First Regiment Michigan Infantry.* Kalamazoo, MI: Ihling Bros. and Everard, 1905.

_____. *Record of Service of Michigan Volunteers in the Civil War 1861–1865—Vol. 44: First Regiment Michigan Sharpshooters.* Kalamazoo, MI: Ihling Bros & Everard, 1905.

Powers, Thomas E., and McNitt, William H. *Guide to Manuscripts in the*

Bibliography

Bentley Historical Library. Ann Arbor, MI: University of Michigan, 1976.
Report of the Committee on the Conduct of the War on the Attack on Petersburg on the 30th Day of July, 1864. Washington, DC: Government Printing Office, 1865.
Romig, Walter. *Michigan Place Names*. Detroit: Wayne State University Press, 1986.
"Traverse City Cemetery Records Book." Traverse City, MI.
University of Michigan—Catalog of Graduates, Non-Graduates, Officers, and Members of the Faculties 1837–1921. Ann Arbor, MI: University of Michigan, 1923.

Letters

Banks, Dr. Margaret Downie, to the Author. Vermillion, SD. 31 January 1991.
Haight, Floyd L., to the Author. Allen Park, MI. 8 November 1986.
Sommers, Dr. Richard J., to the Author. Carlisle Barracks, PA. 22 March 1986.
Walsh, Emily Evans, to the Author. Howell, MI. 19 October 1991.

Index

★ ★ ★ ★ ★

opinion of Hazen Pingree, 505–506

DeLand, Dell Whelan, 47, 347, 353

DeLand, Hooker A., 88, 150; appointed captain, 14; mustered as captain, 37; court-martial, 195–200, 344; post-war activities, 378–380, 428, 449

DeLand, James S., 88, 95, 137, 138, 150, 195, 197, 248, 251, 262, 263, 283, 297, 304, 306, 307, 344, 346, 353, 401, 407, 428, 497; wounded, 210; promoted to lt., 236; appointed capt., 281; wounded, 317; in hospital, 319; cited for bravery, 320; final years, 377, 382

DeLand, William, 5

Delaney house, 343, 370

Dell, Irving R., 388, 422

DeLong, John H., 390, 423

Demarest, George, 404, 413, 423

Demarest, Peter, 423, 444

Deming, Lafayette P., 427

Democratic Expounder, Marshall, MI, 79

Democratic Party, 18, 25, 30, 34, 65, 152, 195, 254, 334–335, 362, 371, 374, 375, 440, 448; newspapers, 78, 79, 269–271

Dennis, James, 397, 428, 495

Dennis, Oscar C., 398, 413, 431

Depew, John C., murder, 80

DePuy, Charles H., 222–223, 224, 227, 290, 349, 368, 403, 431

Desertions, 20–21, 60–61, 62, 75–76, 87, 94, 95, 192, 246, 261, 265, 267, 272, 295, 370, 456–457, 460–461; execution, 248, 497

Detectives, 80–82

Detro, John R., 40–41, 422

Detroit, MI, xvi, 2, 6, 14, 15, 19, 30, 36, 37, 45, 51, 56, 58, 60, 62, 76, 80, 157, 207, 208, 250, 329, 344, 352, 356, 361, 368, 373, 377, 415, 417, 418, 439, 445

Detroit Light Guard, 382

Devan, William, 433

Dewain, John, 431

Dexter, Flavius J., 320, 351, 406, 428

Dibble, George, 433

Dicey, Elmer C., 12, 197, 298, 299, 402, 423, 447, 449; accepted national flag, 43, 59, 62, 64; consolidated regiment into four companies, 190; in command of regiment, 201, 210, 220; captured, 234; recommended for lt. col., 248; in prison camp, 337–338

Dick, Noah, 389, 426

Dickerson, Joseph (Lt. Col.), 340

Dickson, Robert, 428

Dillabaugh, William, 234, 387, 403, 433

Dingman, William, 397, 427, 495

Dinwiddie Court House, Battle of, 314

Disbrow, James, 427

Disease, at Camp Douglas, 69–70, 89; at Annapolis, 95; at Petersburg, 286

District of Columbia, 100, 108

Divine, John, 423

Dixon, Robert, 422

Donnelly, Alexander, 398, 413, 430

Donnelly, Daniel, 430

Doty, William S., 426

Doucette, Simeon, 431

Douglas, Stephen A., 65

Dowagiac, MI, 372, 439

Dowagiac Union School, 33

Doyle, Henry, 422

Draft, in Michigan, 9, 18, 19, 265, 444, 496

Drake, Francis W., 411, 427

March, E. J. (Col.), 176

Marching, 103–104, 106, 107, 108, 109, 113, 114, 115, 124, 125, 126, 127, 129, 165, 166, 167, 168, 169, 175

Mark, John, 429

Marks, Louis, 398, 435, 495

Marlatt, T., 328

Marquette, Frank, 273, 435

Marsh, George C., 320, 406, 425, 489

Marshall, Elisha G. (Col.). *See* Marshall's Provisional Brigade

Marshall, George, 351, 433

Marshall, MI, 66, 250, 293

Marshall's Provisional Brigade, 116, 139, 140, 143, 169

Martin, Horace, 185, 344, 394, 433

Martin, Ira A., 344, 403, 417, 433, 495

Marvin, Lemuel, 433

Mash-kaw, Chic-ah-milgun, 346

Mash-kaw, James, 148, 343, 389, 435

Mash-kaw, John, 148, 343, 389, 435

Masonic Order, 364, 366, 375, 377

Massachusetts Agricultural College, 357

Massachusetts Regiments:
— Battery:
Fourteenth, 140–141, 145, 472
— Infantry:
Fifteenth, 198
Thirty-fifth, 257
Thirty-sixth, 257
Fifty-fifth, 249
Fifty-seventh, 356, 411
Sixty-first, 294

Mathews, Charles W., 390, 429

Mathews, Thomas (Capt.), 266, 291

Matthews, Lewis, 412, 430

Maule, James, 412, 423

McArthur, Samuel, 417, 430

McBride, Neil, 429

McCall, Thomas D., 280, 405, 423

McCann, John, 313, 430, 507

McClellan, George B. (U.S. Maj. Gen.), 191, 268, 269, 270, 271

McClellan, Ralph, 206, 299, 423

McClellan, Robert, 425

McClelland, William S., 34

McConnell, James, 425

McCormick, M., 76, 436

McCoy, Michael, 417, 429

McCreery, Charles (Capt.), 328

McCullouch, Samuel, 429

McElroy, James N. (Col.), 129, 130, 131, 133. *See also* Ohio regiments: Sixtieth Infantry

McFarland, David, 398, 433

McFarland, John, 433

McGivern, John, 405, 428

McGraw, John, 397, 413, 429

McIntosh, John (Justin), 417, 426

McIntyre, Herman P., 433

McKay, Robert, 411, 422

McKeel, Oscar, 240, 403, 425, 461, 489

McLane, James, 432

McLane, Thomas, 398, 414, 432

McLaughlen, Napoleon B. (Col.), 300, 302

McLaughlin, Thomas, 409, 432

McLelland, Benjamin, 295

McLelland, Frank, 429

McLoud, Daniel M., 388, 426

McMahon, Alexander, 422

McMinnville, TN, 5

McNeil, William B., 409, 430, 490

McNett, Jacob (surgeon), 22, 34, 43, 59, 97, 421

McQueen, William, 423

McWilliams, Edmund, 293, 295

Meacham, David R., 426

Meade, George G. (U.S. Maj. Gen.), 94, 111, 214, 215, 231, 232, 240, 329, 479

Meade, Henry, 428

TITLES IN THE
GREAT LAKES BOOKS SERIES

Let the Drum Beat: *A History of the Detroit Light Guard*, by Stanley D. Solvick, 1988

An Afternoon in Waterloo Park, by Gerald Dumas, 1988 (reprint)

Contemporary Michigan Poetry: *Poems from the Third Coast*, edited by Michael Delp, Conrad Hilberry, and Herbert Scott, 1988

Over the Graves of Horses, by Michael Delp, 1988

Wolf in Sheep's Clothing: *The Search for a Child Killer*, by Tommy McIntyre, 1988

Copper-Toed Boots, by Marguerite de Angeli, 1989 (reprint)

Detroit Images: *Photographs of the Renaissance City*, edited by John J. Bukowczyk and Douglas Aikenhead, with Peter Slavcheff, 1989

Hangdog Reef: *Poems Sailing the Great Lakes*, by Stephen Tudor, 1989

Detroit: *City of Race and Class Violence*, revised edition, by B. J. Widick, 1989

Deep Woods Frontier: *A History of Logging in Northern Michigan*, by Theodore J. Karamanski, 1989

Orvie, The Dictator of Dearborn, by David L. Good, 1989

Seasons of Grace: *A History of the Catholic Archdiocese of Detroit*, by Leslie Woodcock Tentler, 1990

The Pottery of John Foster: *Form and Meaning*, by Gordon and Elizabeth Orear, 1990

The Diary of Bishop Frederic Baraga: *First Bishop of Marquette, Michigan*, edited by Regis M. Walling and Rev. N. Daniel Rupp, 1990

Walnut Pickles and Watermelon Cake: *A Century of Michigan Cooking*, by Larry B. Massie and Priscilla Massie, 1990

The Making of Michigan, 1820–1860: *A Pioneer Anthology*, edited by Justin L. Kestenbaum, 1990

America's Favorite Homes: *A Guide to Popular Early Twen-*

tieth-Century Homes, by Robert Schweitzer and Michael W. R. Davis, 1990

Beyond the Model T: *The Other Ventures of Henry Ford*, by Ford R. Bryan, 1990

Life after the Line, by Josie Kearns, 1990

Michigan Lumbertowns: *Lumbermen and Laborers in Saginaw, Bay City, and Muskegon, 1870–1905*, by Jeremy W. Kilar, 1990

Detroit Kids Catalog: *The Hometown Tourist*, by Ellyce Field, 1990

Waiting for the News, by Leo Litwak, 1990 (reprint)

Detroit Perspectives, edited by Wilma Wood Henrickson, 1991

Life on the Great Lakes: *A Wheelsman's Story*, by Fred W. Dutton, edited by William Donohue Ellis, 1991

Copper Country Journal: *The Diary of Schoolmaster Henry Hobart, 1863-1864*, by Henry Hobart, edited by Philip P. Mason, 1991

John Jacob Astor: *Business and Finance in the Early Republic*, by John Denis Haeger, 1991

Survival and Regeneration: *Detroit's American Indian Community*, by Edmund J. Danziger, Jr., 1991

Steamboats and Sailors of the Great Lakes, by Mark L. Thompson, 1991

Cobb Would Have Caught It: *The Golden Years of Baseball in Detroit*, by Richard Bak, 1991

Michigan in Literature, by Clarence Andrews, 1992

Under the Influence of Water: *Poems, Essays, and Stories*, by Michael Delp, 1992

The Country Kitchen, by Della T. Lutes, 1992 (reprint)

The Making of a Mining District: *Keweenaw Native Copper 1500–1870*, by David J. Krause, 1992

Kids Catalog of Michigan Adventures, by Ellyce Field, 1993

Henry's Lieutenants, by Ford R. Bryan, 1993

Historic Highway Bridges of Michigan, by Charles K. Hyde, 1993

Lake Erie and Lake St. Clair Handbook, by Stanley J. Bolsenga and Charles E. Herndendorf, 1993

Queen of the Lakes, by Mark Thompson, 1994

Iron Fleet: *The Great Lakes in World War II*, by George J. Joachim, 1994

Turkey Stearnes and the Detroit Stars: *The Negro Leagues in Detroit, 1919-1933*, by Richard Bak, 1994

Pontiac and the Indian Uprising, by Howard H. Peckham, 1994 (reprint)

Charting the Inland Seas: *A History of the U.S. Lake Survey*, by Arthur M. Woodford, 1994 (reprint)

Ojibwa Narratives of Charles and Charlotte Kawbawgam and Jacques LePique, 1893–1895. *Recorded with Notes by Homer H. Kidder*, edited by Arthur P. Bourgeois, 1994, copublished with the Marquette County Historical Society

Strangers and Sojourners: *A History of Michigan's Keweenaw Peninsula*, by Arthur W. Thurner, 1994

Win Some, Lose Some: *G. Mennen Williams and the New Democrats*, by Helen Washburn Berthelot, 1995

Sarkis, by Gordon and Elizabeth Orear, 1995

The Northern Lights: *Lighthouses of the Upper Great Lakes,* by Charles K. Hyde, 1995 (reprint)

Kids Catalog of Michigan Adventures, second edition, by Ellyce Field, 1995

Rumrunning and the Roaring Twenties: *Prohibition on the Michigan–Ontario Waterway*, by Philip P. Mason, 1995

In the Wilderness with the Red Indians, by E. R. Baierlein, translated by Anita Z. Boldt, edited by Harold W. Moll, 1996

Elmwood Endures: *History of a Detroit Cemetery*, by Michael S. Franck, 1996

Master of Precision: *Henry M. Leland,* by Ottilie M. Leland with Minnie Dubbs Millbrook, 1996 (reprint)

Haul-Out*: New and Selected Poems,* by Stephen Tudor, 1996

Kids Catalog of Michigan Adventures*,* third edition,
    by Ellyce Field, 1997

Beyond the Model T*: The Other Ventures of Henry Ford,*
    by Ford R. Bryan, 1997 (reprint)

Young Henry Ford: *A Picture History of the First Forty Years,*
    by Sidney Olson, 1997 (reprint)

The Coast of Nowhere*: Meditations on Rivers, Lakes, and
    Streams,* by Michael Delp, 1997

From Saginaw Valley to Tin Pan Alley*: Saginaw's
    Contribution to American Popular Music, 1890–1955,*
    by R. Grant Smith, 1998

These Men Have Seen Hard Service*: The First Michigan
    Sharpshooters in the Civil War,* by Raymond J. Herek, 1998